mödling	335
tulln an der donau	337
petronell carnuntum and bad-deutsch	
altenburg	339
melk	341
baden	343
krems and stein	344

ESSENTIALS **347**

planning your trip	348
money	348
safety and health	353
getting around	354
keeping in touch	357
climate	359
measurements	360
language	360

GERMANY 101 .... **365**

history	365
politics and government	369
people	369
land	370
media	370
literature	371
film	371
art and architecture	372
etiquette and customs	373
holidays and festivals	374
sports and recreation	375
food and drink	375

BEYOND TOURISM **377**

studying	378
volunteering	381
working	383

INDEX **387**

map index	390

QUICK REFERENCE **396**

RESEARCHER-WRITERS

SOPHIA ANGELIS. Freshman phenom Sophie tore through northeast Germany, holding her own on a team of Harvard grads. While last-minute German lessons helped Sophie navigate small villages and big cities alike, her outdoorsy California spirit and photographic eye are what truly helped her discover the country.

NELSON GREAVES. On the few occasions that Nelson was able to suppress his attraction to Czech women and addiction to Eastern European cuisine, he pumped out copy that left his editors in stitches. Come the fall, the recent Harvard grad will move south of his hometown of Fresno, California, to start writing the screenplays for all of your favorite TV shows.

ANSLEY DAWN RUBINSTEIN. With the help of her ever-present cup of coffee, this Let's Go veteran and recent Harvard grad reenergized our coverage of Vienna. Bound for stardom as a dancer and actress, Ansley will undoubtedly enjoy fame in Hollywood, but she dreams of eventually returning to her previous Let's Go haunts—Australia and the Greek Islands.

XIN (CINDY) WANG. Fresh off a stint as an RW for *Let's Go Boston,* this Geneva (Illinois!) native strapped on a backpack and hopped a plane for her next Let's Go adventure. Even a recently earned Harvard degree won't keep Cindy resting on her laurels; after researching musical traditions in China next year, she's off to Berkeley for grad school.

GERMANY

Anything that ever made it big is bound to attract some stereotypes, and Germany is no different. Beer, crazy deaf composers, robotic efficiency, sausage, Inglourious Basterds—just to name a few. Germany has some of the best collections of art in the world, incredible architecture, and a history that makes it clear no one bosses Germany around. Whether giving the ancient Romans a run for their money or giving birth to Protestantism, Germany has always been a rebel. Even behind its success as a developed country, it hasn't given up that streak.

The damage from World War II still lingers in city skyscapes, and the country is keenly embarrassed of its Nazi and communist pasts. Even though its concrete wall splitting the city has been demolished, Berlin retains a marked difference between east and west, tempering the picturesque castles and churches of earlier golden ages.

Plenty of discounts, cheap eats, and a large young population make Germany an exciting place to visit and study. It's also incredibly accessible for Anglophone visitors, as many Germans have no qualms about slipping from their native tongue into English.The nightlife and culture of Berlin or Munich will grab you and never let you go, while thriving smaller university towns will charm you into wanting to stay another semester.

when to go

Rain is an old friend in Germany. May is an especially cool and rainy month, but much less crowded and often more affordable than the high season. Autumn has similar weather, except that it gets colder faster. June through August is high season, and while the climate is more hospitable, prices on hostels and airfares are jacked. In the wintertime some hostels close and museum hours may be shortened, but skiing and other winter sports make the season a treat for adrenaline junkies. The ski season is spread out from November to April, but the peak time is mid-December through March.

what to do

BUDGET STUDENT TRAVEL

As a wealthy European nation, Germany certainly can make you feel as though you have to tighten your belt to make ends meet. But don't worry, there are plenty of ways to see some of the best attractions without making you or your wallet scrawny.

- **NATIONAL GALERIE:** Thursdays 6-10pm all state galleries are free (Berlin; p. 43).

- **MIKE'S BIKE TOURS:** This company gives hefty discounts for backpackers who want to tour Munich via two wheels (p. 288).

- **HOSTEL DEALS:** Heidelberg, Germany's oldest university town, still makes itself accessible for scholar and budget travelers. **Steffi's Hostel** with free Wi-Fi and breakfast is a dream come true, and the free bike rental was almost too much for our underprivileged research-writers to handle (p. 225). Many university towns have deals like these, so keep your eyes peeled!

- **DÖNERS:** Discover delicious kebabs that go for only €1.50 in a super secret place in **Stuttgart** (p. 241).

top five places to ⬛bear/⬛beer the wurst

5. ZOOLOGISCHER GARTEN: Try Berlin's traditional *currywurst* and watch Knut the polar bear, deemed psychotic for attention by scientists.

4. MUSEUM FÜR MODERN KUNST: Grab a frankfurter before stomaching modern art.

3. FORESTS OF BAVARIA: Snack on weißwurst in peace; the first bear to wander into the forests in 170 years, Bruno, named after an infamous German vagabond, was shot by hunters in 2006 for demonstrating, "a lust for killing."

2. KÖLLNISCHEN PARK: Chew gummy bears—invented by a German—and greet brown bears Schnute and Maxi Follow this with *berliner weisse,* a pale and sour brew from Berlin.

1. STÄDEL MUSEUM : Want to avoid all four of the above? Check this museum out, then head to its celebrated restaurant and café, Holbein's—delicious but so overpriced it might actually have to be the wurst.

PUB CULTURE, NIGHTLIFE, AND BIER!

Germany is made of beer, or it might seem that way in a country overflowing with the famous brew. It might be German culture, or maybe human instinct. (Please, drink responsibly.)

- **HOFBRÄUHAUS:** The famed beer house will have you singing with strangers all night long (Munich; p. 277).

- **A TRANE:** A classier affair, Berlin's hottest jazz club has hosted greats like Herbie Hancock (Berlin; p. 62).

- **OKTOBERFEST:** Do you need an introduction? The festival of brews held annually in—you guessed it—October attracts thousands from all over the world (Munich; p. 286).

- **THE WEINEREI: FORUM:** Pay €2 and then keep sampling and sampling wines at this legendary local joint (Berlin; p. 66).

- **BIERSTUBE:** Dresden has some of Germany's best nightlife and the Bierstube is no exception. As the hours pass away the place becomes a straight-up beer joint with some of the cheapest beer prices in the country (Dresden; p. 131).

MUSIC

Germany and Vienna, Austria have remained centers of musical achievement and innovation, where classical forms and modern creations are blended together in sweet harmony.

- **DONAUINSEL FEST (DANUBE ISLAND FESTIVAL):** The annual festival on Danube Island in Vienna hosts every genre of music imaginable. The best part? Most of the events are free (Vienna; p. 326).

- **TOLLWOOD FESTIVAL:** This festival attracts a young, active German crowd with hundreds of concerts housed in tents (Munich; p. 285).

- **NATIONAL THEATER:** This world-class opera theater sells €9 student tickets 1hr. before the show (Munich; p. 284).

- **GROSSE FREIHEIT 36/KAISERKELLER:** Relax with the classics, from the Beatles, to Prince, to Willie Nelson (Hamburg; p. 104).

---

student superlatives

- **BEST TAKE ON WORSHIP:** The monks at the Andechs monastery serve the holiest—and at 12% alcohol, the most potent—brew in Bavaria.

- **BEST ALL DAY PARTYING:** The annual Bunte Republik Neustadt alternative festival in Dresden means food, music, and beer in the sunshine, dancing, music, and beer in the heat of the night.

- **BEST CINDERELLA MOMENT:** You'll be looking around for your fairy god-mother when you find yourself in Neuschwanstein Castle.

- **BEST CULTURALLY ACCURATE FUN:** A night at Hofbrauhaus, which only serves its own beer.

- **BEST ROUND-THE-CLOCK DILAPIDATED ART:** Schwarzes Café transforms peeling paint into art, especially as you alternate between their all-day breakfasts and all-night drinks.

BEYOND TOURISM

Want to repair damaged historic castles? How about promoting organic farming or championing disability rights? If you're one of those people who can't just hide behind the walls of museums or stroll mindlessly along urban streets, check out the opportunities below.

- **NERDS UNITE:** Experience (IAESTE) offers hands-on technical internships in Germany for undergraduate students (p. 379).
- **THINK ENGLISH IS THE WORLD'S OFFICIAL LANGUAGE?** Consider teaching it in Berlin (p. 384).
- **GREEN LIVING:** German forests and farms need your green thumb (p. 381).
- **SNACKST DU INGELSCH?** Don't understand what that means? You will after an intensive German language program (p. 380).

suggested itineraries

BEST OF GERMANY (1 MONTH)

For the best taste of Deutschland, take these cities by storm. Berlin, Munich, and Köln are the easiest to get lost in, but many of the tinier cities have their own culture and charm. Choose what vibe you want, and get packing.

1. BERLIN: This enormous city has it all—legendary museums, exhilarating nightlife, and some of the must-see highlights of Europe.

2. DRESDEN: Explore this tiny but meticulously-restored walking city.

3. LEIPZIG: Bach's birthplace hosts world-class classical concerts all over the city.

4. WEIMAR: Pay homage to dead famous men like Goethe and Schiller in what was briefly the capital of the Weimar Republic.

5. JENA: The world's most famous optical industry makes this otherwise cutesy and much less touristy town worth the visit.

6. MUNICH: Be amazed by enormous beer gardens and raucous culture in the Bavarian capital.

7. FRANKFURT: This business capital's ultra-modern pace will blow you away.

8. KÖLN: The GLBT nightlife here is unbeatable, and the parades and costume balls make the city crazy fun.

9. DÜSSELDORF: The alternative art scene will make a hipster out of you yet. After all, black-and-white films look better through sunglasses.

10. HAMBURG: The Beatles played here. Isn't that enough?

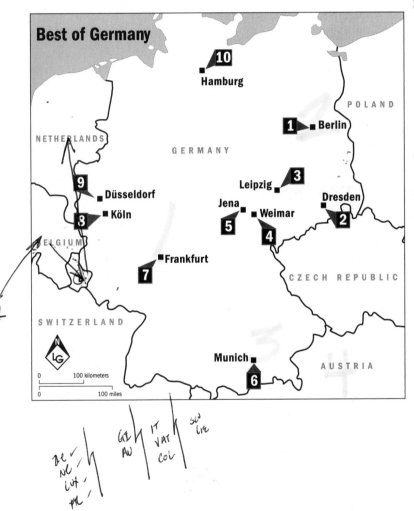

Best of Germany

Hamburg 10

POLAND

Berlin 1

GERMANY

NETHERLANDS

Leipzig 3

Dresden

Düsseldorf 9

Jena Weimar 2

Köln 8

5 4

BELGIUM

Frankfurt 7

CZECH REPUBLIC

SWITZERLAND

Munich 6

AUSTRIA

0   100 kilometers

0   100 miles

SLOSHED AND SCHLOßED (3 WEEKS)

Germany is the place for castles and booze. Plan your travels around that, and you can't go wrong.

1. BERLIN: Party it up at Mitte's techno clubs and in Schöneburg, the unofficial gay district.

2. POTSDAM: Rococo recovery never felt so right at Schloß Sanssouci.

3. DRESDEN: Schloß Moritzburg's Baroque beauty will make you wish weren't broke.

4. NUREMBERG: Take in the city from Kaiserburg's colossal castle walls.

5. MUNICH: Probably the epitome of Slosh and Schloß, Munich is home to Oktoberfest and Schloß Nymphenburg.

6. STUTTGART: Neues Schloß, Schloßgarten, Altes Schloß...So much schloß.

7. HEIDELBERG: Traipse around the romantic, crumbling castle. Go ahead, you know you want to.

8. BONN: The ruins of castle Drachenfels and the intimate local pubs make this a student's dream city.

9. KÖLN: More for the slosh, this industrial city plays host to some wild parties.

discover germany

FEAST IN THE EAST (2 WEEKS)

East Germany gives you a flavor of the USSR in contrast with the wealth of West Germany.

1. BERLIN: Travel west to east to see the differences that remain in the city even after the Cold War.

2. POTSDAM: Now you can get in on Friedrich I's fave hangout, his hunting ground. Let's Go does not recommend using the same manner for putting food on the table.

3. DRESDEN: The gem of the DDR is all about recovery; recover from hunger with some of the best bagels you've ever had.

4. MORITZBURG: Its Schloß will have you imagining what it would be like to feast there.

5. LEIPZIG: Music greats like Bach and Mendelssohn rest in peace here, and the ever-growing city is developing its rapport with the music world. Then venture to Germany's first coffeehouse for a historical treat.

6. WEIMAR: Feast on the landscape of Goethe's old stomping grounds, then eat for real at one of the many affordable places to fill up.

7. JENA: Inexpensive eats make this one of the best feasting cities in Germany, with cafes of studying students at every corner.

Feast in the East

WONDERLAND WANDERS (2 WEEKS)

Sometimes we all just want that fairytale. We can't guarantee you'll find your Prince Charming, but these places are the perfect settings to play out all those Disney dreams.

1. BONN: Beethoven's birthplace hosts an annual fête in his honor, while gold-leaf mosaics dazzle you in the Münsterbasilica (not monster).

2. KÖNIGSSCHLÖßER: You will enter a fairytale. No, really, we're serious.

3. MUNICH: Fests of every taste and a shloß to match. Venture out to Neuschwanstein Castle, a.k.a. Cinderella's home.

4. SPREEWALD FOREST: Lose yourself canoeing through this wondrous forest.

5. POTSDAM: The castle here will have you oohing and ahhing.

6. VIENNA: Palaces and castles and churches, oh my!

discover germany

how to use this book

CHAPTERS

In the next few pages, the travel coverage chapters—the meat of any *Let's Go* book—begin with Berlin. Next up, Hamburg takes the stage. After Hamburg, delve into Dresden, Leipzig, and Weimar-Jena. Then venture into the country's western region, in the cities of Köln, Düsseldorf, and Frankfurt. After that Heidelberg and Stuttgart make their appearance, with Munich closely following at their heels. Our gateway city, which is not located in Germany, but makes a great following trip, is Vienna. From there, you can enjoy both the city and various excursions into the Austrian Alps.

But that's not all, folks. We also have a few extra chapters for you to peruse:

CHAPTER	DESCRIPTION
Discover Germany	Discover tells you what to do, when to do it, and where to go for it. The absolute coolest things about any destination get highlighted in this chapter at the front of all *Let's Go* books.
Essentials	Essentials contains the practical info you need before, during, and after your trip–visas, regional transportation, health and safety, phrasebooks, and more.
Germany 101	Germany 101 is just what it sounds like–a crash course in where you're traveling. This short chapter on Germany's history and culture makes great reading on a long plane ride.
Beyond Tourism	As students ourselves, we at *Let's Go* encourage studying abroad, or going beyond tourism more generally, every chance we get. This chapter lists ideas for how to study, volunteer, or work abroad with other young travelers in Germany to get more out of your trip.

LISTINGS

Listings—a.k.a. reviews of individual establishments—constitute a majority of *Let's Go* coverage. Our Researcher-Writers list establishments in order from **best to worst value**—not necessarily quality. (Obviously a five-star hotel is nicer than a hostel, but it would probably be ranked lower because it's not as good a value.) Listings pack in a lot of information, but it's easy to digest if you know how they're constructed:

ESTABLISHMENT NAME 💳💵♿🚫📶🍸❄⛅▼ type of establishment ❶

Address ☎phone number 💻website

Editorial review goes here.

🧭 Directions to the establishment. ℹ Other practical information about the establishment, like age restrictions at a club or whether breakfast is included at a hostel. $ Prices for goods or services. ⏰ Hours or schedules.

ICONS

First things first: places and things that we absolutely love, sappily cherish, generally obsess over, and wholeheartedly endorse are denoted by the all-empowering 👍**Let's Go thumbs-up.** In addition, the icons scattered throughout a listing (as you saw in the sample above) can tell you a lot about an establishment. The following icons answer a series of yes-no questions about a place:

💳	Credit cards accepted	💵	Cash only	♿	Wheelchair-accessible
🚫	Not wheelchair-accessible	📶	Internet access available	🍸	Alcohol served
❄	Air-conditioned	⛅	Outdoor seating available	▼	GLBT or GLBT-friendly

The rest are visual cues to help you navigate each listing:

☎	Phone numbers	💻	Websites	🧭	Directions
ℹ	Other hard info	$	Prices	⏰	Hours

OTHER USEFUL STUFF

Area codes for each destination appear opposite the name of the city and are denoted by the ☎ icon. Finally, in order to pack the book with as much information as possible, we have used a few **standard abbreviations.** "Strasse" is abbreviated into "str.," while "Platz" is shortened into "pl."

PRICE DIVERSITY

A final set of icons corresponds to what we call our "price diversity" scale, which approximates how much money you can expect to spend at a given establishment. For **accommodations,** we base our range on the cheapest price for which a single traveler can stay for one night. For **food,** we estimate the average amount one traveler will spend in one sitting. The table below tells you what you'll *typically* find in Germany at the corresponding price range, but keep in mind that no system can allow for the quirks of individual establishments.

ACCOMMODATIONS	RANGE	WHAT YOU'RE LIKELY TO FIND
❶	under €15	Campgrounds and dorm rooms, both in hostels and actual universities. Expect bunk beds and a communal bath. You may have to provide or rent towels and sheets.
❷	€15-25	Upper-end hostels or lower-end hotels. You may have a private bathroom, or there may be a sink in your room and a communal shower in the hall.
❸	€26-35	A small room with a private bath. Should have decent amenities, such as phone and TV. Breakfast may be included.
❹	€36-50	Should have bigger rooms than a ❸, with more amenities or in a more convenient location. Breakfast probably included.
❺	over €50	Large hotels or upscale chains. If it's a ❺ and it doesn't have the perks you want (and more), you've paid too much.

FOOD	RANGE	WHAT YOU'RE LIKELY TO FIND
❶	under €5	Probably street food or a fast-food joint, but also university cafeterias and bakeries (yum). Usually takeout, but you may have the option of sitting down.
❷	€5-9	Sandwiches, pizza, appetizers at a bar, or low-priced entrees. Most ethnic eateries are a ❷. Either takeout or a sit-down meal, but only slightly more fashionable decor.
❸	€10-14	Mid-priced entrees, seafood, and exotic pasta dishes. More upscale ethnic eateries. Since you'll have the luxury of a waiter, tip will set you back a little extra.
❹	€15-22	A somewhat fancy restaurant. Entrees tend to be heartier or more elaborate, but you're really paying for decor and ambience. Few restaurants in this range have a dress code, but some may look down on T-shirts and sandals.
❺	over €22	Your meal might cost more than your room, but there's a reason—it's something fabulous, famous, or both. Slacks and dress shirts may be expected. Offers foreign-sounding food and a decent wine list. Don't order a PB and J!

BERLIN

Congratulations on your decision to visit Berlin. Your wussy friends went to Paris. Your snob friends left for London. Your tacky friends chose Florence. And your fat friends stayed home. But you chose Berlin, which makes two things true of you: 1) You're smarter than your friends. 2) You're bad at choosing friends. Everything that rocks in the other European capitals does so in Berlin, but here the beat is faster, the groove is harder, and all of it is covered in more mustard than Mr. French could dream. First, Berlin has normal history; the Prussians ruled from Berlin's canal-lined boulevards, built the Berliner Dom, pimped out opera houses, and collected enough art to make the Louvre green with envy.

But Berlin also has more recent history, part of which was the implosion of its older history in WWII, then there whole "wall" thing when the Soviets cut the city in half. In short, "change" more than anything else continues to define Berlin. As a city simultaneously abandoned and dominated by authority, Berlin became a haven of punks and anarchists in the '70s and '80s. When the wall came down, that sharp culture was suddenly forced to have a playdate with legitimacy as East and West reunited and sought to establish common ground.

In 1999, the German government moved from Bonn to Berlin, and suddenly Berlin's graffiti-filled streets were full of briefcase-carrying bureaucrats. Embracing change and pushing forward has also made Berlin the "cool" capital of Europe.

Your friends are morons.

greatest hits

- **COLD WAR KIDS.** Admire the Berlin Wall murals painted by artists from around the world at the East Side Gallery (p. 49).
- **TAKE ME TO THE RIVER.** Party like T. Pain (on a boat!) with rum and pizza at Club der Visionaere (p.71).
- **SASSY GAY FRIEND.** Take the weekly pub quiz with the hottest members of Berlin's GLBT community at Hafen (p. 63).
- **SHOP IT TO ME.** Barter with bakers and brewers at the biweekly Turkish market (p. 76).

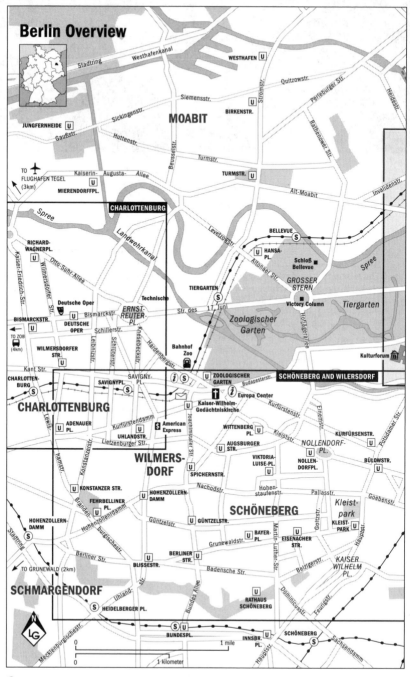

Berlin Overview

MOABIT

CHARLOTTENBURG

TIERGARTEN

SCHÖNEBERG AND WILERSDORF

WILMERS-DORF

SCHÖNEBERG

SCHMARGENDORF

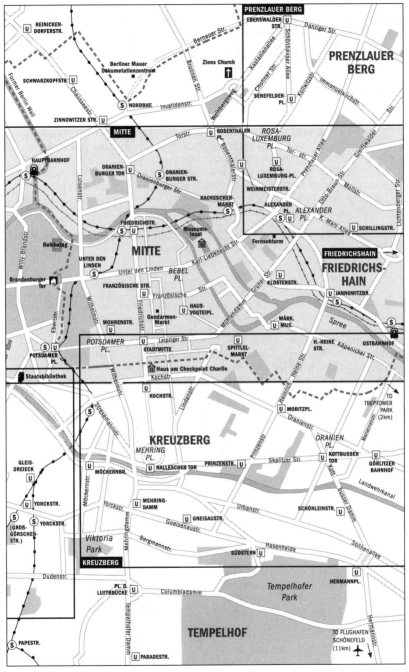

orientation

student life

Hit up the Bahnof Zoo and the schloß in Charlottenburg, but bounce as soon as the sun goes down. Shake the geriatrics, sip wine alongside PYTs at Solsi e Morsi, and befriend the legendary bar owner. Continue to paint the town—or at least Prenzlauer Berg—red at Klub Der Republic, a bar that proves that drinking can be educational, but maybe only if you're studying all of the Soviet-era artifacts hanging on the walls. After your tektonik dance marathon, cool off with some ice cream from Caramello Eis, a student haunt that claims to serve up the best chocolate ice cream in all of Berlin. When your daily schedule begins to reek of LiLo's party addiction, take a shot of culture instead at Berliner Philharmonisches Orchester; standing room at a show costs only €7.

CHARLOTTENBURG

Should you forget that Berlin is an old European capital, venture into West Berlin's Charlottenburg. Originally a separate town founded around the grounds of Friedrich I's palace, it was an affluent cultural center during the Weimar years as well as the Berlin Wall era thanks to Anglo-American support. The neighborhood retains that old-world opulence, from its upscale Beaux-Arts apartments to the shamefully extravagant **Kurfürstendamm,** Berlin's main shopping strip. **Ku'damm,** as the locals call it, runs east to west through southern Charlottenburg. It's also home to Europe's largest department store, **KaDeWe,** which comprises five massive floors that keep patrons dressed to a tee and their pantries similarly so with truffle oil. Close to central Charlottenburg is the large **Bahnof Zoo,** a Berlin family favorite, which may join the Ku'damm (and its never-ending flow of teenagers darting in and out of H and M) as the youngest and liveliest areas in Charlottenburg. Other sights include part of the Tiergarten, the sprawling Zoologischer Garten, the Spree River in the northwest, and the **Shloß Charlottenburg** to the west. Otherwise, the higher neighborhood rents keep out most young people and students, so the Charlottenburg crowd is quiet and somewhat older, and the nightlife options are few and far between.

SCHÖNEBERG AND WILMERSDORF

South of Ku'damm, Schöneberg and Wilmersdorf are primarily middle class, residential neighborhoods, remarkable for their world class mellow cafe culture, bistro tables, relaxed diners, and coffee shops spilling onto virtually every cobblestone street. Nowhere else in Berlin, and perhaps in all of Germany, is the gay community quite as contentedly outrageous as in the area immediately surrounding **Nollendorfplatz.** The gay nightlife scene, ranging from dark and smoky bars to chic and sleek clubs, is diverse in decor and music, but also laid-back and welcoming. To the west lies one of Berlin's most convenient outdoor getaways: **Grunewald,** popular with city-dwellers trading in their daily commute for peaceful strolls with the family dog along pine-lined dirt trails, is reachable by bus and tram in just about 20min.

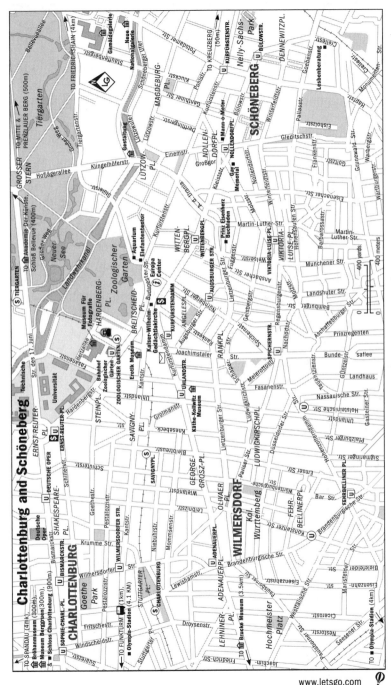

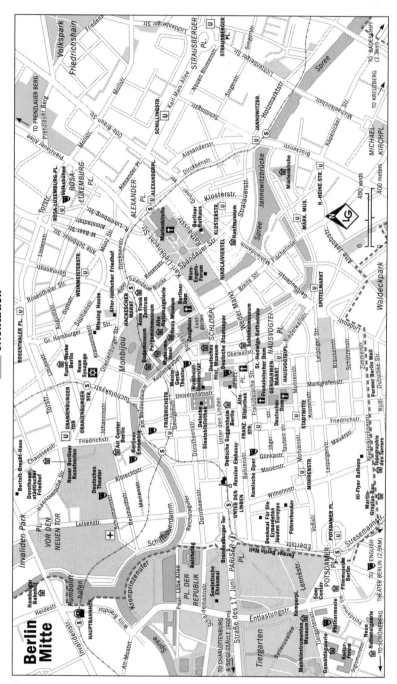

Berlin Mitte

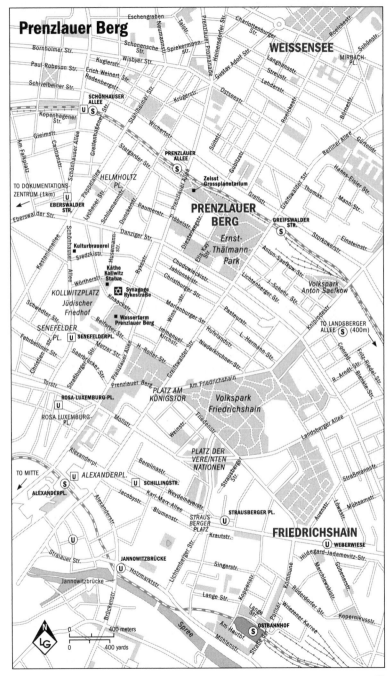

Prenzlauer Berg

MITTE

Mitte is without a doubt the most important district in Berlin. It has the **Brandenburg Gate,** the **Reichstag,** the **Jewish Memorial,** the **Column of Victory,** and the **Berliner Dom.** It has the best cultural institutions; **Museum Island** stacks the world's best musuems practically on top of each other. And somehow Mitte manages to multitask as a center for Berlin hipsterdom as well, with sick clubs, indie movie theaters, excellent food, and more walking plaid than that nightmare where the tablecloths came alive. Then, of course, there's the forest-like **Tiergarten** at the center of Mitte, which shelters sunbathers, barbecuers, and grasping lovers. The main street, **Strasse des 17 Juni,** serves as a a populist gathering place where carnivals, markets, protests, and public viewings of the World Cup take precedent over traffic. However, what's most fun about Mitte is tracing the history of Berlin down its streets and through its old and new buildings (which are often combined). The **Berlin Wall** ran directly through Mitte, and East and West Germany made a habit of comparing the sizes of their manhood over the wall. The communists built the Berlin Fernsehturm (TV Tower) as a sign of dominance—it's still the tallest building in Europe. The Americans responded with Congress Hall, now the House of World Cultures, an architectural wonder that's earned the nickname "pregnant oyster." Elsewhere, at the "Topography of Terror" museum, one of the longest standing stretches of the Berlin Wall streaks above the ruins of Hitler's war offices. And even with all this history to fall back on, Mitte continues to construct and reconstruct icons. The **Berlin Shloβ,** the Hohenzollern Imperial Palace that was destroyed in the 1950s, is scheduled to re-open in 2018.

PRENZLAUER BERG

What was once Berlin's overlooked Beirke, replete with crumbling cement and graffiti-covered Soviet-era buildings, is rapidly transforming into perhaps the trendiest area in the city. Attracted by low rents, students and artists stormed the neighborhood after reunification, giving the area a bohemian vibe with a unique DDR spin. Today, the streets are owned by well-dressed schoolchildren and their young, effortlessly hip parents, and the city blocks are interrupted by countless small parks, playgrounds, and costly secondhand stores. In Prenzlauer Berg, everything used to be something else. Delicious brunches are served every summer in what were once butcher shops, students party in a horse stable turned nightclub, and cheap cocktails are served from a bar countertop in a former linoleum showroom. For this neighborhood, what's cool is ironic, and what's ironic is the bare-bones, stuck in the '70s, USSR cement siding, burnt-orange shag carpeting past. Cafe-bar owners know what's hip, so even as relics of Prenzlauer Berg's are rapidly disappearing, mismatched sofas and floral wallpaper remain the shabby-chic decorating standard. The bar scene is to Prenzlauer Berg as club culture is to Friedrichshain. After dark, Prenzlauer Berg turns into a not-to-be-missed extravaganza of hole-in-the-wall basement concerts, laid-back wine tastings, and trendy, vegan cafes.

Geographically, Prenzlauer Berg is east of the city center, overlapping in some places with Mitte to the west. Cheaper bars cluster around the **Kastanienallee,** while the area around Lettestr. is ideal for checking out the '70s decorating revival. Only two U-Bahn lines and a single S-Bahn line cut through the area, so plan on trams or walking to explore the berg.

FRIEDRICHSHAIN

Friedrichshain's low rents and DDR edge draw a crowd of punk-rock types ever eastward. From the longest remnant of the Berlin Wall that runs along the river to the oppressive, towering architecture of the neighborhood's central axis, **Frankfurter Allee,** the presence of the former Soviet Union is still strong. Nowhere is that hard edge felt as sharply as in Friedrichshain's famous hardcore nightlife monopolizing every

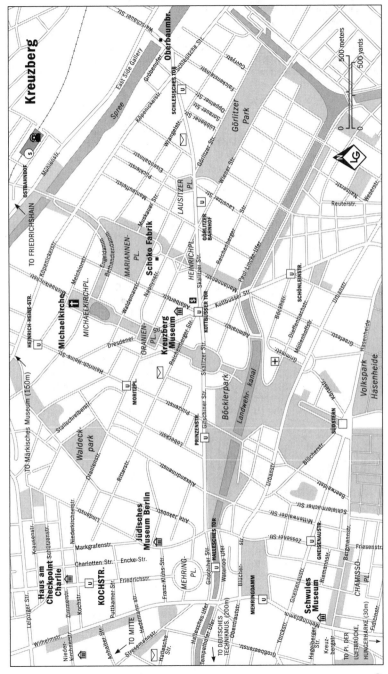

Kreuzberg

rundown train station and abandoned factory along the Spree, turning graffitied cement sheds into wild raves and electro hangouts. However, some locals complain that gentrification has found its way even here, as traditional residential buildings pop up and chic 20-somethings set up shop on the cafe-ridden **Simon-Dach-Strasse** and **Boxhagenerplatz.** But however legitimate those observations may be, Friedrichshain is still wonderfully inexpensive and fantastically out of the ordinary. Travelers should keep an eye out at night, as Friedrichshain is still a little rough around the edges and even desolate in some spots.

close to home

Pensions are family-owned guest houses. They are cheaper than hotels, but more expensive than hostels. Many offer long-term rates.

KREUZBERG

If Mitte is Manhattan, Kreuzberg is Brooklyn. Gritty graffiti covers everything here, and the younger population skulks around chowing down street food good enough for the Last Supper. The parties start later, go later, and sometimes never stop. Kreuzberg once ruled as the center of punkdom and counterculture in Berlin. It was occupied by *hausbesetzer* (squatters) in the 1920s and '70s, until a conservative city government forcibly evicted them in the early '80s. Riots ensued, and during Reagan's 1985 visit to the city, authorities so feared protests in Kreuzberg that they locked down the entire district. While these days find it a bit tamer, the alternative heart of Kreuzberg remains. Underground clubs turn on when the lights go down in abandoned basements, burned-out apartment buildings, and shaky rooftop terraces; the clubs that party the hardest in Berlin all find shelter in Kreuzberg. Kreuzberg is also notably home to Berlin's enormous Turkish population. Döner kebabs, those shawarma sandwich-like miracles, go for €2-3 all across this district, and the Turkish Market along the southern bank of the Landwehrkanal is one of the most exciting, raucous, cheap, and authentic markets in Western Europe. If you want to learn things about Berlin, go to Mitte. If you want to not remember your entire trip, come to Kreuzberg.

accommodations

CHARLOTTENBURG

BEROLINA BACKPACKER — HOSTEL ❷

Stuttgarter Pl. 17 ☎030 32 70 90 72 www.berolinabackpacker.de

This quiet hostel keeps things elegant with pastel walls and bunk-free dorms. Backpackers enjoy the high ceilings and big windows; some rooms even have balconies and intricate molding. Surrounding cafes and close proximity to the S-Bahn make up for its distance from the rush of the city. Communal and private kitchens *(communal €1 per day, private €9.50)* available for use. Relax and enjoy a breakfast buffet *(€7)*, or the "backpackers' breakfast" *(a roll with sausage, cheese and coffee; €3)* in the popular and newly decorated pale blue dining area.

S3, S5, S9, or S75: Charlottenburg. ℹ Internet €0.50 per 15min. Wi-Fi included. $ 5 bed dorms €10-13.50; singles €29.50-35.50; doubles €37-47; triples €39-64; quads €46-60. ⏰ Reception 24hr. Check-out 11am.

A AND O HOSTEL
🚫💳🚫♿ HOSTEL ❶

Joachimstaler Str. 1-3 ☎030 809 47 53 00 💻www.aohostels.com

On a busy, commercial street, A and O may not have an ideal location unless you plan on frequenting the Erotik Museum 40m away, but it has reliable rooms and close proximity to the Bahnhof Zoo transit hub. The lobby and bar are packed nightly, as is the roof patio despite its resembalence to a dilapidated mini-golf course. Rooms have metal bunks, big windows, personal lockers, and ensuite baths.

🚇 30m from Bahnhof Zoo. ℹ Wi-Fi €5 per day. Breakfast buffet €6. Linens €6. $ 8-10 bed dorms from €10; smaller dorms from €15. Doubles from €25; singles from €39. Prices may change significantly in busy months. ⏰ Reception 24hr.

FRAUENHOTEL ARTEMISIA
💳🚫♿📶 HOTEL ❹

Brandenburgische Str. ☎030 873 89 05 💻www.frauenhotel-berlin.de

This elegant hotel for women only was the first of its kind in Germany. A quiet rooftop terrace with sweeping views of Berlin is adjacent to a sunny breakfast room. Rooms are spacious, with large windows and molding around the ceiling. Named after Italian painter Artemisia Gentileschi, the hotel hosts rotating art exhibitions.

🚇 U7: Konstanzer Str. ℹ Breakfast buffet €8. Wi-Fi included. $ Singles €49-54, with bath €64-79; doubles €78/78-108. Additional beds for €20. ⏰ Reception daily 7am-10pm.

JUGENDHOTEL BERLIN
💳 HOSTEL ❸

Kaiserdamm 3 ☎030 322 10 11 💻www.sportjugendhotel-berlin.de

Though mostly booked by traveling school groups, Jugendhotel Berlin is a good option for the traveler short on places to stay. Clean rooms with lots of light suffer from an unfortunate lack of decoration and character. All rooms have full baths, and over half have outdoor balconies.

🚇 U2: Sophie-Charlotte-Pl. ℹ Breakfast and bed linens included. Substantial discounts for groups of 10 people or more, email for details. $ Singles €36-€46; doubles €33; triples €29-30. ⏰ Reception 24hr.

CITY PENSION BERLIN
💳📶 PENSION ❸

Stuttgarter Pl. 9 ☎493 03 27 74 10 💻www.city-pension.de

In exchange for the extra euros, travelers at City Pension get an ensuite bath, television, and large rooms sans bunk beds. Near the S-Bahn and accentuated with elegant molding and watered glass, City Pension is a fancier non-hostel option for group travelers that can keep you all under budget.

🚇 S3, S5, S7, or S75: Charlottenburg, or U7: Wilmersdorfer Str. ℹ Wi-Fi and breakfast included. $ Singles €54; doubles €76; 3-bed rooms €89; 4-bed €104; 5-bed €120. ⏰ Reception 24hr.

HOTEL PENSION CITYBLICK
💳📶 PENSION ❸

Kantstr. 71 ☎030 32 30 32 82 💻www.hotel-cityblick.de

The value of proximity to public transportation can never be underestimated. There's that and more, including rich ochre decor, surprisingly large rooms, and exposed timbers. An adjacent restaurant clinches the deal. The eating area is warm and friendly. Just be aware that prices may vary steeply from one week (or even one day) to the next. To avoid surprises, email ahead to verify costs at hotel-cityblick@gmx.de.

🚇 S3, S5, S7 or S75: Charlottenberg, or U7: Wilmersdorferstr. $ Singles from €45; doubles from €60; triples from €80; quads from €90. ⏰ Reception 8am-10pm.

SCHÖNEBERG AND WILMERSDORF

JUGENDHOTEL BERLINCITY
💳♿📶 HOSTEL ❸

Crellerstr. 22 ☎030 78 70 21 30 💻www.jugendhotel-berlin.de

Located on a quiet street and bordered by trees, this Jugendhotel Berlincity

has first-class rooms, but no dorms. This hostel is a splurge for solo travelers and small groups (think arching-brick-ceilings-and-dark-wood-floors kind of splurge), and usually larger groups get more reasonable rates. The hostel has a strict no smoking and no alcohol policy.

🚇 U7: Kleistpark. ℹ Wi-Fi €1 per 30min., €5 per day. Sheets and breakfast included. Ⓢ Singles €38, with bath €52; doubles from €60/79; triples €87/102; quads €112/126; quints €124/150; 6-person rooms €146/168. ⏰ Reception 24hr.

JETPAK

👍⊗ HOSTEL [1]

Pücklerstr. 54 ☎030 83 25 💻www.jetpak.de

JetPAK is way out in the boonies; if you're even remotely concerned about having a somewhat central location, think hard before booking here. That said, there's a lot that sets this hostel apart, and might make it worth the walk, bus, or train. Converted from an old German army camp, the hostel has been warmed up with colorful walls and comfortable beds and sofas, and is now more convincing as a summer camp. With showers heated by the hostel's own solar panels, this JetPAK is also one of Berlin's most environmentally conscious places to kick back and reap the benefits of nature.

🚇 U3: Fehrbelliner Pl. or U9: Güntzselstr., then bus #115 (dir. Neurippiner Str.): Pücklerstr. Follow the signs to Grunewald, and turn left on Pücklerstr. Turn left again when the JetPAK sign directs you, just before the road turns to dirt. ℹ Breakfast, linens, and Internet included. Ⓢ 8-bed dorms €14; doubles €23.

ART-HOTEL CONNECTION

👍⊗▼ HOTEL [4]

Fuggerstr. 33 ☎030 210 21 88 00 💻www.arthotel-connection.de

Recently redecorated with deep purple walls, crystal chandeliers, and dark wood floors, this hotel is (almost) nothing but class. A gay hotel that describes itself as "hetero-friendly," Art-Hotel boasts some of the most sophisticated style in Schöneberg. But lest we get too serious, this hotel also offers "playrooms," with slings and other sex toys.

🚇 U1, U2 or U15: Wittenbergpl. Ⓢ Mar-Oct singles €48; doubles €64; "playrooms" €99. Nov.-Feb. €43/59/89. ⏰ Reception 8am-10pm.

JETPAK CITY HOSTEL

👍⊗ HOSTEL [2]

Pariserstr. 58 ☎030 784 43 60 💻www.jetpak.de

There's nothing like large rooms with pine bunks, large windows, and brightly colored walls to lessen the institutional hostel feel. Owned by the same people who started the JetPAK in Grunewald, this hostel is much more central and practical for the city traveler, if not quite so one-of-a-kind. But after all, real estate hints at the importance of "location, location, location." The bathrooms are newly tiled, and the common room has couches and a foosball table. Most JetPAK travelers book ahead of time online.

🚇 U3 or U9: Spichernstr. ℹ Linens included. Most breakfast items, including croissants, €1. Ⓢ 8-bed dorms from €18; 6 bed dorms from €19; 4 bed dorms from €20. ⏰ Reception 8am-midnight.

JUGENDGÄSTEHAUS CENTRAL

👍♿ HOSTEL [2]

Nikolsburger Str. 2-4 ☎030 873 01 88 89 💻www.jugendgaestehaus-central.de

With a little more charm than the average *jugendgästehaus*, a few fun murals brighten this otherwise sparse hostel. The common room has a pool and foosball table and a TV for guests. A friendly, English-speaking staff that's actually helpful makes this otherwise ordinary hostel, usually reserved by groups, a slightly better option for backpackers.

🚇 U9: Güntzelstr. ℹ Sheets €2.50 for stays of less than 3 nights. More than 3 nights, sheets included. Ⓢ Mar-Oct €24 with breakfast included, with half-board €28, with full board €30. Nov-Feb €20/24/26. For a single room, add €5.50 per night. ⏰ Reception 24hr.

JUGENDHOTEL "VIER JAHRESZEITEN" HOSTEL ❷

Bundasallee 31a ☎030 873 30 14 💻www.jugendhotel-4j.de

These rooms may be a little lacking in character with white walls and sparse decoration, but we always fall hard for bathrooms that actually have baths! Two rooms share a bathroom, with three common rooms and eating spaces on the first floor. Mostly popular with school groups, but also takes in a fair number of backpackers.

U7 to "Güntzelstr." [i] Breakfast and sheets included. $ Doubles €22.50; 6-bed rooms €22.50 per night. ⏰ Reception 24hr.

CVJM JUGENDGÄSTEHAUS HOSTEL ❷

Einemstr. 10 ☎030 26 49 10 88 💻www.cvjm-jugendgaestehaus.de

From the outside, CVJM, a YMCA hostel, is sterile and plain. The interior is slightly warmer and always well-cleaned, with pine beds and large windows, if still lacking creative decoration. But there's not much to criticize about the top-floor common room, which has an open fireplace and views of Berlin. Hostel is usually booked for school groups. Quiet hours from 11pm.

U1, U3, U4, or U9: Nollendorfpl. [i] Breakfast, Wi-Fi, and linens included. Lunch €3.20 extra. $ Mar-Oct singles €35; doubles €27.50; 3-bed rooms €25.50; 4-bed rooms €24.50. ⏰ Reception M-F 9am-6pm.

ARTA LENZ HOTEL HOTEL ❸

Xantener Str. 8 ☎030 88 91 79 24 💻www.arta-lenz-hotel.de

Arta Lenz Hotel is a step up from most of the surrounding hostels in comfort, but far from opulent. A few rooms, including reception and the main entryway, reflect West Berlin's affluent past and the wealth on the nearby Kurfürstendamm, with granite walls, dark wood paneling, and marble floors. The rooms also have high ceilings with simple decorative carving around the top, but underwhelm with bland furnishings. Still, especially for groups of multiple travelers, Arta Lenz offers reliable, clean rooms for a very reasonable cost. Call ahead or check the website for prices: they can vary significantly.

U7 to "Adenauerpl." [i] Breakfast included. Internet €5 per day. $ Singles from €39; doubles from €49; triples from €59; quads from €69. ⏰ Reception 24hr.

OLIVAER APART HOTEL HOTEL ❸

Konstanzer Str. 1 ☎030 885 86 0 💻www.olivaer-apart-hotel.de

With all new, sleek modern furniture, and dark wood paneling on ground floor walls, Olivaer is certainly more refined than any hostel in Schöneberg. That said, its rooms lack character, with nondescript white wallpaper, red carpeting, and simple beds. Rooms are all well-maintained, and bathrooms are decorated with marble tiled floors and shower stalls. And after a day of walking all over decadent *shloßes*, who couldn't use some trodding on marble? Sometimes "third beds" are fold out couches; check by email or phone, or at reception to find out what you're getting. Prices vary, so call ahead.

U7 to "Adenauerpl." [i] Breakfast included. Internet access for a fee. $ Singles from €39; doubles from €49; triples from €59; quads from €79; quints from €99.

MITTE

Travelers with a limited number of nights should especially think about paying the few extra bucks a night for a place in Mitte. Most of the hostels are nice, and a few of them are literally minutes away from major sights.

CIRCUS HOSTEL HOSTEL ❷

Weinbergswet 1A ☎030 20 00 39 39 (Skype: circus-berlin) 💻www.circus-berlin.de

A cushy place with luxurious beds in the hippest part of Mitte, Circus has a chill cafe, a great bar with nightly specials, DJs, and a pimping karaoke night. Wi-Fi only works well in rooms, and the lack of a "chill-out area" leaves more net-addicted guests wanting, but forgive us for nitpicking. Breakfast is generous and all you can eat, and the mattresses are like clouds. Rooms come with a load of "extras"; the podcast audio tours, jogging route maps, quality food recommendations, and outstandingly helpful staff really do make a difference.

➡ U8: Rosenthaler Pl. ℹ Linens included. Segways €35 per day. Bikes €12 per day. Breakfast €5. Towels €1. Luggage lockers €10 deposit. $ 8- to 10-bed dorms €19; 4-bed dorms €23. Singles €43; doubles €28. ⏰ Reception 24hr.

★ HELTER SKELTER
💻🚬📶🍸 HOSTEL [1]

Kalkscheunenstr. 4-5 ☎030 28 04 49 97 🖥www.helterskelterhostel.de

The receptionist's warning: "The bar's open all day, but if you're too drunk at breakfast, we cut you off." A bit dirty, a bit worn, but that's just because every night here is wild. If hostel-wide drinking games and late nights are your thing, then take a chance on this place, and years from now you'll remember it as a Berlin highlight.

➡ U6: Oranienburger Tor. From the station, head south on Friedrichstr. and take a left on Johannisstr. The hostel is on the 3rd fl. through a courtyard. Follow the signs. ℹ Linens, towel, coffee, tea, and Wi-Fi included. Breakfast €3 (free for guests staying longer than 3 days). Smoking allowed in common area. Kitchen available. First 10min. on computer free, €1 per 30min. after. Key deposit €5. $ Megadorm €10-14. Singles €34; doubles €22-27. ⏰ Reception 24hr. Check-in 2pm. Check-out noon.

BAXPAX DOWNTOWN HOTEL/HOSTEL
💻♿📶🍸 HOSTEL, HOTEL [2]

Ziegelstr. 28 ☎30 27 87 48 80 🖥www.baxpax.de

Baxpax Downtown has a bag full of fun hostel tricks. Two above ground pools are revealed in the summer (one on the lower patio, the other on the roof, where, by the way, there's a sweet minibar). Downstairs has its own bar, where a giant stuffed moose head keeps court. The hangout room has a pinball machine, and the patio has a bizzare 6m long bed in case you want to get weird with your friends.

➡ U6: Oranienburger Tor. From the station, head south on Friedrichstr., then turn left on Ziegelstr. ℹ Key deposit €5. Linens €2.50. Towel €1, free in doubles and singles. Breakfast €5.50. Laundry self-service €5, full-service €8. Non-smoking. $ 20-bed dorms €10-31; 5-bed dorms with private shower €16-36. Singles €29-92; doubles €54-132. ⏰ Reception 24hr. Check-in 3pm. Check-out 11am.

WOMBAT'S CITY HOSTEL
💻♿📶🍸☀ HOSTEL [2]

Alte Schönhauser Str. 2 ☎030 84 71 08 20 🖥www.wombats-hostels.com

Mod, spotless, comfortable, with a rooftop bar and terrace—if Wombats is wrong, we don't want to be right. Hotel-like amenities exclude the possibility of clutch deals, but relax on the beanbags in the lobby and consider that you get what you pay for—that is, except for your first drink at the bar, which is free. The apartments with mini kitchens are nice enough to live in long-term.

➡ U2: Rosa-Luxemburg-Pl. ℹ Linens, lockers, luggage storage, and Wi-Fi included. Towel €2, free in doubles and apartments. 8 Internet stations; €.50 per 20min. Breakfast €3.70. Laundry €4.50. Guest kitchen. Non-smoking. $ 4- to 6-bed dorms €20-24; doubles €58-70; apartments €40-50 per person. ⏰ Reception 24hr. Check-in 2pm. Check-out 10am.

CITYSTAY
💻♿📶☀ HOSTEL [2]

Rosenstr. 16 ☎030 23 62 40 31 🖥www.citystay.de

Besides being the most centrally located hostel in Berlin, a beautiful, well-kept courtyard and an expansive cafe lounge separate this hostel from the pack. Rooms are nice enough with huge windows and adequate beds. But you know what's really nice? A 2min. walk to Museum Island and Unter der Linden.

➡ U5, U8, S5, S7, S9, S75: Alexander Pl. ℹ Laundry €5. 5 computers in lobby; €3 per hr. Lockers

€10 deposit. Sheets €2.50, free with ISIC. Towel €5 deposit. 2 women-only dorms. Ⓢ 8-bed dorms €17; 4-bed dorms €21; doubles €50, with private shower €65. ⏰ Reception 24hr. Check-in 2pm. Check-out 10am.

ST. CHRISTOPHER'S 💳♿📶🍸🧺 HOSTEL [2]

Rosa Luxembourg Str. 41 ☎030 81 45 39 60 🖥www.st-christophers.co.uk

It's rare you find a hostel bar with drinks as cheap as €1 Jager shots, but St. Christopher's delivers this and, subsequently, many a wild night. The Wi-Fi-equipped bar, lobby, and loft spaces blow most hostels out of the water. Rooms are spacious and clean and smell nice, though the same can't always be said of your roommates.

🚇 U2: Rosa-Luxemburg-Pl. i Breakfast, luggage storage, lockers, and linens included. Towels €1. Internet €2 per hr. Non-smoking. Ⓢ Prices change in real time based upon availability. Dorms €12-20; doubles €35-50; quads €60-96. ⏰ Reception 24hr. Check-in 2pm. Check-out 10am. Bar open daily until 3am.

BAXPAX MITTE 💳📶🍸 HOSTEL [2]

Chausseestr. 102 ☎30 28 39 09 65 🖥www.baxpax.de/mittes-backpacker

Baxpax Mitte rewards travelers who favor flavor over luxury. A group of traveling artists spread their love over the rooms to create a series of themed sanctuaries like the Garden of Eden, which has carpet-lined walls, or the Four Elements room with floors of water, beds of fire, earth tracked in by your dormmates, and air of air. The poetry room continues to develop as guests add their own original works: "Let's Go knows/That it should stick/To prose." No beds are actually made of fire.

🚇 U6: Zinnowitzer Str. i Guest kitchen available. Linens €2.50. Key deposit €10. Towel €1. Full service laundry €7. Breakfast €5.50. 2 Internet kiosks €2 per hr. Happy hour at small in-house bar 7-8pm. Non-smoking. Ⓢ 7- to 9-bed dorms €13-19; 4-bed dorms €19-26. Singles €37-39; doubles €58-62, with private toilet €46-68. ⏰ Reception 24hr. Check-in 3pm. Check-out 11am.

HEART OF GOLD HOSTEL 💳♿📶 HOSTEL [1]

Johannisstr. 11 ☎030 29 00 33 00 🖥www.heartofgold-hostel.de

With a rundown *The Hitchhiker's Guide to the Galaxy* theme, Heart of Gold Hostel makes a bunch of references to its source material that most travelers won't get. Don't worry—not everyone can appreciate literature. The dorms aren't very plush, but enormous windows and wild space-themed rooms will distract you from that.

🚇 S1, S2, S25: Oranienburger Str. Or U6: Oranienburger Tor. i Wi-Fi, lockers, and towel included. Breakfast €3.50, free for guests staying more than 3 days. Laundry €4. Key deposit €5. Linens deposit €5. Padlock deposit €10. Ⓢ Megadorms €22; 4-bed dorms €12. Singles €40; doubles €60. ⏰ Reception 24hr. Check-in 2pm. Check-out noon.

CITY HOSTEL BERLIN 💳♿📶🍸🧺 HOSTEL [2]

Glinka Str. 5-7 ☎030 238 86 68 52 🖥www.cityhostel-berlin.com

City Hostel Berlin feels a little old and institutionalized for having only been around a few years. Although it can't produce an awesome social environment, the beds are nice and the bathrooms are clean. A nice little bar with cheap and delicious snacks stays open late but doesn't exactly encourage revelry. Great "family rooms" with a bunk and a double bed available.

🚇 U2: Mohrenstr. i 6 Internet stations €0.50 per hour. Breakfast, luggage storage, safe box, Wi-Fi, lockers, linens, and towels included. Bike rental available. Ⓢ Dorms €17-22; doubles with shower €48-54. ⏰ Reception 24hr. Check-in 3pm. Check-out 10am. Bar open 6pm-late.

THREE LITTLE PIGS HOSTEL 🚫💳🚭🍸 HOSTEL [2]

Stresemannstr. 66 ☎030 32 66 29 55 🖥www.three-little-pigs.de

An enormous 100-year-old former abbey serves as this hostel's lobby. Pushed back from the road through a series of courtyards, Three Little Pigs feels removed from

berlin

the bustle of the city. Sturdy benches and long oak tables make it feel more like a medieval drinking hall than a hostel. Rooms and mattresses could be plusher but are entirely adequate, and the outdoor terrace is heaven on warm days.
🚇 S1, S2, or S25: Anhalter Bahnhof. ℹ Wi-Fi and lockers included. Laundry €5. Bike rental €12 per day. 4 computers with Internet access €2 per hr. Breakfast €5. Linens €2.50. Towel €1. Guest kitchen. Parking facilities available. [$] 6- to 8-bed dorms €11-17; Singles €34-36; doubles €44-48. ⏰ Reception 24hr. Check-in 3pm. Check-out 11am.

PRENZLAUER BERG

👍 PFEFFERBETT
♿ 📶 🍸 HOSTEL [2]

Christinenstr. 18-19 ☎030 93 93 58 58 💻www.pfefferbett.de

This old, 19th-century brick building is tasteful with a modern edge. The lobby's towering ceilings are supported by brick arches, and the garden out back has a patio popular for socializing. Bathrooms are newly tiled, and spacious rooms have a fun style, with thick stripes running around the walls. Lounge room has a pool, foosball table, and fireplace.
🚇 U2: Senefelderpl. ℹ Breakfast items from €1. Linens €2.50. [$] Mar-Oct 8-bed dorms €16; 6-bed €20; 4-bed dorms with bath €25; singles with bath €58; doubles with bath €78. Nov-Feb 8-bed dorms €12; 6-bed €15; 4-bed dorms with bath €20; singles with bath Nov-Feb €47; doubles with €64. ⏰ Reception 24hr.

👍 EAST SEVEN HOSTEL
♿ 📶 🍸 HOSTEL [2]

Schwedter Str. 7 ☎030 93 62 22 40 💻www.eastseven.de

Orange and olive walls make this retro hostel a cool, bunk-free place to stay. The indoor lounge area with comfortable sofas and the back patio with a grill are well-used hangouts for backpackers who appreciate cold beer specials *(€1)*. Rooms are spacious, with hardwood floors, old windows, and subtle-hued stripes that would make Martha Stewart proud.
🚇 U2: Senefelderpl. ℹ Free Wi-Fi; Internet terminals €0.50 per 20min. Linens included. Bike rental €10 per day. [$] Mar-Oct 8-bed dorms €18; 4-bed dorms with bath €22; singles €38; doubles €26; triples €22. Nov-Feb 8-bed dorms €14; 4-bed dorms with bath €19; singles €31; doubles €22; triples €19. ⏰ Reception 7am-midnight.

ALCATRAZ
📶 HOSTEL [2]

Schönehauser Allee 133A ☎030 48 49 68 15 💻www.alcatraz-backpacker.de

Alcatraz is hardly an inescapable prison, but you probably wouldn't mind spending a life sentence here. This hostel's graffiti-chic, spray-painted exterior is as lively as the sociable "chill out room," fully stocked with a foosball table and television. Alcatraz has 80 beds in carefully decorated rooms that contrast the chaos of the common areas. All rooms have ensuite baths, big windows, light yellow walls, and pine bunks.
🚇 U2: Eberswalder Str. ℹ Wi-Fi included. Fully equipped kitchen. Linens €2. Bike rental €10 per day. [$] Mar-Oct 8-bed dorms €16; 4-bed €18; singles €40; doubles €50; triples €69. Nov-Feb 8-bed dorms €13; 4-bed dorms €15; singles €35; doubles €44; triples €57. ⏰ Reception 24hr.

LETTE'M SLEEP HOSTEL
♿ 📶 HOSTEL [2]

Lettestr. 7 ☎030 44 73 36 23 💻www.backpackers.de

Located opposite a small park and between the popular bars of the lively Helmholtzpl., this brightly painted hostel is situated perfectly in the middle of Prenzlauer Berg's afternoon and early evening cafe scene. The big kitchen, complete with comfy red couches, a television, and a selection of DVDs, is home base for the hostel's young backpackers. Rooms are spacious and well-lit, with personal lockers and sinks in every room.
🚇 U2: Eberswalder Str. ℹ Linens and Wi-Fi included. [$] Apr-Oct 4- to 7-bed dorms €17-23; doubles with sheets and a small kitchenette €55; triples €60. Nov-Mar 4- to 7-bed dorms €11-20; doubles with sheets and a small kitchenette €40; triples €60. ⏰ Reception 24hr.

MEININGER

♨ ♿ (ᵖ) HOTEL ❸

Schönehauser Allee 19

🖳 www.meininger-hotels.com

Meininger is having an identity crisis; the establishment self-identifies as a hotel but charges by the person to fill up its dorms. Decorated in red and white, this neat and clean ho(s)tel is all reliability. Boasting bright white walls, spotless rooms, lots of windows, and just-outside proximity to the U-Bahn station, you really can't lose. Special deals for families.

☦ *U2: Senefelderpl.* ⓘ *Free Wi-Fi, or €1 per 20min. at terminals. Breakfast €5.50. Sheets includ-ed. All bathrooms ensuite.* ⓢ *3- to 6-bed dorms €28; women-only or small dorms €19; singles €52; doubles €70. Children 6-12 pay 50% of per person fee.* ⌚ *Reception 24hr. Check-out 1pm.*

AURORA-HOTEL

● ⊘ HOSTEL ❸

Pappelallee 21

☎030 46 99 59 30 🖳 www.aurora-hostel.com

There's not much to set this small hostel apart, other than an unbeatable loca-tion. Walls are white and generally lack decoration, and linoleum floors don't lend character, but this spotless hostel has one quirk: guests can pick a colored light bulb to shine in their window, making the outside of the hostel its own aurora by night.

☦ *U2: Eberswalder Str.* ⓢ *3-bed dorms €64.50; singles €30; doubles €49.* ⌚ *Reception 8am-10pm.*

FRIEDRICHSHAIN

Friedrichshain has built a reputation for itself as Berlin's neighborhood for inexpen-sive student-friendly housing. Luckily, travelers will enjoy the same wide range of youthful, cheap options for accommodations.

ALL IN HOSTEL

♨ ♿ (ᵖ) HOTEL ❶

Grünberger Str. 54

☎030 288 76 83 🖳 www.all-in-hostel.com

A bright, open lounge with a welcoming staff make you feel right at home. Rooms have crowded bunks but compensate with high ceilings and big windows. The location is unbeatable—right in the thick of Friedrichshain's popular cafes and bars on a quiet, arboreal street. The crowded lounge area, with big, comfortable couches, is great for socializing.

☦ *U5: Franfurter Tor.* ⓘ *Wi-Fi €1 per hr., hostel terminal €1 per 20min. Breakfast €5. Sheets €3 for 1st night only.* ⓢ *10-bed dorms €10; 6-bed dorms with bath €18. Singles with bath €39; doubles with bath €44.* ⌚ *Reception 24hr.*

GLOBETROTTER HOSTEL ODYSSEE

● (ᵖ) HOSTEL ❶

Grünberger Str. 23

☎030 29 00 00 81 🖳 www.globetrotterhostel

Right in the middle of Friedrichshain's bars and restaurants, Globetrotter Od-yssee is decorated with quirky medieval statues and vaulted ceilings. Muraled walls and rock music in the lounge (furnished with a pool table) give the hostel an East Berlin edge.

☦ *U5: Franfurter Tor.* ⓘ *Free Wi-Fi, hostel terminals €0.50 per 20min. Breakfast €8. Sheets €3 deposit. Credit card min. €25.* ⓢ *Mar-Oct 8-bed dorms €13.50; 6-bed €15.50; 4-bed €17.50; 3-bed €19.50; singles €36; doubles €47. Nov-Feb 8-bed dorms €10; 6-bed €12; 4-bed €14; 3-bed €16; singles €29, doubles €39.* ⌚ *Reception 24hr.*

U INN BERLIN HOSTEL

● ⊘(ᵖ) HOSTEL ❷

Finowstr. 36

☎030 33 02 44 10 🖳 info@uinnberlinhostel.com

This small hostel has only 40 beds and is set off a quiet street in Friedrichshain. Rooms are spacious, with pine bunks and brightly colored walls. U Inn Berlin doesn't consider itself a party hostel; there's a no-alcohol policy, and quiet hours start at 10pm. This hostel's speciality is creating a community for its small number of guests, with events like free German cooking lessons every Friday at 7pm.

☦ *U5: Franfurter Tor.* ⓘ *Linens €2. Breakfast €2. Hostel terminals €1 per 20min. €0.50 daily* supplement to pay for "greening" the cleaning supplies and buying fair-trade, organic coffee. *$ Apr-Oct 8-bed dorms €15; 5-bed €18; 4-bed €19; 3-bed €23; singles €29; doubles €50. Nov-Mar 8-bed dorms €13; 5-bed €16; 4-bed €17; 3-bed €21; singles €25; doubles €46. ⏰ Reception 7am-1am.*

PEGASUS HOSTEL BERLIN HOSTEL ❶

Str. der Pariser Kommune 35 ☎030 297 73 60 💻www.pegasushostel.de

Set around a courtyard with picnic tables, this hostel has a laid-back atmosphere, but is full of young energy. Towering orange and yellow walls are decorated with canvases of student artwork. There are private lockers in all the rooms. The top floor rooms include loft beds, set right underneath large skylights.

🚇 U5: Weberwiese. i Linens included. Breakfast €6. $ 8- to 10-bed dorms €13; 6-bed €15; quads from €68; triples from €57. Prices vary significantly; call or email ahead to confirm. ⏰ Reception 24hr.

A AND O HOSTEL HOSTEL ❶

Boxhagener Str. 73 ☎030 80 94 7 54 00 💻www.aohostels.com

With over 450 beds, this A and O feels like more like a self-sufficient youth community than a hostel. A bright, airy lounge and bar have their own, separate building with foosball and pool tables. Travelers sleep in towering buildings that surround a courtyard. The backyard has a tar volleyball court and single basketball hoop for pick-up games. This A and O might still have some of that chain-hostel look with pre-fab beds and minimal decoration on the walls, but a few quirky touches, like student-made statues in the living area, give it more character.

🚇 U5: Frankfurter Allee. Alternatively, S3, S5, S7, S9 or S75: Ostdreuz. i Breakfast €4. Sheets €3 1st night. Wi-Fi €1 per hr., €8 per week. $ 4- to 8-bed dorms from €10; singles from €19. Prices vary significantly; in the high season, dorms cost as much as €20 per person. Additional €2 for ensuite bath. ⏰ Reception 24hr.

SUNFLOWER HOSTEL HOSTEL ❶

Helsingforser Str. 17 ☎030 44 04 42 50 💻www.sunflower-hostel.de

This relaxed, eclectic hostel is decorated in dark blue and vivid orange with vines hanging from the ceiling and a small pond with running water in the lounge. The spotless rooms with high ceilings, striped walls, big windows and personal lockers are a marked contrast to the studied chaos of the common areas. The staff invites guests to ask about Berlin; use them as a great resource for Friedrichshain nightlife. This hostel is close to the action on the river but farther away from cafes and bars in the Simon-Dach area.

🚇 U1, S3, S5, S7, S9 or S75: Warschauer Str. i Breakfast €3. Laundry €4.50. Linens and padlocks €3 deposit. $ 7- to 8-bed dorms €10-14.50; 5- to 6-bed dorms €12.50-16.50. Singles €30-36.50; doubles €38-46.50; triples €51-61.50; quads €60-79.50. ⏰ Reception 24hr.

EASTERN COMFORT HOSTEL HOSTEL ❷

Mühlenstr. 73-77 ☎030 66 76 38 06 💻www.eatern-comfort.com

Stop flipping copies at Kinko's and grab your swim trunks and your flippy-floppies. This hostel is straight flowing on the Spree on the deep blue East Berlin side of the river. Guests rent rooms in cabins, with fold-down beds in dorm rooms and portals for windows. The truly adventurous can rent a tent and sleep on the top deck for the cheapest view of the big blue watery road. Every Wednesday, travelers enjoy a Language Party, where guests get together to experience the hostel's international clientele.

🚇 U1, S3, S5, S7, S9, or S75: Warschauer Str. i Wi-Fi included. Breakfast €4.50. Internet €3 per hr. Linens €5. 2-night bookings only on the weekends. $ 4- or 5-bed dorms €16; 4-bed dorms with bath €19. Singles with bath €50; doubles with bath €58; triples with bath €69. Tents €12. ⏰ Reception 8am-midnight.

OSTEL

⚓(•) HOSTEL ❷

Wriezener Karree 5

☎030 25 76 86 60 ◼www.ostel.eu

No, it's not a typo. The oddly abbreviated "Ostel" is also distinctive for a lime green exterior in a newly constructed, stucco-sided, small high-rise, built close to the river but far from Friedrichshain's restaurants and bars. This recently-decorated hostel prides itself on its "DDR Design," but unless that's code for a business-hotel vibe, we're a little lost. Pre-fab beds and small stripes of wallpaper decorate this neat and clean hostel's walls. Some rooms have balconies.

🚇 *S3, S5, S7, S9, or S75: Ostbahnhof.* *i* *Linens and towels included. Breakfast €6.50.* Ⓢ *8-bed dorms €15; singles €33; doubles €54.* ⏲ *Reception 24hr.*

KREUZBERG

Accommodations in Kreuzberg tend to a bit grungier than other parts of the city, but the hostels also have a much better sense of community. Staying in Kreuzberg lets travelers live in a rich community while still being close to the city's major sights.

▨ METROPOL HOSTEL

⚓&♼ HOSTEL ❷

Mehringdamm 32

◼www.Metropolhostel-berlin.com

The newest addition to the Kreuzberg hostel scene wasn't entirely finished when *Let's Go* stopped by, but the results thus far are pretty promising. The hallways feel a bit like a hospital, but the rooms themselves sometimes verge on near-hotel accommodations. Superb mattresses, clean floors, newly painted walls, and spotless bathrooms all work to this end. Oh, and those century-old-looking doors are actually 100 years old. The building is a historical site and the doors cannot be replaced.

🚇 *U6 or U7: Mehringdamm.* *i* *Shower and toilet in every room. Breakfast, linens, lockers, luggage storage, safe box, and towels included.* Ⓢ *6-to 10-bed dorms €9-14; singles €39-49; doubles €49-50.* ⏲ *Reception 24hr. Check-in 2pm. Check-out 10am.*

HOSTEL X BERGER

⚓⊗(•)♼ HOSTEL ❶

Schlesischestr. 22

☎030 69 53 18 63 ◼www.hostelxberger.com

For the quickest jump to the coolest clubs in Berlin, no one outdoes Hostel X Berger, located right along the canal. While the accommodations are far from new, the rooms somehow feel relaxed, like you've already lived there. A foggy downstairs smoke room with a pool table works like an underground club, while a quiet study upstairs makes good space to work. Rooms are also designed to let you play hard, with a late check-out time and free coffee for the after-party blues.

🚇 *U1: Schlesisches Tor. From the U-bahn, head south on Schlesischestr.* *i* *Luggage storage and Wi-Fi included. 2 computers with free Internet. Linens €2. Towel €1. Laundry €4. Lock rental €1. Key deposit €6. Guest kitchen open until 9:30pm.* Ⓢ *4-bed dorms €17-18; 16-bed dorms €11-12. Singles €32-36; doubles €40-46.* ⏲ *Reception 24hr. Check-in 2pm. Check-out 2pm.*

BAXPAX KREUZBERG

⚓&(•)♼⚐ HOSTEL ❷

Skalitzer Str. 104

☎030 69 51 83 22 ◼www.baxpax.de

This old-school backpacker hostel offers far from the royal treatment, but a weary traveler will find a bed, lively drunk guests, and staff accustomed to drunk guests. Rooms are themed around countries—someone literally sleeps in a VW bug in the German room. A rooftop terrace connected to the guest kitchen is brilliant in the daytime but unfortunately closes at 10pm. Shoddy Wi-Fi is a major turn-off, but the signal is enough to check mail. Staff wakes you up if you sleep past check-out...not that we would know.

🚇 *U1: Görlitzer Bahnhof.* *i* *Breakfast options €1-2.50. Linens and towel €2.50. Internet €2 per hr. Laundry €7. Lockers, luggage storage, and safebox included. Guests can smoke in the common room after 6pm.* 💲 *32-bed dorms €9-14; 8-bed €10-17; 4-bed €14-20. Singles €26-37; doubles with bath €24-30.* ⏰ *Reception 24hr. Check-in 3pm. Check-out 11am.*

HOSTEL 36 ROOMS 🚫💳 🚫♿ 📶 🍸 HOSTEL [1]

Spreewaldpl. 8 ☎030 53 08 63 98 💻www.36rooms.com

Nice large rooms and a beautiful outdoor patio are somewhat robbed of fun by the hostel's no-outside-alcohol policy. Guests can beer it at the hostel bar or wait until Thursday, Friday and Saturday, when one of Kreuzberg's hippest underground clubs rocks in the hostel's basement. Hot travelers can dip in the wave pool across the street at the hostel's discounted price *(€2 per hr.)*. Old World rooms have chandeliers and great views of the nearby park. Unfortunately some also have an Old World smell.

🚇 *U1: Görlitzer Bahnhof.* ℹ *Locker rental €2. Linens and towel €2.50. Bike rental €10 per day. Key deposit €10.* 💲 *8-bed dorms €14-17; 4-bed €18-21. Singles €35-39; doubles €50-58.* ⏰ *Reception 24hr. Check-in 1pm. Check-out 11am. Patio and kitchen open until 10pm.*

COMEBACK PACKERS HOSTEL 🚫💳 🚫♿ 📶 🍸 HOSTEL [1]

Alabertstr. 97 ☎030 60 05 75 27 💻www.comebackpackers.com

As you climb the fish-smelling stairs, you'd never guess that this relaxed hostel waited at the top, just chilling there. The large common room feels more like your mother's kitchen and stays open all night. Guests can jump out the windows... onto the roof for a smoke or some sun at the picnic tables. The showers are pretty exposed—as in, people will definitely see you naked, and you definitely should not pee because everyone will know, and it will be embarrassing. Anyway—beds are adequate and tend to not be bunked. Rooms are large, wood-floored, and climb-on-the-roof-able, but otherwise unremarkable. The only remarkable thing is the goose lamp in the goose room. It's a goose. But it's also a lamp. Staff has a very German sense of humor.

🚇 *U1 or U8: Kotbusser Tor.* ℹ *Coffee, linens, and Wi-Fi included. Key deposit €10. Full-service laundry €5. Towel €2. Continental breakfast (€3) must be requested.* 💲 *Dorms €14-20.* ⏰ *Reception 24hr. Check-in 3pm. Check-out 1pm.*

MEININGER 💳 ♿ 🍸 HOSTEL [2]

Hallesches Ufer 30 ☎030 66 63 61 00 💻www.meininger-hotels.com

Meininger might not be the cheapest hostel around, but it provides top-notch service. Most impressive is that Meininger balances hip with professionalism. Graffiti-lined walls lead to a quaint guest kitchen that never closes, all-you-can-eat breakfast is served on a beautiful roof terrace, and a relaxed bar/workspace serves up drinks daily from 7pm. The beds don't break any comfort records, but the rooms definitely beat the average: each has a TV and carpets are all unstained. Potsdammer pl. and many of the great sites in lower Mitte are just a hop away, assuming you have developed hopping muscles.

🚇 *U1 or U6: Hallesches Tor.* ℹ *Linens and lockers included. Late riser fee €5. Breakfast €4. Laundry €5. Towel €1, plus €5 deposit. Lock deposit €5.* 💲 *8-bed dorms €18-21; 4-bed €23-24. Singles €49-55; doubles €66-72.* ⏰ *Reception 24hr. Check-in 2pm. Check-out 10am. Late check-out 1pm. Roof terrace open until 10pm.*

ALETTO'S 💳 ♿ 🍸 🍳 HOSTEL [2]

Tempelhofer Ufer 8-9 ☎030 25 93 04 80 💻www.aletto.de

In spite of a logo that resembles a horned dildo, Aletto keeps it clean for groups of travelers. Even though its rooms come in denominations for one to eight people, each room is private and must be booked in its entirety. The Hostel Oscar nominees for Best Amenities at an Aletto hostel in Kreuzberg are: large free breakfast, starring eggs; the mini-cinema, starring free DVD rentals; and the snappy common spaces, starring free Wi-Fi, a full service bar, and a foosball table. Matresses are a cut above average, and proud pictures of the horned dildo enchant every room.

🚉 U1 or U6: Hallesches Tor. ℹ Linens, luggage storage, and towels included. ATM available. Internet €2 per hr. $ All prices are per room. 4-bed dorms €16-29; 6-bed €90-156. Singles €35-55; doubles €39-75. ⏰ Reception 24hr. Check-in 2pm. Check-out noon.

BERLIN BOUTIQUE HOSTEL 💳🚭📶🍸 HOSTEL ❶

Gneisenaustr. 109-110 ☎030 69 81 92 37 🖥www.boutique-hostel.de

If boutiques are small and fancy, then this tiny hostel lives up to at least half of its name. With only 32 beds, Boutique lacks a sense of real hostel community, and even though it's small, it could benefit from a few more toilets and showers. Additionally, if you need a lot of help in life (which you won't because you bought this really comprehensive travel guide), the lack of 24hr. reception can be a bummer. But for travelers who don't care, the rooms are cheap, clean, and even have some charm, with tall French doors and high ceilings in some of them. A small lounge area has a DVD collection and a flatscreen TV.

🚉 U6 or U7: Mehringdamm. ℹ Luggage storage and Wi-Fi included. Irons and hair dryers available at front desk. $ 12-bed dorms €12-13; 6-bed €14-15. Doubles €50-60. ⏰ Reception 8am-11pm. Check-in 2pm. Check-out noon. Travelers can arrange for late arrival.

CHARLOTTENBURG

Most of Berlin's sights are located outside of residential Charlottenburg, closer to the center of the city. That said, Charlottenburg has certain sights that recommend themselves to the traveler with more than a day or two to spend in Berlin. Unique museums, grand palaces, and one of the world's most historic stadiums are spread out all over the neighborhood.

KÄTHE-KOLLWITZ-MUSEUM — MUSEUM

Fasanenstr. 24 ☎030 32 69 06 00 www.kaethe-kollwitz.de

Through both World Wars, Käthe Kollwitz, a member of the Berlin Sezession (Secession) movement and one of Germany's most prominent 20th century artists, protested war and the situation of the working class with haunting sketches, etchings, sculpture and charcoal drawings of death, poverty, and starvation. The series of works entitled, "A Weaver's Revolt," on the second floor are the drawings that skyrocketed Kollwitz to fame. The death of the artist's own son, who was killed in Russia during WWII, provides a wrenching emotional authenticity to her depictions of death, pregnancy, and starvation, and her own revealing self-portraits.

U1: "Uhlandstr." $ Admission €6, students €3. Open daily 11am-6pm.

SCHLOß CHARLOTTENBURG — PALACE

Spandauer Damm 10-22 ☎030 320 9275

This expansive Baroque palace, commissioned by Friedrich I in the 1600s as a gift for his wife, Sophia-Charlotte, stands impressively at the end of a long treelined walkway on the outer north end of Charlottenberg. The Schloß is made up of several parts. **Altes Schloß,** the oldest section (marked by a blue dome in the middle of the courtyard), has rooms chock full of historic furnishings (much of it reconstructed due to war damage) and elaborate gold guilding. **Neuer Flügel** (New Wing), includes the marble receiving rooms and the more somber royal chambers. **Neuer Pavillion** houses a museum dedicated to Prussian architect Karl Friedrich Schinkel. Other sections include the **Belvedere,** a small building housing the royal family's porcelain collection, and the **Mausoleum,** the final resting place for most of the family. Behind the palace extends the exquisitely manicured Schloßgarten, full of small lakes, footbridges and fountains.

Bus #M45 from Bahnhof Zoo to Luisenpl./Schloß Charlottenburg or U2: Sophie-Charlotte Pl. $ Altes Shloβ €10, students €7; Neuer Flügel €6/5; Belvedere €2/1.50; Mausoleum free. Audio tours available in English included. Altes Shloβ open Apr-Oct Tu-Su 10am-6pm; Nov-Mar Tu-Su 10am-5pm. Neuer Flügel open year-round M and W-Su 10am-5pm. Belvedere and Mausoleum open Apr-Oct daily 10am-6pm, Nov-Mar daily noon-5pm.

MUSEUM BERGGRUEN — MUSEUM

Schloßstr. 1 ☎030 326 95 80

Think Picasso is a jerk whose art didn't deserve the hype it got? This intimate three-floor museum will put away your anti-Picasso sentiments. The first and second floor are Picasso-packed, with added bonuses of French Impressionist Matisse's art and African masks. The third floor showcases paintings by Bauhaus teacher Paul Klee and Alberto Giacometti's super-skinny sculptures of human forms.

Bus #M45 from Bahnhof Zoo to Luisenpl./Schloß Charlottenburg or U2: Sophie-Charlotte Pl. $ €12, €6 students, children free. Audio guide included. Open Tu-Su 10am-6pm.

BRÖHANMUSEUM — MUSEUM

Schloßstr. 1A ☎030 32 69 06 00 www.broehanmuseum.de

If you're wondering where all the stuff you couldn't sell at your great-aunt's estate sale went, here it is. The Bröhanmuseum showcases epic brös ißing brös... Just kidding, we mean Art Nouveau and Art Deco paintings, housewares, and furniture. Along with figurines and lampshades that resemble knicknacks you sneered at (and now regret not buying) at neighborhood garage sales, the ground floor also pairs several groupings of period furniture with paintings from the same era (1889-1939). The first floor is a small gallery dedicated to the Modernist Berlin *Sezession* painters, though occasionally upstaged by oddly chosen shocking green walls, and the top floor houses special exhibitions.

Bus #M45 from Bahnhof Zoo to Luisenpl./Schloß Charlottenburg or U2: Sophie-Charlotte Pl. The museum is next to the Bergguen, across from the Schloß. $ Admission €6, students €4. ⏰ Open Tu-Su 10am-6pm.

OLYMPIASTADION STADIUM

Olympischer Pl. 3 (Visitor Center) ☎030 25 00 23 22 🖥www.olypiastadion-berlin.de

This massive Nazi-built stadium comes in a close second to Tempelhof Airport in the list of monumental Third Reich buildings in Berlin. It was erected for the infamous 1936 Olympic Games, in which African-American track and field athlete Jesse Owens won four gold medals. Hitler refused to congratulate Owens, who has since been honored with a Berlin street, Jesse-Ownes-Allee and his name has been engraved into the side of the stadium with the other 1936 gold medal winners. The six stone pillars flanking the stadium were originally intended to signify the unity of the six "tribes" of ethnicities that Hitler believed fed into true German heritage. Recent uses have included the 2006 World Cup final. The independently operated **Glockenturm** (bell tower) provides a great lookout point and houses an exhibit on the history of German athletics.

S5, S7, or U2: Olympia-Stadion. For Glockenturm, S5 or S7: Pichelsburg. $ €4, students €3. Tour with guide €8, students €7, children under 6 free. ⏰ Open daily Mar 20-May 9am-7pm, June-Sept 15 9am-8pm, Sept 16-Oct 31 9am-7pm, Nov-Mar 19 9am-4pm.

KAISER-WILHELM-GEDÄCHTNISKIRCH (MEMORIAL CHURCH) CHURCH

Centre of the Breitscheidpl. ☎030 218 5023

This partially destroyed church was left standing after World War II as a reminder of the devastation of war. With gaping holes where the large circular stained glass used to fit, this is a moving testament to the price Germany paid. Part neo-Romanesque and Byzantine style, part war-ravaged, cracked colorful mosaics line the interior, which you can compare to a small exhibit that shows the church in happier days and horrific photos of the city in the wake of WWII. Across from Memorial Church stands the New Church, constructed in 1992 with a plain exterior and blue stained glass interior.

On the Kurfürstendamm in the centre of the Breitscheidpl. ⏰ Exhibit open M-Sa 10am-4pm. Church open daily 9am-7pm.

ZOOLOGISCHER GARTEN ZOO

8 Hardenberg Pl. ☎030 25 40 10 🖥www.zoo-berlin.de

Germany's oldest zoo houses around 14,000 animals of 1500 species, most in open-air habitats connected by winding pathways under dense cover of trees and brush. While you're there, pay your respects to the world-famous polar bear **Knut,** or he may go nuts. Originally deemed the cutest polar bear alive, Knut has been diagnosed by animal specialists as a psychopath addicted to human attention. Luckily, he's still pretty cute.

U2 or U9: Zoological Garten, or S5, S7 or S75: Bahnhof Zoo. Main entrance is across from the Europa Center. $ €12, students €9, children €6. Combination to zoo and aquarium €18/14/9. ⏰ Open daily from 9am-7pm (last entry 6pm). Animal houses open 9am-6pm.

AQUARIUM

Budapester Str. 32   ☎030 25 40 10 💻www.aquarium-berlin.de.

Within the walls of the zoo, but independently accessible, is an aquarium with three floors of fish, reptiles, amphibians and insects. Highlights include the pychadelic jellyfish and the slimey carp petting zoo.

⚐ *U2 or U9: Zoological Garten, or S5, S7 or S75: Bahnhof Zoo.* Ⓢ *€12, students €9, children €6. See above for aquarium-zoo combination tickets.* ⌚ *Open daily 9am-6pm.*

BEATE UHSE EROTIK MUSEUM

MUSEUM

Joachimstalerstr. 4   ☎030 886 06 66 💻www.erotikmuseum.de

The world's largest sex museum contains over 5,000 sex artifacts from around the world. Attracting a quarter of a million visitors per year, it is Berlin's fifth most popular tourist attraction. Visitors come to see erotica ranging from explicit carvings on a 17th century Italian deer-hunting knife to a 1955 calender featuring Marilyn Monroe in her birthday suit. A small exhibit describes the life of Beate Uhse, a pilot-turned-entrepeneur who started Europe's first and largest sex-shop chain, then decided to get historical about the whole thing and founded the museum.

⚐ *S5, S7 or S75: Bahnhof Zoo.* Ⓢ *€14 per person, €25 couples. €10 students with ID, or with WelcomeCard. Make it an orgy (€10 per person for groups of 10 and over), or bring grandpa (€10 seniors).* ⌚ *Open daily 9am-midnight.*

SCHÖNEBERG AND WILMERSDORF

Schöneberg sights are a mix of gorgeous parks and whatever cultural bits and pieces ended up in this largely residential neighborhood. Travelers with limited time in Berlin should note that attractions here are few and far between, and aren't easily and efficiently visited.

▨ GRUNEWALD AND THE JAGDSCHLOß

⊛ PARK

Am Grunewaldsee 29 (Access from Pücklerstr.)   ☎030 813 35 97 💻www.spsg.de

This 3 sq. km park, with winding paths through wild underbrush, gridded pines, and a peaceful lake, is popular dog-walking turf and a great change from the rest of the bustling Berlin. About a 1km walk into the woods is the **Jadgschloß**, a restored royal hunting lodge that houses a gallery of portaits and paintings by German artists like Graff and Cranach. The house is the picture of understated elegance, surrounded by even more blooming botany. The one-room hunting lodge is worth skipping, unless you find pottery shards particularly gripping. Instead, walk around the grounds, or take a hike north in the forest to **Teufelsberg** ("Devil's Mountain"), the highest point in Berlin, made of rubble from World War II piled over a Nazi military school.

⚐ *U3 or U7: Fehrbelliner Pl., or S45 or S46: Hohenzollerndamm then bus #115 (dir. Neuruppiner Str. of Spanische Alle/Potsdamer): Pücklerstr. Turn left on Pücklerstr. following the signs and continue straight into the forest to reach the lodge.* ⓘ *Check the Jadgschloß visitor's center for a map.* Ⓢ *Admission to the hunting lodge €4, €3 students. Tours in German offered on the weekends €1.* ⌚ *Open Tu-Su 10am-6pm.*

BRÜCKE MUSEUM

MUSEUM

Bussardsteig 9   ☎030 831 20 29 💻www.brueckemusuem.de

This museum displays an uncommon collection of Brücke art, German impressionism inspired by its French contemporaries. The brief *Die Brücke* ("The Bridge") stylistic period was characterized by bright, fierce colors. The Brücke Museum building, inside the Grunewald forest, is a work of contemporary art itself. The staff loves the collection (which says something), and often rotates special exhibitions displaying pieces related to the Brücke period, including the obvious French Impressionist works, but also world art, such as African craft works.

🚇 U3 or U7: Fehberlliner Pl., then bus #115 (dir. Neuruppiner Str. to Spanische Allee/Potsdammer): Pücklerstr. $ €4, €3 students. For a ticket including special exhibits, €5/4. ⏰ Open M and W-Su 11am-5pm.

GAY MEMORIAL — MEMORIAL

Just outside the Nollendorf U-Bahn station

Blink and you might miss it. This unassuming, unmarked memorial is shaped like a Crayola crayon, and striped with as many colors as a box of the art supply. The small monument commemorates the homosexuals killed in World War II.

🚇 U1, U3, U4, or U9: Nollendorfpl.

ST. NORBERT KIRCHE CEMETERY — CEMETERY

Access from Belzinger Str., between Martin-Luther-Str. and Eisenacher Str.

Sunken in a few feet from street level and walled off by unlocked gates, this enchanting cemetery brings R.I.P. to the living. With a mix between manicured shrubs and a patch of wild, over-grown ivy in front of every tomb, a quick stop here on a busy day is beautiful. An adjoining children's playground outside the gates brightens things up. We wouldn't say this is worth a trip itself, but the cemetery is good for a stroll after stepping out of one of Schöneberg's popular cafes.

🚇 U7: Eisenacherstr. ⏰ Gate usually locked by 6pm.

VIKTORIA-LUISE-PLATZ — PARK

On Motzstr., where it intersects Winterfeldstr.

This relaxed hangout is just a block south of the lively scene on Fuggerstr. Named after the daughter of Wilhelm II, this park channels the extravagance of an older bourgeois Berlin. A large central fountain is encircled by hedges, and a semi-circular stone-worked arch with detailed columns marks one end. This is a favorite summer picnic spot for locals, thanks to the city-maintained gardens.

🚇 U4: Viktoria-Luise-Pl.

APOSTLE PAULUS KIRCHE — CHURCH

Klixstr. 2 (Grunewaldstr.) ☎030 781 12 80 💻www.apostel-paulus-gemeinde.de

Apostle Paulus Kirche is the best known and perhaps most architecturally significant church in all of Schöneberg. Black and dark green brickwork intricately patterns the exterior a series of gothic arches. The church is often used by community choirs and a range of other performers who visit for the acclaimed acoustics.

🚇 U7: Eisenacher Str. ℹ Check website for information on upcoming events. $ Church only open during service hours; Su at 10am, meditative morning prayers every M from 9:15-9:30am.

MITTE

Like any KFC, Mitte contains 95% good stuff and 5% crap. Stick with the recommendations, and you'll be fine. You're on your own with KFC.

✔ PERGAMON MUSEUM — 🎟♿ MUSEUM

Am Kupfergraben 5 ☎0302 090 55 77 💻www.smb.museum

If it kept its two main exhibits, the Pergamon temple and the Ishtar Gate, the rest of this museum could show off cotton balls and it'd still be worth it. The museum reconstructs the Pergamon temple nearly to its full size, and the battle mural on the wall displays jagged toothed snakes ripping off heroes' arms while titans rip lions' mouths apart. The Mesopotamian Ishtar Gate, reconstructed tile-by-original-tile, rises 30m into the air, then stretches 100m down a hallway. You'll hardly believe it.

🚇 U2, U5, U8: Alexanderpl. $ €10, students €5. Free Th after 6pm. ⏰ Open M-W 10am-6pm, Th 10am-10pm, F-Su 10am-6pm.

✔ TOPOGRAPHY OF TERROR — ♿🍸 MUSEUM

Niederkirchner Str. 8 ☎0302 545 09 50 💻www.topographie.de

This exhibit opened May 2010 and looks at the origins, development, and deployment of Nazi terror from 1930 to 1946. This detailed, personalized, fair, and informative exhibition provides one of the best insights into Nazi strategies and the extent of the horror. No detail (or image) is deemed off-limits, and travelers with weak stomachs are warned. That said, the conclusions of this exhibit are so incredibly important and so poorly understood that a trip here should really be considered a must. A bookshop, cafe, and library take up the bottom floor, while a segment of the Berlin Wall and the excavated foundations of Hitler's old terror headquarters fill out an enormous, otherwise empty, courtyard.

U2: Potsdamer Pl. From the Metro, head east on Leipziegerstr. and take a right on Wilhelm-Leipziegerstr. The exhibit is directly across from the Hi-Flyer. $ Free. ⏰ Open daily 10am-8pm.

MEMORIAL TO THE MURDERED JEWS OF EUROPE — ♿ MEMORIAL

Cora-Berliner-Str. 1 ☎0302 639 43 11 💻www.stiftung-denkmal.de

Imposing concrete blocks equidistant from each other commemorate the Jews who were killed by the National Socialists. If you're looking for reflection or somberness, you won't find it aboveground, where kids play hide and seek, tourists nap on blocks, and policemen from the nearby American embassy work in a paranoid frenzy to keep cars from stopping. See the memorial quickly, then head below ground for a moving, informative exhibit on the Jewish history of WWII. Especially devastating is the "family" room, which presents pre-war Jewish family portraits and then investigates the individual fates of the family members. The last room continuously plays one of thousands of compiled mini-biographies of individuals killed in the Holocaust. To read the bios of every murdered Jew would take over six years.

U2: Potsdamer Pl. From the Metro, walk north on Ebertstr. $ Free. ⏰ Open daily Apr-Sept 10am-8pm; Oct-Mar 10am-7pm.

HOMOSEXUAL MEMORIAL — ♿ MEMORIAL

On Ebertstr. 💻www.stiftung-denkmal.de/en/homosexualmemorial

While Berlin now accepts homosexuality like few places do in the world, it wasn't so until 1969, before which homosexuality was illegal under a law passed by the Nazis. As a result, homosexuals were not included in many memorials against Nazi violence. This memorial, which opened in 2008, consists of a giant block with a screen that plays a video of two men kissing on loop—though part of the memorial, this video is set to change every two years.

U2: Potsdamer Pl. From the Metro, walk north on Ebertstr. The memorial will be on your left, in the garden. ⏰ Open 24hr.

HOUSE OF WORLD CULTURES — ♿ 🍸 EXHIBIT HALL

John-Foster-Dulles-Allee 10 ☎3039 78 70 💻www.hkw.de

Originally built by the Americans to show off to the nearby East Berliners, the House of World Cultures now hosts festivals, movie screenings, lectures, and an incredible anarchist bookstore in a bizarre structure that's been affectionately called "The Pregnant Clam." The formless statue in the pool out front becomes a butterfly when you view its reflection.

U55: Bundestag. From the Metro, head southwest down Paul Löbe Allee. $ Free. Event prices vary. ⏰ Open daily 10am-7pm. Exhibitions open M 11am-7pm, W-Su 11am-7pm.

NEUES MUSEUM — ♿ MUSEUM

Bodestr. 1 💻www.neues-museum.de

One of the top museums in the city, this collection of Egyptian and Greek antiquities goes beyond what you'd expect. Mummies abound, sarcophogi run rampant, and somewhere in it all, that famous bust of Nefertiti—yeah, that one—sits glowing in her own room. The building was heavily damaged in the war, and this new New Museum does a brilliant job of incorporating the old structure into a fantastically modern creation. To avoid the lines, reserve a ticket online.

🚇 U6: Friedrichstr. S5,S7,S75,or S9: Hackescher Markt. *i* Tickets correspond to a time, and after they've been purchased visitors must return at the time printed on their ticket. No line Th 6-8pm. 💲 €10, students €5. Free Th after 6pm. 🕐 Open M-W 10am-6pm, Th-Sa 10am-8pm, Su 10am-6pm.

SOVIET MEMORIAL
♿♨ MEMORIAL

Str. des 17 Juni

WWII tanks and anti-aircraft guns flank this memorial built by the Soviets in 1945. It is estimated that between eight to 10 million Soviets died fighting in the war, including 80,000 who died in the Battle of Berlin.

🚇 Bus #100: Pl. der Republik. Head south through Tiergarten to Str. des 17 Juni and take a right. 💲 Free. 🕐 Open 24hr.

BRANDENBERG GATE
♿ GATE

Pariser Pl. ☎0302 263 30 17

During the day, tourists swarm this famous 18th-century gate; the wise traveler will return at night to see it lit in a blaze of gold. Friederich Wilhelm II built the gate as a symbol of military victory, but Germans these days prefer to shy away from that designation, you know, because of WWI and, uh, WWII. A system of gates once surrounded it, but today only this most famous gate remains.

🚇 U55: Brandenburg Tor. 💲 Free. 🕐 Open 24hr.

HUMBOLDT UNIVERSITY
♿ UNIVERSITY

Unter den Linden 6

Home to some of the greatest thinkers of the modern age, including Freud and Einstein, this university is closed to the public and doesn't make much of a sight touring-wise, but it's neat to stop by and feel like you're somehow being involved in something. During the day, vendors sell used books out in front. Maybe you'll find Einstein's old unread copy of *The Mayor of Casterbridge*.

🚇U2: Hausvogteipl. From the Metro, walk north along Oberwalstraße.

THE KENNEDYS
🚶♿ MUSEUM

Pariser Pl. 4A ☎030 20 65 35 70 🖥www.thekennedys.de

A mostly photographic exhibit of this family that had such strong ties to Berlin. Incomprehensibly, this musuem has a book of its entire exhibit in the lobby and bookstore. Just look through this and save the money. The museum also features various temporary exhibitions.

🚇 Bus TXL 100/200. 💲 €7, students €3.50. 🕐 Open daily 10am-6pm.

VICTORY COLUMN
🚶⊗♈ MONUMENT

Großer Stern 1 ☎030 391 29 61 🖥www.monument-tales.de

This 27m tall monument celebrates Prussia's victory over France in 1880. The statue of Victoria at the top is made of melted-down French cannons, and during WWII, Hitler had the statue moved to its present location to increase its visibility. The column is under renovation; an exhibition that examines the significance of various "monuments" built throughout the world is expected to be finished in 2011.

🚇 U9:Hansapl. *i* Present your ticket at the cafe to get a €0.50 discount on all drinks. 💲 €2.20, students €1.50. 🕐 Open Apr-Oct M-F 9:30am-6:30pm, Sa-Su 9:30am-7pm; Nov-Mar M-F 10am-5pm, Sa-Su 10am-5:30pm.

NEUE WACHE
♿ MEMORIAL

Unter den Linden 4 ☎030 25 00 25

This building was built as a guard house for the nearby city palace (hence, "New Watch"). The building has been used as a number of memorials since then, and in 1969 the remains of an unknown soldier and an unknown concentration camp victim were laid to rest here. Since 1993 the Neue Wache has served as the central memorial of the Federal Republic of Germany for the Victims of War and Tyranny. A statue of a mother holding her dead son stands alone in the center of an enormous empty room.

U2: Hausvogteipl. From the Metro, walk north along Oberwalstr. $ Free. ⏰ Open daily 10am-6pm. The interior of the monument is still visible when the building's gate is closed.

BEBELPLATZ
♿ SQUARE

Bebelpl.

In 1933, a crazed group of Nazi students raided the Humboldt library and burned over 20,000 volumes of "un-German" books written by Jews, communists, and homosexuals. A plaque displays Heinreich Heines's prophetic words: "Only where they burn books, will they eventually burn people." Visitors can look down through a glass window into a library full of empty white shelves. It's spooky.

U2: Hausvogteipl. From the Metro, walk north along Oberwalstr.

SCHLOßPLATZ
♿ SQUARE

Schloßpl.

Schloßplatz manages to be a sight where castles themselves are feuding. The Berliner Schloß, the Hohenzollern imperial palace stood on this spot until the communists tore it down in 1950 to build the Palast der Republick. After reunification, the Palast der Republick was torn down, this time to make way for a replica of the Berliner Schloß. The new building will house the collections of Humboldt University among other exhibitions. Construction is set to start in 2013 and finish in 2019. Currently, the field sits open in some parts, while others are under excavation. A nearby visitors center has German-only information on the forthcoming building.

U2: Hausvogteipl. From the Metro, walk north along Oberwalstr. and take a right on Französische Str. Continue it across the canal bridge. ⏰ Visitors center open daily 10am-6pm.

FERNSHEHTURM
TOWER

Panoramastr. 1A ☎030 242 3333 www.tv-turm.de

At 368m, the Fernshehturm, literally "TV Tower," trumps all other sky-ticklers in the EU. It's shaped like a lame 1950s space probe on purpose; commies wanted folk to think of Sputnik when they saw it. In the DDR's defense, it wasn't its biggest miscalculation. This supposed "triumph of Soviet technology" was actually completed by Swedish engineers when construction faltered. Elevators now shoot more than a million people each year to a height of 200m where they can dig a 360° panorama, grab a drink at the bar, or stomach an incredibly pricey meal. The height plays especially well in Berlin, which has few tall buildings.

U2, U5, U8: Alexanderpl. $ €10.50, under 16 €6.50. ⏰ Open daily Mar-Oct 9am-midnight; Nov-Feb 10am-midnight.

ROTES RATHAUS
CITY HALL

Rathausstr. 15 ☎0309 02 60

This imposing red brick structure looks like the world's most intense East Coast private high school, but it used to be the East Berlin City Hall and now houses the Berlin Senate. Senate? In Berlin? But Berlin's a city! Well, actually, traveler, Berlin is one of the 16 states that make up the Federal Republic of Germany. Each district of Berlin has a mayor, and individual state senators who conduct business at the Rotes Rathaus.

U2: Klosterstr. From the Metro, head north.

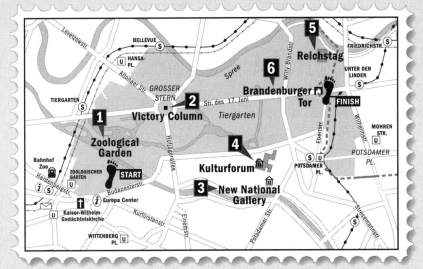

tiergarten

1. ZOOLOGICAL GARDEN. The oldest and most popular zoo in Germany is home to almost 1,500 species of flora and fauna. Frederick William IV, King of Prussia, donated animals from the pheasantry and menagerie of the Tiergarten to comprise the zoo's starter collection.

2. VICTORY COLUMN. Heinrich Strack designed the column to commemorate Prussian victory in the Danish-Prussian War. The 35-ton bronze statue of Victoria was later added to celebrate victories in the Austro-Prussian and Franco-Prussian Wars. The Prussians won a lot of wars.

3. NEW NATIONAL GALLERY. The "temple of light and glass" houses a collection that ranges from early modern art to pieces from the 1960s—not just light and glass. Plan ahead if you're hoping to see a particular work; when temporary exhibitions are on show, the permanent collection is closed.

4. KULTURFORUM. This building complex—comprised of the Philharmonic Hall, the Musical Instrument Museum, and the Chamber Music Hall—is the perfect place to get your groove back.

5. REICHSTAG. After German reunification, intensive restoration brought the meeting place of the German Parliament to its present-day splendor. Climb to the roof and peer through the building's 1200-ton glass dome to witness some democracy.

6. BRANDENBURGER TOR. On November 9, 2009, 1000 foam dominoes were lined up along the former route of the Berlin Wall, and converged here to celebrate the "Festival of Freedom"—the 20th anniversary of the wall's fall.

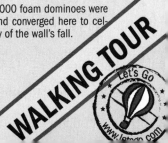

MARIENKIRCHE
🚫♿ CHURCH

Karl-Liebknecht-Str. 8 ☎0302 500 25 🖥www.marienkirche-berlin.de

The oldest still-standing medieval church in Berlin (est. 1270) has one of the most frightening murals you'll ever see: a line of saints and kings perform the dance of death alongside a line of skeletons who look more like space creatures from *The X-Files*. There's a Dan Brown novel here waiting to be written.

🚇 U2, U5, U8: Alexanderpl. $ Free. ⏰ Open daily in summer 10am-9pm; in winter 10am-6pm.

SAINT HEDWIG'S CATHEDRAL
🚫♿ CATHEDRAL

Hinter der Katholischen Kirche 3 ☎0302 03 48 10 🖥www.hedwigs-kathedrale.de

Named after Harry Potter's owl (not really), the biggest and oldest Catholic cathedral in the city also looks like no cathedral you've seen before. Round like a *yurt*, this church's altar is actually a level down, while the seats are located on the ground level. The interior has also been recently renovated with a cool Space-Age roof and hanging sets of 10 glowing balls that make the place feel like something out of Kubrick. Still, the place is rich in history, having been established as a haven for Catholics by Frederick II in 1773.

🚇 U2: Hausvogteipl. From the Metro, walk north along Oberwalstr. Look for the copper dome. $ Free. ⏰ Open M-F 10am-5pm, Sa 10am-4:30pm, Su 1-5pm.

REICHSTAG
💳♿🍸 PARLIAMENT

Pl. der Republik 1 ☎0302 273 21 52 🖥www.bundestag.de

Visitors to the German parliament building can climb the roof's 1200-ton glass dome that looks down into the main chamber as a symbol of the "openness" of German democracy. It also serves to focus sunlight into the government chambers via an aggressive spire of mirrored fragments that juts down toward the floor. A free, automated audio tour tracks your movements up and down the nearly 300m ramp. Stop off at the very top for a swell view of the Berlin skyline and to marvel at the fact that this dome—and therefore the Reichstag—has no roof. Rain, snow, and sleet all fall into the building and land in a giant "cone" located on the dome's floor. Visitors can trek around the roof terrace to avoid the solar panels that make the Reichstag the world's only zero-emission congress. Across the way stand a series of futuristic government offices that have been affectionately termed "the Washing Machine." If viewing democracy makes you hungry, stop at the restaurant located on the roof.

🚇 Bus #100: Pl. der Republik. $ Free. ⏰ Open daily 8am-10pm.

SHLOß BELLEVUE
PALACE

Spreeweg 1 ☎0302 00 00

This palace, home of the German president, was the first Neoclassical building in Germany. What? That doesn't excite you? Then try this: when there's a gala, watch from the street as the privileged drink cocktails.

🚇U9: Hansapl. From the Metro, head east past the Victory Column. ⏰ Never open to you.

HI-FLYER BALLOON
💳♿🍸 HOT-AIR BALLOON

Wilhelmstr. ☎0302 266 788 11 🖥www.air-service-berlin.de

The best thing that can be said about the Hi-Flyer Balloon is that it actually gets cooler as you approach it. What looks like an annoying, touristy balloon becomes a pretty enormous, annoying, touristy balloon. Even so, if you want a 15min. trip 150m into the air, this balloon obliges. Always call ahead to see if weather conditions allow for flying.

🚇 U6: Kochstr. $ €19, students €13. ⏰ Open daily Apr-Oct 10am-10pm; Nov-Mar 11am-6pm.

BERLINER DOM
🚫💳♿ CHURCH

Am Lustgarten ☎0302 026 91 19 🖥www.berlinerdom.de

You'll probably spend the whole time thinking how big a bowl of cereal the inverted dome would make; in other words, it's a fantastically enormous dome and a ridiculously beautiful church. "Dom" means cathedral in German; since this 1905 church belongs to the Protestants, it's technically not a cathedral, but in terms of grandeur it blows away most cathedrals you've seen. A museum upstairs shows various failed incarnations of the church, and if you climb some sketchy-feeling backstairs, you can actually get to a roof terrace lookout. Don't forget the basement with the most luxurious crypt you've ever seen, housing the ghosts of lightweights like the Hohenzollern kings.

U2, U5, U8: Alexanderpl. $ €5, students €3. ⏰ Open Apr-Sept M-Sa 9am-8pm, Su noon-8pm; Oct-Mar Ma-Sa 9am-7pm, Su noon-7pm.

ALTES MUSEUM ♿ MUSEUM

Am Lustgarten 🖥www.smb.museum

A newly organized collection of Roman and Estruscan antiquities now takes up the entire first floor of this incredible musuem. Though this museum's cool in another context, those who've seen its flashier cousins, the Pergamon and the Neues, might be a bit disappointed. Check it if you've got the time; skip it if you don't.

U2, U5, U8: Alexanderpl. $ €8, students €4. Free Th after 6pm. ⏰ Open M-W 10am-6pm, Th 10am-10pm, F-Su 10am-6pm.

ALTE NATIONAL GALERIE ♿ GALLERY

Bodestr. 1-3 ☎0302 090 55 77 🖥www.smb.museum

This fantastic, small collection of mostly German art does special justice to masters like Adolph Menzel. While the building also houses several Monets, Van Goghs, and some Cézannes, the wealth of the place is in its German collection. Music fans will note the famous portrait of Richard Wagner.

U2, U5, U8: Alexanderpl. $ €8, students €4. Free Th after 6pm. ⏰ Open M-W 10am-6pm, Th 10am-10pm, F-Su 10am-6pm.

BODE MUSEUM ♿ MUSEUM

Am Kupfergraben 1 ☎0302 090 55 77 🖥www.smb.museum

Though interesting to some folk, the Bode Museum largely contains medieval art and Christian iconography, and if we have to explain to you why this is cool, you probably won't find it cool. The gorgeous building, which looks like it's floating on the water, is worth a free entrance on a Thursday night, but unless 100 depictions of Christ is your thing, your time's better spent elsewhere.

U2, U5, U8: Alexanderpl. $ €8, students €4. Free Th after 6pm. ⏰ Open M-W 10am-6pm, Th 10am-10pm, F-Su 10am-6pm.

AKADEMIE DER KÜNSTE ♿ MUSEUM

Pariser Pl. 4 ☎0302 005 70 🖥www.adk.de

Exhibits rotate every two months in this eye-pleasing modern museum that serves as the headquarters for the Akademie der Künste, an society of famous German artists. Exhibits tend toward the bold and progressive in media ranging from photo to design to traditional painting. Incredibly, the walls of this exhibit hall are the original 17th-century pieces, and the modern hall has been built around it.

Bus #100 or #200 to Brandenburg Tor. $ €5, students €3-4. Free 1st Su of the month. ⏰ Open Tu-Su 11am-10pm.

TIERGARTEN ♿ 🍸 PARK

Tiergarten

Stretching from the Brandenburg Gate in the east to the Bahnhof Zoo in the west, this Balrog-sized park is at the heart of Berlin and contains some of its most famous iconic monuments including the Column of Victory and the Soviet

War Memorial. Str. des 17 Juni bisects the park from east to west, and frequently hosts parades or celebrations. During the 2010 World Cup, the city blocked off the entire street from June to July and presented the World Cup on 10 enormous screens to daily hordes of thousands of fans. It was drunk and it was loud. The park also contains some beautiful paths and gardens that can offer solace from the hipster invasion.

✠ *Bus #100 or #200: Brandenburg Tor.*

DOROTHEEN MUNICIPAL CEMETERY   ♿ CEMETERY
Chausseestr. 125

Hegel, one of the most important historians of the 19th century, lies dead here along with Bertold Brecht, who might be the most important playwright of the 1900s. If graves don't get your blood running, this body grove also makes a great park. A map near the entrance points out graves of interest.

✠ *U6: Oranienburger Tor. From the U-Bahn, head north on Chausseestr.* ☒ *Open daily 8am-dusk.*

UNTER DER LINDEN   ♿ STREET
Unter Der Linden

Many of Berlin's most famous sites, including Bebelplatz, the Neue Wache, and the Berlin Opera House, lie along this wide boulevard, which dates back to the 16th century, when it was a palace path leading to the royal hunting grounds. The street gets its name from the rows of linden trees that run through the middle. Today, the path makes perfect grounds for biking, especially at night, while during the day small cafes and ice-cream shops feed the mostly tourist crowd roaming the grounds. The statue of Frederick the Great starts the row of trees, and nothing less than the Brandenburg Gate ends it. If you're lucky—and somewhat unlucky—a group of drunk Aussies will pedal by on the 10-person

bicycle-beer bar that runs up and down this street.

🚌 *Bus #100 or #200: Brandenburg Tor.*

TACHELES

⊕⊘♀ GALLERY

Oranienburger Str. 53

An unforgettable experience day or night, this bombed-out department store has become a living, breathing street-art metropolis. Bars, galleries, a movie theater, faux beach exterior, and sculpture garden/workshop all exist where every available space is covered in graffiti art, human piss, or both. *But it's worth it.* Seating options in the outside bars range from lifeguard towers to forklifts.

🚇 *U6: Oranienburger Tor.* Ⓢ *Free to enter; most galleries cost €1-5.* Ⓞ *Open 8am-late.*

CENTRUM JUDAICUM: NEW SYNAGOGUE

⊕⊘ SYNAGOGUE

Oranienburger Str. 28-30 ☎88028 316 🖳centrumjudaicum.de

The New Synagogue, built in 1866, was once one of the most awesome Jewish temples in Europe, with 3200 seats and a 50m dome. Almost completely destroyed, first by Nazi violence, then by American bombs, after 1989 the building's exterior and dome were restored, and the building became the museum, cultural center, and miniature synagogue that it remains today. The exhibit on the original synagogue is small and only justified by a pre-existing interest in the building's history. The dome, too, disappoints somewhat, and most visitors will be satisfied with a strut past the front.

🚇 *U6: Oranienburger Tor.* **i** *Information in English.* Ⓢ *Permanent exhibition €3, reduced €2. Dome €1.50, reduced €1.* Ⓞ *Open Apr-Sept M 10am-8pm, Tu-Th 10am-6pm, F 10am-5pm, Su 10am-8pm; Oct and Mar M 10am-8pm, Tu-Th 10am-6pm, F 10am-2pm, Su 10am-8pm; Nov-Feb M-Th 10am-6pm, F 10am-2pm, Su 10am-6pm.*

POTSDAMER PLATZ

♀ SQUARE

Potsdamer Pl.

Berlin's answer to Times Sq. feels like the inside of the Death Star, since an enormous antenna-like spoke sticks down from what seems a giant satellite dish. This new commerical center of Berlin sees fancy tourist-heavy restaurants serve unexciting food beside a fountain that actually is exciting. The square additionally has three movie theaters, a Sony Design store, and a museum dedicated to German film history.

🚇 *U2: Potsdamer Pl.* Ⓢ *Free.* Ⓞ *Hours vary.*

NEUE NATIONAL GALLERIE

🍴♿♀ MUSEUM

Potsdamer Str. 50 ☎0302 66 42 45 10 🖳www.smb.museum

The be-all end-all of early 20th-century painting in Berlin, this museum's building is almost as famous as its collection. Strange temporary exhibits live upstairs in the so-called "Temple of Light and Glass" designed by Mies van der Rohe, while the basement holds a treasure trove of primarily German paintings and sculptures. Works by Edward Munch, Franz Marc, and Max Ernst are just a few of the highlights. Sadly, in the 1930s, key works were labeled "degenerate" by the Nazis and have since disappeared from the collection. Missing works appear as black-and-white photocopies and are still hung throughout the gallery.

🚇 *U2: Potsdamer Pl.* **i** *Audio tour included in the price of admission.* Ⓢ *€10, students €5. Free Th after 6pm.* Ⓞ *Open M-W 10am-6pm, Th 10am-10pm, F-Sa 10am-6pm.*

MUSEUM FOR FILM AND TELEVISION

🍴♿ MUSEUM

Potsdamer Str. 2 ☎30 300 903 0 🖳www.deutsche-kinemathek.de

A fun little exhibit on the history of German cinema, with a special emphasis on the work of Fritz Lang and Marlene Dietrich. Not a must-see, but the production photos and set drawings of *The Cabinet of Dr. Caligari* and *Metropolis* are worth the admission price alone. Film buffs will be rewarded, and film gruffs will still find a few things to tickle them. A TV library lets visitors watch old German TV. If you thought their *wars* were crazy...

U2: Potsdamer Pl. $ €5, students €3. Audio tour €4/3. Open Tu-W 10am-6pm, Th 10am-8pm, F-Su 10am-6pm.

ZIONS CHURCH CHURCH

Zionskirchstr. 44 ☎0308 870 98 70 www.zionskirche-berlin.de

This quiet little church in North Mitte suffered damage and looting after the war and only recently have modest renovation efforts begun. While the 140-year-old church may not have the history of some of Berlin's houses of worship, its neglect makes a visit here all the more worthwhile. A beautiful tower rises high from a natural hill while the church's interior remains unadorned, empty, and candlelit.

U8: Roenthaler Pl. From the Metro, head northeast on Weinbergsweg. $ Free. Open daily 9am-7pm.

BERTOLD BRECHT HAUS MUSEUM

Chausseestr. 125 ☎030 200 57 1844 www.adk.de

Bertold Brecht revolutionized theater with such masterworks as the *Three Penny Opera*, and this tour lets you glimpse into his personal life. While Brecht only lived (and died) here from 1953 to 1956, the same is true of his other addresses—Brecht "changed countries as often as shoes," so don't feel like you're getting a raw deal. Preserved by his wife, the Brechtian actress Helen Weigel, Brecht's apartment (two studies and the bedroom where he croaked) contains his library and other small artifacts of note. Come with an English-speaking crew so they do the tour in English; otherwise you'll be stuck reading along and wondering if the Germans are mocking you each time they laugh.

U6: Oranienburger Tor. From the U-Bahn, head north on Chausseestr. The house will be on your left. There isn't a good sign or anything, so look for the address. i All tours are guided. $ €4, students €2.50. Tours every 30min. Tu 10-11:30am, 2-3:30pm. W 10-11:30am. Th 10-11:30am, 5-6:30pm. F 10am, 10:30am, and 11:30am. Sa 10-noon, 1-3:30pm. Su 11am, noon, 1, 2, 3, 4, 5, and 6pm.

HACKESCHER MARKT ♿🍸 SQUARE

Hackescher Markt

Grungy electric didgeridoo acts rock off against angsty singer/songwriters who trade chords with father/son jazz duos. Vendors hawk wares and street artists juggle fire in this beautiful square that runs along the train tracks. Tons of outdoor restaurants. Plaid is everywhere and there's an American Apparel for kids. Yikes.

S5, S7, S9, S75: Hackescher Markt.

HAMBURGER BANHOFF MUSEUM ♿🍸 MUSEUM

Invalidenstr. 50-51 ☎03039 78 34 39 www.hamburgerbahnhof.de

This modern art museum does a good job of mixing traditionally recognized modern masterworks (Andy Warhol, etc.) with whacked out temporary exhibitions. Maybe you'll enter a room where clowns throw basketballs at you from TV screens. Maybe you find a room filled with a large black tunnel and you'll feel sorry for the security guard who works here alone with this tunnel. While you should avoid getting his job, the museum itself is massive, stretching the entire length of the old station house. If modern art even slightly tickles you, this joint's worth a look.

S5, S7, S9, or S75: Hauptbahnhof. $ €12, students €6. Open Tu-F 10am-6pm, Sa 11am-8pm, Su 11am-6pm.

DEUTSCHER DOM

MUSEUM

Gendarmenmarkt 1-2 ☎0302 273 04 31 🖥 www.bundestag.de

Originally an 18th-century Protestant church, this building was completely destroyed during the war. It has now been rebuilt and houses a museum of German government called "Milestones, Setbacks, Sidetracks." The exhibit is only in German, and though the free English audio tour helps, the main enjoyment of this building comes from considering its estimation of Nazi dictatorship as a "setback" and looking up the narrow belltower from the lobby.

U2: Hausvogteipl. $ Free. ⏰ Open daily Oct-Apr 10am-6pm; May-Sept 10am-7pm.

GENDARMENMARKT

SQUARE

Gendarmenmarkt

The plaza that includes the Deutscher Dome also contains Koncerthaus Berlin, where the Berlin Philharmonic Symphony plays, and the Französischer Dom, an 18th-century church built for French Huguenots (Protestants). In July, the Berlin Symphony Orchestra plays free night concerts outside, while the tower of the Französischer Dom provides a view of the city. Easily one of the most beautiful squares in Europe. For a kick, read some of the menus of the fancy cafes around the square that try to be "bourgeois hip" and offer such pairings as currywurst and champagne.

U2: Hausvogteipl. $ Französischer Dom Tower €2.50. ⏰ Tower open daily 10am-6pm.

CURRYWURST MUSEUM

MUSEUM

Schützenstr. 70 ☎0308 871 86 30 🖥 www.currywurstmuseum.de

The hilarious Currywurst Museum expertly traces the origins of this Berlin treat from a small kitchen in Germany to the mouths of Berliners everywhere. Exhibits are very hands-on (squeeze a ketchup bottle and it sings to you) and sometimes mouths-on, since each ticket comes with a sample of the wurst in question. A gift shop sells sausages, hats, shirts, spices, and more. Good story and great resource for the currywurst scholar.

U2, U6: Stadtmitte. $ €11, students €7. Entrance includes a cup of currywurst. ⏰ Open daily 10am-10pm.

PRENZLAUER BERG

BERLINER MAUER DOKUMENTATIONZENTRUM

MUSEUM, MONUMENT

Bernauer Str. 111 ☎030 464 1030 🖥 www.berliner-mauer-dokumentationzentrum.de

A remembrance complex, museum, chapel, and entire city block of the preserved Berlin Wall, two concrete barriers separated by the open *Todesstreife*, or death strip, come together in a memorial to "victims of the communist tyranny." The church is made of an inner oval of poured cement walls, lit from above by a large skylight, with gaps that look out over a field of tall grasses and poppies. The museum has assembled a comprehensive collection of all things Wall. Exhibits include photos, film clips, and sound bites. Climb up a staircase to see the wall from above.

U8: Bernauer Str. $ Free. ⏰ Open Tu-Su Apr-Oct 9:30am-7pm; Nov-Mar 9:30am-6pm.

JÜDISCHER FRIEDHOF

CEMETERY

On Schönehauser Allee; enter by the Lapidarium

Prenzlauer Berg was one of the major centers of Jewish Berlin during the 19th and early 20th centuries. The ivy-covered Jewish cemetery contains the graves of Giacomo Meyerbeer and Max Liebermann and is studded by impressively high, dark tombs under towering old trees. Nearby, **Synagogue Rykstrasse** *(Rykestr. 53)* is one of Berlin's loveliest synagogues. It was spared on *Kristallnacht* thanks to its inconspicuous location. Unfortunately, visitors are not allowed in, as the synagogue still operates as a school.

✈ *U2: Senefelderpl.* Ⓢ *Free.* 🕐 *Open M-Th 8am-4pm, F 8am-1pm.*

KOLLWITZPLATZ

PARK, MONUMENT

Directly below Wörther Str.

This little triangle of greenery is one big playground, with toddlers climbing over tree stumps, jungle gyms, and even the lap of Käthe Kollwitz's statue. Close by, a magical little playground with a small bridge, stream, and willow trees is another popular destination for young moms with energetic kids. Non-parents are drawn by the upscale market on Saturdays, where vendors sell everything from boar meat sausage to handmade ravioli.

✈ *U2: Senefelderpl.* Ⓢ *Free.*

ZEISS-GROSSPLANETARIUM

PLANETARIUM

Prenzlauer Allee 80 ☎030 421 84 50 💻www.astw.de

In 1987 this planetarium opened as the most modern facility of its kind in the DDR. Compared to its peers in the West, it seems about as technologically advanced as a tricycle, but it can still show you the stars. No exhibits here, only shows; check the website or call in advance for times.

✈ *S8, S41, S42, or tram M2: Prenzlauer Allee. From the stop, the planetarium is across the bridge.* Ⓢ *€5, students €4.* 🕐 *Open Tu 9am-noon, W 9am-noon and 1:30-3pm, Th 9am-noon, F 7-9pm, Sa 2:30-9pm, Su 1:30-5pm.*

KULTURBRAUEREI

COMMUNITY SPACE

Schönehauser Allee 36 ☎030 44 43 56 20 💻www.kulturbrauerei-berlin.de

A former brewery, the Kulturbrauerei now calls itself the "cultural melting pot" of a diverse Berlin. Home to offices, restaurants, and a cinema, this old brick building tower and courtyard hosts community events, including salsa lessons and local theater performances. For the traveler, this space might be best enjoyed as a brief peek at the interesting architecture.

✈ *U2: Senefelderpl.*

WASSERTURM PRENZLAUER BERG

PARK, WATER TOWER

Berlin's oldest water tower was built to supply the rapidly growing population of workers in Prenzlauer Berg with water. Below the tower were the homes of the former machinery operators, still occupied today as apartments. The area around the tower has since been converted into a park with excellent views of Prenzlauer Berg, the TV Tower, and suntanning Germans.

✈ *U2: Senefelderpl. Between Knaackstr. and Belforter Str. in Kollwitzkiez*

FRIEDRICHSHAIN

🏛 VOLKSPARK

PARK

Volkspark is the second-largest park in Berlin and its oldest. This 52-hectare park is too big to feel crowded, even with masses of dog-walkers and suntanners filling the paths and grassy lawns. Since opening in 1840, monuments and memorials have been added here and there around the green spaces. In 1913 the **Fairy Fountain** was added, representing 10 characters from the book *The Brothers Grimm.* The rubble from two bunkers that were bombed and destroyed in World War II was piled into a war monument in 1950, now called **Mont Klemont,** and is sometimes used as a platform for open-air concerts and movie screenings in the summer. Statues that commemorate the Polish soldiers and German antifascists were built in 1972.

✈ *S8 or S10: Landsberger Allee. Alternatively, U5: Strausbgr. Pl. Bounded by Am Friedrichshain to the north, Danziger Str. to the east, Landsberger Allee to the south, and Friedenstr. Str. to the south.*

palace prowl

Come for the beer. Come for the bratwurst. Come for the museums. Come for the music. There are, at last count, a million reasons to come to Berlin. But palaces just aren't one of them. Berlin has about as many royal castles in its city limits as, say, Philadelphia.

And what is perhaps slightly odd by American standards is absolutely shocking by castle-crowded, palace-packed European city ones. Don't get me wrong—Berlin is full of Baroque, Romantic, and otherwise intricately detailed, elaborate buildings of the first class. It's just that almost none of them were built by or lived in by kings.

I had no idea where all the palaces went. Until today. When I found them. All of them. In a single 600-acre space.

Potsdam. There, I said it—now you know. The castles are in Potsdam. It was here, about a half hour from the city center, that Friedrich II built himself a gilded playground of incredible schloßes, Chinese teahouses, windmills, and whatever the heck else he wanted (being king, you see, he didn't have to worry about permits). And all these stunning buildings are in a single royal park: the **Sanssouci.** Bike paths and walking trails weave through the beautifully planned park, filled with meadows of tall grasses, jasmine bushes, towering chestnut trees...and then wham! All of a sudden you're standing at the front door of a palace. It's unbelievable. It's breathtaking. It's the most wonderful feeling of discovery and awe and reverence for what are, I can guarantee you, some of the most beautiful buildings you'll ever see. It's Disneyland with palaces instead of rides, bike paths instead of lines, and (it is Germany, after all), overpriced beer instead of overpriced ice cream.

Sophia Angelis

EAST SIDE GALLERY — MONUMENT

Along Mühlenstr. 🖥www.eastsidegallery.com

The longest remaining portion of the Berlin Wall, this 1.3km stretch of cement slabs has been converted into the world's largest open-air art gallery. The Cold War graffiti wasn't preserved; instead, the current murals were painted by an international group of artists who gathered in 1989 to celebrate the end of the city's division. One of the most famous contributors is artist Dmitri Wrubel, who depicted a wet kiss between Leonid Brezhnev and East German leader Eric Honecker. The stretch of street remains unsupervised and, on the Warschauer Str. side, open at all hours, but vandalism is surprisingly rare.

🚉 U1, U15, S3, S5, S6, S7, S9, or S75: Warschauer Str. Alternatively, S5, S7, S9, or S75: Ostbahnhof. From the stops, walk back toward the river. $ Free.

STASI MUSEUM — MUSEUM

Ruschestr. 103, Haus 1 ☎030 553 68 54 🖥www.stasimuseum.de

The Lichetenberg suburb harbors perhaps the most hated and feared building of the DDR regime: the headquarters of the East German secret police, the **Staatssicherheit** or **Stasi.** During the Cold War, the Stasi kept dossiers on some six million of East Germany's own citizens, an amazing feat and a testament to the huge number of civilian informers in a country of only 16 million people.

On January 15, 1990, a crowd of 100,000 Berliners stormed and vandalized the building to celebrate the demise of the police state. Since a 1991 law made the records public, the "Horror Files" have rocked Germany, exposing millions of informants and wrecking careers, marriages, and friendships at every level of German society. Officially known today as the **Forschungs-und Gedenkstätte Normannenstrasse,** the building retains its oppressive Orwellian gloom and much of its worn 1970s aesthetic. The exhibit displays the extensive offices of Erich Mielke, the loathed Minister for State Security from 1957 to 1989, a large collection of tiny microphones and hidden cameras used for surveillance by the Stasi, and a replica of a Stasi prison cell.

❦ U5: Magdalenenstr. Ⓢ €4, students €3. Exhibits in German; English information booklet €3. Open M-F 11am-6pm, Sa-Su 2-6pm.

KARL-MARX-ALLEE   STREET

Formerly known as Stalinallee, this was the main drag of the East German Potempkin Village, where party members staged elaborate military parades. Built in the early 1950s, it is flanked by hideous gray pre-fab buildings and wedding-cake style "people's palaces" at Strausberger Pl. Covered in gleaming white plastic tiles and aluminum railings dyed gold, these "palaces" were clearly designed to impress. At the end of Strausberger Pl., the two Stalin-styled **Frankenfurter Tors** flank the street.

❦ U5: Strausbgr. Pl. or Frankfurter Tor. Starting at the intersection of Karl-Marx-Allee and Litchtenbergger Str., and running to the intersection of Karl-Marx-Allee and Petersburger Str.

KREUZBERG

While sights don't quite compare to the grand historical scope of Mitte, there is still a fair amount to see in this more real section of town. The greenery in itself is an amazing sight.

▨ DEUTSCHES TECHNIKMUSEUM BERLIN   ✈♿♈ MUSEUM
Trebbiner Str. 9   ☎03090 25 40 ◧www.sdtb.de

Don't tell the National Air and Space Museum about this place. With 30 full-sized airplanes, 20 boats—including a full-sized Viking relic—and a train from every decade since 1880, this museum could be a city in itself. Most impressive are the large mechanical demonstrations conducted throughout the day. The museum also has a garden with two windmills and a brewery.

❦ U1 or U2: Gleisdreieck. *i* Many exhibits in English. Ⓢ €4.50, students €2.50. Open Tu-F 9am-5:30pm, Sa-Su 10am-6pm.

OBERBAUMBRÜCKE   ♿ BRIDGE

Twin brick towers rise from this double-decker bridge that spans the Spree River. Once a border crossing into East Berlin, it now connects Kreuzberg to Friedrichshain. Residents of the rival neighbohoods duke it out on the bridge every July 27, when thousands of people chuck rotten vegetables at each other.

❦ U1 or U15: Schlesisches Tor.

MOLECULE MAN   ♿ STATUE
Between the bridges Elsenbrücke and Oberbaumbrücke

It's a bird! It's a plane! It's a statue that looks like three men hugging! "Molecule" refers to the porous grating the statue is constructed from, and "Man" refers to the junk between its legs. Designed by American artist Jonathan Borofsky in 1999, the 30m tall statue sitting in the middle of the river symbolizes unity.

❦ S8, S9, S41, S42, or S85: Treptower Park.

ARENA POOL   ●⊗♈ POOL
Eichenstr. 4   ☎03053 320 30 ◧www.arena-berlin.de

In the summer it's a pool floating in the river. In the winter it's a sauna. Year-round, it's awesome. Arena Pool has a bar, club, party boat, and enough Speedo-clad German men to forever give you nightmares.

⚑ S8, S9, S41, S42, or S85: Treptower Park. *i* Admission warrants unlimited pool entrance and access to bar and locker room. Ⓢ Adults €4, students €3. ⌚ Open daily 8am-late.

TEMPELHOFER PARK
                                                            ♿ ♨ 🐕 PARK
At Columbiadamm and Tempelhofdamm   ☎03070 09 06 88 🖳www.gruen-berlin.de

This expansive park was an airport, and also the drop point for the Berlin Air-lift, until 2008 when it closed forever. In 2010, the space was converted into a park where runways became jog trails and beer gardens replaced those weird caterpillar-like cart things that hold your luggage.

⚑ U6: Pl. der Luftbrücke. *i* The dog that you brought with you on your backpacking trip must stay on a leash. Ⓢ Free. ⌚ Open dawn-dusk.

CHECKPOINT CHARLIE
                                                        ♿ HISTORIC SIGHT
Zimmerstr. and Friedrichstr.

This tourist trap once had significance as the entrance point into the Ameri-can sector from East Berlin. For reasons unknown to Let's Go, it has recently become a prime tourist destination, where buses of photo-snapping lemmings buy into this scheme. Germans in American uniforms stand in the middle of the street and charge you €3 to take a picture of them; this is the most lucrative business since prostitution. A set of placards along Kochstr. provide a somewhat interesting history on the checkpoint and the various escapes it saw. Skip the musuem.

⚑ U6: Kochstraße Ⓢ Free. ⌚ Open 24hr.

BERGMANSTRASSE
                                                                 ♿ STREET
Bergmanstr. between Merringdamm and Zorrenstr.

A bubbling commercial street where street vendors mix with specialty restau-rants, hip clothing stores, and a series of conspicuous Whole Foods knock-off stores.

⚑ Pl. der Luftbrücke. From the U-bahn, head north up Merringdamm.

JEWISH MUSEUM
                                                 ✍♿♨🐕 MUSEUM
Lindenstr. 9-14   ☎0302 599 33 00 🖳www.jmberlin.de

Modern, interactive exhibits treat subjects ranging from explanations of the Torah to the philosophies of Moses Mendelssohn to the anatomy of Jewish dis-crimination under Charles V. Architect Daniel Libeskind designed the museum's building to reflect the discomfort, pain, and inherent voids in Jewish history. While most attempts at "conceptual buildings" suck grandly, this one amazingly succeeds and the effect is moving, disorienting, and thought-provoking. No two surfaces are parallel to each other; the floor is uneven, and the doors and win-dows seem like portals from a nightmare.

⚑ U1 or U6: Hallesches Tor. From the station, head east on Gitschinerstr. and take a left at Lin-denstr. Ⓢ €5, students €2.50. Audio tours €2. ⌚ Open M 10am-10pm, Tu-Su 10am-8pm. Last entry 1hr. before close.

SCHWULES MUSEUM (GAY MUSEUM)
                                                            ♨ MUSEUM
Mehringdamm 61   ☎0306 959 90 50 🖳www.schwulesmuseum.de

This little indie-feeling museum is actually state-supported, making it the world's only state-funded exhibit on homosexual persecution. Temporary exhibits take up over half of the museum, and displays are far from extensive, but the museum does offer a history rarely presented. The permanent exhibit focuses on German homosexual history from 1800 to the present.

⚑ U6 or U7: Mehringdamm. From the station, head south on Merhringdamm. The museum will be through a courtyard on your left. *i* English exhibit guide available. Ⓢ €5, students €3. ⌚ Open Tu-F 2-6pm, Sa 2-7pm.

sights • kreuzberg

rule of thumb

While ordering beer (or anything else), be careful which finger you use to indicate "one." As you may have seen in *Inglourious Basterds,* Germans use the 👍 **thumb** to ask for one, while adding the pointer finger means two. Simply holding up the second finger may earn you some confused looks from the occasional bartender.

CHARLOTTENBURG

Charlottenburg's history of wealth and opulence is still visible to the visitor in the upscale Ku'damm or in its elegant hotels. It's not surprising that inexpensive meals are difficult to come by. In north Charlottenburg, the neighborhood called Moabit (right next to Mitte) is home to strong Middle Eastern and Asian ethnic communities. For cheap, authentic Turkish or Vietnamese food, it may be worth the trip of 20min. from the Zoo.

👍 **SCHWARZES CAFE** — 🍸 BAR, RESTAURANT 3

Kantstr. 148 — ☎030 313 80 38

Pharmacies, grocery stores, and even whole neighborhoods might close down at night, but Schwarzes Cafe will still be open. Drink absinthe after dark inside the frescoed walls of the area's most popular boho cafe. The artistically peeling paint on the floors will increasingly bewilder as the absinthe gets to your head. Chase it down with breakfast when the sun comes up, or at a mere bohemian hour: all meals are served around the clock.

S3, S5, S7, S9, or S75: Savignypl. $ Weekly specials €7-13 served 11:30am-8pm. Breakfast €5-8.50. Cash only. ⏰ Open M 24hr., Tu 4am-10am, W-Su 24hr.

ABBAS — MIDDLE EASTERN 1

Huttenstr. 71 — ☎030 34 34 77 70

Abbas and the restaurants around it belong to Arabic and Asian immigrants attracted by the area's low rent. This sprawling sweet and nut shop sells a wide range of authentic Middle Eastern desserts on the cheap, from chocolate-covered lentils to pistachio-cashew pastries. Try its specialty baklava *(€1.30 for 2 pieces).*

Bus M27: Turmstr./Beusseistr. $ Cash only. ⏰ Open M-Th 10am-5pm, F and Sa noon-8pm.

MARIBEL — 🍸 RESTAURANT, BAR 3

Kantstr. 70 — ☎030 31 00 48 73 www.restaurant-maribel.de

A lovely corner restaurant with floor-to-ceiling French doors that open onto the sidewalk on sunny days, Maribel is one of the best deals for families and those with exceptionally big appetites. For Saturday and Sunday brunch *(10am-4pm),* enjoy an all-you-can-eat spread of sophisticated cheeses (sophisticated can also mean pungent), sauteed vegetables, breads, pastries, salami, and smoked salmon *(adults €9.50, ages 7-14 €4, children under 6 free).* Breakfast *(including omelettes, €4.80)* served daily until 4pm. Lunch menu served from 11:30am to close.

U7: Wilmersdorfer Str., or S3, S5, S7 or S75: Charlottenburg. $ Entrees €7-11. ⏰ Open M-Sa 9am-1am, Su 10am-1am.

PARIS BAR — 🍸 BAR, RESTAURANT 4

Kantstr. 152 — ☎030 313 80 52

One of former West Berlin's favorite gathering places is still a hot spot for hip artists, popular politicians, uber-celebs being "normal people," and students who can only afford the desserts. With warm lighting, dark wood, and a well-stocked bar, this restaurant is an option for any budget—just supplement a dish off the starter menu with some dirt-cheap döner later.

U1: Uhlandstr. $ Soups from €5.50; starters €6.50-14.50; entrees €12-25. Open daily noon-2am. Kitchen closes at 1am.

MENSA TU — CAFETERIA 1

Hardenbergerstr. 34 ☎030 939 39 74 39

It's a cafeteria, but the Hardenbergerstr. Mensa offers the cheapest hot meal around, with three-entree choices as well as vegetarian options. And our favorite part: your portion size is as much food as you can fit on a plate. Accordingly, it's overrun by university students. A slightly higher-priced cafeteria is downstairs; avoid it.

U2: Ernst-Reuter-Pl., bus #245: Steinpl., a 10min. walk from Bahnhof Zoo. $ Meals €3-4, students €2-3. Downstairs cafeteria open M-F 11am-2:30pm. Upstairs open M-F 11:30am-3:30pm, coffee bar M-F 11am-6pm, and cake shop M-F 7:30am-2:30pm.

LA PETIT FRANCE CROISSANTERIE — CAFE 1

Nürnberger Str. 24A ☎017 817 11 38 26

Fresh, inexpensive lunches are sometimes difficult to come by in sprawling Charlottenburg. This pocket-sized French bistro has some stellar baguettes and classic Francophone music to transport you across the Rhein. Try the small baguettes with a variety of toppings, including tomato, mozzarella and basil *(€2.50; large €3.30)*. Or try a light quiche and salad combo *(€4.50)*.

U3 to Ausgburger Str. Open M-Sa 8am-6:30pm.

FAM DANG — THAI AND VIETNAMESE 1

Hutten Str. 5 ☎030 75 56 75 26

Located in a predominantly Vietnamese area, Fam Dang's bright rooms, outdoor patio, and ridiculously inexpensive daily menu make it a must. The highlight is the standing soup menu, with large bowls of Thai and Vietnamese favorites *(€5)*. The entree menu rotates daily, but prices are in the same ballpark.

Bus M27: Turnstr./Beusselstr. $ Entrees €5 or less. Open M-F 11:30-9pm, Sa 2pm-9pm.

SCHÖNEBERG AND WILMERSDORF

Schöneberg's relaxed cafe culture is best experienced around the intersection of **Maaßenstrasse** and **Winterfeldstrasse.** More popular cafes and inexpensive restaurants crowd the **Akazienstrasse,** from the U-Bahn station at Eisenacherstr., to Hauptstr.

CAFE BILDERBUCH — CAFE 2

Akazienstr. 28 ☎030 78 70 60 57 www.cafe-bilderbruch.de

Even if you couldn't eat here, Cafe Bilderbuch's antique cabinets, fringed lamps, deep-cushioned sofas, and adjoining library would still make this a place to visit. Fortunately, their unbeatable Sunday brunch buffets *(€8)* have us shoving grandmothers out of the way to get in the door. The dinner specials *(€5-8.50)* are always affordable and never stuffy.

U7: Eisenacher Str. i Free Wi-Fi. $ Soup from €3.70. Salads from €6. Entrees €8. Coffee €1.50. Open M-Th 9am-1am, F-Sa 9am-2am, Su 10am-1am. Kitchen closes Su-F 11pm, Sa midnight.

BAHARAT FALAFEL — TURKISH 1

Winterfeldtstr. 37 ☎030 216 83 01

This isn't your average *döner* stand. First, because it doesn't serve *döner*. Second, because this vegetarian Turkish restaurant makes all its falafel fried to order, in fluffy pita with lots of tomatoes, lettuce, and mango or chili sauce *(€3-4)*. Wash Baharat's plates, with hummus, tabouleh, and salad, all down with fresh-squeezed *Gute Laune Saft (good-mood juice, €1-2)*. Indoor seating with bright walls and flowers on the table, or an outdoor bench under a striped awning.

U1, U3, U4 or U9: Nollendorfpl. $ Entrees €6-8. ⏰ Open M-Sa 11am-2am, Su noon-2am.

✓ HIMALI

TIBETAN, NEPALESE ❷

Crellerstr. 45 ☎030 78 71 61 75 www.himali-restaurant.de

Nepali and Tibetan classics are cooked up and served piping hot from a tandoori oven. Food is never short on spices, either in quantity or variety, which are grown and ground by hand. This restaurant offers a huge range of vegetarian dishes, curried or grilled, with tofu, vegetables and *naan* with your choice of seasonings. The Nepali tea *(€2.50)* is to die for.

U7: Kleistpark. $ Entrees €6.50-10. ⏰ Open daily noon-midinight.

DOUBLE EYE

CAFE ❶

Akazienstr. 22 ☎017 94 56 69 60 www.doubleeye.de

For coffee purists, this is an inexpensive way to enjoy the best kind of brew. This coffee bar is packed all day with locals, who come for the no-syrup-added, only-best-quality-cream daily brews. Baristas prepare each espresso with surgical precision and take pride on their top quality "latte-art" designs traced into the inch deep foam. They've got victory plaques behind the bar to back up that smack.

U7: Eisenacher Str. $ Cappuccinos €1.80. Macchiatos €2. ⏰ Open daily 8:45am-5:30pm, Sa 9am-6pm.

CAFE BERIO

VIENNESE ❷

Maaßenstr. 7 ☎030 216 19 46 www.cafe-berio.de

French doors open to the streets and let passerby look in on this constantly jam-packed Viennese-style cafe. Frequented by a mostly gay clientele, Cafe Berio is a favorite stop-off point before a night of clubbing. The two-floor cafe is best known for their breakfast menu *(€3-11)*, two-for-one happy hour drinks *(M-Th and Su 7pm-midnight, F-Sa 7-9pm)*, and obscenely extensive menu of dessert options, with cakes and tortes *(from €2)*.

U1, U3, U4, or U9: Nollendorfpl. $ Entrees €5-9. ⏰ Open M-Th 8am-midnight, F-Sa 8am-1am, Su 8am-midnight. Kitchen open daily 8am-11pm.

CAFE EINSTEIN

CAFE ❹

Kurfurstenstr. 58 ☎030 261 5096 www.cafeeinstein.com

Cafe Einstein is Berlin's premiere Viennese coffeeshop, and an obligatory stop for tourists and intelligent, good-looking Let's Go travelers alike. Large windows ingeniously look out onto Einstein's private garden, which you can enjoy along with splurge-worthy home-roasted coffee *(cappuccino €4.30, milchkaffee €3.80)*. A small cake or torte is the least expensive way to enjoy the cafe's wood paneled and detailed molding, and will set you back about €4.

U1, U3, U4, or U9: Nollendorfpl. $ Entrees €14.50-22. Breakfast from €5.80, €12.80 for a Sunday brunch bar. Mixed drinks at the bar Lebensstern from €9. ⏰ Open daily 6am-1am. The bar Lenesstern is open 7pm-late.

BAR TOLUCCI

TUSCAN ❷

Eisenacher Str. 86 ☎030 214 16 07 www.bar-tolucci.de

With stone-oven cooked pizzas *(from €5.50)* and outdoor seating on wood-slated bistro tables along the quiet streetcorner, this restaurant is casual eating and generous portions at their finest. Surround yourself with photographs from Italian filmmaker Bertolluci's films with the inside seating, or seclude yourself in the small garden.

🍴 *U7: Eisenacher Str.* 💲 *Pizzas €5.50-8.20. Entrees €6-7.* 🕐 *Open daily noon-1am, garden noon-midnight. Oven in use M-F from 5pm, and Sa-Su from noon.*

YOGI-HAUS
🍴♈️⛄️ INDIAN ❷

Belziger Str. 42 ☎030 782 92 23 🖥www.restaurant-yogihaus.de

In an ethnic food scene dominated by Turkish cuisine, Yogi-Haus is a welcome deviation from the *döner* and falafel norm. Find it tucked in-between a gaggle of cafes next to a small park. The two outdoor seating patios overlooking trees and quiet roads may help you connect with your inner yogi. The authentically Indian cuisine will definitely jumpstart your discovery of the stomach *chakra*.

🍴 *U7: Eisenacher Str. The restaurant is on the corner of Ecke Eisenacher Str.* 💲 *Traditional Indian soups €2.30-3.10. Vegetarian entrees €4.80-6.50. Chicken and lamb curry dishes €5.50-8.* 🕐 *Open daily noon-midnight.*

SEILDS
🍴♈️⛄️ ROMANTIC ❹

Gotenstr. 1 ☎030 78 09 79 97 🖥www.seilds-berlin.de

This airy, out of the way restaurant oozes romance. Outside, the triangular patio shaded by trees makes an ideal chill-out date after a particularly bad argument. Inside, local art on red walls and candlelight sets the scene for a *Lady and the Tramp* sequel. If you're looking to lighten your wallet, this is a good place to indulge.

🍴 *S1: Julius-Leber-Brücke.* 💲 *Soups from €6, weekly specials €10-19. Beer from €2.80.* 🕐 *Open M-Sa noon-1am, Su 9-1am.*

VIET RICE
🍴 VIETNAMESE ❶

Martin-Luther-Str. 99 ☎152 03 11 00 63 🖥www.vietrice.de

This stark Vietnamese restaurant may have tried and failed to make itself "elegant," but the food is still great and incredibly cheap. Uncomfortable seating and too many tables can make sit-down meals a nightmare, but as an upscale takeout place, without the extra cost, Viet Rice is unbeatable. A short menu includes many Vietnamese staples, like veal soup with coriander *(€5)*. Watch your food being made in the large, updated kitchen.

🍴 *U4: Rathaus Schöneberg.* 💲 *Full entrees €3.60-5.60.* 🕐 *Open daily 11:30am-11pm.*

MITTE

BERLINER MARCUS BRÄU
🍴♿️♈️ GERMAN ❷

1-3 Münzstr. ☎0302 47 69 85 🖥www.marcus-brau.de

This corner shack's been brewing its own beer and liqueurs since before its country tried to conquer the world. The liqueurs, especially the coffee liqueur, taste as good as your mom smells, assuming she smells great. The food isn't exactly free, and the decor isn't exactly Ritz Carlton, but it's authentic, hearty, and German. Try the beer *(from €3 for 5L)*; it's among the best in the city.

🍴 *U2, U5, U8, S5, S7, S9, or S75: Alexanderpl.* 💲 *Entrees €7.50-9. Drinks €1-7.* 🕐 *Open daily noon-late.*

GOOD MORNING VIETNAM
🍴♿️♈️⛄️ VIETNAMESE ❷

Alte Schonhauser 60 ☎030 30 88 29 73 🖥www.good-morning-vietnam.de

The name is great. Explanation for the name is even better: "A yesterday's movie title, a salutation that reminds us of the past, a past full of starvation and war..." Brimming with such great food, this restaurant is hardly about starvation. Entrees *(€7)*, are cheaper than much-hyped Monsieur Vuong's down the street, and include crispy duck, mango chicken skewers, and tofu platters.

🍴 *U2: Rosa-Luxemburg-Pl.* 💲 *Entrees €7-7.50.* 🕐 *Open daily noon-midnight.*

MONSIEUR VUONG
🍴♿️♈️⛄️ VIETNAMESE ❸

Alte Schonhauserstr. 46 ☎030 99 29 69 24 🖥www.monsieurvuong.de

Other people will be talking about it, and the food is good, but don't feel like

food . mitte

you must make it to this wildly popular Vietnamese bistro. The menu changes every two days, keeping a crew of regulars coming back to try the forthcoming noodle and rish dishes, but popularity has unnecessarily jacked up the prices. The only exception is the fantastic and reasonable Vietnamese coffee *(€2)* made with condensed milk and a little bit of love.

✈ *U2: Rosa-Luxemburg-Pl.* ⓘ *Only the outdoor seating is wheelchair-accessible.* Ⓢ *Entrees €7.40-9.80.* ⌚ *Open daily noon-midnight.*

DOLORES BURRITOS
Rosa-Luxemburg-Str. 7

🌐♿ MEXICAN FUSION ❶
☎030 28 09 95 97

Modeled after the Mexican fusion of Baja Fresh or Chipotle, this "California Burrito" shop sells hulking tubes under €5. While we won't go as far as calling these suckers "Californian," the place does a good job of supplying a real spread of chipotle chicken *(€1)*, spiced *carnitas (€1.30)*, and vegetables *(€0.80)* and lets you combine them in burrito *(€4)*, bowl *(€4)*, or quesadilla *(€3.70)* form. The staff could be nicer, but with the rush of students they're dealing with, you hardly blame them.

✈ *U2, U5, U8, S5, S7, S9, or S75: Alexanderpl.* Ⓢ *Burritos around €5; prices vary depending on your ingredients.* ⌚ *Open M-Sa 11:30am-10pm, Su 1-10pm.*

TIPICA
Rosenstr. 19

📶♿ MEXICAN ❶
☎030 25 09 94 40 🖥www.tipica.mx

Tipica is built around a "do-it-yourself" taco menu. Large portions of meat, cilantro, onion, and lime come with four tortillas; you add the sides and salsas to roll your own creations. The meats get crazy, even including a veal taco, but the portions are large, and friends like to come and mix and match. Get any meat Alcurbie style—fried with peppers, onions, and bacon—for no extra charge.

✈ *S5, S7, S9, or S75: Hackescher Markt. From the station, head east and turn right at An der Spandauer Brucke immediately after the Markt. Follow it 100m or so as it curves around to the right.* ⓘ *Only outdoor seating is wheelchair-accessible.* Ⓢ *Tacos €4-7. Sides €2. Salsas €1.* ⌚ *Open M-Th 11am-11pm, F-Sa 11am-1am, Su 11am-11pm.*

ARAB ESKE
Kastanienallee 59

♿🍴♿ LEBANESE ❶
☎030 44 01 27 70 🖥www.arabeske.berlin.de

A solid meal at a great price with no frills and one thrill (the salad dressing! No joke, it kills). Safe bets include shawarma *(€5.50)*, which comes with hummus and salad. Vegetarians can find comfort in falafel *(€4)* and the fact that they only indirectly contribute to the deaths of millions of innocent animals.

✈ *U8: Rosenthaler Pl. From the U-Bahn, head northeast up Weinbergsweg.* Ⓢ *Entrees €4-6.* ⌚ *Open daily 11am-late.*

HUMBOLDT UNIVERSITY NEW LIBRARY
Geschwister-Scholl-Str. 1

🌐♿🍴 CAFETERIA ❶
☎03020 939 93 99

In the thick of Mitte tourist mecca—where a cup of coffee costs €4—sits the quiet, seemingly off-limits library of Humbodlt University. You'll find no one but students inside this tiny cafeteria (conveniently located before the security checkpoint) that has the lowest prices anywhere in central Berlin. Bockwurst *(€1.50)*, salads with chicken and egg *(€1)*, and coffee *(€0.60-2)* must be state-subsidized at these prices. They even have a tray of powders for constructing your very own "curry bockwurst."

✈ *U6: Friedrichstraße. From the station, take Friedrichstraße north and take a right just past the tracks.* Ⓢ *Entrees €1-2.* ⌚ *Open M-F 9am-8pm, Sa-Su noon-5pm.*

FASSBENDER AND RAUSCH CHOCOLATIERS
Charlottenstr. 60

♿🍴 CHOCOLATERIE ❶
☎0302 045 84 43 🖥www.fassbender-rausch.de

To prepare for his fall into Wonka's chocolate river, Augustus Gloop jumped into

berlin

F and R's chocolate volcano (real), took a ride on their chocolate *Titanic* (real, though it might be the *Lusitania*), and commented on the Baroque idealism of their chocolate Berliner Dom. A stimulating, bustling, enormous chocolate house where every inch is filled with confections so delicious, they're physically arousing. Truffles *(€0.50-0.80)* come in 100 flavors, and it's hard to go wrong with any of them.

U2 or U6: Stadmitte. $ Chocolate €0.50-300. ⏰ Open M-Sa 10am-8pm, Su 11am-8pm.

GALERIA GOURMET—GALERIA KAUFHOF ♿ GROCERIES ❷

Alexanderpl. 9 ☎0302 474 30 💻www.galeria-kaufhof.de

The entire bottom floor of this seven-story department store devotes itself to laying out the anatomy of the German diet. Take this time to spy all the whacked-out foods the Germans enjoy at this Deutsche version of Whole Foods, like 10 types of pickled herring, more sausages than you thought the world had pigs, and a great assortment of relatively cheap German wine *(€2-200)*. Sandwiches *(€4-6)*, warm sausages *(€2-5)*, and other prepared food can be taken to nearby Alexanderpl. and enjoyed from a bench.

U2, U5, or U8: Alexanderpl. $ Prepared food €4-8. ⏰ Open M-W 9:30am-8pm, Th-Su 9:30am-10pm.

CURRY 61 ♿ CURRYWURST ❶

Oranienburgerstr. 6 ☎0302 636 99 41 💻www.curry61.de

There's a horde of currywurst stands across this city, but God did not make them all equal. Curry 61 is your best bet in Mitte since the supposed originator of currywurst mysteriously went out of business for a few months. Try the **spicy with skin.**

S5, S7, S9, or S75: Hackescher Markt. $ Currywurst €1.70. ⏰ Open M-Sa 11am-1pm.

ROSENTHAL GRILL ♿🍸 CAFE ❶

Torstr. 125 ☎0302 83 21 53

Outstanding deals and quality Berlin street food at a nice outdoor cafe. Big eaters: an entire chicken costs €5. Döner kebabs (which are like a gyro, but made with cabbage) and pizzas are also great.

U8: Rosenthaler Pl. $ Menu €1-6. ⏰ Open 24hr.

PRENZLAUER BERG

W-IMBISS 🍸 VEGETARIAN ❶

Katanienallee 49 ☎030 48 49 26 57

Maybe it's Indian food, or maybe it's Mexican. We can't really tell, but one thing we do know: this food is good. W-Imbiss specializes in fusing ethnic food types to make something interestingly novel, and damn good. Their specialty is the *naan* pizza—freshly baked bread in a tandoori oven spread with anything from pesto to avocado to chipotle sauce and served piled high with arugula and feta or mozzarella. W-Imbiss also sells cold wraps and quesadillas to an international crowd.

U8: Voltastr. $ Pizza €2-5.50. Wraps €4-5. ⏰ Open May-Aug daily noon-midnight; Sept-Apr daily 12:30-11:30pm.

HANS WURST 🍸 VEGAN ❷

Dunckerstr. 2A ☎030 41 71 78 22

This small cafe serves only organic, vegan foods with no flavor enhancers. Readings, DJs, and acoustic concerts spice up the evenings in this minimally decorated, laid-back venue. The menu changes daily, with seasonal and innovative offerings. Try the tofu burger on toast with original, spicy sauces.

U2: Eberswalder Str. Or M10: Husemannstr. $ Entrees €3.70-8. Tofu burger €4. ⏰ Open M-Th noon-midnight, F-Sa noon-late.

DAS FILM CAFE 🚭🍸⛅ BURGERS, THEATER ❷

Schliemannstr. 15 ☎030 810 11 90 50 💻www.dasfilmcafe.de

Das Film Cafe serves up homemade burgers to fans hungry for a good meal and even better movies. This cafe has two screenings a night in a small, high-resolution theater downstairs, usually around 8pm and 10pm, and prides itself on selecting films with an international, independent flair. Films are never dubbed over and are usually shown in English.

🚇 U2: Eberswalder Str. $ Tickets €4.50, students €4. Burgers €7. Hummus plates €5.50. Cappuccino €2. ⏰ Open M-F 2:30pm-late, Sa-Su 11:30am-late.

THE BIRD 🚭🍸⛅ BURGERS ❷

Am Falkpl. 5 ☎030 51 05 32 83

With a bar made of old wood and exposed brick walls, this seemingly quintessential European restaurant is anything but. Opened by two New York transplants, The Bird makes some of the only honest-to-goodness, criminally huge burgers in Berlin. Everything is made from scratch daily, including the sauce for the aptly named "napalm wings." Locals appreciate "Angry Hour," 6-8pm, when all beer is buy one, get one free.

🚇 U8: Voltastr. $ Burgers €9-12. Wings €6. ⏰ Open M-Sa 6pm-late, Su noon-late.

CAFE RESTAURANT MIRÓ 🚭🍸⛅ MEDITERRANEAN ❷

Raumerstr. 29 ☎030 44 73 30 13 💻www.miro-restaurant.de

Cafe Miró captures the essence of the Mediterranean, whose food it proudly serves in a candlelit, pillow-laden room. Brick walls and cobalt blue details set the scene for your love affair with feta and oregano. The Greek omelettes *(€5.20)* are incredibly popular.

🚇 U2: Eberswalder Str. $ Entrees €8.50-15.50. Appetizers and salads €4-9. Soups €3.20-3.70. Su brunch €8. ⏰ Open M-F 3pm-late, Sa-Su 10am-late. Brunch Su 10am-4pm. Kitchen open until midnight.

LIEBLING 🚭🍸⛅ CAFE ❶

Raumer Str. 36A ☎030 41 19 82 09

This corner cafe is all elegance, with a little edge. An alternative crowd chills out and sips on gin and coffee in the completely white-on-white interior plastered with mosaic tile. Enjoy a typically-Berlin *milchkaffee* on a bistro table on a quiet street or stick around 'til dark to watch the chairs fill with guests sipping aperitifs and liquor.

🚇 U2: Eberswalder Str. $ Milchkaffee €2.50. Apertifs €2.50-4. Mixed drinks €2-3.50. ⏰ Open M-F 9am-late, Sa-Su noon-late.

BABEL 🚭⛅ MIDDLE EASTERN ❶

Kastanienalle 33 ☎030 44 03 13 18

With the exception of Che Guevara's portrait, which hangs over the front door, Babel is a perfect Middle Eastern eatery. Locals obsessed with the falafel keep this neighborhood joint busy at all hours, eating at outside packed tables or inside under dangling garlic. Scarf down some döner to the beat of Middle Eastern tunes.

🚇 U8: Bernauer Str. $ Falafel €3-6. ⏰ Open daily 11am-2am.

SOUPANOVA 🚭🍸⛅ SOUP ❶

Stargader Str. 24 💻www.soupanova.de

Creative soups here begin with a broth base from a variety of choices, including Thai coconut milk and miso. Then add tofu, wonton, or chicken to make it a meal. Full of vegetarian options and zany floral patterns.

🚇 U2: Eberswalder Str. $ Soup €4-5. ⏰ Open daily 6pm-late.

CAFE IMNU 🚭🍸⛅ CAFE ❷

Lychener Str. 41 ☎0304 471 88 98

Located just across from one of Prenzlauer Berg's best-known parks, Cafe ImNu is a serene place to enjoy an early breakfast or midday meal. Juices are squeezed fresh to order, including the sweet strawberry-kiwi-banana blend *(€3.80)*. The vegetarian breakfast comes with pasta, mozzarella, tomatoes, pesto, yogurt, honey, and a garden salad.

🚇 U2: Eberswalder Str. $ Breakfast €5.10-8. Baguette sandwiches €3.20-4.10. ⏰ Open daily 8am-7pm.

FRIEDRICHSHAIN

Friedrichshain is famous for its inexpensive, student-centered living, and its restaurants, bars and cafes don't disappoint. In the area bounded by Frankfurter-Allee to the north, Jennerstr. to the east, Simon-Dach-Str. to the west, and Wühlschischerstr. to the south, streets overflow with bistro tables, outdoor umbrellas, and cheap food.

👍 FRITTIERSALON

🚭🍸⛅ GERMAN ❶

Boxhagener Str. 104 ☎030 25 93 39 06

Yes, we know, ever since you set foot in Berlin, you've been drowning in bratwurst, currywurst, and fried potatoes. But for anyone in Friedrichshain, this all-organic "frying salon" is unique enough to merit a visit. In addition to a traditional prize-winning Berliner currywurst, this restaurant serves a number of German classics with a twist: try the wheat-based vegetarian currywurst or bratwurst or a hamburger or veggie burger with strawberries and avocado. All sauces and french fries are homemade, and all dishes are cooked to order.

🚇 U5: Frankfurter Tor. $ Bratwurst and currywurst €2.20. Burgers €6. ⏰ Open M 6pm-late, Tu-F noon-late, Sa-Su 1pm-late.

👍 CARAMELLO EIS

🚭⛅ ICE CREAM ❶

Wühlischerstr. 31 ☎030 50 34 31 05 💻www.caramello-eis.de

Caramello Eis scoops some of the best ice cream in town all night long to a following of devoted students. All of Caramello's ice cream is handmade, organic, and vegan. Don't leave Friedrichshain without trying the dark chocolate *eis* with chili powder; the staff says it's the best chocolate ice cream in all of Berlin, and we're not about to argue.

🚇 U5: Frankfurter Tor. $ Cones €1. ⏰ Open daily 11am-late.

AUNT BENNY

🚭📶⛅ CAFE ❶

Oderstr. 7 ☎030 66 40 53 00

Frequented by moms who take their children to the playground across the street, students who love Wi-Fi, and anyone who's serious about the art of making carrot cake, this cafe is always buzzing with energy. Regulars are almost aggressive with their enthusiasm for the cafe's *bricher-muesli*—a kind of Swiss cereal, containing nuts, fresh apples, and oats, soaked overnight, served with yogurt, and usually sold out by 4pm.

🚇 U5: Frankfurter Allee. $ Smoothies €4.20-4.80. Bagels €1.60. Coffee €1.60. Su brunch €8. ⏰ Open Tu-F 9am-7pm, Sa-Su 10am-7pm.

HOPS AND BARLEY

🚭🍸⛅ MICROBREWERY ❶

Wühlischstr. 22/23 ☎030 29 36 75 34 💻www.hopsandbarley-berlin.de

This microbrewery makes its own cider, pilsner, and lager on site for hordes of thirsty locals. The bar gets particularly packed for German club football games, when the bar opens early *(3pm)* and stays open late. The guys here also make their own bread daily, so no German, or wandering traveler, has to drink good beer on an empty stomach.

🚇 U5: Frankfurter Allee. $ 0.3L beer €1.90. 0.5L beer €2.80. ⏰ Open 5pm-late.

INTIMES KINO-CAFE

🚭🍸⛅ CAFE ❷

Boxhagener Str. 107 ☎030 29 66 64 57

A portrait on the wall pays homage to Che Guevara, for a reason that the staff either doesn't know or won't tell. A large photograph of Havana that looks weirdly like East Berlin covers another wall. A large variety of vegetarian entrees (more than just pasta!) and outdoor tables overrun with locals in the summertime make this restaurant a standout.

🚇 U5: Frankfurter Tor. $ Vegetarian casseroles and gratin €7-9.10. Tarte flambées €4.50-7. ⏰ Open daily 10am-midnight.

YOBARCA — 🚫⛅ FROZEN YOGURT [1]

Simon-Dach-Str. 40 — ☎0170 969 97 37 💻www.yobarca.com

This is the first frozen-yogurt place opened in Friedrichshain, and while the locals might still be figuring it out, we love it. Try toppings from blueberries and blackberries to pineapple and passion-fruit sauce. Started by an Italian ice-cream maker, this froyo cafe is outfitted in shocking yellow walls and chairs strewn around a small patio on a busy, shaded Friedrichshain street.

🚇 U5: Frankfurter Tor. $ Small yogurt with 1 topping €2.50. Bubble tea €2.50. Extra toppings €0.50. ⏰ Open daily 10am-10pm.

CAFE CORTADO — 🚫🍸⛅ CAFE [1]

Simon-Dach-Str. 9

Flowers and boardgames on breezy patio tables and a cozy, sofa-covered back-room draw a young crowd with a taste for international coffee blends. Cafe Cortado's mosaic bar serves up Turkish and Portuguese coffee by day and beer and cocktails by night. A variety of chai teas and a berry torte, made fresh daily, are favorites.

🚇 U5: Frankfurter Allee. $ Beer €3. Mixed drinks from €6. ⏰ Open M-F 9am-9pm, Sa-Su 9am-midnight.

LEMONGRASS — 🚫🍸⛅ THAI [1]

Simon-Dach-Str. 2 — ☎030 20 05 69 75

Located on a popular street with shops and restaurants, this criminally cheap Thai restaurant serves up classic favorites in a relaxed, green-striped kitchen. Bistro tables crowd the outdoor patio, and small tables inside look over the kitchen. Portions are huge, so pick your view and relax while enjoying authentic Asian specialities.

🚇 U5: Frankfurter Tor. $ Soups from €2.80. Entrees €6.50-8. ⏰ Open daily noon-midnight.

STRANDGUT BERLIN — 🚫🍸⛅ RESTOBAR [1]

Mühlenstr. 61 — ☎030 70 08 55 66 💻www.strandgut-berlin.com

There's something a little inauthentic about sitting on a beach next to the Spree, but we're not letting that keep us from enjoying a little piece of paradise (however contrived) in the middle of Berlin. Imported sand and lounge chairs line the river, shaded by trees and umbrellas. A beach-house-style bar and restaurant serve up quick, cheap food to frighteningly pale Germans working on their tan.

🚇 U1, S3, S5, S7, S9 or S75: Warschauer Str. $ Beer €3. Mixed drinks €6. Soda €2. Hamburgers €3.50. Salads €2. ⏰ Open M-F 10am-10pm, Sa-Su 10am-4pm. Restaurant open noon-late.

DER FLIEGENDER TISCH — 🚫🍸⛅ ITALIAN [2]

Mainzer Str. 10 — ☎030 02 97 76 48

This cozy candlelit eatery serves inexpensive Italian food to local devotees. The pizza is cooked fresh in a Dutch oven. The restaurant's fans swear by their risotto *(€5.60-6.50)*. Meals are served on small, crowded tables in a darkened room with a central bar and understated Tuscan decor.

🚇 U5: Samariter Str. $ Pizza €5. Pasta €4.30-6.60. ⏰ Open daily 5pm-midnight.

KREUZBERG

Good food lives and dies all over Kreuzberg, but the best food is stacked up in the area near **Oranienestrasse.**

👍 CAFE MORGANLAND 🥬🚭🍸☀ CAFE [1]
Skalitzer Str. 35 ☎03061 132 91 💻www.cafemorgenland.eu

Its Parisian breakfast—a fresh butter croissant, a large dish of perfect vanilla custard with fresh fruit, and the best milk coffee you've ever had—breaks the laws of economics. The all-you-can-eat brunch buffet *(€9.50)* on the weekends will literally make your jaw drop: eight types of meat, five types of bread, 15 spreads, sausages, eggs, curries, potatoes, fish, vegetables, fruits—it's paradise. Solid international fare fills out the rest of the menu.

🚇 U1: Görlitzer Bahnhof. $ Entrees €5-15. ⏰ Open daily 10am-1am.

👍 RESTAURANT RISSANI 🥬🚭🍸 MIDDLE EASTERN [1]
Spreewaldpl. 4 ☎3061 62 94 33

A lot of döner kebab places around town call themselves authentic. Well, Rissani doesn't serve döners—they call them chicken shawarma sandwiches—but they're twice as delicious and half as expensive *(€2)*. Dinner plates, with shawarma, falafel, tabbouleh, hummus, and salad will make you forget your bad day.

🚇 U1: Görlitzer Bahnhof. From the station, head east down Skalitzer str. and take a right at Spreewaldpl. $ Entrees €2-5. ⏰ Open M-Th 11am-3am, F-Sa 11am-5am, Su 11am-3am.

👍 MUSTAFAS 🥬♿🍸 MIDDLE EASTERN [1]
Mehringdamm 32 💻www.mustafas.de

Some say that this place serves up the best döner kebabs in the city—that's debatable, but what's not is that Mustafas has the best *durum (shawarma burrito with sauce; €4)* in the city. It tastes like the best thing in the world stuffed with the second-best thing in the world. Vegetarians who usually scrounge through various falafel options will rejoice over the delicious grilled vegetables in the veggie *durum (€3.10)*. If you want to check it out yourself, their website has a live webcam.

🚇 U6 or U7: Mehringdamm. $ Entrees €2.50-5. ⏰ Open 24hr.

👍 HENNE ALT-BERLINER WIRTSHAUS GASTSTÄTTEN 🥬🚭🍸☀ GERMAN [2]
Leuschnerdamm 25 ☎3061 477 30 💻www.henne-berlin.de

Henne provides the most German experience imaginable. An antler-lined parlor crammed with plaid tablecloths, sturdy German damsels hauling mugs of beer, and a menu that consists of a single dinner: a piece of bread, creamy potato salad, and enormous, perfectly crispy, internationally renowned chicken that will forever redefine "fried food." The chicken skin whispers as you crunch it, "I'm better than the girls you'll miss out on by eating me and gaining weight." She only speaks the truth.

🚇 U1 or U8: Kottbusser Tor. From the station, head northwest on Oranienstr. Take a right at Oranienpl. ℹ Reservations needed for outdoor seating. $ Entrees from €8. ⏰ Open Tu-Sa 7pm-late, Su 5pm-late.

CURRY 36 🥬♿🍸☀ CURRYWURST [1]
Mehringdamm 36 ☎0302 51 73 68 💻www.curry36.de

The best currywurst in Berlin means the best currywurst in the world. Be brave: take it with ketchup, fries, and an enormous glob of mayo.

🚇 U6 or U7: Mehringdamm. $ Currywurst €1.50. ⏰ Open M-F 9am-4am, Sa 10am-4am, Su 11am-3am.

SK KREUZBERG FOOD 24 GMBH 🥬♿🍸 STREET FOOD [1]
Schlesischestr. 1-2 ☎0306 107 60 00

Home of the amazing €1.50 personal pizza and the €3 impersonal pizza (so cold), SK gets flooded by post-clubbers and pre-clubbers every evening. Heftier dishes come in the form of pastas and sandwiches *(€3-5)*. No need to look further; this

is the cheapest drunk food in Kreuzberg.
🚇 *U1: Schlesisches Tor.* $ *Entrees €1-5.* ⏰ *Open 24hr.*

SANTA MARIA MEXICAN ❷
Oranienstr. 170 ☎0309 221 00 27 💻asmarias.de
A few bites of fare from this Mexican bistro will cause a riot in your mouth. *Choriqueso (€6.50)* is a pot of melted cheese and sausage...just think about that for a second. The standard issue grub like fat Mexican sandwiches *(€6)*, tacos *(€3-7)*, Coronas *(€2.50)*, and margaritas *(€5)* are also on hand. A popular evening hangout for expats.
🚇 *U8: Moritzpl. From the U-bahn, head southeast on Oranienstr.* $ *Entrees €5-8.* ⏰ *Open daily noon-midnight.*

AMAR ♿🍸 INDIAN ❸
Shloβstr. 50 ☎0306 956 66 73 💻www.amar-berlin.de
Always pleasant and always packed, Amar has classy, flashy Indian food, even if it's not the world's cheapest. For Indian in Kreuzberg, there isn't a better combination of taste and price. Curries come in separate metal pots to guests packed into every outdoor table. Vegetarians have a huge variety of cheese, vegetable, and curry dishes *(€5.70-8)* to choose from. Many guests use this place as a jumping-off point to the best nearby clubs in Berlin.
🚇 *U1: Schlesisches Tor.* $ *Entrees €4-10.* ⏰ *Open M-Th 11:30am-1am, F-Sa noon-2am, Su 11:30am-1am.*

nightlife

CHARLOTTENBURG

Charlottenburg's quiet cafes and music venues cater to the 30-something set. Great for a mellow evening, or a chance to hear the city's best jazz, but the real parties are eastward. The Ku'damm is best avoided after sunset, unless you enjoy fraternizing with drunk businessmen.

A TRANE 🍸 BAR AND CLUB
Bleibtreustr. 1 ☎030 313 25 50 💻www.a-trane.de
Small in size, big on talent. Hanging black and white photographs of jazz greats, some who even performed at A Trane (like legends Herbie Hancock and Wynton Marsalis), look down on crowded tables filled with jazz enthusiasts. First-class musicians still entertain guests on a quiet street corner.
🚇 *S3, S5, S7, S9, or S75: Savignypl.* $ *Cover €7-15, students €5-13. Sa from 12:30am no cover.* ⏰ *Open M-Th and Su 9pm-2am, F-Sa 9pm-late.*

CASCADE 🍸 CLUB
Fasanenstr. 81 ☎030 31 80 09 40 💻www.cascade-club.de
The walk down to the large basement club is bookended by steps flooded by flowing water, hence the name Cascade. With a high cover, this club might be a bit of a splurge, but in return travelers get a dance floor of underlit blocks (à la **John Travolta**), a wall-to-wall bar, and a young crowd–there might even actually be dancing! There are ways to get around the high admission price; stop by on a Friday and pick up a voucher for free entry, good the next evening, or next weekend.
🚇 *U1: Uhlandstr.* $ *Cover €10. Beer €3.50, shots €4.* ⏰ *Open F-Sa 11am-late.*

SALZ 🍸 CLUB
Salzufer 20 ☎017 02 83 35 04 💻www.salz-club.de
You'll have to go a little out of your way to find more upbeat and youthful bunch in low-key Charlottenburg. And by that we mean a 20-minute walk from the

nearest U-Bahn station. But if you're looking to stay "in the neighborhood" and see someone dancing under the age of 32, this is the place to go. Exposed brick walls keep the disco-ball-lit floor looking classy at this salt-warehouse turned techno club. Out front find a beautiful patio lit with multi-colored lights and tiki torches.

🚇 U2: Ernst-Reuter-Pl. Walk down Str. des 17 Juni to Satzufer. Turn left and walk along the river to Salz. *i* Check the website for music schedules. Ⓢ No cover. 🕐 Open F-Sa 8pm-late.

QUASIMODO

⊛⊗Ⴘ CLUB

Kantstr. 12A ☎030 312 80 86 ▣www.quasimodo.de

The upside is that Quasimodo showcases live music in a variety of genres, including soul, R and B, and jazz, nearly every night of the week. The downside is that the older crowd sometimes gives the club a kind of office-party energy. Spacious basement room with large bar and stage.

🚇 U2, S5, S7, S9, or S75: Zoologischer Garten. *i* Check the website for music schedule. Ⓢ Drinks €2.50-4.50. Cover for concerts €8-30, cheaper if reserved in advance. 🕐 Open daily 1pm-late.

ANDA LUCIA

♥Ⴗᛠ BAR, RESTAURANT

Savignypl. 2 ☎030 54 02 71 ▣www.andalucia-berlin.de

So you're wandering around the streets of Berlin after hours, thinking, "Hey, you know what I'm in the mood for? A little Latin flavor! I wonder where I could get nosh on tapas and show off my salsa at 2am!" Don't say we don't know our readers. And we've found the perfect place for you. Anda Lucia may not have a dance floor, but that doesn't keep the guests and staff from dancing around tables to salsa tunes blasting late into the heat of the night. Outdoor patio seating for those on a dance siesta and in the mood for a late night tapas (€3.70-4.10).

🚇 S5, S7, or S75: Savignypl. Ⓢ Wines from €4 a glass. Tequila €3. 🕐 Kitchen open 5pm-midnight. Tapas bar open 5pm-late.

SCHÖNEBERG AND WILMERSDORF

Schöneberg is still Berlin's unofficial gay district, full of GLBT nightlife. We've picked some of our favorites, but the neighborhood is full of outrageously popular bars and clubs that serve a vibrant gay community. From what we can tell, there aren't happier partiers in all of Berlin.

▨ HAFEN

⊛Ⴘ▼ GAY BAR

Motzstr. 19 ☎030 211 41 18 ▣www.hafen-berlin.de

Nearly 20 years old, this bar has become a landmark for Berlin's gay community. The sign outside may only specifically invite "drop dead gorgeous looking tourists," but you'll find plenty of locals all along the spectrum of attractiveness. The mostly male crowd spills out onto the streets during the summer. The weekly pub quiz, Monday at 8pm, is wildly popular (first Monday of the month in English), and every Wednesday features a new DJ. On April 30th, Hafen hosts their largest party of the year, in honor of the Queen of the Netherlands. They promise us that the "Queen" makes an appearance.

🚇 U1, U3, U4 or U9: Nollendorfpl. Ⓢ No cover. 🕐 Open daily 8am-4am.

▨ PRINZKNECHT

⊛Ⴘ▼ GAY BAR

Fuggerstr. 33 ☎030 23 62 74 44 ▣www.prinzknecht.de

Prinzknecht serves a mostly male clientele from a huge central wooden bar. Even with so many bar stools and couches, the bar fills up way past capacity on event nights, and people begin to resemble waves on the street. Check the website for upcoming events, including an incredibly popular ▨ABBA night.

🚇 U1 or U2: Wittenbergpl. Ⓢ No cover. 🕐 Open M-F 2pm-3am, Sa and Su 3pm-3am.

SLUMBERLAND ◉🍸⛅ BAR

Goltstr. 24 ☎030 216 53 49

So normally we like a little more authenticity in our bars, but we're not going to pretend that we don't appreciate this island escape in the middle of land-locked Berlin, and the locals aren't either. So what if you didn't come to Germany for the reggae and palm trees? Try a mixed drink *(€5)* on a sandy floor, with rotating African art exhibits on the walls.

🚇 U1 , U3, U4 or U9: Nollendorfpl. $ Most drinks €2-5. ⏰ Open M-Th and Su 6pm-2am, F 6pm-4am, Sa 11am-4pm.

BEGINE 🍸▼ LESBIAN BAR

Potsdamer Str. 139 ☎030 215 14 14 🖥www.begine.de

In a neighborhood dominated by male gay clubs, Begine is a welcome retreat for women. Named after a now-defunct Lesbian WC, Berlin's biggest lesbian community center has a popular, low-key cafe/bar with comfortable sofas, live music, and readings at night.

🚇 U2: Bülowstr. $ No cover. ⏰ Open M-F 5pm-late, Sa 3pm-late, Su 7pm-late.

ALT BERLINER BIERSALON ◉🍸⛅ BAR

Kufürstendamm 225 ☎030 884 39 90 🖥

The Alt Berliner Biersalon may cater to an older crowd on most nights, but from October to May, this is one of the best spots in Schöneberg to watch a German football match. For all its West Berlin wood-paneled opulence, the atmosphere is far from stuffy. With rowdy crowds and plenty of TV screens, you'll be right in the middle of the action, or just living vicariously through athletes while chugging down beer.

🚇 U1 or U9: Kufüstendamm. $ Beer €3-4.50. ⏰ Open 24hr.

HELLE WELT ◉🍸▼ GAY BAR

Motzstr. 5 ☎030 21 91 75 05

Even with the addition of two enormous, quiet sitting rooms, the 20-something clientele still pack the bar and take over the street. The fur-covered wall, chandeliers, and well-directed mood lighting don't keep this sophisticated-looking club from being relaxed. Though it has a mostly male crowd during "prime time," more women show up in the early evening, on weekdays, and in the morning.

🚇 U1, U3, U4, or U9: Nollendorfpl. $ No cover. ⏰ Open daily 6pm-4am, sometimes later.

XARA CAFE AND LOUNGE ◉🍸⛅▼ HOOKAH BAR

Maaßenstr. 7 ☎030 30 10 47 77

In an area dominated by high energy nightlife, this bar offers up mellow with a hookah side. Serving inexpensive crepes and baguettes by day, this cafe turns into a relaxed lounge at night, with outdoor seating overlooking a popular street. Comfortable chairs are grouped around tables with hookah, popular with a younger crowd.

🚇 U1, U3, U4 or U9: Nollendorfpl. $ Crepes from €2, baguettes from €3.20. Hookah €8 per pipe. Cocktails €6.10-8.80. Beer €2.60-3.50. Shots €2.90-5.50. ⏰ Open daily from 9am-late. Happy hour Su-Th 7pm-10pm, cocktails €4.

MAXXX ◉🍸▼ GAY BAR

Fuggerstr. 34 ☎030 21 00 52 89 🖥www.maxxx-berlin.de

A smoky, dark-green interior with a simple bar draws a mostly male, leather-clad crowd for some unexpected chill-out conversation. Maxxx has inexpensive drinks and ready-to-talk bartenders. During the day, the bar doubles as a cafe.

🚇 U1 or U2: Wittenbergpl. $ Beer from €2.50. ⏰ Open daily noon-3am.

MITTE

BANG BANG CLUB
CLUB

Neue Promenade 10 ☎030 604 053 10 www.bangbangclub.net

Hiding beneath the S-bahn tracks in groovy, smoky caverns of arched brick, the Bang Bang club plays it cool without being snooty. Weave through the tight hallways and dance the night away with Berliners.

S5, S7, S9, S75: Hackescher Markt. U. $ Admission free-€20. Usually open F-Sa 10pm-late. Check website for details.

COOKIES
CLUB

Friedrichstr. 158 ☎030 274 929 40 www.cookies-berlin.de

Hot, sweaty, sexy, and packed, Cookies jams in a former Stasi bunker that operates as a restaurant during the day. Locals claim that this party originally started in some guy's basement before moving to hip venues. The party don't start till 1am, so save your tears if you show up alone at midnight. Entrance can be a little exclusive—don't dress up, dress down—so it helps if you know the name of the DJ playing that night.

U6: Französische Str. From the U-bahn, head north. $ Admission €5-15. Club open Tu 10:30pm-6am, Th 10:30pm-6am.

KAFFEE BURGER
CLUB

Torstr. 58-60 ☎030 280 46 49 5 www.kaffeeburger.de

Those looking to groove can jam at this artsy dance club while those looking to chill can hop next door to the "Burger Bar." Despite looking a little like your grandma's living room, things get wild here later in the evenings. Weekly programs include poetry readings, film screenings, and drunken sloppiness.

U6: Rosa-Luxemburg-Pl. $ Cover M-Th €1, F-Sa €5, Su €1. Open M-F 8pm-late, Sa 9pm-late, Su 7pm-late.

CLARCHENS BALLHAUS
CLUB

Auguststr. 24 ☎030 282 92 95 www.ballhaus.de

For travelers who enjoy the type of dancing that gets worse as the night wears on, this 1930s-style ballroom has cha cha, salsa, and other programs Mondays through Thursdays and Sundays. Friday and Saturday see DJs playing "hipper" music. Come early for a drink in the beautiful patio garden.

U8: Rosenthaler Pl. $ M-Tu, Su programs €8, students €6, F-Sa €3. Open daily 10am-late. Dance programs start at 8pm.

WEEK-END
CLUB

Alexanderpl. 5 www.week-end-berlin.de

Not the cheapest place in the world, but the only experience of its kind in Berlin. Come for good music and the chance to see the sun rise over the city from Berlin's only real skyscraper. A night you'll remember.

U6: Alexandr Pl. $ Admission €10-20. Open F-Su 11pm-late.

8MM BAR
BAR

Schönhauser Allee 177 ☎030 405 006 24 www.8mmbar.com

A dimly lit, low-key hipster bar where you can chat about how ironic you are or just play a round of pool, just 'cause. Crowd levels vary randomly, but when it's bustling, it's bustling.

U2: Senefelderpl. $ Beer €2.50-6. Mixed drinks €4-7. Open M-Th 8pm-late. F-Su 9pm-late.

KIT KAT CLUB
CLUB

Köpenicker Str. 76 ☎030 7871896 www.kitkatclub.org

A visit here is an unforgettable experience. Everyone is decked out in straps, chaps, and leather. If you're scared of penises, don't come.

◆ U8: Heinrich Heinestr. *i* Fetish dress code strictly enforced. Ⓢ Admission €5-10. ◲ Open F-Sa (sometimes Su) 11pm-late.

ZAPATA

●& ¥△ BAR

Oranienburger Str. 54   ☎030 281 6109 █www.cafe-zapata.de

The hippest of the bars at Tacheles, Zapata has parties every night of the week with some of the biggest DJs in town. Anyone trying to keep it "clean" and "tame" should definitely stay home, as Zapata's crowd spills into the attached faux-beach, and dirt and broken glass become as much a part of the experience as the music and the dancing. The outdoor sculpture garden bores images into your mind that may never leave. Guests willing to climb can enjoy cocktails from on top of a forklift.

◆ U6: Oranienburger Tor. Ⓢ Admission €5-10. ◲ Club open daily 10pm-late.

DELICIOUS DOUGHNUTS

●⊗¥ CLUB

Rosenthaler Straße 9   ☎0302 809 92 74 █www.delicious-doughnuts.de

No, it's not a donut shop. Yes, it's a hip backpacker hangout. Not tons of room to dance here, but plenty of room to relax, talk, drink, and smoke. If your friends are boring, you can escape to the pinball machine. A small steel ball is friend enough for anyone.

◆ U8: Roenthaler Pl. Ⓢ Cover €5-10. ◲ Open daily 10pm-late.

TAPE

●⊗¥ CLUB

Heidestr. 14   ☎0308 48 48 73 █www.tapeberlin.de

The huge open spaces of this converted warehouse keep it cool when the party gets hot. And it does frequently. Party starts (and goes) very late.

◆ U8: Rosenthaler Pl. Ⓢ Admission varies. ◲ Open F-Sa 11pm-late.

CCCP KLUB

●⊗¥ CLUB

Torstr. 136   ☎030 99194904 █www.cojito.de/cccpclubbar.5653.htm

This Soviet-themed bar shows off a bunch of communist relics including flags, maps, and a stuffed badger, undoubtedly of the communist persuasion. Down drinks at the perfect bar and show Richard Nixon who's boss. Unfortunately, the drinks are not provided free according to need, but the downstairs club does feel unpretentious and of the people.

◆ U8: Rosenthaler Pl. Ⓢ Cover varies with party. ◲ Open Tu-Th 6pm-late, F-Sa 10pm-late.

PRENZLAUER BERG

Far less techno and far more laid-back than other parts of Berlin, Prenzlauer Berg's trendy cafes and late-night restaurants each have a devoted local following. Opt for bars over clubs in this part of town.

▨ THE WEINEREI: FORUM

●¥△ BAR

Veteranenstr. 14   ☎030 440 6983

This unmarked wine bar has gone from a local secret to a local legend, catapulted by its comfortable elegance and unique paying system. Pay €2 for a glass, sample all the wines, and then sample again, and again, and before leaving, pay what you think you owe. Enjoy your vintage at an outdoor table, on an indoor sofa, or in the downstairs wine cellar (by request).

◆ U2: Senefelderpl. Ⓢ Depends on how drunk you get. ◲ Open M-Sa 10am-late, Su 11am-late.

▨ SOLSI E MORSI

●¥△ BAR

Marienburger Str. 10   It's not often that an owner becomes as loved as his bar, but Johnny Petrongolo is that rare exception. Buzzing about tables, opening wine bottles, and handing out plates of free parma ham, cheese, bread and olives, Johnny and his familial staff have won over the hearts of their young regulars, and ours as well. If you're not sure where to start, let the Petrongolos help you pick your wine.

◆ U2: Senefelderpl. Ⓢ Wine from €3 a glass. ◲ Open daily 6pm-late.

KLUB DER REPUBLIC (KDR)

CLUB

Pappelallee 81

There are few museums that have as many authentic Soviet artifacts as KDR has hanging on its walls. Once the showroom of the DDR carpet and linoleum supplier, KDR kept the old formica bar and leaded glass, and added lamps from the original Palast Republik, collected as the building was being torn down. The furniture is from the DDR landmark Cafe Moscow. DJs play every night to a mixed crowd attracted by the club's no cover policy.

U2: Eberswalder Str. Turn into what looks like a deserted parking lot and climb the metal stairs. $ Drinks €5, beer €4. ⏰ Open from "dark to light." In more definite terms, that's around 9pm in the summer, in the winter 8pm-late.

INTERSOUP

BAR

Schliemannstr. 31 ☎030 23 27 30 45 www.intersoup.de

With worn '70s furniture, retro floral wallpaper, and soup specials, this is your East-Berlin Soviet-era grandmother's living room turned ironic. Named after the DDR-era general store Intershop, Intersoup has been keeping things quintessentially Prenzlauer Berg-esque and getting quite the local following doing it. The upper level always has a DJ, but the real highlight is the downstairs **undersoup,** where international bands perform every night at 10pm, in genres from folk to rock, to an audience seated in comfortable mix-matched chairs covered in lurid orange and olive patterns. There's almost never a cover.

U2: Eberswalder Str. $ Soup €4.50-5. ⏰ Open M-Sa 6pm-3am, Su.

WOHNZIMMER

BAR

Lettestr. 6 ☎030 445 5458

Wohnzimmer means "living room," and it's not hard to see why this bar goes by that name, given its wide wood-planked floors, and glassware cabinets along the walls of the bar. Settle into a velvety Victorian sofa with a mixed drink among a diverse crowd. Wohnzimmer is a favorite of hip 20-somethings and an older crowd who could have furnished the bar with relics from their garage sales.

U2: Eberswalder Str. $ Cocktails €4-5. Beer €2.50-3. ⏰ Open daily 9am-4am.

DR. PONG

BAR

Eberswalder Str. 21

In the middle of a concrete room with peeling paint, and under falling fluorescent lights, stands a single ping-pong table, the centerpiece of this minimalist bar. Intense hipsters ring the table, gripping their paddles. All are welcome, including beginners and the severely intoxicated.

U2: Eberswalder Str. $ Drinks €2-5.50. ⏰ Open M-Sa 8pm-late, Su 6pm-late.

PRATER GARTEN

BEER GARDEN

Kastanienallee 7-9 ☎030 448 5688 www.pratergarten.de

Locals and travelers of all ages eat and drink at sprawling picnic tables under a canopy of chestnut trees. Set just off a busy street, the peaceful ambiance of the hundreds of small hung lights is perfect as either a stop-off between clubs, or as the setting for a whole evening of relaxed conversation and good beer. Prater Garten, arguably the prettiest beer garden in Berlin, also has an outdoor theater and television.

U2: Eberswalder Str. $ Bratwurst €2.50. Beer €2.50-3.50. ⏰ Open in good weather Apr-Sept daily noon-late.

WHITE TRASH FAST FOOD

BAR

Schönehauser Allee 6-7 ☎030 50 34 86 67 www.whitetrash-fastfood.com

Guarded by two gilded lions out front, four levels of kitsch at White Trash Fast Food provide endless visual entertainment. Fish tanks, rabbit skins, rocking horses, and movie memorabilia cover the bar. Drinks come with honest, English explanations: the Zombie will "blast your head into 1000 pieces!" International rock bands play to a packed crowd in this I-Spy paradise.

🚇 U2: Senefelderpl. $ Specialty drinks from €8. ⏰ Open M-F 12pm-late, Sa-Su 6pm-late.

SCOTCH AND SOFA ● 🍸 ⛅ BAR

Kollwitzstr. 18 ☎030 44 04 23 71

Exactly what the name promises. This bar channels gold-foiled '70s glamour in the Sean-Connery-as-James-Bond tradition, and serves up classic drinks on vintage sofas. Far from stuffy, Scotch and Sofa relaxes to some mellow, big-band tunes, and grand French doors open up to a quiet street lined with patio seating.

🚇 U2: Senefelderpl. $ Scotch from €5. Happy hour daily 6pm-7pm, when the cocktail of the day is €3.80. ⏰ Open daily 6pm-very late.

MORGENROT ● 🍸 ⛅ BAR

Kastanienallee 85 ☎030 44 31 78 44 💻www.cafe-morgenrot.de

This little cafe is trying to save the world, and they're having a great time doing it. Owned by a five person work collective, Morganrot makes vegan, organic, fair-trade food by day *(including a weekend brunch buffet where guests pay only what they can afford from €4)*, and serves up frosty vodka shots at night. Deep teal walls and climbing plants on the outside pull in crowds off Kastanienallee.

🚇 U2: Eberswalder Str. $ Shots €2. ⏰ Open Tu-Th noon-1am, F-Sa 11am-3am, Su 11am-1am.

DUNCKER ● 🍸 ⛅ CLUB

Dunckerstr. 64 ☎030 445 9509 💻www.dunckerclub.de

Suits of armor, chainmail, and retro bead curtains hang from the high ceilings of this horse-stable-turned-club. Trees and climbing ivy cover the outside of the building, and form a canopy over the back patio. Duncker heats up at about 1am, when it draws an intense crowds with its insider vibe. Ring the bell for entry.

🚇 S8, S41, or S85: Prenzlauer Allee. ℹ M-Tu goth, Th live bands. $ Cover M €2.50, F €4, Sa €4.50, Su €2.50. Th free. F-Sa all drinks max €2. ⏰ Open M-Tu, Th-Su 8pm-late.

FISHING FOR COMPLIMENTS ● 🍸 ⛅ BAR

Kastanienallee 23 ☎030 51 05 76 86

By day, Fishing for Compliments eagerly seeks your compliments with its fish and chips. But on weekend nights, this becomes one of the coolest fried food places around. The staff opens the front wall up to the street, and sets up a stereosystem that blasts music onto Kastanienallee.

🚇 U2: Eberswalder Str. $ Fish and chips €3.50. Beer €2-3. ⏰ Open M-F noon-11pm, Sa-Su noon-late.

CAFE NEMO ● 🍸 ⛅ BAR

Oderberger Str. 46 ☎030 4 48 19 59

Woven reed mats line the walls of this south-of-the-border bar, and model ships hang from corners of the ceiling. With some quirky murals of inexplicably blue men on the walls, Cafe Nemo manages to avoid being kitschy while still creating a Central American vibe. The outside patio gets crowded early, as does the back room pool and foosball table.

🚇 U2: Eberswalder Str. $ Beer €1.80-3. Mixed drinks €4-5. ⏰ Open M-Sa 6pm-late, Su 4pm-late.

FRIEDRICHSHAIN

When people think of Berlin techno clubs, they're picturing Friedrichshain. You won't find more legendary converted factory or warehouse clubs in any other neighborhood in Germany, and maybe even all of Europe. Most of these raging dance venues are spread out along the river and railroad tracks, between the car dealerships and empty lots on **Mühlenstrasse.** More low-key, but equally popular bars are clustered around **Simon-Dach-Strasse.** In fact, even as we've recommended our favorite laid-back and hoppin' bars below, you really can't go wrong with any place along **Simon-Dach.**

ASTRO-BAR

BAR

Simon-Dach-Str. 40 — www.astro-bar.de

This popular bar gets back to the basics with cheap prices and generously poured alcohol. A DJ plays vinyl records every night starting at 10pm, featuring classics like the Stones and the Beatles, along with some newer indie tracks. Run by a bunch of guys who like their music, love their whiskey *(€4),* and decorate the back of their bar with Transformers nailed to the wall.

U5: Frankfurter Tor. $ Beer from €2.50. Mixed drinks from €5. Open 6pm-late.

ABGEDREHT

BAR

Karl-Marx-Allee 150 — ☎030 29 38 19 11 www.abgedreht.net

This no-frills bar is located right next to Frankfurter Tor, so you can soak up Soviet ambiance while you practically sit on the laps of locals. Sheet music papers the walls, and leather couches are clumped around antique sewing tables. This bar caters to the 30+ crowd, and is a little removed from most of the action on Simon-Dach, but if you're looking to drink a beer with a view of the DDR main street, this is the place to go.

U5: Frankfurter Tor. $ 0.5L beer €3-4. Open daily 5pm-late. Happy hour 7-9pm, cocktails from €5.

SANITORIUM 23

BAR

Frankfurter Allee 23 — ☎030 42 02 11 93 www.sanatorium23.de

If you're looking to experience the techno scene, but don't know if you're ready for the Mühlenstr. madness, get your feet wet at Sanitorium 23. This bar plays relaxed tunes to guests that lounge on sleek couches and chaises. With globe lights suspended from the ceiling, Sanatorium 23 still manages to be a laid-back hangout.

U5: Frankfurter Tors. $ Cocktails €6-8. Beer €3.20. Open M-Th 4pm-2am, F-Sa 4pm-4am, Su 4pm-2am.

RED ROOSTER

BAR

Grünbergerstr. 23 — ☎030 29 00 33 10 www.redrooster.de

This bar is a favorite of locals and travelers alike. The Red Rooster is linked to the hostel next door, and an international crowd of backpackers lounge on the outdoor patio and porch swing. From behind an old wood countertop and under exposed brick ceilings and pipelines, bartenders serve up cider and Czech beers from the tap. For the particularly outgoing or desperate backpacker, "perform 4 stay" events invite you to sing for a free beer—or even a free bed!

U5: Frankfurter Tor. $ Beer from €2.50-3. Open M-Th 5pm-1am, F-Sa 5pm-3am, Su 5pm-1am.

JÄGERKLAUSE

BAR, BEER GARDEN

Grünbergerstr. 1 — ☎0176 222 86 892 www.jaegerklause-berlin.de

Jägerklause is frequented by pin-up stylers, leather-clad bikers, and the old-T-shirt, ripped-jeans crowd. Hence the mounted antlers with disco ball combo. This bar is known for its large beer garden lined with tall shrubs, where guests can lounge in canvas chairs under strands of outdoor lights, while bratwurst and steaks are grilled on a barbeque. The connected pub has a dance floor, and usually features live bands on Wednesdays.

🚇 U5: Frankfurter Tor. ⏰ Biergarten open 3pm-late. Pub open 6pm-late.

PAUL'S METAL ECK BAR

Krossener Str. 15/Simon-Dach-Str. ☎030 201 16 24 💻www.paules-metal-eck.de

Metal hits from the last 50 years are blasted on speakers with videos showing performances of all the best bands. A pierced and tattooed staff serves over 12 varieties of beer from 10 different countries to an international crowd of hardcore fans in this bar outfitted with dart boards and pool tables.

🚇 U5: Frankfurter Tor. $ Beer €2.50-4.50. ⏰ Open daily 1pm-late, usually around 5am-8am.

HABERMEYER BAR

Gärtnerstr. 6 ☎030 29 77 18 87

Habermeyer's retro stylings, and soft red lighting from funky lamps compliment New Wave DJ sessions. The foosball table in the back lends a competitive edge to an otherwise relaxed bar. The young regulars enjoy conversation on low, loungy chairs.

🚇 U5: Samariterstr. $ Mixed drinks €6-7.40. ⏰ Open daily 7pm-late.

ROSI'S CLUB

Revaler Str. 29 💻www.rosis-berlin.de

This always crowded, outdoor club is blocked from the street with bamboo matting. A series of buildings "decorated" with graffiti frame a courtyard full of picnic tables and strung lights. This laid-back river club plays mostly techno and rock music.

🚇 U1 or S3, S5, S7, S9, or S75: Warschauer Str. $ Cover €3-7. ⏰ Open Th-Sa 11pm-late.

CASSIOPIA CLUB, BEER GARDEN, RESTAURANT, MUSIC VENUE

Revaler Str. 99 ☎0302 936 29 66

A sprawling nightlife oasis in an abandoned train factory, this all-in-one entertainment complex is its own self-sufficient entertainment community. Outdoor couches and a climbing wall let you take a break from the indoor dance floor. The multiple bars in the beer garden cater to a mostly student crowd. Occasionally, the club hosts concerts, usually starting around 8pm.

🚇 U1 or S3, S5, S7, S9, or S75: Warschauer Str. $ Cover €5-7. Beer €2.50-3. Vodka €2.50. ⏰ Open W-Sa 11pm-late.

K-17 CLUB

Pettenkoferstr. 17 ☎💻www.k-17.de

This towering club has a dance floor and bar for each of its four floors. Students crowd the courtyard of this out-of-the-way, underground techno club, and colored lights shine on the graffitied exterior walls. Concerts are usually hosted once a week; keep an eye on the website for dates and prices.

🚇 U5: Frankfurter Allee. Once you're on Pettenkoferstr., keep an eye out for signs; the club is off the road, on your right. $ Cover €6. Beer €2.50. Vodka and coke €3.50. ⏰ Open F-Sa 10pm-late.

ASTRA CLUB

Revaler Str. 99 ☎0302 005 67 67 💻www.astra-berlin.de

This converted warehouse by the train tracks is now home to one of the largest dance floors on Revaler. Themed parties draw in big crowds of mixed-age clubbers, from 20-somethings to 40-year-olds, depending on the night, and keep the mood relaxed even while the music blasts. Live bands perform almost weekly. Check the website for performance schedules.

🚇 U1, S3, S5, S7, S9, or S75: Warschauer Str. $ Cover €4-7. ⏰ Open 11:30pm-late.

KREUZBERG

👍 CLUB DER VISIONAERE
👥🚭🍸⛅ CLUB

Am Flutgraben 1 ☎030 695 189 44 💻www.clubdervisionaere.com

Though this river-front cabana/bar/club/boat is packed, the experience is worth the sweaty armpits. A mini-indoor club has a DJ spinning, but the fun is outside with rum-based drinks, feet dipped in the river, and large pizzas *(€8)*. This club is like a mix of the Bayou, New York, and Cancun. One of the best experiences you will have anywhere. So relaxing, so engaging, so Berlin.

🚶 U1: Schlesisches Tor. From the U-bahn head southeast on Schleissichestr. $ Admission €4-15. ⏰ Open daily 10pm-late.

👍 WATERGATE
👥🚭⛅🍸 CLUB

Falckensteinstr. 49 ☎030 61 28 03 96 💻www.water-gate.de

This ultra-exclusive club lights up the river with an eye-popping display of lights, but from the street, not even a sign marks its entrance. You'll have to rely on the enormous line of partiers who've come for a club that lives up to its reputation. Tired guests can "chill out" on the floating dock, while raging rhinos can tear up one of two dance floors. The place won't get packed until 2am—but then it roars until the sun shushes it down. Groups of more than two should pretend like they're separate, and couples should pretend like they're single—seriously.

🚶 U1: Schlesisches Tor. Head toward the bridge. It's the unmarked door at the top of those stairs immediately before the river. $ Cover €8-20. Mixed drinks €6.50. ⏰ Open W 11-late. F and Sa midnight-late.

LUZIA
👥🚭⛅🍸 BAR, CAFE

Oranienstr. 34 ☎030 611 074 69 💻www.luzia.tc

An artsy cafe and bar full of slightly older chums. The patio is most popular in the summer. Try inside for a little privacy, say, inside this place's person-sized doll-house, or in one of the lofts that you climb a ladder to get to.

🚶U1, U8: Kotbusser Tor. From the U-bahn head northeast up AldabertStraße and turn left on Oranienstr. $ Beer €3-6. Mixed drinks €6-8. ⏰ Open daily noon-late.

FARBFERNSEHER
👥🚭🍸 BAR

Skalitzer Str. 114

During the day, you wouldn't think twice about this abandoned office building, but when the sun goes down, this ultra-chill, miniature night club goes up. The whole place has a more relaxed feel than nearly most in Berlin, and its small size means the parties feel both active and intimate without ever being overpowering. Young locals sway to DJs, smoke out front, or talk in the back with friends. They're trying to keep it super-local here, so avoid wearing your fanny pack.

🚶U1, U8 to Kotbusser Tor. From the U-bahn head east down Skalitzer Str. $ Cover €1 (or free with drink purchase). ⏰ Open Sept to mid-July W-Su 10pm-late.

CLUB TRESOR
👥♿🍸⛅ CLUB

Köpenicker Str. 70 ☎0306 290 87 50 💻www.tresorberlin.com

Tresor has an act that starts at 7am. Starts. At. 7am. Multiple DJs spin nightly in this enormous converted warehouse that now houses Berlin's first official Techno Club. The downstairs houses a store, mini-cafe, and men's and women's bathrooms that are literally just cubbies in one long wall. A huge outdoor garden makes space for breaks, while inside, projectors shoot images on every wall, an advanced lighting system disorients and intoxicates, and a killer sound system makes aural magic.

🚶 U8: Heinrich Heinestr. $ Admission €8-15. ⏰ Usually open W, F, Sa 10pm-late.

MAGNET CLUB
🍸⛅ CLUB, MUSIC VENUE

Falckensteinstr. 48 ☎030 44008140 💻www.magnet-club.de

This club's guests break down into two groups: cool locals who come for the

DJs and frequent live bands, and angry tourists who got rejected from Watergate Club next door. Bands play on a short, shallow stage that makes them seem like they're dancing in the crowd. An additional dance floor with separately spinning DJ, and an outdoor chillspace that feels like a converted construction sight, allow guests choose their own experience.

🚇 U1: Schlesisches Tor. Head toward the bridge. An "M" hangs above the door. $ Admission €5-10. ⏰ Usually open Tu-Su from 8pm. Check online for exact schedule.

HEINZ MINKI 🚫💳♿🍸⛅ BEER GARDEN

Vor dem Schlesischen Tor 3 ☎030 6953-3766 💻www.heinzminki.de

A beautiful garden large enough for your group to have some privacy even in a very full, very public place. Lanterns and outdoor music make nights here feel like a drawn-out Fitzgerald novel, without the deep-seated ambiguities and obligatory death. Various booths around the garden serve pizza *(€3),* bratwurst *(€2.50)* and other snacks *(€1-7).* Stealthier guests can steal a bite from the fruit trees spread throughout the garden.

🚇 U1: Schlesisches Tor. $ Beer €2-5. Mixed drinks €5-9. ⏰ Open daily 10pm-late.

ARENA CLUB 🚫💳🚫♿🍸⛅ CLUB

Eichenstr. 4 ☎030 533 20 30 💻www.arena-club.de

This awesome indoor/outdoor complex has a swimming pool in the river during the summer, a faux beach that sells drinks, and dance floors ranging from epic to legendary. A ticket into one of the clubs gets you access to the pool-and-beach bar.

🚇 U1: Schlesisches Tor. From the U-bahn head south on Schlesischestr. across both canal bridges. The Arena complex is the large industrial set of buildings on your left after the 2nd bridge. $ Vary. ⏰ Party hours vary but usually Th-Su from 10pm.

SO36 🚫💳🚫♿🍸▼ BAR, CLUB, MUSIC VENUE

Oranienstr. 190 ☎030 61 40 13 06 💻www.so36.de

SO36 sees itself less as a club, though it's a great club, and more as an organization with an attitude. The various parties, live bands, and cultural presentations that go on here attract a mixed gay/straight clientele whose common demoninator is that they like to party hardy. Gayhane, a gay cabaret that performs the last Saturday of every month, has become a staple of the Berlin gay scene, and can get pretty epic. Remember how *Cabaret* takes place in Berlin? Well, this lives up to that reputation.

🚇 U1, U8: Kottbusser Tor. $ Vary. ⏰ Opening times vary, but usually open F-Sa 10pm-late.

ROSES 🚫💳🚫♿🍸▼ GAY BAR

Oranienstr. 187 ☎030 6156570

Mostly gay men and a few lesbians hang out in this little bar that has fuzzy pink walls and a fuzzy pink ceiling. The bar's small size keeps the energy level high, and the endless assortment of wall trinkets (glowing mounted antlers, glowing hearts) will keep you curious.

🚇 U1, U8: Kottbusser Tor. $ Beer €3. Mixed drinks €4-6. ⏰ Open daily 9pm-late.

FESTAAL KREUZBERG 🚫💳♿🍸⛅ CLUB, MUSIC VENUE

Skalitzerstr. 130 ☎030 611013-13 💻www.festsaal-kreuzberg.de

Live bands play regularly in this punkish old-school former movie theater. The type of place that feels perfectly worn-in but not yet old or dirty. After the concerts, local partygoers spill into the courtyard for more drinks, smokes, and some good ol' post-production chatting. Some nights feature poetry readings, screenings, or art performances.

🚇 U1, U8: Kotbusser Tor. From the U-bahn, head east on Stalitzerstr. $ Tickets €5-20. ⏰ Hours vary. Usually open F-Sa from 9pm. Check website for details.

BIERHIMMEL ⊛♿🍸☀▼ CAFE, BAR

Oranienstr. 183 ☎030 6153122

A relaxing gay-friendly cafe that draws a good mix of gays, lesbians, and straight people. Many have a drink or two here before heading out to more wild adventures like Roses and SO36 next door. The barstaff requests that only nice people who understand tipping stop by.

🚇 U1, U6: Kotbusser Tor. $ Mixed drinks €4-6. Coffee €1-4. ⏰ Open daily 1pm-late.

CLUB MONARCH ⊛⊘🍸 BAR, CLUB

Skalitzerstr. 134

Few clubs fit the word "fun" as well as Club Monarch. A great mixture of old and young, gay and straight, creepers and guys you'll hook up with fill out this small bar above Kaiser's supermarket. A large window gives you a nice view of the U-Bahn and solid DJs keep the party pumping. Smaller crowds are made of regulars and a few foreigners. Parties won't shake out your molars, but they might loosen your bicuspids.

🚇 U1, U8: Kotbusser Tor. Go through the door into the staircase next to Kaiser's. $ Cover €1. Mixed drinks €4-7. ⏰ Open Tu-Sa 10pm-late.

KLEINE REISE ⊛⊘🍸 CLUB

Spreewaldpl. 8

This little underground club, which looks like a bombed-out middle school locker room, spins from the basement of a hostel. Not a place to rage your ass off, but a fantastically hip hangout where you can meet future friends, chat with current friends, or get "friendly" in one of the natural dark spaces in this crumbling basement. The €2 Jager shots are nice, and the robots marching on the window sill are special, indeed.

🚇 U1: Görlitzer Bahnhof. $ Admission €3. ⏰ Open Th-Sa from 10pm.

arts and culture

MUSIC AND OPERA

BERLINER PHILHARMONIKER MITTE

Herbert-von-Karajan-Str. 1 ☎030 25 48 89 99 💻www.berlin-philharmonic.com

It may look strange from the outside, but acoustically, this yellow building is pitch-perfect; all audience members hear the music exactly as it's intended to reach their ears. The Berliner Philharmoniker, led by the eminent Sir Simon Rattle, is one of the world's finest orchestras. It's tough to get a seat; check 1hr. before concert time or e-mail at least 8 weeks in advance.

🚇 S1, S2, or S25 or U2: Potsdamer Pl. $ Tickets from €7 for standing room, from €13 for seats. ⏰ Open July-early Sept. Box office open M-F 3-6pm, Sa-Su 11am-2pm.

DEUTSCHE STAATSOPER MITTE

Unter den Linden 7 ☎030 203 545 55 💻www.staatsoper-berlin.de

The Deutsche Staatsoper is East Berlin's leading opera theater. Though it suffered during the years of separation, this opera house is rebuilding its reputation and its repertoire of classical Baroque opera and contemporary pieces.

🚇 U6: Französische Str. Or bus #100, 157, or 348: Deutsche Staatsoper. $ Tickets €50-160; students €12, if purchased 30min. before shows and ½-price on cheaper seats for certain performances. ⏰ Open Aug to mid-July. Box office open daily noon-7pm, and 1hr. before performances.

DEUTSCHE OPER BERLIN MITTE

Bismarckstr. 35 ☎030 34 38 43 43 💻www.deutscheoperberlin.de

The Deutsche Oper is Berlin's newest opera house. If you have the chance, don't pass on a cheap ticket to go see one of Berlin's best performances.

🚇 U2: Deutsche Oper. $ Tickets €12-118. 25% student discounts. ⏰ Open Sept-June. Box office open M-Sa 11am until beginning of the performance, or 11am-7pm on days without performances; Su 10am-2pm. Evening tickets available 1hr. before performances.

FILM

Finding English films in Berlin is anything but difficult. On any night, choose from over 150 different films, marked **O.F.** or **O.V.** for the original version (meaning not dubbed in German), **O.m.U** for original version with German subtitles, or **O.m.u.E.** for original film with English subtitles.

KINO BABYLON
⊗⊛🍸 MITTE

Rosa-Luxemburg-Str. 30 ☎030 242 59 69 💻www.babylonberlin.de

A spunky little independent film house with a commitment to quality films, Kino Americans and Berliners alike who flock here for pure film culture. Occasional summer screenings happen outdoors on the beautiful Rosa-Luxemburg-and an epic screening of Rocky Horror Picture Show goes down regularly here.

🚇 U2: Rosa-Luxemburg-Pl. $ Tickets €4-8. ⏰ Schedules change daily. Check website for details.

IMAX 3D SONY CENTER
🎟♿🍸 MITTE

Potsdamer Str. 4 ☎030 230 979 50 💻www.cinestar-imax.de

A big, commercial theater that shows new releases as early as you'll find them anywhere in Berlin. 3D costs extra, but can you really put a price on a dimension?

🚇 U2: Potsdamer Pl. $ Tickets €7-13. ⏰ 1st showing at noon. Last showing at 11pm.

CENTRAL KINO
⊛♿🍸☀ MITTE

Rosenthaler Str. 39 ☎030 28599973 💻kino-central.de

A small theater right in the middle of hip Mitte, this place shows indie American, German and international films, mostly in their original format with German subtitles. While the screens aren't huge, the theater makes up for it with style. One of the theaters is even outside.

🚇 U8: Weinmeisterstr. $ €6.50, students €6. ⏰ Open daily before the 1st movie, noon-3pm.

ARSENAL
KREUZBERG

In the Filmhaus at Potsdamer Pl. ☎030 26 95 51 00 💻www.fdk-berlin.de

Run by the founders of Berlinale, Arsenal showcases indie films and some classics *(€6.50)*. Frequent appearances by guest directors make the theater a popular meeting place for Berlin's filmmakers.

🚇 U2, S1, S2, or S25: Potsdamer Pl.

FILMKUNSTHAUS BABYLON
MITTE

Rosa-Luxemburg-Str. 30 ☎030 242 59 69 💻www.babylon-berlin.de

This *haus* shows classics like *Goodfellas* in the main theater and global art films in the intellectual Studiokino. Most English-language films not dubbed in German.

🚇 U2: Rosa-Luxemburg-Pl. Entrance on Hirtenstr. $ Main theater M-W €5.50, Th-Su €6.50.

THEATER

ENGLISH THEATER BERLIN
🎟♿🍸 KREUZBERG

Fidicinstr. 40 ☎030 693 56 92 💻www.etberlin.de

For over 20 years Berlin's only all English-language theater has been defying German-language totalitarianism with everything from 10-minute short festivals to full length productions. Leave your *umlauts* at home.

🚇 U6: Pl. der Luftbrücke. $ €14, students €8. ⏰ Box office opens 1hr. before show time. Shows are at 8pm unless otherwise noted.

DEUTSCHES THEATER

♥♿🍴 MITTE

Schumann Straße 13a   ☎030 28 44 10 📧www.deutschestheater.de

Built in 1850, this world-famous theater that legendary director Max Reinhardt once controlled is still a cultural heavy hitter in Berlin. Performances tend to be in German, and they tend to change frequently, so check the website for details. *U6: Oranienburger Tor. From the U-bahn, head south on Friederichstraße, take a right on Reinhartße and another right on Albrecthstr. Ⓢ €5-30. ⌚ Box office open M-Sa 11am-6:30pm, Su 3-6:30pm. Shows are at 8pm unless otherwise noted.*

VOLKS BÜHNE

♥♿ MITTE

Linienstraße 227   ☎030 24 06 55 📧www.volksbuehne-berlin.de

Recently re-opened after a renovation, this imposing theater that looks straight from a Utopian sci-fi thriller delivers on its promise of "art for the people." While the enormous stage goes quiet during the summer, from Septemner to May it is alive with concerts, theatrical shows in German and English, and touring performances and festivals. Before and after the shows, crowds gather in the beautiful plaza to smoke and talk. *U2: Rosa-Luxemburg-Pl. Ⓢ Tickets €6-30. Students get 50% discount. ⌚ Box office open daily noon-6pm and 1hr. before performances. Shows are at 8pm unless otherwise noted.*

BERLINER ENSEMBLE

MITTE

Bertolt-Brecht-Pl. 1   ☎030 28 40 81 55 📧www.berliner-ensemble.de

The theater, established by Brecht, is enjoying a renaissance under the leadership of Claus Peymann. Hip repertoire with the like of Heiner Müller, young playwrights, and Brecht. Some of the plays are in English. *U6 or S1, S2, S5, S7, S9, S25, or S75: Friedrichstr. Ⓢ Tickets €2-30; students €7. ⌚ Box office open M-F 8am-6pm, Sa-Su 11am-6pm, and 1hr. before shows.*

shopping

CLOTHING

Department Stores

KADEWE

♥ CHARLOTTENBURG

Tauentzienstr. 21-24   ☎030 212 10

You'll find a thousand things you can't live without, and absolutely nothing you can afford. But you'll have a great time looking. KaDeWe is Berlin's Harrod's, with the stylish extavagance of Chanel, Prada, and Cartier flashing out from every window display. And even if most of us will never actually shop in the KaDeWe, watching the people who do is almost as fun as window shopping. *U1, U2, or U3: Wittenbergpl. ⌚ Open M-Th 10am-8pm, F 10am-9pm, Sa 9:30am-8pm.*

Secondhand

MACY'Z

WILMERSDORF

Mommsenstr. 2   ☎030 881 13 63

Mommenstr. is Berlin's secondhand designer-label mecca, and Macy'z may have the best collection around. Everything the store carries is less than two years old, and designed by the biggest names in the industry: It's 🔖Gucci bags and Prada shoes, for half the original price or less. Just to clarify, half-price on a Burberry coat might still set you back €500. But for the truly devoted, a (very relative) deal can be found. *U1: Uhlandstr. ⌚ Open M-Sa noon-6:30pm, Su noon-4pm.*

CACHE-COEUR PRENZLAUER BERG

Schönehauser Allee 174 ☎030 44 35 49 62

Prenzlauer Berg is full of costly vintage clothing shops, but dedicated shoppers can still find a deal. Cache-Coeur is a women's vintage clothing store that specializes in clothing from the 1950s-70s, but carries pieces from the '20s-'40s as well. All clothing is tailored before it goes on the rack, so no rips or tears. The owner has painstakingly selected only the most beautiful pieces, and sells at very reasonable prices. Most dresses, for example, fall between €50-125.

🚇 *U2: Senefelderpl.*

GARAGE SCHÖNEBERG

Ahornstraße 2 ☎302 11 27 60

The Garage is one of Berlin's cheapest secondhand clothing stores, and with one of the biggest selections. About a third of the items are fix-priced, but the rest is sold by the kilo, for €15 per kg. Über cheap deals like that mean mostly basic items; but, as always, shoppers with a little more time and energy might be able to find something out of the ordinary.

🚇 *U1, U2, U3, U4, or U9: Nollendorfpl.*

JEWELRY

MICHAELA BINDER 💳♿ MITTE

Gipsstr. 13 ☎030 2838 4869 💻www.michaelabinder.de

There's plenty of great street jewelry all over the city; most of it can be found near the cash registers at T-shirt stores. But for the big spenders who need real valuables to boost their self esteems, this Mitte jeweler does beautiful rings, bracelets, and necklaces with textbook Berlin understatement.

🚇 *U8: Weinmeisterstr.* [S] *Pieces from €60.* ⏰ *Open Tu-F noon-7pm, Sa noon-4pm.*

FLEA MARKETS

👍 **ARKONAPLATZ** 🌿♿🍸☀ PRENZLAUER BERG

Arkonapl. ☎786 9764

Craftsmen sell jewelry. Farmers juice oranges. That guy down the street hawks his CDs from a towel. Arkonaplatz brings out the weird, the old, the desperate, and everyone who wants their stuff. The market's enormous size makes the junk spread incredible: DDR relics, massive rolls of fabric, pictures of vendors' babies, antique space hats? Stick around in the afternoons when the unnamed Irish man comes by with a karaoke machine on his bike. He's been doing it for years now.

🚇 *U8: Bernaurstr.* ⏰ *Open Su 9am-6pm.*

👍 **TURKISH MARKET** 🌿♿🍸☀ KREUZBERG

Along the south bank of the Landwehrkanal

Fruit vendors shout to passersby about their fruit, bakers shout about their baking, clothing dealers shout about their clothing. The Turkish Market is not just an amazing place to find great deals on fruit and clothing, it's one of the best experiences of the entire city. The fruit stands have fruits you've never seen, and they only cost €1. The clothing stands have deals like three pairs of socks for the price of one. On top of this, musicians play at the ends of the market. Not exactly a "flea" market, but an incredible market, and one you won't forget.

🚇 *U1: Kottbusser Tor. From the U-bahn, head south toward the canal.* ⏰ *Open Tu and F noon-6pm.*

👍 **MAUERPARK FLEA MARKET** PRENZLAUER BERG

On Eberswalderstr.

The Mauerpark Flea Market is the biggest and best-known in all of Berlin. A labyrinth of booths and stalls sells everything from hand-ground spices to used clothing to enamel jewelry to potted plants. Hoards of bargain hunters, hipsters, and gawking tourists crowd the park, drinking fresh-squeezed orange juice and listening to the street musicians who swarm the market. Like all secondhand stores in Prenzlauer Berg, Mauerpark is rarely dirt-cheap. You can still find good values, but expect slightly higher prices.

U2: Eberswalderstr.

STRASSE DES 17 JUNI
●&♿♿☕ MITTE

Str. des 17 Juni

A large but touristy market, Straße des 17 Juni gets a lot of people looking for the "authentic Berlin flea market experience." But it's a little like tasting a McDonalds cause you heard Americans made good hamburgers. Check it out if you're in the area, but if you don't want to experience trashy, unpredictable flea markets of Berlin, steer clear.

Take the S-Bahn to Tiergarten. ☒ Open Sa-Su 11am-5pm.

PREUSSENPARK FLEA MARKET
● WILMERSDORF

On the corner of Brandenburgische Str. and Hohenzollerndamm

The Preußenpark flea market is smaller and less varied than the Mauerpark one to the east, but the prices are a lot cheaper. Clothing is rarely more than €10, and usually less. Some handmade crafts and original paintings, and a large selection of antique maps and prints. Preußenpark is a great place to find vintage jewelry and woodblock prints.

U3 or U7: Fehrbelliner Pl. ☒ Open Sa-Su 10am-4pm.

AM KUPFERGRABEN
● OUTSKIRTS

On Am Kupfergraben, across from the Bodemuseum

Stroll along Museum Island while you shop at secondhand tents. For the location, there may be no better flea market in Berlin. Though the selection is relatively small, Am Kupfergraben's flea market has a wide variety of antique and old books and maps, as well as some works by new, young artists. A requisite collection of *steins* rounds out this quintessentially Berlin market.

S3, S5, S7, or S75: Hackeshire Markt. ☒ Open Sa-Su 10am-5pm.

BOOKS

ST. GEORGE'S BOOKSTORE
● PRENZLAUER BERG

Wörtherstr. 27 ☎0308 179 83 33

You'll be hard-pressed to find a better English-language bookstore on the continent. St. George's owner makes frequent trips to the UK and US to buy up loads of titles so that his customers can find any book they're looking for, and then some. Over half of the books are used and extremely well-priced *(paperbacks €4-6)*, with a number of books for just €1. This shop also carries new books and can order absolutely any title they don't already carry. If you're looking for travel reading material, there's absolutely no better place to go in Berlin. Pay in euro, British pounds, or American dollars (oh my!).

U2: Senefelderpl. ☒ Open M-F 11am-7pm, Sa 10am-4pm.

HUNDTHAMMERSTEIN
☕ PRENZLAUER BERG

Alte Schoenhauser Str. 23/24 ☎0302 345 76 69 ■www.hundthammerstein.de

This medium-sized book store has a large English section of literature, poetry, non-fiction, and trash literature. Almost half the books are in English, which is rare for Berlin. Racy books like *The Giant Book of Penises* sit behind the counter. If you ask, they'll let you take a peek.

U8: Winmeisstr. ☒ Open M-Sa 11am-8pm.

shopping • books

MUSIC

SPACE HALL
♦⊗♨ KREUZBERG

Zossenerstr. 33, 35 ☎306947664 ▣www.spacehall.de

They don't make them like this in the States no more. The CD store is two doors down from the vinyl store. The vinyl store just keeps going, with a "bunker" vibe and a courtyard where DJs sometimes spin and sample turntables. They also have an inspiring collection of rubber duckies.

₮ *U7: Gneisenaustr.* 🕑 *Open M-W 11am-8pm, Th-F 11am-10pm, Sa 11-8pm.*

MELTING POINT
♦& PRENZLAUER BERG

Kastanienallee 55 ☎030 44047131 ▣www.meltingpoint-berlin.de

An unassuming little pod with vinyl and CD collections, this little joint gets frequented by Berliner DJs and other members of Berlin's popping club scene. Don't come here for the White Album.

₮ *U8: Rosenthaler Pl. From the U-bahn walk nort east up Weinbergsweg, which will turn into Kastanienallee.* ⑤ *Records €5-30.* 🕑 *Open M-Sa noon-8pm.*

HARDWAX
●⊗ KREUZBERG

Paul-Lincke-Ufer 44a ☎030 611 301 11 ▣www.hardwax.com

This record shop lies hidden, pushed back from the street, up a graffiti-covered stairwell to the third floor of a space that could as easily be a garage or a storage shed. Instead, records that set the latest trends in Berlin line the walls, and a staff that lives and breathes this music stands by to (if they must) help out clueless tourists.

₮ *U1 or U8: Kottbusser Tor. From the U-bahn, head south on Kottbusserstr. Take a left just before the canal.* ⑤ *Records €5-30.* 🕑 *Open M-Sa noon-8pm.*

FRANZ AND JOSEF SCHEIBEN
⊛ PRENZLAUER BERG

Kastanienallee 48 ☎030 417 146 82

This is secondhand vinyl at its best. With a huge collection of used records that spills out of the shop and onto the street outside, Franz and Josef may specialize in '80s rock and punk, but they carry much more. Records sell for as low as €1, but prices vary in a store that sells some true antiques; the owner will tell you to expect to pay somewhere between €1 and €1000 for your vinyl. Thankfully, almost all the records fall pretty close to that first marker.

₮ *U2: Senefelderpl.* 🕑 *Open M-Sa 1pm-8pm.*

FIDELIO
⊛ SCHÖNEBERG

Akazienstr. 30 ☎030 781 97 36

For those looking to get in touch with their classier side, Fidelio is the place to go. An extensive selection of classical, jazz, and world music lines the walls and spills out of low bookcases. If you've only just recently been inspired to give Wagner a listen, the staff here are more than happy to point newcomers in the right direction. Fidelio sells primarily CDs, with some vintage vinyl on the side. Prices are generally standard; there's a wide range, but albums usually fall in at about €12.

₮ *U7: Eisenacherstr.* 🕑 *Open M-F 11am-7pm, Sa 10am-3pm.*

berlin

essentials

> ## baby, you called?
> The phone code for Berlin is ☎030.

PRACTICALITIES

- **TOURIST OFFICES:** Now privately owned, tourist offices provide far fewer free services than they once did. ◾www.berlin.de has quality information on all aspects of the city. **EurAide** sells rail tickets, maps, phone cards, and walking-tour tickets. (☎1781 828 2488 ♐ *In the Hauptbahnhof, across from the McDonald's.*) **Tourist Info Centers.** (*Berlin Tourismus Marketing GmbH, Am Karlsbad 11, 10785. Office located on the ground floor of the Hauptbahnhof. The entrance is on Europl.* ☎030 25 00 25 ◾www.berlin-tourist-information.de* ⅈ* Service in English. Siegessäule, Sergej, and Gay-Yellowpages have gay and lesbian event and club listings.* ⑤ *Reserve rooms for a €3-6 fee. Transit maps free; city maps €1. The monthly Berlin Programm lists museums, sights, restaurants, and hotels, as well as opera, theater, and classical music performances, €1.75. Full listings of film, theater, concerts, and clubs in German Tip, €2.70, or Zitty, €2.70. English-language movie and theater reviews are in Ex-Berliner €2.* ✪ *Open daily 8am-10pm.*) **Alternate location.** (*Brandenburger Tor* ♐ *S1, S2, or S25 or bus #100: Unter dne Linden. On your left as you face the pillars from the Unter den Linden side.* ✪ *Open daily 10am-6pm.*)

- **TOURS: Terry Brewer's Best of Berlin** is legendary for vast knowledge and engaging personalities, making the over 6hr. walk well worth it. (*Tours leave daily from in front of the Bandy Brooks shop on Friedrichstr.* ☎0177 388 1537 ◾www.berwersberlintours.com. ♐ *S1, S7, S9, S75, or U6: Friedrichstr.* ✪ *10:30am.* ⑤ *€12.*) **Sinful Berlin** tour meets for some good (not so clean) fun and includes entrance to Europ's largest erotic museum. (✪ *Th and Sa 8pm.*) **Insider Tour** offers a variety of fun, informative tours that hit all the major sights. More importantly, the guide's enthusiasm for Berlin is contagious, and their accents span the English-speaking world (we'll be honest, we always fall for a good accent). (☎030 692 3149 ◾www.insidertour.com ⅈ *Offers tours of Nazi Berlin, Cold War Berlin, Potsdam, and a Berlin Pub Crawl as well as daytrip tours to Dresden.* ⑤ *€12, under 26 or with a WelcomeCard or ISIC €10. Bike tours €20/18.* ✪ *Picks up daily Apr-Oct 10am, 2:30pm at the McDonald's outside the Zoo Station, 30min. later at the Coffeemamas at "Hackescher Markt"; Nov-Mar 10am from the Zoo Station and 10:30am at "Hackescher Markt" only. Bike tours meet by the Coffee Mamas at "Hackescher Markt." June-Sept 10:30am and 3pm. Tours last 4hr.*) **Original Berlin Walks** offers a range of English language walking tours, including "Infamous Third Reich Sites," "Jewish Life in Berlin," "Nest of Spies," and "Discover Potsdam." (☎030 301 9194 ◾www.berlinwalks.de ⑤ *Discover Berlin Walk €12, under 26 €10, WelcomeCard and ISIC €9.* ✪ *Tours meet Apr-Oct 10am, 2:30pm at the taxi stand in front of Bahnhof Zoo and at the Hackescher Markt Häagen-Datz 10:30am, 3pm; Nov-Mar 10am at the taxi stand and 1-:30am at Hackescher Markt.*) **New Berlin** offers free tours on a tip-only basis, which means some pandering from the guides, of Berlin's biggest sights, and special tours (Sachsenhausen, Third Reich tour, pub crawl, etc.) for a fee. Backpackers with little cash are encouraged to take the tour but occasionally dislike the cursory nature of the set-up. (☎030 51

05 00 30 🖥www.newberlintours.com ℹ A new bike tour daily at 11am, 2pm in front of the Postfurhramat, on the corner of Oranienburgerstr. and Tucholskystr., S-Bahn: Oranienberger Str. $ With bike rental €15, without bike rental €12. ⏰ Tours leave daily from the Brandenburg Gate Starbucks at 11am, 1, 4pm, and the Zoologischer Garten Dunkin' Donuts at 10:30am, 12:30, 3:30pm.)

- **STUDENT TRAVEL OFFICES: STA** books flights and hotels and sells ISICs. *(Dorotheenstr. 30 ☎030 20 16 50 63 🚇 S3, S5, S7, S9, S75, or U6 to Friedrichstr. ⏰ Open M-F 10am-7pm, Sa 11am-3pm.)* **Second location.** *(Sleimstr. 28 🚇 S4, S8, S85, or U2: Schönhauser Allee. ⏰ Open M-F 10am-7pm, Sa 11am-4pm.)* **Third location.** *(Hardenbergerstr. 9 🚇 U2: Ernst-Reuter-Pl. ⏰ Open M-F 10am-7pm, Sa 11am-3pm.)* **Fourth location.** *(Takustr. 47 ⏰ Open M-F 10am-7pm, Sa 10am-2pm.)*
- **CURRENCY EXCHANGE AND MONEY WIRES:** The best rates are usually found at exchange offices with *Wechselstrube* signs outside, at most major train-stations, and in large squares. For money wires through Western Union, use **ReiseBank.** *(Hauptbahnhof ☎030 20 45 37 61 ⏰ M-Sa 8am-10pm.)* **Second location.** *(Bahnhof Zoo ☎030 881 7117.)* **Third location.** *(Ostbahnhof ☎030 296 4393.)*
- **LUGGAGE STORAGE:** *(🚇In the Hauptbahnhof, in "DB Gepack Center," 1st fl., East side. $ €4 per day.)* Lockers also in Bahnhof Zoo, Ostbahnhof, and Alexanderpl.
- **INTERNET:** Free Internet with admission to the **Staatsbibliothek.** During their renovation, Staatsbibliothek requires a €10 week-long pass to their library. *(Potsdamer Str. 33 ☎030 26 60 ⏰ Open M-F 9am-9pm, Sa 9am-7pm.)* **Netlounge** *(Auguststr. 89 ☎030 24 34 25 97 🖥www.netlounge-berlin.de 🚇 U-Bahn: Oranienburger Str. $ €2.50 per hr. ⏰ Open daily noon-midnight.)* **Easy Internet** has several locations throughout Berlin *(Unter den Linden 24, Rosenstraße 16, Frankfurter Allee 32, Rykestraße 29, and Kurfürstendamm 18).* Many cafes throughout Berlin offer free Wi-Fi.
- **POST OFFICES: Main branch.** *(Joachimstaler Str. 7 ☎030 88 70 86 11 🚇 Down Joachimstaler Str. from Bahnhof Zoo and near Kantstr. ⏰ Open M-Sa 9am-8pm.)* **Tegel Airport** *(⏰ Open M-F 8am-6pm, Sa 8am-noon.)* **Ostbahnhof.** *(⏰ Open M-F 8am-8pm, Sa-Su 10am-6pm.)*
- **POSTAL CODE:** 10706.

EMERGENCY!

- **POLICE:** *(Pl. der Luftbrücke 6. 🚇 U6: Pl. der Luftbrüche.)*
- **EMERGENCY NUMBERS:** ☎110. **Ambulance and Fire** ☎112. **Non-emergency advice hotline:** ☎030 46 64 46 64.
- **MEDICAL SERVICES:** The American and British embassies list English-speaking doctors. The **emergency doctor** *(☎030 31 00 31 or ☎01804 2255 2362)* service helps travelers find English-speaking doctors. **Emergency dentist.** *(☎030 89 00 43 33.)*
- **CRISIS LINES:** English spoken at most crisis lines. **American Hotline** has crisis and referral services. *(☎0177 814 15 10.)* **Poison Control.** *(☎030 192 40.)* **Berliner Behindertenverband** has advice for the handicapped. *(Jägerstr. 63d ☎030 204 38 48 🖥www.bbv-ev.de ⏰ Open W noon-5pm and by appointment.)* **Deutsche AIDS-Hilfe.** *(Wilhelmstr. 138 ☎030 690 0870 🖥www.aidshilfe.de.)* **Drug Crisis.** *(☎030 192 37 ⏰ 24hr.)* **Women's Resources.** Frauendrisentelefon Women's crisis line. *(☎030 615 4243 🖥www.frauenkrisentelefon.de ⏰ Open M*

and Th 10am-noon, Tu-W, F 7pm-9pm, Sa-Su 5pm-7pm.) **Lesbenberatung** offers lesbian counseling. *(Kulmer Str. 20 ☎030 215 2000 💻www.lesbenberatung-berlin.de.)* **Schwulenberatung** offers gay men's counseling. *(Mommenstr. 45 ☎030 194 46 💻www.schwulenberatungberlin.de.)* **Maneo.** Legal help for gay violence victims. *(☎030 216 3336 💻www.maneo.de ⏰ Open daily 5pm-7pm.)* **LARA.** Sexual assault help. *(Fuggerstr. 19 ☎030 216 88 88 💻www.lara-berlin.de ⏰ Open M-F 9am-6pm.)* **Children's emergency helpline.** *(☎030 610 061.)*

GETTING THERE

By Plane

Capital Airport Berlin Brandenburg International (BBI) will open in the southeast Berlin in 2012. Until then, **Tegel Airport** will continue to serve travelers. *(Take express bus #X9 or #109 from Jakob-Kaiser Pl. on U7, bus #128 from Kurt-Schumacher-Pl. on U6, or bus TXL from Beusselstr on S42 and S41. Follow signs in the airport for ground transportation. ☎49 30 6091 2055 💻www.berlin-airport.de.)*

By Train

International trains *(☎972 226 150)* pass through Berlin's **Hauptbahnhof**and run to: **Amsterdam, NTH** *($ €130. ⏰6½hr., 16 per day)*; **Brussels, BEL** *($ €165⏰ 7hr., 14 per day)*; **Budapest, HUN** *($ €165 ⏰ 13hr., 4 per day)*; **Copenhagen, DNK** *($ €155⏰ 7hr., 7 per day)*; **Paris, FRA** *($ €200 ⏰ 9hr., 9 per day)*; **Prague, CZR** *($ €80 ⏰5hr., 12 per day)*; **Vienna, AUT** *($ €155 ⏰ 10hr., 12 per day)*.

By Bus

ZOB is the central bus station. *(Masurenallee 4. 🚉 U2: Kaiserdamm. Alternatively, S4, S45, or S46: Messe Nord/ICC. ☎030 301 30 80 ⏰ Open M-F 6am-9pm, Sa-Su and holidays 6am-8pm.)*

GETTING AROUND

By Bike

The best way to see Berlin is by bike. Unless your hostel's out in the boonies, few trips will be out of cycling reach, and given that U-Bahn tickets verge on €3 and that the average long-term bike rental costs €8 per day, pedaling your way is just a better deal.

FAT TIRE BIKE RENTAL MITTE

Alexanderpl. ☎030 24 04 79 91 💻www.berlinfahrradverleih.com

Rents bikes for half- and full-days.

🚉 East location U2: Alexanderpl. Directly under the TV Tower. West location U2 or U9: Zoological Garten. $ €7 per ½-day (up to 4hr.), €12 per day. ⏰ Open May-Oct 15 daily 9:30am-8pm; Oct 16-Nov and Mar-Apr daily 9:30am-6pm.

The BVG

The heart of Berlin's public transportation system is the U-Bahn and S-Bahn Metro trains, which cover the city in a spidery and circular patterns, respectively. Trams *(Straßenbahn)* and buses (both part of the U-Bahn system) scuttle around the remaining city corners. *(BVG's 24hr. hotline ☎030 194 49 💻www.bvg.de.)* Berlin is divided into three transit zones. Zone A has central Berlin, including Tempelhof Airport. The rest of Berlin is in Zone B; Zone C consists of outlying areas, including Potsdam and Oranienburg. An AB ticket is the best deal, since you can later buy extension tickets for the outlying areas. A one-way ticket is good for 2hr. after validation. *($ Zones AB €2.10, BC €2.50, ABC €2.80, under 14 reduced fare, under 6 free.)* Within the validation period, the ticket may be used on any S-Bahn, U-Bahn, bus, or tram.

Most train lines don't run Monday through Friday 1-4am. S-Bahn and U-Bahn lines do run Friday and Saturday nights, but less frequently. When trains stop, 70 night buses take over, running every 20-30min. and tending to follow major transit lines; pick up the free Nachtliniennetz map of bus routes at a **Fahrscheine und Mehr** office. The letter "N" precedes night bus numbers. Trams also continue to run at night.

Buy tickets, including monthly passes, from machines or ticket windows in Metro stations or from bus drivers. **Be warned:** machines don't give more than €10 change, and many machines don't take bills, though some accept credit cards. Validate your ticket by inserting it into the stamp machines before boarding. Failure to validate becomes a big deal when plainclothes policemen bust you and charge you €40 for freeloading. If you bring a bike on the U-Bahn or S-Bahn, you must buy it a child's ticket. Bikes are forbidden on buses and trams.

Single-ride tickets are a waste of money. A **Day Ticket** (*Ⓢ AB €6.10, ABC €6.50*) is good from the time it's stamped until 3am the next day. The BVG also sells **7-day tickets** (*Ⓢ AB €26.20, ABC €32.30*) and **month-long tickets** (*Ⓢ AB €72, ABC €88.50*). Another option are the popular tourist cards: the **WelcomeCard** (sold at tourist offices) buys unlimited travel (*Ⓢ AB 48hr. €17, ABC €19; 72hr. €23/26*) and includes discounts on 130 city sights. The **CityTourCard** is good within zones AB (*Ⓢ 48hr. €16, 72hr. €22*) and offers discounts at over 50 attractions.

By Taxi

Taxis: Call 15min. in advance. Women can request female drivers. Trips within the city cost up to €30. (*☎030 26 10 26, ☎0800 263 0000 toll-free.*)

excursions

SPREEWALD AND LÜBBENAU ☎03542

About 100km southeast of Berlin, the Spree River splits into an intricate maze of small streams and canals, weaving between meadows, forests, and farmland that were once home to the **Sorbs**, Germany's native Slavic minority. In broad terms, the 1000 sq. km of this area is termed the **Spreewald** (*Spree Forest*), and, of the many small villages scattered around the area, the most famous is **Lübbenau.**

Spreewald is a popular daytrip destination for Berliners seeking their pastoral-idyllic fix in its hiking trails, gondola rides, and kayaks. Tourists drift down scenic canals lined with thatched roofs and birch trees, catching glimpses of the wildlife. For quaint German towns, Lübbenau simply can't be beat. Even as it's increasingly corrupted by the knick-knack shops that sell decorated eggs and jars of pickles, there is still something refreshingly authentic about the ambience. Many of the buildings from the original Sorb settlement have either been preserved or recreated, and the virtue of simplicity and wholesome living are echoed in the rough-hewn wood siding and bare floors of the homes. And however tourist-oriented the city centers may be, there's no denying the incredible beauty of the Spreewald landscape. Vast meadows of tall grasses and pockets of densely packed birches make for an endlessly refreshing view as you tramp across hiking trails or paddle through streams in your canoe.

A small second town, officially considered part of Lübbenau, is 3km away from city center. **Lehde** is truthfully less of a town, and more of a sight; it's here that you'll find a higher concentration of preserved homes clustered together in a densely forested area.

Accommodations

The only things outnumbering gondolas in Lübbenau are the **hotel pensions** literally shoulder-to-shoulder along cobblestone streets, and sometimes on top of each other. Just five minutes of walking through the streets of Lübbenau will bring you in contact with seven or so pensions, each almost identical in price, appearance, and location. Expect to pay €45-55 for a double room, or, at the slightly lower end of the spectrum, about €20 per person. Your best bet is to check out the comprehensive catalog of pension listings available in the tourist office; in the busy summer months, it's likely that your decision will be determined by availability. Though there's little diversity in accommodation options, we've listed the least expensive hostels in Lübbenau, as places you might want to contact first when inquiring about a room. Or go **camping;** there may be no better place than Spreewald to dust off your tents and break out the mosquito repellent.

CAMPINGPLATZ AM SCHLOSSPARK — CAMPGROUND ❶

Schlßbezirk 20 ☎03542 35 33 💻www.spreewaldcamping.de

125 tent plots with cooking and bathing facilities on site, as well as a convenience store, make this beautiful campground a little more comfortable to boot.

➔ From the tourist information office, follow Ehm-Welk-Str. to the left, as it turns into Schloßbezirk. $ €6 per person; 2- to 4-person bungalows €20-50. ⏰ Reception 7:30am-12:30pm and 2-10pm.

PENSION SCHERZ — PENSION ❷

Bergstr. 9A ☎03542 465 78 💻www.pensionscherz.de

Coral walls and mismatched lawn furniture give this pension the feel of a laid-back family lake house. This pension might be worth checking first because of its low prices and wonderfully kind staff.

➔ From the tourist information office, walk down Ehm-Welk-Str. until it turns into Karl-Marx-Str. Turn right onto Bergerstr. The pension is at the end of the street. ℹ Breakfast included. $ Singles €38; doubles €45. Per-person rates €19-24 per night.

PENSION AM ALTEN BAUERNHAFEN — PENSION ❸

Stottof 5 ☎03542 29 30 💻www.am-alten-bauernhafen.de

Pine paneled walls and red-checked curtains make this pension an unusually well-decorated riverside retreat. The outdoor patio backs right up to a canal, and guests lounge in the shade. Prices vary, so check ahead.

➔ From the tourist information office, follow Ehm-Welk-Str. as it turns into Karl-Marx-Str., and then turn left onto Stottof. The pension will be on your left. $ Doubles from €44; triples from €55; 4-person rooms €50-80.

Sights

Luckily for travelers, Lübbenau's biggest sight is always free and open. **Spreewald Forest's** winding paths and quaint canals are yours for the taking, so explore the woods at will. If you're looking to relax and enjoy a view of Spreewald in true Sorb fashion, and don't mind the company of many a senior citizen, gondola rides are the way to go. Tours of the forest (in German) depart from the **Großer Hafen** (larger port) and the **Kleiner Hafen** (smaller port). The Großer Hafen, along Dammstr. behind the church, offers a wider variety of tours, including 2-3hr. trips to Lehde. The boats take on customers starting 9-10am and depart when full (about 20 passengers) throughout the day. **Genossenschaft der Kahnfährleute** *(Dammstr. 77a. ☎03542 22 254 💻www.grosser-hafen.de $ €8.50, children €4.25; 3hr. €10/5; 5hr. tour of the forest €13/6.50. ⏰ Open Mar-Oct daily 9:30am-6pm)* is the largest gondola company in Lübbenau. They offer 2hr. round trips to Lehde. From the Kleiner Hafen, less-touristed but nearly identical wilderness trips are run by the **Kahnfährmannsverein der Spreewaldfreunde** *(Spreestr. 10a. ☎03542 40 37 10 $ €8-20, children €4-10. ⏰ Open Apr-Oct daily 9am-6pm).*

There's no better view of Lübbenau than from the river, and perhaps no better way than on a kayak or canoe. Where gondola rides are restrictive for those looking to explore on their own, paddling your own boat lets you wander through streams and canals as you please. Kayaks, canoes, and paddleboats can be rented from the **Campingplatz Am Schloßpark** (above) for €5 per hr. *(single person)*, or €15 per day. **Kajak-Sports.** *(Dammstr. 76a. ☎03542 37 64 💻www.bootsverleih-richter.de $ Single paddleboats for €5 per hr., €14 per day. Doubles for €6 per hr., €15 per day. Kayaks for €9 per hr., €12 for 2 hr., €18 per day. ⏰ Open daily from 9am.)*

FREILANDMUSEUM LEHDE (OPEN-AIR MUSEUM LEHDE) MUSEUM

Located in Lehde, behind the aquarium. ☎03542 24 72 🖥www.freiland-museum-lehde

Lehde itself is a sight to see. Just 3km away from Lübbenau along a tree-shaded path, this UNESCO-protected landmark is accessible by foot, boat, or bike. The Freilandmuseum is a small community of recreated houses and workshops with exhibits that illustrate the 19th century lifestyle of the Sorbs, when whole families slept in one room, and newlyweds would go out back for a literal "romp in the hay." Though the unfortunately creepy mannequins performing typical Sorbian tasks are more off-putting than enlightening, the overall effect of this small cluster of buildings is pleasant; the buildings are authentically constructed, and the handicraft is observable in the rough timbers lining the walls and the uneven clay-brick floors. Artisans have set up workshops in some the buildings, making pots and decorative eggs in the Sorbian tradition.

⇞ Follow the signs from Altstadt or Groß Harbor to Lehde. $ €5, students €4, children under 16 €1. ⏰ Open daily Apr-Sept 10am-6pm, last entry 5:30pm; Oct 10am-5pm.

SPREEWALDMUSEUM MUSEUM

Topfmarkt 12 ☎03542 24 72 🖥www.spreewald-web.de

While community history museums often fall flat, Spreewaldmuseum rotates fascinating exhibits on clothing, yarn-spinning, art, and toys from the beautiful Spreewald region. The thatched roofs of Lehde are captured in oil on hanging canvases, and intricately woven dresses, antique looms, and, of course, original steins with Sorbian history are on display on the upper levels. Aside from the requisite uninteresting pottery shards, this museum does an excellent job of capturing the history of a fascinating culture whose influence still permeates Lübbenau. Visit here before the Freilandmuseum, to gain a little more knowledge and perspective on the Sorbs as you walk through the reconstructed houses in Lehde.

⇞ From the tourist information office, follow Ehm-Welk-Str. to just before it turns into Karl-Marx-Str. $ €4, students €3, children under 16 €1. ⏰ Open Apr-mid-Oct Tu-Su 10am-6pm.

Food

Although virtually every restaurant in Lübbenau caters to tourists, with moderately overpriced menus and hordes of 60-year-olds crowding outdoor patios, there's still pleanty of cheap food available. Check out the *Imbiße* (snack bars) and stands that line the **Großer Hafen,** and other main town squares. The local specialties are pickles and fresh fish, so if you're itching to eat like the Sorbs, go for one of those. The irrepressible bratwurst is a good fallback for a filling meal, and the sausage-and-beer combo feels fitting in this quintessentially German town.

Essentials

Practicalities

- **TOURIST OFFICE:** *(Ehm-Welk-Str. 32. ☎03542 4 66 47 ⏰ Open M-F 10am-5pm.)*

Getting There

Lübbenau is a 2hr. bus and train ride away from Berlin, through beautiful farmland and pine forests. Don't let the distance scare you; the trip is pleasant. Take the **Regional Express, line 2** toward **Königs Wusterhausen.** Trains run every 2hr. from Zoologischer Garten, Berlin Hauptbahnhof, and Berlin Ostbahnhof *(tickets €13).* At Königs Wusterhausen you'll need to transfer to a bus; exit the train station, turn right, and then take the first right about 30m from the train station, and walk under the bridge. **Bus B,** the second leg of the the trip, departs from there (dir. Lübbenau). Lübbenau is about 1hr. from the station, the last stop on the bus line.

Getting Around

There's not much to be said for internal transportation in little Lübbenau. Buses run M-F early morning-3pm *(single ride €1.30)*, but luckily, you won't need them. The whole area is easily covered on foot, or, if you prefer, on bike. Bike rentals are all over the city; expect to pay €8-10 for a day rental. For rentals, try **Kowalsky's**, near the train station *(Poststr. 6. ☎03542 28 35 $ €8 per day. ⏰ Open M-F 9am-12:30pm and 2-6pm, Sa 9am-noon, Su call in advance)*, or **Michael Metzdorf**, across from the tourist office.

POTSDAM ☎0331

Imagine Disneyland. Now swap out the the rollercoaster rides for exquisite old palaces, the long lines for winding gravel pathways, and the acres of concrete parking lots for fields of tall grass, towering trees, and serene lakes. That's Potsdam. Just an S-Bahn ride away from a decidedly un-royal Berlin, Potsdam is the glittering city of Friedrich II, and one of our candidates for the most beautiful towns on earth. If you have the time, low cost and accessibility make Potsdam an absolute must-see for anyone visiting Berlin. The extraordinary sights are concentrated in the Park Sanssouci, which overflows with yellow ochre palaces and perfectly manicured gardens. You can barely walk 10m without hitting your head on a hanging crystal chandelier. The smaller Neuer Park to the north is also home to beautiful palaces and monuments, and has the added advantage of a lakeside setting.

Accommodations

Budget options are extremely limited in Potsdam. Luckily, it's easy to commute from your hostel in Berlin, meaning you most likely won't need to find accommodations.

JUGENDHERBERGE POTSDAM (HI) HOSTEL [1]

Schulstr. 9 ☎0331 581 31 00 www.jh-potsdam.de

The closest hostel is one S-Bahn stop before Potsdam. Far less sterile than many HI hostels, Jugendherberge is warmed up with pine bunks and light yellow walls, even if it still mostly lacks decoration and character. Rooms are a little crowded, but clean and neat, with personal lockers and ensuite baths.

*S7: Babelsberg. **i** Breakfast and linens included. Wi-Fi €2 per hr. $ Dorms from €15, over 27 €18; singles €31.50/34; doubles €26.5/29.50. ⏰ Reception 24hr.*

CAMPINGPLATZ SANSSOUCI-GAISBERG CAMPGROUND [1]

An der Pirschhiede 41 ☎0331 951 09 88 www.campingpark-sanssouci-potsdam.de

Located on the banks of the beautiful Templiner See, this campsite is far removed from the sights in Potsdam. The *campingplatz* isn't a convenient place from which to explore Potsdam or Berlin, but its relaxed, lake-side living style might make it a destination itself.

*S7: Potsdam Hauptbahnhof, then tram #91:Bahnhof Pirschheide. Call 8:45am-10:45am, or 5:30-9pm for free shuttle to the campsite from "Pirschheide." **i** Internet €2 per day. $ €12.30 per person. ⏰ Phone reception 8am-1pm and 3-8pm.*

Sights

The **Premium Day Ticket** will get you into all the sights in the Parks *(€19, students €14)*, and the **Day pass** will get you in everywhere except the Shloβ *(€14/10)*. The **Premium Family Ticket** is good for two adults and up to three children *(€49)*, as is the **Family ticket without Schloß** *(€24)*.

Park Sanssouci Sights

If you only go one place in Potsdam, make it **Park Sanssouci.** The park's full of winding paths and yellow palaces that will keep you wandering in awe for days, and more small palaces, monuments, and little teahouses than you could imagine. Next to the Schloß Sanssouci, the collection of Caravaggio, van Dycke, and Reubens crowd the wall of an exquisitely guilded **Buildergalerie.** *(☎0331 969 4181 $ €3, students €2.50. Audio guide €1. ⏰ Open Apr-Oct Tu-Su 10am-5:30pm.)* The stunning

Sizilianer Garten (Sicilian Garden) is next door. Overlooking the park from the north, the pseudo-Italian **Orangerie** is famous for its 67 dubious Raphael imitations that replace originals swiped by Napoleon. Climb to the top of the tower for a view of the whole park *($ Tours €3, students €2.50. Tower only €2. ⏰ Open mid-May to mid-Oct Tu-Su 10am-12:30pm and 1-5pm).* Romantic **Schloß Charlottenhof,** whose park surroundings were a Christmans gift from Friedrich Wilhelm III to his son Friedrich Wilhem IV, flows from landscaped gardens to grape arbors *($ €4, students €3. ⏰ Open May-Oct Tu-Su 10am-6pm).* Nearby is the **Römische Bader** (Roman bath), which sits beside a reedy pond with small bridges. The park's single and mystifyingly Asian-inspired building, the **Chinesisches Teehaus,** is complete with a parasol-laden Buddha on the rooftop and 18th-century Chinese pottery inside *($ €3, students €2.50. ⏰ Open May-Oct. Tu-Su 10am-6pm).*

PARK SANSSOUCI — PARK

Access the park from Hegelallee, Weinbergstr., or Gregor-Mendal-Str. ☎0331 969 4200

Schloß Sanssouci's 600-acre "backyard" puts Versailles to shame. The park is done in two distinct styles; half is Baroque, with geometric paths intersecting at topiaries and statues of nude nymphs. The other half is a rolling, almost-but-not-quite-natural landscape of wheat fields, rose trellises, and lush, immaculate gardens. There may be no more magically beautiful garden than this one; be warned that once you start walking, you may never want to leave. For information on the park's many attractions, from Rococo sculptures to beautiful fountains, head to the visitors center next to the windmill, behind the Schloß.

🚌 Buses #606, #612, #614 or #692: Luisenpl. Nord/Park Sanssouci. $ Free. ⏰ Open daily Mar-Oct 8am-10pm; Nov-Feb 9am-8pm.

SHLOß SANSSOUCI — PALACE

Off Zur Historischen Mühle ☎0331 696 42 00

The park's main attraction, the turquoise-domed *schloß Sanssouci* sits atop a terraced hill, looking out over fountains and manicured gardens. Designed in 1747, the palace is small and airy, with ethereal paintings and carvings of the Greek gods in pinks and light greens. Frescoes of Dionysus are right at home in a breezy palace, whose name is French for "without worry." The brainchild of Friedrich, the Francophile, Sanssouci also has the small, exotically decorated **Voltairezimmer** (Voltaire Room), outfitted with carved reliefs of parrots and tropical fruit that climb around walls and down the chandelier. The library reveals another of Friedrich's eccentricities: whenever he wanted to read a book, he had a copy printed for each of his palaces--*en français*, of course. Also on display is Andy Warhol's magnificently magenta-and-lime modern interpretation of the king's portrait.

🚌 Bus #695 of X15: Schloß Sanssouci. $ Admission €12, students €8. Audio guide (available in English) and ticket to the Buldergalerie included. ⏰ Open Tu-Su Apr-Oct 10am-6pm, last entry 5:30pm; Nov-Mar 10am-5pm, last entry 4:30.

NEUES PALACE — PALACE

Located on Lindenavenue ☎0331 96 94 361

Because sometimes one beautiful royal palace just isn't enough. Friedrich the Great built Sanssouci's fourth and largest palace in celebration of the Prussian victory in the Seven Years' War. And because nothing says masculine-military-power like pale magenta, Neues Palace is an expansive, 200-room, proudly pink *schloß*, featuring royal apartments, festival halls, and the impressive Grottensaal, whose shimmering walls are covered with seashells.

🚌 X5: Neues Palace. $ €5, students €4. Audio guide €1. ⏰ Open Apr-Oct M and W-Su 10am-6pm, last entry 5:30pm; Nov-Mar 10am-5pm, last entry 4:30pm.

Other Sights

NEUER GARTEN GARDEN

Schloß Cecilienhof ☎0331 969 42 44

Borded by Holy Lake on the east, and Am Neuen Garten on the west

Neuer Garten, the smaller, less-attraction-packed counterpart to Park Sanssouci that lies to the east, is all free-flowing meadows and beautiful lake beaches. Scattered through the park are several royal residences, including the **Schloß Cecilienhof.** Built in the style of an English Tudor manor, this *shloß* houses exhibits on the Potsdam Treaty, signed at the palace in 1945. Visitors can see the table where the Big Three bargained over Europe's fate, and stand in the room Stalin used as his study. The garden also contains the centerpiece of the park, the **Marmorpalais** (Marble Palace). Classically designed from rust-colored marble, the palace also has a concert hall. Also in the Neuer Garten is the inexplicable **Egyptian pyramid** once used for food storage. At the far north end of the lake, beachgoers bare all, and relieve themselves of the summer humidity in the cool water.

🚌 Bus #692: Schloß Cecilianhof. $ Garden free. Schloß Cecilienhof €5, students €4. Marmorpalais €4/3. ⏰ Schloß Cecilienhof open Apr-Oct Tu-Su 10am-6pm; Nov-Mar 10am-5pm. Marmorpalais open Apr-Oct Tu-Su 10am-5pm; Nov-Mar Sa-Su 10am-4pm.

Food

Altstadt is overflowing with lovely cafes and restaurants, but unfortunately, high prices come with the territory. For fresh produce, try the **flea market** in Bassinpl *(open M-F 9am-6pm),* or stock up at the massive **Kaufland** grocery store in the Hauptbahnhof *(open daily 6am-8pm).* For budget options, your best bet is to try ethnic eateries.

SIAM 🌱🍸☀ THAI ❶

Friedrich-Ebert-Str. 13 ☎0311 200 9292

For large portions and low prices, Siam is the place to go. Admittedly, it's more than a little strange to watch Thai specialties being cooked up in a bamboo-covered kitchen, with a view of such a quintessentially old European street. But if you embrace the irony, you'll leave Potsdam with a full stomach and wallet.

🚌 Trams 92 or 96: Brandenbergerstr. $ Entrees €4.70-8. ⏰ Open daily 11:30am-11pm.

KASHMIR HAUS 🌱🍸☀ INDIAN ❷

Jägerstr. 1 ☎0331 870 9580

This understated Indian restaurant is removed from the touristy bustle. The weekday lunch special is a fantastic deal, and includes vegetarian options. On a hot day, cool down with mango or lychee smoothies *(€2.50).*

🚌 Trams 92 or 96: Nauener Tor. ℹ Lunch special served 11am-4pm. $ Lunch special €4.50-6.50. ⏰ Open M-F 11am-11pm, Sa-Su 11am-midnight.

CAFE HEIDER GERMAN ❸

Friedrich-Ebert-Str. 29 ☎0331 270

If you're looking to spend a little extra for a German meal in this most European of cities, one of your cheapest options is Cafe Heider. Breakfasts run from €4-7.80, and entrees from €8-15. Eat on the expansive patio overlooking Nauen Gate.

🚌 Trams #92 or 96: Nauener Tor. $ Homemade ice cream €1.30 per scoop. ⏰ Open M-F 8am-midnight, Sa 9am-midnight, Su 10am-midnight.

Essentials

Practicalities

- **TOURIST OFFICES:** *(in the S-Bahn station. ⏰ Open M-Sa 9:30am-8pm, Su 10am-4pm.)* **Second location.** *(Brandenbergerstr. 3 in the city center. ⏰ Open Apr-Oct M-F 9:30am-6pm, Sa-Su 9:30am-4pm; Nov-Mar M-F 9:30am-6pm, Sa-Su 9:30am-*

2pm.) Both offices sell **city maps** for €1 (if you don't already have a good map of the parks, you'll definitely want to pick this up), and book rooms for free with cooperating hotels. The tourist offices run 2hr. tours of the Old Town in English and German; inquire at the office *([$]€8 ⏰ departs May-Sept daily 3pm).* They also lead 3½hr. tours of Sanssouci Park *(1½hr. without Sanssouci Palace)* daily at 11am, departing from Potsdam Hauptbahnhof. Reservations required *([$] €27, without Sanssouci Palace €16).*

- **POST OFFICE:** *(Pl. der Einheit. ⏰ Open M-F 9am-6:30pm, Sa 9am-1pm.)* **Postal Code:** 14476.

Getting There

Getting to Potsdam is wonderfully simple. Take the **S7** toward Potsdam *(40min.)*, or the **RE1** from most major stations, including Berlin Ostbahnhof, Friedrichstr., Alexanderpl., Hauptbahnhof, or Zoologischer Garten *(25min.)*. You'll need to buy a ticket for Zones A, B, and C *(€2.40 single ticket)*, or if you already have a day or week-long pass for Zones A and B, supplement it with an extra ticket to Zone C *(€1.40)*.

Getting Around

Public Transportation: Potsdam is in **Zone C** of Belrin's BVG transit network, so all main-city prices are the same. Special Potsdam-only passes can be purchased on any bus or tram *(€1.40 valid 1hr., €4 all-day)*. The **Berlin Welcome Card** is also valid in Potsdam.

Bike Rental and Tours: Potsdam is best experienced by bike. If you choose to rent for the day, be sure to request a map, outlining the best route to see all the sights on wheels. From the Griebnitzsee station, pay to take your bike on the S-Bahn *(special bike pass €1.20 at any BGV ticket office)*. **Potsdam Per Pedales.** *(Main location at Rudolf-Breitscheid-Str. 201, in the "Griebnitzsee" S-Bahn station or on the S-Bahn platform at Potsdam Hauptbahnhof. ☎0331 784 0057 💻www.pedales.de ℹ Bike tours in English (reserve ahead) and German. [$] Rentals €10, €8.50 for students. Bike tours €10.50, €8.50 students. Audio guide €6. ⏰ Open 9:30am-7pm.)* **Cityrad.** *(Right across from the Babelsbergerstr. exit of the Hauptbahnhof. ☎0177 825 47 46 💻www.cityrad-rebhan.de [$] €11 per day. ⏰ Open Apr-Oct M-F 9am-7pm, Sa 9am-8pm.)*

HAMBURG

Hamburg is a city of paradoxes. One of the most historic port cities in northern Europe, Hamburg is over 100km from the North Sea. Considerably nearer is the city of Lübeckm another maritime metropolis. Combined the two are the highlights of northernmost Germany.

greatest hits

- **PLENTY OF FISH IN THE SEA.** Devour generous helpings of Spanish- and Portuguese-inspired seafood at La Sepia (p. 102).

- **EVERYTHING'S COMING UP ROSES.** Wander through the largest Japanese garden in Europe at Planten un Blomen (p. 97).

- **ALIVE, ALIVE OH.** Grab a Guinness and chat it up with some of the funniest bartenders this side of the Chunnel at Shamrock Irish Bar (p. 105).

- **SKY BLUE SKY.** Oogle Dutch, Flemish, and French artwork or the sweeping views from the balcony at Jenisch Haus (p. 101).

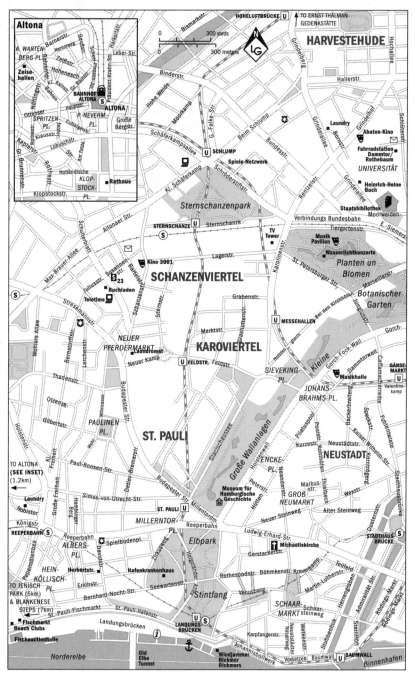

hamburg

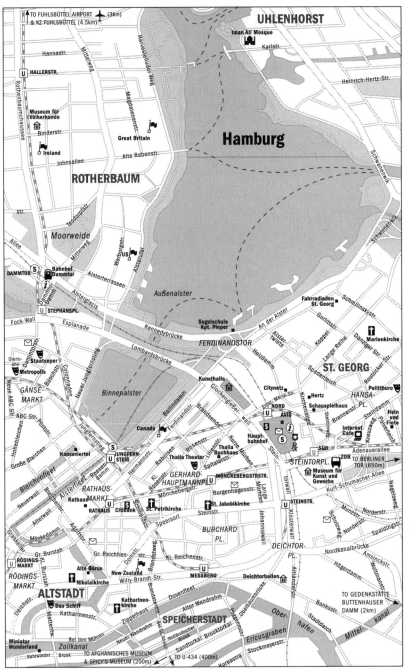

Hamburg

Hamburg is home to some phenomenal budget accommodations. Young back-packers gather daily at Instant Sleep before heading out to the city's attractions, and again at night to meet up with fellow bar crawlers. Schanzenstern Übernach-tungs-und Gasthaus proves to be another happening hostel, sharing a block with an indy film theater; sip come cappuccinos with your dormmates at the adjoining cafe. After your caffeine jolt, take advantage of the city's student discounts: €5 will buy you into Museum für Kunst und Gewerbe, an art museum featuring everything from traditional photography to a collection of over 430 historical keyboard instru-ments. Finish the day at Cafe Gnosa with a couple of cocktails. Or drink 10. And then rejoice that the cafe also serves up specialty cakes—the perfect drunk food.

hamburg

A city of old money, beautiful churches, and an extravagantly ornate **Rathaus** are mere miles away from camps of the homeless and unemployed set up under stone bridges. Some of Germany's renowned orchestras and symphonies share a 3km radius with the unapologetically trashy strip joints and erotic shops on the infamous **Reeperbahn.** The only constant is the Elbe, tying Hamburg to the world. Massive commercial ships and a crane-studded industrial district just across the Elbe from Hamburg bring global products and people. Portugese and Turkish immigrants coalesce in the west, in Altona and Schanzenviertel, and tapas bars and falafel stands stand side-by-side with Irish pubs and German breweries. Hamburg's notable **Altstadt,** recognizable by its mammoth churches and towering spires, is split by canals, streams, and bridges at every bend. A total of 2,479 bridges connect Hamburg, out-bridging Venice.

Any visitor will note the tragedies left by the Great Fire of 1842 and the devastat-ing Allied WWII bombing. In a single night in July of 1943, air raids simultaneously leveled the city and killed over 50,000 tenants in the crowded buildings lining the waterfront. As a result, many of the architectural masterpieces that once filled the city are lost. Fortunately, a massive 1960s reconstruction effort restored many of Hamburg's beloved buildings, including the **Große Michaeliskirche,** an aqua-blue and gold-gilded oceanic masterpiece of a church. In shocking contrast to this opulence are the coal-black ruins of St. Nikolai, whose dark Gothic spire is a reminder of the cost of war. Despite it's cautioning remembrances, Hamburg has seen changes like the St. Georg district, which today is home to a flourishing gay community. And, of course, Hamburg is incomplete without **The Beatles.** The music legends performed here pre-fame, and so the city has become a magnet for independent musical art-ists.

ORIENTATION

Hamburg lies on the northern bank of the **Elbe** river, 100km south of the North Sea. The city's **Altstadt,** full of old buildings and mazes of canals, lies north of the Elbe and south of the **Alster lakes.** Of the two Alster lakes, **Binnenalster,** the much smaller of the two, is located in the heart of the Altstadt, bordered by Jungfernstieg to the south and Ballindamm to the West. The much larger **Außenalster,** popular for sailing in the summer and skating in the winter, is slightly further north, just separated from the Binnenalster by the **Kennedybrücke.** Five beautiful churches, whose spires spear the Hamburg skyline, outline Hamburg's Altstadt. Anchoring the center of the Altstadt is the palacial **Rathaus,** the ornate town hall, and **Rathaus market,** home to political

protests and farmers' markets alike. **Alsterfleet canal** bisects the downtown area and separates Altstadt on the eastern bank from the Neustadt on the west. The city's best museums, galleries, and theaters are located within these two districts.

The **Hauptbahnhof** lies at the eastern edge of the city center, along Steintorwall. Starting from the Kirchenallee exit of the Hauptbahnhof, Hamburg's unofficial gay district, **St. Georg,** follows the **Lange Reihe** eastward, where quiet cafes populate the streets. Outside the Hauptbahnhof's main exit on Sheintorwall is the **Kunstmelle** (Art Mile), a row of museums extending southward from the Alster lakes to the banks of the Elbe. Perpendicular to Seintorwall, **Mönickebergstraße,** Hamburg's most famous shopping street, runs westward to the **Rathause,** which connects the city center to the train station. The Neustadt's **Hanseviertel,** between Rathausmarkt and Gänsemarkt, is full of shops, galleries, and auction houses. Hanseviertel is striped with canals, giving the area a Venetian glamour.

Just south of the Rathaus, **St. Pauli** houses large stretches of walkways along the industrial Elbe, the **Landungsbrücke,** and the weekly Hamburg **fischmarkt.** Also in St. Pauli is the infamous **Reeperbahn,** running parallel to the river, packed with strip joints and erotic shops. To the north of St. Pauli, students and academics inhabit the **Dammtor** district, home to Hamburg's university and the Planten un Blomen botanical gardens. The city's wealthiest neighborhoods, including **Winterhunde** and **Harvesthude,** are just opposite Dammtor on the shores of the lake. Farther west, **Schanzenviertel** is a more liberal community of students, artists, and sizable immigrant populations. Here, rows of street-art-covered restaurants and a busy late-night bar scene impart the area's new-found edge. On the westernmost side of Hamburg, **Altona** celebrates with a nightlife and restaurant scene similar to Schanzenviertel. The area was an independent city ruled by Denmark in the 17th century before eventually being absorbed by Hamburg. Altona's pedestrian zone, the **Ottenser Hauptstrasse,** runs west from the Altona station. To the far east of Hamburg lies one of the city's most important, if distant sights. The former concentration camp, **KZ Neuengamme,** is now a memorial to victims of forced labor in World War II. On the extreme opposite side of the city past Altona, **Klein-Flottbek** has two of Hamburg's most beautiful museums, set in the scenic **Jenisch Park** along the Elbe.

ACCOMMODATIONS 🏠

👍 INSTANT SLEEP
⊕🚭📶🍸 HOSTEL ❶

Max-Brauer-Allee 27 ☎040 43 18 23 10 💻www.instantsleep.de

Bright, spotless dorms, colorful murals, and personal lockers in every room for safety ensure what the name promises. The real highlight, which causes more staying up than the opposite, is the common room complete with foosball table, hammocks, benches, and a comfortable loft for lounging. A young backpacking crowd gathers here every morning and evening for socializing.

🚇 U3, S11, S21, or S31: Sternschanze. ℹ Sheets included. Free Wi-Fi and Internet at guest terminals. $ Dorms €16.50; singles €31; doubles €45; triples €62. ⏰ Reception W-Sa 8am-2am, Su-Tu 8am-11pm. Check-in 3-8pm; call ahead if you're arriving outside these hours. Check-out 11am.

👍 SCHANZENSTERN ÜBERNACHTUNGS-UND GASTHAUS
⊕♿📶🍸 HOSTEL ❷

Bartelsstr. 12 ☎040 439 84 41 💻www.schanzenstern.de

In the middle of the upbeat Schanzenviertel, this guesthouse has bright, hotel-like rooms on the upper floors of a converted pen factory. Big windows look out over the red-tiled rooftops of Hamburg, and the hostel shares a block with an independent film theater. The hostel owns a laid-back adjoining cafe with a shady courtyard and porch swings. All showers ensuite.

🚇 U3, S11, S21, or S31: Sternschanze. ℹ Breakfast €4.50-6.50. Laundry €5. Sheets included. Free Internet terminals for guests, Wi-Fi €2 per hr. $ Dorms €19; singles €38.50; doubles €54; triples €64; quads €78; quints €95. ⏰ Reception 6:30am-2am. Check-out 11am.

SCHANZENSTERN ALTONA
⊕♿📶 HOSTEL ❷

Kleiner Rainstr. 24-26 ☎040 39 91 91 91 💻www.schanzenstern-altona.dess

On a quiet residential street, this bright hostel is filled with light from the common area's full wall of windows looking over the adjacent courtyard. Spacious rooms with pine beds and ensuite baths.

🚇 S1, S2, S3, S11 or S31: Altona. ℹ Wi-Fi €2 per hr., Internet on guest terminals free. Sheets included. Breakfast €6.50. $ Dorms €19; singles €44; doubles €59-69; triples €74; quads €84; apartments €79-100. ⏰ Reception 7am-11pm. Check-out 11am.

JUGENDHERBERGEN HAMBURG (HI)
⊕♿📶 HOSTEL ❷

Alfred-Wegener-Weg 5 ☎040 31 91 0 37 💻www.jugendherberge.de/jh/hamburg-stiftang

So close to the harbor, you could (almost) jump out your window and go for a swim. The panorama dorm can't be beat for views, though it's closely seconded by the lounge area, which looks out on the water from a wall of floor to ceiling windows. Request a view; not all rooms have a good one. Rooms are small but comfortably furnished, with checked sheets and yellow walls.

🚇 S1, S3 or U3 tp: Landungsbrücken. ℹ Internet terminals €1 per 10 min. Breakfast and linens included. $ Panorama dorm €19.90; dorm with ensuite bath €22.90; doubles €59.90; triples €74.70; quads €99.60; quint €123.50; 6-bed room €148.20. ⏰ Reception 24hr.

MEININGER
💳♿📶🍸 HOSTEL ❶

Goetheallee 11 ☎040 414 31 40 08 💻www.meininger-hotels.com

Just a short walk from the S-Bahn, all of central Hamburg's sights are easily accessible from this slightly out-of-the-way hostel in Altona. Rooms are newly painted, and decorated in deep burgundy and white, with high ceilings and privacy curtains in dorms. All rooms have television and ensuite baths. The common room and adjoining bar are popular hang-outs for guests, equipped with foosball and pool tables.

➜ S1, S2, or S3: Altona. ℹ Sheets and Wi-Fi included. Internet terminals €2 per hr. Breakfast €6.50. Ⓢ Prices vary. Dorms range from €10-25, singles from €35-79. ⏰ Reception 24hr. Check-out 10am.

A AND O HOSTEL HAUPTBAHNHOF 💳♿📶🍸 HOSTEL ❶

Amsinckstr. 2-10 ☎040 644 21 56 00 💻www.aohostels.com

A far better choice than its sister hostel on Reeperbahn, this A and O is light and bright, with spacious rooms and big windows. Large televisions and a pool table in the common area make it a gathering place for backpackers and traveling groups alike. Even more popular is the lobby bar with drinks *(from €2)*, open 24 hours. A free English walking tour leaves daily from the hostel entrance.

➜ From the Hauptbahnhof, go south on Klosterwall, cross Deichtorpl., and then follow Deichtorpl. west as it turns into Amsinckstr. ℹ Wi-Fi €1 per hr. Breakfast €4. Sheets €3. Ⓢ Prices vary. 8-10 bed-dorms from €12; 4-6 bed dorms from €15; doubles from €25; singles from €39. ⏰ Reception 24hr. Check-out 10am.

BACKPACKERS ST. PAULI 🚫💳🚫♿📶🍸 HOSTEL ❷

Bernstorffstr. 98 ☎040 23 51 70 43 💻www.backpackers-stpauli.de

A creative maroon and pink mural of Hamburg's canal scene dresses up a funky lounge area, complete with bar and television, but the fun decor doesn't extend to the rooms. Light cream walls and black furnishings, including personal lockers in all rooms, make up the clean but bare dorms. An outdoor courtyard has a firepit and barbeque for guest use. This hostel is about an eight minute walk from the nearest S-Bahn station.

➜ S1, S2 or S3: Reeperbahn. ℹ Free Internet on guest terminals. Breakfast €4. Bedsheets €2. Ⓢ 8-bed dorms from €19.50; 6-bed dorms from €23; 4-bed dorms from €24; triples from €25; doubles from €30. ⏰ Reception 8am-midnight. Check-in from 3pm-1am; call ahead for other arrivals.

CAMPINGPLATZ BUCHHOLTZ 🚫💳♿ CAMPGOUND ❶

Kieler Str. 374 ☎040 540 45 32 💻www.camping-buchholz.de

Less of a campground and more of a glorified parking lot, Campingplatz Buchholtz—though mostly filled with RVs—can offer you some room to pitch a tent, but not much in the way of nature or scenery. About 30 plots in a gravel and cement paved area lined with trees and surrounded by residential houses, just off a busy road. The campground also runs a bed and breakfast.

➜ S1, S2, or S3: Altona, then bus #183: Basselweg (20min., 2-3 per hr., 5am-midnight). Follow the bus 100m; the campground is just off the busy street on your right. ℹ Quiet hours 10pm-7am. No tent rental. Ⓢ €5.50 per tent. Bed and breakfast singles with bath €60; doubles €70. ⏰ Reception M-Th 8am-12:30pm and 3-7pm, F-Sa 8am-noon and 2-7pm, Su 8am-12:30pm and 3-7pm.

ARCADE HOSTEL 🚫💳🚫♿📶 HOSTEL ❸

Kieler Str. 385 ☎040 54 48 14 💻www.arcade-hostel-hamburg.de

This hostel is all chic hotel-elegance. About 20 min. outside Altona, Arcade compensates with sleek dark wood, cool gray granite, red walls, and warm lighting. Bedrooms have newly painted beige walls, black furniture and televisions. You might think of Arcade as more of a low-end hotel than a hostel

➜ S1, S2, or S3: Altona, then bus #183: Basselweg (20min., 2-3 per hr., 5am-midnight). Follow the bus 200m, the hostel is across the street, on your left. ℹ Sheets and Wi-Fi included. Breakfast €6. Ⓢ Singles with shower €35-45, with ensuite bath €46-58; doubles with shower €46-58, with ensuite bath €65-85. ⏰ Reception M-F 6am-10pm, Sa-Su 7:30am-10pm.

A AND O HOSTEL REEPERBAHN 💳♿ HOSTEL [1]

Reeperbahn 154 ☎040 644 21 04 56 00 💻www.aohostels.com

This hostel's interior design choice in the middle of Reeperbahn's erotic shops and strip clubs, is just as seedy. Exposed piping, bare walls, flourescent lighting and linoleum floors don't do much in the way of charm or warmth. With A and O's often low prices, expect to get what you're paying for.

🚉 S1, S2 or S3: Reeperbahn. ℹ Sheets €3, breakfast €4. $ Dynamic prices, call ahead to check. 8-10 bed-dorms from €12; 4-6 bed dorms from €15; doubles from €25; singles from €39. ⏰ Reception 24hr. Check-out 10am.

HOTEL KÖNIGSHOF NOVUM 💳🚭📶 PENSION [4]

Pulverteich 18 ☎040 284 07 40 💻www.hotel-koenigshof-novum.de

Large rooms on a quiet street in Hamburg's gay-friendly neighborhood. The atmosphere is relaxed and professional, with big windows and bright decor. In-room amenities include a television, radio, and phone. For perfect peace and privacy, and a place to stay in a welcoming area of town, this could be worth the extra euros.

🚉 Take Adenauerallee, which runs past the southern end of the Hauptbahnhof, and turn left onto Kreuzweg. Turn right onto Pulterteich. ℹ Free Wi-Fi. Sheets included. $ Prices vary. Singles from €50; doubles from €60; triples from €80. ⏰ Reception 24hr.

HOTEL ANNENHOF 🍴🚭 PENSION [3]

Lange Reihe 23 ☎040 24 34 26 💻www.hotelannenhof.de

There's nothing understated about the bright teal and coral walls, or the feet of intricate white molding running around the ceiling of every room, but Hotel Annenhof still manages elegance and excellence. To experience old Hamburg's old money years with a twist, there's no better place than this pension. Rooms

are large and well-lit with large windows and hanging chandeliers.

From the Hauptbanhof, take Ernst-Mecke-Str. (on the north side of the station), and follow it as the street turns into Lange Reihe. i Sheets included. $ Singles €40; doubles €70; triples €100. ⏰ Reception open M-F 8am-8pm, Sa-Su 9am-6pm.

SIGHTS

PLANTEN UN BLOMEN — BOTANICAL GARDEN

Bordered by An der Verbindungsbahn to the north, Gorch-Fock-Wall to the south, and St. Petersburgerstr. to the west. ☎040 428 23 21 25 🖥www.plantenunblomen.hamburg.de

This perfect mix of manicured gardens, tranquil lily-pad laden ponds, and wide expanses of grassy lawns is enjoyed by newspaper readers, picnickers, and sun worshippers alike. Wander for miles through scenic paths overgrown with lavender bushes, or sit on white wooden chairs under the shade of towering chestnut trees. Planten un Blomen also contains the largest **Japanese Garden** in Europe, a rose garden with over 300 varieties of blooms, and a botanical garden with an exotic variety of plants. Children or the young at heart can play on three playgrounds, a water slide, trampoline, minigolf, or water-jet soccer. For the more serious Harry Potter enthusiast, a giant, though inanimate chess set is the arena of many a blood-thirsty competition. Daily performances by groups ranging from Irish step dancers to Hamburg's police choir fill the outdoor Musikpavillion at 3pm from May to September. The nightly **Wasserlichtkonzerte** draws crowds to the lake with choreographed fountains and underwater lights.

S21 or S31: Dammtor. ⏰ Open May-Sept 7am-11pm, Oct-Apr 7am-8pm. Japanese Garden open Mar-Oct M-F 9am-4:45pm, Sa-Su 10am-5:45pm; Nov-Feb M-F 9am-3:45pm, Sa-Su 10am-3:45pm. Wasserlichtkonzerte May-Aug. nightly 10pm, Sept. 9pm.

MUSEUM FÜR KUNST UND GEWERBE — MUSEUM

Steintorpl. 1 ☎040 42 81 34 🖥www.mkg-hamburg.de

This museum of applied arts sets the tone for it's collection with a hammock hanging between two fake palms in a plexiglass bubble suspended above the entrance. Quirky Art Nouveau pieces will have you asking, "Is this art?," but enjoying the absurdity of foam cactuses all the same. More conventional and equally impressive are the extensive photography exhibits on the first floor, featuring post-war German photographers. Another hall contains over 430 historical keyboard instruments including harpsichords, clavichords, and hammer-klaviers all the way up to the modern piano, and another exhibit traces the history of porcelain through region, which an expansive array of Asian pottery.

Walk 1 block south from the Hauptbahnhof. $ €8, students €5, children under 18 free. ⏰ Open Tu-Su 11am-6pm, Th from 11am-9pm.

HAMBURGER KUNSTHALLE (HALL OF ART) — ART MUSEUM

Glockengießerwall ☎040 428 13 12 09 🖥www.hamburger-kunsthalle.de

It would take days to fully appreciate all the world-class art displayed in the expansive Kunsthalle, one of the best art museums in Germany. The collection is organized chronologically. Old Masters and 19th century work is on the upper levels, prints and drawings downstairs, and a contemporary art collection is in the adjacent Galerie der Gegenwart. An impressive French Impressionist and German Realist collection is a can't-miss, especially the gigantic Renoir canvases. The revolving exhibitions in the Galerie der Gegenwart are one of the museum's biggest highlights.

Turn right from the "Sitalerstr./City" exit of the Hauptbahnhof and cross the street. The Kunsthalle is identifiable by its domed ceiling. $ €10, €5 students, under 18 free. ⏰ Open Tu-W 10am-6pm, Th 10am-9pm, F-Su 10am-6pm.

RATHAUS — TOWN HALL

Accessible from Bergerstr. ☎040 428 31 24 70

With more rooms than Buckingham Palace, the 1897 Hamburg Rathaus, which replaced the one that was burned down in the Great Fire of 1842, is an ornate stone-carved monument to Hamburg's long history as a wealthy port city. Its lavish chambers, accessible only through a worthwhile guided tour, are furnished with expansive murals and mind-blowingly designed chandeliers. The building still serves as the seat of both city and state government, while the Rathausmarkt out front hosts a slew of festivities, from political demonstrations to medieval fairs.

U3: Rathaus. ⓢ Tours €3. 🕒 Only accessible on a tour. English tours run M-F at 11:15am, 1:15pm and 3:15pm, Sa 11:15 and 1:15, and Su 11:15am, 1:15pm, 3:15pm, and 5:15pm. Tours don't run on days that the state government convenes, so call ahead.

GROSSE MICHAELISKIRCHE
CHURCH

Englishe Planke 1 ☎040 376 78 0 🖥www.st-michaelis.de

The towering steeple of the Grosse Michaeliskirche is one of the most recognizable features of Hamburg's skyline. The church has been destroyed and rebuilt more times than Bill Clinton's reputation. To guard against further catastrophe, a larger-than-life statue of St. Michael stands holding his spear over Satan, trapped below his foot. The inside of the church is painted a stunningly bright white with aqua- and gold-guilded accents and a shell motif. A visit inside the church is a must, but don't expect to get much praying done amid the throngs of tourists. Pass on the lower crypt; it's mostly just plaques describing the church's history. Use the elevator *(€3)* to cut the 462-stair climb to the top of the tower for an incredbile view of Hamburg.

S1, S3 of U3: Landungsbrücken. ⓢ Church free with €2 suggested donation. Tower €3.50, students €3, children under 12 €2.50; crypt €3/2.50/2, combined ticket €5/4/3. ⏰ Open daily May-Oct 9am-8pm, Nov-Apr 10am-6pm. Organ music daily Apr-Aug at noon. Crypt open June-Oct daily 11am-4:30pm, Nov-May Sa-Su 11am-4:30pm.

DEICHTORHALLEN HAMBURG ART MUSEUM

Deichtorstr. 1-2 ☎040 32 10 30 💻www.deichtorhallen.de

Hamburg's contemporary art scene thrives in these two former fruit markets, which house rotating photography, painting, sculpture, and film installations. The south hall features photography, while the north hall divides its attention between several creative mediums. Both halls are worth the trip, but check ahead to find what exhibit you'll be visiting—some are more "experimental" than others.

🚇 U1: Steinstr. Follow signs from the U-Bahn station. $ Each building €7, students €5, families €9.50. Combination ticket to both halls €12/8/16.50, or €4.50 Tu after 4pm. Under 18 free. ⏰ Open Tu-Su 11am-6pm.

NIKOLAIKIRCHE CHURCH

Willy-Brandt-Str. 60 ☎040 37 11 25

In one of the most powerful war memorials in the country, the blackened ruins of Nikolaikirche shape the Hamburg skyline and stretch over the remnants of the former church's interior. Bombed in World War II, the empty holes that used to hold stained-glass windows and soot-blackened stones that visitors face as they ride the glass elevator up to the top of the skeletal spire are a striking testament to the destruction warfare causes. The view from the top is a stunning panorama of this beautiful city.

🚇 U3: Rödingsmarkt. $ Elevator €3.70, €2.90 students, children under 16 €2. ⏰ Elevator open daily May-Sept 10am-8pm, Oct-Apr 10am-5pm.

ST. PETRI KIRCHE CHURCH

Mönckebergstr.

The oldest parish church in Hamburg has records dating back to 1195. Destroyed, in the 1843 fire along with most of Hamburg, it was rebuilt two years later. The interior is cool and darkly lit, refreshingly simple and minimalist, with white brick and high vaulted ceilings with black ribbing. Free organ music concerts happen about three to four times a week. Check the schedule outside for events. Sunday services start at 10am.

🚇 U3: Rathaus. ⏰ Open M-Tu 10am-6:30pm, W 10am-7pm, Th 10am-6:30pm, and F 10am-6:30pm, Sa 10am-5pm, Su 9am-9pm.

FISCHMARKT FISH MARKET

Große Elbstraße 137 ☎040 38 01 21 💻www.fischmarkt-hamburg.de

A Hamburg tradition since 1703, the Sunday morning Fishmarkt is an anarchic mix of vocal vendors hawking fish, produce, flowers, and clothing. Early risers mix with Reeperbahn partyers fresh from a long night out at clubs and bars. Make yourself the least conventional breakfast you'll ever have: fish and beer just as the sun's coming up. Everything's delicious and cheap. Bands of all genres entertain shoppers with loud rock music from the stages of the beautiful three-story brick and stained-glass fish auction hall, but the real action is outside.

🚇 S1, S3, or U3: Landugsbrücken. ⏰ Open Apr-Oct Su 5-9:30am, Nov-Mar Su 7-9:30am.

ST. PAULI LANDUNGSBRÜCKEN HARBOR

Across St. Pauli Hafenstr. from the U-Bahn and S-Bahn station

Hamburg's harbor, the second largest port in Europe, is full of lit-up ships and partyers off the Reeperbahn by night. During the day, though crowded by tourists, these piers provide exceptional views of the harbor, and are the starting point for most cruises and tours. Kapitän Prüsse gives tours of the harbor departing every 30min. from Pier 3 (*☎040 31 31 30 💻www.kapitaen-pruesse.de. 1hr.*

$ Tours in German only; €14, ages 5-14 €7. ⏰Open daily in summer 11am-5pm, in winter 9pm-4pm). **HADAG** offers elaborate cuises of outlying areas from Pier 2 *(☎040 311 70 70* ***i*** *Times and prices vary by cruise).* **Rainer Abicht** offers similar tours from Pier 1 departing every 30min. *(☎040 317 82 20 🖥www.abicht.de. $ From €14, children €7. ⏰Open daily 10am-6pm.)* Docked at Pier 1 is the tri-masted, 97m long ★**Windjammer Rickmer Rickmers.** Constructed in 1896, the ship has been renamed five times and served many different roles before finally coming to rest in the harbor as a green-hulled museum. All quarters have been painstakingly restored to their original 1890s condition. The ship also houses a large history exhibit, complete with a cafe. *(☎040 319 59 59 $€3, students €2.50, families €7. ⏰ Open daily 10am-5:30pm.)*
🚆 S1, S2, S3, or U3: Landungsbrücken.

ALSTER LAKES — LAKES

Just north of downtown, the Alster river flowing from Schleswig-Holstein branches out into the two Alster lakes before converging with the Elbe. Follow the elegant promenades around the **Binnenalster** *(🚆 U1, U2, S1, or S3: Jungfernstieg),* or join the joggers and bikers near the larger Außensalster *(🚆 S21 or S31: Dammtor).* Rent a sailboat, row boat, or windsurf board and enjoy the water on sunny days. **ATG Alster-Touristik GmbH** leads 50min. tours of the lakes *(☎040 357 42 40 🖥www.alstertouristik.de. $Adults €11, children €5.50. ⏰Tours every 30min. Mar-Oct 10am-6pm, Nov 11am-4pm every 30min, and 5pm. Available in English).*

ALTER ELBETUNNEL — TUNNEL

Starts at the domed building in the Ladungsbrücken

Construction of the Alter Elbetunnel was completed in 1911, when it became the shortest connection between St. Pauli and the opposite side of the Elbe in Steinwerder. The tunnel runs 23.5m below the river's surface, and 426 m in total length. Cross the tunnel for a view of Altstadt and the Hamburg skyline, but not much else; the other side of the Elbe is industrial, so unless you're a cement pipe and crane-lift enthusiast, a quick look at the city should be all you need.
🚆 U3, S1, S2, or S3: Landungsbrücken. $ Free. ⏰ Open all hours to pedestrians and cyclists.

HAMBURGER MUSEUM FÜR VOLKERKUNDE — MUSEUM

Rothenbaumchaussee 64 ☎018 05 30 88 88 🖥www.voelkerkundemuseum.com

From African masks to an entire Maori house, this museum of world cultures is an anthropologist's paradise. The exhibit on nationalism and the creation of a European culture is especially interesting in the light of the current European Union political situation. Along with impressive English documentation, the museum's geographic and thematic organization makes browsing a breeze.
🚆 U1: Hallerstr. $ €7, students €3.50, under 18 free. ⏰ Open Tu-Su 10am-5pm.

Outside Central Hamburg

Hamburg's sights are fascinating and varied, but many of the most unique attractions are located away from the city center; making it to one of these can carve out a good chunk of your day.

KZ-GEDENKSTÄTTE NEUENGAMME — CONCENTRATION CAMP

Jean-Dolidier-Weg 75 ☎040 428 13 15 00 🖥www.kz-gedenkstaette-neuengamme.de

Between 1938 and 1945, this concentration camp held 110,000 people as forced laborers. Close to half the occupants died from overwork or execution. Walk around the camp buildings, from the cafeteria to the dorms to the work-camps, and the thoughtful, well-presented and heart-wrenching exhibits of Neuengamme's former prisoners. Several paths lead from the meticulously labeled multilingual main exhibition, which features recorded stories from survivors and a series of red photo albums, each detailing the life of one of Neuengamme's victims. Outside, follow a path through to the brick-making factory, labor barracks, and war memorials.

🚌 *S21: Bergedorf (about 20min.), then bus #227 or #327: KZ-Gedenkstätte, Aussellung (about 35min.). Buses leave the train station and the camp every 30min., Su every 2hr.* $ *Free.* ⏰ *Museum and memorial open Apr-Sept M-F 9:30am-4pm, Sa-Su noon-7pm; Oct-Mar M-F 9:30am-4pm, Sa-Su noon-5pm. Paths open 24hr. Tours in German Su noon and 2:30pm.*

JENISCH HAUS — ART MUSEUM

Baron-Voght-Str. 50 ☎040 82 87 90 💻www.altonaermuseum.de

Situated in the middle of a peaceful park that looks out onto the Elbe, this bright white museum is just as beautiful as its stunning art collection. A variety of Flemish, Dutch, and French paintings from the 18th and 19th centuries are impeccably displayed on sky blue walls in galleries with large windows. And it would be easy to mistake the view from one of the balconies over the park for an oil-painted masterpiece.

🚌 *S1: Klein Flottbek. Go left on Jürgensallee, then right on Baron-Voght-Str. The park where the museum is located is on the lefthand side, about 10min. down.* $ *€5, students €3.50.* ⏰ *Open Tu-Su 11am-6pm.*

ERNST BARLACH HAUS — ART MUSEUM

Baron-Voght-Str. 50a ☎040 82 60 85 💻www.barlach-haus.de

Also in Jenischpark, Ernst Barloch Haus is the simple, single story contemporary art sister museum to Jenisch Haus. Revolving exhibits show more recent art, like Picasso and Barlach. The center room is separated from the rest of the museum by sound-proof glass doors, and a glass roof looks up at the sky. The perfect peace and quiet of the space make it perfect for getting truly lost in beauty.

🚌 *S1; Klein Flottbek. Go left on Jürgensallee, then right on Baron-Voght-Str. The park where the museum is located is on the lefthand side, about 10min. down.* $ *€6, students €4.* ⏰ *Open Tu-Su 11am-6pm.*

BOTANICAL GARDENS — BOTANICAL GARDEN

Directly across from the "Klein Flottbek" S-Bahn station

If you're near Klein Flottbek, the botanical gardens are a must-see. Winding paths take you through bamboo forests and lavender gardens to a tranquil lake, complete with several small docks outfitted with benches and pergolas with climbing vines. Elderly Hamburgers stroll through the Grüne Garten, the bloom-less portion of the expansive park, or walk hand-in-hand through the rose trellises.

🚌 *S1: Klein Flottbek.* $ *Free.* ⏰ *Open daily 9am-10pm.*

GEDENKSTÄTTE BULLENHUSER DAMM — MEMORIAL

Bullenhauser Damm 92 ☎040 428 13 10 💻www.kz-gedenkstaette-neuengamme.de

The Janusz-Korczak School and its adjoining rose garden serve as a memorial to the 20 Jewish children who underwent "medical testing" at KZ Neuengamme and were murdered on April 20, 1945, only hours before Allied troops arrived in Hamburg. Visitors are invited to plant a rose in memory of the victims, whose photographs line the fence of the flower garden. Inside the school, a small exhibition tells the victims' story.

🚌 *S21: Rothenburgsort. Follow the signs to Bullenhuser Damm along Ausschläger Billdeich, over the bridge. The garden is on the left side of the intersection with Grossmannstr.; the school is through the garden's leftmost gate.* $ *Free.* ⏰ *Rose garden open 24hr. Exhibition open Su 10am-5pm.*

U-434 — SUBMARINE

Vermannstr. 23c. ☎040 32 00 49 34 💻www.u-434.de

After being decommissioned in 2002, the world's largest non-nuclear sub was purchased from the Russian navy and towed to a remote Hamburg harbor. Here, this piece of Cold War history is now open to curious tourists. The 90m long ship and its 84-man crew were stationed off the American coast on reconnaissance missions from 1976-1978, after which this ship served on patrols of the North Sea. The maze of pipes and instruments will fascinate the mechanically-inclined and terrify the claustrophobic. Prepare to squeeze through small hatches and wait in narrow halls behind tourist traffic. U-434 is only worth the trip if you've got a submarine fetish or don't mind cramped spaces.

🚶 Hitch a ride with the red double-decker Stadt Rundfahrt tour bus (€2.50 each way) from St. Pauli Landungsbrücken; call ☎040 792 8979 for details. The 25min. walk from U1: Messberg along pedestrian-unfriendly streets is not recommended. $ €8, students €6, families €18. Tour €3, in German only. ⏰ Open Apr 1-Oct 3 M-Th 10am-6pm, F-Su 9am-7pm; Oct 4-May 31 daily 10am-6pm.

HAGENBECK'S TIERPARK — ZOO AND AQUARIUM

Lokstedter Grenzstr. 2 — ☎040 450 00 10 🖥www.hagenbeck.de

Founded in 1907 by the eccentric exotic animal enthusiast, Carl Hagenbeck, today the park is equal parts zoo and theme park. Zoo purists won't be impressed by the flocks of tourists feeding vegetables to the elephants by hand, or the contrived aquarium complete with plastic stalagtites and fake rock. Quirky touches abound, from the red and gold Chinese teahouse to the adjacent pond full of recreated prehistoric animals.

🚶 U2: Hagenbeck's Tierpark. $ Zoo €16, Aquarium €13, combined ticket €25, under 16 €11/9/16, family ticket (2 adults and 2 children) €49/39/69. ⏰ Open daily 9am-6pm.

FOOD

LA SEPIA — SEAFOOD [1]

Schulterblatt 36 — ☎040 432 24 84 🖥www.la-sepia.de

This Spanish and Portugese restaurant serves some of the most affordable and generously served seafood in town. See your meal prepared in front of you fresh from the harbor. The lunch special *(€4-6)* is a steal; try the grilled salmon, served with potato soup and a heaping side of (more!) potatoes and vegetables.

🚶 U3,S11, S21, or S31: Sternschanze. $ Entrees €7.50-22. ⏰ Open daily noon-3am.

HATARI PFÄLZER CANTINA — GERMAN [2]

Schanzenstr. 2 — ☎040 43 20 88 66

This eclectic restaurant is decorated with Chinese dragons and hunting trophies. A young student crowd flocks to this busys street corner for hamburgers *(€7.30-7.90)* and people watching. Hatari also serves German specialties, including the misleadingly-named French pizza, a Bavarian dish of thin cooked dough spread with cream and piled with toppings.

🚶 U3 or S11, S21, or S31: Sternschanze. $ Entrees from €7. ⏰ Open noon-late.

HIN AND VEG — VEGETARIAN [1]

Schulterblatt 16 — ☎040 594 534 02

If you've been holding back on trying the meat-heavy German classics, this is your chance to fill up on some Deutschland staples served up by an Indian owner. Hin and Veg is a completely meat-free restaurant that serves up vegetarian versions of *currywurst (€3)* and *döner (€4)*, all with vegan sauces.

🚶 U3, S11, S21, or S31: Sternschanze. $ South Asian specialties €5.50-8.50. ⏰ Open M-Th 11:30am-11:30pm, F-Sa 11:30am-midnight, Su 12:30pm-10pm.

OMAS APOTHEK — FUSION [2]

Schanzenstr. 87 — ☎040 43 66 20

Omas serves up large meals at low prices in a retro-themed bar, outfitted with floral wallpaper and the apothecary drawers that give the restaurant its name. The food is as eclectic as the decor: a mix of German, Italian, and American cuisine, and some of the friendliest bar staff on Schanzenstraße, draws in a relaxed crowd of all ages. A popular pick is the breakfast platters, served M-F 9am-noon, and Sa-Su 9-3pm *(€7.30, students €6.30).*

🚇 U3, S11, S21, or S31: Sternschanze. $ Schnitzel platter €7.50. Hamburger and fries €6.60. ⏰ Open daily 9am-1am, F-Sa until 2am or later.

HOFFSKI MÜSLI BAR ❀🍸 CEREAL [1]

Bartelsstr. 8 ☎040 79 69 68 78

A wholesome change from the German diet, this cereal bar lets you design your own perfect bowl of nuts, grains, cornflakes, chocolate chips, and even the fierce German gummy bears. Also enjoy the *bircher müesli*, a Swiss morning specialty of cereals soaked over-night in yogurt. Antique white chairs and dark wood floors with gilded accents give this cafe an elegant touch, while keeping the vibe relaxed and low-key.

🚇 U3, S11, S21, or S31: Sternschanze. $ €1.80 for 100 grams, about €3 for a large bowl. ⏰ Open M-F 8:30am-7pm, Sa 10am-5pm, Su 11am-4pm.

TRANSMONTANA ❀🍸☁ PORTUGUESE [1]

Schulterblatt 86 ☎040 439 74 55

Transmontana serves up all tapas all the time to a local following that can't get enough of this Portuguese snack bar. Sandwiches, grilled on fresh bread with serrano ham, chorrizo, tomatoes, and lettuce, are one of the best deals on popular Schulterblatt. Get a real taste of Portugal from the pastries, especially the flavorful *natas*.

🚇 U3 or S11, S21, or S31: Sternschanze. $ Sandwiches €2.10. Natas €1. ⏰ Open M-Sa 7am-10pm, Su 8am-10pm.

BALUTSCHISTAN 🎟🍸 PAKISTANI [2]

Bahrenfelderstr. 169 ☎040 390 22 29

Pakistani owners cook up authentic Middle Eastern specialities for diners seated at thickly brocaded chairs. In an area crowded with ethnic eateries, Baluschistan stands out with its fantastic tandoori dishes and tasteful wood carved doorways and hanging tapestries. Try the *Kofta curry lichi* (vegetable balls in curry with sweet lichee fruit and almonds) or the pink, nutty *doodh* soda.

🚇 S1, S2, S3, S11, or S31: Altona. $ Lunch plates €5-6. Entrees €8-15. ⏰ Open daily noon-midnight.

GEO PIZZA AUS DEM HOLZBACKOFEN ❀☁ PIZZA [2]

Beim Schlump 53 ☎040 45 79 29

This popular pizza joint is low-key despite the marble counters on the bar and dark wood walls. Students from the nearby university flock to Geo for the *flammkuchen* special, huge plate of thinly cooked dough spread with cream and piled high with olives, tomatoes, spinach, and salami. Ingredients are fresh, and pizzas are cooked up in a big brick dutch oven.

🚇 U2 or U3: Schlump. $ Flammkuchen €7. ⏰ Open M-Th 11am-midnight, F 11am-1am, Sa 10am-1am, Su noon-1am.

MENSA ❀🍸 CAFETERIA [1]

Von-Melle-Park 5 ☎040 45 03 95 81 💻www.studierendenwerk-hamburg.de

Anything but fancy, this student cafeteria draws swarms of budget-conscious youngsters with big appetites. Pack as much food as you can onto your plate and enjoy cheap prices when you flash that plastic (translation: student ID).

🚇 S21 or S31: Dammtor, then bus #4 or 5: Staatsbibliothek (1 stop). Turn right into the courtyard past the bookstore, Heinrich-Heine Buchandlung, on Grindelallee. $ Entrees €3-3.50. Non-students add an additional €1. ⏰ Open M-Th 10am-4pm, F 10am-3:30pm. Limited summer hours.

KUMPIR ❀🍸☁ SPUDS [1]

Schanzenstr. 95 ☎040 43 09 76 04

Kumpir does one thing, and one thing only—baked potatoes. That is, we think they're baked potatoes; it's hard to tell under the mountain of salad and vegetables and meat piled on top.

✵ *U3 or S11, S21, or S31: Sternschanze.* ⑤ *€3-4 per spud.* ⌚ *Open M-Th and Su noon-midnight, F-Sa noon-1am.*

CAFE ORIENTAL
⊛ ❦ ⌂ CAFE ❶

Markstr. 21A
☎040 42 10 29 95

It's hard to miss this magenta-colored restaurant, even under the thick cover of an ivy trellis. Deep red and purple walls lit by golden lanterns make this bar a stand-out in an area full of ethnic eateries. Cafe Oriental serves mostly drinks, and a few small entrees. Their specialty is *Yogitee (€2.80)*, honey tea with piles of cinnamon-dusted milk foam.

✵ *U2: Feldstr.* ⑤ *Wraps €3.50, warm sandwiches €2.50. Cocktails €6, beer €2.80-3.* ⌚ *Open daily noon-1am, later on weekends.*

NIGHTLIFE
🛑

Reeperbahn and St. Pauli

ROSI'S BAR
⊛ ⌂ BAR

Hamburger Berg 7

On a strip of almost-identical bars running along the Hamburger Berg, Rosi's stands out with a playlist of mostly soul music, and a 60-year history of serving up drinks to thirsty Hamburgers and Hamburgerins. Rosi, the one-time wife of Tony Sheridan who began managing the bar at 18, still runs it with her son. Wood paneled walls are dressed up with a single disco ball. DJs almost every night starting at 11pm.

✵ *S1, S2, or S3: Reeperbahn.* ⑤ *Beer €2.50, cocktails €5.* ⌚ *Open Su-Th 9pm-4am, F-Sa 9pm-6pm.*

BARBARABAR
⊛ ❦ BAR

Hamburger Berg 11
☎016 090 36 15 19 💻www.barbarabar.de

Hamburger Berg is full of laid-back retro bars. Think every-night DJs, cheap(ish) drinks, and sagging sofas. Barbarabar stays true to this form. Its foosball table is a big hit with a crowd of young students, where matches can get almost as heated as the deep red wallpaper. Music is mostly pop, with a tad of electro on the side.

✵ *S1, S2, or S3: Reeperbahn.* ⑤ *Beer €2.40, mixed drinks about €5.* ⌚ *Open daily 8pm-late.*

MELANIE BAR/MOLOTOW
⊛ ❦ BAR, CLUB

Spielbudenpl. 5
☎040 31 08 45 💻www.molotowclub.com

Class is relative, right? Then even Melanie Bar, and its downstairs nightclub, Molotow, are the height of sophistication, compared to their strip-club neighbors. Quirky decor, with red and orange lights, forest murals on the walls, worn couches from the 70s and hanging plastic vines from the ceiling make this feel like the Brady Bunch's hunting lodge gone nightclub. Live bands perform everything from indie to punk rock, from beat to 1960s acoustic revival.

✵ *S1, S2, or S3: Reeperbahn.* ⑤ *Cover for Molotow €3-4, live bands €8-15.* ⌚ *Open F-Sa 11pm-late, from 8pm for concerts.*

GROSSE FREIHEIT 36/KAISERKELLER
⊛ ❦ CLUB

Große Freiheit 36
☎040 317 77 80 💻www.grosse-freiheit36.de

If you must go, then go. The Beatles played here during their now legendary Hamburg years, but little of that 1960s ambiance remains. You won't find any young locals here; just throngs of tourists. To its credit, Große Freiheit still manages to pull in some impressive musical acts, from Prince to Willie Nelson. Check the website for show schedules.

✵ *S1, S2, or S3: Reeperbahn.* ⑤ *Cover €5-6, live bands €10-30.* ⌚ *Live bands and DJs perform almost every day. Check the website for complete schedule.*

St. Georg

👍 CAFE GNOSA
⊛🍸⛅▼ CAFE, GAY BAR

Lange Reihe 93 ☎040 24 30 34 💻www.gnosa.de

A Hamburg institution, if an unconventional nightlife pick. More cafe than bar, Cafe Gnosa has been serving up drinks and city-famous cakes in a well-lit, quiet restaurant since WWII. Hamburg's first gay bar has a laid-back, yet sophisticated atmosphere, with damask walls and revolving art exhibitions in the back room. Free gay publications like *hinnerk* and *Hamburg's Gay Map* available.

🚏 Follow Ernst-Mecke-Str. from the north entrance of the Hauptbahnhof as it turns into Lange Reihe. $ Beer €2.50, mixed drinks €5.5-7.50. Cakes €3-5. ⏰ Open daily 10am-1am.

KYTI VOO
⊛⛅▼ GAY BAR

Lange Reihe 82 ☎040 28 05 55 65 💻www.kytivoo.de

This large and relaxed gay bar keeps things upbeat with quiet electro beats and strategic red lights and disco balls. The outdoor seating area under a large awning is a popular place to drink for a young, mellow crowd.

🚏 Follow Ernst-Mecke-Str. from the north entrance of the Hauptbahnhof as it turns into Lange Reihe. $ Espresso €1.60. Beer €2.90. Cocktails €5.50-8. ⏰ Open M-F 9am-open end, Sa-Su 10am-late.

CUBE
⊛🍸⛅ BAR

Lange Reihe 88 ☎0173 313 6632

This chic bar in the heart of St. Georg takes its name seriously. Outfitted in an all-cube theme, from the low stools to the bar to the hanging lights, Cube plays light techno beats to a mixed crowd.

🚏 Follow Ernst-Mecke-Str. from the north entrance of the Hauptbahnhof as it turns into Lange Reihe. $ Beer €3. Cocktails €5.50-7.50. ⏰ Open daily from 7pm-late. M-Tu, Su happy hour all night, cocktails €5. W-Sa happy hour until 10pm.

Schanzenvtiertel

SHAMROCK IRISH BAR
🍸⛅ BAR

Feldstr. 40 ☎040 43 27 72 75

This is about as Irish as it gets outside of Dublin. Three smoky, dark wood rooms are filled to capacity with a young, often English-speaking crowd. Irish football banners hang from the ceiling, and some of the funniest bartenders this side of the Channel fill up huge steins while Celtic tunes, big band music, and classic rock keep the atmosphere upbeat.

🚏 U3: Feldstr. $ Beer €3.50. Guinness €3.80. ⏰ Open M-Th 6pm-late, F 5pm-late, Sa-Su noon-late.

YOKO MONO
⊛🍸 BAR

Marktstr. 41 ☎040 43 18 29 91 💻www.yokomono.de

Plywood tops the counter of this smoke-filled, no-frills bar. Busy with a young, alternative crowd, Yoko Mono boasts a popular pool table and DJs most nights. Let vinyl booths and rock music throw you back to a different decade.

🚏 U3: Feldstr. $ Beer €2.80, wine €2.50. ⏰ Open daily noon-2am or later.

GOLDFISCHGLAS
⊛🍸 CLUB, BAR

Bartelstr. 30 ☎017 93 90 06 48

Despite this nightlife destination's name—Fishbowl—here's little room to swim, or even breathe, in this packed bar. A swanky professional-heavy crowd sips drinks while backed up against deep-red walls. A downstairs dance floor with DJ is open Th-Sa.

🚏 U3, S21, or S31: Sternstanze. $ Cocktails around €6. ⏰ Open M-W noon-2am, Th noon-3am, F-Sa noon-5am, Su noon-2am.

SOFABAR (OR SUB, OR ZOÉ II) ✪🍸 BAR

Neuer Pferdemarkt 17

About 15 mismatched sofas crowd the floor of this large bar, but that's not enough for Sofabar's devoted fans. A young crowd packs every couch, aisle, and window sill in this classically shabby-chic bar, where half-stripped wallpaper never looked so fashionable.

🚇 U3, S21, or S31: Sternstanze. $ Beer €2.80. Mixed drinks €5.50-8. ⏰ Open daily 9pm-late.

BEDFORD CAFE 🍸⛅ BAR

Schulterblatt 72 ☎040 43 18 83 32

Loud music blasts in this upbeat, crowded bar. Ornate moldings and chandeliers lend the bar elegance, without making it stuffy. Hipsters pack the tables inside and out, and drinks are served from a beautiful old wood and glass bar.

🚇 U3, S21, or S31: Sternstanze. $ Salads and sandwiches €3.30-4.80. Beer €2.40-3.40. Mixed drinks €5-6. ⏰ Open daily 10am-late.

BP1 🍸⛅ BAR

Schulterblatt 74 ☎040 432 29 96

Social bar-hoppers float between the casual BP1 and its neighboring Bedford Cafe. Floor to ceiling windows open up in the front for a thankful breeze that cools down a packed house that spills out onto the street. It's all about the new music and funky wallpaper here, with experimental DJs supplying the soundtrack nightly. Performance schedule on the website.

🚇 U3, S21, or S31: Sternstanze. $ Beer €2.50. Mixed drinks €5-7.50. ⏰ Open daily 9pm-late.

MOBILE BLUES CLUB 🍸⛅ MUSIC BAR

Corner of Schulterblatt and Max-Bauer-Allee ☎017 687 23 27 61 💻www.mobile-blues-club.de

Some of Hamburg's freshest indie tunes are played in this small mobile home. With no cover, you can support bluegrass, alternative, and jazz musicians as they perform on a closet-sized stage at one end of the home. Crowds congregate on the small adjacent lawn, lit with hanging bulbs and furnished with patio chairs. Check the website for performance schedules.

🚇 U3, S21, or S31: Sternstanze. $ Beer €2.40. No cover for bands. ⏰ Open W-Sa from 1pm-late.

Altona

FABRIK 🍸⛅ CLUB

Barnerstr. 36 ☎040 39 10 70 💻www.fabrik.de

This former weapons factory now only kills on the dance floor. For years, crowds have packed the two level club, complete with a rusted crane on the roof, to hear big-name rock acts and an eclectic mix of other bands, with styles ranging from Latin to punk. Check the website ahead of time for a schedule of events; the club also hosts a "Gay Factory" night each month.

🚇 S1, S3, or S31: Altona. $ Cover €7-8. ⏰ Music nearly every night, starting at 9pm. Live DJ most Sa nights at 10pm.

AUREL ✪🍸⛅ BAR

Bahrenfelder Str. 157 ☎040 390 27 27

This laid-back bar draws the ultimate "mixed crowd." Students rub shoulders with architects who sit side-by-side with artists and travelers. But the real appeal is the international vibe; bartenders are from France, US, and England, and their guests are from all around the world. Aurel gets its fair share of locals as well, who come for the mojito happy hour *(daily from 9pm)* and the relaxed feel.

🚇 S1, S3, or S31: Altona. $ Beer €2.90. Mixed drinks €6-8. ⏰ Open daily from 10am-3am.

IMOTO ✪🍸⛅ BAR

Bahrenfelder Str. 88 ☎017 17 77 07 70

A wall-to-wall lounging sofa is packed with young people looking to re-live (or, rather, like the first time) the 70s. Cool geometric pyramids cover the ceiling and vinyl-covered window seats, probably helped along by happy hour *(daily until 10pm, cocktails €5)*, set the groove for nightly DJs..

✚ *S1, S3, or S31: Altona.* Ⓢ *Beer €2-3. Mixed drinks €5.50-7.* ⓩ *Open daily 7pm-late.*

INSBETH
⬤⁽ᵒ⁾ 𝗬 ⟋ BAR
Nöltingstr. 84   ☎040 390 1924

If simplicity is a virtue Insbeth is absolutely sinful. A ceiling covered with small lightbulbs is overwhelmed by the masses of colorful Christmas lights hanging around the bar. Seating is a mix of old theater seats, velvet, gilded couches, and outdoor seats under the canopy of (you guessed it) more Christmas lights.

✚ *S1, S3, or S31: Altona.* Ⓢ *Beer €1.90-3.90. Mixed drinks €5.40.* ⓩ *Open daily 9am-late.*

REH
⬤⁽ᵒ⁾ ⟋ BAR
Nöltingstr. 84   ☎040 99 99 22 09

Reh is all quiet elegance, with deep green walls and shimmering gold ceilings. Oversized candelabras hang from the high ceiling, and a mixed crowd sips mojitos underneath.

✚ *S1, S3, or S31: Altona.* Ⓢ *Beer €2.40-3.50. Mixed drinks €6-8.* ⓩ *Open daily 9am- around 1am-4am. Happy hour daily 6-9pm.*

LAUNDRETTE
⬤ 𝗬 ⟋ BAR, LAUNDROMAT
Ottenser Hauptstr. 56   ☎040 51 90 82 43 🖳www.laundrette.dk

Exactly as advertised: a bar and a laundrette. Light green walls with deep burgundy accents and state-of-the-art laundry machines in the back mean you can get sloshed and washed at the same time. DJs on Th-Sa from 9pm usually play stoner rock and 80s independent tunes.

✚ *S1, S3, or S31: Altona.* Ⓢ *Most drinks €4.50-8.50. Beer €2.40-3.40.* ⓩ *Open M-Th 8am-midnight or later, F 8am-2am or later, Sa 9am-late, Su 9am-midnight. Washing machines turned off around 8pm so the spin cycle doesn't compete with the DJ's.*

CAFÉ TREIBEIS
⬤ 𝗬 ⟋ BAR
Gaußstr. 25   ☎040 39 33 57 🖳www.cafetreibeis.de

An eclectic interior draws a crowd to match. This smoky bar has a few ironic touches, like a leopard-print and sequin-covered sofa, that keep the atmosphere light-hearted, while rock classics blast in the background. The outdoor patio has barbeque Thursdays May-Oct., a favorite with Altona locals. DJs every Friday night.

✚ *S1, S3, or S31: Altona.* Ⓢ *Beer €2.50-3.40. Mixed drinks €4-5. Tequila shots €2.* ⓩ *Open M-Sa 5pm-late.*

ARTS AND CULTURE

STATSOPER
OPERA
Große Theaterstr. 36   ☎040 35 68 68 🖳www.hamburgische-staatsoper.de

The Statsoper was opened in 1678 as the first theater in Hamburg for aristocrats and nobles. Today, it houses one of the best opera companies in Germany as well as the national dance powerhouse, the John Neumeier Ballet company. And with low prices, we lowly peasants can still get a seat.

✚ *U2: Gänsemarkt* Ⓢ *Tickets starting from €8.* ⓩ *Box office open M-Sa 10am-6:30pm and 90min. before performacnces.*

DEUTSCHES SCHAUSPIELHAUS
THEATER
Kirchenallee 39.   ☎040 24 87 13 🖳www.schauspielhaus.de

This theater produces contemporary international works mixed with Shakespeare and Sophocles. Its quirky off-beat plays, and the tried-and-true classics, are usually performed in German.

✚ *Located diagonally across from the Hauptbahnhof.* Ⓢ *Student prices from €7.50.* ⓩ *Box office open M-Sa 10am-7pm, or during showtimes.*

HAMBURG SYMPHONIKER ORCHESTRA

Rothenbaumchaussee 77. ☎040 44 02 98 🖳www.hamburgersymphonkier.de

The Hamburg Symphoniker performs at the Hamburg Musikhalle *(Johannes-Brahms-Pl. 20, ☎040 34 69 30 🖳www.musikhalle-hamburg.de)*, which is is home to many of Hamburg's great orchestras, including the Philharmonie *(🖳www.elbphilharmonie.de)* and the Norddeutscher Rundfunk Symphony *(🖳www4.ndr.de)*.

🚇 U2: Gänsemarkt. $ Tickets from €8. ⏰ Box office open M-F 10am-6pm.

SHOPPING

Hamburg is the place to go for new music. The stomping ground for the Beatles still brings in talented, little-known musicians strumming on big-time dreams. Hamburg is full of fantastic record shops that showcase new talent.

If you're looking to take home something other than tunes, you can't go wrong with the boutiques crowding the **Schanzenstraße.** For women's clothing especially, this street is brimming with mid-priced buys and good quality, high fashion clothes, even if the price tags aren't dirt cheap.

HANSEPLATTE 💿 RECORD STORE

Neuer Kamp 32 ☎040 285 701 93 🖳www.hanseplatte.de

This record store is located right next to the popular indie performing venue, Knust. Hanseplatte specializes in local bands, so whatever genre of Hamburg musicians took your fancy, you'll be able to find them here.

🚇 U3, S21, or S31: Sternstanze. $ Records from €5, but prices vary considerably. ⏰ Open M-F 11am-7pm, Sa 10am-6pm.

BURNOUT RECORDSTORE 💿 RECORD STORE

Beim Grünen Jäger 21 ☎040 43 18 31 26 🖳www.burnoutrecords.de

Burnout's collection of punk rock, hardcore, and alternative music couldn't have less in common with its name. Browse through stacks of 50s and 60s tunes, surf and stoner rock, some secondhand, in this edgy store. The passionate and upbeat staff is willing to point you in the right direction.

🚇 U3, S21 or S31: Sternstanze. $ Records from €4. ⏰ M-F 11:30-7pm, Sa 12-6pm.

MICHELLE RECORDS 💿 RECORD STORE

Gertrudenkirchof 10 ☎040 32 62 11 🖳www.michelle-records.de

Michelle is Hamburg's oldest record store, and still carries an impressive selection of mostly indie and underground CDs and vinyl. The staff is extremely helpful with navigating you through all kinds of new music. "Secret performances" still happen at Michelle's; visit the store to see when independent bands are performing.

🚇 U3: Mönckebergstraße. $ Secondhand vinyl from €1. ⏰ Open M-F 11am-7:30pm, Sa 11am-7pm.

ESSENTIALS

Practicalities

- **TOURIST OFFICES:** Hamburg's main tourist offices supply free English-language maps and pamplets. All sell the **Hamburg Card** (see "Getting Around.") The **Hauptbahnhof** office books rooms for a €4 fee. *(In the Wandelhalle, the station's main shopping plaza, near the Kirchenallee exit. ☎040 30 05 12 01. 🖳www.hamburg-tourism.de ⏰ Open M-Sa 9am-7pm, Su 10am-6pm.)* The **Sankt Pauli Landungsbrücken** office is often less crowded than the Hauptbahn office. *(Between piers 4 and 5. ☎040 30 05 12 03. ⏰ Open Oct-May daily 10am-5:30pm; Apr-Sept M, W, Su 8am-6pm, Tu and Th-Sa 8am-7pm.)*
- **TOURS: Top-Tour Hamburg** offers double-decker bus tours. If a sight requires a little further exploration, you can hop off anytime for a look and jump back on the

next bus. Tours depart from the Kirchenallee exit of the Hauptbahnhof for land-lubbers (Top-Tour) and the St. Pauli Landungsbrücken for the nautically inclined (Maritim-Tour); combine the two in an all-encompassing Gala Tour. *(☎040 641 37 31. 🖳www.top-tour-hamburg.de ℹ English-language tours available upon request. $ €15, students €13, children free. ⏰ Buses leave every 30min. daily Apr-Oct 9:30am-5pm; fall and winter tours every 1hr. 10am-3pm.)* **Strattreisen Hamburg** offers offbeat 1-2hr. themed walks, with titles like "Reeperbahn by Night," "Merchants and Catastrophes Downtown," and "Neon-Lights, Seedy Bars, and Catholics in St. Pauli." *(Kuhberg 2. ☎040 430 3481. 🖳www.stattreisen-hamburg.de ℹ Most tours are offered in German; however, English language tours are also given on a less frequent basis. $ €7-46. ⏰ Call ahead for times.)* See Hamburg with a water-bird's eye view on a 50min. boat rides around the lakes with **Alster-Touristik.** *(On Jungfernstieg by the Außenalster. ☎040 357 4240. 🖳www.alstertouristik.de $ €10, under 16 €5. Group discounts available. 🚇 U1, U2, S1, or S3: Jungfernstieg; follow the swan signs. ⏰ Tours leave daily late Mar-Oct every 30min. 10am-6pm.)*

hamburg hotline

The English speakers on the **Hamburg Hotline** *(☎040 30 05 13 00)* book rooms *(€4 fee)*, sell event tickets, and answer questions.

- **CONSULATES: Canada** *(Ballindamm 35, between Alestertor and Bergstr. ☎040 460 02 70. 🚇 U1, S1, S2, or S3: Jungfernstieg. ⏰ Open M-F 9:30am-12:30pm.)* **Ireland** *(Feldbrunnerstr. 43. ☎040 44 18 61 13. ⏰ Open M-F 9am-1pm.)* **New Zealand** *(Domstr. 19, on the 2nd fl. of block C of Zürich-Haus. ☎040 442 55 50. 🚇 U1: Messberg. ⏰ Open M-Th 9am-1pm and 2-4:30pm.)* **UK** *(Harvesthuder Weg 8a. ☎040 448 03 20. 🚇 U1: Hallerstr. ⏰ Open M-Th 9am-4pm, F 9am-3pm.)* **US** *(Alsterufer 27/28. ☎040 41 17 11 00. 🚇 S11, S21 or S31: Dammtor. ⏰ Open M-F 9am-noon.)*
- **CURRENCY EXCHANGE: ReiseBank** arranges money transfers for Western Union, cashes traveler's checks. *(2nd fl. of the Hauptbahnhof near the Kirchenallee exit. ☎040 32 34 83. ℹ ReiseBank also has branches in the Altona and Dammtor train stations as well as in the Flughafen. $ 1.5% commission, charges €6.50 to cash 1-9 checks, €10 for 10 checks, and €25 for 25 checks, and exchanges currency for a fixed charge of €3-5. ⏰ Open daily 7:30am-10pm.)* **Citibank** cashes traveler's checks, including AmEx. *(Rathausstr. 2 ☎040 30 29 62 02. 🚇 U3: Rathaus. ⏰ Open M-F 9am-1pm and 2-6pm.)*

save the bills

For better rates, try one of the dozens of exchanges and banks (most of which are open M-F 9am-5pm) near the Hauptbahnhof or downtown.

Emergency!

- **POLICE:** *(From the Kirchenallee exit of the Hauptbahnhof, turn left and follow signs for "BGS/Bahnpolizei/Bundespolizei." ☎110. ℹ Another branch is located on the Reeperbahn at the corner of Davidstr. and Spielbudenpl. and in the courtyard of the Rathaus.)*

- **FIRE AND AMBULANCE:** ☎112.
- **PHARMACIES: Senator-Apotheke.** *(Hachmannpl. 14. ☎040 32 75 27 ℹ English-speaking staff. ⏰ Open M-F 8am-6:30pm, Sa 9am-1pm.)* **Hauptbahnhof-Apotheke Wandelhalle.** *(In the station's upper shopping gallery. ☎040 32 52 73 83. ⏰ Open M-F 7am-8pm, Th-F 7am-10pm, and Sa-Su 8am-9pm.)*
- **INTERNET ACCESS: Internet Cafe** offers one of the best deals in town. *(Adenauerallee 10, directly across from the ZOB. ☎040 28 00 38 98. $ €0.75 per 30min. ⏰ Open daily 10am-11:55pm.)* **Teletime** doubles as a hookah bar at night. *(Schulterblatt 39. ☎040 41 30 47 30. $ €0.50 per 15min. ⏰ Open M-F 10am-10pm, Sa-Su 10am-7pm.)* Free Wi-Fi is available in **Wildwechsel** *(Beim Grünen Jäger 25. ⏰ Open daily from 4pm)* and at **Altan Hotel** *(Beim Grünen Jäger 23. ⏰ Open 24hr.).* **Staats- und Universitätsbibliothek** has computers on the 2nd fl., but internet access is limited to library cardholders; some temporary internet access for non-cardholders may be arranged. *(Von Melle-Park 3. ☎040 428 38 22 33. 🖥www.sub.uni-hamburg.de $ Library card €5 per month or €15 for 6 months. ⏰ Open to the public M-F; hours vary by department, but generally 10am-6pm.)*
- **POST OFFICE:** At the Kirchenallee exit of the Hauptbahnhof. *(⏰ Open M-F 8am-6pm, Sa 8:30am-12:30pm.)*
- **POSTAL CODE:** 20099.
- **HOME SHARE: Mitwohnzentrale Homecompany.** *(Schulterblatt 112. ☎040 194 45. 🖥www.hamburg.homecompany.de ⏰ Apartments available for 1 month or more. Passport and deposit of 1-2 months' rent required. 🚇 U3, S21, or S31: Sternschanze. Then follow the Schulterblatt under the bridge. ⏰ Open M-F 9am-1pm and 2-6pm, Sa 9am-1pm.)*
- **BOOKSTORES: Thalia-Buchhandlungen** is one of the city's largest bookstores. *(Spitalerstr. 8. ☎040 48 50 11 22. 🖥www.thalia.de 🚇 U2: Mönckebergstr.)* **Europa Passage** offers the city's biggest English language selection. *(Ballindamm 40. ☎309 549 80. 🚇 U1, U2, S1 or S3: Jungferstieg.)* **Heinrich-Heine Buchhandlung** has an excellent travel section and a decent selection of English-language novels. *(Grindelallee 26-28. ☎040 441 13 30. 🖥www.heinebuch.de ⏰ Open M-F 9:30am-7pm, Sa 10am-4pm.)*
- **LAUNDROMAT: Schnell und Sauber** *(Neuer Pferdemarkt 27. $ Wash €3.50 for 6kg or €7 for 12kg. Dry €0.50 per 10min. 🚇 U3: Feldstr. ⏰ Open daily 7am-10:30pm.)* Or enjoy a beer while laundering at **Loundromatte.**
- **GLBT RESOURCES:** St. Georg is the center of the gay community. **Cafe Gnosa** offers delicious refreshments and several free publications concerning Germany's gay community. *(Lange Reihe 93.)* **Hein unt Fiete,** a self-described switchboard, gives advice on doctors, disease prevention, and tips on the gay scene. *(Pulverteich 21. ☎040 24 03 33. 🚇 Walk down Steindamm away from the Hauptbahnhof, turn right on Pulverteich and look for a rainbow-striped flag on the left. ⏰ Open M-F 4-9pm, Sa 4-7pm.)* **Magnus-Hirschfeld-Centrum** offers daily film screenings, counseling sessions, and a gay-friendly evening cafe. *(Borgweg 8. ☎040 27 87 78 00. 🚇 U3: Borgweg.)* **Dementy** operates hotlines for gays and lesbians. *(☎040 27 87 78 01. ℹ* Gay hotline *☎040 279 0069 ⏰ Open M and Th-F 2-6pm, Tu-W 2-6pm and 7-10pm.* Lesbian hotline *☎040 279 0049, W 7-9pm. ⏰ Open M-Th 5pm-11pm, F 5pm-late, Su 3-10pm.).*

Getting There

By Plane

Air France *(☎01805 83 08 30)* and **Lufthansa** *(☎01803 80 38 03)*, among other airlines, service Hamburg's **Fuhlsbüttel Airport** *(☎040 507 50)*. **Jasper Airport Express** buses *(☎040 22 71 06 10 🖥www.jasper.de)* run from the Kirchenallee exit of the Hauptbahnhof directly to the airport *($ €5, under 12 €2. ⏰ 25min., every 10-15min. 4:45am-7pm, every 20min. 7-9:20pm)*. Alternatively, you can take U1,S1, or S11 to Ohlsdorf, and then an **express bus** to the airport *($ €2.60, children 6-14 €0.90. ⏰ Every 10min. 4:30am-11pm, every 30min. 11pm-1am)*. The same modes of transporation are available from the airport to the center of the city.

By Train

The **Hauptbahnhof,** Hamburg's central station, has connections to: **Berlin** *($ €56. ⏰ 2hr.)*; **Copenhagen, Denmark***($ €80.⏰ 4.5hr.)*, **Frankfurt** *($ €150. ⏰ 5hr.)*; **Hanover** *($ €55.⏰ 1.5hr.)*; **Munich** *($ €185. ⏰ 7hr.)*. Be advised that prices may vary depending on day of travel, time of year, and proximity of purchase date to travel date. The efficient staff at the **DB Reisezentrum** sells tickets *(⏰ Open M-F 5:30am-10pm, Sa-Su 7am-10pm)*, which are also available at the ticket machines located throughout the Hauptbahnhof and online at **🖥www.db.de. Dammtor** station is near the university, to the west of Außenalster; **Harburgdorf** is to the southeast. Most trains to and from Schleswig-Holstein stop only at **Altona,** while most trains toward Lübeck stop only in the Hauptbahnhof. Frequent locals trains and the S-Bahn connect the stations.

By Bus

The **ZOB** terminal is across the Steintorpl. from the Hauptbahnhof *(⏰ Open M-Th 5am-10pm, F-Sa 5am-midnight, Su 5am-10pm)*.

Ride Share

Mitfahrzentrale Citynetz, Ernst-Merke-Str. 12-14. *(☎040 194 44 🖥www.citynetz-mitfahrzentrale.de $Prices vary by driver. ⏰ Open M-F 9:30am-6:30pm, Sa 10am-2pm.)*

Getting Around

By Public Transportation

HVV operates the efficient U-Bahn, S-Bahn, and bus network. Short rides within downtown cost €1.65, one-way in greater Hamburg €2.60; 1-day pass €5.60, 3-day pass €15.90. Passes are available for longer, though anything over a week requires a photo. Frequent riders can bring a photo or take one in the nearby ID booths for €5. The **Hamburg Card** provides unlimited access to public transportation, reduced admission to museums, and discounts on souvenirs, restaurants, theater, and bus and boat tours for groups of 1 adult and up to 3 children under 15. *(Available at tourist offices and in some hostels and hotels. $ €8 per day, €18 for 3 days, €33 for 5 days.)* The Group Card provides the same benefits for up to 5 people of any age *($ 1-day €11.80, 3-day €29.80, 5-day €51)*.

By Ferry

HADAG Seetouristik und Fährdienst AG, St. Pauli Landungsbrücken *(☎040 311 7070)*. Most locals suggest taking the HVV-affiliated ferries in lieu of the expensive tour boats for an equally impressive view of the river Elbe. Departing every 15min. from the docks at St. Pauli to 21 stops along the river. Full circuit lasts 75min. Price included in HVV train and bus passes; €2.60 for a new ticket.

By Taxi

All Hamburg taxies charge the same rates. **Taxi Hamburg,** *(☎040 666 666)*. **Das Taxi,** *(☎040 22 11 22)*. **Autoruf,** *(☎040 44 10 11)*. Normally about €2.40 to start, then €1.75 or less per additional km.

By Car Rental

Avis. (✚ In the Hauptbahnhof near track #12 on the Spitalerstraße side. ☎040 32 87 38 00, international ☎018 05 55 77 55 🖥 www.avis.de **i** Lower prices online. Ⓢ Cars from €242 per week, with insurance and 24hr. emergency assistance. 🕐 Open M-F 7:30am-9pm, Sa 8am-6pm, Su 10am-6pm.) Lower prices online at **Hertz.** (Kirchenallee 34-36✚ Across the Kirchenallee from Ernst-Merck-Str. ☎040 280 1202, international ☎01805 33 35 35 🖥 www.hertz.de **i** Lower prices online. Ⓢ Cars from €243 per week, including insurance. 🕐 Open M-F 7am-7:30pm, Sa 8am-4pm, Su 10am-4pm.) **Europecar.** (Holstenstr. 156✚ U3: Feldstr. ☎040 306 8260 🖥 www.europecar.de **i** Lower prices online. Ⓢ Cars from €245 per week. 🕐 Open daily 24hr.)

By Boat Rental

Die Segelschule Pieper. (An der Alster/Atlantickstieg ✚ Directly across form the Hotel Atlantic at the intersection of Holtzdamm and the An der Alster on the Außenalster. ☎040 24 75 78 🖥www. segelschule-pieper.de **i** Must be 14+ to rent. Ⓢ Pedalboats and rowboats for €12-13 per hr., and sailboats for up to 6 people for €16-19 per hr. 🕐 Open May-Sept daily 10am-9pm.)

By Bike Rental

Hamburg is very bike-friendly, with wide bike lanes built into most sidewalks. **Fhrrandstation Dammtor/Rotherbaum.** (Schlüterstr. 11. ☎040 41 46 82 77, Ⓢ €3 per day. 🕐 Open M-F 9am-6pm.) **Fahrandladen St. Georg.** (Schmilinskystr. 6. ✚Off the Lange Reihe near the Außenalster. ☎040 24 39 08 Ⓢ €8 per day, €56 per week with a €50 deposit. 🕐 Open M-F 10am-7pm, Sa 10am-1pm.)

lübeck   ☎0451

Lübeck is a perfectly medieval town, with two specialties: churches and marzipan. These specialties make strange but enjoyable bedfellows. Travelers can enjoy the sweetest indulgences in one of Germany's best confectionaries, and then repent for their gluttony in the cavernous interior of a colossal kirche. Lübeck was also home to creative giants Thomas and Horace Mann, and Günter Grass. Today their immaculately restored homes are impressive museums of these men's literary and artistic geniuses. Though not all of Lübeck's buildings are as well preserved, and massive chain stores and horrid '70s era architecture have crept into the streets, Lübeck retains a distinctly ancient feel. Once the capital city of the Hanseatic League, Lübeck basks in the medieval ambiance and munches on marzipan.

ACCOMMODATIONS   🔟

RUCKSACK HOTEL   ⊛⊗⊕ HOSTEL
Kanalstr. 70   ☎0451 70 68 92 🖥www.rucksackhotel-luebeck.de

A member of a collective of communal, eco-friendly shops, this painstakingly decorated hostel boasts beautiful double rooms in an international theme celebrating India, China, and Brazil. Rucksack's dorms are also warm and comforatble, in deep yellows and outfitted with pine bunks, that attract a young, artistic crowd—many of the musicians that come to play in Lübeck stay here.

✚ Bus #1, 11, 21, or 31: Katharineum. **i** Sheets and Wi-Fi included. Ⓢ 6- to 8-bed dorms €13; 4-bed dorms €15; doubles €18; singles €25. 🕐 Reception open daily 10am-1pm, and 5pm-8pm.

SLEEP-IN (CVJM)   ⊛
Große Petersgrube 11   ☎0451 719 20 🖥www.cvjm-luebeck.de

This lodge, run by a Christian organization, has exposed brick walls and heavy timbers on the ceilings that keeps things cozy. Pine bunks with checked sheets look out over brick townhouses on a narrow street. All rooms have ensuite baths, and the quiet downstairs pub is complete with television, piano, and jazz music.

i Sheets included. *i* Breakfast €4. Ⓢ 4- to 8-bed dorms €20; 2-person apartments from €60. 🕐 Reception 8am-8pm. Check-in before 7pm.

SIGHTS

MARIENKIRCHE
Schüsselbuden

CHURCH
☎0451 39 77 00

In a skyline riddled with steeples, Marienkirche still manages to dominate the sky-scape. Construction of the church began around 1200 in the Romanesque style, but it was completed as a Gothic cathedral in 1350. This huge building sustained heavy damage during WWII—a giant bronze bell, warped and splintered, lies embedded in the shattered marble floor where it fell during the air raids of 1942. Gape at pictures of the church's famous Tonentanzbild, an elaborate mural depicting the "dance of death" in the left apse, where the original, lost in the fire that followed the air attacks, once stood. To the left of the pews is the church's newly restored astronomical clock. Outside, a sculpture of the devil shares a seat with photo-happy tourists. Legend has it that Satan helped build the church, thinking it would be a bar. When he realized his mistake, locals stopped him from destroying the church by building a bar across the street.

i Free tours in German daily in June-Sept. at 12:15pm. Tower tours June-Sept W and Sa 3:15pm, Apr-Oct Sa 3:15pm. Ⓢ Suggested donation €1. Tower tours €4, students €3. 🕐 Open daily in summer 10am-6pm, in winter 10am-4pm.

KUNSTHALLE ST. ANNEN
Sankt-Annen-Straße 15

ART MUSEUM
☎0451 122 41 34

St. Annen is a fantastic blend of the oldest and the newest in art. Sacred illustrations from this one-time monastery is displayed in what remains of the original building. For a truly medieval experience, don't miss the statue of St. George and the Dragon. Adjacent are four floors of roving exhibitions of world class contemporary art. The two exhibits are included in the cost of a ticket, and are best enoyed together.

[$] €5, with special exhibitions €7. Students €2.50/3.50. ⏰ Open Tu-Su 10am-5pm.

PETRIKIRCHE CHURCH

Schüsselbuden 13 ☎0451 777 67 💻www.st-petri-luebeck.de

If you were expecting a dark medieval church, prepare yourself for a sunny surprise. Petrikirche's interior, with its towering arches and impressive altar, is painted entirely bright white. Canvas sails hanging from the ceiling add a stunning contemporary touch to an ancient church. An elevator rises 50.5m to the viewing platform inside the 13th century steeple for a sweeping, windy view of Altstadt and Lübeck's spire-filled skyline. The church nave occasionally exhibits modern art—check website for details.

[$] Requested donation €1. Tower €3, students €2. ⏰ Open Tu-Su 11am-4pm. Tower open daily Apr.-Oct. 9am-9pm; Mar. and Nov. 11am-5pm; Dec. 9am-7pm.

GÜNTER GRASS-HAUS MUSEUM

Glockengießerstr. 21 ☎0451 122 42 30

The former house of acclaimed author Günter Grass is now a tribute to his masterful skill in writing, sketching, and sculpting, with over 1,100 pieces of his work. Come here to learn more about the life of this Nobel laureate's politically charged, creative career. Though the impressive museum has many highlights, be sure to look out for the watercolors from Grass' series of paintings entitled "20th century," with one watercolor for each year.

[$] €5, with special exhibit €7. Students €3.50/€2.50. ⏰ Open daily Apr.-Dec. 10am-5pm; Jan.-Mar. 11am-5pm.

WILLY-BRANDT HAUS LÜBECK MUSEUM

Königstr. 21 ☎0451 122 42 50 💻www.willy-brandt-luebeck.de

Willy Brandt was mayor of West Berlin when the Wall was built, and then later Chancellor of West Germany. In his former house in his hometown Lübeck, visitors can walk through exhibits detailing his illustrious career, captioned in English and German. For German history fans, the museum also provides an interesting look at the turmoil that beset the country from the Weimar years all the way through the Cold War.

[$] Free. ⏰ Open Jan-Mar Tu-Su 11am-5pm, Apr-Dec M-Su 11am-6pm

RATHAUS TOWN HALL

Breite Str. 62 ☎0451 12 20

Lübeck's beloved city hall, at the center of Altstadt, is something of a haphazard ode to a variety of architectural styles. The original building, constructed in the 13th century, was built from red and black glazed brick. New wings were added in the 14th and 15th centuries. The building's courtyard is now a venue for flower, produce, and jewelry vendors, and serves as spill-over seating from the nearby cafes. Admission with tours only, offered in German.

[$] M-F €4, €2 students, Sa-Su €4, students €3. ⏰ Tours M-F at 11am, 12pm, and 3pm. Sa-Su at 1:30pm.

THEATERFIGURENMUSEUM MUSEUM

Kolk 14 ☎0751 786 26 💻www.tfm-luebeck.com

The world's largest private collector of puppets converted his hobby into a foundation at this museum, which displays puppets from around the world and across centuries. Over 1,200 exquisitely detailed hand, string, shadow, and stick puppets from Germany to China pack the museum's five floors. Puppets range from the whimsical to the somewhat grotesque; small children might find some of the figures frightening.

Ⓢ €5, students €3, children €2. 🕐 Open daily Apr-Sept 10am-6pm; Oct 10am-4pm; Nov-Mar 10am-3pm.

DOM
CHURCH

Domkirschhof ☎0751 747 04

A tribute to Henry the Lion, Lübeck's oldest church was built in 1173, complete with a lion statue guarding the exterior. This church is shocking for its sheer size; colossal white-washed pillars create a cavernous interior with enough beautiful carving and stained glass as an art gallery. To the right of the altar, tombs are marked by fantastic marble statues and gilded wrought iron. The back window of stained glass is a contemporary masterpiece, mixing old with new after some destruction during the WWII bombing and a subsequent restoration.

Ⓢ Free. 🕐 Open daily 10am-6pm.

MUSEUM BEHN-UND DRÄGERHAUS
MUSEUM

Königstr. 21 ☎0751 122 4148

This 18th-century house keeps a large collection of paintings and sculptures from the 19th-century through today, focusing on Romantic and Nazarene art and featuring works by Edvard Munch and sculptor Ernst Barlach. The museum also includes less fascinating exhibits of 18th- and 19th-century furnished rooms.

Ⓢ €5, with special exhibits €7. Students €2.50/€2.50. 🕐 Open daily 10am-5pm.

BUDDENBROOKHAUS
MUSEUM

Mengstr. 4 ☎0751 122 41 92 🖳www.buddenbrookhaus.de

Author Thomas Mann, winner of the 1929 Nobel Prize in literature, set his novel *Buddenbrooks* in this house, where he and his brother were raised. The house was built in 1758, and converted into a museum in 2000 as part of The Expo 2000 World Literature Project. Today, the permanent exhibit reproduces the novel as a walk-in story, allowing readers to wander through the scenes of the novel in their original setting. Additional exhibits detail the life of the Mann brothers.

Ⓢ €5, with special exhibits €7. Students half price. 🕐 Open daily 10am-6pm, Jan-Mar 11am-5pm.

FOOD

▨ I. G. NIEDEREGGER MARZIPAN CAFE
✎ ⵂ CAFE, BAKERY ❶

Breitestr. 89 ☎0751 530 11 26

Lübeck is the best German town for eating marzipan, and Niederigger is its best confectionery. Sample marzipan-flavored ice cream, or buy candies shaped like pigs, jellyfish, or the town gate. Don't leave without trying the marzipan cream cake. All treats are cheaper to-go than in the cafe, but the ambiance might be worth the extra €0.50. The upstairs Marzipan Salon, a free exhibit on the history of the almond-sweet, is worth skipping.

Ⓢ Cakes €2.20-3. 🕐 Open M-F 9am-7pm, Sa 9am-6pm, Su 10am-6pm.

CAFE AFFENBRAT
⊛ ⵂ CAFE ❷

Kanalstr. 70 ☎0751 721 93

A vegetarian cafe and biergarten, Affenbrot is part of the same co-op as the Rucksack Hotel. Students frequent this popular haunt with bright purple and neon green decor. A large sunroom is the perfect place to enjoy a fresh pizza, with pesto and feta cheese *(€7.50)*. Menu rotates to include seasonal ingredients.

⌖ Take bus #1, 11, 21, or 31: Katharineum. Ⓢ Sweets €4.50-8.50 🕐 Open daily 9:30am-11:30pm. Kitchen open 9:30am-10:30pm.

KURBIS
⊛ ⵂ⌖ GERMAN ❷

Mühlenstr. 9 ☎0751 707 0126

Wood-beamed ceilings and deep yellow walls in a comfortable bar with lots of booth seating. The kitchen serves up inexpensive German classics and popular *Pfanne*, enormous pan-fried meals served piping hot and topped with melted cheese *(€6.90-8.90)*.

$ Currywurst and fries €4.90. Wienerschnitzel €5.90. ⏰ Open M-Tu and Th noon-10pm, F-Sa noon-midnight. Kitchen closes 30min. earlier.

ESSENTIALS

Practicalities

- **TOURIST OFFICE:** Holstentorpl. 1, next to the Holstentor. *(☎045 188 22 33. $City maps €1. Internet access €3 per hr. Happy Day Card, €7 for one day, €14 for three days, provides unlimited access to public transportation and discounted admission to many of Lübeck's museums. ⏰ Open June-Sept. M-F 9:30am-7pm, Sa 10am-3pm, Su 10am-2pm; Oct.-Nov. and Jan-May M-F 9:30am-6pm, Sa 10am-3pm; Dec. M-F 9:30am-6pm, Sa 10am-3pm.)*
- **POLICE:** Mengstr. 18-20. ☎110.
- **FIRE:** ☎112.
- **AMBULANCE:** ☎0451 192 22.
- **PHARMACY: Adler-Apotheke.** *(Breite Str. 71. ☎0451 798 85 15. After-hours after hours 045 17 10 81. ⏰ Open M-F 8:30am-7pm, Sa 9am-6pm.)*
- **INTERNET ACCESS: Handy-Shop Lübeck.** *(Königstr. 111. ☎0451 409 97 70. $ €1 per hr.)*
- **POST OFFICE:** *(Königstr. 44-46. i 24hr. ATM accessible at this location. ⏰ Open M-F 8:30am-6:30pm, Sa 8:30am-1pm.)*
- **POSTAL CODE:** 23552.

Getting There

By Train

Every hr. to: **Berlin** *($ €78. ⏰ 3.5hr.)*; **Hamburg** *($ €18. ⏰ 45min.)*; **Rostock** *($ €23. ⏰ 2hr.)*.

Getting Around

By Taxi

Catch a taxi just outside the train station *(☎0451 811 22)*.

By Ferry

Many ferries run waterfront tours on **An der Obertrave** and **An der Untertrave.** Quant-Linne, An der Obertrave cruises around the Altstadt and harbor from the bridge in front of the Holstentor. *(☎0451 777 99 🖥www.quandt-linie.de. $ €8, students €6.50. ⏰ Open May-Oct. daily every 30min. 10am-4pm; less frequent during low season.)*

By Public Transportation

Altstadt is more easily seen on foot, but public buses are well-networked around the outside of the city. The **ZOB** (central bus station) is across from the train station. To reach the Lübeck airport, take bus #6 (dir.: Blankenese/Seekamp) to Flughafen. Direct questions to the LVG Service Center, am ZOB *(☎0451 888 2828 $ Single ride €1.60-2.60. Day pass €7. ⏰Open M-F 5am-8pm, Sa-Su 9am-4pm)*.

DRESDEN, LEIPZIG, AND WEIMAR-JENA

Dresden, Leipzig, Weimar and small, nearby Jena are united only in geographical proximity and a common history of Soviet occupation as a part of former East Germany. Each one on its own offers the traveler something unique, but together they're a mosaic of German culture, history, and yes, some of the wildest nightlife around. In other words, let's check your wanderlust symptoms, and prescribe you a piece of the East German experience.

The castle-gazer and the club-hopper will find their fill of both beautiful architecture and bass-blasting nightlife in the "Florence on the Elbe," **Dresden,** an up-and-coming city whose strong student population is infusing life into a town that's on its way to reclaiming its former glory. **Leipzig,** too, has seen its share of reconstruction in the past two decades. Leipzig is a retreat for the incurable bistro enthusiast, or the musician with the classical bug. Leipzig's pedestrian-dominated cobblestone streets and elegant facades are squeezed into a bounded city center just one kilometer in diameter that somehow includes refined restaurants and quirky student bars alike. And for those suffering from chronic sophisticated bohemianism, **Weimar's**

greatest hits

- **ON THE ROCKS.** Mosh at an epic concert or sip a mixed drink in the lounge of the Industriegelände's Washroom in Dresden's Neustadt (p. 131).

- **BACK TO BACH.** Hear Bach's masterpieces performed at Leipzig's Thomaskirche, where Johann spent the last 27 years of his career (p. 141).

- **WHOSE HOUSE?** Explore Bauhaus, where crafting and fine art techniques converged to form an influential current in modern design (p. 152).

- **ALL THAT JAZZ.** Catch local or traveling musicians at Blue Note Dresden—one of the best jazz bars in Germany (p. 132).

117

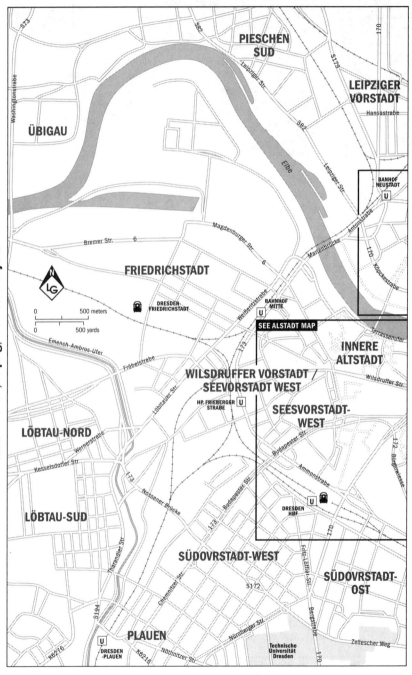

dresden, leipzig, and weimar-jena

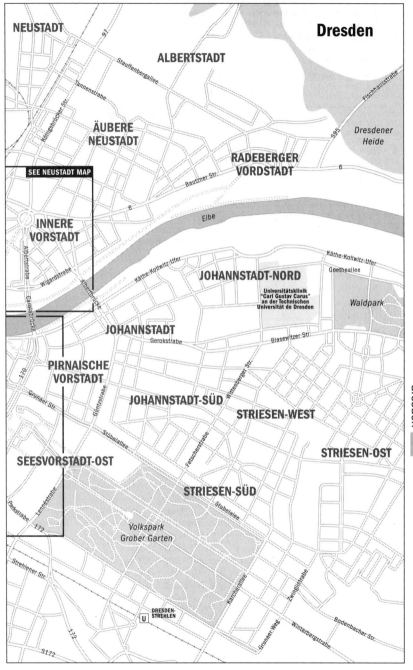

Dresden

dresden

rich literary and artistic history is an unparalleled cure. Home to **Goethe** and **Schiller,** and birthplace of Bauhaus Modernism, this little town is charmingly, nauseatingly cute. Narrow stone pathways weave between colorful cottages, most of which were blessedly spared destruction during the first and second World War. Nearby **Jena,** a town whose lifeblood is its students and (get this) its thriving optical industry, is prescribed in small doses as a complement to Weimar's more geriatric scene.

student life

Beach, booze, and bargain bites: three things that young people can universally agree to love. Dresden, Leipzig, Weimar, and Jena offer up solid servings of all of the above. Grab some shades and head to Puro Beach or City Beach in Dresden—two sandy-floored bars that will transport you to paradiße. After getting your tan on, what's left to do but get your rage on? Alternative students chill on every windowsill and stairway in Jena's aptly named Studentenhaus Wagner, a laid-back bar with a live music soundtrack. Unfortunately, classes are probably cluttering your party schedule. The morning after you earn an A+ in flip cup, grab some inexpensive breakfast at Weimar's AAC before lab, or stick around (too hungover for class?) and hear Bauhaus professors lecture about art in English.

dresden ☏0351

In 1945, a two-night-long Allied air raid completely destroyed Dresden, killing between 25,000 and 50,000 Germans. Until the reunification of Germany in 1989, many of the historic buildings burned in the bombing were left untouched as a monument to the war. As striking as these ruins must have been, we're thrilled the city of Dresden ultimately decided to reconstruct its stunning riverside view (with substantial help from the German and British national governments.) With the ongoing, incredibly successful restoration of the Dresden landscape, "Florence on the Elbe" has resurrected its old Baroque beauty, and given rise to a vibrant youth culture. With world-class museums, operas, and palaces to fill your day, and nightclubs and bars busy late into the night, we suggest you come for the *Kirches* and stay for the *Klubs* (or vice versa).

ORIENTATION

Dresden is located about 60km northwest of the Czech border and 200km south of Berlin, with its population of 500,000 heavily concentrated around the banks of the **Elbe.** The river bisects the city, with **Neustadt** to the north, and **Altstadt** to the south. **Hauptbahnof,** which is located in Alstadt, is linked to the **Altmarkt** (with its beautiful historic buildings) by **Prager Strasse,** a pedestrian zone lined with shops and fountains. **Altmarkt** is connected to Neustadt by **Austusbrucke,** the Elbe's central walking bridge, which links Alstadt to Neustadt's pedestrian walkway, **Haupstrasse.** Most of Dresden's historic sights are located along the Elbe, with the majority found in Altstadt. Neustadt is the younger, more alternative side of Dresden, full of hostels, inexpensive restaurants, and unbeatable nightlife.

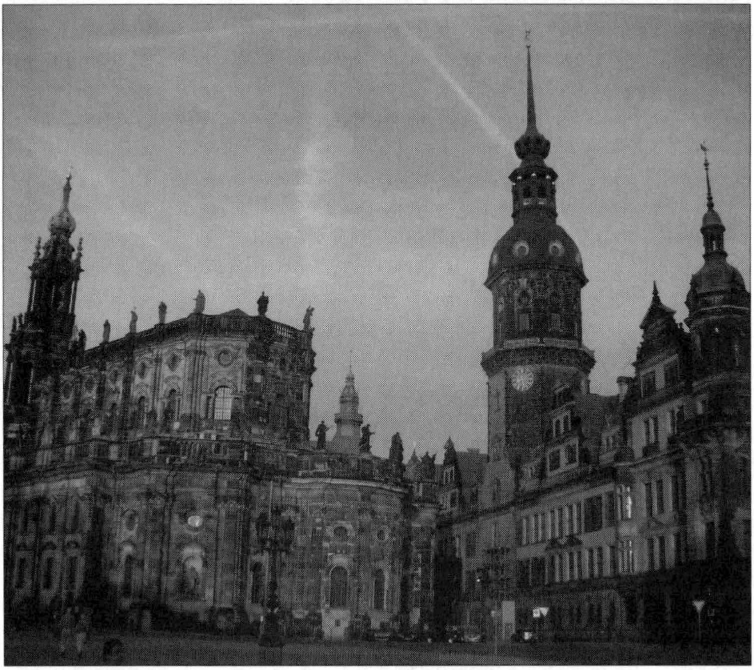

ACCOMMODATIONS

With the Hauptbahnhof and river sights located in Altstadt, it may be tempting to book your stay on the south side of the river. However, far more hostels, with lower prices and a more youthful clientele, are in the Neustadt. Public transportation makes everything easily accessible from either side of the river, so don't let proximity keep you from finding your bunk to the north of the Elbe.

Altstadt

JUGENDGÄSTEHAUS ⊛ HOSTEL [2]

Masternistraße 22 ☎0351 49 26 20 🖥www.dresden.jugendherberg.de

Jugendgästehaus, a member of Hosteling International, is one of few hostels located in Dresden's Altstadt, and, at just a 7min. walk away, is the closest to Dresden's historic river sights. The hostel's interior is admittedly asylum-esque, with stark white walls, fluorescent lighting and hospital waiting room furniture. Rooms have either two or four beds, and are mostly popular with families.

➹ From the (H) at Post Platz, follow Feiberger to Maternistr. ***i*** *Ensuite full bath is available for an extra €4.50.* *$ May-Oct with breakfast from €21.25, with either lunch or dinner €26.75, with lunch and dinner €32.25. Nov-Apr from €20.25.* *⏰ Reception 24hr.*

CITY HERBERGE 🚬📶 HOSTEL, HOTEL [3]

Lingnerallee 3 ☎0351 485 99 00 🖥www.cityherberge.de

If you are set on staying in the Altstadt, this is the place to do it. From the outside the building looks a bit like an insane asylum, and it's located across from a happening skate park, but the rooms themselves are cozy, comfortable, and can be personalized based on your budget. The hostel rooms share toilets on the floor while the hotel-style rooms come with a bathroom and amped-up decor

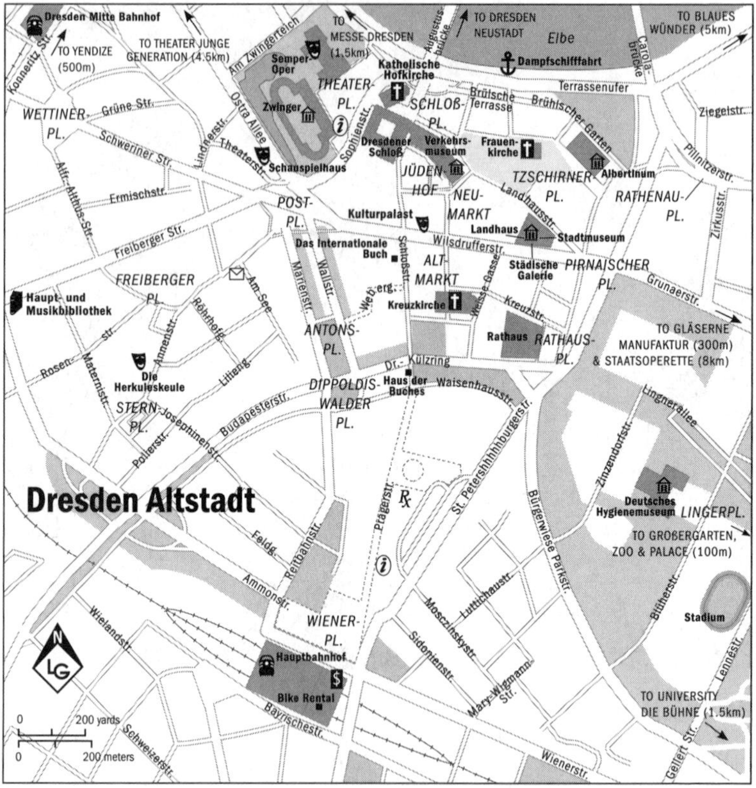

(like paintings and fluffier pillows). Suitable for all age groups; the great lobby area is stocked with board games.

🚊 Tram 7 or 12: Pirnaischer Pl. From the stop, walk down St. Petersburger Str. toward the Rathaus (City Hall with the big tower). ℹ Breakfast and internet access included. $ Basic rooms €16-35; standard €21-42; comfort €30-56. ⏰ Reception 24hr.

JH RUDI ARNDT — HOSTEL ❷

Hübnerstr. 11 — ☎0351 471 06 67 💻www.jh-rudiarndt.de

JH Rudi Arndt is located in a leafy residential area and feels more like a personal home than a typical backpacker hostel. Cozy up in a bunk, pop some fresh popcorn in the lobby, and grab a drink at the downstairs bar. However, if you plan on stumbling home after a long night out in Neustadt, think twice before you book your accommodation here, because it's not easy to get to.

🚊 Tram 3 or 8: Nürnberger Place. From the stop, continue down Nürnbergerstr. in the direction of the tram, then take a right on Hübnerstr. The hostel will be down the street on the right. ℹ Reservations recommended. Breakfast included. Towel rental €1. Youth hostel membership (YHI card) required. Internet €1 per hr., €2.50 per 3 hr. $ Ages 27+ €19.55-21.05 per night; ages 13-27 €16.05-17.55 per night; ages 2-12 €9.60-10.50 per night. Payment upon arrival.

A AND O DRESDEN — HOSTEL, HOTEL ❶

Strehlener Str. 10 — ☎0351 46 92 71 59 00 💻www.aohostels.com

The Dresden location of the large A and O chain, this hostel and hotel takes in

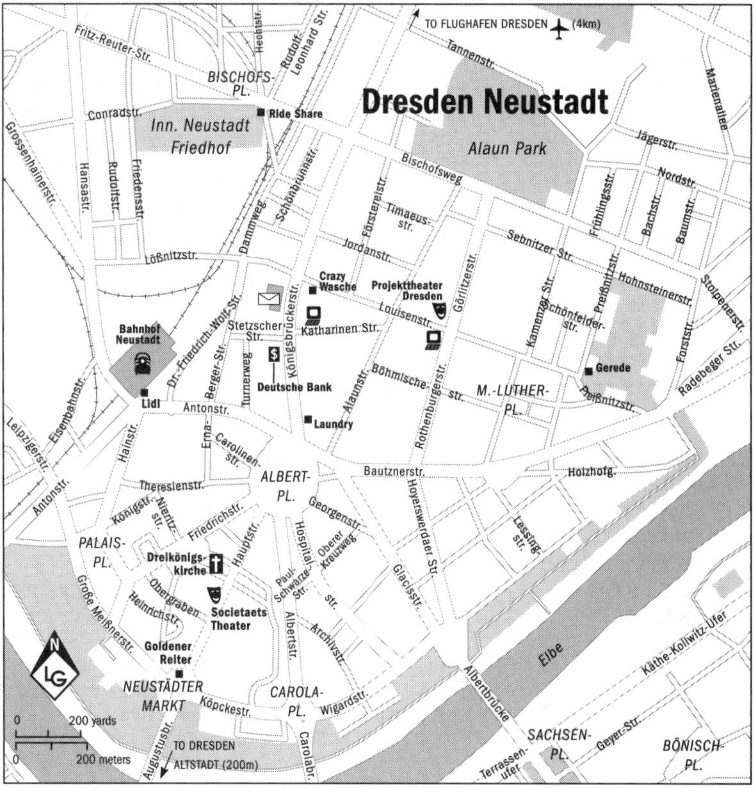

and spits out guests like a revolving door—it has all the bare necessities, but none of the personal touch. It has about 15 stories of both hostel and hotel-style rooms, so you will undoubtedly find some new friends to explore the city with.

🚏 Bus #66: Uhlandstr. You can also walk from the main station down Strehlener Str. ℹ Breakfast buffet €4. Linens included. Internet available. $ 4- to 6-bed dorms €13-15; 8- to 10-bed dorms €12-13; singles from €39; doubles from €50. ⏰ Reception 24hr.

Neustadt

LOUISE 20 — HOSTEL, PENSION ❶

Louisenstr. 20 ☎0351 889 48 94 💻www.louise20.de

The golden hardwood floors and dainty glass canisters with cereal conjure feelings of comfort, with impeccable cleanliness and in-room sinks to match. You may feel so at home that you don't want to leave, except to find nourishment in the conveniently located restaurant and bar called Planwirtschaft below. Luckily, the location provides easy access to trams to the Altstadt while also centrally located amidst Neustadt restaurants, shops, and bars.

🚏 Tram 7 or 8: Louisenstr. ℹ Breakfast €5.50. Linens included with ISIC card. Group discounts available. $ 5-bed dorm €14-17; 3-4 bed room €16-18; singles €29-35; doubles €38-46. ⏰ Reception daily 7am-11pm. If arriving earlier or later with a reservation, arrange in advance.

HOSTEL MONDPALAST

圏(ℙ)Ÿ HOSTEL ❶

Louisenstr. 77   ☎0351 563 40 50 ▣www.mondpalast.de

This place is seriously cosmic. Hostel Mondpalast (Moon Palace) is nestled smack in the middle of of Neustadt's restaurant and nightlife district, and serves a mostly young clientele. The hostel has a bar and restaurant on its lower level (happy hour prices all day long for guests!). Rooms are constellation-themed, with pine beds, private lockers, and stellar murals.

✦ *Tram 7: Louisenstr.. From the stop, walk along Louisenstraße to Mondpalast, on the left. Or, tram 11: Pulsnitzer Straße. From the stop, turn left onto Louisenstr.* ⓘ *Breakfast €6. In-room shower and bathroom available, usually for an extra €6-8. All guests required to pay for linens, €2 (one time charge). Fully equipped kitchen. Wi-Fi included.* Ⓢ *8-10 bed rooms €14; 5-6 bed rooms €16; single €34; doubles €39.* ⏰ *Reception Apr-Oct 24hr.; Nov-Mar call ahead for hours. Check-out noon.*

KANGAROO STOP

圏க(ℙ)Ÿ HOSTEL ❶

8-10 Erna-Berger Str.   ☎0351 314 34 55 ▣www.kangaroo-stop.de

Kangaroo Stop, with its Rainbow Snake mural and hammock-heavy lounge room, might belong to Dresden's biggest Aussie-ophile. It also has some of the cheapest beds in Dresden, and its garden and outdoor fire-pit make for great late-night sing-alongs. It's about a 6min. walk from Neustadt's shops and restaurants.

✦ *Neustadt. From the station, walk about 3min. down Antonstr. toward Albertpl. Turn left on Erna-Berger. It's easy to miss, but there are signs to tell you if you've gone too far.* ⓘ *Wi-Fi included. Fully equipped kitchen. Laundry facilities available.* Ⓢ *10-bed dorms €12.50; 5-6 bed dorms €15; singles €33; doubles €40.* ⏰ *Reception 24hr.*

LOLLI'S HOSTEL

✦(ℙ)Ÿ HOSTEL ❶

Görlitzer Str. 34   ☎0351 810 84 58 ▣www.lollishome.de

This hostel is perfect for the homesick, travel-weary backpacker. Laid-back Lolli's Homestay has a living room and fully-equipped kitchen popular with guests, who often share meals together. Lolli's is just seconds away from Neustadt bars, restaurants, and nightlife, with low prices even in high season.

✦ *Tram 7: Bischofsweg. From the stop, turn right on Bischofsweg, take the 3rd street on the right, and walk about 100 yards.* ⓘ *Wi-Fi included. Sheets €2, or free if you stay 4 nights or more.* Ⓢ *8-bed room €13; 4-bed room €28; singles €30; doubles €44. On F and Sa, all beds cost an extra €2.* ⏰ *Reception 24hr.*

MEZCALERO BED AND BREAKFAST

✦(ℙ)Ÿ BED AND BREAKFAST ❷

64 Konigsbrucker Str.   ☎0351 81 07 70 ▣www.mezcalero.de

Stucco walls and beautiful Spanish tile make Mezcalero a *paraíso pequeño* in Neustadt. Large windows frame beautiful views. Rooms have 1-7 beds, and are most commonly booked by groups or families.

✦*Tram 7: Bischofsweg. From the stop, walk about 50 yards along Konigsbrucker to Mezcalero.* ⓘ *Breakfast €6.50. Wi-Fi included. Book in advance, rooms fill up quickly. Ensuite baths can be reserved for about €6 extra.* Ⓢ *4-bed dorm €19; 7-bed dorm €17; singles €30; doubles €48.* ⏰ *Reception 24hr. Check-out noon.*

PENSION RASKÖLNIKOFF

✦⊗ PENSION, BED AND BREAKFAST ❹

Bömische Str. 34   ☎0351 804 57 06 ▣www.raskolnikoff.de

Hidden behind the shabby exterior of a 173-year-old house, this pension has only six simple and clean rooms, which retain their character with exposed stone walls and slanted ceilings. With no dorms in sight, these rooms are better suited as apartment rentals for introverted couples. The multiple locked doors offer tight security, and there is no regular reception—be careful not lose your key!

✦ *Tram 11: Martin-Luther Str. From the stop, walk up Martin-Luther Str. and turn left on Bomische. The pension will be on the left, and the rooms are above the RasKölnikoff restaurant and gallery in the same building.* ⓘ *Reservations required, e-mail pension@raskolnikoff.de.* Ⓢ *Single €40; double €52; larger room for 3 or more people €60 per night, min. 2-night stay.*

SIGHTS

We'd tell you that there's too much for a traveler to see in just a few days, but fortunately for you and your weary feet, many of Dresden's major sights are clumped close together on the beautiful scenic banks of the Elbe. With the **Royal Cathedral** right next to the **Royal Palace** right next to the **City Opera House,** the original city-plan was either drawn up by the incurably lazy for their own convenience, or the admirably considerate for ours. Most of the places to see are in the Altstadt, but there's plenty to keep you busy in the Neustadt as well.

Altstadt

FRAUENKIRCHE CHURCH

Neumarkt ☎0351 656 06 🖥www.fauenkirche-dresden.de

Frauenkirche (Church of Our Lady) was first bombed and destroyed in 1945. Originally left in ruins as a monument to the terrors of war, it was decided after the German reunification that the church would be rebuilt, incorporating the black, burned stones from the old church into the new, lighter stones. Because the British financed a substantial portion of the reconstruction, Dresden now regards the church as a symbol of reconciliation. Unfortunately, the light blue, green, and pink painted interior seems to be visually more symbolic of an Easter egg or a Miami condo than the mended relations between previously warring states. Visitors can see Altstadt from the top of the dome.

🚋 Tram 1, 2, 4, or 12: Altmarkt. Tram 3, 6, 7 or bus 75: Pirnaischer Platz. $ €8. ⏰ Open Mar-Oct M-Sa 10am-6pm, Su 12:30-6pm. Nov-Feb M-Sa 10am-4pm, Su 12:30-4pm. Weekend times restricted due to rehearsals.

DRESDENER RESIDENZ SCHLOSS ROYAL PALACE

Taschenberg 2 ☎0351 49 14 20 00 🖥www.skdmuseum.de

Originally built as a residential palace for Saxony's Wettin dynasty of electors (you can see their portraits in the palace's Gallery of Electors, if you're curious), it was ruined in the 1945 Allied bombing. Currently, the palace is being restored as a museum, with four different exhibits open at different times and for different admission prices. High on the list of those to see are both the New and Historic Green Vaults, which have recently found a home back in the palace. The **Historic Green Vault,** a collection of Augustus the Strong's jewelry, ivory carvings, and intricate work by goldsmiths, might be worth the admission fee. The **New Green Vault,** is a smaller exhibit, but less of a hassle to visit, and features a separate part of Augustus's treasure collection. Visitors can also visit the **Rüstdammer** (Armory), **Münzkabinett** (Coin Cabinet), and **Kupferstich-Kabinett** (Cabinet of Prints and Drawings).

🚋 Tram 4, 8 or 9: Theaterpl. ℹ Historic Green Vault ticket reservation at least one day prior to visit. Reservations can be made online at www.dresden.de.). No reservations necessary for the New Green Vault. $ Historic Green Vault €10, including audio tour. Children under 7 free. New Green Vault €6, students €3.50. ⏰ Historic Green Vault open M and W-Su 10am-7pm, last entry 6pm. New Green Vault open M and W-Su 10am-6pm.

KATHOLISCHE HOFKIRCHE CATHEDRAL

Schloβpl. ☎0351 484 48 12 🖥www.kathedrale-dresden.de

Katholische Hofkirche (the Catholic Court Cathedral) adjoins the palace. Though destroyed in 1945, it was quickly restored to near perfect condition, with a striking bright white marble interior. The cathedral still displays its original organ on the second floor, which, having miraculously survived the bombing, represents the last surviving work of world-famous organ-builder Gottfried Silbermann. Because the church is still very much used by worshippers, remember to behave respectfully (confessionals aren't photobooths, folks).

🚋 Tram 7, 8 or 9: Theatpl. ℹ Guided tours M-Th 2pm, F-Su 1pm, Sa 1pm. $ Free. ⏰ Open M-Tu

9am-6pm, W-Th 9am-5pm, F 1-5pm, Sa 10am-5pm, Su noon-4pm.

SEMPERBAU MIT ZWINGGER — MUSEUM

Theaterpl. 1 ☎0351 491 46 22 🖥www.skd-dresden.de

Contains collections including the **Gemäldegalerie Alte Meister** (Old Masters Picture Gallery). The Old Masters Gallery has large, tightly packed canvases reaching from the ground to the high ceilings, often organized by artist. Walk past **Canaletto's** paintings of Venice, or Carriera's room of portraits on the third floor. Don't miss Canaletto's 18th century iconic paintings of the Dresden waterfront to see how successful the reconstruction of Altstadt has been. Other works by **Raphael, Botticelli, Titian, Rembrandt,** and **Correggio** also make this worth the visit. Part of the **Rüstkammer** (armory) collection is also housed here, in addition to the **Porzellansammlung** (porcelain collection), the largest ceramics collection in the world, with over 20,000 works. A porcelain aficionado, the display traces pottery specimens from the Ming Dynasty to Japanese Imari wares from the early 17th and 18th centuries.

🚋 Tram 7, 8 or 9: Theaterpl. The Zwingger is right across from the Hofkirche. $ Gemäldegalerie Alte Meister €3, students €2, entire collection €10/7.50. Under 16 free. ⏰ Open Tu-Su 10am-6pm.

BRÜHLSCHE TERRACE — WALKWAY

The Brühlsche Terrace, or the "Balcony of Europe," is the 500m long stretch along the Altstadt side of the Elbe, starting at the **Schloβpl.** (Castle Square), and ending at the **Brühlsche Garten.** Situated at the top of an old Renaissance fort, you can also see the **Academy of Fine Arts,** and its glass tower affectionately referred to as the "lemon squeezer," and the **Lipiusbau,** an alternative contemporary art spot next to the Albertinum. The city suggests that, at the end of your walk, you search for the legendary thumbprint of Augustus the Strong, embedded somewhere along the balustrade handrail. Get lucky and you might catch a fireworks display over the Elbe!

🚋 Trams 3 or 7: Synagoge. $ Free. ⏰ Open 24hr.

DIE GLÄSERNE MANUFAKTUR (THE TRANSPARENT FACTORY) ♿❄☀ — FACTORY

Lennestr. 1 ☎01805 89 62 68 🖥www.glaesernemanufaktur.de

Join a guided tour through this glass extravaganza that houses the Volkswagen's Phaeton, and watch men in white moon-suits piece the luxury cars together by hand. Each Phaeton on the assembly line is unique, and will eventually be delivered to its owner through an elaborate display in which the car ascends into the room on a platform. If cars aren't your thing, the almost transparent building is still a spectacle. At the end of the tour, there is a parked Phaeton to play with (no test driving allowed). Be sure to sit in the driver's seat and turn on the back massager.

🚋 Tram 12 or 13: Strassburger Platz. ℹ The factory is occasionally open for independent exploration, but the areas for independent visit are restricted. $ €4, students, seniors, disabled €2. Family card €10 (two adults, up to 5 children). Group discounts available. ⏰ English tours daily at noon and 3pm, but hours and tours subject to change; call in advance to confirm and reserve.

GROSSER GARTEN ♿☀ — PARK

Entrance on Lennestr.

This is the city's best and most expansive green space, with bike and rollerskating paths, hidden fountains, and a Baroque-style palace with a sculpture exhibit. Sit on a bench in the sun with a good book, or explore the botanic gardens and kite meadow. Take a sip from the fountain of youth and hop on the kiddy train that makes loops through the park.

🚋 Tram 10 or 13: Grosser Garten. $ Free. ⏰ Open dawn to dusk.

DEUTSCHES HYGIENE MUSEUM ♿☀ — MUSEUM

Lingnerpl. 1 ☎0351 484 64 00 🖥www.dhmd.de

Sex, drugs, and rock 'n' roll...OK, not the drugs and rock 'n' roll part, but definitely the sex. With an area devoted (somewhat graphically) to sexuality, this museum explores everything that makes us human from "Living and Dying" to "Eating and Drinking" to "Sexuality." The permanent exhibit also boasts the "Transparent Man," a glass figure with illuminated organs. Taking advantage of the interactive nature of this museum, clusters of children are everywhere poking, prodding, pressing, and giggling at things. The temporary exhibits are spectacular; "What is Beautiful?" is open until January 2011; also new in 2011 is "Images of the Mind," which examines humans' relationship to the arts and sciences.

🚋 Tram 1, 2, 4, or 12: Deutsches Hygiene Museum. Or, Tram 10 or 13: Grosser Garten. ℹ Many descriptions are in English. $ €7, students €3, family ticket (2 adults, 2 children) €11, under 16 free. F from 3pm free. ⏰ Open Tu-Su 10am-6pm. Closed Jan 1 and Dec 24-25.

ALBERTINUM MUSEUM MUSEUM

Georg-Treu-Pl. 2 💻www.skdmuseum.de

This newly-renovated museum should not be missed. Although formerly an arsenal, this museum could not hold off the flood of 2002, and the current multi-million-euro project will fortify the building entirely against any future floods. In the past, the Albertinum housed art from the 19th and 20th centuries in the Alte Meister Galerie (Old Master's Gallery) and classical sculpture in the Skulpturen-sammlung (Sculpture Gallery). The new museum promises to restore these, as well as reveal new works, creating a bridge between many genres and their eras.

🚋 Tram 4, 8, 9: Theaterpl. From the stop, walk along the Bruhlsche Terrace. Or, tram 3 or 7: Synagogue. $ €8, students €6, groups (10+) €7 per person. ⏰ Open daily 10am-6pm.

KREUZKIRCHE CHURCH

An der Kreuzkirche 6 ☎0351 439 39 20 💻www.kreuzkirche-dresden.de

Not as flashy as the Frauenkirche, the Kreuzkirche actually feels like a church. In other words, there are no tourists and camera flashes. The interior has been left plain after five fires, and the simple stone-based pillars and white walls exude a pleasant calm. The view from the tower is the cheapest view in the city, but there is no elevator to the top. On Sunday mornings, the famous Dresden Boy's Choir performs as part of the church service.

🚋 Tram 1, 2, or 4: Altmarkt. From the stop, the church is through the square; look for the really big tower. $ Church free. Tower €2.50, students and children €2, family €5. ⏰ Open M-Sa 10am-6pm, Su noon-6pm.

SEMPEROPER ♿🍸 OPERA HOUSE

Theaterpl. 2 ☎0351 796 63 05 💻www.semperoper-erleben.de

If you don't have an opportunity to see a performance here, the next best thing is to take a tour of the Semperoper, Dresden's claim to fame in the world of art and music. The tour takes you first through the hand-painted golden lower foyer, then to the upper foyer and vestibule made entirely of artificial marble. The highlight is the dazzling auditorium, with its hanging chandelier, sweeping gold curtains, and maximized acoustics.

🚋 Tram 4, 8, or 9: Theaterpl. $ English tours generally at 3pm. $ €8, students €4. Photos €2. ⏰ Check daily schedule outside the front doors for hours.

NEW SYNAGOGUE SYNAGOGUE

Hasenberg 1 ☎0351 656 07 20 💻www.freundeskreis-synagoge-dresden.de

Although the Jewish community has been present in Dresden since 1206, this New Synagogue (built after the war) looks more like something from the space age—the building is a sandstone-colored cube with no windows. According to historical accounts, the Star of David on the portal was rescued by a lone fire-man on the Night of Broken Glass, when Nazis organized fires throughout the country and forbade everyone from putting them out.

🚋 Tram 3 or 7: Synagogue. $ €4, student €2.50. ⏰ Open M-Th and Su noon-6pm.

Neustadt

DREIKÖNIGSKIRCHE (CHURCH OF THE MAGI) — CHURCH

Hauptstr. 23 ☎0351 812 41 00

Only the original clock and bell tower, designed in 1730, survived the 1945 Dresden bombing, but a new structure has been built around it to allow church services to continue. Climb to the top of the bell tower, up a dizzying series of spiral staircases, to see panoramic views of all of Dresden.

🚋 Tram 8: Neustädter Markt. $ Admission to the tower €1.50, children €1. Church service free. ⏰ Tower open Mar-Oct Tu 11:30am-4pm, W-Sa 11am-5pm, Su 11:30am-5pm. Nov-Feb W noon-4pm, Th-F 1pm-4pm, Su 11:30am-4:30pm.

GOLDEN REITER (GILDED HORSEMAN) — STATUE

This gold-plated August the Strong faces the Augustusbrücke on Neustädter Markt. Some locals find the statue of a "fat man on a fat horse" unappealing and gaudy, but there's something to be said for large gold equine statues...probably. Augustus' commendatory suffix has two suggested derivations. First, it alters his physical strength, supposedly displayed by his indented thumbprint on the **Brühlsche Terrasse.** Since the thumprint was made after his death, this would indeed be quite a show of strength. Second, it speaks to his his virility—legend has it that he fathered 365 children, though the official tally is 15.

🚋 Tram 8: Neustädter Markt. $ Free.

ALAUNPARK — PARK

On sunny days, families have picnics, children eat ice cream, students study on the grass, and everyone else runs around playing soccer and frisbee. This expansive park occasionally hosts a local produce market during the summer, and is always a perfect place to bring a meal and take a stroll.

🚋 Bordered by Bischofsweg, Alaunstr., Kamenzer Str. and Tannenstr. $ Free.

ELBEWISEN (ELBE MEADOW) — ⛅🍸 GREENSPACE

The strips of grass that run alongside the Elbe through the city center offer another chill hangout for enjoying the nice weather. With the city's Baroque skyline as the ultimate backdrop, people picnic, tan, sleep, and read. Be sure to bring a blanket, sunscreen, and some cash to grab a beer at one of the *biergartens* that line the meadow. In July and August, movies are screened on the river banks as part of an outdoor film festival.

🚋 Tram 4, 8, or 9: Neustadter Markt. From the stop, walk down the stairs at the beginning of the bridge. $ Free. ⏰ Open daily in sunshine.

BAROQUE QUARTER — ♿🍸⛅ SQUARE

Konigstr., Obergraben, Heinrichstr., Rahnitzgasse

Another vision of King Augustus the Strong, the Baroque Quarter was built after a fire in 1685 and has been fairly untouched even after the bombings of WWII. The facades have been slightly spruced up, and these buildings now house luxury hotels, expensive boutiques, and art galleries. The Rodeo Drive of Dresden, if you will.

🚋 Tram 7 or 8: Albertpl. From the stop, walk down Konigstr., then turn left onto the smaller side streets. $ Free.

KUNSTHAUS DRESDEN — ♿ MUSEUM

Rahnitzgasse 8 ☎0351 804 14 56 💻www.kunsthausdresden.de

Tucked away in the corner of the Baroque Quarter, this venue has been a center for contemporary art since 1989 and continues to hold challenging exhibits that include videos, pictures, performances, and installations. Themes cover current reigional and international events related to the world of art. Bring along a friend for lively debate.

🚊 Tram #8: Neustadter Markt. From the stop, walk past the golden rider back along Pragerstr. Turn left on Heinrichstr. under the overpass, then again left. It will be on the corner next to the small garden with benches. [S] €3, students €2. ⏰ Open Tu-F 2-7pm, Sa-Su noon-8pm. Hours may vary according to current exhibitions and events.

FOOD

Dresden is full of inexpensive and great tasting food. Affordable restaurants in Altstadt are difficult to come by; travelers will have to sacrifice their budgets and eat alongside masses of tourists to enjoy a meal with great views of reconstructed Baroque buildings. Luckily, markets are open relatively frequently in the summer months in **Altmarkt,** where good food is available for a lot less. Neustadt, however, has a wide range of eateries with plenty of low-budget options. Make sure you pick up a free *Dresden by Locals* map in any hostel or tourist office to see a long listing of places Dresdeners go to be fed and watered.

Altstadt

Restaurants around the Altstadt market let visitors in on the incredible views of the Frauenkirche and the Elbe. Unfortunately, these places are expensive and overrun by hoards of tourists. If you're looking to stay on a budget, your cheapest options are the *bratwurst* stands scattered around the **Markts,** which sell their fare for €2-3. It's usually safe to bet that at least one vendor will be on **Münzgasse,** which runs from the river to the Frauenkirche. Restaurants in the area, which have similar prices and serve similar crowds, apparently attempt to differentiate themselves by emulating different countries, which makes them look slightly ridiculous in such a quintessentially German *platz.*

CAFE AHA — 💳♿⛅ CAFE, VEGETARIAN [2]

Kreuzstr. 7 — ☎351 496 0673 💻www.ladencafe.de

If your German meat-heavy diet is starting to take a toll on your arteries, you will breathe "aha" with relief at the veggies here. The meals are mostly vegetarian, the products are organic, and the outdoor seating beneath the Kreuzkirche is the table to grab. The Saxon potato soup *(€4)* is a local specialty, while the classic Spinach lasagna is another favorite *(€9).*

🚊 Tram 1, 2, or 4: Altmarkt, next to Kreuzkirche. [S] Soups and salads €4-10. Entrees €5-11. Desserts €2-4. ⏰ Open daily 10am-midnight.

AUGUSTINER AN DER FRAUENKIRCHE — 💳🍸⛅ GERMAN [2]

An der Frauenkirche 16/17 — ☎0351 48 28 97 💻www.augustiner-dresden.de

If you feel like splurging on one of the Altmarkt restaraunts, consider eating at Augustiner an der Frauenkirche. With outdoor seating only about 50 yards from the Frauenkirche, and an extensive beer and liquor menu, it might be worth the extra cost. Entrees include pan-seared mushrooms with bread dumplings *(€10.80),* beer stew (bet you didn't see that one coming) with carrots and dumplings *(8.80),* and schnitzel with salad and fried potatoes *(€15).*

🚊 Tram 1, 4, 8, 9, 11, or 12: Postpl. [S] Beer €3.20-€6.40. Entrees €8-15. ⏰ Open daily 10am-1pm.

RAUSCHENBACH DELI — 💳♿🍸⛅ CAFE, BAR [2]

Weissegasse 2 — ☎0351 821 27 60 💻www.rauschenbach-deli.de

Breakfast, lunch, dinner, drinks—Rauschenbach Deli is a classic of the Weissegasse cafe row at any time of day, and doesn't seem quite as touristy as the surrounding restaurants. The ample outdoor seating, also in the shadow of Kreuzkriche, is the perfect place to people-watch as you sip a beer *(€2.20)* and snack on mozzarella sticks *(€3.50).*

🚊 Tram 1, 2, or 4: Altmarkt, next to Kreuzkirche. [S] Breakfast €4-7. Salads and pasta €7-11. Entrees €13-15. Ice cream €4-7. ⏰ Open M-W 9am-midnight, Th 9am-1am, F-Sa 9am-2am, Su 9am-midnight.

🔲 HOT SPOON
⊕& CAFE ❶

Konigsbrucker Str. 74   ☎0351 89 96 08 75 ▣www.hotspoon.de

A large yellow spoon with a smiley face will lead you to this soup-happy haven. Inside, the lime green walls, hanging lanterns, and black and white checked floor look like something from *Alice in Wonderland*. The soup is served in brightly colored bowls from a large pot-shaped counter. The Italian tomato soup *(small €2.60, medium €3.70, large €4.20)* has basil, fresh hunks of mozzarella, and bow-tie pasta. Vegans can delight in Russian borscht *(€2.60/3.70/4.20)* with mushrooms, tomatoes, potatoes, and sauerkraut. Menu changes frequently.

⧲ *Tram 7 or 8: Bischofsweg.* ℹ *Another branch located at Kunsthandwerkerpassage 9 is open 11:30am-4pm.* ⓢ *Small soups €2.30-2.70, medium €3.60-3.80, large €4.10-4.30.* 🕐 *Open M-F 11:30am-11pm, Sa-Su noon-11pm.*

BAGEL'S DRESDEN
⊕Ψ♨ BAGELS, SANDWICHES ❶

Louisenstr.77   ☎0152 06 84 65 84 ▣www.bagels-dresden.de

Bagel's Dresden offers huge bagels for very little. Try the Italian bagel, with salami, fresh balsamic cheese, and olive spread, or the Torro, with pesto, pastrami, and camembert. *Bier und bagel*, you ask? Just add an extra €1.80-2.

⧲ *Tram 7: Louisenstr. From the stoop, walk along Louisenstr. to Mondpalast, on the left. Or, tram 11: Pulsnitzer Str. Turn left onto Louisenstr.* ⓢ *Bagel sandwiches from €3.80.* 🕐 *Open daily noon-1am.*

CAFÉ KOMISCH
⊕♨ CAFE ❶

Bischofsweg 50

Café Komisch is both a cafe and ice cream *(eis)* parlor. The cafe has indoor seating and inexpensive drinks, but the outdoor ice cream window is the local hotspot, with lines sometimes stretching around the block. Get the soft ice cream in orange or banana, and happily lick away as you make your way across the street to Alaunpark.

⧲ *Tram 7: Bischofsweg. From the stop, follow Bischofsweg for about 3 minutes to the café.* ⓢ *Small ice cream €1.30, large €2. Cappuccino €1.80. Espresso €1.* 🕐 *Coffee shop open M-F 3-6:30pm, Sa-Su 2-6:30pm. Ice cream window open daily 10am-10pm. Winter hours subject to change.*

CURRY UND CO.
⊕Ψ♨ CURRYWURST ❶

Louisenstr. 62   ☎0152 07 08 54 02 ▣www.curryundco.com

A local favorite, Curry und Co. serves inexpensive *currywurst*, french fries and beer. On Friday and Saturday nights, the outdoor service window becomes a popular watering hole for young people in between clubs. Full meals are offered: "Economy Class" *(currywurst and fries; €3.50)* to "First Class" *(currywurst, fries and champagne; €15.50)*.

⧲ *Tram 7: Louisenstr. From the stop, walk along Louisenstr. to Mondpalast, on the left. Or, tram 11: Pulsnitzer Str.. Turn left onto Louisenstr.* ⓢ *Currywurst €2.20. French fries €1.70. Beer from €1.80.* 🕐 *Open M-W 11am-10pm, Th 11am-noon, F-Sa, 11am-2pm, Su 11am-10pm.*

BLUMENAU
✒ CAFE ❷

Louisenstr. 67   ☎0351 802 65 02 ▣www.cafe-blumenau.de

Grab one of the many newspapers lining the counter on the way in, and pretend to read German as you settle into a perfect breakfast nook. The waitress will probably figure it out when you can't read the menu or order, but it will be entertaining nonetheless. The daily specials, served 9am-4pm, are by far the best value, including the ham, cheese and chive omelette *(€5)* with toast and side salad. The luxurious coffee menu, including *milchkaffee* with white chocolate *(€2.70)* will dazzle your taste buds—or perhaps just burn them off if you choose the *milchkaffee* with chili *(€2.70)*.

🚏 Tram 7 or 8: Louisenstr. $ Breakfast €5.80-7. Entrees €6-12. Mixed drinks €4.80-8. ⏰ Open M-Th 8:30am-1am, F 8:30am-3am, Sa 9am-3am, Su 9am-1am.

NIGHTLIFE

Dresden's nightlife scene is one of the best in Germany. Bars and small live music venues overflow with students and locals in the Neustadt every Friday and Saturday, and often on other days of the week as well. Farther up, about 15 minutes by tram *(Tram 7 or 8: Industriegeländ)* stands a crowded block of industrial buildings turned nightclubs, with more dance floors and bars than we care to count, and the occasional, unbeatable, rave concert.

Altstadt

BIERSTUBE
🍴♿🍸☁ BAR

Bergstr. 1 ☎0351 47 16 09 🖥www.klubneuemensa.de

Bierstube roughly translates to "beer living room," which pretty much sums up this student hangout. The beer is oh-so-cheap *(0.5L for €1.90)* and the heaping meals fill the stomachs of procrastinating students who drink, smoke, and play cards, before reluctantly returning to the library. Or not.

🚏 Tram 8 or 66: Nurnberger Str. At the intersection, walk down Bergstr. away from the city. It will be on the left amidst the other campus buildings. $ Entrees €2-5. Beer from €2. ⏰ Open M-F 9am-1am, Sa noon-1am, Su 5pm-1am.

CLUB AQUARIUM
🍸☁ BAR, MUSIC VENUE

St. Petersburger Str. ☎0351 497 66 70 🖥www.club-aquarium.de

Once located on the rooftop of the student dorm at the same address, this student bar had to move to the basement because of noise complaints, just in time for the flood of 2002. During the flood, the bar was filled with water (and fish), and thus Aquarium was born. Now the venue is a student hotspot during the week for strong, cheap drinks like a classic gin and tonic *(€2.80)*. There are often live acts and game nights.

🚏 Tram 3, 7, 8, 9, or 11: Walpurgistr. $ Beer and mixed drinks €2-8. ⏰ Open M-F 1pm-1am.

BÄRENZWINGER
🍸☁ BAR

Brühlscher Garten 1 ☎351 79 27 85 27 🖥www.baerenzwinger.de

With the entrance beneath the old cannon gate (where cannons were rolled into the fort), this student club has been around since the 1960s and offers a place to drink for cheap the whole week long. Watch sports games on the big screen, or have a laugh playing drunk Yahtzee as you sip even more cheap beer.

🚏 Tram 3 or 7: Synagogue. $ Beer €1.80-3. Snacks €1.50-3. ⏰ Open daily 7pm-late.

Neustadt

WASHROOM
🍴🍸 CLUB, LOUNGE, MUSIC VENUE

Hermann-Mende-Str. 1 ☎0351 80 44 41 57 08 🖥www.washroom.de

Part of the Industriegelände community, the Washroom is part lounge, part dance club, and part concert venue (on certain nights). If you can, try to catch a hip-hop, techno, or rap concert at the Washroom—the price is well worth the experience. When the performers take a break, jump around to the electro music under blue, red, and black lights.

🚏 Tram 7 or 8: Industriegeläende. Follow the flashing lights and blaring bass. $ Concert tickets from €8, but the cost varies depending on the performer. Cover €5-10 without show. Beer and mixed drinks from €2.50. Keep an eye out for €1 drink nights. ⏰ Hours vary; generally open F-Sa 10pm-4am.

STRASSE E
🍴🍸 CLUB

Werner-Hartmann-Str. 2 ☎0351 213 85 30 🖥www.strasse-e.de

Strasse E, another Industriegalaende club, is a three-story, six-floor dance club (including one outdoors). The club gets packed even before midnight with both young people and middle-aged auto-designers by day/dance divas by night types. Come to watch (and join) Germans get their groove on—some better than others—to electro and rock music.

🚋 *Take the 7 or 8: Industriegelaende.* ⑤ *Cover around €8.* ☼ *Open F-Sa 10pm-5am.*

ROSIS AMÜSIERLOKAL
●✹ BAR, MUSIC VENUE

Eschenstr. 11 ☎0351 880 76 31 ▣www.rosis-dresden.de

Rosis has built itself an excellent reputation as a venue for live performances. This club has no cover, and so, huge numbers of people crowd the small stage where indie, rock, and alternative bands play almost every night. Deep booths surround a central bar, with a small dance floor in front of the stage.

🚋 *Tram 7: Louisenstr. From the stop, walk up Königsbrucker Str. toward Scheunenhofstr. Continue past Schwepnitzer Str. to Eschenstr. Walk 2 blocks to Rosis.* ⑤ *Beer €2.20. Vodka €3.20.* ☼ *Open daily 10pm-late.*

KATY'S GARAGE
●✹ BAR, CLUB

Alaunstr. 48 ☎0351 656 77 01▣www.katysgarage.de

Katy's Garage is one of the livelier clubs in central Neustadt, with a young crowd and live music every night. The club is small in size, with a lounge, foosball and pool tables, a bar, and a small dance floor and stage. Monday is student night, with no cover and cheap drinks *(beer and wine €1.50)*, Tuesday has "core" music (hardcore, metal, the like), Wednesday is alternative, and Thursday and Friday are indie or reggae, Saturday disco.

🚋 *Tram 7 or 8: Louisenstr. From the stop, follow Louisenstr. to Alaunstr. Katy's Garage is on the corner.* ⑤ *Vodka €4. Beer €2.50. Cover €3-4. No cover, and discounted drinks, before 10pm.* ☼ *Open daily 8pm-late.*

BLUE NOTE DRESDEN
●✹ JAZZ BAR

Görlitzer Str. 2b ▣www.jazzdepartment.com

Blue Note is a small, mellow jazz bar in the heart of Dresden, featuring live music by local performers and traveling groups almost every night. With no cover for local bands, this smoky, dark bar is often crowded with regulars.

🚋 *Tram 7: Lousinstr. From thes top, walk along Louisenstr. to Görlitzer.* ⑤ *€5 cover when popular musicians perform. Make sure to tip the newer artists! Gin €3.50. Brandy €5. Löbauer Pilsner .3L €2.* ☼ *Open daily 10pm-5am.*

HEBEDA'S
Ⓧ✹◉ BAR

Rothenburger Str. 30 ☎0351 895 10 10▣www.hebedas.de

This small, smoky bar is "the best place to go when you don't know where else to go," as put by one local. It becomes packed at the beginning of the night with 20-somethings that booze up before hitting the larger clubs of Neustadt. Seating is scarce, so arrive early or try out your moves on the dark dance floor in back. The vending machine on the way to the bathrooms sells trinkets made by local artists.

🚋 *Tram 13: Rothenburger Str.* ⑤ *Beer €2-5. Mixed drinks €4-8.* ☼ *Open daily 8pm-5am.*

SPUTNIK 2.0
Ⓧ✹◉ BAR, CLUB

Schlesischer Pl. 1 ▣www.neustadtsputnik.de

Descend beneath Neustadt's train station to the old cellars that have been converted into a dance floor, bar, and various seating areas to rest your weary legs after you bust a move. Don't be put off by the slightly younger crowd and awkward dancers mid-floor trying to wiggle to the illusive rock beat. Just go with it. Fridays are known to be the happening nights at Sputnik.

🚋 *Tram 11: Neustadt Station.* ℹ *Check the website for the upcoming DJ schedule.* ⑤ *Beer and mixed drinks €3-5. Cover €2.* ☼ *Open F-Sa 10pm-5am.*

ALTES WETTBÜRO
Ⓧ✹♨◉ CLUB

Antonstr. 8 ☎0351 658 89 83 ▣www.altes-wettbuero.de

The best part about this club is the music, whose deep base literally shakes the building from the inside out. Hip hop, rap, experimental, funk, and rock are all the norm. On warm summer nights, relax with a drink in the beer garden.

Tram 7, 8, or 11: Albertpl. From the stop, walk down Antonstr. toward Station Neustadt. $ Beer and mixed drinks €2-7. ⏰ Open Th-Sa 8pm-late. Occasional Tu openings as well.

LEBOWSKI'S

🍸 BAR

Gölitzer Str. 5 — 💻www.dudes-bar.de

The Big Lebowski is on a constant loop, and your intake of drinks should be, too. Make your way through the entire list from the White Russian original *(€4.70)* to the Dudes 43 *(€5.40)*, and don't be surprised if you stay here all night.

Tram 13: Rothenburger Str. $ Beer €3. Infamous White Russians €4.50-€5.40. Mixed drinks €5-8. ⏰ Open daily 7pm-5am.

ARTS AND CULTURE

Entertainment

SÄCHSISCHE STAATSOPER (SEMPER OPER)

🎟 OPERA HOUSE

Theaterpl. 2 — ☎0351 491 10 💻www.semperoper.de

The ornate Baroque Semper Oper offers visitors one of the best cultural experiences in Dresden. For as little as €8, you can see operas, ballets, and concerts, including performances by the Staatskapelle Dresden, the city's premier orchestra in the beautiful city theater.

Tram 4, 8, or 9: Theaterpl. The box office is located across from the Semper Oper. [i] Order tickets online at www.semperoper-erleben.de. Guided tours of the opera house are the only way to see the interior without attending a performance. $ Tours €8, students €4. ⏰ Tours M-F 1:30-3:30pm, Sa-Su 8:30am and 1:30pm-3:30pm; schedule varies greatly, so call ahead to confirm. Box office open M-F 10am-6pm, Sa-Su 10am-1pm, and 1hr. before the show starts.

KULTURPALAST

🎟 PERFORMANCE VENUE

Schloßstr. 2, am Altmarkt — ☎0531 48 66 66 💻www.kulturpalast-dresden.de

This stark, industrial building might seem uninspired from the outside, but the Kulturpalast is home to the **Dresdener Philharmonie** *(☎0351 486 63 06 💻www.dresdenerphilharmonie.de)* and a large variety of other performances, including hip-hop, classical and American popular music.

Tram 8, 11, 12: Postpl. [i] The box office is located in the same building, adjacent to tourist information. ⏰ Box office open M-F 10am-7pm, Sa 10-6pm, Su 10am-3pm.

STAATSOPERETTE DRESDEN

🎟 OPERETTAS, MUSICALS

Staatsoperette Dresden — ☎0351 20 79 90 💻www.staatsoperette-dresden.de

This small performance venue is about a 35-min. tram ride away from central Dresden, but if you're looking for a change of scenery or a certain musical (or operetta, as it were), it could be worth the trek. Be sure to take a look at the Himmelfahrtskirche, just across the street, to make your trip complete.

Tram 6: Altleuben. $ Tickets vary in price. Students generally €8-24. ⏰ Box office open M 10am-4pm, Tu-F 10am-7pm, Sa 4-7pm, Su 1hr. before curtain.

STAATSSCHAUSPIEL

🎟 THEATER

Theaterstr. 2 — ☎0351 491 35 55 💻www.staatsschauspiel-dresden.de

With four different venues at two locations in the city, this theater offers contemporary comedies, as well as works by Shakespeare and Chekhov. The main location at Theaterstr. 2 is more expensive; the second venue Kleines Haus has cheaper shows.

Tram 8, 11, 12: Postplatz. From the station,walk down Ostra-Allee, left on Theaterstr. $ Tickets €9-20. ⏰ Box office open M-F 10am- 6:30pm, Sa 10am-2pm.

Recreation

PURO BEACH
♿ ☕ ⛱ POOL, BAR
Leipziger Str. 15
☎0351 215 27 71 💻www.puro.de
Where the wanna-be beach babes of Dresden come to see and be seen; wear your sparkly bikini, flex your abs, and lay out stylishly on the large cushions under sweeping white umbrellas. The small pool even has a waterfall.

🚋 *Tram 11: Antonstr. From the stop, walk toward the bridge, down the stairs, and follow the path along the Elbe.* Ⓢ *Mixed drinks €2-7.* 🕐 *Open daily 11am-late; the party continues at the neighboring club, Pier 15.*

CITY BEACH DRESDEN
♿ ☕ ⛱ BEACH, BAR
Leipziger Str. 31
☎0152 24 39 43 04 💻www.citybeachdresden.de
The down-to-earth brother of Puro Beach, City Beach Dresden is the summertime hang-out for locals with an expanse of sand, beach beds, and picnic tables. Get a group together and reserve a beach volleyball court—once play begins it almost feels as though you are on the beaches of California.

🚋 *A little past Puro Beach, also on the path along the Elbe.* Ⓢ *Mixed drinks €2-5. Beach volleyball court €10-15* 🕐 *Open daily 10am-dusk.*

Festivals

STRIEZELMARKT (CHRISTMAS MARKET)
♿ ☕ ⛱ FESTIVAL
Altpl.
💻www.dresden.de
The Christmas Market in Dresden began in 1434, and remains one of the most popular in the entire country. Stroll from stall to stall browsing the trinkets with a cup of *glühwein* (mulled wine) and a hunk of *christstollen* (Christmas cake) in hand.

🚋 *Tram 1, 2, 4: Altmarkt.* 🕐 *December.*

SHOPPING

TRANQUILLO
⊛ CLOTHING
Louisenstr. 45
☎0351 25 09 10 94 💻www.fabulous-tranquillo.com
Bags, clothes, and even seat cushions are all Indian-inspired, with bright blocks of color and various fabrics. Your new jacket with sideways zippers or warm fleece coat with colored pockets will likely be accompanied by a spicy scent of incense. Check out the sale room in the back for the best deals.

🚋 *Tram 7 or 8: Louisenstr.* 𝒊 *Second location at Rothenburger Str. 14.* 🕐 *Open M-F 11am-8pm, Sa 10am-6pm.*

ART+FORM (ART UND FORM)
⬦ GALLERY
Bautzner Str. 11
☎0351 003 13 22 💻www.artundform.de
The primary business of this art shop is framing and matting paintings and pictures. Handmade paper and high-end pens (read: overpriced office supplies) are also available here. The real draw of Art und Form is the gallery. Check out paintings by contemporary German artists including Kammerer, Koch and Klose.

🚋 *Tram 3, 6, 7, or 9: Albertpl.* 🕐 *Open M-F 10am-8pm, Sa 10am-6pm.*

THALIA BOOKS
⬦ BOOKS
24 Altmarkt
☎0351 65 64 60 💻www.thalia.de
Although there are branches all over the city, the large store at the Altmarkt location has the largest selection of English language (as well as Russian, Spanish, Dutch, and Italian for over-achievers) books in the entire city. Crime, travel, fiction, and beyond—from Bill Bryson to *Twilight*.

🚋 *Tram 1, 2, or 4: Altmarkt.* Ⓢ *English language books €8-12.* 🕐 *Open M-Sa 10am-8pm.*

DROP-OUT RECORDS
⊛⊗ MUSIC
Alaunstr. 43
☎0351 804 28 62 💻www.drop-out-records.de
This local favorite specializes in vinyl records, and the collection is a mix of new

and secondhand, including reggae, house, punk, and lots of alternative. You can pick up a hookah water pipe as you exit through the neighboring tobacco shop, THC, but trust us, the records will be easier to fit in your suitcase.

Tram 11: Albertpatz. From the stop, walk up Alaunstr. Or, tram 7 or 8: Louisenstr. i Enter through the neighboring tobacco store. $ Secondhand and new records and CDs €3-15. ⏰ Open M-F noon-8pm, Sa 11am-5pm.

ESSENTIALS

Practicalities

- **TOURIST OFFICES:** The tourist office staff books rooms (from €25) for free and sells the Dresden City Card and the Dresden Regio Card (see below). *(General information ☎0351 49 19 21 00. Room reservations ☎0351 49 19 22 22. Group tours ☎0351 49 19 21 00. Advance ticket purchases ☎0351 49 19 22 33. 💻www.dresden-tourist.de $English language city guides €.50. Audio-walking tour in English €7.50 for 4hr. ⏰ Open M-F 10am-6pm, Sa-Su 10am-4pm.)*
- **TOURS: Stadtrundfahrt** double-decker bus tours include 30min. walking tours of the Zwinger Palace and Fauenkirche. Stay onboard for the 90min tour, or go freestyle and jump on and off as you please at any of the 22 stops. *(Depart from Theaterpl. ☎0351 899 56 50 💻www.stadtrundfahrt.de $ Day pass €20, children €1. ⏰ Tours Apr-Oct 9:30am-5pm every 15-30min., Nov-Mar 9:30am-3pm every 30-60min.)*
- **CURRENCY EXCHANGE:** Western Union money transfer service is available at **ReiseBank.** *(Located in the Hauptbahnhof. ☎0351 471 21 77 $ min. €2 max. €10 fee for any exchange, plus 2.5% charge on the amount exchanged. ⏰ Open M-F 8am-8pm, Sa 9am-6pm, Su 10am-6pm.)* **Deutsche Bank.** *(Located on the corner of Königsbrücker Str. and Katharinenstr. in the Neustadt. ☎0351 482 40 💻www.db.com ⏰ Open M-Tu 9am-1pm and 2-6pm, W 9am-1pm, Th 9am-1pm and 2-7pm, and F 9am-1pm and 2-4pm.)*
- **LUGGAGE STORAGE:** Lockers are located in all train stations. Follow suitcase symbol. *($ €3-4 per 24hr.)*
- **HOME SHARE: Mitwohnzentrale** offers flats available in outer districts from €150 per month. *(Dr.-Friedrich-Wolf-Str. 2, on Schlesischer Pl. ☎0351 194 30 💻www.dresden- mitwohnzentrale.de ⏰ Open M-F 10am-8pm, Sa-Su 10am-2pm.)*
- **GLBT RESOURCES: Grenede.** *(Prießnitzstr. 18. ☎3051 802 22 51. Counseling ☎0351 804 44 80 💻www.gerede-dresden.de ⏰Open M-F 8am-5pm.)*
- **WOMENS RESOURCES: Frauenzentrum "sowieso" (Frauen für Frauen)** specializes in addressing sexual harassment and assault, eating disorders, and employment. *(Angelikastr. 1. ☎0351 804 14 70 💻www.frauenzentrumsowieso.de Tram 11: Angelikastr., or walk 30min. up Bautzner Str. from Alpertpl. ⏰ Open M, W, and F 9am-3pm, Th 9am-6pm. Advice in person or by phone M, W, F 9-11am, Th 3-6pm. Psychologist by appointment M-F or walk-in Th 3-6pm.)*
- **LAUNDROMATS: Eco-Express.** *(2 Königsbrücker Str., on Albertpl. $ Wash €1.90 before 11am, €2.40 after 11am. 14kg machine €5. Dry €0.50 per 10min. Soap €0.30. ⏰ Open daily 6am-11pm.)* Staff books rooms *(from €25)* for free and hands out city map.
- **INTERNET ACCESS:** Mondial. *(Rothenburgerstr. 43. Enter on Louisenstr. ☎0351 896 14 70 i Wi-Fi available. $ €2 per hour. ⏰ Open M-F 10am-1am, Sa-Su 11am-1am.)* **Haupt- und Musikbibliothek.** *(Freiberger Str. 35, in World Trade Center. ☎0351 864 82 33 i Some English books. Free internet 30min. at a time.*

Music scores, CDs and DVDs. Bring a passport to check out items. 🕐*Open M-F 11am-7pm, Sa 10am-2pm.)*

- **POST OFFICE:** *(* Königsbrücker Str. 21-29. ☎0180 304 05 00r *i* Western Union available. Wheelchair accessible. 🕐 *Open M-F 9am-7pm, Sa 10am-1pm.)* An alternate branch is located in the Altstadt. *(Wilsdruffer Str. 22* 🕐 *Open M-Sa 10am-7pm.)*

- **POSTAL CODE:** 01099.

Emergency!

- **EMERGENCY NUMBERS: Police:** ☎110. **Ambulance and Fire:** ☎*112.*

- **LATE-NIGHT PHARMACY: Saxonia Apotheke Internationale.** *(Prager Str. 8a.* ☎*0351 490 49 49* 🖥*www.saxoniaapotheke.de i Carries international medicines. The Notdienst sign outside lists rotating 24hr. pharmacies.* 🕐 *Open M-F 9am-8pm, Sa 9:30am-5pm.)*

Getting There

By Plane

The **Dresden Airport** information desk *(*☎*0351 881 33 60* 🖥*www.dresden-airport.de)* is reachable by public transit on the S-Bahn, line S2, which leaves every half hour, 4am-11:30pm. The shuttle *(tickets €1.90)* will pick up or drop off at Dresden-Neustadt and most Dresden hotels *(15min.),* or the Dresden Hauptbahnhof *(20min.).*

By Train

Dresden has two main stations: the **Hauptbahnhof** (south of Altstadt), and **Bahnhof-Dresden-Neustadt,** across the Elbe on the western edge of the Neustadt. A third station, **Dresden Mitte,** lies between the two but is rarely used because of its location. Trains to: **Bautzen** (💲 *€10.50.* 🕐 *1 hr., every hour);* **Berlin** (💲 *€37.* 🕐 *3hr., 1 per hr.);* **Budapest, Hungary** (💲 *€103.* 🕐 *11hrs., 3 per day);* **Frankfurt am Main** (💲 *€87.* 🕐 *4hr., every hr.);* **Görlitz** (💲 *€19.* 🕐 *1hr., every hr.);* **Leipzig** (💲 *€21.* 🕐 *1hr., 1-2 per hr.);* **Munich** (💲 *€101.* 🕐 *7hr., 1-2 per hr.);* **Prague** (💲 *€31.* 🕐 *2hr., 7 per day).*

Getting Around

By Tram

Dresden is largely a walking city, and there aren't many places you'll need to go that you can't get to on foot. For trips across the city, use the tram system *(Single ticket €1.90; 4-trip card €4; one-day ticket €5; one-week travel pass €14.50).* Tickets are available from **Fahrkarten** dispensers at major stops, and on trams. Validate your tickets in the red boxes onboard the tram. For information and maps, visit 🖥www.vvo-online.de, or try the **Service Punkt** stands in front of the Hauptbahnhof or at Postpl., Albertpl., and Pirnaischer Pl. Most major lines run every 10min. or so during the day, and every 30min. after midnight—look for the moon sign marked "Gute-Nacht-Linie."

city cards

Tourist cards can be purchased at the tourist office, online *(*🖥*www.dresden-tourist.de),* or at DVB transportation centers.

The **Dresden City Card,** valid for 48 hours (21€), includes unlimited free travel by public transit and free admission to numerous museums (including the Old Master's Gallery and the New Green Vault in the Royal Palace).

The **Dresden Regio Card,** valid for 72 hours (€32), includes all of the above benefits, plus free travel on public transit with partner companies in the Dresden (Oberelbe) region, and price discounts on many sights and participating restaurants around the region.

By Metro

The **S-Bahn,** or suburban train, travels along the Elbe from **Meißen** to the **Czech border.** Buy tickets from the Automaten and validate them in the red machines at the bottom of the stairwells to each track.

By Taxi

☎0351 211 211 or ☎888 88 88.

By Car

Sixt-Budget (☎*1805 25 25 25*) is located at Hamburger Str. 11, is open M-F 6am-10pm. Sa-Su 8am-noon.

By Bike

Bike rental is available at all train stations. **German Bahn** at Neustadt station and Hauptbahnhof offers bikes for €8 per day. (☎*1805 15 14 15.* ☼ *Open M-Sa 6am-8pm, Su 8am-8pm.*)

By Ferry

Sächsische Dampfschiffart (☎*0351 86 60 90* ▣*www.sächsische-dampfschiffart.de*) offers daily cruises on steamers along the Elbe, usually departing from the terrace bank in Dresden, to destinations including **Pillnitz** and **Bad Schandau.** *(Office and info desk open M-Th and Su 8am-6pm, F-Sa 8am-7:30pm.)*

Ride Share

Mitfahrzentrale. *(Dr.-Friedrich-Wolf-Str. 2, on Schlesischer Pl., across from Bahnhof Neustadt.* (☎*0351 194 40* ▣*www. mitfahrzentrale.de* ☼ *Open M-F 9am-8pm, Sa-Su 10am-4pm.)*

moritzburg ☎0352

Moritzburg, a former residence of artist Käthe Kollwitz, is best known for its beautiful Baroque Schloß Moritzburg. Located outside of Dresden, it is a great daytrip if you've got the extra time.

ORIENTATION

Moritzburg's tourist office is at Schloßallee 3b, just before the bus station.

SIGHTS

SCHLOSS MORITZBURG
PALACE

BarockSchloß Moritzburg ☎0352 07 87 30 ▣www.schoss-moritzburg.de

Never one for subtlety, Augustus the Strong tore down a small palace in 1723 and replaced it with the Schloß Moritzburg, a titanic Baroque hunting lodge. The sprawling golden Schloß, with turrets on all four sides, stands at the end of Moritzburg's main street, Schloßallee, on a tree lined island in the middle of a man-made lake. Each of the museum's rooms is named after its contents. The *Federzimmer* (feather room), with its feather-woven canopy and tapestries, might fail at irony (it supposed to be inspired by an inverted featherbed), but certainly succeeds at extravagance. Upstairs, look for the 8000-year-old fossil antlers of the now extinct giant red deer in the Stone Hall and the 66-point (if we measure generously) "Moritzburger" in the Hall of Monstrosities.

ⓢ *Palace grounds free, interior and exhibition €6.50, students €3.50. Feather room is €3.50 extra. Guided tours in German. Audio tours in English €2.* ☼ *Open daily Apr-Oct 10am-5:30pm; Nov-Dec 10am-4pm; Jan Sa-Sun 10am-4pm; Feb-Mar Tu-Su 10am-4pm. Last entry 30min. before close.*

FASANENSCHLÖSSCHEN
PALACE

☎0352 07 87 36 10

A 30min. walk from the main palace, the Fasanenschlößchen (Little Pheasant Palace), was built by the great-grandson of August, Friedrich Augustus III. Girded by tall Hedges and crumbling statues, the pink hunting lodge is a monument to elegant restraint, if not hunterly masculinity. A small manmade cove was once used by bored, rich princes for make-believe ship fights. A path loops around the wild game reserve, connecting the *Fasanenschlößchen* and the schloß. Walk around the schloß and take the path bordering the lake to the right, and follow signs.

ℹ *Tours May-Sept 10am-6pm, Apr. and Oct. 10am-5pm.* $ *€4. Tours €5.*

FOOD

ADAM'S GASTHOF — GERMAN

Markt 9 ☎0352 07 85 70 💻www.adamsgasthof.com

If you don't succeed in killing your own dinner, consider checking out this place for a consolation meal. With most of the restaurants crowding the castle on the expensive end, Adam's Gasthof always offers the inexpensive, if unoriginal, freshly grilled bratwurst.

$ *Bratwurst €2.* ⏰ *Open daily 11am-late.*

ESSENTIALS

Getting There

Take bus #326 from Bahnhof-Neustadt to Moritzburg, Schloß *($€3.70 each way. ⏰25 min., M-F every 30 min. 5:15am-11:25pm, Sa-Su every hr. 8am-11pm).* Be sure to buy your return ticket before you leave. Return trips from "Moritzburg Markt" on Markstr. can be difficult to find. If facing the palace, turn left and walk until the first street. Turn right and walk about 50 yd.

leipzig ☎0341

Leipzig is a growing town, with a similarly expanding array of festivals and events that make it a hub for Germany's alternative culture. From Indie music festivals to the world's largest Goth celebration, Leipzig's Baroque architecture buzzes with a significantly less traditional crowd. That said, Leipzig residents are very proud of their cultural roots, and Bach and Mendelssohn are enshrined at every cafe and street corner. Thanks to these two composers, classical music is big here, with church perfomances offering musically inclined travelers world-class concerts for free. Architecturally, Leipzig is stunning. Its ornate facades and cobblestone streets, often completely devoted to pedestrian traffic, inspired Goethe to call this town a "little Paris." In warm weather, you can enjoy the scenery under restaurant umbrellas that cover many of the smaller streets. And, of course, there's more to German history than the evolution of the modern brew. Try educating yourself about DDR history in one of Leipzig's many museums that chronicle German's era as part of the Socialist east, from the propaganda to the secret police.

Oh wait! We just re-read that last sentence and realized we were dangerously close to discounting the importance of German beer. Bring in a keg, we have some atonement to do! Leipzig's university, **Leipzig Universität,** should help us with that; it attracts young people from all over Germany to enjoy an education in a city with a low cost of living, and student-filled bars and clubs all week long. So wash down all that culture and history with some inexpensive brews. It's good for the digestion.

ORIENTATION

Leipzig's **Innenstadt,** where the traveler will find most of Leipzig's sights and museums, is contained within a one-kilometer wide ring, surrounded by wide streets on all sides. The city is anchored by the **Hauptbahnhof** train station to the north and **Thomaskirche** to the west. The inside of the ring is split by smaller, mostly-pedestrian roads lined with the crowded, elaborate buildings. Parks border the center on the east and the

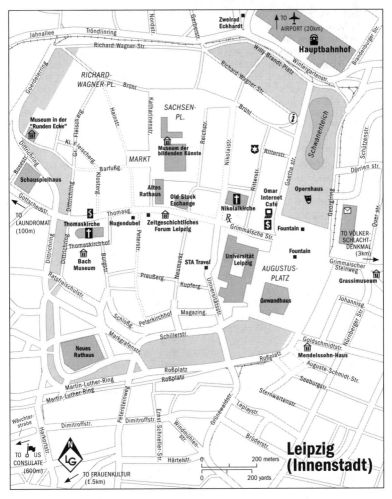

Leipzig
(Innenstadt)

south, with **Clara Zetkin Park,** the city's largest, located to the east just off **Martin Luther Ring.** The main hubs of the Innenstadt are located in the **Markt** and close to **Grimmais-chestrasse,** which cuts the city in half from west to east, with a high concentration of restaurants and bars just outside the ring, on **Gottschedstrasse** Outside the Innenstadt, prices get less expensive, geared toward Leipzig Universität students. The university buildings are scattered throughout the city, but most campus activity is concentrated in the southeast of Innenstadt, with a ribbon of funky college nightclubs, bars, and restaurants winding down **Karl-Liebknecht-Strasse.**

ACCOMMODATIONS

Leipzig's tourists are often accommodated by an uncomfortably large proportion of chain hotels, like Best Western and Mariott, scattered throughout the city. The best places to stay are, of course, Leipzig's youth hostels. Be sure to check ahead for festivals that might crowd out hostel rooms; serveral times a year Leipzig is booked to capacity.

HOSTEL SLEEPY LION

HOSTEL ❶

Käthe-Kollwitz-Str. 3 ☎0341 993 94 80 📧www.hostel-leipzig.com

Chillax, 🎵bro. This hostel is a laid-back favorite for international backpackers. Personal showers are in every room—bet you're feeling more hygienic just thinking about it. The large rooms with pine beds and personal lockers are spacious enough for the lion in you. Get your foos on in the lounge to an upbeat soundtrack. Hostel Sleepy Lion will move to a wheelchair-accessible building at Jacobstraße 1 in January of 2011.

🚶 10 min. walk from the station; follow Richard-Wagner-Str., then turn left on Gordelerring. Follow Gördelerring until Käthe-Kollwitz-Str. veers to the right. Or, take tram 1 or 14: Gottschedst. 🛈 Sheets €2.50. Breakfast €3.50. Bike rentals €5 per day. Wi-Fi included. 💲 8-bed dorms €14; 6-bed rooms €16; 4-bed rooms €17; doubles €21; singles €29.50. 🕐 Reception 24hr.

CENTRAL GLOBETROTTER

HOSTEL ❶

Kurt-Schumacher-Str. 41 ☎0341 149 89 60 📧www.globetrotter-leipzig.de

Run by the same owners as the Sleepy Lion, Central Globetrotter is close to the train station, if a little farther from the nightlife (located right next to a smoke shop—compensation for the extra hike). Large, well-sofa-ed lounge rooms, patio out back, and big bedrooms with personal lockers line the halls. Leave your mark by stickering your hometown on the cool map upon departure.

🚶 From the train station, take the west exit and turn right onto Kurt-Schumacher-Str. 🛈 Wi-Fi included. Sheets €2.50. Breakfast €3.50. 💲 8-bed dorms €14; 6-bed rooms €16; 4-bed rooms €17; singles €29.50; doubles €21. 🕐 Reception 24hr.

A AND O HOSTEL

HOSTEL ❶

Brandenburger Str. 2 ☎0341 25 079 49 📧www.aohostels.com

With bright rooms and big windows, this hostel is located just outside the Innenstadt, conveniently near the train station. It's about as close to everything as the Central Globetrotter, but with less character. If you're looking for an upgrade, the A and O chain houses hotel rooms in the same building.

🚶Exit the Hauptbahnhof from the east side. The hostel is across Brankenburger Str. 🛈 TV in every room. Wi-Fi €1 per hour. Breakfast €6. 💲 4-6-bed dorms €13; doubles with ensuite shower and bed linens €25; singles with ensuite shower and linens €39. Group discounts available. 🕐 Reception 24hr. Check-out at 10am.

HOSTEL ABSTEIGE

HOSTEL ❷

Harkortstr. 21 ☎0341 640 67 47 📧www.absteigeninleipzig.de

A 10-minute walk from the city center, Hostel Absteige is located right next to a beautiful park in a quiet neighborhood. The historic building has large, wood doors, high ceilings, and wide hallways. Foosball tables and a record player liven up the common space. Spacious doubles have ensuite baths, sofas, big windows, and televisions. The hostel is adjacent to **Duke's Bar** (open daily 6pm-late), where guests get 20% off drinks in the small courtyard or inside bar.

🚶 From the Hauptbahnhof, take trams 2, 8, or 9: Neues Rathaus. From the stop, walk up Martin Luether Ring to Harkortstr. The hostel entrance is around the corner of Harkortstr. on Str. D. 17 Juni. 🛈 Linens €3. Wi-Fi included. 💲 3-8-bed dorms €15; doubles €50 per room. 🕐 Reception 10am-10pm.

HOTEL-PENSION WEISSES ROSS

HOTEL PENSION ❸

Auguste-Schmidt-Str. 20 ☎0341 960 59 51 📧www.weisses-ross-leipzig.de

If your political connections aren't getting you a room at a booked hostel, and your godfather is otherwise occupied, try finding a bed at Weißes Roß. With carved staircases and banisters, this hotel links to a dark wood bar and restaurant. Rooms are small and warm, with light yellow walls, red bedding, and wood frames.

🚶 Tram 6, 8, 10, or 11: Augustuspl. From the stop, head toward Johannispl. on Grimm. Steinweg, *and take Nümberger Str. to Auguste-Schmidt-Str. $ Apr-Oct singles €28; doubles €42. Nov-Mar singles €35; doubles €55. ⏰ Reception daily 5-10pm.*

IBIS HOTEL 🛏 HOTEL ❸

Brühl 69 ☎0341 218 60 💻www.ibishotel.com

If you find yourself out of budget options, the Ibis is a relatively low priced, centrally located chain hotel that's worth a look. Clean, if unoriginal rooms (read: prefab funiture and bed linens), and close to the train station. Only double rooms are available, but an extra cot can be brought in for a fee.

 # From the Hauptbahnhof, cross the road to Richard-Wagner-Str. Keep going straight on Nikolaistr., then turn left onto Brühl. The hotel is on your left. $ Doubles €59-69, depending on availability. Extra fold out bed €15. ⏰ Reception 24hr.

CAMPING AND MOTEL AM AUENSEE 🌳 CAMPSITE ❶

Gustav-Esche-Str. 5 ☎0341 465 16 00 💻www.camping-auensee.de

If you hear the call of the wild (or feel your wallet tightening), this out-of-the-way campsite is set in the abundantly forested suburb of Warhten, about 20 minutes outside the town. Though serenely close to nature, it also means that the campsite is an infrequently running bus ride and tram trip away from town. But the cabins are decorated with red-checked curtains, if you like that whole Little Red Riding Hood look.

 # Tram 10 or 11: Annaberger Str. Change to bus #80: Auensee. ℹ Public showers €0.75. $ €6 per person, €3.50-5 per tent; 1-bed cabins with shower €29; 2-bed €39; small bungalows (walls and a roof) from €22; €7 for additional beds. ⏰ Reception daily May-Sept 7:30am-1pm and 2-9:30pm, Nov-Apr 8am-1pm and 2-7:30pm.

SIGHTS 👁

Leipzig was once home to maestros Bach and Mehndelsson. Don't worry, the town hasn't forgotten. The city still celebrates an illustrious musical history, with some fine art and beautiful churches thrown in for good measure.

THOMASKIRCHE CHURCH

☎0341 22 22 40 💻www.thomaskirche.org

Johann Sebastian Bach spent the last 27 years of his career serving as the church's cantor, until his death in 1750. Lest we miss that minute detail, a statue in his likeness marks the outside of the church. Both the interior and exterior of the church are beautifully simple, with light walls and deep red ribbing along the ceiling. An absolute don't-miss for any trip to Leipzig is the Sunday service *(9:30am)*, when musicians and vocalists perform Bach's classics to the congregation. It's worth sitting through a whole sermon in German to hear Bach's music performed exactly the way he experienced it himself. The **Thomanerchor**, once directed by Bach, is one of Europe's most prestigious boy's choirs; if you're lucky, they might be performing at the Sunday morning service.

 # Down Thomasgrasse from the Altes Rathaus. $ Free. Thomanerchor performances €2. ⏰ Open daily 9am-6pm. Choir concerts F 6pm and Sa 3pm.

VÖLKERSCHLACHTDENKMAL (MONUMENT TO BATTLE OF NATIONS) 🌳⊗

Prager Str. ☎0341 961 85 38 💻www.völkerschlachtdenkmal.de

In 1813, over 120,000 soldiers died in the Battle of Nations, a six-day struggle that turned the tide against Napoleon and ultimately determined many of Europe's national boundaries as they stand today. Exactly a century later, a group of city planners were faced with a Herculean task of their own: how to memorialize such a battle. We're not sure who first floated the idea of a Mesopotamian ziggurat, or who stuffed the ballot box to make that the winning design; either way, this curiously Aztec-ian building, with a cavernous interior and towering statues of fallen soldiers now stands as a memorial to the high price of these Germans' success. Using the free "elevator," the climb to the top (and to unbeatable city views) is 364 steps. An additional mechanical boost *(€1)* is also available. On the ground the Forum 1813 museum describes the battle with paintings and soldier's uniforms.

🚏 Tram 15: Völkerschlachtdenkmal. From the stop, take the street on the right and follow the hand-railed path up to the left. $ Monument €6, students €4. Museum €3/2. English language audio tour €1. ⏰ Museum and memorial open daily Apr-Oct 10am-6pm, Nov-Mar 10am-4pm.

BACH MUSEUM LEIPZIG

🚫💳 🚫♿ MUSEUM

Thomas Churchyard 15/16. ☎0341 913 72 02 💻www.bach-leipzig.de

The Bach Museum's informative exhibits emphasize his role as choir director, teacher, and city musician, focusing on the composer's life and work in Leipzig, where he wrote his *Mass in B minor* and both the *St. John* and *St. Matthew Passions.* The museum plays host to concerts during the fall

🚏 Tram 9 or bus #89: St. Thomas Church ℹ Tours F 3pm and Sa 11am; customized group tours available. $ €6, groups of 10 or more €5 per person, students €4,children under 16 free. First Tu of the month free. ⏰ Open Tu-Su 10am-6pm.

MUSEUM IM GRASSI

MUSEUM

Johannispl. 5-11 ☎0341 222 91 00 💻www.grassimuseum.de

The Museum im Gassi houses three distinct exhibits, each more charming than the next. The **Museum für Musikinstrumente** *(Musical Instrument Museum. ☎0341 973 07 50; 💻mfm.uni-leipzig.de)* displays a stunning collection of antique instruments from the 16th century Renaissance, with pianos, violas, harps, and experimental hybrid organ-keyboards that never caught on (for obvious reasons, as you'll see). Make sure you visit the upstairs **klanglabor** (noise laboratory) and be as enthusiastic with the percussion instruments as the 7-year-olds. Next stop: everywhere. If you don't have time for an 80-day trip around the world, walk through the **Museum für Völkerkunde** *(☎0341 97 31 1000)* to see a display of global crafts—beaded, woven, carved, painted, sculpted, and magically conjured (the last is an informed guess). Learn how the swastika appeared in its original Indian context, how to stay warm in Siberia, and how best to float on the Tigris. For a compelling display of European artisanry, including a selection of 🍺**steins,** visit the **Museum für Angewandte Kunst** (Applied Arts Museum). If your grandmother were queen of Germany, France, and England, for the past four centuries, this would be her two-story, carefully organized attic. Pick up an English guide at the exhibition entrance.

🚏 From Augustuspl., take Grimmailscher Steinweg across Georgiring for 200m. $ Museum für Musikinstrumente €4, students €2. Museum für Völkerkunde €4, students €2; special exhibitions €4/€2. Museum für Angewandte Kunst €5, students €3.50; special exhibition €6/4; joint permanent and special €8/5.50; first W of the month free. Völkerkunde and Angewandte Kunst combination ticket €8, students €6. All 3 €12/9. English audio tour €1. ⏰ Open Tu-Su 9am-6pm.

MUSEUM DER BILDENDEN KÜNSTE LEIPZIG (LEIPZIG FINE ARTS MUSEUM)

♿ MUSEUM

Katharinenstr. 10 ☎0341 21 69 90 💻www.mdbk.de

From the outside, this plastic-sided museum might look like the worst kind of architectural faux-pas. But step inside, and you'll see what the abundance of natural light does for Leipzig's premier art collection. With towering ceilings and sunlight flooding every floor, Museum der Bildenden Künste does its masterpieces justice. The first and second floors display the standing exhibits, including works by local German masters such as Böckstiegal. Be sure to see Gundig's politically charged *Victims of Fascism.* The third floor and basement levels both show revolving exhibits, specializing in contemporary and experimental work.

🚏 Enter from Brühl, Reichstr., and Katharinenstr. Even the most directionally challenged can't miss this big, clear-sided building. $ Permanent exhibit €5, students €3.50. Special exhibits €8/€5. Combination ticket €10. ⏰ Open Tu and Th-Su 10am-6pm, W noon-8pm.

MUSEUM IN DER "RUNDEN ECKE" (MUSEUM IN THE "ROUND CORNER") MUSEUM

Dittriching 24 ☎0341 961 24 43 🖥www.runde-ecke-leipzig.de

The East German Staatssicherheit, or simply Stasi, was the largest per capita secret police force in world history. Over 91,000 employees produced miles of paper and mountains of cassettes and photographs in their attempts to keep tabs on suspected "enemies of the state." In 1950, the "Runden Ecke" (which we'll keep putting in "quotation marks" because they do, even though it's "annoying") became the Stasi district headquarters. When the citizens wrested the building away from Stasi hands during the Peaceful Revolution, they preserved and put on display most of the tools used to play Big Brother, including disguise kits, document destroyers, and concealed audio recorders. The archive, including citzen profiles with everything from handwriting samples to scents (no, we're not kidding), is the largest of its kind in Germany. The museum staff also give tours of a bunker nearby (for Stasi refuge in the event of tension) that contains an exhibit detailing the organization's unrealized plans. Every Saturday at 2pm a tour departs from the door of St. Nikolai's Church, stopping at major landmarks of the Peaceful Revolution.

ℹ Ask for an English handout (€0.50) at the office, or an English audio tour (€3). Bunker tours are 1-4pm on the last Sa and Su of the month. $ Free. Tours €3, students €2. ⏰ Open daily 10am-6pm. Tours in German 3pm, in English for groups by appointment.

ZEITGESCHICHTLICHES FORUM LEIPZIG (FORUM FOR CONTEMPORARY HISTORY) MUSEUM

Grimmaischetr. 6 ☎0341 222 00 🖥www.hdg.de

So chances are you've heard about WWII. In fact, chances are you've heard about it a lot. But the oft neglected second act of Germany's dramatic 20th century history is the period of division that plagued the country for decades. This museum takes the visitor through an extensive collection of propaganda posters, period vehicles, busts of Stalin, newspapers, and illicit typewriters, eventually culminating in an incredibly moving film tribute to the fall of the Berlin Wall. Whether you've seen the footage of friends and family reunited for the first time in years once, twice, or a thousand times, it's worth seeing again in a place overflowing with Cold War culture. For the non-sprechen-ing traveler, this museum can sometimes be a little confusing with so many audio displays, but the visual impact is still profound.

🚶 Just off Markt, in a glass-sided building. ℹ 1½hr. tours in German Sa 3pm, Su 11am. $ Free. ⏰ Open Tu-F 9am-6pm, Sa-Su 10am-6pm.

MENDELSSOHN-HAUS MUSEUM

Goldschmidt-str. 12 ☎0341 127 02 49🖥www.mendelsson-stiftung.de

Seafoam green never looked so good. Interesting interior color choice is the least of what this beautiful house offers the musically inclined traveler. From this house, composer Felix Mendelssohn-Bartholdy led a Bach revival in Leipzig for the two years he lived here (1845-1847), conducting performances at the Gewandhaus. Some rooms have been furnished to appear as Mendelssohn knew them, while others house exhibits on his life and work. The Musiksalon hosts the annual Leipzig Piano Summer series and Mendelssohn Festival. Small chamber concerts, €12, €8 students.

🚶 Take Rosspl, a piece of the Innenstadt's outer ring, south away from the Opernhaus, then a left down Goldschmidtstr. $ €3.50, students €2.50. ℹ Musiksalon 1hr. concerts Su 11am. ⏰ Open daily 10am-6pm.

FOOD

As a university town, Leipzig has good quality (if sometimes well-hidden) inexpensive places to eat. As with most of Leipzig, prices drop outside the Innenstadt, so a trip outside the city center might get you a better meal for a little less. There are also two grocery stores, an **Aldi** and a **Rewe**, located on the bottom floor of the Hauptbahnhof. A large **farmer's market** is set up on Markt. every Tuesday and Friday from 10am-5pm.

MAZA PITA — MIDDLE EASTERN, VEGETARIAN 1

Neumarkt 9 ☎0341 99 88 999

For the traveler trying to tighten their wallet and their waistband, Maza Pita is a fresher, healthier, and, frankly, better tasting alternative to the classic *döner* fallback. With a more inventive menu full of vegetarian options, try the Gemüse Pita (cooked zucchini, mushrooms, and bellpeppers with hummus, grilled in a pita), or Pita Falafel (falafel with salad greens, vegetables, and sesame sause). Right across from the university, Maza Pita is frequented by college students fed up with their cafeteria fare. In the basement, you'll find a **CopyTel,** with internet, copy machines, and telephones.

From Grimmaischestr., walk up Neumarkt. Maza Pita is across from the University building, on your right. $ Pitas from €2.50. Open M-F 10am-7pm, Sa 10am-4pm.

BELLINI'S — CAFE 2

Barfussgässchen 3-7 ☎0341 961 76 81

No trip to Leipzig is complete with enjoying a cup of coffee under a 50 meter stretch of crowded bistro tables and umbrellas on the **Barfussgässchen.** Especially enjoyable at night, this stretch of cafes is serenely peaceful, while buzzing with energy. If this seems like a contradiction, pocket your note to the editor, and go check it out. Of course, such an excellent location comes with a higher pricetag; if it's a little out of your budget, enjoy a cup of coffee around 10pm to enjoy the experience.

The short Barfussgässchen connects Markt on one side, and Klosterg. on the other. $ Soups from €4. Baguette sandwiches €5.50-6.50. Entrees €9.50-11.50. Coffee €2.10. Open daily noon-late.

LUISE — RESTO BAR 2

Bosestr. 4, corner of Bosestr. and Gottschedstr. ☎0341 961 14 88 www.luise-leipzig.de

With Luise's immense windows on one of Leipzig's most popular streets, you can sit back, enjoy a meal, and subtly people-watch. Small tables crowd the interior, but students take their meals outside; try the asparagus creme soup *(€4.30)*—a local specialty. A large bar sees some action at night.

Tram 1 or 14: Gottschedstr. i Happy hour (all drinks—except shots—€1.50 off) M-Th 10pm-midnight, F-Sa 11pm-1am, Su 10pm-midnight. $ Sweet breakfast crepes €5.70. Entrees €6.50-13.50. Open daily 9am-late.

COFFE BAUM — CAFE 1

Kleine Fleischergasse 4 ☎0341 961 00 60 www.coffe-baum.de

Pop quiz: Where was Germany's first coffee house? If you guessed Kleine Fleischergasse 4 (and we're betting you did), then you get a cookie, or a small parade! Opened in 1720, this historic coffee shop once provided Leipzig intellectuals and creative giants with caffeination for inspiration. Enjoy a basic (but historic!) cup of coffee, or try one with Grand Marnier (they don't make 'em like that at Starbucks!).

From Markt, walk through Barfußgäschen to Fleischergasse. Cafe Baum is on the corner, by the fountain. $ Coffee €2. Cappucino for €2.55. Mexican coffee with chocolate €4.50. Cakes €3.50. Open daily 11am-midnight.

AUERBACHS KELLER — GERMAN 5

Grimmaischestr. 2-4

So let's consider a hypothetical. You've saved up your dinner funds for a few nights, skipping meals and reading Goethe's *Faust* late into the night. You finish, put down your book, and think: "Gosh, I'm really hungry. And inspired to enjoy my meals in a cellar with historic literary significance!" Well good news: we've got your place. Auerbachs Keller, first opened in 1525, is a palatial, vaulted-ceiling basement wtih liberal red and gold accents. In *Faust*, Mephistopheles tricks some drunkards here before carrying Faust away on an enchanted beer barrel. And if this sounds like something that could have happened last night through your own drunken haze, maybe consider trying it sober (just to shake things up). Scenes from the book are painted around the ceiling of the restaurant.

✵ *Go inside the glass tunnel, where all the shops are located off Grimmaistr. The restaurant is down the first staircase.* ⓘ *Historic wine room (where Luther himself drank some not-so-holy wine) open M-Sa 6pm-midnight.* Ⓢ *Appetizers €12-25. Entrees €26-32.* Ⓞ *Open daily 11:30am-midnight. Kitchen open 11:30am-10pm.*

LA GROTTA
⊛ ⅄ ⌂ PIZZERIA ❷

Ratsfreischulstr. 6-8 ☎0341 962 99 74 ▣www.lagrottaleipzig.de

This pizzeria, owned by an Italian immigrant, serves huge, thin crust pizzas fresh out of a woodburning oven to diners seated outside, or in one of the many small cozy rooms inside the restaurant. One pizza (with spinach, parmesan, ricotta and tomatoes) can easily serve two. La Grotta is also connected to a bar, and specialty *eis* shop, which serves basic ice cream to delicious rarities.

✵ *Take Burgerstr. toward the cinema. At the cinema, hook around the block to Ratsfreischulstr.* Ⓢ *Pizzas €8-10.* Ⓞ *Open daily 11am-late.*

ALADIN DÖNER
⊛ ⌂ DÖNER ❶

Burgerstr. 12 ☎0170 97 66 67 07

Let chicken kebab and Turkish yogurt take you to a whole new world. And failing that, the university student consensus is that you've at least still got the best döner in town. We'd blow the copyright whistle on the huge creepy Aladdin mural on the wall, but then we risk losing that fantastic falafel. You may think it's over, but it ain't over; free cups of tea come at the end of your meal.

✵ *Just south of Thomaskirche, on the corner with Ratsfreischulstr.* Ⓢ *Döner kebab €3. Vegetarian falafel €2.50.* Ⓞ *Open M-W 10am-11pm, Th-Su 10am-1pm.*

100 WASSER CAFE
✎ ⅄ ⌂ RESTO BAR ❷

Bargussgasse 15 ☎0341 215 79 27

It's shaggadelic, baby! Thought you could get away from mirror mosaics and groovy murals just because it's not 1960? Think again, Foxy Cleopatra. Outdoor seating lets you show off your bellbottoms to passers-by. Do I make you randy, baby?

✵ *On the corner of Barfussgasse and Fleischergasse.* Ⓢ *Baguette sandwiches €4.10. Salads €4.10-7.80. Pesto pasta €5.10. Mixed drinks €5.90.* Ⓞ *Open daily from 8am-late. Kitchen open M-Th 8am-midnight, F-Sa 8am-1am, Su 8am-midnight.*

SAN REMO PIZZERIA
⊛ ⅄ ⌂ PIZZERIA ❷

Nikolaistr. 1 ☎0341 211 17 72 ▣www.san-remo.leipzig.de

Outdoor seating and a view of Nikolaikirche can make an ordinary eating experience a little more special. Freshly made pizzas *(with salami, tomatoes, and oregano; €5.60)* are a family favorite. Get your buzz on with the massive mixed ice cream sundae with liquor, pralines, and chocolate chips *(€5.80).*

✵ *On the corner of Nikolaistr. and Grimmaischustr., right across from the Nikolai church.* Ⓢ *Pizzas from €5.20. Pasta €5.20-€6.90. Ice cream from €5.70.* Ⓞ *Open M-Sa 9am-6pm.*

NIGHTLIFE

If you're looking for the low-down on Leipzig's nightlife, be sure to pick up *Kreuzer* to find all the city's local bars, clubs, and events. Be absolutely sure to check out the restaurants on **Barfussgässchen,** a small street so full of bistros there's only a small walking path left unclaimed by tables and chairs. After 10pm on almost every summer night all the seats are occupied. Outside the Innenstadt, the bars are no less crowded, and a little less expensive. Just across Dittrichring on **Gottschedstr.** and **Bosestr.**, a slightly younger crowd celebrates... well, we're not sure exactly what, but by 11pm, it definitely seems like everyone's out for some kind of occasion. **Kart-Liebknecht-Str.** hosts Leipzig's alternative scene, with more distinctive, if more spread out, bars, strung together by hanging lights and crowds of students on busy nights. Take tram #11 (dir.: Markkleeburg-Ost) or #10 (dir.: Lößnig) to "Südpl."

MORITZBASTEI — 🍸 CLUB

Universitätsstr. 9 ☎0341 70 25 90 💻www.moritzbastei.de

University students spent 8 years excavating this series of medieval tunnels. And it may have been the most productive thing they did at college. Mortizbastei is a subterranean dancer's paradise, filled with cafes, hammocks, and dance floors. Set under beautiful high vaulted stone and brick ceilings, this may be the most historic place you ever take a shot. The Wednesday and Saturday **All You Can Dance** disco blasts music ranging from metal to minimal techno. On disco nights, **Cafe Barbakan,** located inside the Moritzbastei *(☎0341 702 59 30),* gives the clubber a chance to rest before getting back to the dance floor to bust some more moves.

🚋 Tram 9, 15 or 16: Roßpl. The club is located behind the university tower. ℹ An open-air movie theater screens indie and foreign films July-Aug daily at 10pm, weather permitting. $ Cover after 11pm €4, students with ID €2.50; slightly more for concerts. Movie tickets €5, students €4. ⏰ Club open W and Sa from 10pm. Office on street level open M-F 10am-6pm. Cafe Barbakan open M-Sa 10am-late, Su 9am-late.

NIGHT FEVER — 🍸 CLUB

Gottschedstr. 4 ☎0341 149 99 00 💻www.night-fever.net

Pay your respects to disco-god John Travolta (whose likeness is painted on the wall) by bringing your best disco moves to Night Fever's dance floor. With colorful lights and no shortage of disco balls, moonwalk the night away to super-fly music from 70s and 80s. On Tuesday, enjoy some liquid courage on the cheap.

🚋 Tram 1 or 14: Gottschedstr. $ Beer from €1.30. Wine from €1.50. Mixed drinks from €2.10. ⏰ Open Tu and F-Sa from 10pm.

CAFE SPIZZ — 🍸 BAR AND CLUB

Markt 6 ☎0341 960 80 43 💻www.spizz.org

Cafe by day, club by night, and a little of both in the evening. The bar takes up two storefronts on the popular and beautiful Barfussgässchen, with tables spilling out into the market square. Big jazz names show up occasionally for weekend concerts, while Wednesday "Boogie Night" features live bands and piano music (no cover).

🚋 Located on the corner of Markt and Barfussgässchen. $ F-Sa cover €3; all my ladies free F before 1am. Martinis €3. Vodka from €2. ⏰ Open W and F-Sa 10pm-late.

LA BOUM — 🍸 BAR

Karl-Liebknecht-Str. 43 ☎0341 149 42 21

Located on this student-dominated night street, La Boum has a large front deck that looks out over the *strasse.* Popular with young locals (who apparently dig the disco), La Boum is decorated with hanging Moroccan lanterns and the ever-popular disco ball.

🚋 Tram 9, 10, or 11: Südpl. $ Beer €2.10-3. Martinis €3.20. Specialty drinks, including the tequilla mixes, from €5.50. ⏰ Open M-F 5pm-late, Sa-Su 3pm-late.

SOL Y MAR — 🍸 RESTO BAR

Gottschedstr. 4 ☎0341 961 57 21 💻www.solymar-leipzig.de

Feed (and water) your inner sophisticate at this upscale bar and restaraunt. Even those traveling on a budget can afford a light meal in this relaxed restaurant, where pale fabric drapes across the walls and ceiling, lit from above and below with artistically placed lighting.

🚋 *Tram 1 or 14 to Gottschedstr.* Ⓢ *Risotto €5.90-9.90. Pasta €4.50-7.10. Mixed drinks €5.50.* ⏰ *Open daily 9am-late.*

kabaret

Kabaretts are a German form of political satire. Keepin' it to real Deutsche form, the Germans took out all the fun French showiness of cabaret, and kept it intellectual. Boo. But yay for stimulating intelligence. Right?

STUK
⏏️ ❤️🚫 CLUB

Nürnbergerstr. 42   ☎0341 993 86 92 🖥www.stuk-leipzig.de

In the basement of a secluded, nondescript building, StuK (Leipziger Studentenkeller) is full of young regulars and free-flowing alcohol. This basic club has a dance floor lit with flashing lights and a bar, but on a Tuesday night, it's one of the few places open late. Students are drawn by cheap drinks and low cover. Check the website for a calender of events, including cocktail evenings and beer and game nights.

🚋 *From Augustuspl., walk down Grimm Steinweg and turn right onto Nürnbergerstr. Follow the street to number 42, on your right.* Ⓢ *Cover €2, students €1. Shots €1. Mixed drinks €2.50. Beer €1.50.* ⏰ *Open M and F as a pub 8pm-1am, Tu for dancing 9pm-3am.*

SCHAUHAUS
❤️⏏️ CLUB

Bosestr. 1   ☎0341 960 05 96 🖥www.shauhaus-leipzig.de

If dance floors were filled with water, this would be a kiddie pool, and (judging from the dance moves) a few of these kids would be drowning. Drawing in the younger crowd, 18-year-olds (and younger, we're afraid) are attracted by the low cover and obscenely cheap drinks, served in a no-frills, drink-this-out-of-a-trough kind of way.

🚋 *Tram 1 or 14: Gottschedstr. From the stop, the entrance is around the corner from Bosestr., on Dittrichring.* Ⓢ *Cover €0.75 after 11pm. F drink €20 worth of alcohol for €8, Sa drink €30 for €10.* ⏰ *Open Tu-Su for discos.*

ARTS AND CULTURE
🎵

🖼 GERWANDHAUS ORCHESTER
CLASSICAL MUSIC

Augustuspl. 8   ☎0341 127 02 80 🖥www.gewandhaus.de

The Gewandhaus Orchester is a major international orchestra that's been performing since 1843. Check the website for performance dates.

🚋 *Take trams 4, 7, 10, 11, 15, or 16: Augustuspl.* Ⓢ *Tickets €9-26. To get a €9 ticket, show up a half hour before the show to claim any unclaimed seats. Most concerts are 20% off for students.* ⏰ *Box office open M-F 10am-6pm, Sa 10am-2pm, 1hr. before perfomances.*

OPERA
OPERA

Augustuspl. 12   ☎0341 126 12 61 🖥www.oper-leipzig.de

With world-class performances (if not world-class architecture), the Leipzig opera entertains sophisticates and students alike, with inexpensive seats available for every performance. During the summer season, ballets, and international music concerts make a show at the Opera an *event*.

🚋 *Tram 4, 7, 10, 11, 15, or 16: Augustuspl.* Ⓢ *Tickets €12-33, students 30% off.* ⏰ *Counter and phone lines open M-F 10am-8pm, Sa 10am-6pm, and 1 hr. before performances.*

KELLERTHEATER
CONTEMPORARY THEATER

Augustuspl. 12   ☎0341 126 12 61 🖥www.kellertheater.at

Kellertheater, located in the basement of the Opera, is an experimental theater

leipzig • arts and culture

venue. To enter, go around the side of the Opera (along Georgiring).
🚊 *Tram 4, 7, 10, 11, 15, or 16: Augustuspl.* Ⓢ *Tickets €11, students €5.* 🕐 *Box office open M-F 10am-8pm, Sa 10am-6pm.*

ACADEMIXER   KABARETT
Kupfergasse, right by the university   ☎0341 21 78 78 78 🖳www.academixer.com
A student *kabaret*, the academixer performs a political or social satire every night (in German). Started in 1966, this troop performs in a basement theater with 200 chairs surrounding a simple stage.
Ⓢ *Tickets from €10.* 🕐 *Shows daily 8pm. Box office open daily 10am-8pm.*

LEIPZIGER PFEFFERMÜHLE   KABARETT
Gottschedstr. 1   ☎0341 960 31 96 🖳www.kabarett-leipziger-pfeffermuehle.de
Leipzig's oldest kabaret (running since 1954) pulls talent from all around Saxony for satirical performances in German.
Ⓢ *Tickets Su-Th €20, F-Sa €22.* 🕐 *Performances daily 8pm. Box office open M-F 10am-8pm, Sa 3-8pm, and Su 6pm-8pm.*

SCHAUSPIELHAUS   THEATER
Bosestr. 1   ☎0341 126 81 68 🖳www.schauspiel-leipzig.de
This theater shows everything from the classics to experiemental student plays to concerts.
Ⓢ *Tickets from €7-17. Check the schedule for the monthly Theatertag, when all tickets are €5.55.* 🕐 *Box office open M-F 10am-7pm, Sa 10am-1pm, and 1½ hr. before performances.*

SKALA   CONTEMPORARY THEATER
Gottschedstr. 16   ☎0341 126 81 68 🖳www.skala-leipzig.de
Run by the Schauspielhaus, skala is a venue for contemporary performances.
🚊 *Tickets available at Bosestr. 1.* Ⓢ *Tickets from €7-17. Check the scheudle for the monthly Theatertag, when all tickets are €5.55.* 🕐 *Box office open M-F 10am-7pm, Sa 10am-1pm, and 1½ hr. before performances.*

SHOPPING   🕮

Most of Leipzig's Innenstadt shopping is dominated by chain stores, with few locally owned, one-of-a-kind businesses. That said, there's still might be some history to that third H and M you've walked by: the arched passages that run through the middle of city blocks were actually originally intended to be shopping malls; **Auerbachs Keller,** off of Grimmaischestr., is the oldest mall in the city. To find a more unusual souvenir of your time in Leipzig, go outside the city center to **Peterssteinweg,** (off Roßpl), and check out these shops. (Take trams #2 or #8 to Neues Rathaus. Peterssteinweg is past Martin Luther Ring, on the way to Roßpl.)

WÖRTERSEE DE CONNEWITZER   ⊛ BOOKS, ART
Peterssteinweg 7   ☎0341 224 87 83
A new and used bookstore, this shop is unique for the student art it displays and sells. Creative and colorful graphic prints are hung around the walls, screen-printed by artists at the *Hochschule für Grafik und Buchkunst Leipzig* (Academy of Visual Arst Leipzig).
🚊 *Take trams 2 or 8: Neues Rathaus. Peterssteinweg is past Martin Luther Ring, on the way to Roßpl.* Ⓢ *Prices vary by size and quantity of prints made. Prints 1m by 1m from €18.* 🕐 *Open M-F 10am-5pm, Sa 10am-2pm.*

SÄCHSISCHE PFEIFENSTUBE   ✎ CRAFTS
Peterssteinweg 5   ☎0341 212 49 38 🖳www.pfeifenstube.de
This workshop offers a chance to watch a master craftsman carve pipes in the centuries-old tradition, sanding and oiling with original tools and materials from a workbench in the front of the store.
🚊 *Trams 2 or 8: Neues Rathaus. Peterssteinweg is past Martin Luther Ring, on the way to Roßpl.* Ⓢ

Pipes €19-350. ⏰ Open M-F 10am-5pm.

MUSIKHAUS KIETZ — MUSIC

Peterssteinweg 3 ☎0341 301 46 27 🖥www.musikhauskietz.de

Musikhaus has been in business for 16 years, and has accumulated an extensive collection of vinyl records, including some new, but mostly the more interesting labels from the DDR era. About 80% of the records are secondhand.

🚏 Tram 2 or 8: Neues Rathaus. Peterssteinweg is past Martin Luther Ring, on the way to Roßpl. $ Vinyl €1-19. ⏰ Open M-Sa 10am-8pm.

ESSENTIALS

Practicalities

- **TOURIST OFFICE:** Staff books rooms, sells theater tickets, and hands out several free English maps. *(Richard-Wagner-Str. ☎0341 710 42 65 🖥www.leipzig.de 🚏 From the Hauptbahnhof, walk across Willy-Brandt-Pl. and take Goethestr. toward the left; the office on the first corner. $ Walking-tour map €2. ⏰ Open M-F 9:30am-6pm, Sa 9:30am-4pm, Su 9:30am-3pm.)*
- **TOURS:** Offered by the tourist office. *(Richard-Wagner-Str. ☎0341 710 42 65 ℹ 2hr. long. $ Bus tours €13. Walking tours €7-8. ⏰ German bus tours daily at 10:30am and 1:30pm. In English at 1:30pm. Walking tours in German M-F at 3pm, Sa-Su at 2pm.)*
- **CONSULATES: U.S.** *(Wilhelm-Seyferth-Str. 4. ☎0341 21 38 405 🚏 Cross the Innenstadt ring behind the Neues Rathaus and follow Tauchinitzstr. wuntil Weilhelm-Seyferth-Str. comes up on the left. The entrance is through Grassistr., the next street to the left. ⏰ Open M-F 9am-5pm.)*
- **CURRENCY EXCHANGE: Commerzbank.** *(Thomaskirchof 22, across the street from the church on the western side of the Innenstadt. ☎0341 141 50 ⏰ Open M 9am-4pm, Tu 9am-6pm, W 9am-4pm, Th 9am-6pm, F 9am-1pm.)* **Citibank** *(Goethestr. 1, just before the Opernhaus on the eastern side.)* Both have 24hr. ATMs.
- **WOMENS RESOURCES: Fauenkultur,** a center for art, meetings, and leisure, runs evening women's cafe; call for schedule. *(Windscheidstr. 51. ☎0341 213 0030 🖥www.frauen-kultur.leipzig.de.)* 🚏 Take tram 9, 10, or 11: Connewitz, Kreuz. From the stop, make a right onto Selneckerstr. and turn right again onto Windscheidstr. The building is located in 1st alley on the right. *(⏰ Office open M-F 9am-2pm, later for afternoon events.)*
- **GLBT RESOURCES: AIDS-Hilfe** features a popular cafe and distributes the magazine *genenpol. (Ossietzkystr. 18 ☎0341 232 31 27 🚏Tram 1: Ossietzkystr./Gorkistr. ⏰ Office open M 10am-6pm, Tu 10am-10pm, W 10am-6pm, Th 10am-10pm, F 10am-2pm. Cafe open Tu, Th 5-10pm.)*
- **HOME SHARE: Mitwohnzentrale.** *(Richard-Wagner-Str. 🖥www.mitwohnzentrale.de ℹ Home share services offered only online.)*
- **LAUNDROMAT: Maga Pon.** *(Gottschedstr. 11. ☎0341 337 3782 ℹ Detergent complimentary. $Wash €3.80. Dry €1.80.)*
- **EMERGENCY NUMBERS: Police:** ☎110. **Fire and Ambulance:** ☎112.
- **INTERNET ACCESS: Intertelcafe.** *(Reichstr. 16 and Am Bruehl 64. ☎0341 225 5402 $ €2 per hr.)*

Getting There

By Plane

Flughafen Leipzig-Halle (☎0341 24 11 55) on Schkeuditzg., is 20km from Leipzig with international service throughout Europe. Outbound trains stop at the airport. *(From the Hauptbahnhof,* Ⓢ *€3.40.* ⌚ *15min., 2 per hr. 3:30am-12:10am.)*

By Train

Trains pull in to **Hauptbahnhof,** the central station at the north end of Leipzig. Trains to: **Berlin** (Ⓢ €43. ⌚ 2.5hrs., 1 per hr.); **Dresden** (Ⓢ €29. ⌚ 1.5hr., every hr.); **Frankfurt** (Ⓢ €72. ⌚ 3.5hr., every hr.); **Munich** (Ⓢ €89. ⌚ 5hr., every 2hr.). The "Service Point" counter near track 14 is the quickest source of information and itineraries. For tickets, use **Automaten** (don't forget to validate at the small box on the entrance to the platform), or the **Reisezentrum** (travel center) on the ground floor near the main entrance.

Getting Around

By Tram and Bus

Information (☎0341 194 49). Trams and buses cover the city; the hub is in front of the Hauptbahnhof. None of the trams and buses run through the center of Innenstadt; instead, they all circle around, with the exception of bus 89, which runs through the middle, from the Hauptbahnhof, via Thomaskirche. A **Kurzstrecke** ticket covers up to 4 stops (€5.60); a regular ticket covers a single trip (€2). A **Tageskarte** (day card) is valid until 4am the day after purchase (€5). Tickets available from the tourist office, the Mobi Zentrum on Willy-Brandt-Platz in front of the train station *(open M-F 8am-8pm, Sa 8-10am. Credit cards accepted),* some trams, and Automaten. Validate all tickets on board. Night buses (look for the "N" prefix and bat silhouette at the stop) leave from the Hauptbahnhof 1:11am, 2:22am, and 3:33am, Sa-Su also 1:45am and 3am, along most daytime routes.

By Taxi

Call ☎0341 48 84 or toll-free ☎0800 800 42 33 for taxis.

By Car

Sixt has an office in the Hauptbahnhof at track 6. *(*☎*0341 26 988 11* ▣*www.sixt.de.* ⌚ *Open M-F 7am-10pm, Sa 8am-6:30pm, Su 10am-6pm.)* More offices at the airport.

Ride Share: Mitfahrzentral. *(Goethestr. 7-10, past the tourist office.* ☎*0341 194 40.)*

---

leipzig card

The **Leipzig Card** is good for trams and buses within the city, discounts on city tours, museum admissions, and some restaurants. *(*Ⓢ *1 day until 4am €9, 3 day €18.50, 3-day group ticket for 2 adults and 3 children €34.)*

---

weimar ☎03643

In its prime, Weimar, a small German town of 64,000, was a watering hole for cultural icons such as Goethe, Schiller, and Johann Gottfried von Herder (grandfather of the Romantics) whose fame still draws thousands of visitors to the city. In 1999, Weimar was declared the cultural capital of all of Europe, and, for the occasion, underwent extensive restoration (think prom queen the night before the formal), making it one of the most renovated cities in the former DDR. Despite the fact that Goethe's name is stamped on every storefront, restaurant window, and child in town, Weimar should also be appreciated for its brief history as the capital and namesake of the Weimar Republic, Germany's first attempt at a democratic state after WWI, and as the birthplace of the Bauhaus architectural and artistic movement, whose Bauhaus Universität still brings the city bohemian energy.

ORIENTATION

Tell any German that you've just come from Weimar, and they'll respond knowingly, nodding with eyebrows raised; "Ah, yes. Weimar, the cultural capital of Germany. Did you enjoy it? And did you, by chance, notice all the *culture*?" Why yes, thank you, you'll respond. All that culture kind of hit me over the head, now that you mention it. In fact, will you please serve me the house lager in a crystal flute? I'm afraid that culture has rubbed off on me a bit. "Ah, yes," your new German friend will respond. "All that culture is wonderful." You both will lean back in your chairs, unconsciously extending your pinkies and reminiscing on the refinement and, dare we say, *culture*, of this small German town.

A series of open squares strung together by side streets make up Weimar's city center, which contains most of the sights. From the train station, Carl-Ausust-Allee stretches downhill past the Neues Museum to Karl-Liebknect-Str., which leads into Goethepl. From there, Theaterpl. is down Wielandstr. to the left, and the Marktpl. is a short walk from Theaterpl. down Schillerstr. Winding streets that intersect at odd angles and change names frequently can make the city difficult to navigate without a map—pick one up at a tourist office *(€0.20)*.

ACCOMMODATIONS

LABYRINTH HOSTEL

HOSTEL [1]

Goethepl. 6 ☎03643 81 18 22 🖥www.weimar-hostel.com

Travelers weary of sterile HI hostels will find something a little cozier in this place hidden a few yards off the street. With a clean, well-maintained kitchen and common room, recently updated bedrooms, and student art covering the walls, Labyrinth Hostel may be the best value in town.

➜ Follow K.-Liebknecht-Str. from Carl-August-Allee as it turns into Goethepl. The hostel is a few buildings down from the post office, opposite the green space. i Breakfast €3. Bed linens €2. $ Apr-Oct 8-bed rooms €14; 6-bed €17; 4-bed €20; singles €40; doubles €46. Nov-Mar 8-bed rooms €13; 4-bed rooms €20. Singles €23; doubles €40. Sa-Su add €1 to each room price. ⏰ Reception 8am-9:30pm.

HABABUSCH HOSTEL

HOSTEL [1]

Geleitstr. 4 ☎03643 85 07 37 🖥www.hababusch.de

Central location? Yes. Fully equipped kitchen? Yes. Ironic? Umm... yeah, actually. Showers have car-wash hoses and squeegies, and an overly large candelabra dominates the lounge area. Nights and mornings can get very cold, so double up on blankets if possible. Reserve singles and doubles ahead in the summer. Run by art students who rarely keep regular hours at reception.

➜ From Theaterpl. follow Zeughot, the narrow, downhill road to the right of the Bauhaus museum. The hostel is marked by a large fountain. $ 7-bed dorms €10; 4-bed €12. Singles €20; doubles €30-36. ⏰ No fixed reception hours.

JUGENDHERBERGE GERMANIA (HI)

HOSTEL [2]

Carl-August-Allee 13 ☎03643 85 04 90 🖥www.djh-thueringen.de

This hostel is close to the train station but far removed from downtown; travelers pulling in late will find a convenient bed. Not too high on charm, this hostel's rooms are clean, but full of pre-fab furniture and white walls. A large breakfast room for guests is on the ground floor.

➜ From the train station, walk straight down Carl-August-Allee. The hostel is on your right. i Breakfast included. Internet €2 per hr. $ Dorms €23, under 27 €20. ⏰ Reception 24hr.

JUGENDHERBERGE

Humboldtstr. 17   ☎03643 85 07 92 ■www.jugendherberge.de

A member of HI, this big, turn-of-the-century brownstone located about 6min from the city center primarily hosts school groups. Fluorescent lighting, linoleum floors, and little decor make this hostel seem impersonal and sterile.

⚡ *From Wielandpl. in the south end of Weimar, follow Humboltstr. from where it forks off of Steubenstr. to the hostel.* ⓘ *Internet access €0.10 per min.* ⓢ *Doubles or 8-bed dorms with breakfast 1 night €27, 3 nights €24 per night; with full board 1 night €31, 3 nights €28 per night.* ⌚ *Reception 24hr.*

SIGHTS

For such a small town, Weimar has a ton of fascinating cultural history. Of course, as the hometown of Goethe and Schiller, this city will always belong to its poets (to whom every overpriced restaurant is forever indebted). But don't forget to explore the relics of Weimar's impressive artistic and political legacy as well. If you plan on enjoying more than a few of the city's historical sights, consider buying the **Weimar-Card** *(€12)* that gives 24hr. of free access to all museums that belong to the Klassik Stiftung Weimar. (Available at tourist offices, or participating museums).

🏛 PARK AN DER ILM AND GARTENHAUS

🏛 MUSEUM

Theaterpl.   ☎03643 54 33 57

Get lost in this sprawling park's extensive pathways and many bridges. Landscaped by (you guessed it) Goethe, Park an der Ilm is a living testment to the poet's remarkable artistic skill. Perhaps less artistic are the fake ruins built by the Weimar shooting club, located on the Schloßmuseum side of the river, about 200 meters from the main bridge. But should you manage to forget what you've read here, we hope that the discovery of 100-year-old ruins (presto!) right in the middle of a manicured park warms your heart. Goethe's Gartenhaus, away from the river, and toward the far slopes, was the poet's first Weimar home, and his later retreat from the city. Enjoy the gardens, or see the house's spartan and well-restored interior.

⚡ *Accessible from just about anywhere, the main bridge (Sternbrücke) crosses a stream just behind the Schloß.* ⓢ *Gartenhaus €4.50, reduced €3.50, with WeimarCard free.* ⌚ *Gartenhaus open daily Apr-Oct 10am-6pm; Nov-Mar 10am-4pm.*

🏛 BAUHAUS MUSEUM

♿ MUSEUM

Theaterpl.   ☎0364 54 59 61 ■www.uni-weimar.de/bauhausspaziergang.

Forget about Goethe. Let's talk about Gropius. Walter Gropius, the German architect and visionary responsible for opening the Bauhaus art school in Weimar, is considered to be one of the first Modernists. His students and fellow teachers forever changed the modern aesthetic, and the Bauhaus museum has succeeded in archiving many of Weimar's revolutionary Modernist's first works. For art enthusiasts and history buffs alike, this is a must-see. Catch an informative film (German with English subtitles) for more background on this artistic movement. Check with the ticket counter for screening times.

⚡ *In the Theaterpl., directly across from the Deutsches National Theater.* ⓢ *€4.50, reduced €3.50, free with WeimarCard. Museum tours Su 11am €2, students €1.50.* ⌚ *Open daily 10am-6pm.*

GOETHES WOHNHAUS

MUSEUM

Frauenplan 1   ☎03643 545 400 ■www.swkk.de

If you still haven't figured out that Goethe lived in Weimar, we recommend psychotherapy. But don't let the Goethe-mania keep you away from this museum. Unlike the countless German towns that leap at any excuse to put up a plaque on every rock the poet tripped over on his way from Weimar to Düsseldorf, **Goethes Wohnhaus** is the real thing. Goethe paced these floors, wrote at this desk, ate at

dresden, leipzig, and weimar-jena

that table, and presumably stubbed his toe on that stair (let your imagination run wild) during the 50 years he lived at this house in Weimar. The rooms are crammed with Italian sculptures, including a rather garish 4ft. tall replica of the goddess Juno's head, favorite books, and over 18,000 cabbage-like rocks. The entry hall and frescoes were inspired by his visits to Italy. Goethe's easy-to-miss yellow buggy is stashed in the barn under the house. To preserve the exhibit's authenticity, no explanatory signs are posted in the Goethehaus, so grab an English audio tour. The rest of the Goethe-Nationalmuseum consists of an exhibit on Weimar's history.

⇞ South of Markt. From Markt., follow Freuegtorstr. past Schillerstr. to Goethe's Wonhaus. ***i*** *Expect to wait on summer weekends.* *$ €8.50, reduced €7, students €2.50, with WeimarCard free. English audio tours €1.* *⏰ Open Apr-Sept Tu-F 9am-6pm, Sa 9am-7pm, Su 9am-4pm; Oct Tu-Su 9am-6pm; Nov-Mar Tu-Su 9am-4pm.*

SCHLOSSMUSEUM MUSEUM

Burgpl. 4 ☎03643 545960 🖥www.swkk.de

The collection at the palace is organized roughly chronologically by floor, with Baroque art and Russian religious icons on the first floor, 17th- and 18th-century German paintings, mostly romantic landscapes, on the second, and a bit of skin for the ambitious visitor on the third. The third floor displays more modern work, mostly German Impressionism with a sprinkling of Rodin and Monet. Be sure to find Kristian Kersting's series of four progressive paintings, each depicting a different German of a distinct social strata, all working at their desks.

⇞ The left of the Marktpl. Enter the archway and head through the courtyard. *$ €6, reduced €5, students €2.50, with WeimarCard free.* *⏰ Open Tu-Su Apr-Oct 10am-6pm, Nov-Mar 10am-4pm.*

SCHILLERS WOHNHAUS MUSEUM

Schillerstr. 12 ☎03643 54 54 01 🖥www.swkk.de

There must be something in Weimar's water. It was while living here, close to the Goethehaus, that Schiller wrote many of his noteable works, from *William Tell* to *The Maid of New Orleans*, which are now on display along with a selection of his plays. We surmise that the 1970s-looking replicas of original wallpaper on the top floors are secretly an ode to the Bradyhaus.

⇞ From Markt head south on Freuegtorstr. to Schillerstr. ***i*** *All explanatory plaques in German.* *$€5, €4 reduced, €2 students, free with WeimarCard. English audio tours €1.* *⏰ Open Apr-Sept Tu-F 9am-6pm, Sat 9am-7pm, Su 9am-6pm; Oct Tu-Su 9am-6pm; Nov-Mar Tu-Su 9am-4pm.*

NEUES MUSEUM WEIMAR MUSEUM

Weimarpl. 5 ☎03643 545 400 🖥www.swkk.de

The former Grand Ducal Museum, Neues Museum houses one of the most extensive and varied collections of art in Weimar, including contemporary art and French Impressionism. On the second floor, don't miss the series of canvases by Weimar-born painter Max Thedy, whose paintings of dark, empty rooms show his unique mastery of light. The basement floor houses a collection of Bauhaus-Univerisität Weimar works.

⇞ From the train station, head south on Carl-August-Allee. The musuem is at the end; enter on the south side from Weimarpl. *$ €3.50, reduced €2.50, students €1.50, with WeimarCard free.* *⏰ Open Tu-Su Apr-Oct 11am-6pm, Nov-Mar 11am-4pm.*

HERZONGIN ANNA AMALIA BIBLIOTHEK MUSEUM

Pl. der Demokratie 1 ☎03643 545200 🖥www.swkk.de

Goethe's old intellectual batting cage is located on the way to the park from the Markt. After outgrowing the palace, the *bibliothek* was relocated to its own building, built around the stunning light blue and gilded Rococo Hall. As pennance for something awful you did in your previous life, you are required to wear large one-size-fits-all slippers over your shoes, and shuffle around with embarrassing clumsiness to see the inspiration to Weimar's intellectual masters.

✈ *From Theaterpl., go west on Windischerstr. to Pl. der Demokratie.* ℹ *Limited tickets, so reserve ahead. Audio tours in English included.* Ⓢ *€6.50, reduced €5.50, students €3.* ⏲ *Open Tu-Su 10am-2:30pm.*

NIETZSCHE ARCHIV
MUSEUM

Humboldstr. 36 ☎03643 54 51 💻 www.swkk.de

Nietzsche-enthusiasts delight. *Nietzsche ist tot*, but the home he stayed in for three years while recovering form mental and physical illness still displays the philosopher's work. His sister's totalitarian control over the documents contributed to the Nazis' misuse of Nietzsche's philosophy, to horrifying ends. On display is a history of the archive, many portaits (and a death mask) of the man and his famous mustache, documents in his own hand, and an enviable flat designed by Henry can de Velde.

✈ *The Archiv is located relatively far from central Weimar. If you want to spare your legs the big hill, take the #6 bus to W.-Kütz Str.* Ⓢ *€2.50, reduced €2, students €0.50, with WeimarCard free.* ⏲ *Open Apr-Oct Tu-Su 1-6pm.*

FOOD 🎏

Anything with "Goethe" in the name is pretty much off-limits to the budget traveler. Food in Weimar is generally very expensive, but there are a few ways to get around the high cost. For groceries, try the produce market at the Marktpl. *(open M-Sa 6am-4pm)*, or supermarkets **Rewe** *(located on the bottom floor of the Goethe, Kaufhaus in Theaterpl. Open M-F 7am-10pm, Sa 7am-8pm)* and Na Kauf, on the corner of Fauenplan and Steubenstr *(open M-F 7am-11pm, Sa 7am-8pm).* Another cheap option are the many *döner* places around Weimar, serving Turkish beef pitas and vegetarian falafel. These restaurants are all great, inexpensive finds. So "goethe" crazy, and eat yourself happy.

🏴 CREPERIE DU PALAIS
🍴🍸🗑 RESTAURANT ❶

Am Palais 1 ☎03643 40 15 18

French expats serve delicious sweet and savory crepes big enough for a traveler-sized appetite. With potted plants and big windows, and service on a tree-shaded terrace outside, Creperie du Palais might be one of the best places to enjoy a French specialty outside of Paris. Try a buckwheat gallette for lunch or dinner *(with cooked ham €2.70; with Roquefort cheese, creme fraiche, and walnuts €5.10)*, or a crepe for dessert *(with banana, chocolate and coconut €3.30; with pears, almond cream, and chocolate sauce €4.30).* Or both. Or both and then some.

✈ *From Theaterpl., take the narrow road Zeughof down a slight slope. The creperie is about 15m down.* Ⓢ *Crepes from €2.50.* ⏲ *Open daily 11am-11pm.*

🏴 AAC
📶((•))🍸🗑 CAFE ❶

Burgpl. 1-2 ☎03643 85 11 61 💻www.acc-cafe.de

In addition to this cafe's wrap-around, I-Spy mecca of a photo collage, ACC offers incredible, relatively inexpensive, high-quality, filling food. Eat gourmet for a fraction of the cost. Inexpensive breakfasts *(baguette with butter, jam, ham, and coffee; €4.50)*, entrees *(toasted, unleavened bread with tomatoes, mozzarella, and balsamic vinagrette; €5.20)*, and drinks make this a popular place for Weimar students. On Mondays, professors from Bauhaus lecture about art in English. Free Wi-Fi, even after hours.

✈ *Located directly across Burgerpl. from the Schloß.* Ⓢ *Coffee €1.60. Cappuccino €2. Entrees from €5.* ⏲ *Open daily 11am-1am.*

BAUHAUS CAFE
🍴 CAFE ❶

Marienstr. 3 ☎01781 13 05 65

Serves foot-long, toasted baguette sandwiches with pesto, tomatoes, as well as large cookies *(€1)* for the traveler with a sweet tooth, and coffee *(€1)* for the traveler just off a bad stay at a hostel. There's limited seating; either take one of five bar stools, or get your food to go.

➡ *From Wielandpl., follow Marienstr. 15m to Bauhaus Cafe.* $ *Sandwiches from €2.30.* ⏰ *Open M-F 9am-6pm.*

TEE BOUTIQUE — CAFE, STORE ❶

Windischenstr. 23 ☎03643 90 51 77 🖥www.teeboutique.de

The Tee Boutique sells and serves a wide variety of specialty loose leaf teas. Inspired by the mystical ginkgo tree immortalized in one of Goethe's poems, this shop carries a large number of original ginkgo blends.

➡ *From Theaterpl, go west on Windischenstr.* $ *Most teas are €3-3.60 per 100g, with some as high as €7.20.* ⏰ *Open M-F 10am-6pm, Sa 10am-2pm.*

RESIDENZ-CAFE — RESTAURANT ❷

Grüner Mark. 4 ☎0364 35 94 08 🖥www.residenz-cafe.de

Weimar's oldest restaurant, located just across from the Schloβmuseum off on the corner of Burgpl., is a little more expensive, but the history and prime outdoor seating might make it worth the splurge.

ℹ *Credit card min. €20.* $ *Spaghetti bolognese €7.40. Vegetarian gnocchi €8. Beer €2.* ⏰ *Open daily 8am-1am.*

NIGHTLIFE

By 9pm Weimar's streets may be empty, but there are still a few student hangouts that keep going late into the evening.

STUDENTEN CLUB KASSETURM — CLUB

Goethepl. 10 ☎03643 85 16 70 🖥www.kasseturm.de

The oldest student club in Germany serves cheap drinks on two floors of 500-year-old tower. Concave stone ceilings make the basement bar and the second-floor dance floor perfect for a medieval knight out.

➡ *Located in Goethepl. greenspace, accross from the post office.* ℹ *Disco W at 10pm.* $ *On nights with live performances, cover €3-5. Shots €1-€1.20. Beer €2.50.* ⏰ *Open M-Sa from 6pm, Sun from 2pm. Close around 2pm or later.*

WUNDERBAR — BAR, CLUB

Gerberstr. 3 ☎03643 51 44 76 🖥www.gerberstrasse.net

This former squatter's home now provides shelter to social outcasts of a different kind: the pierced, tattooed rebels of quaint little Weimar. With graffiti-covered walls and motorcycles suspended from the ceiling, Wunderbar could be the aesthetic brainchild of Bob Marley and the KGB. Even on weekday nights, the bar is packed.

➡ *From Goethepl., go east on Graben until it turns into Gerberstr.* $ *Cover €5. Beer €1.30-2. Mixed drinks €2.30.* ⏰ *Bar open M-Sa 8pm-late.*

STUDENTEN CLUB — CLUB

Schützengasse 2 ☎03643 90 43 23 🖥www.schuetzengasse.de

A student hangout with nightly themes. The Monday film club shows German and English movies *(8pm-midnight or later)*. Tuesday Club Nights have live music and a cocktail special *(9pm-midnight or later)*. Wednesdays are game night *(7:30pm-midnight or later)*. Thursdays see salsa dancing *(6:30pm-2am)* and a tequila shot special *(€1)*. Friday is dance party night *(9pm-late)*. Saturdays involve dancing with live bands *(9pm-late)*. If you can't find one night you like, you don't like fun.

➡ *Located right off Theaterpl.* $ *Cover €5, students €3. Beer €1-2.10.*

SHOPPING

Ever the tourist's city, Weimar's litle shops and boutiques are often expensive, and aren't always very unique. But for visitors that look hard enough, there's always something to be found that's in budget and out of the ordinary.

WERKSTATTGALERIE VIVIAN SÄNGER — CLOTHING

Marktstr. 11 — ☎03643 90 69 73

Unless you're traveling on your recent million-dollar lottery winnings, you probably won't find anything to take home at Werkstattgalerie Vivian Sänger. But if you can stand to just browse, this isn't a place to miss. Designer and seamstress Sänger works right in her shop, making beautiful dresses, felt hats, and jewelry.

#On Marktstr., close to the intersection of Geleitstr. $ Most clothing from €120. ⏰ Open M-F 10am-3pm and 5-6pm, Sa 11am-3pm.

MINERALIEN UND FOSSILCENHANDBURG — FOSSILS

Schillerstr. 18

We can't believe this shop exists. Right in the middle of high-end cafes and a few doors down from Schillerhaus, this oddly oriented shop carries geodes, fossilized shells, dead starfish, dried seed pods, and even preserved insects. Even if these don't offer the average traveler much in the way of cultural relics or Weimar mementos, Mineralien is certainly refreshing for its originality.

#From Markt., go south on Freuegtorstr. to Schillerstr. $ Geodes and fossils €3.50-€14. ⏰ Open M-Sa 10am-6pm, Su noon-6pm.

ESSENTIALS

Practicalities

- **TOURIST OFFICES: Weimar Information.** *(Markt. 10, across from the Rathaus. ☎03643 74 50 💻www.weimar.de ℹ 2hr. Walking tours, in German, leave the office daily at 10am and 2pm. A separate desk supplies information on Buchenweld, and another on the classical museums of the city. $ Maps €0.20. Brochure detailing major sights €0.50. Books theater tickets and books rooms free. Tours €7, with Weimar Card €3.50, students €4, children under 14 free. Audiovisual iGuide in English €7 for 2hr., €7.50 for 4hr. ⏰ Open Apr-Oct M-Sa 9:30-7pm, Su and holidays 9:30-3pm; Nov-Mar M-F 9:30am-6pm, Sa-Su 9:30-2pm.)*
- **CURRENCY EXCHANGE:** Four banks with **24hr. ATMs** are spread out on Schillerstr. and Frauentorstr., with many more located around the city. **Deutsche Bank.** *(on Frauenstr. 3. ☎01818 10 00 💻www.deutsche-bank.de $* €5.50 fee for any exchange. *⏰ Open M 9:30-1pm and 2-4pm, Tu 9:30am-1pm and 2-4pm, W 9:30-1pm, Th 9:30am-1pm and 2pm-4pm, F 9:30-1pm.)* **Commerzbank, Postbank,** and **Sparkasse** all have locations on the same two streets.
- **LAUNDROMAT: SB-Waschsalon.** *(Graben 47, a few blocks from Goethpl. $ Wash €3.50. Dry €0.50 per 15min. ⏰ Open M-Sa 8am-10pm. Last wash 8:30pm.)*
- **PHARMACY: Stadt Apotheke.** *(Frauenstr. 3 ☎03643 20 20 93 ℹ Has a Notdienst (emergency service) buzzer. ⏰ Open M-F 8am-7pm, Sa 9am-2pm.)* **Apotheke.** *(Goethepl. 6, right next to post office. ☎03643 20 20 93 ⏰ Open M-F 7:30am-8pm, Sa 9am-4:30pm.)*
- **INTERNET: Roxanne.** *(Markt. 21 in the Markpl. $ Bar, cafe, and Internet access €2 per hour. ⏰ Open M-Sa from 10am, Su from 1pm.)* **ACC.** *(Burgpl. 1-2 ☎03634 40 15 81 💻www.acc-cafe.de ⏰ Open daily 11am-1am.)*
- **POST OFFICE:** *(Am Goethepl. 7-8. ⏰ Open M-F 9am-6:30pm. Sa 9am-12pm. 24hr. ATM.)*
- **POSTAL CODE:** 99421.

Getting There

Trains to: **Dresden** *($ €45. ⏰ 2hr., every hr.);* **Berlin** *($ €55. ⏰ 2½hr., every hr.);* **Erfurt** *($ €7.50. ⏰ 20min., every hr.);* **Jena** *($ €5. ⏰ 20min., 2-3 per hr.);* **Leipzig** *($ €25. ⏰ 1hr., every hr.).*

Getting Around

Most of Weimar is easily walkable, and its windy streets are easier to navigate than its infrequently-running bus system. Be sure to pick up a map with the bus routes *(€0.20)* at any tourist office. *(Single tickets €1.90; 4-trip card €4; 1-day ticket €5.)* Buy tickets at tourist offices, the main ticket office on Goethepl., or at news-stands with green and yellow "H" signs. Tickets must be validated on buses. If you're getting off of a train at Hauptbahnhof, buses #9, #6, #7, and #3 will all take you to Goethepl., close to the center of town.

jena ☎03641

Unlike many tourist hotspots, Jena (YEH-nah) is enjoyed more by its locals than by visitors. In any market and on every strasse, crowds of university students and residents make tourists the minority, and without a gift shop or pair of lederhosen in sight, Jena gives the traveler a chance to experience life as a real Deutschland-er. That said, we like our towns out of the ordinary, and Jena's illustrious and proud history as the founder of the optical industry (oh come on now, you're impressed!), celebrated at every street corner with eyeglass shops, puts it squarely in the category of absurd. Even more central to Jena is its university. Once the premier college in all of Germany, the Universität still gives Jena a vibrant student population that fuels some of the best nightlife and inexpensive eats around.

ORIENTATION

With students and locals outnumbering tourists at every corner, Jena is a place to experience what it really means to be a German. Germany *Behind the Beer Stein*, if you will, or *The Real Life of Germany: Confessions of a Jena Student*.

But navigating through Jena can be something of an obstacle course. Some tourists might throw up their hands in despair, retreat into the nearest pub, and not emerge until Oktoberfest. And while this solution has a certain appeal, we can assure you that Jena is conquerable, even for the poorest of navigators. The Salle River runs through the eastern part of the city, coursing more to the west in southern Jena. At the center of the city are the Planetarium and other major sights that can be reached by traveling east-west on Fürstengraben, one of the biggest streets in Jena. Running south of Fürstengraben is Leutragraben, which leads to a seven-direction star of streets that take you to many of the other major city sights. Enter the Jena Tourist Information office, where every traveler should pick up a free map *(or a more detailed version, €0.50)*.

ACCOMMODATIONS

Jena's hostels don't offer all-night reception, so plan to arrive during the day to book a room. You also may want to check with the tourist office in Markt, which has free brochures that include listings from private homes renting rooms *(starting at €25 per night)*.

ALPHA ONE HOSTEL ❶

Lassallestr. 8 ☎03641 59 78 97 🖥www.hostel-jena.de

Clean, inexpensive rooms make Alpha One a good option for the budget traveler, and its location close to the university means you'll always have a drinking buddy. Hostel reception is on the fourth floor, with big rooms on the well-lit floor below; through the immediate streets are quiet.

➜ From Johannispl., follow Bachstr. as it turns into Semmelstr. The hostel is on the corner of Semmelstr. and Lassallestr. ℹ Breakfast €3.50. Sheets included. Internet €1 per hour; no Wi-Fi. $ 6-bed dorms €15; 4-bed €17. Singles €25; doubles €40. ⏰ Reception 7am-10pm.

MEHR GENERATIONEN HAUS JENA

HOSTEL ❶

Erfurter Str. 52 ☎03641 35 27 10 🖥www.ueag-jena.de

About a 10min. walk from the center of town, this big yellow house is worth the little added daily exercise. Rooms are bright and well-lit with big windows, light yellow walls, and pine beds. Common rooms with large, comfortably cushioned red sofas, and small balconies on every floor complete the homey vision of this hostel.

 # From the Botanical Gardens, go west on Str. des 17 Juni as it turns into Humbodtstr, and then into Erfurterstr. i Free internet on the house computers. Sheets €3.50 for the first night. Breakfast €3.70. $ 10-bed dorms €12.50; singles €17.50; doubles €15.50. ⏰ Reception M-F 7:15am-4pm.

IB JUGENDGÄSTENHAUS

HOSTEL ❷

Am Herrenberge 3 ☎03641 68 72 30

Unless you're training for a walkathon or you're on the run from the police, the IB Jugendgästenhaus has a less than ideal location. Don't try to reach it on foot; follow the bus directions below. Stay in large rooms with pre-fab furniture and big windows looking out onto beautiful, forested Jena hills while you plan your escape route. Common rooms with TV on every floor.

 # Bus #10, #13, or #40: Zeiss-Werk. Follow the bus as you get off and take a right on Muehlenstr., going uphill until it turns into Am Herrenberge (about 15min.). i Wi-Fi €1 per hour. Prices include sheets and breakfast. $ 3- to 4-bed dorms €20.70 1st night, €18.60 subsequent nights; singles €29. Full ensuite baths available for €22.50. ⏰ Reception M-F 24hr., Sa-Su 7-11am and 5-10pm.

SIGHTS

CAMSDORFER BRÜCKE

BRIDGE, PARK

When Napoleon crossed this bridge during his European conquests, he was so taken with Camsdorfer Brücke that the decided he wanted one too. And since he couldn't fit it conveniently on the back of his horse, he had a replica built when he returned to Paris. The less than Napoleonic traveler, more interested in scenery than territorial conquest, will find something here too. Take a stroll along the banks of the Salle on either side of the bridge. Some visitors may consider another important landmark to be of even greater historical significance: the world's first frat-house, the **Grüne Tanne,** (located at 1 Wenigenjear) founded in 1815, is immediately across the river, and continues to fulfill its original purpose by serving brews and wines to thirsty travelers.

 # Follow Steinweg over the Salle river.

ST. JOHN CEMETERY

CEMETERY, CHURCH

Push through any one of the small gates surrounding the St. John Cemetery (Johannisfriedhof) and enjoy the thrill of discovery. Excuse us while we gush, but are there many things better than finding a secret garden, with overgrown ivy and winding paths leading through an old cemetery, all surrounding a mystical centuries-old church, the Friedenskirche? Just answer three questions to enter. What is your quest? What is your name? And what is your favorite color?

 # On the corner of Str. des 17. Juni and Philosophenweg. ⏰ Gates open 8am-10pm.

ZEISS-PLANETARIUM

PLANETARIUM, LIGHT SHOW

Am Planetarium 5 ☎06341 88 54 88 🖥www.planetarium-jena.de

This is not the world's oldest planetarium you were expecting to see. Unless, of course, you were expecting a laser-light show set to Pink Floyd music, in which case we applaud your psychic abilities. A large round sphere shoots lasers out of different, small lenses onto a concave screen on the ceiling. We can't imagine that this is what Zeiss had in mind when he was holding glass pieces against the grindstone, but hey—everyone likes Pink Floyd, right?

$ Admission €9 for musical, €8 for scientific; students €7.50/6.50. Comination Optical Museum

and science show ticket €11/9. ⏰ *Check the poster on the gate or the website for event times, usually 11am-7:30pm. Ticket office open Tu-F 10am-2pm and 7-8pm, Sa 1pm-9:30pm, Su 1-7:30pm, and 30min. before all shows. Shows 30-75min. long.*

STADTKIRCHE ST. MICHAEL — CHURCH

Kirchepl. ☎03641 44 33 84 🖥www.stadtkirche-jena.de

The Stadkirche St. Michael is beautifully authentic and simple, in very much the same condition now as it was during the Reformation, when Martin Luther preached here twice. The church also houses Luther's tombstone, designed by Cranach the Elder, conspicuously missing from Luther's grave in Wittenberg. Evidently, a battle interrupted the stone's shipment, though Wittenbergers find the story hard to swallow. We prefer not to get in the middle of it.

🧭 *Located just north of Markt, on Kirchepl.* $ *Free.* ⏰ *Open M 12:30-5pm, Tu-Sa 10-11:45am and 12:30-5pm.*

ROMANTIKERHAUS — MUSEUM

Unterm Markt. 12a ☎06341 44 32 63 🖥www.jena.de

This small museum manifests Jena's pride in its intellectual history. Owned by philosopher and fiery democrat Johan Fichte from 1794-99, it hosted the poetic, philosophical, and musical shenanigans of the early Romantics. Rather than preserving the original furnishings, the town uses the house to teach visitors about Romantic history, with rotating exhibits and some supplemental information in English. Perhaps overly inclined toward the metaphysical, the museum indulges in a figurative representation of the progression of Romanticism, with a stairwell painted "in yellow shades intensifying gradually until obtaining a golden tint at the third level, to represent the Golden Age," and an oddly placed wasp's nest, whose "fragments illustrate the dispute within the Jena circle of certain contemporaries."

🧭 *From Markt, follow Unterm Markt (street) to the museum.* $ *€4, seniors €3, students €2.50.* ⏰ *Open Tu-Su 10am-5pm.*

OPTISCHES MUSEUM (OPTICAL MUSEUM) — MUSEUM

Carl-Zeiß-Pl. 12 ☎06341 44 31 65 🖥www.optischesmuseum.de

To the visually challenged (and we don't mean the horribly unattractive), celebrate your savior! Carl Zeiss, the inventor of the optical lens, once called Jena home, and Jena has been benefiting from the association ever since. Now a world center for camera, telescope, eyeglass, and medical lenses, this museum outlines the history of the field of optometry, staring with a replica of Zeiss' original workshop in the basement. Be sure to check out the holograms on the bottom floor for a sober (we assume) trip. The first floor details the life of Carl Zeiss, and the history of the camera lens. The third floor, replete with occassional, mystifying space-age sound effects and murmured shuttle launch instructions in German, features the planetary applications of Zeiss's work.

🧭 *Head south on Johannispl. to Krautgasse. Turn left onto Carl-Zeiss-Str. and follow it to Carl-Zeiß-Pl. 12.* $ *€5, students and seniors €4. English audio tours €1, deposit €5; borrow an informational pamphlet in English for €4.50.* ⏰ *Open Tu-F 10am-4:30pm, Sa 11am-5pm.*

FOOD

Like most college towns, Jena has great, inexpensive restaurants. If you're looking for the basics, there's an **Aldi** supermarket in the basement of Neue Mitte shopping center *(Open M-Sa 8-10pm)* and a **Spar** on Löbderstr *(Open M-F 7am-10pm, Sa 7am-6pm)*. There's also a fresh **produce market** in front of the Rathaus *(Open Tu, Th-F 6am- 5pm)*.

CAFE IMMERGRÜM — CAFE, RESTAURANT ❶

Jennergasse 6 ☎03641 44 73 13

With comfortable chairs and couches, warm lighting, and laid-back music, this cafe and restaurant is popular with local students and families. Don't miss out on an inexpensive menu with some made-in-house favorites, including the *Fladen-*

brot (€3). Lots of vegetarian options, including pastas and baguette sandwiches. If the weather's good, enjoy eating outside this big yellow house on the umbrella and tree-shaded patio.

➡ From Johannispl., follow Johanisstr. to Jennergasse, on your left. Where Jennergasse splits, take the fork to your left. $ Sandwiches €3.50-4.80. ⏰ Open M-Sa 11am-1pm, Su 10am-2:30pm.

CAFE STILLBRÜCH
🌐🍸⛅ RESTAURANT [2]

Wagnergasse 1-2 ☎03641 82 71 71

The cafe's three stories, connected by spiral staircases and tables tucked away in little nooks, are a perfectly cozy place to enjoy a meal. Cafe Stillbrüch is on one of Jena's most picturesque cobblestone roads, and, with outdoor seating, you can be right in the middle of the best scenery. The house specialty, *Pfannengerichte (piping hot meals served in a small cooking pan; €7-10)* will leave you and your wallet full.

➡ From Johannispl., follow Wagnergasse to Stillbrüch. $ Pastas €5.60-7. ⏰ Open daily 9am-1am.

GRÜNOWSKI
🌐🍸⛅ CAFE [1]

Schillergässen 5 ☎03641 44 66 20 💻www.gruenowski.de

On a warm day, try a fruit-blended milkshake *(€2.50)* or sparkling mango juice *(€2)* on the tree shaded patio under umbrellas and outdoor lights. This old, graffittied building is full of exposed character, and a wild exterior make it a unique place to eat a meal. Grünowski serves light meals, including soups and pastas.

➡ From Johannispl., go south on Westbahnhofstr. (in some places called Schiller Levt.) to Schillergässen. $ Entrees €3-6.50. Beer €2.50. ⏰ Open M-Sa from noon, Su from 2pm.

FRITZ MITTE
🌐⛅ RESTAURANT [1]

Corner of Johannispl. and Wegergasse ☎03641 30 98 98

From a serving window in a lime-green shack, Fritz Mitte serves currywurst and french fries with a variety of dipping sauces to local students looking for a quick snack or meal. We might not go crazy for seven varieties of mayonnaise-based french-fry toppings, but hey, we're not European. And we won't judge.

$ Currywurst €2. Fries €1.60-2. ⏰ Open M-Th 10am-11pm, F-Su 10am-midnight.

NIGHTLIFE

Every student understands that Fridays deserve their own celebration. During their brief visits, Fridays need to feel special. We live in perpetual fear that a Friday will feel neglected, and decide not to come back again next week. For these reasons, it is imperative to throw parties, and no one understands this like Jena students. To do your part to save our weekends, you can start by picking up a monthly *Blitz Guide* from the tourist office to see what special events are scheduled.

FIDDLER'S GREEN
🌐🍸⛅ BAR

Bachstr. 39 ☎03641 51 57 88 💻www.irishpub-jena.de

If you're looking for a fun night, definitely start with Wagnergasse. The street, busy during the day, practically vibrates with energy at night. Excellent restaurants line the narrow cobblestone walkway, dominated by bistro tables and happy diners. This pub is a great place to start, or finish up the night. With Guinness glasses and bottles lining the wall behind the bar, outdoor seating on a patio right on the corner of Wagnergasse, and football playing on the TV inside, Fiddler's Green is a surprisingly authentic Irish experience in the middle of Germany. And, if you'll allow us to be honest: no one knows their way around the bottle like the Irish.

➡ Located right off Johannispl. $ 0.5L beer €2-2.50. ⏰ Open 5pm-late. Happy hour 5-6pm.

STUDENTENHAUS WAGNER
🌐🍸 BAR

Wagnergasse 26 ☎06341 47 21 53 💻www.wagnerverein-jena.de

Located off Wagnergasse in a large graffitted house, the young rebel seems to have taken over. With alternative students hanging off every window sill and sitting on every stairway, the whole house has a *Home Alone* feel. With considerably more edge and considerably fewer Christmas sweaters, of course. The Studentenhaus also hosts plays, live music, and film screenings. In addition to the unofficial schedule (months worth of concert and performance posters) papering their outside gate, the website has a more accurate, if less creative, way to view the upcoming events.

⇄ From Johannispl., follow Wagnergasse about 40m. Take the stairs up past a wooden gate to the Studentenhaus. ⏰ Open M-F 11am-1am, Sa-Su 7:30pm-1am.

SHOPPING

As a residential city, most of Jena's stores are familiar to foreign travelers. If you're in a shopping mood, try the Goethe Galerie for everything from clothing to books to electronics, or the **Neue Mitte** shopping center just across the street. If you're looking for something out of the ordinary, try looking on **Unterm Markt** for some smaller shops.

EINE-WELT-LADEN JENA — 🌍 FAIR TRADE

Unterm Markt 13 — ☎03641 636 95 04 💻www.eine-jena.de

What's bad for the wallet could be good for the earth! Picking up some fair trade coffee, tea, jewelry, bags, or crafts may just be your contribution to saving humanity.

⇄ From Markt., follow Unterm Markt to Eine-West-Laden. $ Wallets from €15. Necklaces from €13. ⏰ Open M-F 10am-6pm, Sa 10am-2pm.

ESSENTIALS

Practicalities

- **TOURIST OFFICE:** *(Markt 16. ☎03641 49 80 50 💻www.jena.de $ Free maps, leads city tours in German €5, and books private rooms for free. Free listings for privately rented rooms, from €20. JenaCard for 48hr. of free public transportation, a free tour, and free and reduced entry to Jena's sights and museums €9. ⏰ Open M-F 10am-7pm, Sa-Su 10am-4pm.)*
- **CURRENCY EXCHANGE:** 24hr. ATMs and Sparkasse banks are located frequently around the city. **Sparkasse.** *(Filiale-Ludwig-Wimar Gasse 5. ⏰ Open M-F 9am-6pm. 24hr. ATM outside.)* **Deutsche Bank** *(Schloßgasse 20. Located between Eichpl. and Marktpl., beside the Rathaus)* has a 24hr. ATM.
- **PHARMACIES:** Pharmacies have many locations around town. Should you need to find one quickly, here are a few addresses that should help. **Geothe-Apotheke.** *(Weigelstr. 7, located in front of the church. ☎03641 45 45 45 ⏰ Open M-F 8am-8pm, Sa 8am-4pm.)* **Flora-Apotheke.** *(Löbderstr., by the Rathaus. ☎03641 45 95 00 ℹ Lists signs of rotating 24hr. pharmacies in front window. Notdienstrglacke (emergency) buzzer. ⏰ Open M-F 8am-6:30pm, Sa 8am-1pm.)*
- **LAUNDROMAT AND INTERNET:** *(Wagnergasse 11. ☎03641 63 88 84 ℹ J. Kinski's is the only place to find free Wi-Fi in Jena. Also a bar and laundromat. $ €2.50 for a wash, dry €0.50 per 10min. ⏰ Open M-Sa 11am-late. No drying after 10pm.)*
- **POST OFFICE:** *(Englepl. 8. ⏰Open M-F 9am-6:30pm, Sa 9am-1pm.)*
- **POSTAL CODE:** 07743.

Getting There

By Train

Stop at any of Jena's three stations: **Bahnhof Jena-West** (mostly trains to/from Dresden and Erfurt), **Jena Saalbahnhof** (trains to/from Berlin and Munich), and **Bahnhof Jena-Paradies** (where trains going through the Saalbahnhof station will also often stop).

Make sure you check online to find which station to leave from.

Trains to: **Leipzig** (ⓢ €25. ⏰ 1hr., every hr.); **Dresden** (ⓢ €43. ⏰ 2hr., every hr.); **Berlin** (ⓢ €57. ⏰ 2½hr., every hr.); **Munich** (ⓢ €79. ⏰ 4½hr., every hr.)

Getting Around

By Public Transportation.

Jena is a walkable city, and may even be easier to navigate by foot than by bus. Bus/tram tickets are €1.90, bought and validated aboard each bus or tram. All public transportation is centered around the "Zentrum" stop.

By Bike

The main bike rental is **Kirscht Fahrrad.** (Löbdergraben 8. ☎03641 44 15 39 ⓢ €15 for the 1st day, €10 per additional day. ⏰ Open M-F 9am-7pm, Sa 9am-4pm.)

KÖLN AND DÜSSELDORF

In 1946, the victorious Allies attempted to expedite Germany's recovery by merging the traditionally distinct regions of Westphalia, Lippe, and the northern Rheinland, bringing the industrial nucleus of post-war Germany under one government. This gave rise to the Land von Kohle und Stahl (Land of Coal and Steel), feeding the great German Wirtschaftswunder, the rapid economic expansion after WWII. A dense concentration of highways and rail lines connect the most heavily populated and economically powerful region in Germany, though interestingly, less than 25% of the land is actually used for industry; the rest is dedicated to forestry and agriculture.

Despite the industrial boom, the region still retains many of its own unique traditions, whether the original Kölsch dialect or drinking beer from tiny 0.2L glasses to retain its freshness. The region was the birthplace of both Beethoven and Marx, and the city of Bonn was the center of the West German government for almost half a century. Nordrhein-Westfalen boasts astounding river scenery, majestic cathedrals, and world-class museums.

But for all the solemnity of impressive art exhibits and ancient cathedrals, the Nordrhein-Westfalen region hasn't forgotten how to have a good time. At night, the 260 bars, coffee shops, and brewing houses located in Düsseldorf's Altstadt are said

greatest hits

- **MAN V. FOOD.** Master the art of competitve schnitzel eating and get your name on the wall of fame at Bei Oma Kleinmann (p. 174).

- **MAN V. WILD.** Test out gear in environment and weather simulation chambers at Globetrotter Ausrüstung (p. 178).

- **DESIGN STAR.** Sip a cocktail on Annabel's floral bed or lounge with a brew in JoJo's vintage mini-bus at Die Wohngemeinschaft (p. 176).

- **WORK OF ART.** Marvel at everything from antique glasswork to intricate locks at Museum Für Angewandte Kunst (p. 171).

to make up the "longest bar in the world." But indulge with caution: to order a Kölsch beer, the traditional Köln brew, in a Düsseldorf bar is a burn to the locals. Please. Here, we drink Altbier, doncha know?

köln *cologne* ☎0221

The Roman city of Colonia made headlines many times in history before becoming a staple of Germany travel guides. Housing valuable relics of the Three Kings, Köln first made its name as a hubbub of pilgrimage activity. Later, its port along the Rhein made it a commercial entrepeneur's dream city. In the 18th century, Farina's invention of the fragrant Eau de Cologne made Köln citizens, and then the rest of the world, smell nice. Finally, in 1880, the City's Dom was completed.

Today, pilgrims take the form of chatty tourists who leave with suitcases full of perfume and dozens of photos of the Dom (in their defense, it's pretty incredible). Yet the city still clings to its roots, and the many archaeological excavation sites around the Altstadt attest to Köln's obsession with historical preservation. True to form, many Kölners also converse with each other in the city's own dialect, called *Kölsch*—which, coincidentally, is also the name of the city's own beer, made exclusively in breweries with a clear view of the Dom. With all that *Kölsch* and a robust nightlife scene fueled by students from Germany's largest university, you're bound to have a good time.

ORIENTATION

The Rhein River runs north-south through the middle of the city, though most of the river runs to the west. There, a long semi-circular street comprised of **Hansaring, Hohenzollernring, Hohenstaufenring, Sachsenring,** and **Ubierring,** divides the city's **Altstadt** inside the ring along the river and the **Neustadt** outside. On the other side of the river is **Deutz,** home to Köln's trade fairs.

Altstadt-Nord

The beloved Dom is the heart of the Altstadt-Nord, next door to the Hauptbahnhof. Bounded by the Deutzer Brücke to the south, this part of town is one-third historical sights, one-third shopping malls, and one-third overpriced German brewhouses.

Altstadt-Sud

Admittedly, there's not much in this part of town—yet. While the **Schockoladen Museum** remains this quarter's greatest asset, recent construction along the banks of the Rhein have transformed the formerly defunct **Rheinhaufen** harbor into a posh new residential area. The three inverted L-shaped apartment buildings, called the **Kranhaus (Crane House),** have brought the city some modern architectural street cred.

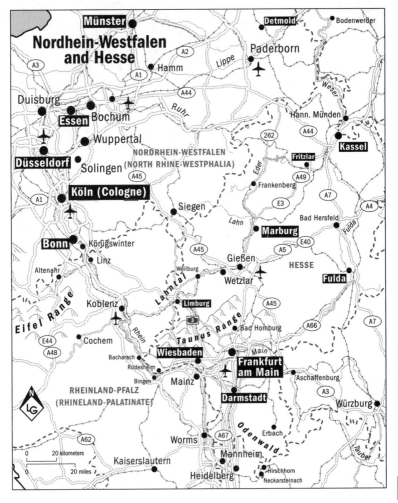

Neustadt

The western end of this part of town is the university. You'll find plenty of cheap eats and student-friendly nightlife in the area around **Zülpicher Platz.** Along the north-western end, the **Belgisches Viertel** neighborhood is populated by chic boutiques and designer furniture stores, along with a few of the city's more upscale bars.

ACCOMMODATIONS

Köln's hotels raise rates from March to October, when trade winds blow convention-ers into town. The hotel haven is **Brandenburger Strasse,** on the less busy side of the Hauptbahnhof. Looking for last-minute deals during **Karneval** is foolish—book up to a year ahead and expect to pay a premium.

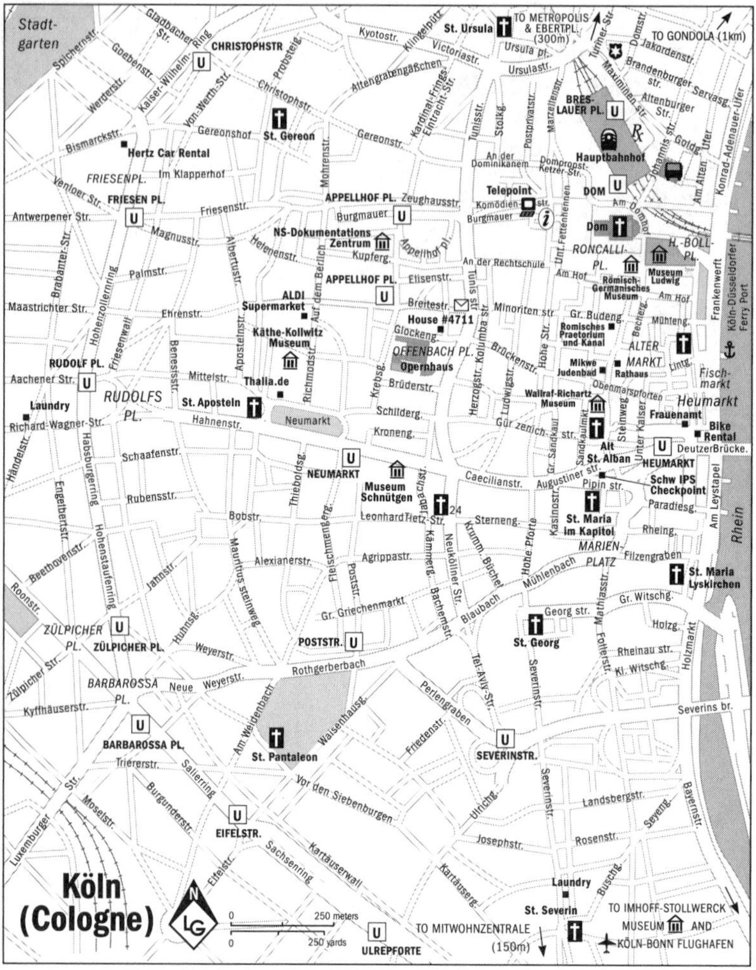

Altstadt-Nord

STATION HOSTEL FOR BACKPACKERS

💳🚭📶 HOSTEL ❷

Marzellenstr. 44-56 ☎0221 912 53 01 💻www.hostel-cologne.de

The most conveniently located hostel in Köln also boasts the best atmosphere, with chalkboards telling you about all the goings-ons around the city and knowledgeable staff quick to help you with whatever you need. The dorms are often not bunked, meaning you don't have to fumble around ladders in the middle of the night.

⇟ From the Hauptbahnhof, take the Dompropst-Ketzer-Str. exit with the Dom to the left and the Rolex building to the right, and turn right behind the Rolex building onto Marzellenstr. ***i*** *Linens and Wi-Fi included.* *$ 6-bed dorms €17; singles €32-39; doubles €44-55; triples €66-75; quads €80-88; quints €90.* *⏰ Reception 24hr. Check-in 3pm. Check-out noon.*

HOTEL IM KUPFERKESSEL

💳🚭📶 HOTEL ❸

Probsteigasse 6 ☎0221 270 79 60 💻www.im-kupferkessel.de

This small family-run hotel has been delighting guests for over 35 years. The rooms are spotless and cozy with simple, if slightly bland, decor. A location close to the Dom makes this an affordable steal for hostel-hoppers looking for some peace and quiet.

✈ *U12 or U15: Christophstr./Mediapark, then head east on Christophstr. and turn left onto Probstigasse.* ℹ *Breakfast and Wi-Fi included. Free beds for children under 12.* ⑤ *Singles €36, with bath €49; doubles with bathroom €76.* ☼ *Reception M-F 7am-8pm, Sa-Su 8am-8pm.*

JUGENDHERBERGE KÖLN-DEUTZ (HI)   ➴ &. ⑽❄   HOSTEL ❷

Siegesstr. 5   ☎0221 81 47 11 🖃www.koeln-deutz.jugendherberge.de

Though this hostel is a little impersonal, you're always guaranteed clean and accessible rooms with great amenities: rooms come with spacious individual lockers and safes, as well as separate showers and toilets for maximal efficiency. The lobby has a 24hr. convenience store, and there's even a ticket office on the third floor.

✈ *U1 or U9: Deutzer Freiheit, then head up to the walkway and turn right toward Siegesstr. Continue half a block on Siegesstr. to hostel on left.* ℹ *Breakfast and linens included.* ⑤ *Dorms €20-27; singles €30-45; doubles €50-65; quads €80-107.* ☼ *Reception 24hr.*

STAPELHÄUS'CHEN DAS KLEINE   ⑳⑫   HOTEL ❸

Fischmarkt 1-3   ☎0221 272 77 77 🖃www.koeln-altstadt.de/stapelhaeuschen

Housed in a former fish market, this hostel has small yet solid, un-fishy rooms with unbeatable views for the price: you'll either get a coveted panorama and the noise of the Rhein, or, on the other side, the walls of the lovely Groß St. Martin Cathedral.

✈ *From the Dom, head toward the Rhein and then head south on Am Frankenturm. That will turn into Am Bollwerk, which finally turns into Mauthgasse. Hotel is located at the intersection with Lintgasse.* ℹ *Breakfast included. Some rooms with private bath.* ⑤ *Singles €40-85; doubles €68-148.* ☼ *Reception 6am-11pm.*

köln • accommodations

Altstadt-Sud

👍 HOSTEL KÖLN
💳♿📶❄☁ HOTEL [3]

Marsilstein 29 ☎0221 998 77 60 💻www.hostel.ag

Sleek rooms, friendly reception, and a great location by Neumarkt make this hostel a great deal for travelers. Although it's called a hostel because of the multiple-bed rooms, the place actually functions like a hotel: if you book a dorm you have to book the entire room. So come with friends, and enjoy your free breakfast on the rooftop balcony with some great views.

*🚇 U1, U3, U4, U7, U9, U16, or U18: Neumarkt, then head west and turn left onto Im Lach and right onto Marsilstein to hostel on right. **i** Breakfast, linens, and towels included. Free Wi-Fi and computers for guest use. [$] 3- to 8-bed dorms from €24; singles from €45; doubles from €60. ⏰ Reception 24hr. Check-in 3pm. Check-out 11am.*

Neustadt

MEININGER CITY HOSTEL
💳🚭📶🍸 HOSTEL [2]

Engelbertstr. 33-35 ☎0221 355 33 20 14 💻www.meininger-hostels.com

This trendy hostel boasts a game room, lounge, cinema, and bar, along with a breakfast room decorated with chandeliers and velvet wallpaper. Rooms are quiet and clean, if not small, and all come with private bathrooms.

*🚇 U1, U7, U12, or U15: Rudolfpl., then exit station, turn left (south) onto Habsburgstr., right on Lindenstr., and left on Engelbertstr. **i** Breakfast €4.50. Linens included. Towels available with deposit. Free Wi-Fi in lobby; €5 per day in room. [$] 8-bed dorms from €19; 3- to 6-bed dorms from €25; women-only 6-bed dorms €22; singles from €49; doubles from €68. ⏰ Reception 24hr. Check-in 3pm. Check-out 10am.*

BLACK SHEEP HOSTEL
💳♿📶 HOSTEL [2]

Barbarossapl. 1 ☎0221 30 29 09 60 💻www.blacksheephostel.de

Don't be deterred by the slightly hidden location—Black Sheep Hostel is cute, cozy, and homey in all the right ways. Each room has a different theme and decor, like the "**dragon** room" or the "sheep room," and the sunny communal kitchen is a great place to meet fellow travelers.

*🚇 U12, U15, U16, or U18: Barbarossapl. Look for the McDonald's, and enter through the door on the left side. **i** Breakfast included. Linens €2, free for stays over 3 nights. Free Wi-Fi and computers for guest use. [$] 8-bed dorms €18.50; 6-bed dorms €20; singles and doubles €25; quads €23. ⏰ Reception daily 8am-11:30pm. Check-in should be arranged in advance. Check-out 11am.*

PENSION JANSEN
🐾🚭 PENSION [3]

Richard-Wagner-Str. 18 ☎0221 251875 💻www.pensionjansen.com

Brightly colored and tastefully decorated rooms abound at this chic little pension located on the third floor of an apartment building. Enjoy a well-balanced breakfast (included) in the cute dining room before launching your full-scale assault on the town.

🚇 U1, U7, U12, U15: Rudolfpl., then walk south 1 block to Richard-Wagner-Str. and head west for two blocks to pension on right. [$] Singles €35-48; doubles €70-100; triples €105-140. Discounts for longer stays. ⏰ Reception daily 8-10am and by appointment. Check-in arrange in advance. Check-out 11am.

SIGHTS 👁

Altstadt-Nord

👍 DOM
💳♿❄ CATHEDRAL

💻www.koelner-dom.de

This towering structure, which took over 600 years to build, has defined Köln with its colossal spires since its completion in 1880. A canopied ceiling towering 44m above the floor, and 1350 sq. m of exquisite stained glass casting a harlequin display of colored light, the cathedral is the perfect realization of High Gothic style. Despite the endless construction that guarantees constant scaffolding along the ornate exterior, thousands of visitors flock to this landmark daily.

Begin your tour at the plaza out front where a conglomeration of street performers and camera-touting tourists interact. Directly opposite the front door, a scale replica of the cathedral's crowning pinnacles lets you marvel at their size. Enter the church and head to the choir, keeping to the right-hand side. The stained-glass window in the South Transept might look a little different than the others; called the **"pixel window"** by some, this piece of modern art was created in 2007 to replace the original destroyed in World War II, using a computer program to position squares of 72 different colors for a mystical effect. As you walk farther toward the back of the cathedral, a small chapel houses a **15th-century triptych** painted by Stephen Lochner to represent the city's five patron saints: St. Ursula and her bevy of female attendants (a whopping 10,000 virgins, according to legend) dominate the left wing; St. Gereon is on the right; in the center, the Three Kings pay tribute to a newborn Christ. Continue along the back of the church to take a peek at the **Shrine of the Three Kings** inside the iron gates. On the left side of the choir is the **Chapel of the Cross,** which holds the 10th-century **Gero Crucifix,** the oldest intact sculpture of *Christus patiens* (a crucified and deceased Christ with eyes shut). Nearby, a doorway leads outside and a right turn will get you into the cavernous **Schatzkammer** (treasury), which holds clerical relics: thorn, cross, and nail bits, as well as liturgical vestments and pieces of 18 saints.

To ascend the tower, go back outside and turn left to head down the stairs. 15min. and 509 steps (100m) are all it takes to scale the **Südturmb** (south tower) and catch an impresive view of the city and river below, as well as a birdseye view of the inside of the cathedral itself. Catch your breath at the **Glockenstube** (about ¾ of the way up), a chamber for the tower's nine bells. Four of the bells date from the Middle Ages, but the 19th-century upstart known affectionately as **Der Große Peter** (at 24 tons, the world's heaviest swinging bell) is loudest.

⚑ *By the Hauptbahnhof.* ℹ *The Dom Forum (located across the street, ☎0221 92584720 💻www.domforum.de) organizes guided tours in English M-Sa 10:30am and 2:30pm, Su 2:30pm, €6, students €4. A 20min. film shown inside the Dom Forum building also gives an introduction to the cathedral, in German M-Sa noon, 1:30pm, 3pm, 4:30pm, Su 3pm and 4:30pm; in English M-Sa 11:30am and 3:30pm, Su 3:30pm; €2, students €1.* Ⓢ *Entry free. Schatzkammer €4, students €2; tower €2.50/1; combined €5/2.50.* ⌚ *Church open daily May-Oct 6am-9pm, Nov-Apr 6am-7:30pm. Schatzkammer open daily 10am-6pm. Tower open daily May-Sept 9am-6pm, Oct and Mar-Apr 9am-5pm, Nov-Feb 9am-4pm.*

⬛ MUSEUM LUDWIG
Heinrich-Böll-Pl.

♦⟨♿⟩❄ MUSEUM

☎0221 22 12 61 65 💻www.museum-ludwig.de

This attractive museum features works by virtually every big-name artist of the 20th century, with displays of pop art, photography, and one of the world's largest Picasso collections. The museum also houses sculptures by artists more known for their paintings, including Picasso, Lichtenstein, and Warhol.

⚑ *Behind the Dom to the right and the Römisch-Germanisches Museum.* ℹ *Audio tour €3, or download the entire thing online before you go.* Ⓢ *€10, students €7. First Th of the month ½-price after 5pm.* ⌚ *Open Tu-Su 10am-6pm, first Th of the month 10am-10pm.*

⬛ KOLUMBA
Kolumbastr. 4

♦⟨♿⟩⬧ MUSEUM

☎0221 933 19 30 💻www.kolumba.de

This enormous concrete building, constructed over the ruins of the Gothic cathedral St. Kolumba, is the art museum of the archbishop of Köln. On the ground floor, a cavernous room reveals the cathedral's excavation, where a bridge guides you along the rubble. Elsewhere in the museum, ancient relics and church artifacts are juxtaposed with modern secular works, all of them dramatically presented. Art aside, a gorgeous reading room with high-backed and comfortable leather chairs on the top floor invites you to sit and contemplate the art, or to peruse through their collection of art books and German literature.

✈ *U3, U4: Appellhofpl., then walk through the Opern Passage and turn left onto Glockengasse and go a block past 4711.* *i* *Free guidebooks available in English.* Ⓢ *€5, students €3, under 18 free.* 🕐 *Open M-Th 9am-noon and 2-6pm, F 9am-noon.*

RÖMISCH-GERMANISCHES MUSEUM
MUSEUM

Roncallipl. 4   ☎0221 221 24438 ▣www.museenkoeln.de/roemisch-germanisches-museum/

A third-century Dionysus Mosaic, discovered in 1941 during the excavation of an air raid shelter, forms the foundation for this extensive collection. Three floors of artifacts including ancient toys, 13th-century ⟏jugs, and Roman statues illuminate Köln's history as a Roman colony. Don't miss the New Media section on the top floor, where you can virtually cruise through a three-D model of Roman Köln.

✈ *Behind the Dom to the right.* *i* *Abridged information in English.* Ⓢ *€6, students €2. First Th of each month free.* 🕐 *Open Tu-Su 10am-5pm, first Th of the month 10am-10pm.*

EL-DE HAUS (NS-DOKUMENTATIONSZENTRUM)
MUSEUM

Appellhofpl. 23-25   ☎0221 2212 6332 ▣www.museenkoeln.de/ns-dok

The city's former Gestapo headquarters now educates visitors on the city's history under Nazi rule. Prison cells in the basement, once overcrowded with political wrong-doers and wrongly accused bystanders, have been meticulously preserved, and impart harrowing first-hand accounts of torture that prisoners inscribed into the walls. The inscriptions also include poems of protest, simple calendars, love letters, and self-portraits. The top floors exhibit stories and artifacts from Köln under the Third Reich.

✈ *U3, U4, U16, or U18: Appellhofpl., then follow the signs.* *i* *English explanations in the downstairs jail, but not in the upstairs exhibits. Audio tour €2.* Ⓢ *€3.60, students €1.50.* 🕐 *Open Tu-Su 11am-5pm.*

ARCHAEOLOGICAL SITES
MUSEUM

Kleine Budengasse 2 and Rathauspl.   ☎0221 221 23332 ▣www.museenkoeln.de

While World War II managed to destroy the city's Altstadt, reconstruction struck a silver lining and managed to unearth a wealth of buildings and artifacts from the city's Roman days. The **Praetorium** is the site of the former governor's mansion, dating back to first century, and you can take a walk through the ruins along the constructed bridge. Nearby, the **Archäologische Zone** is your chance to see a real-live archaeological site in action; a full-blown museum covering the site and its artifacts is planned for 2012. In the meantime, you're welcome to walk around the premises. In the middle of the Archäologische Zone under the glass pyramid is a Jewish **Mikvah,** a ritual bath, built in the 8th century.

✈ *From the plaza to the right side of the Dom, walk south down Unter Goldschmied and look to your left for the Praetorium. For the Archäologische Zone, continue south and look for the big white tent and the big hole in the ground by the Rathaus.* Ⓢ *Praetorium €2.50, students €1.50, under 18 free.* 🕐 *Praetorium open Tu-Su 10am-5pm. Last entry 30min. before close. Mikvah accessible with a key from the Praetorium box office (deposit required). Archäologische Zone only accessible on a guided tour every F 2pm, but tours are limited to 25 people so reserve in advance by calling ☎0221 221 33422 M-F 10am-noon.*

WALLRAF-RICHARTZ-MUSEUM
MUSEUM

Obenmarspforten   ☎0221 221 21119 ▣www.wallraf.museum

A stunning collection of works from medieval times to the mid-20th century are displayed in four high-ceilinged floors of this recently renovated museum. In 1998, the museum reached international headlines when it was discovered that one of their Monets, *On the Banks of the Seine by Port Villez*, was in fact a forgery. That said, the museum has five other (authentic) paintings by Monet, including an original of Monet's *Waterlilies*, one of the few in the world to be displayed in its original matte condition.

🏃 *From the Dom's right-hand plaza, walk south along Unter Goldschmied to museum on the left.* ℹ️ *All explanations in English.* 💲 *€9.50, students €7.50.* 🕐 *Open Tu-W 10am-6pm, Th 10am-10pm, F 10am-6pm, Sa-Su 11am-6pm.*

MUSEUM FÜR ANGEWANDTE KUNST
An der Rechtschule   ♠♿✺ MUSEUM
☎0221 221 26735 💻www.museenkoeln.de

This fascinating museum looks at the intersection between art and utility, displaying furniture, utensils, and other items from the Baroque to the present. Start your tour of the permanent collection upstairs, where the ornate patterns inherent to ancient articles eventually peter out to the simple, well-defined lines of the Jugendstil (Art Deco). Downstairs, follow the timeline as various art movements are juxtaposed around world events, and learn about the design evolution of radios, chairs, coffeemakers, and other everyday household items.

🏃 *With the Dom at your back, walk south along Unter Feltenhennen and turn right at the restaurant Campi am Funkhaus.* ℹ️ *All explanations in English.* 💲 *€4.20, students €2.60.* 🕐 *Open Tu-Su 11am-5pm.*

DUFTMUSEUM IM FARINA HAUS
Obenmarspforten 21   ♠⊗✺ MUSEUM
☎0221 3998994 💻www.farina.eu

The brand Farina probably suffered from a poor marketing department, which is why so few people have ever heard the name. However, they do have the distinction of actually being the *original* Eau de Cologne, no matter what 4711 claims. Concocted by John Maria Farina in 1709, the perfume had nearly 90 years of history before 4711 stole the show, and today the company is run by eighth-generation Farinas. This museum, with its comprehensive guided tours, gives a thorough introduction to the history of cologne, with an obvious bent on the scent created by Farina. Admission also includes a small sample of the perfume.

🏃 *Across the street from the Wallarf-Richartz Museum.* 💲 *€5.* 🕐 *Open M-Sa 10am-6pm, Su 11am-4pm, though the museum is often closed for private tours. Check the calendar on the website for the times of public English-language tours.*

GLOCKENGASSE 4711
Glockengasse 4   ♠⊗✺ MUSEUM, SHOP
☎0221 27 09 99 10 💻www.4711.com

No visit to Köln is complete without a visit to the company that turned the city name into a household one. The ingredients for 4711, known by its vintage turquoise and gold label that has remained unchanged over the years, were presented to its first manufacturer, Wilhelm Mühlens, on his wedding day in 1792. Once also prescribed as a potable curative containing 80% alcohol, today it is treasured merely for its scent, whose name comes from Mühlens's residence which had been re-christened "4711" under a Napoleonic order that assigned each house a unique number to make things easier for the occupying forces. The home now functions as a boutique, where a faux faucet fountain in the corner spews the scented water a-plenty and elegantly attired attendants dole out small samples. The tiny free museum also contains company artifacts, and the giant tapestry on the wall was made to commemorate the re-opening of the building in 1964. Stop by on the hour to listen to gimmicky chimes of the *glockenspiel*.

🏃 *U3 or U4: Appellhofpl., then walk through the Opern Passage and turn left onto Glockengasse.* 💲 *Free, though souvenirs will cost you plenty.* 🕐 *Open M-F 9am-7pm, Sa 9am-6pm.*

KÄTHE KOLLWITZ MUSEUM
Neumarkt 18-24   ◉♿✺ MUSEUM
☎0221 227 2899 💻www.kollwitz.de

The sketches and paintings of Käthe Kollwitz, a brilliant anti-war activist, depict the haunting sorrow and suffering of a world ravaged by war. After enjoying relative fame in the wake of the First World War, Kollwitz succumbed to forced obscurity in the wake of the Third Reich until her death in 1940. For 25 years, the Käthe Kollwitz Museum has sought to raise her oevure back into the limelight it deserves. Housed on the top floor of a bank, the museum contains over 270 of Kollwitz's drawings, 500 of her prints, and all of her posters and sculptures. Dark and deeply moving images chronicle the struggle of daily life and pains of personal loss against the stark black-and-white landscape of early 20th-century Berlin.

U1, U3, U4, U7, U9, U16, or U18: Neumarkt, then walk through the Neumarkt Passage to the elevator in the atrium and take it to the 4th floor. $ €3, students €1.50. ⏰ Open Tu-F 10am-6pm, Sa-Su 11am-6pm.

Altstadt-Sud

SCHOKOLADEN MUSEUM — MUSEUM

Am Schokoladenmuseum 1a ☎0221 931 88 80 💻www.schokoladenmuseum.de

Yes, it's every child's dream: a full-blown chocolate museum and factory! Yet beyond the demonstrations of how to make hollow chocolate balls and the mesmerizing packaging machine, the museum is surprisingly thorough and some sections even downright academic. The anthropologists will appreciate the numerous profiles of cocoa farmers, the activists the explanations of fair trade, and the economists the charts and figures of global chocolate price-setting. Much more than just a fun excuse to immerse yourself in chocolate, the museum is a great opportunity to learn just about everything (and then some) about your favorite food. Be sure to stop at the gold fountain, which spurts a stream of free samples.

Bus #106 to Schokoladen Mueum, or walk south along the Rhein past the Deute Brucke and turn left onto the small footbridge. i All explanations in English. $ €7.50, students €5. ⏰ Open Tu-F 10am-6pm, Sa-Su 11am-7pm. Last entry 1hr. before close.

DEUTSCHES SPORT AND OLYMPIA MUSEUM — MUSEUM

Im Zollhafen 1 ☎0221 33 60 90 💻www.sportsmuseum.info

Race through the history of German sportsmanship and the Olympic games in this interactive museum. Hands-on exhibits include a pommel horse, bicycle wind tunnel, boxing ring, and tiny turf soccer field on the roof. Extended exhibits also highlight the design and events of Germany's own Olympic games, 1936 in Berlin and 1972 in Munich. There's plenty of German memorabilia (think old sneakers and tennis racquets) displayed as well. No air conditioning means that it gets quite stuffy.

Bus #106 to Schokoladen Museum, or walk south along the Rhein past the Deute Brucke and turn left onto the small footbridge. The museum is behind the Schokoladen. i Labels in English. $ €6, students €3. ⏰ Open Tu-F 10am-6pm, Sa-Su 11am-7pm.

MUSEUM SCHNÜTGEN — MUSEUM

Cäcilienstr. 29-33 ☎0221 22 12 36 20 💻www.museenkoeln.de/museum-schnuetgen

This museum opened in a brand new space in October 2010, showcasing one of the world's largest collections of medieval art from the early Middle Ages to the end of the Baroque period. With over 5000 Romanesque and Gothic stone sculptures and 2000 works in silver, gold, ivory, and bronze, this museum is a bastion of ecclesiastical art from its very beginnings. Also included is an extensive collection of stained glass windows, tapestries, and priestly fashions.

U1, U3, U4, U7, U9, U16, or U18: Neumarkt, then head east a tiny bit on Cäcilienstr. $ €5, students €3. ⏰ Open Tu-W 10am-6pm, Th 10am-8pm, Su 10am-6pm.

Neustadt

The Romanesque period saw the construction of 12 churches in a semi-circle around the Altstadt, each containing the holy bones of saints to protect the city. Though dwarfed by the splendor of the Dom, these churches attest to the glory and immense wealth of what was once the most important city north of the Alps. The most memorable church, owing to its glorious imprints on the city skyline, is the **Groß St. Martin**. Near the Rathaus and the Altstadt, the church was re-opened in 1985 after near destruction in WWII. The interior is tiled with mosaics from the Middle Ages, and crypts downstairs house an esoteric collection of stones and diagrams *(An Groß St. Martin 9 ☎0221 257 79 24 Ⓢ Church free. Crypt €0.50. Ⓣ Open Tu-F 10am-noon and 3-5pm, Sa 10am-12:30pm and 1:30-5pm, Su 2-4pm).* In addition, **St. Ursula,** north of the Dom, commemorates Ursula's attempts to maintain celibacy despite her betrothal. This was easier after she was struck by an arrow in 383 AD during an untimely attack in the midst of a Hun siege. Relics and more than 700 skulls line the walls of the Goldene Kammer *(Ursulapl. 24 ☎ 0221 13 34 00 Ⓢ Church free. Kammer €1, children €0.50. Ⓣ Open M-Sa 10am-noon and 3-5pm, Su 3-4:30pm).* The other Romanesque churches include **St. Gereon** *(Gereonsdriesch 2-4),* **St. Cäcilien** *(Cäcilienstr. 29),* **St. Maria im Kapitol** *(Marienpl. 19),* **Alt St. Alban** *(Martinstr. 39),* **St. Maria** *(An Lyskirchen 10),* **St. Georg** *(Georgspl. 17),* **St. Pantaleon** *(An Pantaleonsberg 2),* **St. Severin** *(Im Ferkulum 29),* **St. Kunibert** *(Kunibertsklosterg. 2),* and **St. Apostein** *(Neumarkt 30).*

FOOD

Köln's local cuisine centers on sausage and *rievkooche*, slabs of fried potato to dunk in *apfelmus* (apple sauce). Don't pass through without sampling the city's smooth Kölsch beer, a local favorite whose shield adorns most bars. Local brews include Sion, Küppers, Früh, Gaffel, and Dom. They usually come in small 0.2L glasses for freshness, but don't worry—waiters are quick to refill. Cheap restaurants and cafes packed with students line the trendy **Zülpicher Str** *(U9, U12, U15: Zülpicher Platz).* Mid-priced ethnic restaurants are concentrated around the perimeter of the Altstadt, particularly from **Hohenzollernring** to **Hohenstaufenring**. For groceries, head to **Rewe City** *(Hohenstaufenring 30, by Zülpicher Pl. Ⓣ Open M-Sa 7am-midnight)* or **Aldi Süd** *(Richmodstr. 31, by Neumarkt. Ⓣ Open M-Sa 8am-8pm).*

Altstadt-Nord

▨ FRÜH AM DOM
Am Hof 18

🍴⅙🍸❄☂ GERMAN ❸
☎0221 2613-211 🖵www.frueh.de

It's enormous, it's right across the street from the Dom, and it's always filled with tourists, but even native Kölners will take their out-of-town guests to this massive beer hall for the epitome of the Köln experience. The excellent food is reasonably priced, and the terrace outside offers spectacular views of the Dom.

🍴 *By the south plaza of the Dom. Ⓢ Entrees €4.10-23. Kölsch €1.60. Ⓣ Open daily 8am-midnight.*

SUPASALAD
Getrudenstr. 33 or Friesenwall 7

🍴⅙ SALADS ❶
☎0176 2354 8413 🖵www.supasalad.de

The antithesis of meat-and-potato-packed German cuisine, Supasalad offers fast and healthy options for those looking for a wholesome meal. Choose from one of their pre-made options, or be creative and choose your own mix-ins. Don't miss their freshly pressed juices *(orange, apple, or carrot, €3-3.50).*

🍴 *Getrudenstr.: U1, U3, U4, U7, U9, U16, or U18: Neumarkt, then head in the direction of the St. Apostoles church and turn right onto Getrudenstr. Frisenwall: U3, U4, U5, U12, or U15: Friesen-platz, then head east on Magnusstr., turn left after Alex (restaurant). Ⓢ Salads €4.20-6.50. Panini €3.90-5.50. Ⓣ Open M-F 10am-8pm, Sa noon-8pm.*

köln . food (side tab)

PÄFFGEN-BRAUEREI
💳♿🍸⛅ GERMAN [3]

Friesenstr. 64-66 ☎0221 135461 💻www.paeffgen-koelsch.de

Legendary Kölsch *(€1.40)* brewed on the premises is enjoyed in cavernous halls that seat a whopping 600 people. The distant location from the Dom makes it a little less touristy, but don't expect to be only surrounded by locals. Try the house specialty, the pork knuckle (*schweinehaxe*), for an authentic experience.

🪧 U3, U4, U5, U12, or U15: Friesenpl. Head east on Magnusstr., turn left after Alex restaurant, and then right onto immediately onto Friesenstr. Ⓢ Entrees €8.20-20.50. ⏰ Open daily 11am-midnight.

CAFE STANTON
🚫♿ CAFE [3]

Schildergasse 57 ☎0221 271 0710 💻www.cafe-stanton.de

Located on a quiet side street by the cathedral, Cafe Stanton serves a Monday-Friday business lunch, a whopping entree of the day with a small drink *(€7.50)*. If the portions make you feel a little guilty, know that Cafe Stanton's meals are ecologically conscious. If you read German, check out the margins of the menu, which offer hilarious biographies of people whose names have become daily nouns. Stanton To-Go also offers cheap combo meals for those the run.

🪧 U1, U3, U4, U7, U9, U16, or U18: Neumarkt. Head east on Schildergasse toward Antoniterkirche. Ⓢ Entrees €9.80-18. ⏰ Open M-F 9:30am-1am, Sa 9am-1am, Su 10am-1am. Stanton To-Go open daily at 8am.

Altstadt

TOSCANINI
🚫⊗🍸 ITALIAN [2]

Jakobstr. 22 ☎0221 310 9990

Transport yourself to an Italian country villa with this restaurant, where your food comes out piping fresh from the stone oven. While stone oven pizzas are all the rage in Germany, there are few that do them as well as Toscanini's; try the Rustica *(€8.90)*, a delicious combination of cheeses, serrano ham, and arugula. The subdued ambience means it's nice enough for a date, but casual enough for jeans.

🪧 U3 or U4: Severinstr. Head south down Severinstr. and turn right onto Jakobstr. Ⓢ Entrees €5-20. ⏰ Open M-F noon-3pm and 6-11pm, Sa 6-11pm., Su noon-3pm and 6-11pm.

JONNY TURISTA
💳⊗🍸⛅ TAPAS [3]

Mauritiussteinweg 74 ☎0221 240 7055 💻www.jonny-turista.de

The name might be written in Cyrillic on the menu, but don't be confused—Jonny Turista is an all-out Spanish-style tapas bar. Bring a friend and order all the expensive tapas with the 3-for-€12.40 deal, and dine outdoors in the shadows of the grand Mauritiuskirche.

🪧 U9: Mauritiuskirche. Ⓢ Individual tapas €2-5.20. ⏰ Open daily 11am-late.

Neustadt

👍 HABIBI FALAFEL
🚫⊗🍸⛅ CAFE [1]

Zülpicherstr. 26 ☎0221 271 71 41 💻www.habibi-koeln.de

Cheap and hearty falafel *(€1.50)* and shawarma *(€3)* make this a popular student joint, especially on late nights after a few rounds of drinks. The falafel is always perfectly moist and the meat is perfectly juicy, and all entrees come with a free cup of tea.

🪧 U9, U12, or U15: Zülpicher Pl., then head down Zülpicherstr. to restaurant on right. Ⓢ Entrees €1.50-7.70. ⏰ Open M-Th 11am-1am, F-Sa 11am-3am, Su 11am-1am.

👍 BEI OMA KLEINMANN
🚫⊗🍸 CAFE [2]

Zülpicherstr. 9 ☎0221 23 23 46 💻www.beiomakleinmann.de

Though the dear Oma Kleinmann who founded this popular schnitzel joint passed away in 2009, her spirit lives on. The framed prints of photos and other memorabilia from the '50s attest to the restaurant's vintage character; a plaque of sorts to the left of the bar with names of students who have eaten the most schnitzel attests to the place's popularity. A convivial atmosphere permeates the restaurant, so come by for dinner and a few obligatory glasses of Kölsch.

U9, U12, or U15: Zülpicher Pl., then head down Zülpicherstr. to restaurant on left. ⑤ *Schnitzel €9.90-12.80. Kölsch €1.40.* ⏰ *Open Tu-Su 5pm-1am. Kitchen open 5-11pm.*

CAFE ORLANDO
●●⑧⁽ᵗ⁾ᵞ⏁ CAFE ❷
Engelbertstr. 9 ☎0221 42 34 84 03 ☐www.cafeorlando.de

This small cafe, decorated with a red-and-gold vintage French theme, is filled in the mornings with locals enjoying a lazy breakfast and the morning paper. Slow service make this a poor choice for frenzied see-it-all travelers, but a stop here for some coffee or a superbly fresh fruit bowl will not disappoint.

U9, U12, or U15: Zülpicher Pl., then head down Zülpicher Pl. and turn right onto Engelbertstr. *i* *Free Wi-Fi.* ⑤ *Breakfast €3.30-7.50. Omelettes €5.50-5.80. Pasta entrees €5.50-6.80* ⏰ *Open daily 9am-midnight.*

BARISTA
●⑧ᵞ⏁ CAFE ❶
Kyffhäuserstr. 50 ☎0221 27 16 20 31 ☐www.barista-koeln.de

These down-to-earth coffee snobs will brew you the best cup of joe in Köln, hands down. They take their coffee seriously here. Their breakfast options are surprisingly limited; stop by for some delicious lunchtime pasta instead and use the coffee as an afternoon jolt.

U9: Dasselstr./Bf Süd, then head down Kyffhäuserstr. ⑤ *Entrees €5-6.* ⏰ *Open M-F 9:15am-9pm, Sa 9am-5pm.*

CAFE FEYNSINN
●⑧ᵞ⏁ CAFE ❷
Rathenauplatz 7 ☎0221 240 92 10 ☐www.cafe-feynsinn.de

You can be sure that anything you eat here is organic, fair-trade, and delicious. The owners of this upbeat cafe take pride in doing their part for the economy and the environment; they even traveled to Mexico to visit the farm from where they get their coffee beans.

U9: Dasselstr./Bf Süd, then walk down Meister-Gerhard-Str. for 1 block. ⑤ *Entrees €6-10.* ⏰ *Open M-F 9am-1am, Sa 9:20am-2am, Su 10am-1am.*

GANESHA
●⑧ᵞ⏁ INDIAN ❸
Händelstr. 26 ☎0221 21 31 65 ☐www.ganesha-restaurant.de

This elaborately draped restaurant offers the full spectrum of well-spiced Indian specialties. The *naan*, which comes in five different variations, is thin and crispy rather than thick and chewy. Wash down your meal with some creamy and delicious chai *(€1.80, with honey €1.90)*.

U1, U7, U12, or U15: Rudolfpl., then take Aachenerstr. west and take the 1st left onto Händelstr. ⑤ *Entrees €6.90-14.90.* ⏰ *Open M 6pm-midnight, Tu-Su 12:30pm-3pm and 6pm-midnight. Kitchen open until 30min. before close.*

NIGHTLIFE

For a good time, head over to the Neustadt for your nightlife adventures; the closer to the Rhein or Dom you venture, the faster your wallet will empty and the more tourists you're likely to encouter. After dark in Hohenzollernring, crowds of people move from theaters to clubs and finally to cafes in the early hours of the morning. Students congregate in the **Bermuda-Dreleck** (Bermuda Triangle), bounded by **Zülpicherplatz, Roonstr.,** and **Luxemburgstr.** The center of gay nightlife runs up **Matthiasstr.** to **Mülhenbach, Hohe Pforte, Marienplatz,** and up to the **Heumarkt** area by **Deutzer Brücke.** Radiating westward from Friesenpl., the **Belgisches Viertel** (Belgian Quarter) is dotted with more expensive bars and cafes.

Kölners will often visit four or five establishments in one night, and true to their wanderlust nature, a favorite pasttime includes grabbing bottles of beer at

Köln · nightlife

the numerous small **kiosks** that dot the streets, walking and drinking, then refilling at another kiosk. On summer nights, the **Brüsslerplatz** area in the shadow of the St. Michael Church is always packed with students on the prowl, with rowdiness that the city has imposed heavy fines against (look for the PSCHT! sign).

Alstadt-Nord

🏛 GLORIA ⬧♿♈❄♘▼ BAR, CLUB, CAFE, THEATER

Apostelnstr. 11 ☎0221 66 06 30 🖥www.gloria-theater.com

A former movie theater, this popular local cafe, comedy theater, and occasional club is at the nexus of Köln's trendy gay and lesbian scene. Call or visit the website for a schedule of themed parties, which alternate between gay and mixed.

✈ *U1, U3, U4, U7, U9, U16, or U18: Neumarkt, then walk west toward the St. Apostein cathedral and follow Apostelnstr. as it curves to the right.* ⑤ *Cover €7-30, may include show ticket. Beer €1.60-4.70. Cocktails €6.50.* ⧖ *Open M-Sa 10am-11pm, until 5am on party nights. General ticket office open M-F noon-6pm.*

P9 ⬤⊗♈♘▼ BAR, CLUB

Pipinstr. 9 ☎0221 99 67 69 10 🖥www.p9cologne.de

At P9, the party never stops, literally. With its 23-hour schedule, this is the where the city's young gay and lesbian population end up at 6am when all the other bars close. That's not to say, though, that it doesn't enjoy a lively scene when everything else is open, either. A downstairs disco plays all the hottest beats on Friday and Saturday nights after 10pm, while the ground floor bar is always packed.

✈ *U1, U7, U9: Heumarkt.* ⑤ *Beer €1.40-3. Cocktails €6.* ⧖ *Open daily 6am-5am.*

ZUM PITTER ⬤⊗♈♘▼ BAR

Alter Markt 58-60 ☎0221 258 31 22 🖥www.zum-pitter-cologne.de

Warm evenings bring a primarily gay crowd to the outside patio of this easygoing pub, especially on weekends. During the week, the crowd sitting inside the dramatically red interior, complete with suggestive photographs of male figures, is mostly older, but the mean age lowers during peak times.

✈*In the northeastern end of the Alter Markt, halfway between the Dom and Heumarkt.* ⑤ *Beer €1.60-3. Cocktails €6.50-7.* ⧖ *Open daily noon-1am.*

Neustadt

🏛 DAS DING ⬤⊗♈ CLUB

Hohenstaufenring 30-32 ☎0221 24 63 48 🖥www.dingzone.de

This smoky, eclectic student bar and disco has dirt-cheap specials *(often under €1, F-Sa 10-11pm)* and themed parties parties. The required student ID at the door keeps the age down and the party hopping.

✈ *U9, U12, or U15: Zülpicher Pl.* ⑤ *Cover €3-5. Almost all drinks under €3.* ⧖ *Open Tu 9pm-3am, W 9pm-2am, Th 10pm-3am, F-Sa 10pm-4am.*

🏛 DIE WOHNGEMEINSCHAFT ⬧⊗♈❄ CLUB

Richard-Wagner-Str. 39 ☎0221 39 75 77 18 🖥www.die-wohngemeinschaft.net

Meet your newest housemates, and sit in the rooms of Annabel, Mai Li, Easy, and JoJo at this novelty club, meant to give 20-somethings the nostalgia of dorms and shared apartments. Annabel's cutesy white bed with floral sheets is the perfect setting for a girl-talk, while Mai Li's room has a ping pong table where you can practice her favorite hobby, and the backseat of JoJo's vintage mini-bus is the perfect place for a bit of privacy (ahem).

✈ *U1, U7, U12, or U15: Rudolfpl., then walk south 1 block to Richard-Wagner-Str. and head west.* ⑤ *Beer €1.60. Mixed drinks €5-6.* ⧖ *Open daily 3pm-2am.*

HOTELUX ⬤⊗♈ BAR

Rathenauplatz 22 ☎0221 24 11 36 🖥www.hotelux.de

This hipster bar swathed in red Soviet decor proves that you can indeed get great vodka in Germany. Quirky shots mix the finest of liquors with a variety of add-ins, from strawberry to chili. For a real trip, wash down a chili shot with a honey shot, and savor the salvation that the sweetness brings.

🚇 U9, U12, or U15: Zülpicher Pl., then head down Zülpicherstr. and turn right onto Heinsbergstr. Turn left and right again around the park to bar on the left. $ Shots €2.60-3.80. Cocktails €4.80-6.10. ⏰ Open daily 8pm-late.

SIX PACK 🍸 BAR

Aachener Str. 33 ☎0221 25 45 87 🖥www.gottes.de

Forget taps—here, the beer comes in bottles perfectly lined in the supermarket-style glass refrigerators behind the bar. If you can, plop yourself down on the comfortably worn leather seats, but be warned—this place gets majorly crowded around midnight.

🚇 U1 or U7: Moltkestr., then head east down Aachenerstr. to bar on right. $ Beer €2.60-3. Mixed drinks €6-7.50. ⏰ Open M-Th 8pm-3am, F-Sa until 8am, Su 8pm-3am.

CENT CLUB 🍸 CLUB

Hohenstaufenring 25-27 ☎0221 946 35 42 🖥www.centclub.de

A student disco, the bar features more dance and less talk, with the appeal of enticingly inexpensive drinks. Party under the groovy orange lights and watch the hours zoom by.

🚇 U9, U12, or U15: Zülpicher Pl. $ Cover €3-5, W 9-10pm free. Beer €1-1.80. Cocktails €3. ⏰ Open W-Sa 9pm-late.

GOTTES GRÜNE WIESE 🍸 BAR

Bismarckstr. 53 ☎0221 500 83 53 🖥www.gottesgruenewiese.de

This bar is all about sports played on "God's Green Fields." Yet far from being the stereotypical American sports bar with peanut shells strewn on the floor, this one exudes style, with its leather seats and purple walls. In fact, when games aren't being projected on the back wall, the bar resembles any other upscale bar, but that's no fun—go during a major game and cheer on your favorite team.

🚇 U1 or U7: Moltkestr., then head north on Moltkestr. for 3 blocks. $ Beer €1.50-3.30. Cocktails €5.40-7.50. ⏰ Open daily 6pm-3am.

CAFE MAGNUS ♿🍸 BAR

Zülpicherstr. 48 ☎0221 241469 🖥www.cafemagnus.de

A family-friendly cafe by day, this joint turns into a full-blown bar on weekend nights, with the large drinks menu and cheap and hearty eats making it ideal for groups. Come after 10pm for €4 pizza, pasta, and salads, or join the legions of old friends reconnecting over a scrumptious brunch buffet on Sundays *(€10.80 per person)*.

*🚇 U9: Dasselstraße/Bf Süd. **i** Happy hour daily 6:30-8pm; cocktails €5.50, 10pm-2am €4.50. $ Beer €2.10-2.60. Cocktails €6.50-8.50. ⏰ Open M 9am-1am, Tu-Th 9am-2am, F-Sa 9am-4am, Su 9am-1am.*

ARTS AND CULTURE

Köln explodes with festivity during **Karneval** *(late Jan-early Feb)*, a week-long pre-Lenten "farewell to flesh." Celebrated in the hedonistic spirit of the city's Roman past, Karneval is made up of 50 neighborhood processions in the weeks before Ash Wednesday. The festivities kick off with **Weiberfastnacht** *(Mar 1, 2011; Feb 28, 2012)*, where the mayor mounts the platform at Alter Markt and abdicates city leadership to the city's *Weiber* (a regional, untranslatable, and unabashedly politically incorrect term for women). In a demonstration of power, women then traditionally find their husbands at work and chop off their ties. In the afternoon, the first of the big parades begins at **Severinstor.** The weekend builds up to the out-of-control parade on **Rosenmontag,** the last Monday before **Lent** *(Mar. 7, 2011; Mar. 5, 2012)*. Everyone dresses in costume and gives and gets a couple dozen *Bützchen* (*Kölsche* dialect for a kiss on the cheek).

While most revelers nurse their hangovers on **Shrove Tuesday,** pubs and restaurants set fire to straw scarecrows hanging out of their windows.

For shows, get your tickets from **KölnTicket** *(☎0221 2801 🖥www.koelnticket.de),* which has multiple locations throughout the city, most notably in the basement of the **Tourist Office** in the same building as the **Römisch-Germanisches Museum.**

cheaper melodies

Over the summer, free organ concerts take place every Tuesday night at 8pm and often include performances by guest artists from all around the world. It's always guaranteed to be packed so come at least half an hour early to get a seat. For other concerts in the Dom, visit 🖥www.koelner-dommusik.de.

OPER DER STADT KÖLN AND KÖLNER SCHAUSPIELHAUS 💳♿❄ OPERA, THEATER

Offenbachpl. ☎0221 22 12 84 00 🖥www.buehnenkoeln.de

These two venues, part of the same complex, form Köln's cultural center and are home to the city's opera and theater companies. Both are under plans for major renovation to begin sometime in the next few years, but don't worry—the companies will just move to alternate venues.

🚊 U3 or U4: Appellhofpl. $ Open €10-70, students €10 or 50% off. Schauspielhaus €9-33, students €6. ⏰ Box office open M-F 10:30am-7pm, Sa 11am-4pm.

KÖLN PHILHARMONIE 💳♿❄ ORCHESTRA

Bischofsgartenstr. 1 ☎0221 221 20 40 80 🖥www.koelner-philharmonie.de

This amphitheater is home to the Köln's very own symphony orchestra. During the normal season, come by on Thursdays at 12:30pm for PhilharmonieLunch, a free 30min. concert. When the orchestra goes on break over the summer, the Kölner Sommerfestival takes over, staging opera and popular musicals on tour.

🚊 Behind the Römisch-Germanisches Museum and Museum Ludwig. $ Prices vary for each concert; students get a 25% discount. Tickets includes local public transportation 4hr. before and 4hr. after the concert.

SHOPPING

Köln's main touristy shopping street is the **Hohe Strasse,** running parallel to the Rhein a few blocks inland, where the narrow pedestrian street is lined with miniature versions of international chains. A mix of larger luxury and department stores can be found on the wider pedestrian zones at **Schildergasse** and **Mittelstrasse** around Neumarkt.

GLOBETROTTER AUSRÜSTUNG 💳♿❄ OUTDOOR EQUIPMENT

Richmodstr. 10 ☎0221 277 28 80 🖥www.globetrotter.de

Ever buy a waterproof jacket only to realize that it wasn't actually waterproof? At this four-story wilderness superstore, you'll never have to worry about that. You can don your prospective raincoat and take it through the rain room, where water pours from the ceiling, or try on a parka in the ice-cold cooling chamber. A glass bouldering tunnel is there for your future climbing shoes, and a big pool in the basement lets you paddle around in your dream kayak.

🚊 U1, U3, U4, U7, U9, U16, or U18: Neumarkt, then head north on Zeppelinstr. ⏰ Open M-Th 10am-8pm, F-Sa 10am-9pm.

SATURN 🎧♿❄ MUSIC, ELECTRONICS

Maybachstr. 115 ☎0221 161 60 🖥www.saturn.de

This branch of the German electronics chain claims to have the world's largest music collection, with over a million CDs and 300 listening stations. Test it out for yourself and see if you can find the most obscure record you can think of in this megastore.

🚇 U12 or U15: Hansaring, then look for the giant tower with the Saturn logo. ⏰ Open M-Sa 10am-8pm.

ENGLISH BOOKS AND TEA 🌍♿ BOOKS

Auf dem Rothenberg 9a ☎0221 992 81 02 💻www.englishbooksandtea.de

Forget chains like Thalia and Mayersche—for books in English, visit this charming shop right by the Gross St. Martin. The tight space is laden with new and used bestsellers and classics, with an especially large selection of paperback mysteries and science fiction. Grab yourself one of the black leather seats and ask for a cup of real English tea as you browse through some of your favorites.

🚇 U1, U7, or U9: Heumarkt, then walk toward the Rhein (by the Maredo restaurant) and turn left onto Auf dem Rothenberg. ⏰ Open M-F 11:30am-8pm, Sa 11am-6:30pm.

ESSENTIALS

Practicalities

wil-köln-en

The Köln WelcomeCard, available at the tourist office, hotels, and from travel agents, gives you discounts to a number of sights and includes free public transportation throughout the city. A 24-hour pass is €9, and more expensive options can also get you transport coverage into other regions outside of Köln.

- **TOURIST OFFICE: KölnTourismus.** *(Kardinal-Höffner-Platz 1, right across from the Dom. ☎0221 221 💻www.cologne-tourism.de ℹ The basement contains a souvenir shop and a Ticket Office. Several companies have hop-on hop-off bus tours for about €15; inquire in the tourist office. $ City maps (€0.20) and guides (€0.50) and books rooms for a €3 fee. Do-it-yourself 1.5hr.* **iGuide** *€8 per 4hr. English-language walking tour €9, students €7. ⏰ Open M-Sa 9am-8pm, Su 10am-5pm, to 6pm in summer. 1.5hr. English-language walking tour every Sa at 1pm.)*
- **BUDGET TRAVEL: STA Travel.** *(Zülpicher Str. 178 ☎0221 44 20 11 🚇 U9: Universität. ℹ Sells ISICs and books flights. ⏰ Open M-F 10am-7pm, Sa 11am-3pm.)*
- **CURRENCY EXCHANGE: Reisebank.** *(In the Hauptbahnhof. ⏰ Open daily 7am-10pm.)* Inside the tourist office is also **Exchange.** *(⏰ Open M-F 9am-6pm, Sa 9am-4pm.)*
- **WOMEN'S RESOURCES: Frauenamt.** *(Markmannsgasse 7 ☎0221 26482 ⏰ Open M-F 8am-4pm, Tu 8am-6pm, F 8am-midnight.)*
- **ROOM SHARE: Zeitwohnen** arranges furnished apartments for 1 month to 3 years. *(Konrad-Adenauer-Str. 4 ☎0221 8002340 💻www.zeitwohnen.de ⏰ Office open M-F 9am-6pm.)*
- **LAUNDROMAT: Eco-Express Waschsalon.** *(At the corner of Richard-Wagner-Str. and Händelstr. $ Wash 6-10am €1.90, 10am-11pm €2.50. Soap €0.50. Dry €0.50 per 10min. ⏰ Open M-Sa 6am-11pm.)*
- **GLBT RESOURCES: SchwIPS Checkpoint.** *(Pininstr. 7, just around the corner from Hotel Timp. ☎0221 92 57 68 11 💻www.checkpoint-koeln.de ℹ* **Emergency helpline.** *☎0221 19228. ⏰ Open W-Th 5-9pm, F-Sa 2-7pm, Su and holidays 2-6pm.)*
- **INTERNET ACCESS:** Most cafes have free wireless, including the **Starbucks** in the Hauptbahnhof. **Gigabyte.** *(Across the street from the Hauptbahnhof. $ 24hr.*

internet terminals €2.79 per hr. Wireless €0.50 per hr.)

- **POST OFFICE:** *(Trankgasse 11, right by the Hauptbahnhof. ⏰ Open M-Sa 7am-10pm, Su 8am-10pm.)*
- **POSTAL CODE:** 50667.

Emergency!

- **POLICE** ☎110.
- **FIRE AND AMBULANCE:** ☎112.
- **PHARMACY: Dom Apotheke.** *(In the courtyard between the Dom and the Hauptbahnhof. ⏰ Open M-F 8am-8pm, Sa 9am-8pm.)*

Getting There

By Plane

Köln-Bonn Flughafen. *(Halfway between Köln and Bonn. The S13 runs between the Köln Hauptbahnhof and the airport every 20-30min. 💻www.koeln-bonn-airport.de* ***i*** *Flight information ☎02203 4040 0102.)*

By Train

The Köln **Hauptbahnhof** is centrally located right by the Dom in the Altstadt-Nord. Trains to: **Berlin** *($ €60-115. ⏰ 5-8hr., 1-2 per hr.);* **Frankfurt** *($ €30-90. ⏰1-3hr., 2 per hr.);* **Bonn** *($ €7-12. ⏰ 0.25-1hr., 4-5 per hr.);* **Munich** *($ €70-150. ⏰ 5hr., 2 per hr.);* **Amsterdam, NED** *($€30-55. ⏰ 3-4hr., 2 per hr.);* **Brussels, BEL** *($ €40-80. ⏰ 2-4hr., 13 per day);* **London, GBR** *($ €70-130. ⏰ 5hr., 7 per day);* **Basel, CHE** *($ €60-140. ⏰ 4-6hr., 1 per hr.);* **Vienna, AUT** *($ €60-180. ⏰ 8-12hr., 1 per hr.).*

Getting Around

By Public Transport

Köln's buses, trams, and subways are served by the KVB, or Kölner Verkehrs-Betriebe *(💻www.kvb-koeln.de)*. A short ride (less than 4 stops) is €1.60, kids 6-14 €0.90. A ride anywhere in the city is €2.40, kids €1.20, and the prices increase with farther distance. You can also get 4 tickets at a time for a cheaper price *(€8.60, kids €4.50)*, or get a day ticket *(€7.10, €10.40 for up to 5 people)*. Validate your tickets at the start of your trip by getting them stamped in the rectangular box. If you're caught without a ticket, you face an immediate €40 fine.

By Ferry

Köln-Düsseldorfer. *(☎0221 2088318 💻www.k-d.com* ***i*** *Boats leave from the dock in the Altstadt halfway between the Deutzer and Hohenzollern bridges. Offers trips up and down the Rhein. $ A trip all the way to the end at Mainz is €52.50, with return €58.50. Trips to Bonn €12.80/€14.90. Students ½-price with ID. 1hr. panoramic cruises up and down the Rhein along the Köln area €7.80 per person. 2hr. afternoon cruises €11.10. ⏰ 1hr. panoramic cruises daily Apr-Oct at 10:30am, noon, 2, and 6pm. 2hr. afternoon cruises leave at 3:30pm.)*

By Gondola

Kölner Seilbahn sells gondolas trips on the Rhein from the Zoo to the Theinpark across the river. *(Rhiehlerstr. 180, U18: Zoo/Flora. ☎0221 547 4184 💻www.koelner-seilbahn.de $ €4, children ages 4-12 €2.40; round trip €6/3.50. ⏰ Open Apr-Oct daily 10am-6pm.)*

By Bike

Kölner Fahrradverleih rents bikes. *(Makmannsgasse, in the Altstadt. ☎0171 629 87 96 💻www.koelnerfahrradverleih.de $ €2 per hr., €10 per day, €40 per week. ⏰ Open daily 10am-6pm.)*

By Car

Ride Share: CityNetz Mitfahrzentrale. *(Maximinenstr. 2. ☎0221 19444 ⏰ Open M-F 9am-6pm, Sa-Su 10am-2pm.)*

bonn ☎0228

Known derisively for the past 50 years as the *Hauptdorf* (capital village), Bonn (pop. 319,800) was basically a non-entity before falling into the limelight by chance. Konrad Adenauer, the Federal Republic's first chancellor, resided in the suburbs, and the occupying Allied powers made Bonn the "provisional capital" of the Western Occupation Zone before naming it capital of the fledgling Republic. Today, the Bundestag stands as a vestige of bygone years. The summer of 1991 brought headlines of "Chaos in Bonn" as Berlin fought to reclaim the seat of government, but Berlin won by the narrowest of margins, and in 1999, the Bundestag packed up and moved east. Though Berliners joke that Bonn is "half the size of a Berlin cemetery and twice as dead," it has the perfect combination of history and progressive optimism, with a sparkling Altstadt and a forward-thinking university.

ACCOMMODATIONS

In case you haven't gotten your fill of Bonn's lovely museums, spend an extra night at one of the smaller hotels in town; the HI hostel *(Jugendgästehaus Bonn-Venusberg, Haager Weg 42 ☎0228 28 99 70 ▣www.bonn.jugendherberge.de)* is located about 20min. outside of the city, so you might as well spend just a little extra getting a room closer to the sights. These two hotels are located right next to each other and are usually filled with business travelers during the week, so make sure to book early.

DEUTSCHES HAUS
✦⊗⊗ HOTEL ❸

Kasernenstr. 19-21   ☎0228 633 777 ▣ www.hotel-deutscheshaus.net

On a quiet residential street connecting busy squares (Münsterpl. and Berlinerpl.), this value hotel offers lightly furnished rooms with TVs. Enjoy breakfast in a tulip-filled room.

✠ *U61, U65: Wilhelmsplatz, then walk south along Kölnstr. and turn right onto Kasernenstr.* **i** *Breakfast included. Wi-Fi €1 per hr., €1.80 per 2hr.* ⓢ *Singles €35-79; doubles €65-91; triples €110-130.* ⓩ *Reception 5am-midnight. Check-in noon. Check-out 11am.*

HOTEL BERGMANN
⊛⊗⊗ PENSION ❸

Kasernenstr. 13   ☎0228 633 891

Next to Deutsches Haus, this hotel offers elegant accommodations in four well-decorated rooms of a 19th-century home.

✠ *U61 or U65: Wilhelmsplatz, then walk south along Kölnstr. and turn right onto Kasernenstr.* **i** *Breakfast included. Free Wi-Fi.* ⓢ *Singles €35; doubles €60.* ⓩ *Reception by appointment (reserve in advance). Arrange check-in and check-out at reservation.*

SIGHTS

Bonn is a museum-lovers' paradise. In addition to the ones listed below, the **Museum Alexander König** *(☎0228 912 20 ▣www.zfmk.de* ✠ *Adenauerallee 160* ⓢ *€3, students €1.50.* ⓩ *Open Tu-Su 10am-6pm, W until 9pm)* is Bonn's natural history museum, with taxidermy galore in recreated "natural" habitats, and the **Frauenmuseum** *(Im Krausfeld 10 ☎0228 69 13 44 ▣www.frauenmuseum.de* ⓢ *€4.50, students €3.* ⓩ *Open Tu-Sa 2-6pm, Su 11am-6pm)* is the first and still the only museum in Germany that celebrates the lives and works of women.

🖾 BEETHOVENHAUS
✦⊗❀ MUSEUM

Bonngasse 20   ☎0228 981 7525 ▣www.beethoven-haus-bonn.de

Attracting music aficionados of all sorts, Beethoven's birthplace hosts a fantastic collection of the composer's personal effects, with over 1000 manuscripts, primitive hearing aids, and his first viola. The Haus also hosts the annual Beethoven Festival *(mid-Sept-mid-Oct)*. The first fête, in 1845, was a riot—**Franz Liszt** brawled with French nationalist **Louis Berlioz** while King Ludwig's mistress

Lola Montez table-danced. Besides the artifacts, a digital studio, with computers and headphones for guest use, provides access to numerous digital scores and recordings, along with the chance to send some musical e-cards to friends. In the basement, the Stage for Musical Visualization depicts characters and scenes from Beethoven's opera *Fidelio* as psychedelic dots and waves on a three-D stage; don the glasses and use the interactive portals to move the characters around.

🪧 U62, U65, U66, or U67: Beethovenhaus. i An included brochure explains most exhibits. Audio tour €2. $ €5, students €4. ⏰ Open Apr-Oct M-Sa 10am-6pm, Su 11am-6pm; Nov-Mar M-Sa 10am-5pm, Su 11am-5pm. Last entry 25min. before close.

👍 HAUS DER GESCHICHTE (MUSEUM OF HISTORY) 🎟♿❄ MUSEUM

Willy-Brandt-Allee 14 ☎0228 9165 212 💻www.hdg.de/bonn

Beginning in the broken landscape of 1945 and culminating in a chronicle of modern issues, this museum studies a nation grappling with its past and future. Along the way, enjoy the artful exhibits, including Konrad Adenauer's first Mercedes, rubble from the Berlin Wall, the first German green card granted to a foreigner, and a genuine moon rock.

🪧 U16, U63, U66, U67, or U68: Heussallee/Museumsmeile. i Explanations only in German. English audio tour, free with deposit. English guidebook €6. $ Free. ⏰ Open Tu-Su 9am-7pm.

BONNER MÜNSTER 🎟♿❄ CHURCH

Willy-Brandt-Allee 14 ☎0228 9858815 💻www.bonner-muenster.de

Three stories of arches within arches yield to a gorgeous gold-leaf mosaic inside this impressive basilica. A 12th-century cloister is laced with crossways and passages branching off under the doorway labeled Kreuzgang. Keep an eye out for the incongruous blue-red windows, designed by Expressionist Heinrich Campendonk.

🪧 From the Hauptbahnhof, go straight ahead and turn right at In der Sürst. $ Free. ⏰ Open daily 7am-9pm, with breaks for mass. Cloister open M-Sa 10am-5:30pm, Su 1-5:30pm.

KUNSTMUSEUM BONN 🎟♿❄ MUSEUM

Friedrich-Ebert-Allee 2 ☎0228 776260 💻www.kunstmuseum-bonn.de

Unveiled in 1992, this immense building designed by Berlin architect Axel Schultes houses an impressive collection of 20th-century German art. Highlights include the genre-defying canvases by Richter, cameo works by Warhol and Duchamp, and an extensive selection of oils and sketches by local Expressionist August Macke.

🪧 U16, U63, U66, U67, or U68: Heussallee/Museumsmeile. i Explanations only in German. English audio tour (free with deposit) or an English guidebook €6. $ €7, students €3.50. ⏰ Open Tu 11am-6pm, W 11am-9pm, Th-Su 11am-6pm.

KUNST UND AUSSTELLUNGSHALLE 🎟♿❄ MUSEUM

Friedrich-Ebert-Allee 4 ☎0228 91710 💻www.bundeskunsthalle.de

This modern hall has no permanent art collection. Scheduled shows vary widely, and the hall hosts films, concerts, and theatrical performances. The striking building is a defining element of the Bonn skyline with its three sharp cone spires and 16 columns flanking the Ausstellungshalle, designed to represent Germany's federal states.

🪧 U16, U63, U66, U67, or U68: Heussallee/Museumsmeile. $ Single exhibit €8, students €5. All three exhibits €14/9. All exhibits €5 the last 2hr. before close. ⏰ Open Tu-W 10am-9pm, Th-Su 10am-7pm, last entry 30min. before close.

ARITHMEUM 🎟♿❄ MUSEUM

Lennéstr. 2 ☎0228 73 87 90 💻www.arithmeum.uni-bonn.de

The Arithmeum displays a hands-on history of calculators with detailed explanations of how each thing works. Finagle your way with Napier's rods, try your hand at Pascal's adding machine, and scratch your head trying to figure out how Poleni's weighted wheel machine works. The sheer size of those old calculators will make you grateful for your trusty pocket-sized TI-83. Also on display are pieces of modern art and, on the other end of the spectrum, silicon chips.

*U16, U63, U66, U67, or U68: Juridicum, then head north on Adenauerallee and turn left onto Am Hofgarten. **i** English explanations available from the placards in the red bins. $ €3, students €2. ⏰ Open Tu-Su 11am-6pm.*

FOOD

For some fresh meats and veggies, head to the Markt at the Rathausplatz, which teems with haggling vendors and determined customers. At the end of the day, voices rise and prices plummet *(Open M-Sa 8am-6pm)*. Also in the Markt is the **Bönnsche Imbiss** *(open M-F 5pm-9pm, Sa 11:30am-7pm, Su 1pm-7pm)*, Bonn's tastiest currywurst *(with fries, €2.20)*. For a really cheap eat, head to **Sterntor Snack** *(Vivatsgasse 12, by the Sterntor)* for some filling 50-cent slices of pizza.

CARL'S MENSA-BISTRO — CAFETERIA ❶

Nassestr. 15

Cheap restaurant-quality meals are served here right next to the university's cafeteria, and is always populated by students looking for deals. Daily specials, rotating weekly Mondays through Thursdays, have generous servings *(€3-4)*.

U61 or U62: Königstr., then head northeast on Königstr. and turn right onto Kaiserstr.; restaurant is at the intersection of Kaiserstr. and Nasserstr. $ Entrees €3.20-4.70. ⏰ Open M-Th 10:30am-4:30pm, F 10:30am-3pm. Kitchen open M-Th 11am-4pm, F 11am-2:45pm.

CAFE BLAU — ♿ ❄ CAFE, BAR ❷

Franziskanerstr. 9 ☎0228 650717

During mealtimes, crowds of students spill onto the streets outside this turquoise cafe that plays electronic, funk, and soul. If you can get the attention of the waitstaff, you can have your fill of tasty pasta and fresh salad *(€3-6)*. A curtained disco provides a great dance venue.

U16, U63, U66, U67, or U68: Universität or Markt. $ Entrees €4.70-8. Beer €2.30-4. Mixed drinks €5.50-6. ⏰ Open daily 9am-1am.

BIERHAUS MACHOLD — ♿ ❄ GERMAN ❷

Heerstr. 52 ☎0228 9637877 🖳www.bierhaus-machold.com

Located deep within the Altstadt, the Bierhaus Machold is a well-kept local secret. The microbrewery churns out its own beer, which you can sample *(0.25L €2.40)*; the default is the *Dunkles*, but the *Hausspezialität* is lighter and milder. Even better than the beer, if that's possible, is the food, which comes on heaping platters with delicious sauces. Try the *Kutscherpfännchen*, three juicily grilled pork medallions in a mushroom garlic sauce. For the homesick, the burgers are a quite delicious cure.

U61 or U65: Rosenplatz, then head down Heerstr. $ Entrees €8.40-22.90. ⏰ Open M-Sa 5pm-1am, Su 10am-midnight.

OPATIJA — ♿ ❄ CROATIAN ❸

Friedrichstr. 27 ☎0228 638555

Dine in the shadow of the St.-Remigius-Kirche, the site of Beethoven's first organ gig when he was just 10-years-old, at this Croatian restaurant. The soft-spoken waiters hand out the amazing Croatian and German specialities as if you were a long lost family member. The entrees all come with use of the well-stocked salad bar, a respite from the meat-and-potatoes German diet. The *Ćevapčići*, Croatian "sausages" served with fries, are especially tender and delicious.

U62, U65, U66, or U67: Beethovenhaus, then take Wenzelgasse south and turn left at the church plaza. $ Entrees €9.50-22.50. ⏰ Open daily 11am-midnight.

ESSENTIALS

Practicalities

- **TOURIST OFFICES:** The tourist office hands out free maps and offers self-guided mp3 walking tours of the city. *(☎0228 77 5000 🖥www.bonn-region.de ✈ Windeckstr. 1, off Münsterpl. near the Münsterbasilika ⏰ Open M-F 9am-6:30pm, Sa 9am-4pm, Su 10am-2pm.)* The **Bonn Regio WelcomeCard** offers public transit within Bonn as well as free admission or discounts at a multitude of museums *(€9 for 1 day).*

Getting There and Getting Around

Bonn and Köln are bound by the same public transit system, and tickets between the two cities in the local system cost €6.60. **U16** and **U18** connect Köln's Neumarket to Bonn's Hauptbahnhof, taking about an hour; faster trains taking half an hour between the two cities' Hauptbahnhofs run approximately every 20min. Once there, rides on the system cost the same as rides in Köln. Or, consider renting a bike from the **Radstation** by the Hauptbahnhof. *(☎0228 981 4636 $ €7.50 per day. ⏰ Open M-F 6am-10:30pm, Sa 7am-10:30pm, Su 8am-10:30pm.)*

düsseldorf ☎0211

Düsseldorf—a destination for art lovers and barhoppers alike—is perhaps most frequently visited by travelers en route to Amsterdam, Belgium, or larger German cities. Located on the Rhein River, Düsseldorf attracts the diversity and the wealth that comes with being a port city. Nowhere are those attributes as tastefully displayed as in the Altstadt, the city's "Old Side," where ethnic eateries compete with fresh seafood restaurants and wild pubs for space. An incredibly progressive art scene has sprung up along the banks of the Rhein, where world-class exhibits rotate through some of Germany's best modern and contemporary art museums. If canvas and sculpture aren't your thing, you might enjoy yourself better perusing Düsseldorf's hundreds of small, pricey boutiques—tiny triumphs of excess and style.

ORIENTATION

Düsseldorf lies tucked into green hills along the western banks of the **Rhein** river. The largest in a community of small cities connected by the same public transit network, Düsseldorf's city center is at once sprawling and highly concentrated. Largely residential apartment buildings and townhouses crowd most of the city blocks. Most travelers will enter the town from the southeast, through the **Hauptbahnhof,** which is just a few stops away from the Düsseldorf **airport.** Located in the **Stadmitte,** this area is marked by mediocre concrete architecture and a preponderance of pharmacies and magazine stands. On the north end of the city, **Pempelfort** is a similarly residential, if slightly more upscale, where young moms and working professionals enjoy the cafes and low-key restaurants. Close to the center of Düsseldorf, running from east to west, is the **Hofgarten,** Germany's oldest public park. Full of fountains and bike paths, it's a great escape from the uproarious traffic. But chances are that you'll spend most of your time in Düsseldorf in **Altstadt.** The "Old Side" trades automotive congestion for more manageable pedestrian traffic and concrete facades for charming old storefronts. Altstadt is the best place to go for relatively inexpensive food and a good bar scene. Düsseldorf's best attractions, its **art museums,** start in the north end with the **Kunst Palace** and extend southward along the eastern edge of Altstadt, making museum-hopping easier here than just about anywhere else.

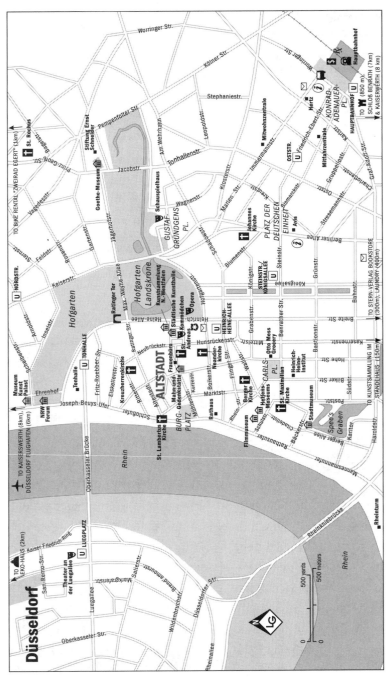

Düsseldorf

düsseldorf . orientation

ACCOMMODATIONS

Budget options in Düsseldorf are extremely limited. Though rooms are usually available, it's advised to book ahead for summer weekends in order to avoid finding yourself in the uncomfortable position of having to pay a higher price for (admittedly very comfortable) hotel rooms.

BACKPACKERS DÜSSELDORF — HOSTEL 2

Fürstenwall 180 ☎0211 302 0848 www.backpackers-duesseldorf.de

This lived-in facility with its youthful, international clientele is close to the city's top sights. Boasting long-term guests and a laid-back staff who enjoys drinking beers with travelers on an outdoor patio, this hostel feels as close to being at home as you can get. The common room, complete with comfortable couches and a temperamental television, is a popular hangout for guests. Rooms have pine bunks and personal lockers.

Bus #725: Corneliusstr. From the stop, follow the bus a block and a half to the hostel. i Sheets, light breakfast, and Wi-Fi included. Fully equipped kitchen. $ 10-bed dorms M-Th and Su €17, F-Sa €20; 6-bed dorms €29/21; 4-bed dorms €22/23. Singles €34; doubles €54. Reception 8am-9pm.

A AND O HOSTEL — HOSTEL 1

Corneliusstr. 9-11 ☎0211 33 994 48 00 www.aohostels.com

Less intimate and social than a private hostel, A and O still provides clean rooms, great proximity to sights, personal lockers, and ensuite baths. Metal bunks and white walls are admittedly low on personality but make for a very low-budget option.

Bus #725: Corneliusstr. i Wi-Fi €5 per 24hr. Internet terminal €2.50 per hr. Breakfast €4. Sheets €3. $ Prices vary, so call ahead. 8- to 10-bed dorms from €12; 4- to 6-bed dorms from

€13. Singles from €39; doubles from €50. ☺ Reception 24hr.

JUGENDHERBERGE DÜSSELDORF (HI)
◉ⓗ☺✦ HOSTEL ❷

Düsseldorfterstr. 1   ☎0211 55 73 10 🖥www.duesseldorf.jugendherberge.de

Walls of windows look out on a tree-lined park right next to the Rhein. This sunny hostel, with bright rooms, personal lockers, and cozy decor, defies the HI stereotype . Special family dorms fit two children (*€14.60 each*) and two adults. Located just across the river, this hostel is just a short tram ride from the sights in Altstadt.

⚡ U70 or U74, U5, U6, or U77: Belsenpl., then bus #832 or 836: Jugendherberge. ℹ Sheets and breakfast included. Wi-Fi €1.50 per hr. Internet terminals €3 per hr. ⓢ 4-bed dorms (separated by gender) €26.80; singles €45; doubles €65. ☺ Reception 24hr.

HOTEL ALT DÜSSELDORF
◆⊗ⓗ☺✦ HOTEL ❸

Hunsrückenstr. 11   ☎0211 13 36 04 🖥www.alt-duesseldorf.de

Located in the heart of the Altstadt, the hotel lobby seating spills into the pedestrian-ridden street, where chairs mix with bistros and barstools from nearby cafes. An older crowd appreciates the ambience of the comfortable lounge. In contrast to the ochre and ivy covered lobby and exterior, bedrooms are small and sparsely decorated, but well-lit with large windows. All rooms have ensuite baths, televisions, and telephones.

⚡ U70, U74, U75, U76, U77, U78, or U79, tram 706, 713, or 715: Heinrich-Heine-Allee. ℹ Breakfast and Wi-Fi included. ⓢ Singles €49; doubles €69; triples €81; quad €104. ☺ Reception 7am-1am.

BEST WESTERN
◆ⓗ☺✦ HOTEL ❹

Harkortstr. 7-9   ☎0211 87 67 74 0 🖥www.ambassador-duesseldorf.bestwestern.de

There's nothing outstanding about this Best Western other than its proximity to the Hauptbahnhof, reliable rooms, and good deals on the weekends. Most guests are of the business-suit variety, drinking cocktails in a quiet hotel bar against a backdrop of inexplicable Tuscan murals. Rooms are sparsely decorated, but have the advantage of television, telephone, and impossibly large ensuite bathrooms.

⚡ Bus #725: Mintroppl. ℹ Breakfast and Wi-Fi included. ⓢ Singles M-Th €75, F-Su €59; doubles €89/69. ☺ Reception 24hr.

HOTEL IBIS
◆ⓗ☺✦ HOTEL ❸

Konrad-Adenauer-Pl. 14   ☎0211 167 20 🖥www.accorhotels.com

For travelers just stopping in at Düsseldorf, Ibis is ideally located inside the Hauptbahnhof. This chain hotel offers cheap, bland rooms to the road-weary just looking for a place to put up for a night or two. Reliability and cleanliness, as well as discounts accessible from the website, make Ibis a good deal. All rooms have a television and telephone.

⚡ Located inside the Hauptbahnhof. ℹ Wi-Fi €9 per day, guest terminals free. Breakfast €10. ⓢ Singles and doubles from €59. Check the website for special deals, including occasional €10 discounts per night. ☺ Reception 24hr.

CAMPINGPLATZ UNTERBACHER SEE
◉ CAMPGROUND ❶

Kleiner Torfbruch 31   ☎0211 899 2038 🖥www.unterbachersee.com

Located on the banks of the beautiful Unterbacher Sea, this campsite offers an entirely different experience of Düsseldorf than the madness of the downtown. Those looking to give their wallets and city-weary feet a break can explore the sea by foot, bike, or boat. Paddleboats, canoes, sailboats and bikes are all available for rent. Slightly less natural (but no less fun) is the mini-golf course on the premises.

⚡ S8, S28 or S68: Düsseldorf Geresheim, then bus #735: Sweeweg. ⓢ €5.50 per person, €6.50 per tent. ☺ Reception M-F 9am-1pm and 3pm-8pm, Sa-Su 9am-8pm.

JUGENDHERBERGE DUISBURG-WEDAU (HI)
®®® HOSTEL ❷
Kalkweg 148E
☎0211 203 72 41 64

"Inconvenient location" doesn't even begin to cover it. This hostel is not in Düsseldorf at all; expect to spend at least 35min. getting yourself from the city to this remote location in Duisberg. For those only staying in Düsseldorf for a flight connection, this might make slightly more sense, but try options in Düsseldorf before venturing out to this hostel.

✇ S1, S21, or RE1: Duisburg Hauptbahnhof, then bus #934 or #944: Jugendherberge. Ⓢ Dorms €17.50; singles €25.20. Surcharge if over 27 €3. 10% discount for stays over 2 nights. ☒ Reception 8am-10pm.

SIGHTS
◉

If you come to Düsseldorf for one thing, make it the art; this city is host to world-class experimental and contemporary art. Almost all the museums are located on the western side of Düsseldorf, along the Rhein.

▨ ST. ANDREAS KIRCHE
CHURCH
Andreasstr. 27
☎0211 136340 ▣www.dominikaner-duesseldorf.de

The ochre St. Andreas Kirche is perhaps the most beautiful church in Düsseldorf. An example of early Baroque architecture, this intricately decorated 1629 masterpiece is covered with quiet whites and gold leaf on the inside. The domed ceiling is a sea of plaster sculpture, with rosettes extending from one gorgeous arch to the other. Don't miss the large oil 1908 painting just left of the alter, entitled *The Martyrdom of St. Andrew.*

✇ U70, U74, U75, U76, U78, U79, tram 706, 713, or 715: Heinrich-Heine-Allee. Ⓢ Free. ☒ Open M-Sa 9am-6pm. Mass Su 11am and 6pm. Free organ concert Su 6:30pm.

▨ K21: KUNSTSAMMLUNG IM STÄNDEHAUS
MUSEUM
Ständehausstr. 1
☎0211 838 16 00 ▣www.kunstsammlung.de

Once home to the *Land*'s parliament, this enormous building reopened in April 2002 as a companion musuem to the **Kunstsammlung Nordrhein-Westfalen,** focusing on experimental and contemporary art from the late 20th century onward. A box fan swinging like an erratic pendulum at the museum entrance sets the tone for some of the world's most progressive art. Exhibits are usually titled in English and German. Tours are occasionally offered in English; if you have the chance, don't pass up an opportunity for a guided tour. The mystifying art suddenly makes more sense.

✇ Tram 704, 709, or 719: Graf-Adolf-Pl. Walk 1 block down Elizabethstr. along the park. The museum is on your right. Ⓢ Prices vary; €6-10, students €4.50-7.50. ☒ Open Tu-F 10am-6pm, Sa-Su 11am-6pm. Open 1st W of the month 10am-10pm; free admission 6-10pm.

KÖNIGSALLEE (KING'S AVENUE)
SHOPPING STREET
End-stopped by Carl-Theodore-Str. to the south and Blumenstr. to the north

If you've managed to block that expensive hostel bill or uncomfortably pricey night out from your memory, Königsallee is the place to give your credit card a workout. The street was so named with the hope of mollifying a humiliated **King Wilhem IV,** who was struck by projectile manure during a visit to Düsseldorf (perhaps the peasants were particularly irritated after being charged €4 for a small cup of coffee). Less assuaging are the exorbitant prices of the Cartier, Chanel, and Prada boutiques that reign supreme here.

✇ U70 or U74-79: Steinstr./Königsallee. Ⓢ No money, no problems.

K20: THE KUNSTSAMMLUNG NORDHEIN-WESTFALEN
MUSEUM
Grabbepl. 5
☎0211 838 11 30 ▣www.kunstsammlung.de

When the K21 ran out of room for its collection, the K20 was constructed to house the overflow. And what an overflow it is: inside this impressive black-glass structure, sunlight floods a world-class display of classical modern art, with works primarily from the early 20th century to 1945. Work by Jackson Pollock, Max Beckmann, Max Ernst, Mark Rothko, and Andy Warhol are don't-miss highlights, as are pieces from Paul Klee, a former professor at Düsseldorf's art academy.

🚇 *U70, U74, U75, U76, U78, U79, Tram 706, 713, or 715: Heinrich-Heine-Allee.* 💲 *€3, students €1.50.* 🕑 *Open Tu-F 10am-6pm, Sa-Su 11am-6pm. 1st W of the month 11am-10pm. Tours in German W 3:30pm, Su 11:30am.*

BENRATH SCHLOß
CASTLE

Benrather Schloßallee 100-106 ☎0211 899 38 32

Man, they don't make them like this anymore. Elector Karl Theodor commissioned the construction of the Benrath Schloß, one of the last examples of Rococo architecture in Western Europe. Think pink, teal, marble floors, and silk curtains.

🚇 *S6: Benrath.* ℹ️ *Only accessible by tour.* 💲 *€7, students €5.* 🕑 *Open from mid-Apr to Oct 10am-6pm; from Nov to mid-Apr 11am-5pm. Tours on the hr.; last one at 5pm, in English if requested.*

MUSEUM KUNST PALACE (PALACE OF ART)
MUSEUM

Ehrenhof 4-5 ☎0211 899 24 60 🖳www.museum-kunst-palast.de

The Kunst Palace is divided into two distinct segments. Its standing exhibition includes a collection of glasswork dating from antiquity to modernity and a display of some astonishingly intricate locks. The other branch of the museum hosts incredible rotating contemporary art exhibits. Collections are wonderfully thorough, taking up a whole floor of a large gallery space, and include arrays of paintings from around the world but with a unifying theme, giving displays an international edge.

🚇 *U78 or U79, Tram 701 or 715: Nordstr.* 💲 *Permanent collection €2.50, students €1. Special exhibits €9/4.* 🕑 *Open Tu-W 11am-6pm, Th 11am-9pm, F-Su 11am-6pm.*

NRW FORUM
ART MUSEUM

Ehrenhof 2 ☎0211 892 66 90 🖳www.nrw-forum.de

For world-class art that's (shockingly) not oil-based, the NRW Forum is the place to go. Fantastic photography and film exhibitions from the last 20 years make this museum a must-see for anyone interested in, well, photography or film. Exhibits rotate. When English-speaking artists are featured, short documentaries and plaques (also in English) provide background to the exhibited pieces.

🚇 *U78, U79, Tram 701 or 715: Nordstr.* 💲 *€5.80, students €3.80.* 🕑 *Open Tu-Su 11am-8pm, F 11am-midnight.*

HEINRICH-HEINE-INSTITUT
MUSEUM

Bilker Str. 12-14 ☎0211 89 99 29 02 🖳www.duesseldorf.de/kultur/heineinstitut

The birthplace and homestead of the influential German romantic, Düsseldorf enshrines its native son in the world's only official Heinrich Heine museum. The all-things-Heine theme includes manuscripts, play posters, and drawings, like the entertaining caricatures of Napoleon (exhibit #33) hidden behind a door. Also included in the museum is a less extensive, but still interesting, Schumann exhibit. Explanatory plaques are all in German, so be sure to pick up a free audioguide.

🚇 *U70, U74, U5, U6, U79, Tram 706, 713, or 715: Heinrich-Heine-Allee.* 💲 *€3, students €1.50. Audioguide in English or German free.* 🕑 *Open Tu-F and Su 11am-5pm.*

GOETHE-MUSEUM
MUSEUM

Jakobistr. 2 ☎0211 899 6262

Though Goethe only visited Düsseldorf once, staying for four weeks in 1792, the city still hasn't forgotten. Forever proud of their month-long guest, the city capitalizes on its ties to the famous German poet with the world's largest collection of artifacts relating to his life. Over 1000 manuscripts, first-edition books, and personal letters are on display at the museum. Not to be missed are the stunning illustrations of Goethe's *Faust* by artists Salvadore Dalí and Ernst Barlach.

Tram 707: Schloß Jägerhof. $ €3, students €1.50. Open Tu-F 11am-5pm, Sa 1-5pm, Su 11am-5pm.

STÄDTISCHE KUNSTHALLE ART MUSEUM

Grabbepl. 4 ☎0211 899 62 43 www.kunsthalle-duesseldorf.de

Located just across from the K20 museum, Städtische Kunsthalle houses galleries of rotating modern-art exhibits. Much of the work on display can only be described as experimental (when it can be described at all). Off-kilter and edgy prints and paintings are suspended on towering white walls by binderclips, and the occasional flowerpot is nailed to the side of a gallery.

U70, U74, U75, U76, U77, U76 or U79: Steinstr./Königsallee. $ Admission varies depending on exhibit; usually around €5, students €4. Open Tu-Sa noon-7pm, Su 11am-6pm.

MAHN- UND GEDENKSTÄDTTE MEMORIAL MUSEUM

Mühlenstr. 29 ☎0211 899 62 05

The Mahn- und Gedenkstädtte uses photographs and documents to detail the history of persecuted groups in Düsseldorf. Visitors can begin their tour of the museum by watching an introductory video of interviews with persons persecuted for their religion, class, or politics, and then explore the artifacts in this small museum, of which most are copies of originals. The Gedenkstädtte focuses on Jewish suffering under the Third Reich, and the worker's movement against discrimination. Be sure to check out the permanent exhibit on the Düsseldorf World War II resistance. Supplemental information is available in English, but

explanatory plaques are entirely in German.

🚇 U70, U74, U75, U76, U77, U78, U79, tram 706, 713, or 715: Heinrich-Heine-Allee. $ Free. ⏰ Open Tu-F 11am-5pm, Su 11am-5pm.

HETJENS-MUSEUM MUSEUM

Schulstr. 4 ☎0211 899 4210

Adjacent to the Filmmuseum, the Hetjens-Museum fills four floors with 8000 years of ceramics. Pieces range from the bewilderingly modern to the incredibly ancient. Stark ceramic cylinders that (we can only assume) represent a kind of metaphysical and spiritual continuity between potters across centuries sit between Chinese vases dating back to antiquity. On the first floor, half of an Islamic dome is covered in intricate cobalt and turquoise tiles. Two floors above, a grid of ceramic replicas of rodent skulls symbolizes... something.

🚇 U70, U74, U75, U76, U77, U78, U79, Tram 706, 713, or 715: Heinrich-Heine-Allee. $ €3, students €1.50. ⏰ Open Tu 11am-5pm, W 11am-9pm, Th-Su 11am-5pm.

THEATERMUSEUM MUSEUM

Jägerhofstr. 1 ☎0211 899 46 60 💻www.duesseldorf.de/theatermuseum

This museum documents the history of German theater since the 17th century, with exhibits of photographs, film clips, and theater billings from many of the country's most beloved plays. An exhibit of stage costumes is accompanied by the original sketches by designers that are every bit as artistic as the finished product. No one can fault the museum for lack of explanatory plaques; unfortunately, this information is only in German.

🚇 Tram 707: Schloß Jägerhof. $ €3, students €1.50. ⏰ Open Tu-Su 1-8:30pm.

HOFGARTEN PARK

The oldest public park in Germany is hiding its age well. Beautiful old trees and fountains are linked by winding paths in a large park that dominates the north end of the city center. The Landskrone pond, as popular with swans as it is with the tourists photographing them, sits at the peaceful center of the park.

🚇 U70, U74, U75, U76, U77, U76, U79, Tram 706, 713, or 715: Heinrich-Heine-Allee. Bordered on the east by Pempelforter Str., to the north by Inselstr., to the west by the Altstadt, and to the south by the top of the Königsallee. $ Free.

ST. LAMBERTUS KIRCHE CHURCH

Stiftspl. 7 ☎0211 13 23 26 💻www.lambertuskirche.de

Construction of the St. Lambertus Kirche began in the 14th century, when, apparently, high-quality contractors were as hard to find as they are today. The tower of the church, an iconic part of the Düsseldorf skyline, is decidedly less than vertical. How exactly the spire came to lean so much is unclear, but the most plausible local legend has it that the wood that was used to build the church was wet, and it expanded after it dried, sending the tower off in more creative directions. The church is adjacent to a convent, and nuns frequent the 5pm masses.

🚇 U70, U74, U5, U6, U79, Tram 706, 713, or 715: Heinrich-Heine-Allee. $ Free. ⏰ Open M-Th 8:30am-6pm, F 11am-6pm, Sa 7am-8pm, Su 9am-8pm. Mass M-F 5pm, Su 10:30am.

FILMMUSEUM MUSEUM

Schulstr. 4 ☎0211 899 2232 💻www.filmmuseum-duesseldorf.de

A black interior is filled with old costumes, movie clips, and photographic odes to some of Germany's most important directors and actors. From Chinese paper puppets to the first truck-engine-sized film cameras, this museum chronicles the history of cinema in all its varied forms. The manually gifted can try their hand at the shadow-puppet exhibit, and the sci-fi fanatic can transport herself into space using greenscreen technology.

🚇 U70, U74, U75, U76, U77, U78, U79, Tram 706, 713, or 715: Heinrich-Heine-Allee. $ €3, students €1.50. ⏰ Open Tu-Su 11am-5pm, W 11am-9pm, Th-Su 11am-5pm.

ST. MAXIMILIAN KIRCHE   CHURCH

Citadellstr. 2   ☎0211 13 16 60 ✉www.maxkirche.de

This church, originally constructed in the 16th century as a Catholic monastery, is already beautiful. But the real draw here is the church's three-century music tradition. The choir stalls date back to the 17th century, and the organ to the 18th. Today, the impressive cloister is the heart of the Düsseldorf Catholic community. Golden angels fly across domed ceilings, and black and white marble checkers the floor.

✚ U70, U74, U75, U76, U78, U79, Tram 706, 713, or 715: Heinrich-Heine-Allee. Ⓢ Free. 🕐 Open M-Tu 10am-12:30pm, and W-F 10am-12:30pm and 3-5pm. Su services 10am.

SCHIFFAHRT-MUSEUM (SHIPPING MUSEUM)   MUSEUM

Burgpl. 30   ☎0211 89 9 41 95 ✉www.schiffahrt-museum.duesseldorf.city-map.de

The tower that now houses a collection of maritime artifacts is all that remains of the Düsseldorf city palace. Exhibits including boat motors, model ships, and periscopes chronicles the development of the city as a major port on the Rhein. The upstairs cafe offers visitors an unobstructed view of Altstadt and an admittedly muddy river.

✚ U70, U74, U75, U76, U77, U78, U79, Tram 706, 713, or 715: Heinrich-Heine-Allee. Ⓢ €3, students €1.50. Free for all daily 5-6pm. 🕐 Open Tu-Su 11am-6pm.

MUSEUM CORPS DE LOGIS   MUSEUM

Benrather Schloßallee   ☎211 899 71 90 ✉www.schloss-benrath.de

The Museum for European Garden Art is located in the east wing of the Schloß Benrath complex, right by the stunning palace gardens. Don't feel guilty about passing over this museum if you're short on time (or cash), but, if you do go, be sure to take a look at the original plans for the Schloß gardens.

✚ S6: Benrath. Ⓢ €7, students €5. Combined ticket with Museum für Naturkinde and Schloß €10/7.50. 🕐 Open from mid-Apr to Oct Tu-Su 10am-6pm, from Nov to mid-Apr 11am-5pm.

MUSEUM FÜR NATURKUNDE   MUSEUM

Benrather Schloßallee   ☎0211 899 72 16

There's something appealingly ironic about a former hunting palace being converted into a museum that celebrates native wildlife. Unfortunately, irony doesn't improve the fact that, ultimately, the Museum für Naturkunde is a lot of stuffed birds. Admittedly, the museum has a few impressive specimens, namely the large stuffed eagles and cranes. But if you're coming to look at the Schloß, you're probably best just sticking to the palace.

✚ S6: Benrather. Ⓢ €7, students €5. Combined ticket for Naturkunde, Corps de Logis, and Schloß €10/7.50. 🕐 Open from mid-Apr to Oct Tu-Su 10am-6pm, from Nov to mid-Apr 11am-5pm.

FOOD

A quick glance at just about any restaurant menu is enough to show you that Düsseldorf is a slight exception to the eat-for-cheap tradition in most German cities; expect to pay around €12 for an entree in a sit-down restaurant, and about €3 for the requisite beer. Avoid the pricier eastern areas in Düsseldorf in favor of the lower prices and better ambience in the **Altstadt,** home to pedestrian-trafficked streets and a view of the river your eyes can feast on. The best deals are on **Berger Straße** and **Bolkingstraße.**

LA COPA   ⬤🍷🛁 TAPAS ❷

Berger Str. 4   ☎0211 323 88 58

This traditional Spanish restaurant serves up over 50 tasty tapas, so you can have a little of everything and forget that it actually adds up to a lot. Small meals at a low cost, but fresh seafood makes this tapas bar a great value. Paella bowls (€15.50) could feed whole villages—definitely not part of the make-my-ex-boyfriend-jealous diet. Try the seafood salad (€6), including octopus and baby squid.

🚇 *U70, U74, U75, U76, U77, U78, U79, tram 706, 713, or 715: Heinrich-Heine-Allee.* $ *Entrees with fish €5-9.50. Tapas €2.50-6.* ⏰ *Open daily noon-midnight.*

FISCHHAUS 🍴🍸⛅ SEAFOOD [3]

Berger Str. 3-7 ☎0211 828 45 64 💻www.fischhaus-duesseldorf.de

More of a *fisch-palast* than *fischhaus*, this expansive restaurant takes up three storefronts on the popular Berger Str. Large seafood entrees are served up fresh from a dizzying array of choices, from scallops to salmon to shrimp. White and black tile with bright blue touches keeps this open-air restaurant feeling light and airy.

🚇 *U70, U74, U75, U76, U77, U78, U79, tram 706, 713, or 715: Heinrich-Heine-Allee.* $ *Fischcreme soup €5.50. Bouillabaisse €7.65. Entrees €9-19.50.* ⏰ *Open daily 11:30am-midnight.*

IM GOLDENEN RING 🍴🍸⛅ GERMAN [2]

Burgpl. 21 ☎0211 87 55 03 33 💻www.im-goldenen-ring.de

In business since 1536, this restaurant and its expansive outdoor seating just by the Rhein are worth a visit. A large brass periscope commands the middle of the restaurant. Try the local specialty, *Düsseldorfter Killepitsche*, cousin to the *Jägermeister*, for €2.90 a shot.

🚇 *U70, U74, U75, U76, U77, U78, U79, tram 706, 713, or 715: Heinrich-Heine-Allee.* $ *Soups €4.90-5.60. German beef-steak with french fries €8. Currywurst with french fries €6.* ⏰ *Open daily 11:30am-midnight or 1am.*

ZUM UERIGE 🍴🍸⛅ MICROBREWERY [1]

Berger Str. 1 ☎0211 86 69 90 💻www.uerige.de

Heavy wood and heavy food fill this microbrewery on the corner of the busy Altstadt. Pub food is served as a complement to the dark house beers, *Uerige (€1.70 for 0.25L)* and *Ueriger Weizen (€2.80).* Beer is poured from oak kegs for diners seated on wooden benches, and stained glass warms up this rustic bar.

🚇 *U70, U74, U75, U76, U77, U78, U79, tram 706, 713, or 715: Heinrich-Heine-Allee.* $ *Smoked bacon and bread €2.80. Black pudding €2.25.* ⏰ *Open daily 10am-midnight. Kitchen open M-F 6-9pm, Sa-Su 11am-4pm.*

BAR AND KÜCHE VENTE 🍴🍸⛅ GERMAN [3]

Lambertstr. 10 ☎0211 566 90 63 💻www.vente-event.de

While most of the restaurants in the Altstadt compete for customers with crowded outdoor seating on pedestrian-trafficked streets, Vente is content to relax on its own quiet alleyway, with a private view of the **Lambertkirche** and its adjacent convent through leaded glass windows. Drinking a beer *(€2.80)* never felt so holy. Outdoor benches are set against ivy-covered walls and under window boxes full of flowers.

🚇 *U70, U74, U75, U76, U77, U78, U79, tram 706, 713, or 715: Heinrich-Heine-Allee.* $ *Entrees €8.50-20. Spargelcreme soup €6. Penne pasta €8.50. Gnocchi with cherry tomatoes €12.50.* ⏰ *Open Tu-Su 5pm-1am. Kitchen open until 11pm.*

LE PAIN QUOTIDIEN 💳🍸⛅ FRENCH RESTAURANT [2]

Berger Str. 35 ☎0211 56 65 72 72 💻www.lepainquotidien.info

Admittedly, Le Pain Quotidien is an international chain—but they do a good job hiding it in Düsseldorf. Warm stucco walls and two floors of open seating in this French-style bistro all center around a large wooden communal table, where strangers can enjoy *tartines* and wine together. But the real highlights of this cafe are the fresh food and relatively low prices.

🚇 *U70, U74, U75, U76, U77, U78, U79, tram 706, 713, or 715: Heinrich-Heine-Allee.* $ *Omelettes €5.45-8.95. Tartines €5-9. Fresh fruit tarts €2.50-4. Wine from €3.50.* ⏰ *Open M-Sa 7:30am-10pm, Su 9am-8pm.*

LIBANON RESTAURANT 💳🍸⛅ LEBANESE [2]

Berger Str. 19-21 ☎0211 13 49 17 💻www.libanon-restaurant.de

Questionable gilding, hanging lanterns, and a generous offering of beaded cushions make this Lebanese restaurant borderline gaudy. Luckily, the homemade hummus and pita *(€5.50)* bring it back to authentic. If you can stomach it, Libanon hosts belly dancing Wednesday-Saturday at 9pm. For a good matinee entree deal *(€9.50)*, eat before 5pm. The adjoining takeout restaurant, **Libanon-Express,** serves falafel *(€2.90)* and taboulleh *(€3.90)*.

🚇 U70, U74, U75, U76, U77, U78, U79, tram 706, 713, or 715: Heinrich-Heine-Allee. [$] Falafel €7.50. Moussakah €7. ⏰ Open daily noon-midnight.

GAGLIARDI MANDELBRENNEREI — ✪☀ SANDWICHES, DESSERT [1]

Kapuzinergasse 2 — ☎0211 86 29 27 31

A creative menu features a mix of inexpensive meals and sweet treats. Cooked-to-order waffles are stuffed with cherries, apples, or strawberries *(€2.50)*, and sweet almonds are soaked in chili pepper, Bailey's, or 👍**rum** *(€2.50 for 100g)*. Toasted *piadina* sandwiches are a quick way to refuel on the cheap in Altstadt. Try it stuffed with mozzarella, tomato, and rucola.

🚇 U70, U74, U75, U76, U77, U78, U79, tram 706, 713, or 715: Heinrich-Heine-Allee. [$] Piandinas from €3.70. Snacks from €2.50. ⏰ Open M-Sa 4pm-3am.

CARLSPLATZ MARKT — ✪🍸☀ OPEN-AIR MARKET [1]

Carlspl.

The least expensive food in Düsseldorf can also be the best. This popular market is full of upscale eats for low prices, from exotic fruit to local favorites (including *Sauerbraten*, or pickled beef). Don't leave without trying a trout or salmon sandwich, the market's specialty.

🚇 U70, U74, U75, U76, U77, U78, U79, tram 706, 713, or 715: Heinrich-Heine-Allee. [$] Peaches €0.80. Fish sandwiches €2-2.40. ⏰ Open M-Sa 9am-8:30pm.

NIGHTLIFE

Düsseldorf's 500 bars are said to make up "the longest bar in the world." We'd like to make an addendum to that: they make for the longest nights too. For wild nightlife and jam-packed bars, look no further than the **Bolkerstraße,** where all of Altstadt seems to gather on Friday and Saturday nights for good beer and good times.

👍 SUB — ✪☀ CLUB

Bolkerstr. 18 — ☎0211 86 58 90 💻www.sub-dc.de

This subterranean club gets packed with partiers early in the night and stays crowded until the early morning. The dance floor, lit up with colored lights from below, is full of young German students showing off their moves underneath flashing overhead lights. Red and blue lights and spinning disco balls make this place a wild party. Shove your way to the back for a double-shot of *Jägermeister* *(€3.50)*, then get back to the dance floor to join the fun.

🚇 U70, U74, U75, U76, U77, U78, U79, tram 706, 713, or 715: Heinrich-Heine-Allee. [$] Beer €2.50. Shots €2.70-3.50. ⏰ Open Th-Sa from 10pm.

KUHSTALL — ✪🍸☀ BAR

Bolkerstr. 35 — ☎0211 21 07 16 85 💻www.kuhstall-duesseldorf.de

The most rambunctious bar on the Bolkerstr. keeps things wild with flashing lights, a crowded bar, and a single (though generally not lonely) pole on the countertop. Kuhstall gets in touch with its rural side, with barn door siding and farmhouse touches, though the disco ball and red and blue lights might confuse Farmer Fritz. Locals and tourists are packed shoulder-to-shoulder, with little room to move but enough time to make some (slurred) conversation.

🚇 U70, U74, U75, U76, U77, U78, U79, tram 706, 713, or 715: Heinrich-Heine-Allee. [$] Beer €2.80. Mixed drinks €6-8.50. ⏰ Open M-Th 6pm-1am, F-Sa 6pm-late, Su 6pm-1am.

ENGEL
🚫🍸⛅ BAR

Bolker Str. 33 ☎0211 862 97 26 💻www.engel-duesseldorf.de

Despite the name, there's absolutely nothing angelic about this bar. Down-to-earth and no-frills, this bar is all about the drinks and the music. Rock blasts for an often leather-clad crowd, but drinkers of all styles and ages get grooving to the upbeat tunes. Expect to see, and join dancing on tables, especially after soccer match victories. If you're in need of a souvenir after a particularly good night, take home a rockin' **bandana** with Engel's guitar ensignia (actually, please don't).

🚉 U70, U74, U75, U76, U77, U78, U79, tram 706, 713, or 715: Heinrich-Heine-Allee. $ Beer €3. Shots from €2.60. ⏰ Open M-Th 6pm-midnight, F-Sa 7pm-late.

MANDALAI
🚫🍸⛅ HOOKAH BAR

Mertensgasse 4 ☎0211 860 66 94 💻www.mandalai.org

Take a break from the wild bar scene to sit back with some hookah on comfortable deep cushions spilling onto the street. The hookah isn't bad, either. Smoke fills the air from midnight until early morning on weekends.

🚉 U70, U74, U75, U76, U77, U78, U79, Tram 706, 713, or 715: Heinrich-Heine-Allee. $ Hookah €8. Beer €3. Mixed drinks €6-8.50. ⏰ Open M-Th noon-1am, F-Sa noon-5am, Su noon-midnight.

HAUSBAR
🚫🍸⛅ BAR

Bolkerstr. 14-20 ☎0211 21 07 44 99 💻www.hausbar-duesseldorf.de

A massive circular bar fills the center of this red-lit hangout on the middle of the Bolkerstr. Disco balls and colored lighting define this upbeat disco with a mixed-age crowd and upscale drinks. Sleek countertops and a wall of windows that open up to an expanse of outdoor seating give this bar a cool, modern edge.

🚉 U70, U74, U75, U76, U77, U78, U79, Tram 706, 713, or 715: Heinrich-Heine-Allee. $ Beer €2.80. Mixed drinks €6.80-8.50. ⏰ Open M-Th 10am-2pm, F-Sa 10pm-late, Su 10am-2pm.

EL PAPAGAYO
🚫⛅ BAR

Mertengasse 2 ☎0211 13 33 30 💻www.elpapagayo.de

If you're hungry for tapas or thirsty for sangria, this Iberian bar is the place to be. A large wooden bar, crowded with young people, fills the center of the first room, and a disco ball and palm fronds hang over the dance floor in the second. Show up early *(8-10pm)* to avoid the cover charge and enjoy cheap drinks. On Monday night, flex the old pipes for some karaoke fun. Freaky Friday is all about hip hop and R and B. Be prepared to show ID to enter.

🚉 U70, U74, U75, U76, U77, U78, U79, Tram 706, 713, or 715: Heinrich-Heine-Allee. $ Cover €3. Beer €2.80. Cocktails €4. ⏰ Open M-Sa 10pm-late.

MOJO-BAR
🚫🍸⛅ BAR

Hunsrückenstr. 16 ☎0211 21 07 07 67 💻www.mojo-bar.de

The modern countertops and contemporary furnishings get a lot less formal when well-watered Germans get up on the back stage for a little karaoke every Friday and Saturday at 9pm. Inexpensive drinks fuel the fun and smooth over that language barrier for *sprechening*-amateurs. Travelers of all countries and locals of all ages enjoy the DJ *(F-Sa)*.

🚉 U70, U74, U75, U76, U77, U78, U79, Tram 706, 713, or 715: Heinrich-Heine-Allee. $ Mixed drinks €5. ⏰ Open M-Th noon-3am, F noon-late, Sa 11-late, Su 11-3am.

LÜLÜ
🚫🍸⛅ BAR

Kurtze Str. 2 ☎0211 69 99 09

French tunes and romantic decor make this bar a favorite with the *frauen*. For a more mellow scene on the Kurtze Straße, claim a seat under vintage glass chandeliers and sip a long drink *(€6.50-8.50)*, or skip the class for expediency with a vodka shot *(€3.50)*. Mismatched chairs and old plaster walls make this a trendy paradise for the ever-shabbily chic.

🚇 U70, U74, U75, U76, U77, U78, U79, Tram 706, 713, or 715: Heinrich-Heine-Allee. $ Beer €2.80. ⏰ Open M-Th 5pm-2am, F 5pm-late, Sa noon-late, Su noon-11pm. Kitchen open until 11pm.

ARTS AND CULTURE

ROBERT-SCHUMANN-SAAL — MUSIC HALL

Ehrenhof 4-5 ☎0211 32 94 43 💻www.robert-schumann-saal.de

This newly constructed, multi-functional chamber hall is integrated into the museum Kunst Palast in Pempelfort. With seating for 850 people, this theater now hosts everything from chamber music to jazz to folk performances.

🚇 U78 or U79: Nord Str. $ Tickets from €10. ⏰ Tickets can be purchased online, from any of the tourist offices, or at the Konzertkasse Tonhalle, open M-F 10am-7pm, Sa 10am-2pm.

DEUTSCHE OPER AM RHEIN — OPERA

Heinrich-Heine-Allee 16a ☎0211 890 82 11 💻www.rheinoper.de

This opulent gold and scarlet theater is an impressive place to catch some of the great classics for a wonderfully affordable price. Düsseldorf's opera company puts on all the classics, from *Tosca* to *Aida*. Operas are, of course, in their original language, subtitled in German; it's generally advisable to brush up on the story line of whatever production you're going to see.

🚇 U70, U74, U75, U76, U77, U78, U79, tram 706, 713, or 715: Heinrich-Heine-Allee. $ Tickets €8-59. ⏰ Box office open M-F 10am-8pm, Sa 10am-6pm, and 1hr. before performances.

BLACK BOX — CINEMA

Schulstr. 4 ☎0211 899 24 90 💻www.duesseldorf.de/kultur/filmmuseum

The wildly popular Black Box shows independent and foreign films to a devoted following of Düsseldorfers. This cinema is affiliated with the Filmmuseum and only shows movies in their original format.

🚇 U70, U74, U75, U76, U77, U78, U79, tram 706, 713, or 715: Heinrich-Heine-Allee. $ €5, students €4. ⏰ Films are shown almost nightly, starting as early as 5pm or as late as 10pm. Tickets available at the door or online.

MARIONETTE THEATER — PUPPET THEATER

Bilker Str. 7 ☎0211 32 84 32 💻www.marionettentheater-duesseldorf.de

Not just for children, the Marionette Theater puts on fantastical performances in German with intricately carved and beautifully painted old puppets. The venue is small and intimate, seating just 100 people in the lovely Palace Wittgenstein. Most performances are on Fridays and Saturdays.

🚇 U70, U74, U75, U76, U77, U78, U79, tram 706, 713, or 715: Heinrich-Heine-Allee. $ Tickets usually around €22, students €20, under 16 €13. ⏰ Box office open Tu-Sa 1-6pm.

SHOPPING

If window-shopping on the **Königsallee** isn't the prescription for your retail fever, try looking in the Altstadt. Like in most of Düsseldorf, don't expect incredibly low prices, but consider these stores with an eye to their good values.

NO. 27 — 👍 SECONDHAND CLOTHING

Wallstr. 27 ☎0172 290 27 51

A rarity in secondhand clothing shops: excellent quality pieces for fair prices. This vintage shop has one-of-a-kind items, purchased by the owner in Amsterdam, London, and Berlin. No. 27 carries a huge selection of men's vintage leather jackets *(from €100)*. Dresses start at €30, but ornately beaded vintage dresses go as high as €110.

🚇 U70, U74, U75, U76, U77, U78, U79, tram 706, 713, or 715: Heinrich-Heine-Allee. $ Leather bags from €39. Women's jackets from €55. ⏰ Open M-Sa noon-7pm.

KAUF DICH GLÜCKLICH BOUTIQUE

Carlspl. 4 ☎0211 86 93 02 91 💻www.kaufdichgluecklich.de

This upscale boutique caters to the young and the fashion-forward. Carrying well-made, unique, and trendy men's and women's clothing, this store makes it tempting to forget your budget and splurge for something special. Luckily, your shopping sins are given reprieve during the summer and winter sales, when a selection of clothing is 50% off.

🚇 U70, U74, U75, U76, U77, U78, U79, tram 706, 713, or 715: Heinrich-Heine-Allee. ⏰ Open daily 10:30am-8pm. Summer sale through much of June and July; winter sale in Jan and Feb.

JOKERS RESTSELLER BOOKS

Mittlestr. 17 ☎0211 1 36 58 36

English bookstores are hard to come by in Düsseldorf. Jokers, a German chain, carries a modest selection of new English novels and a few classics. The one big draw: prices for bestsellers here are way lower than anything you'll find in the US. So stock up on chick-lit, and forgive yourself for abandoning that ambitious reading list.

🚇 U70, U74, U75, U76, U77, U78, U79, Tram 706, 713, or 715: Heinrich-Heine-Allee. $ Novels from €1.50. ⏰ Open Tu-Su 10am-8pm.

FLIPSIDE MUSIC

Wallstr. 37 ☎0211 828 46 36 💻www.flipside-vinyl.de

This independent record store, established in 1998, sells everything from rare albums to new vinyl. Flipside's shelves are stocked with techno, disco, hip hop, soul, jazz, rock, indie—actually, you'll be hard-pressed to find a genre that this store doesn't carry. Faithful locals flock to the store for newly released labels.

🚇 U70, U74, U75, U76, U77, U78, U79, Tram 706, 713, or 715: Heinrich-Heine-Allee. $ Used records from €5; prices vary steeply. ⏰ Open M-F 1-8pm, Sa noon-6pm.

ESSENTIALS

Practicalities

- **TOURIST OFFICES:** A knowledgable office staff offers free copies of the *In Düsseldorf,* event guide, a **Gay Guide** to the city, maps and booking services *(€5 fee during fairs and exhibitions).* Office also sells the **Welcome Card,** good for unlimited public transportation and free or reduced prices at some museums and restaurants. *(Immermannstr. 65b. ☎0211 172 02 28. 💻www.duesseldorf-tourismus.de 🚇 Walk to the right from the train station and look for the Immerhof building. ℹ 12% event ticket fee is better than a 20% surcharge at the door. $ Welcome Card for one person, 24hr. €9, 48hr. €14, 72 hr. €19; for a group, either 3 adults or 2 adults and 2 children, 24hr. €18/28/38. ⏰ Open M-Sa 9:30am-7pm.)* A **second branch** offers similar services. *(Marktpl. 6 ☎0211 720 28 40 ⏰ Open daily from 10am-6pm.)*
- **TOURS: Daily City Tour** leads groups down Königsallee, across the Rhein for a look at the city from across the river, and finishes with a walk through the Altstadt. Tickets are available at the tourist offices. *(Tours depart from the Hauptbahnhof. ☎0211 17 20 28 54. 💻www.duesseldorf-tourismus.de 🚇 Walk to the right from the train station and look for the Immerhof building. ℹ Bus tours in German and English. $ €16.50, ages 6-12 €7. With a boat excursion, tours are €20/9. ⏰ 11:15am.)* **Altstadt Walking Tour.** *(Tours depart from the corner of Marktstr. and Rheinstr. in the Altstadt. ℹ Tours in German and English. $ €10 adults. Children €5. ⏰ Tours run Apr-Oct daily 2:30pm, Nov-Mar Sa 2:30pm. Lasts 90 min., including a 30min. boat excursion.)*
- **CONSULATES: Canada.** *(Benrather Str. 8 ☎0211 17 21 70 ⏰ Open M-F 9:30am-noon.)* **UK.** *(Yorkstr. 19 ☎0211 944 80 ⏰ Open M-Th 8:30am-12:30pm, F 8:30am-12:30pm and 1:30-4:30pm.)* **US.** *(Willi-Becker-Allee 10 ☎0211 788 89 27 ⏰ Open M-F 9am-5pm.)*

- **CURRENCY EXCHANGE: ReiseBank.** (⚡ *Inside the Hauptbahnhof.* 🕐 *Open M-Sa 7am-10pm, Su 8am-9pm.*) **American Express.** (⚡ *Inside the tourist information office on Immermanstr.* 🕐 *Open M-F 9:30-1pm and 1:30-5:30pm, Sa 10am-1pm.*)

- **WOMEN'S RESOURCES: Frauenhaus** offers a hotline service for women. (☎0211 710 34 88. 🖥www.frauenhaus-duesseldorf.de.)

- **GLBT RESOURCES: Cafe Rosa Mund** hosts events for gays and lesbians. (*Lierenfeldstr. 39.* ☎0211 99 23 77. 🖥www.rosamund.de) **Aids-Hilfe Zentrum** provides a hotline service. (*Oberbilker Allee.* ⚡ *U77: S-Bhf. Oberbilk.* Ⓢ *Hotline €0.12 per min.* 🕐 *Open M-Th 10am-1pm and 2-6pm, F 10am-1pm and 2-4pm. Hotline open M-F 9am-6pm.*)

- **LAUNDROMAT: Waschwerk.** (*Talstr. 10.* ⚡ *Walk to the right from the train station and look for the Immerhof building.*Ⓢ *Wash €3.50, soap €0.50, dry €0.50 per 11min.* 𝒊 *Free Wi-Fi available.* 🕐 *Open M-F 7am-8:30pm, Sa 8am-6pm.*)

- **POST OFFICE:** (*Konrad-Adenauer-Pl, to the right of the tourist office.* 🕐 *Open M-F 8am-6pm, Sa 9am-2pm. Limited service M-F 6-8pm.*)

- **POSTAL CODE:** *40210*

Emergency!

- **POLICE:** (*Heinrich-Heine-Allee 17 or Konrad-Adenauer-Pl. 11 in the Hauptbahnhof.* ☎0211 870 9113. *Emergency* ☎110.)

- **FIRE AND AMBULANCE:** ☎112.

- **PHARMACY: Apotheke Im Hauptbahnhof.** (☎0211 115 00. *Emergency* ☎0211 01 15 00. 🕐 *Open M-F 7am-8pm, Sa 8am-8pm.*)

Getting There

By Plane

The main airport, **Flughafen Düsseldorf,** is accessible from the city via the S11 and a Lufthansa shuttle (*approx. 10min.*). Call ☎0211 421 2223 for flight information. (🕐 *Open daily 5am-12:30am.*) **Düsseldorf Weeze** is serviced by budget airlines, including **Ryanair.** Shuttles to and from the airport (*€14*) run irregularly, about every 1hr. 30min from Düsseldorf. Buy tickets on the bus, but check the departure schedules ahead of time (🖥www.airport-weeze.de).

By Train

From **Berlin** (Ⓢ *€102.* 🕐 *4hr., 1 per hr.*); **Frankfurt** (Ⓢ *€75.* 🕐 *2hr., 2 per hr.*); **Hamburg** (Ⓢ *€84.* 🕐 *4hr., 1 per hr.*); **Munich** (Ⓢ *€129.* 🕐 *5-6 hr., 2 per hr.*). Less expensive rides depart from **Aachen, Köln** and **Dortmond.** From there, take the **S-Bahn** to Düsseldorf.

Getting Around

Public Transportation

A network of buses, trams, and U-Bahn and S-Bahn lines is integrated into the **VRR system,** connecting Düsseldorf to nearby cities. Single tickets (*€1.30*) are good for travel to destinations within three stops from the station of departure. Less confusing and more practical is the **Tageskarte** (*€5.30*), good for a day of unlimited travel on public transportation, expiring at 3am.

Taxis

Call ☎0211 333 33, ☎0211 999 99, or ☎0211 21 21 21.

Ride Share

Mitfahrzentrale. (*Graf-Adolf-Str. 80* ☎0211 194 40 🕐 *Open daily 9am-7pm.*)

FRANKFURT, THE BERGSTRASSE, AND MARBURG

Frankfurt is many things; a commercial, cosmopolitan capital. Skyscrapers loom over crowded streets and dark-suited stock traders busily jaywalk across avenues. Though Frankfurt has a reputation for being the most Americanized city in Europe, the government works to preserve the city's rich history.

This 80km "mountain road" spans the two provinces of **Hesse** and **Baden,** stretching from Heidelberg to the south all the way to Darmstadt in the north. The mild Mediterranean climate, with long summers and mild winters, makes it ideal for growing grapes, almonds, and other fruits, while its mountaintop castles and glorious churches easily accessible by car, foot, bike, or rail. By car, take the road B3, which snakes through all the major towns. ◳www.diebergstrasse.de. For an overview of the region, pick up *Holiday Route* at the Heppenheim Tourist Office, a quick guide to all the cities along the road.

greatest hits

- **BUTTERFLY KISSES.** Emerge from Cocoon Club as a drunken butterfly after spending the night wrapped in some German hottie's arms (p. 210).

- **GARDEN-VARIETY.** Bask in the sun at Palmengarten—a city park garnished with everything from palm trees to Venus Fly Traps (p. 205).

- **ON THE SAUCE.** Get saucy with some of the region's most renowned Apfelwein at Adolf Wagner (p. 209).

- **ROOM FOR SQUARES.** Window shop for quirky, modern furniture at Museum für Angewandte Kunst (p. 206).

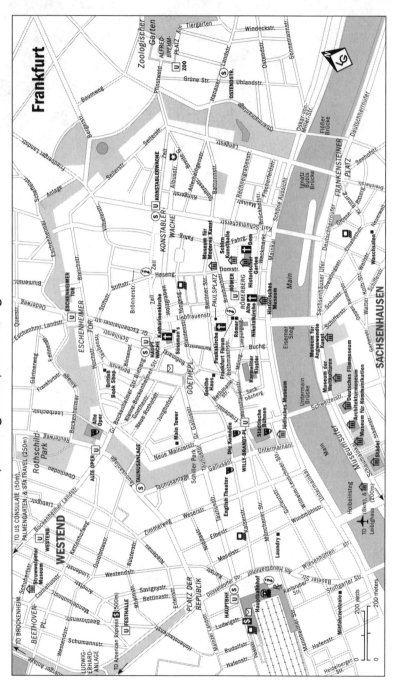

Frankfurt

frankfurt ☎069

Forget the cobblestone roads and half-timbered houses of Germany back in the day: this city on the banks of the Main River is one big financial center, with enough skyscrapers to earn it the nicknames "Mainhattan" and "Bankfurt." Legend has it that the city was auspiciously founded when Charlemagne and his Franks were fleeing the Saxons; they saw a deer crossing the Main River in a shallow *Furt* (ford) and followed it to safety on the opposite bank, and that very spot is where they founded Frankfurt. In 1356, Frankfurt rose to prominence when the Golden Bull of imperial law made it the site of emperors' elections and coronations until the Holy Roman Empire dissolved. Trade fairs—mass conglomerations of merchants all bartering with each other—regularly took place in the city. Fast forward to the 21st century; Frankfurt now houses the EU's bank, marked by an enormous statue of the euro symbol.

ORIENTATION

The Main River runs east to west through Frankfurt, conveniently splitting it into two parts, though most of the city is located in the north.

North of the Main

The city center is called the **Innenstadt,** the site of the Römerberg and the spired Dom. Its northern end is the city's commercial district, with high-class shops and restaurants stretching along the **Zeil** between the subway stops **Hauptwache** and **Konstablerwache.** Immediately west of that, around **Taunusanlage,** is the city's financial district. To the west lies the **Hauptbahnhof,** surrounded by cheap restaurants and the city's red light district. In the northwest corner is Bockenheim, home to students and the wallet-friendly eateries that join them. Some of the city's most upscale and exclusive nightlife can be found along **Hanauer Landstrasse** in the east side of the city, amid automobile dealerships.

South of the Main

Immediately south of the Main is the **Museumsufer,** a network of museums stretching along Schaumankai running along the river. Collectively, the neighborhood to the south is known as **Sachsenhausen.** In the middle around **Schweizer Platz,** you'll find a collection of age-old Apfelwein eateries, while to the east by **Frankensteiner Platz** is a hopping nightlife district, with bars and throngs of young people.

frankfurt . orientation

ACCOMMODATIONS 🏠

As the financial center of Europe, Frankfurt doesn't really offer deals, and hotels are often full of bankers and businessmen. The **West End/Bockenheim** area has affordable options in a quiet setting, though nightlife is more accessible from accommodations in **Sachsenhausen** and near the **Hauptbahnhof.**

North of the Main

👍 FRANKFURT HOSTEL 💳🚭📶🍸 HOSTEL, HOTEL [2]

Kaiserstr. 74 ☎069 247 51 30 💻www.frankfurt-hostel.de

A convenient location and great prices attract young internationals to this bustling hostel, where new friends hang out in the sunny pastel-colored rooms or the homey lobby. Nab a seat on the balcony and people-watch on the Kaiserstr. below. For a cheap meal, take advantage of the free pasta for guests on Saturday evenings, and free tastings of Frankfurt's signature green sauce on Thursdays.

⇄ From the Hauptbahnhof, head along Kaiserstr. to the hostel on the left. i Breakfast and Wi-Fi included. $ Singles and doubles €59; 3-10 bed dorms €19-22. ⏰ Reception 24hr. Check-in 2pm. Check-out 11am.

FIVE ELEMENTS 💳🚭📶🍸 HOSTEL [2]

Moselstr. 40 ☎069 24 00 58 85 💻www.5elementshostel.de

This posh hostel right by the Hauptbahnhof offers a bunch of student-friendly amenities, including a 24hr. bar with stylish leather cube seats and a bike rental. Rooms are also stylishly decked in stainless steel bunks with personal reading lamps and under-bed lockers. All this makes it worth overlooking the fact that this hostel is smack-dab in the middle of Frankfurt's red light district—just don't speak to those strangers outside late at night.

⇄ From the Hauptbahnhof, walk down Kaiserstr. and then turn left onto Moselstr. i Towels and Wi-Fi included. Linens €1.50. Breakfast €4. Laptops available to borrow with deposit. $ 5-7 bed dorms from €18; singles €40; doubles from €50; quads from €88. ⏰ Reception 24hr. Check-in 4pm. Check-out noon.

MEININGER'S HOSTEL AND HOTEL 💳🚭📶🍸❄ HOSTEL, HOTEL [2]

Europaallee. 64 ☎030 66 63 61 00 💻www.meininger-hotels.de

This colorful building has some of the most luxurious hostel accommodations in town, with superbly clean rooms featuring flatscreen TVs and phones in each room. Though mostly populated by businessmen coming into town for trade fairs at the Messe immediately next door, the rooms are a real steal during quieter times.

⇄ S3, S4, S5, or S6: Messe, then walk south toward a blocky multi-colored building. i Breakfast €7.50. Linens and Wi-Fi included. $ 3-6 bed dorms €19-28; singles from €52; doubles €70. ⏰ Reception 24hr. Check-in 3pm. Check-out 10am.

CITY CAMP FRANKFURT 🚭📶🍸 HOSTEL, HOTEL [2]

An der Sandelmühle 35b ☎069 57 03 32 💻www.city-camp-frankfurt.de

A little outside of town, though close to the U-Bahn, the City Camp Frankfurt has plenty of tree-lined spots and a DSL hotspot for internet-aholics.

⇄ U1, U2, or U3: Hedderheim. Exit through the unmarked exit farthest from the street and turn left until you get to the Sandelmühle sign. Turn right, cross the stream, and turn left to campground ahead. i Wi-Fi €4 per day. Restaurant on-site. $ €6.50, children 2-14 €2.50. Tent €4. Showers €1.10. ⏰ Reception M-F 9am-1pm and 4-5pm, Sa-Su 10am-1pm and 5-8pm. Check-out 4pm.

South of the Main

👍 HAUS DER JUGEND (HI) 💳♿📶🍸 HOSTEL [2]

Deutschhernufer 12 ☎069 610 01 50 💻www.jugendherberge-frankfurt.de

Bright and cheery, though with a slight institutional feel common with HI hostels, the Haus der Jugend is situated right by the nightlife frenzy of Sachsenhausen and packs in a whole ton of amenities. Ask the helpful staff for recommendations if you're at a loss for what to do, and don't forget to spend some time playing with the giant chess set!

Bus #46: Frankensteiner Pl., then backtrack a tiny bit to the hostel. ℹ Breakfast and linens included. Wi-Fi €5 per day. Laundry €2. $ 8- to 10-bed dorms €18; singles €36.50; doubles €53-63; triples €63-76.50; quads €84-102. ⏰ Reception 24hr. Lock-out 2-6:30am; call for service. Check-in 1pm. Check-out 10am.

SIGHTS

Beneath the daunting skyscrapers that define the Frankfurt landscape are several historic sights, all of which have undergone some degree of reconstruction since the Altstadt's destruction in 1944. Old and new come to a head in the conflicted metropolis—some attractions reflect the city's increasingly contemporary identity and others remain as relics of a bygone Frankfurt. The city's museums are its most prized cultural possessions, all of them exceptionally well-done though their sheer number is enough to leave any tourist overwhelmed. Consider getting a **Frankfurt Card** or a **Museumsufer Ticket** for some steep discounts.

North of the Main

★ MUSEUM FÜR MODERNE KUNST — MUSEUM

Domstr. 10 ☎069 21 23 04 47 www.mmk-frankfurt.de

Blocks from the Dom, this highly stylized postmodern "slice of cake" building provides a fitting setting for the modern art within. The museum rotates its permanent collection of European and American art, and prides itself on special exhibits of new and unknown artists and forms. Small balconies on the top floor also offer spectacular views of the Dom.

U4 or U5: Römer/Dom. From the station, walk to the curvy building 1 block north of the Dom. ℹ Explanations offered in English. $ €8, students €4. Free admission last Sa of month. ⏰ Open Tu 10am-6pm, W 10am-8pm, Th-Su 10am-6pm.

RÖMERBERG — SQUARE

A voyage through Frankfurt should begin in this central area of the Altstadt, among the half-timbered architecture and medieval-looking fountains that appear on all postcards of the city. The Statue of Justice, with its delicate scales, stands in the center of the square to celebrate the 13 coronations of German emperors once held in the city. Once spouting wine, today she only offers shade to the plethora of pigeons perched at her feet.

U4 or U5: Dom/Römer.

RÖMER — CITY HALL

Römerberg 25

At the west end of the Römerberg, the gables of Römer have marked the site of Frankfurt's city hall since 1405. It was also the original stop on the Main for the merchants who began the city's long trade tradition. Today, the building's upper floors are open to the public. Visit the **Kaisersaal,** a former imperial banquet hall adorned with portraits of 52 German emperors, from Charlemagne to Franz II. Be forewarned, however, that private events held in the Römer close the building to the public entirely.

U4 or U5: Dom/Römer. $ €2. ⏰ Open daily 10am-1pm and 2-5pm.

ARCHÄOLOGISCHER GARTEN — ARCHAEOLOGICAL SITE

Between the Dom and the rest of the Römerberg are the Schirn Kunsthalle and a plantless "garden" of crumbled building foundations dating back to the 2000-year-old Roman settlement. Three sets of ruins, from the first century BC and the ninth and 15th centuries CE, were uncovered during excavations in 1953. Today, they are preserved in a well-maintained urban garden landscape.

Over the summer, theater performances often take place on scaffolding straddling the garden.

U4 or U5: Dom/Römer. From the stop, head toward the Dom.

DOM CHURCH

Dompl. 14 ☎069 13 37 61 84 www.dom-frankfurt.de

East of the Archäologischer Garten stands the only major historical building in the city center that escaped complete destruction in WWII. The seven electors of the Holy Roman Empire chose emperors here, and the Dom served as the site of coronation ceremonies from 1562 to 1792. The **Dom Museum** inside the main entrance has architectural studies of the Dom, intricate chalices, and the ceremonial robes of imperial electors. The **Haus am Dom,** across the courtyard from the church itself, also houses a branch of the museum.

U4 or U5: Dom/Römer. [$] Cathedral free. Dom Museum €3, students €2. Tours €3, students €2. ⏰ Cathedral open M-Th 9am-noon and 2:30pm-8pm, F 2:30-8pm, except during services. Tours in German Tu-Su 3pm. Museum open Tu-F 10am-5pm, Sa-Su 11am-5pm. Haus am Dom open M-F 9am-5pm, Sa-Su 11am-5pm.

GOETHEHAUS HOUSE

Großer Hirschgraben 23-25 ☎069 13 88 00 www.goethehaus-frankfurt.de

The house in which the father of Faust was born was meticulously reconstructed after its WWII destruction and has since been preserved as a shrine to the author, with all of his family's fine furnishings on display. Wind your way up the four stories of sitting rooms, bedrooms, and writing chambers and learn more than you ever thought possible about the childhood home of Germany's most beloved literary giant. The memorable writing chamber, puppet-show room, and personal library should not be missed. If you still want more, the neighboring **Goethe Museum** promises to offer obsessed fans a more in-depth look at the author's life when it reopens after an extensive renovation in early 2011.

U1, U2, U3, U4, or U5: Willy-Brandt-Pl. From the stop, follow the signs. i English placards available. [$] €5, students €2.50. Interactive audio tour €3. ⏰ Open M-Sa 10am-6pm, Su 10am-5:30pm.

MAIN TOWER OBSERVATION DECK OBSERVATION DECK

Neue Mainzer Str. 52-58. ☎069 36 50 47 40 www.maintower.de

Vistors will agree that a trip to the top of Frankfurt's only observation deck is a must. Take the elevator to the 54th floor and walk three floors up to the outdoor observation deck, where your 250m height will let you see for miles (kilometers) on end. You can also sip a cocktail *(from €4)* at the bar just one floor below.

S-bahn: Taunusanlage. From the stop, walk along Junghofstr. and then turn right onto Neue Mainzer Str. [$] €5, students €3.50. ⏰ Ground floor exhibit open M-F 8am-8pm, Sa-Su 10am-5pm. Platform open in summer M-Th 10am-9pm, F-Sa 10am-11pm, Su 10am-9pm; in winter M-Th 10am-7pm, F-Sa 10am-9pm, Su 10am-7pm. Restaurant and bar open Tu-Th 5:30pm-1am, F-Sa 5:30pm-2am.

SCHIRN KUNSTHALE MUSEUM

Römerberg ☎069 299 88 20 www.schirn-kunsthalle.de

With no permanent exhibits, the Schirn morphs up to 10 times a year to accommodate every imaginable genre, from sedate Baroque painting to experimental photodocumentary. The museum's objective remains the same: to create an array of art experiences for the masses. Accordingly, the Schirn holds a variety of art classes for children, adults, and families.

U4 or U5: Römer/Dom. From the stop, walk toward the round building nestled at the southeast side of the square. [$] Prices vary; admission generally €8, students €6. ⏰ Open Tu 10am-7pm, W-Th 10am-10pm, F-Su 10am-7pm.

HISTORISCHES MUSEUM

🍴♿🍸 MUSEUM

💻www.historisches-museum.frankfurt.de

Perched at the southern end of the Römerberg, the Historiches Museum seeks to preserve the city's long and storied past. See treasures from old Frankfurt, learn about life in the city during the Middle Ages, and visit more contempoary exhibitions on the ground floor.

🚇 U4 or U5: Römer/Dom. $ €4, students €2. Free last Sa of month. €2 admission 1hr. before close. ⏰ Open Tu 10am-6pm, W 10am-9pm, Th-Su 10am-6pm.

PALMENGARTEN

🍴♿ BOTANICAL GARDEN

Siesmayerstr. 61 ☎069 21 23 39 39 💻www.palmengarten.frankfurt.de

Palm trees flank the entrance to Frankfurt's botanical garden, a constant source of pride and joy for Frankfurters, who flock to flower beds to smell the roses, to the greenhouses to observe the Venus Fly Traps, and to the lush green fields to sunbathe on the surprisingly comfortable lawn chairs. Stop by the pond and marvel at the immense fish, and forget that you're in the middle of one of Germany's most metropolitan cities.

🚇 U6 or U7: Westend. From the station, turn on Bockenheimier Landstr. away from the Block House and turn right onto Siesmayerstr. $ €5, students €2. ⏰ Box office open Mar-Oct 9am-6pm, Nov-Jan 9am-4pm. Entrance on Siesmayerstr. open until 2hr. after box office closes.

IG FARBENHAUS

♿ MEMORIAL

Grüneburgplatz 1 ☎069 79 83 22 28 💻www.wollheim-memorial.de

A prime example of Bauhaus architecture, this mammoth office building was the largest office building in Europe until the 1950s. This complex housed the headquarters and research offices of IG Farben, a group of chemical companies that included the drug company Bayer and the film company Agfa. During World War II, this building was also the site of product development for a variety of chemicals used by the German forces, including Zyklon B, the notorious gas used in concentration camp gas chambers. Plaques throughout the building, now home to the humanities and cultural studies departments of the Goethe-Universität, trace the building's history, while a small house to the side houses the **Wollheim Memorial.** Marked only by the numbers 107984, the prisoner number of concentration camp survivor Norbert Wollheim, the room features two TV screens with interactive video exhibits giving first-hand accounts from prisoners in IG Farben during the war.

🚇 U6 or U7: Westend. From the station, take bus #36: Uni Campus Westend. Or, from Westend, walk north onto Myliusstr., then turn right onto Grunebergweg and continue until you see a gated parking lot on the left. Walk into the parking lot and the building will be on the right, with the memorial on the left. $ Free. ⏰ Open 24hr.

SENCKENBERG NATURMUSEUM

🍴♿🍸 MUSEUM

Senckenberganlage 25 ☎069 754 20 💻www.senckenberg.de

Natural history is revealed in this museum in the form of fossils, with larger-than-life dinosaurs standing guard in the main hall and a number of smaller fossils from the Messel Pit historic site. Don't miss the giant anaconda fossil (who knew that a snake would have so many bones?) snaking its way through the ground floor, or the lifelike landscape dioramas with taxidermic animals on the top floor.

🚇 U4, U6, or U7: Bockenheimer Warte. $ €6, students €3. ⏰ Open M-Tu 9am-5pm, W 9am-8pm, Th-F 9am-5pm, Sa-Su 9am-6pm.

JÜDISCHES MUSEUM

🍴♿🍸 MUSEUM

Untermankai 14-15 ☎069 21 23 50 00💻www.juedischesmuseum.de

This museum includes a comprehensive history of Jewish life in Frankfurt, displaying furniture and silverware and other artifacts.

U1, U2, U3, U4, or U5: Willy-Brandt-Platz. From the station, walk toward the river and turn right. ℹ English notebooks with explanations available. English audio tour also available. $ €4, students €2. Admission to both the Jüdisches Judengasse €5, students €2.50; last Sa of month free. ⏰ Open Tu 10am-5pm, W 10am-8pm, Th-Su 10am-5pm.*

JUDENGASSE ♿ 🍸 MUSEUM

Kurt-Schumacher-Str. 10 ☎069 297 74 19

This museum includes original excavation sites from 18th-century Jewish ghettos, while immediately outside the museum is a monument inscribed with the individual names of Frankfurt Jews that died in the Holocaust.

 # Tram 11 or 12: Börneplatz. From the station, walk toward the river down Kurt-Schumacher-Str. Alternatively, U4 or U5: Dom/Römer. From the station, walk past the Dom, turn left onto Fahrgasse, then right onto Dominikanergasse to the end. ℹ English audio tour available. $ €2, students €1. Admission to both Judengasse and Jüdisches (see above) €5, students €2.50; free last Sa of month. ⏰ Open Tu 10am-5pm, W 10am-8pm, Th-Su 10am-5pm.

EXPLORA MUSEUM

Glauburgpl. 1 ☎069 78 88 88 💻www.explora.de

Obsessed with optical illusions, magic eyes, or 3D pictures? Explora's the place for you, with a large collection of all things weird and wacky. Start your adventure on the ground floor at the basin with handles; wet your hands in the basin and rub the handles for a cool sound and for the water to fizz. Then take your 3D glasses up through the museum's three floors and try to spot all the incarnations of each image, many of which are actually of naked women. Unless you're into optical illusions, it's probably not worth the high price of admission.

 # U5: Glauburgstr. From the station, walk 3 blocks west and turn left onto Lortzingstr. $ €14, students €10. ⏰ Open Tu-Su 11am-6pm.

South of the Main

Museumsufer

The Museumsufer (that's Museums-ufer, not Museum-sufer, and most definitely and most unfortunately not Museum-surfer) is a strip along the southern bank of the Main that hosts an eclectic range of museums mostly housed in opulent 19th-century mansions. The sheer diversity of topics covered in the museums means that there's something for everyone, from film to anthropology to impressionist art. The Museumsufer is also home to Frankfurt's **Museumsuferfest,** a huge cultural celebration held every August with art showings, music, and general revelry among the Main. To get there, take the U1, U2, or U3 to Schweitzer Pl. and then walk north toward the river. Alternatively, take bus #46 from the Hauptbahnhof, which runs along the Museumsufer.

MUSEUM FÜR ANGEWANDTE KUNST ♿ 🍸 MUSEUM

Schaumankai 17 ☎069 21 23 40 37 💻www.angewandtekunst-frankfurt.de

With an impressive display of art spanning over 5000 years, the modern wing of the museum is perhaps the most fun, with plenty of quirky chairs and lamps and other simple household items that highlight the evolution of industrial design. The futuristic new building is also connected to the original villa via a bridge on the second floor, inside of which furnished rooms represent unique styles and time periods.

 # On the eastern end of the Museumsufer, by the Eierner Steg footbridge. $ €8, students €4. ⏰ Open Tu 10am-5pm, W 10am-9pm, and Th-Su 10am-5pm.

STÄDEL ♿ 🍸 MUSEUM

Holbeinstr. 1 ☎069 696 05 09 80 💻www.staedelmuseum.de

The crown jewel of the Museumsufer presents seven centuries of art, from Old Masters like Botticelli, Rembrant, and Vermeer, to the fathers of modern art including Monet, Renoir, and Picasso. The permanent collection will be closed until summer 2011 for a top-down renovation, which will result in more space to house the museum's expanded modern art collection. In the meantime, rotating temporary exhibits are on display.

⚑ *By the Holbeinsteg, the colorful suspended footbridge.* ℹ *All captions in English. All prices and hours are set to change once the permanent collection reopens.* Ⓢ *€12, students €10, under 12 free. Audio tours €4, students €3.* ⏲ *Open Tu 10am-8pm, W-Th 10am-10pm, and F-Su 10am-8pm.*

LIEBIEGHAUS
⚑ & ♿ MUSEUM

Schaumankai 71 ☎069 650 04 90 ◻www.liebieghaus.de

The impressive building and gardens contain classical, medieval, Renaissance, Baroque, and Rococo statues, friezes, and other sculptures. A climb up the tower also leads you to several rooms still furnished in the house's original style, full of cozy nooks and outstanding views of the Main.

⚑ *Next door to and west of the Städel.* Ⓢ *€9, students 7, under 12 free. Audio tours €4, students €3.* ⏲ *Open Tu 10am-6pm, W-Th until 10am-9pm, F-Su 10am-6pm.*

DEUTSCHES FILMMUSEUM
⚑ & ♿ MUSEUM

Schaumankai 41 ☎069 961 22 00◻www.deutschesfilmmuseum.de

Observe the progression of film from a 19th-century obsession with optical illusions to the first pictures by the Lumière Brothers. Under renovation until spring 2011, the new museum promises more space and a larger soundproof theater.

⚑ *By the Untermainbrücke.* ℹ *Hours and prices will be set when the museum reopens.*

MUSEUM FÜR KOMMUNIKATION (MUSEUM FOR COMMUNICATION)
⚑ & ♿ MUSEUM

Schaumainkai 53 ☎069 606 00 ◻www.mfk-frankfurt.de

Guarded by a mounted knight made of old radios and TVs, this museum focuses on the importance of communications technology. Go behind the scenes of the post office, learn how telegraphs and telephones work, and trace the rise of radio, television, and the internet. Special exhibits also display forms of communication mixed in with the world of art.

⚑ *Next door to and west of the Film Museum.* ℹ *Explanations in German, but a laminated book at each section gives explanations in English. Audio tour €1.50, or you can download everything at the website for free and listen on your own mp3 player.* Ⓢ *€2.50, under 6 €1.* ⏲ *Open Tu-F 9am-6pm, Sa-Su 11am-7pm.*

MUSEUM GIERSCH
⚑ & ♿ MUSEUM

Schaumankai 83 ☎069 63 30 41 28 ◻www.museum-giersch.de

The youngest member of the Museumsufer, the Museum Giersch opened in 2000 to house exhibits usually from private collections that would otherwise never be displayed to the public. While the focus is on visual art, the museum also displays scultpures, graphic art, and photography depending on the exhibit itself.

⚑ *At the western end of the Museumsufer, closest to the Friedensbrücke.* Ⓢ *€5, students €2.50.* ⏲ *Open Tu-F noon-7pm, F noon-5pm, Sa-Su 11-5pm.*

MUSEUM DER WELTKULTUREN (MUSEUM OF WORLD CULTURES)⚑ & ♿ MUSEUM

Schaumankai 29-37 ☎069 212 359 13 ◻www.mwk-frankfurt.de

A treasure trove of indigenous art from all around the world, the Museum der Weltkulturen seeks to promote global understanding through displays of international creations. A new building set to open by 2012 will finally house the entirety of the museum's permanent collection, which is currently displayed on a rotating basis.

Ⓢ *Prices vary with individual exhibits, usually €3-4 for each, students €1-2.* ⏲ *Open Tu 10am-5pm, W 10am-8pm, Th-Su 10am-5pm.*

frankfurt • sights

FOOD

Frankfurters love sausages and beer, but they have their own regional specialties as well. Feast on *Handkäse mit Musik*, a gel-like translucent yellow cheese with a strong flavor, served with vinegar and topped with onions. *Grüne Sosse*, or green sauce, is actually a white sauce made green with borrage, sorrel, chives, and other assorted green herbs and served with peeled potatoes and boiled eggs. Wash both of these specialties down with *Apfelwein* (also called *Ebbelwoi*), apple wine, poured from a blue and white porcelain *Bembel* into small 0.3L *Geripptes* glasses. Portions of apple wine should never exceed €2 and are regularly enjoyed in **Sachsenhausen,** the old district on the southern side of the Main.

The most reasonably-priced meals can be found around the Hauptbahnhof, with a large variety of ethnic (mostly Asian) eateries, and in the university district of Bockenheim (take U4, U6 or U7: Bockenheimer Warte). A number of inexpensive food carts and stands populate the Zeil as well as the large shopping district around Hauptwache. For cheap do-it-yourself meals, keep your eyes peeled for **Penny Markt** *(e.g. Hanauer Landstr. 1-5, right off the Zeil. ⏰ Open M-Sa 7am-10pm)* or **Aldi Süd** *(e.g. Darmstädter Landstr. 10, in Sachsenhausen. ⏰ Open M-Sa 8am-8pm).* At Hauptwache, the **Galeria Kaufhof** *(Zeil 116-126. ⏰ Open M-W 9:30am-8pm, Th-Sa 9:30am-9pm)* also has a grocery store in the basement.

North of the Main

👍 DAS LEBEN IST SCHÖN — 💳🚭🍸❄☀ ITALIAN [2]

Hanauer Landstr. 128 ☎069 43 05 78 70 💻www.daslebenistschoen.de

This restaurant proclaims "life is beautiful," and looking upon the portraits on the walls, one can't help but agree. A bite of the piping hot pastas or freshly baked pizzas will confirm the sentiment. A summer patio is decorated with nautical themes.

🚊 Tram 11: Schwedlerstr, then keep heading west for a ½-block. $ Entrees €6.80-16.80. ⏰ Open M-Th 11:30am-midnight, F 11:30am-1am, Sa noon-1am, Su 6pm-midnight.

👍 KLEINMARKTHALLE — 🚭♿🍸 MARKET [1]

Hasengasse 5 ☎069 21 23 36 96 💻www.kleinmarkthalle.de

Make your own lunch in this three-story warehouse of bakeries, butchers, and produce stands. Cutthroat competition among the many vendors keeps prices low. Find enough meat to feed a small nation, though most of it is raw.

🚊 U4 or U5: Römer/Dom, then head toward the Dom and continue north about a ½ block past the Museum für Moderne Kunst. ⏰ Open M-F 8am-6pm, Sa 8am-4pm.

IMA MULTIBAR — 💳🚭🍸☀ WRAPS [2]

Kleine Bockenheimer Str. 14 ☎069 90 02 56 65 💻www.ima-multibar.de

One of the only affordable eateries by the opulent Goethestr., IMA Multibar serves up delicious and hearty wraps and salads to throngs of shoppers and young professionals. The fast-paced (pay up at the front) and hip (check out the bathroom sinks) combo makes for a popular spot both for lunch and for nighttime drinks.

🚊 U6 or U7: Alte Oper, then head west on Kalbacher Gasse, turn right onto Goethestr., then turn left into the small back alley. $ Wraps €7.50-9. Salads €4.50-12. ⏰ Open M-W 11am-10:30pm, Th-Sa 11am-1:30am. Kitchen open M-W 11am-9:30pm, Th-Sa 11am-midnight.

CAFE LAUMER — 💳♿🍸☀ CAFE [2]

Bockenheimer Landstr. 67 ☎069 72 79 12 💻www.cafe-laumer.de

Dine like a local on the outdoor patio or backyard garden of this celebrated cafe in the West End, only a few blocks from the university. Young business-men on their lunch break enjoy the hearty special of the day *(€6.40-9.80)* while neighborhood residents read the newspaper, drink a cup of coffee *(€2.20),* and eat generous slices of cake *(€2.40-3.20).*

🚇 U6 or U7: Westend, then head east on Bockenheimer Landstr. to restaurant on right. [$] Entrees €4.60-9.80. ⏰ Open M-F 9am-8pm, Sa 8:30am-7pm, Su 9:30am-7pm.

JADE-MAGIC WOK ⊛♿🍸⛅ CHINESE [2]

Moselstr. 25 ☎069 27 13 59 88

This cozy little Chinese restaurant not far from the Hauptbahnhof serves up cheap and tasty meals. Try the entrees with *Sa-Cha Soße,* a flavorful difficult-to-describe Chinese sauce. The recommended specials have plenty of entrees for only €5.

*🚇 From the Hauptbahnhof, walk straight down Kaiserstr. and turn right onto Moselstr. **i** If you speak Chinese with the owners, they're likely to give you free dessert. [$] Entrees €4.10-12.50. ⏰ Open daily 11:30am-11pm.*

CONRAD'S 💳♿🍸⛅ GERMAN [3]

Gross Eschenheimer Str. 3 ☎069 28 53 38

They might claim to be known for their rump steak, but save yourself the money and get one of the inventive schnitzel variations instead—there's an entire page of them, with everything from cheese schnitzel to schnitzel with onions. The outdoor patio offers great views of the Katherinenkirche in Hauptwache, and the bilingual menus make it quite touristy, but it's worth the indulgence.

🚇 U1, U2, U3, U6, U7, or S1-9: Hauptwache, then head to the intersection between the Galeria Kaufhof and the movie theater. [$] Entrees €8-33.

BEST WORSCHT IN TOWN ⊛♿❄⛅ SNACKS [1]

Grünebergweg 37 ☎069 72 11 69 💻www.snack-point.de

This cartoon-ish chain in Frankfurt is known for making some of the spiciest *worscht* (known elsewhere through Germany as *wurst*) in town. Its "heaven and hell" posters show you your options, from the angelic "Cheesy Style" to the Lucifer-infused "F***ing Burning Injection." Standing tables only.

*🚇 U1, U2, or U3: Grünebergweg, then head west on Grünebergweg to stand on left. **i** Other location at Bergerstr. 80, open M-Sa 11am-11pm. Others throughout town, as well. [$] Currywurst creations €2.50-7.30. ⏰ Open M-F 9am-7pm, Sa noon-6pm.*

South of the Main

ADOLF WAGNER 💳♿🍸⛅ GERMAN [3]

Schweizer Str. 71 ☎069 61 25 65 💻www.apfelwein-wagner.de

Saucy German dishes and some of the region's most renowned *Apfelwein* keep patrons of this famous corner of old Sachsenhausen jolly. Sit with storied regulars and try some of the *Grüne Sosse* that you keep hearing about. Head inside for classic German decor, or stay outside for prime people-watching.

*🚇 U1, U2, or U3: Schweizer Platz, then head south on Schweizerstr. to restaurant on left. **i** English menu available. [$] Entrees €7.30-13. 0.3L Apfelwine €1.60. ⏰ Open daily 11am-midnight.*

NIGHTLIFE

If you're just looking for a low-key night with a few drinks, head to Sachsenhausen on the southern side of the city. Head between **Bruckenstrasse** and **Dreieichstrasse** for an authentic German experience, with rowdy pubs and taverns specializing in local *Apfelwein* (also known as *Ebbelwoi*). The complex of cobblestone streets centering on **Grosse** and **Kleine Rittergasse** teems with cafes, bars, restaurants, and Irish pubs. While nightlife can be fickle, Frankfurt has thriving clubs and prominent DJs, mostly between **Zeil** and **Bleichstrasse** and the nearby **Hanauer Landstrasse.** In general, things don't heat up until after midnight. Wear something dressier than jeans and sneakers if you want to get past the picky bouncers.

North of the Main

👍 COCOON CLUB
💳⊗🍸❄ CLUB

Carl-Benz-Str. 21 ☎069 90 02 00 💻www.cocoonclub.net

Oozing with ultra-hip coolness, this popular club epitomizes trend-setting design with intergalactic decor, curvy walls, fluorescent pods, and "membranous" separators. Dress well to get past the bouncers.

🚇 U11, U12: Dieselstr., then walk down Carl-Benz-Str. until you get to the club. $ Cover €15. ⏰ Open F-Sa 9pm-6am.

👍 PULSE AND PIPER RED LOUNGE
💳⊗🍸❄⛅▼ BAR, CLUB

Bleichstr. 38A ☎069 13 88 68 02 💻www.pulse-frankfurt.de

An all-in-one with two dance halls, two lounges, a restaurant, and a summer beer garden, Pulse is swanky and chic. Despite its size, the club manages to maintain a cozy feel as bartenders warmly greet regulars on their way in. A smoking section, Piper, comprised of a separate bar and lots of lounge space is one of the largest public smoking areas in Frankfurt. Although officially a gay club, Pulse enjoys a mixed clientele, especially at their restaurant.

🚇 U1, U2, or U3: Escehenheimer Tor, then move 1 block north and 2 blocks west on Bleichstr. i Martini M, all martinis €5. Happy hour Th, all cocktails €6.50. $ Restaurant entrees change monthly, generally €6-22. Beer €2.80-4. Cocktails €8-10. ⏰ Pulse open M-Th 11am-1am, F 11am-4am, Sa noon-4am, Su noon-1am. Piper Lounge (entry within Pulse) open daily at 6pm and closes with Pulse. Kitchen open until 11pm.

ODEON
💳⊗🍸❄⛅ CLUB

Seilerstr. 34 ☎069 28 50 55 💻www.theodeon.de

Housed in a former art gallery that may have well been a palace, Odeon exudes both class and character, though it is still much more down-to-earth than some of the Frankfurt's more exclusive clubs. Head over on student night Thursdays, where your €3 entry fee also gets you unlimited visits to the delicious midnight buffet.

🚇 U4, U5, U6, U7, or S1-9: Konstablerwache, then head north on Kurt-Schumacher-Str. and turn right onto Seilerstr. Look for the villa with the pillars and the octopus-esque carving on the door. i M hip-hop and R and B, F 27+ nights, Th-Sa house music. $ Cover €5, Sa €8. Beer €3. Cocktails €8. All drinks ½-price until midnight. ⏰ Open M, Th-Sa 10pm-4am.

KING KAMEHAMEHA CLUB
💳⊗🍸❄ CLUB

Hanauer Landstr. 196a ☎069 48 00 37 54 💻www.king-kamehameha.de

The King of all Frankfurt clubs, King Kamehameha Club (or "King Ka" as the locals call it) is luxuriously classy, with stern bouncers at the door guarding their clientele against blasphemous flip-flop-clad commoners. Inside, a two-story lounge also includes a performance space for their in-house cover band, while a canopied outdoor area is more reminiscent of an upper-class Hawaiian beach club. Prices aren't cheap, but King Ka is the place to see and be seen; customers have included Rihanna and members of the German national soccer team.

🚇 Tram 11: Schwedlerstr, then keep heading west for a ½ block. The club is located behind the restaurant Das Leben ist Schön; look for the big smokestack. $ Cover Th 9-10pm free, after 10pm €8, F-Sa €10. Beer €4-5. Mixed drinks €9-12. ⏰ Open Th 9pm-4 or 5am, F-Sa 10pm-4 or 5am.

JAZZKELLER
💳♿🍸❄ JAZZ CLUB

Kleine Bockenheimer Str. 18a ☎069 28 85 37 💻www.jazzkeller.com

Founded in 1952, Jazzkeller is the oldest jazz club in Germany and has hosted a large number of jazz masters, including **Louis Armstrong** and **Dizzy Gillespie.** Wednesday nights are reserved for jam sessions by local groups, while Friday nights are the DJ-ed "Swingin'-Latin-Funky" dance nights. Live performances take place the other nights of the week.

🚇 U6 or U7: Alte Oper, then head west on Kalbacher Gasse, turn right onto Goethestr., then turn left

into the small back alley. Ⓢ *Cover W and F €5, €12-20 on other nights.* ☕ *Open W-Th 9pm-late, F 10pm-3am, Sa 10pm-late, Su 8pm-late. Opening time subject to change.*

SWITCHBOARD
⊕⊗♀▼ CAFE

Alte Gasse 36 ☎069 29 59 59 🖳www.ad36.de

More a community center than an actual club, Switchboard is Frankfurt's go-to for the gay and lesbian community. An information center in the basement has walls filled with free pamphlets, and the bartenders (all volunteers) are also extremely knowledgable about the city's sexual health resources. Although much of the clientele is older, many students also go for the homey atmosphere.

⚲ *U1, U2, or U3: Eschenheimer Tor, then move with traffic down Bleichstr. for 3 blocks and you'll see it on the right.* ⓘ *2nd floor has counseling offices, schedule appointments in advance by phone. Anonymous AIDS testing M 5-7:30pm, €15.* Ⓢ *Beer €2.30-3.20. Shots €1.80. Long drinks €5.80.* ☕ *Open M-Th 7pm-midnight, F-Sa 7pm-1am, Sa-Su 7pm-11pm.*

South of the Main

SAM'S SPORTSBAR
♥♿♀❄♨ BAR

Kleine Rittergasse 28-30 ☎069 66 36 90 20 🖳www.samssportsbar.de

The American theme of this bar might seem like a turn-off, but the low drink prices excuse any kitsch. With €4 cocktails all day and €1 shots after midnight, Sam's is the cheapest bar in the popular Sachsenhausen district, and you'll always find it brimming with young people. Its signature burgers were voted the best in Frankfurt, though in Germany, that statement doesn't go quite as far as it would in America.

⚲ *Bus #46 (from the Hauptbahnhof) or Tram 14: Frankensteiner Pl., then head down Frankensteinerstr. which turns into Kleine Rittergasse.* Ⓢ *Beer €2.50-4.10. Mixed drinks €7-8. Entrees €6-29.* ☕ *Open M-W 4:30pm-1am, Th 4:30pm-2am, F 4:30pm-4am, Sa noon-4am, Su noon-1am.*

ARTS AND CULTURE
🔊

Frankfurt has a large variety of venues that bring you everything from opera to musical theater, rock bands to symphony orchestras. Tickets can be bought from Frankfurt Ticket (☎069 1340-400 🖳www.frankfurt-ticket.de ☕ Open M-F 9am-8pm, Sa 9am-7pm, Su 10am-6pm), or at its office on the B level of the Hauptwache U-Bahn station (open M-F 10am-6pm, Sa 10am-4pm).

Stadtische Buhnen

This modern complex in the financial Willy-Brandt-Platz is home to two main companies: the **Oper Frankfurt** and the **Schauspiel.** Both also hold regular performances in the **Bockenheimer Depot,** a converted train depot (Carlo-Schmid-Platz 1, take the U4, U6, or U7: Bockenheimer Warte. ☎069 134 0400 🖳www.bockenheimer-depot.de).

OPER FRANKFURT
♥♿❄ OPERA

Untermainanlage 11 ☎069 134 04 00 🖳www.oper-frankfurt.de

The new digs of Frankfurt's renowned opera company are situated by the financial district, and the chunky building suits the modern interpretations performed within. Check out the big cloud sculpture that drapes around the lobby.

⚲ *U1, U2, U3, U4, or U5: Willy-Brandt-Platz, then head toward the big euro statue.* ⓘ *Tickets include use of local public transit 5hr. before the performance until the transit shutdown.* Ⓢ *Tickets €9-130, students ½-price.* ☕ *Box office open M-F 10am-6pm, Sa 10am-4pm.*

SCHAUSPIEL
♥♿❄ THEATER

Neuer Mainzer Str. 17 ☎069 134 04 00 🖳www.schauspielfrankfurt.de

Frankfurt's premier theater company puts on about 25 productions a year, many of them experimental. The complex consists of three venues: the **Schauspielhaus** is the largest theater stage in all of Germany, the **Kammerspiele** is kept completely black to prevent distractions, and the **Box** is an intimate venue with only 66 seats.

🚇 U1, U2, U3, U4, or U5: Willy-Brandt-Pl., then head toward the river on Neuer Mainzer Str. ℹ Tickets include use of local public transit 5hr. before the performance until the transit shutdown. $ Tickets €10-44, students €6-10. ⏰ Box office open M-F 10am-6pm, Sa 10am-4pm.

Other Venues

THE ENGLISH THEATRE — 💳♿❄ THEATER

Gallusanlage 7 ☎089 242 316 20 💻www.english-theatre.org

The largest English-language theater in continental Europe, the English Theatre has 300 seats and puts on between 6-8 shows per season, ranging from dramatic tragedies to light-hearted musicals.

🚇 U1, U2, U3, U4, or U5: Willy-Brandt-Pl., then walk past the Euro statue and turn right onto Gallusanlage. $ Tickets generally €21-34, student tickets (not available for Sa performances) €14-23. ⏰ Performances Tu-Sa 7:30pm, Su 6pm. Box office open M noon-6pm, Tu-F 11am-6:30pm, Sa 3pm-6:30pm, Su 3pm-5pm.

ALTE OPER — 💳♿❄ CLASSICAL MUSIC

Opernpl. 1 ☎069 134 03 75 💻www.alteoper.de

Once an ornate opera house, performances here now mostly consist of classical music rather than opera. Although Frankfurt does not have its own symphony orchestra, the city is often a tour stop for internationally renowned orchestras, including the New York Philharmonic and the Berlin Philharmonic. The hall is also home to the Sir Georg Solti Conducting Competition, held every other October.

🚇 U6 or U7: Alte Oper. $ Shows vary in price, students under 27 pay ½-price. ⏰ Box office open M-F 10am-6:30pm, Sa 10am-2pm.

DIE KOMÖDIE — 💳♿❄ THEATER

Neue Mainzer Str. 14-18 ☎069 28 43 30 💻www.diekomoedie.de

This cozy little theater produces lighter theatrical fare, with all productions in German.

🚇 U1, U2, U3, U4, or U5: Willy-Brandt-Pl., then walk toward the river along Neue Mainzer Str. $ Tickets generally €20-30. ⏰ Box office open M-F 9am-5pm.

SHOPPING

Being the cosmopolitan city that it is, Frankfurt has a large contingent of upscale shopping areas scattered throughout the city. Most notably, the super-expensive name brand stores are concentrated on **Goethestr.,** accessible through the **Hauptwache** U-Bahn and S-Bahn stops. **Zeil,** another large shopping street, stretches east-west throughout the city, starting at Hauptwache and ending at **Konstablerwache.** For the ultimate shopping mall experience, head to the **Zeilgalerie** *(Zeil 112-114, by Hauptwache. ☎069 92073499 ⏰ Open M-Sa 10am-8pm),* if not for shopping then for the sheer splendor of the curvy glass building and the rooftop terrace with its gorgeous views of the city.

BRITISH BOOK SHOP — 💳 BOOKS

Börsenstr. 17 ☎049 28 04 92 💻www.british-bookshop.de

This one-room shop features English books and periodicals in every genre from classics to popular novels to nonfiction. A bargain bin with paperbacks has cheap reads for only €2, while a bulletin board (in the window, facing the street) has listings for jobs and other ads targeted to the English-speaking crowd.

🚇 U1, U2, or U3: Eschenheimer Tor, then walk against traffic on Hochstr. and turn left onto Börsenstr. ⏰ Open M-F 9:30am-7pm, Sa 9:30am-6pm.

HUGENDUBEL — 💳♿🍸 BOOKS

Steinweg 12 ☎01801 48 44 84 💻www.hugendubel.de

Germany's largest bookstore chain also has an outpost in Frankfurt, with a large room of foreign-language (read: mostly English) books for the city's many im-

migrants. Enjoy free Wi-Fi and a chance to relax on the signature red couches.
🚇 U1, U2, U3, U6, U7, or S1-6: Hauptwache. ⏰ Open M-F 9:30am-8pm.

VIEUX PONT — SECONDHAND CLOTHING

Fahrgasse 1 ☎069 29 80 17 20

A well-kept collection of clean secondhand clothing for men and women, mostly Italian name brands but also includes some well-known American and other international brands. If you get a chance, chat with the Italian owner Rami, a hilarious conversationalist.

🚇 U4 or U5: Dom/Römer, then head toward the Alte Brücke. ⏰ Open M-F 10am-7pm, Sa 10am-5pm.

FREEBASE RECORDS AND SNEAKERS — MUSIC, CLOTHING

Peterstr. 2 ☎069 13 37 62 55 🖥www.freebase-records.de

A popular base for Frankfurt's stylish skateboarder population, Free Base is both a record store selling mostly house, techno, and hip hop, as well as a sneaker shop with ultra-fluorescent creations that you didn't realize people actually wore.

🚇 U1, U2, or U3: Eschenheimer Tor, then follow traffic down Bleichstr. for 3 blocks until you see the shop on your left. ⏰ Open M-F 11am-8pm, Sa 11am-6pm.

CDS AM GOETHEHAUS — MUSIC

Am Salzhaus 1 ☎069 13 37 62 55 🖥www.cdsamgoethehaus.de

Just like the illustrious Goethe himself, this music store attached to his former home also exudes a sense of academic high-mindedness. Recordings sold are mostly classical and jazz, although the store also offers a few audiobooks and DVDs. The store also serves as a home base for the classical music community in Frankfurt, organizing concerts in the Goethehaus and other venues.

🚇 U1, U2, U3, U4, or U5: Willy-Brandt-Pl. From there, follow the signs to Goethehaus. ⏰ Open M-F 10am-7pm, Sa 10am-6pm.

ESSENTIALS

Practicalities

- **TOURIST OFFICE:** *(☎069 21 23 88 00 🖥www.frankfurt-tourismus.de 🚇 In the Hauptbahnhof near the main exit, next door to the car rental. $ Brochures, tours, and maps €0.50-1. Books rooms for a €3 fee, free if you call or email ahead. ⏰ Open M-F 9:30am-5:30pm, Sa-Su 9am-6pm.)* **Alternate location.** *(Römerberg 27 ℹ Books rooms. ⏰ Open M-F 9:30am-5:30pm, Sa-Su 10am-4pm.)*
- **TOURS:** *($ Afternoon tours €26, students €21, under 12 €10. 25% discount with a Frankfurt-Card. Evening tours €16, students €12, under 12 €5. ⏰ Afternoon tours depart daily 10am and 2pm (in winter 2pm) from the Romerberg tourist office, 15min. later from the Hauptbahnhof tourist office. Tours available in 14 different languages and last 2½hr. Evening tours (1½hr.) depart from the Hauptbahnhof at 5:45pm.)*

high culture, low budget

The Frankfurt Card, available at tourist offices and travel agencies, allows unlimited travel on trains and buses including the airport line. It also gives 20-50% discounts on numerous museums, the Palmengarten, city tours, river cruises, and free drinks with meals at select restaurants *(Tickets 1-day €8.90, groups of up to 5 adults €18. 2-day €12.50/26)*. The MuseumsuferTicket gets you into 34 of the city's museums for 2 days *(€15, students €8, family €23)*.

- **BUDGET TRAVEL: STA Travel.** *(Bergerstr. 118 ☎069 904 36 970 ▣www.statravel. de ♯ U4: Höhenstr., then walk with the flow of traffic down Bergerstr. i Books national and international flights and sells ISICs. ✆ Open M-F 10am-7pm, Sa 10am-4pm.)*

- **CONSULATES: Australia.** *(Neue Mainzer Str. 52-58, 28th fl. ☎069 90 55 80 ✆ Open M-Th 9am-4:30pm, F 9am-4pm.)* **US.** *(Gießenerstr. 30 ☎069 753 50 ✆ Open M-F 8am-4pm. Closed holidays and the last Th of the month.)* **Ireland.** *(Gräfstr. 99 ☎069 977883883 ✆ Open by appointment only.)*

- **CURRENCY EXCHANGE:** At any bank. Banks in the airport and the **ReiseBank** at the Hauptbahnhof *(☎069 24278591 ✆ Open daily 7:30am-9pm)* have slightly worse rates but, unlike most banks, stay open during the weekend. **Deutsche Bank.** *(♯ Right across the street from the Hauptbahnhof.)* **American Express.** *(Theodor-Heuss-Allee 112 ☎069 9797 1000 ✆ Open M-F 9:30am-6pm, Sa 10am-2pm.)* Germany's only remaining American Express branch exchanges currency, handles travelers' checks, and arranges hotel and rental car reservations.

- **GLBT RESOURCES:** The **Switchboard** contains a gay information center. *(Alte Gasse 36 ☎069 29 59 59 ▣www.ag36.de ♯ Take the U- or S-Bahn to Konstablerwache.)* It also has the **Cafe der AIDS-Hilfe Frankfurt,** a popular bar/cafe run by the local AIDS foundation. *(i Anonymous AIDS testing M 5-7:30pm, €15. ✆ Open Sept-June M-Th 7pm-midnight, F-Sa 7pm-1am, Su 2-11pm; Jul-Aug M-Th 7pm-midnight, F-Sa 7pm-1am, Su 7-11pm.)* Another solid resource is the **AIDS Anoyme Beratungsstelle.** *(AIDS Anonymous Information Center ☎069 21243270 ▣www.gesundheitsamt. stadt-frankfurt.de.)*

- **LAUNDRYMAT:** *(SB Waschsalon, Wallstr. 8 ♯ Near Haus der Jugend in Sachsen-hausen. Ⓢ Wash €3.50, dry €0.50 per 10min. ✆ Open daily 6am-11pm.)*

- **INTERNET:** Plenty of Internet-Telefon stores can be found on Kaiserstr., directly across from the Hauptbahnhof. **CyberRyder** *(Töngegasse 31 Ⓢ Internet €1.30 per 15 min. Drinks €1.50-3. ✆ Open M-F 9:30am-10pm, Sa 10am-10pm, Su noon-9pm)* boasts itself as Frankfurt's 1st internet cafe. CyberRyder has computers and Wi-Fi in a cozy cafe setting.

- **POST OFFICE:** *(inside the Hauptbahnhof, opposite track 16. ✆ Open M-F 7am-7pm, Sa 9am-4pm.)*

- **POSTAL CODE:** 60313.

Emergency!

- **EMERGENCY:** ☎110.

- **FIRE AND AMBULANCE:** ☎112.

- **DISABLED TRAVELERS:** A guide to accessible public transportation is available at the Tourist Information offices.

- **PHARMACY: Apotheke im Hauptbahnhof.** *(train station's Einkaufspassage ☎069 23 30 47 ♯ Take the escalators heading down toward the S- or U-Bahn trains, then turn left. ✆ Open M-F 6:30am-8pm, Sa 8am-9pm, Su 9am-8pm.)*

Getting There

By Plane

The largest and busiest airport in Germany, Frankfurt's **Flughafen Rhein-Main** *(☎0180 537 24636)* is the gateway to Germany for thousands of travelers from all over the world. From the airport, S-Bahn trains S8 and S9 travel to the Frankfurt Hauptbahnhof every 15min. *(Ⓢ Tickets €3.80. Buy from the green Fahrkarten machines before boarding.)* Most public transportation and trains to major cities depart from **Airport Terminal 1.**

Take the free bus *(every 15min.)* or walk through the skyway to reach the terminal from the main airport. Taxis to the city center *(around €20)* can be found outside every terminal

By Train

The Hauptbahnhof is located in the west side of the city, close to the river: 0180 519 4195; www.bahn.de for reservations and information. Trains leaving from Frankfurt include those to **Berlin** *($ €90-150. ⏰4 hr., 2 per hr.);* **Köln** *($ €30-90. ⏰1-2hr., 3 per hr.);* **Munich** *($ €40-90.⏰ 3-4hr., 2-3 per hr.);* **Heidelberg** *($ €16-26.⏰ 1-1.5hr., 2-3 per hr.);* **Dresden** *($ €60-110. ⏰ 5-8hr., every hr.);* **Amsterdam, NED** *($ €49-140. ⏰ 4-5hr., every 2 hr.);* **Paris, FRA** *($ €59-140. ⏰ 4-5hr., 6 per day);* **Basel, CHE** *($ €60-100.⏰ 3hr., 1 per hr.).*

By Ride Share

Mitfahrenzentrale *(Stuttgarterstr. 12. Take a right on Baselerstr. at the side exit of the Hauptbahnhof (track 1) and walk 2 blocks toward the river. ☎069 19440 💻www.mfz.de ⏰ Open M-F 9:30am-5:30pm, Sa 10am-2pm)* arranges rides to Berlin *(€20),* Munich *(€15),* Köln *(€11),* Amsterdam *(€20),* Vienna *(€24),* and other cities.

hesse ticket

If you're traveling with a group of friends, or even with just yourself and plan on doing a lot of public transportation, get the €31 Hesse Ticket, which allows up to 5 people to travel on all public transportation in Hesse for a day.

Getting Around

By Public Transportation

Buy your tickets from the green-blue Fahrkarten machines immediately before boarding; tickets are automatically validated upon purchase and are valid for 1hr. Check first if your destination qualifies for a "short ticket" by looking through the stops at the top of the machine, and then punch in the appropriate number before selecting the type of ticket you want. For rides within Frankfurt, use the code "50." *($ €2.30. ⏰ Open M-F 6-9am and 4-6:30pm and Sa-Su all day €2.40, children €1.40. Short rides €1.50, children €1. Day tickets €6, children €3.60, group of up to 5 adults €9.50.)* Failure to buy a ticket results in an immediate €40 fine, and Frankfurt is notorious for checking, especially during rush hour.

By Taxi

☎069 23 00 01, ☎069 23 00 33, or ☎069 79 20 20.

By Car Rental

At the Hauptbahnhof by the Reisezentrum, you'll find the offices of **Avis** *(☎0180 55577 ⏰ Open M-F 7am-9pm, Sa and holidays 8am-5pm, Su 10am-4pm),* **Europcar** *(☎0180 58000 ⏰ Open M-F 7am-8pm, Sa 8am-7pm, Su 8am-7:30pm),* **Hertz** *(☎01805 333535 ⏰ open M-F 7am-9pm, Sa-Su and holidays 8am-5pm),* and **Sixt** *(☎0180 5252525 ⏰ Open M-F 6:30am-9pm, Sa 8am-5pm, Su and holidays 8am-7pm).*

By Boat

Several companies offer Main tours, departing from the Mainkai on the northern bank near the Romerberg. **KD.** *(☎069 285728💻www.k-d.com $ €7.80 per person. ⏰ 1hr. round trips aboard the MS Palladium daily between Apr and Oct at 10:30am, noon, 2, 3:30, 5, and 6:30pm.)* **Primus-Linie** *(☎069 1338370 💻www.primus-linie.de)* cruises to a variety of towns along the Main, making for great day trips.

By Bike

Deutsche Bahn (DB) runs the citywide bike rental, **Call a Bike.** Look for the bright red bikes with the DB logo on street corners throughout the city. Retrieve unlocking code by phone or online *(☎0700 05225522 🖥www.callabike.de).* Bikes are €0.10 per min., €15 per day. Another similar company is **NextBike,** but you must return bikes to specific locations throughout the city *(🖥www.nextbike.de $ Bikes are €1 per hr., €8 per day).*

heppenheim ☎06252

If you want a nice hike around Heppenheim whilst learning abut the wine culture, pick up an English-language map of the UNESCO Geo-Naturpark Bergstrasse (titled *Adventure Trail Wine and Rocks*). If you're lucky enough to come by in the week between June and July, you'll witness a rollicking wine festival, the **Bergstrasser Weinmarkt,** on the permises.

ORIENTATION

From the train station, walk straight ahead along Bahnhofstr. and cross the street onto the pedestrian and commercial zone of Friedrichstr. and follow the signs through the half-timbered houses to the **Altstadt** and the **Markt.** The gorgeous **Rathaus** was built in 1551, and its glockenspiel chimes daily at 8, 11:45am, 3, 6, and 10pm. Across from it is **Liebig-Apotheke,** named after the chemist Justus von Liebig who spent part of his apprenticeship there. Liebig is credited with being the "father of fertilizer" discovering that nitrogen is essential for making healthy fruits and vegetables for your chomping pleasure.

SIGHTS

WEIN UND STEIN (WINE AND ROCKS) TRAIL

Darmstadterstr. 56 ☎06252 79 94 24 🖥www.bergstraesserwinzer.de

This 6.9-km trail that circles through the surrounding mountains. Use the English-language pamphlet from the tourist office to orient youself; the trail is marked by 68 descriptive plaques, but all of them are in German. Make sure to stop at the **Bergstrasser Winzer eG,** a wine shop that sells a host of local varieties with tastings and plenty of helpful information.

⏰ Bergstrasser Winzer eG open M-F 8:30am-7pm, Sa 9am-4pm.

FOOD

GOLDENER ENGEL GERMAN [3]

Großer Markt 8 ☎06252 25 63 🖥www.goldener-engel-heppenheim.de

For a grand German experience, pause here for lunch. Sit on the terrace and listen to the trickling fountain with the 18th-century statue of the Virgin Mary.

$ Entrees €9.90-15.50.

BISTRO ECKSPERIMENTE GERMAN [2]

Marktstr. 15 ☎06252 65 74 🖥www.biomarkt-hp.de

This casual eatery serves up homemade organic foods from a daily rotating menu.

$ Entrees €5-10. ⏰ Open M-W 11am-2:30pm, Th-F 11am-2:30pm and 7pm-10pm, Sa 10am-2pm.

Practicalities

- **TOURIST OFFICE:** *(Großer Markt 1* ☎*06252 130* 🕐 *Open M-F 10am-5pm, Sa in Apr-Sept 10am-4pm)* Has information for both Heppenheim and the Bergstrasse region, with free maps, guides, and suggestions for how to navigate your way around.

Getting There

Start your day by taking the train out to **Heppenheim.** *(💲 €13.35 from Frankfurt. Enter "4560 " into the blue machines. 🕐 1 hr., 1 per hr.)*

darmstadt

Another worthy destination along the Bergstr. is the modern city of Darmstadt, though this locale is much more known for its Jugendstil Art Nouveau architecture and technical university than any age-old charm. Juxtapose the landscape of the grapevines with a visit to this city, which offers a young population and a contemporary feel. One of the world's heaviest elements (atomic number 110) was created in Darmstadt and appropriately named the *Darmstadtium;* appropriately, the city's conference center also bears that name.

ORIENTATION

To get to the tourist office from the Hauptbahnhof, take trams 209 or bus K, F, or H.

SIGHTS

🖼 MATHILDENHÖHE   COMPLEX

Olbrichweg 13   ☎06151 132778 🖥www.mathildenhoehe.info

The mecca of Darmstadt's Jugendstil architecture, this artist colony on a hill west of the city was founded by Grand Duke Ernst Ludwig in 1899. The Duke fell in love with Jugendstil and invited seven artists to build a "living and working world" of art, financing the transformation of the urban landscape into the predecessor to Art Deco. Jugendstil architecture aims to beautify functional, everyday objects and to emphasize natural shape and organic lines. While the Jugendstil school formally disbanded after WWII, the city has committed itself to the upkeep of the resplendent environs of the Mathildenhöhe's museums, chapels, and fountains.

🏃 *Walk east for 10min. from the Luisenpl. along Erich-Ollenhauer-Promenade, or take bus F: Mathildenhöhe. Take a right on Lucasweg.*

HOCHZEITSTURM   TOWER

Resembling a monstrous jukebox or vertical glove, the Hochzeitsturm (Wedding Tower) atop the Mathildenhöhe was designed by Joseph Maria Olbrich and presented to Ernst Ludwig in 1908 as a wedding present from the city. Don't miss the beautiful mosaics in the lobby or the sundial on the side, and climb up the 48m tower for a view of Darmstadt.

💲 *€3, students €2, under 12 free.* 🕐 *Open Mar-Oct Tu-Su 10am-6pm.*

MUSEUM KÜNSTLERKOLONIE   MUSEUM

To the southeast of the tower houses Art Nouveau furniture and modern art, as well as a history of the Jugendstil movement in Darmstadt. A rotating temporary exhibition in the basement highlights other aspects of modern art and architecture.

💲 *€5, students €3.* 🕐 *Open Tu-Su 11am-6pm.*

AUSSTELLUNGSGEBÄUDE MATHILDENHÖHE — MUSEUM

This large exhibition space is reserved for temporary exhibits, many of them thought-provoking displays with a German theme. Expect the museum to be closed between exhibits.

$ €8, students €6. ⏰ Open Tu-W 10am-6pm, Th 10am-9pm, F-Su 10am-6pm. Last entry 30min. before close.

ORTHODOX RUSSIAN CHAPEL — CHURCH

This gilded onion-domed Russian Orthodox church was imported stone by stone from Russia at the behest of the last Tsar Nicholas II when he married Darmstadt's Princess Alexandra. Its foundations were built on earth from every state in the Russian empire so it would stand on Russian soil. Because of its association with the martyred royal family, the chapel has become a pilgrimage site for Russian Orthodox Christians of the diaspora.

$ Free. ⏰ Open Tu-Sa 10am-1pm and 2-4pm, Su 2-4pm, though times may vary.

WALDSPIRALE (FOREST SPIRAL) — BUILDING

Waldspirale 1

An architectural feat of biomorphic shapes and fanciful colors, this project was originally conceived by famous Austrian architect Friedensreich Hundertwasser on a restaurant napkin. The resulting building was largely faithful to this sketch, rejecting straight lines and instead opting for whimsical, sediment-like coloring. The building, completed just months after the artist's death in 2000, contains apartments, office space, and a restaurant.

🚋 Tram 4, 5, 6, 7, or 7: Röhnring, then walk down Büdingerstr. toward the funky house. $ Free. ⏰ Walk by whenever you want.

RESIDENZSCHLOß DARMSTADT — MUSEUM

Marktpl. 15

The gigantic coral-and-white palace is smack-dab in the middle of the city. Built between 1716 and 1727, it was modeled after Versailles by a wistful Frenchman. Since WWII, the Schloβ has served as a public university library and police station. In recent years, it has also housed an underground student club and beer garden.

🚋 Tram 2, 3, 9, or bus H, L, or F: Schloβ. ⏰ Prices and hours to be determined when the Schloβ reopens.

FOOD

Thanks to all the hungry students, cheap eats are everywhere in Darmstadt. Hit up **Landgraf-George-Str.** around the university to get some excellent €2.50 *döners*. Otherwise, the pedestrian areas around the Marktpl. serve up plenty of food, and even the restaurants with outdoor terraces don't get terribly expensive.

RATSKELLER HAUSBRAUEREI — GERMAN [2]

Marktpl. 8 ☎06151 26444 www.ratskeller-darmstadt.de

Enjoy some of the house-brewed beer from shiny copper vats *(0.25L €1.90)* or some traditional German favorites including wurst and *Handkäse mit Musik*, all for very reasonable prices.

🚋 Tram 2, 3, 9, or bus H, L, or F: Schloβ. $ Entrees €5-14.50. ⏰ Open daily 10am-1am.

NIGHTLIFE

CENTRALSTATION — BAR, MUSIC VENUE

Im Carree ☎06151 80 94 60 www.centralstation-darmstadt.de

Not to be confused with the Hauptbahnhof, CentralStation is one of Darmstadt's premier live music venues, mostly presenting indie and jazz greats. Even if you don't come for a concert, though, grab a drink and sit on the steps of the outdoor bar, with orange "tables" cleverly fashioned around the steps. In addition, a rotating daily menu serves up scrumptious lunch and dinner options.

Tram 2, 3 4, 5, 6, 7, 8, or 9: Luisienplatz. Walk behind the Luisien Center on the side of the tourist office and take a left into the small courtyard. $ Entrees around €8. Beer from €2.80. Cocktails €5.50-8.50. ⏰ Open Tu-Th 11am-1am, F-Sa 11am-3am.

ESSENTIALS

Practicalities

- **TOURIST OFFICE:** *(Luisienpl. 5, by the Luisien Center sign. ☎06151 134513 ⏰ Open M-F 10am-6pm, Sa 10am-4pm, Apr-Oct Su 10am-2pm.)* The transportation hub, and city center are also located at **Luisienplatz,** marked by an enormously towering statue of Ludwig I, the first Grand Duke of Hesse.

Getting There

Darmstadt is easily reached from Frankfurt by frequent trains and the S3, which ends at the Darmstadt Hauptbahnhof *(single ride €7.15).*

marburg ☎06421

The jewel of the Lahn Valley, Marburg was once the capital of Hesse, home of St. Elizabeth, and site of the world's first Protestant university. The university has produced an illustrious list of alumni, including **Martin Heidegger, T.S. Eliot, Richard Bunsen** (as in, the Bunsen burner), and most enchantingly, the **Brothers Grimm.** An age-old Schloβ towers over the student-ridden city, and while the throngs of young people give the town a modern and progressive feel, the historic Altstadt still brims with old-fashioned charm, the characteristic half-timbered houses all largely free of chain stores and kitschy souvenir shops.

ORIENTATION

Steinweg is one of Europe's first pedestrian zones. To get there from the Hauptbahnhof, walk straight ahead on Bahnhofstr. past the bridge, then turn left onto Elisabethstr. Once you pass the Elisabethkirche, turn right and then turn left again quickly into the small alleyway, which will lead you to Steinweg and will take you all the way to the Altstadt. You'll pass by the famed **Elisabethkirche.** There is a **free elevator** that connects Pilgrimstein to the more elevated parts of town located in the Parkhaus Oberstadt by the tourist office.

ACCOMMODATIONS

Although Marburg can definitely be done in a day, fantastic sunrises from the Schloβ terrace make an excellent reason for staying overnight.

JUGENDHERBERGE (HI) HOSTEL ❷

Jahnstr. 1 ☎06421 234 61 www.marburg.jugendherberge.de

A beautiful riverside location close to bike trails and boat rental make this an appealing option for young guests. Rooms are located around a central courtyard offering foosball, ping pong, giant chess, and other sports.

Bus C: Auf der Weide, then backtrack and trun right onto a street that crosses two bridges. [i] Breakfast and linens included. Wi-Fi €10 per 24hr. $ Dorms €20. Single night stay extra €2.50. ⏰ Reception 24hr.

TUSCULUM-ART-HOTEL HOTEL ❸

Gutenbergstr. 25 ☎06421 227 78 www.tusculum.de

Some tourists visit art museums, but here you can pretend you're staying in one. Each room is decorated with a different theme, and the bathroom fixtures can get pretty creative.

⚡ *Take bus #1, 2, 5, or 7: Gutenbergstr.* Ⓢ *Singles €38-54; doubles €68-76.* 🕐 *Reception 4-9pm, call ahead to arrange other times.*

CAMPING: LAHNAUE
⚓⊘(ᵞ) CAMPGROUND ❶

Gutenbergstr. 25   ☎06421 227 78 🖥www.lahnaue.de

A campsite located close to the city center, with two wooden heated cottages for guest use, complete with TV, fridge, and stove. A mini-golf course nearby also helps to pass the time if you need a break from all those castles.

⚡ *Take bus #1, 2, 5, or 7: Gutenbergstr.* 𝒊 *Credit card min. €30.* Ⓢ *€5 per person, children €3. Tents €4. Laundry €6. Cottages €10 per night, with additional €10 per adult, €3 per child.* 🕐 *Reception 8am-8pm in summer; shorter hours at other times of year.*

SIGHTS
🔘

🏯 LANDGRAFENSCHLOß (DUKE'S PALACE)
⚓&♿ ¥ CASTLE

Schloß 1   ☎06421 282 23 55 🖥www.uni-marburg.de/uni-museum/kulturgeschichte

The exterior of this castle, which sits on the Gison cliffs, looks almost as it did in 1500 when it was a haunt of infamous Teutonic knights. In 1529, Count Philip brought rival Protestant reformers Martin Luther and Ulrich Zwingli to his court to convince them to reconcile. Inside, the Schloß has been completely remade into the **Museum für Kulturgeschichte** (Museum for Cultural History), which exhibits Hessian history and art, including shields and ornate crosses. The basement holds a 7th-century skeleton and recently unearthed 9th-century wall remnants. The *Landesherrschaft* (Provincial Rule) floor is a war buff's dream come true, with enough spears and handguns to arm a miniscule army. Behind the Schloß is a quiet garden that provides panoramic views of the city and surrounding valleys, as well as a **Camera Obscura** run by the university physics department. *(🕐 Open Mar-Oct F-Su 2-4pm.)*

⚡ *Follow the signs from the Markt, or take bus #10 to the end.* Ⓢ *Museum €4, students €3.* 🕐 *Open Tu-Su Apr-Sept 10am-6pm, Oct-Mar 10am-4pm. Last entry 30 min. before close.*

ELISABETHKIRCHE
⚓♿ CHURCH

Elisabethstr. 3   ☎06421 655 73 🖥www.elisabethkirche.de

Save some ecclesiastic awe for the oldest Gothic church in Germany, modeled on the French cathedral at Reims. The name of the church honors the town patroness, a widowed child-bride (engaged at 4, married at 14, dead by her 20s) who took refuge in Marburg after the death of her husband, founded a hospital, and snagged sainthood only four years after her death. The **reliquary** for her bones is the centerpiece for the elaborate choir, a church-within-a-church, so overdone it's glorious. The somber brown interior is illuminated by glowing stained-glass windows.

⚡ *From the Hauptbahnhof, walk straight down Bahnhofstr. and then turn left onto Elisabethstr. You can't miss it.* Ⓢ *Church free. Reliquary €2.50, students €1.50. Tours €3.50, students €2.50.* 🕐 *Open daily Apr-Sept 9am-6pm; Oct 9am-5pm; Nov-Mar 10am-4pm. Tours in German M-F and Su 3pm.*

ALTE UNIVERSITÄT
♿ CHURCH, BUILDING

Lahntor 3   ☎06421 991 20

The modern university building was erected in 1871, but the original Alte Universität on Rudolphspl. was built on the rubble of a monastery conveniently empty after Reformation-minded Marburgers ejected the resident monks. The enormous stone building stands at the foot of the big hill, anchoring the Altstadt that spreads up and out behind it. The **Aula**, or main hall, bears frescoes illuminating Marburg's history, but you can only see it by reservation (call in advance). The nearby houses are former fraternities, and the topsy-turvy state of their frames attest to a proud, beer-soaked tradition. Connected is the university's **Lutheran church,** with an Art Noveau style organ.

frankfurt, the bergstrasse, and marburg

⇄ The large building at the intersection of Pilgrimstein and Universitätsstr. Ⓢ Free. ⏰ Hours vary based on class schedules, but generally 9am-6pm.

UNIVERSITÄTSMUSEUM FÜR BILDENE KUNST (UNIVERSITY MUSEUM FOR THE VISUAL ARTS) MUSEUM

Biegenstr. 11 ☎06421 282 23 55 🖥www.uni-marburg.de/uni-museum

The university's impressive collection of 19th- and 20th-century German painting and sculpture is housed in this modest building. Pieces by **Paul Klee** and **Otto Dix** compete with temporary exhibits of provocative modern work and a section on Expressive Realism and the lost generation of artists who thrived during Nazi rule.

⇄ From the tourist office, continue south on Pilgrimstein and turn left onto Biegenstr. Ⓢ €4, students €3. ⏰ Open Tu-Su 11am-1pm and 2-5pm.

MARBURGER KUNSTVEREIN ♿ MUSEUM

Gerhard-Jahn-Platz 5 ☎06421 258 82 🖥www.marburger-kunstverein.de

This modern two-story building hosts a rotating set of temporary exhibits of modern art, many featuring local artists. Catch some great views of the river from the small balcony on the top floor. A small library on the ground floor has books on modern art.

⇄ At Rudolphspl. Ⓢ Free. ⏰ Open Tu 11am-8pm, W 11am-8pm, Th-Su 11am-5pm.

FOOD

For inexpensive eateries, head to the cafes around the Markt, always brimming with students. For some cheap cafeteria food with a stunning view of the Schloβ, head to the **Studentenwerk (Student Union),** Erlenring 5, on the east bank of the river (follow the signs to the **Mensa**). You can pay in cash, and explain to the cashier that you're a student to waive the extra €2 guest charge; the staff at the information booth are particularly friendly and helpful.

BÜCKINGSGARTEN: RESTAURANT AM SCHLOß 🍸 GERMAN ❸

Landgraf-Philipp-Str. 6 ☎06421 136 10

Treat yourself to a fantastic meal after your vertical trek up to the LandgrafenSchloβ. With stunning views of the city, this is a great place to refresh yourself under those golden yellow umbrellas after all that physical endeavor.

⇄ By the LandgrafenSchloβ. Ⓢ Entrees €10-15. Appetizers €4-10. ⏰ Open daily 11:30am-11pm.

CAFE BARFUSS 🍸 CAFE ❷

Barfüβerstr. 33 ☎06421 253 49 🖥www.cafe-barfuss.de

Local students flock to this cozy cafe and sit either indoors amidst the burlap coffee sack decor or outdoors on the sloped Barfüβerstr. The big breakfast menu is served until 3pm, and the unique (if not slightly intimidating) *Fladenbrot*-meets-pizza "Fetizza" is especially delicious. The laid-back staff and the great views make this the perfect cafe to spend an entire afternoon.

⇄ From the Markt, head west toward the Schloβ on Barfüβerstr. Ⓢ Entrees €4.50-12.50 ⏰ Open daily 10am-midnight.

CAFE VETTER 🍸 CAFE ❷

Reitgasse 4 ☎06421 258 88 🖥www.cafe-vetter-marburg.de

Cafe Vetter has been serving up its delicious cakes and chocolate creations for over 100 years. Take advantage of the student breakfast *(€5.60)*, complete with bread wurst, cheese, ham, eggs, jam, juice, coffee or tea, and chocolate and butter spreads. Enjoy the view from the terrace on the edge of the Oberstadt. Cakes, chocolates, marizipans, and gourmet tea are also for sale.

⇄ From the Markt, head east (away from the Schloβ) on Barfüβerstr., then turn right onto Reitgasse. Ⓢ Cakes €2-3. Other "fingerfoods" under €6. ⏰ Open M 9am-6:30pm, Tu 11am-6pm, W-Su 9am-6:30pm.

HUGO'S

CAFE ❷

Gerhard-Jahn-Pl. 21a

☎06421 130 00 ▦www.hugos-marburg.de

Take a break at this popular watering hole right on the river, with a terrace and summer beer garden overlooking the Lahn. An enormous menu offers everything from baguettes to chicken nuggets, but the best attraction is probably their cocktails, which, like their beer, come in normal single-sized portions to 1.5L pitchers.

⌖ From the Deutsche Bank on Rudolfspl., head down Biegenstr. and turn right into the cinema, and walk toward the river. Ⓢ Entrees €4-9.50. 0.3L Beer €2.40. Mixed drinks €4.50-7. ⌚ Open M-F 9am-late, Sa-Su 10am-late.

ARTS AND CULTURE

Marburg's upper village alone has over 60 bars and clubs. Live music, concerts, theater, and movie options appear in the weekly *Marburger Express* (▦*www.marbuch-verlag.de)*, available at the tourist office and at all bars and pubs. Posters plaster the main streets to announce larger events. Tickets are available at a counter in the tourist office. The **Marburger Filmkunsttheater** (Steinweg 4. ☎06421 67269 ▦*www.marburg-erfilmkunst.de)* shows old American hits and more unsual recent releases. One movie per week is shown in its original language. Check out the website or the posters by the door. On the first Sunday in July, costumed citizens parade into the Markt for the rowdy **Frühschoppenfest** (Morning Beer Festival). Drinking officially kicks off at 11am when the brass rooster on top of the Rathaus flaps its wings. Unofficially, the barrels of Alt Marburger Pils are tapped at 10am when the ribald old *Trinklieder* (drinking ballads) commence.

ESSENTIALS

❓

Practicalities

- **TOURIST OFFICE:** Has free maps, books rooms, sells theater tickets, and offers a variety of city tours in German. *(Pilgrimstein 26 ☎06421 991 20 ▦www.marburg.de. Ⓢ Tours €3-5, for English register online. ⌚ Open M-F 9am-6pm, Sa 10am-2pm.)*

- **ATMS: Deutschebank** has 24hr. ATMs located at the corner of Pilgrimstein and Biegenstr., right by the Rudolphspl. bus stop.

- **INTERNET ACCESS: Internet Treff.** *(Pilgrimstein 27, right across the street from the Tourist Office. ☎05421 92 47 05 Ⓢ €3 per hr. ⌚ Open M-Sa 10am-1am, Su noon-midnight.)*

Getting There

Trains connect Marburg and Frankfurt. *(Ⓢ €13.35.⌚ 1-1½ hr.)* Buy your tickets at the blue local machines and punch in the number "05," and use one of the red DB machines to find an appropriate timetables—sometimes the fastest route will include a transfer. Once there, the city center (Marktplatz) can be reached from the Hauptbahnhof from a number of buses *(€1.60)* or a 1.5km walk.

Getting Around

Boats and bikes can be rented from vendors along the western bank of the Lahn, directly across the Erlenring bridge right at the intersection of Pilgrimsweg and Universitätsstr.

HEIDELBERG AND STUTTGART

These two cities in Baden-Württemburg exemplify the perfect mix of old- and new-world charm that encapsulates Germany. On first glance they may seem like complete opposites: **Heidelberg,** founded at the edge of an imposing, decaying schloβ, reeks of traditional charm, with cobblestone streets, old-fashioned buildings, historic pubs, and sacred churches. **Stuttgart,** birthplace of the luxury automobile, gives way to sleek buildings and citizens, all pointing toward modernization and economic prosperity. But don't judge based on first impressions, since Germany is a country full of contradictions. Just take a stroll down Heidelberg's bustling **Haupstrasse,** the main shopping street, and you'll see that those old-fashioned buildings contain modern stores, all vying for equal attention from the thousands of students that pass through Germany's oldest university town. The university also gave birth to some of the world's most prominent technological advances, including spectroscopy, the Bunsen burner, and the Haber-Bosch process of producing ammonia. Stuttgart's cosmopolitan shopping centers are flanked by impeccably preserved ornate palaces and only a few minutes' train ride away is the stately town of **Ludwigsburg,** home to three gorgeous schloβes and their impressively manicured gardens.

greatest hits

- **A WALK IN GOETHE'S SHOES.** Hike up the Philosophenweg around sunset for some gorgeous views of Heidelberger Schloβ (p. 228).
- **WON'T YOU BUY ME A MERCEDES-BENZ?** Drool over a century's worth of gleaming automobiles at the Mercedes-Benz Museum (p. 237).
- **COURTSIDE (S)EATS.** Picnic in the picturesque courtyard of the Hans-im-Gluck fountain with a meal from Deli (p. 241).

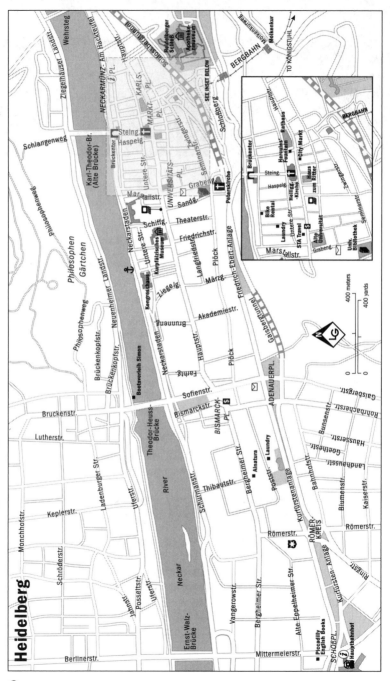

heidelberg and stuttgart

Heidelberg

student life

Heidelberg is home to Germany's oldest and most prestigious university. Explore the Museum der Universität Heidelberg to learn about the institution's history, or hit the town to chill with the institution's students. Veer off the main streets around Universitätspl. for a sampling of cheap international fare, ranging from Malecón's Cuban rice dishes to Raja Rani's Indian chicken korma. Come nightfall, skip the touristy bars along the Hauptstr. and walk one block north to the beer-soaked Unterestr. For the lowdown on nightlife destinations in Stuttgart, pick up Tips'n'Trips from the Tourist Office. Sport a yellow polka-dot bikini to SkyBeach—where young locals drink mojitos or nap in the hammock—or lounge in the canopied beds at Bett where the motto is "Relaxing=Clubbing."

heidelberg ☎06221

Over the years, this sun-drenched town on the Neckar and its crumbling schloβ have beckoned to much of the world's intellectual elite, from **Mark Twain** and **Victor Hugo,** to **Wolfgang von Goethe, Friedrich Holderlin,** and **Robert Schumann.** During the summer, scores of tourists also answer the call, and even off-season the camera-touting legions swarm **Hauptstrasse,** where postcards and T-shirts sell like hotcakes and every sign is posted in four languages. The incessant buzz of tourism, however, does little to detract from Heidelberg's beautiful hillside setting, bustling riverside, and legendary nightlife. In many ways, Heidelberg (pop. 145,000) epitomizes the unique German university town, which combines the crushing weight of history, the fun-loving disaffection of its students, and a ubiquitous effort to market itself to foreigners with pocket-sized souvenirs.

ORIENTATION

About 20km east of the Neckar's confluence with the Rhein, Heidelberg stretches along the river for another several kilometers, with most of the city's attractions in the Altstadt, the eastern quarter of the southern bank. The western edge of the Altstadt is marked by **Bismarckplatz,** home to a bustle of transit activity and the beginning of the **Hauptstrasse,** Heidelberg's main commercial artery, which runs east to west along the Altstadt and, at 1600m, is Europe's longest pedestrian street. Stay off the red bike lanes, used by Heidelberg's large-and-in-charge cyclist population.

ACCOMMODATIONS

STEFFI'S HOSTEL — HOSTEL ❷

Alte Eppelheimerstr. 50 ☎06221 778 27 72 www.hostelheidelberg.de

Walk up to the third floor of this brick building to enter a hostel haven. At Steffi's, rooms are incredibly clean and come with floor-to-ceiling wallpaper depicting scenes from nature—sunny beaches, lush lawns, and green bamboo forests. The kitchen, used daily by Steffi, her husband, and their cute toddler son, is kept well-stocked and impeccably spotless.

From the Hauptbahnhof, take the side exit and walk across the street through the Kurfürstenpassage, then across the street again to the brick building up ahead. Lidl (a grocery store) is on the first floor, and Steffi's on the third. ℹ *Breakfast, linens, towels, Wi-Fi, and bike rental (with €20 deposit) included. 2 computers for guest use.* $ *6-beds €22; 8-beds €20; girls' dorm €22; doubles €26; quads €24. Family rooms also available.* ⏰ *Reception daily 10am-2pm and 4-10pm.*

SUDPFANNE HOSTEL
🍴⊘📶🍸 HOSTEL ❷

Hauptstr. 223 ☎06221 16 36 36 🖥www.heidelberger-sudpfanne.de

The cheapest digs in the middle of town, Sudpfanne offers clean, spacious rooms decked out in snazzy Ikea textiles all within distance of the best bars, restaurants, and sights in Heidelberg. Guests also get a deal at the downstairs Sudpfanne Restaurant, where delicious and hearty meals are offered for only €6.

➜ Bus #33: Neckarmüntzpl. From the station, walk away from the river to Hauptstr. ℹ Reception behind the bar. Linens included. Smaller rooms located in another building a few blocks away from the reception center. Computer and Wi-Fi available. $ Dorms from €16; doubles from €30. Prices negotiable for stays of 3 or more days. ⏰ Reception 11am-midnight.

PENSION JESKE
🍴⊘ PENSION ❷

Mittelbadgasse 2 ☎06221 237 33 🖥www.pension-jeske-heidelberg.de

Small and unassuming, Jeske offers a friendly and welcoming proprietor (the marathon-running Martin), handpainted bedstands and closets, and an unbeatable location only one block from the Marktplatz in the Altstadt. The bathrooms all come with distinct, haphazard tiling that beautifully contrast the bedroom decor. The few rooms in this pension fill up quickly, so make sure to book early.

➜ Bus #33: Rathaus/Bergbahn. From the stop, retrace your steps for a block and turn right onto Mittelbadgasse. Look for the international flags on your left. ℹ Linens included. $ Singles €25; doubles €55; triples €85; quads €100; quints €110. Extra for private sinks and baths. ⏰ Reception 11am-1pm and 5-7pm.

JUGENDHERBERGE HEIDELBERG INTERNATIONAL (HI)
🎫♿📶 HOSTEL ❷

Tiergartenstr. 5 ☎06221 65 11 90 🖥www.jugendherberge-heidelberg.de

Next to the Heidelberg Zoo, this hostel teems with wildlife in the form of schoolchildren. The standard HI rooms, spic-and-span with wavy motifs, and the standard HI amenities, bistro and sunny cafeteria, are supplemented with plenty of outdoor ball-playing space. A handy TouristPoint office provides information on how to explore Heidelberg.

➜ Bus #32: Jugendherberge. ℹ Breakfast and linens included. $ Dorms €23.80 1st night; €20.50 subsequent nights. ⏰ Reception 24hr.

PAPA'S PENSION
🍴♿🍸 PENSION ❷

Fahrtgasse 1 ☎06221 16 50 33 🖥www.hemingways-hd.de/papaspension.html

Situated above the Hemingway's bar, the name of this simple pension pays homage to "Papa" Hemingway and features clean and sunny rooms. The bar can be loud, especially during the summer when the beer garden is in full swing.

➜ From Bismarckpl., head north on Sofienstr. and turn right at the river; you'll see Hemingway's on the right. ℹ Reception in Hemingway's. $ Rooms from €35. ⏰ Reception open M-F 9am-1am, Sa-Su 9am-2am.

CAMPINGPLATZ HEIDELBERG
🍴⊘ CAMPGROUND ❶

Schlierbacher Landstr. 151 ☎06221 80 25 06 🖥www.camping-heidelberg.de

Just a few minutes out of the city by bus, this campground is located along a grassy meadow near the river. Fees are slightly higher than other campgrounds, but they do include showers, and who doesn't like being squeaky clean?

➜ Bus #35: Im Grund. $ €6 per person, children 5-14 €3.50. Car €2.50. Tent €3.50-10. ⏰ Reception 7am-9pm.

CAMPING HAIDE
🍴♿📶 CAMPGROUND ❶

Ziegelhäuserstr. 91 ☎06223 21 11 🖥www.camping-haide.de

Pause to smell the flowers on your way in, and park yourself at a shaded riverside lot. The distance from public transport makes this a poor choice for those on foot, but the peace and quiet makes it ideal for car travelers who don't mind a little distance from the city. An assortment of rustic cabins are also available.

🐝 *Bus #35: Orthopädisches Klinik. From the stop, cross the river, turn right, and walk for about 20 min.* ⓘ *Restaurant on-site. Showers €1. Wi-Fi included.* Ⓢ *€5.40 per person, children 5-14 €2.70. Car €2. Tent €4-7. Cabin single €17; doubles €24; triples €33; quads €40.* 🕐 *Reception daily 8-11am and 4-8:30pm.*

SIGHTS

🖼 **HEIDELBERGER SCHLOß** ⊛ ♿ PALACE

Heidelberg owes its existence to the imposing castle that towers above the town and overlooks the river. Its construction began in the 14th century but the castle was expanded, destroyed, and expanded again over a period of almost 400 years. As a result, the schloß that you see today is an enormous conglomeration of architectural styles including crumbled Gothic and recently refurbished High Renaissance. The terrace and the impressive gardens around the castle (free!) provide the best sunset views of Heidelberg, which you can share with couples who remind you why the phrase "get a room" exists. The inside of the castle can only be seen on a guided tour, but the courtyards alone hold enough intrigue for the cheapskate tourist. Be sure to check out the legendary wine barrels; **Großes Faß**, the largest vat ever to be used, holds nearly 228,000L (that's 55,000 gallons) and is topped with a dance floor. The measly **Kleines Faß**, in comparison, only holds *only* 130,000L. Half the wine in the Faßes would have turned to vinegar by the time anyone drank from it, but with water rumored to carry disease, the citizens of Heidelberg would have each drank about 4L of wine per day. Also in the courtyard is the **Apotheken-Museum** (Pharmacy Museum), where you will learn more than you ever thought possible about pharmaceutical science; the enormous distillation apparatuses displayed might also bring back nightmares from organic chemistry lab.

🐝 *Bus #33: Rathaus/Bergbahn. From the stop, follow the stairs (10 min.) or take the Bergbahn (runs every 10 min.), one of the world's oldest funiculars.* Ⓢ *A combined Bergbahn round trip with castle entry (including the Faßes and the Apotheken-Museum) €5, students €3. 1hr. castle tour €4/€2. Audio tour €4.* 🕐 *Castle grounds open daily 8am-6pm, last entry 5:30pm. Apotheken-Museum open daily 10:15am-6pm, last entry 5:40pm. Tours in German daily every hr. M-F 11am-4pm, Sa-Su 10am; tours in English begin at quarter past the hour every hr.*

UNIVERSITÄT CAMPUS

Heidelberg is home to Germany's oldest (est. 1386) and most prestigious university. The oldest remaining buildings border the stone lion fountain on the *Universitatspl.*, though its campus is scattered all throughout town. The **Museum der Universität Heidelberg** (Grabengasse 1, ☎06221 54 35 93 🖳www.uni-heidelberg.de/einrichtungen/museen/universitaetsmuseum.html) traces the university's long history, and chemistry nerds can feast their eyes on the world's first spectroscope. In the same building lies the magnificent **Alte Aula,** Heidelberg's oldest auditorium. Behind this building is the legendary **Studentenkarzer** (Augustinergasse 2, ☎06221 54 35 54, 🖳www.uni-heidelberg.de/fakultaeten/philosophie/zegk/fpi/karzerhd.html), the jail used until 1914 for rule-breaking students. Its relatively luxurious accommodations and lax rules made imprisonment a goal among students, who made it a point to get incarcerated so that they could spend their days playing hooky and decorating the already-colorful walls of the cells. The gorgeous library, the **Bibliothek** (Plöck 107-109 ☎06221 54 23 80, 🖳www.ub.uni-heidelberg.de), filled with medieval manuscripts in the exhibition halls, offers a quiet place for contemplation.

🐝 *The museum is on the western edge of Universitatspl. The Studentenkarzer is 1 block behind and the Bibliothek 1 block to the right.* ⓘ *The Alte Aula is only available for viewing when not in use by students. Exhibits are in German, but a free English audio tour provides excellent information.* Ⓢ *Museum and Studentenkarzer combined ticket €3, students €2.50. Bibliothek free.* 🕐 *Museum open Apr-Oct Tu-Su 10am-6pm, Nov-Mar Tu-Sa 10am-4pm. Studentenkarzer open Apr-Oct daily 10am-6pm, Nov-Mar M-Sa 10am-4pm. Bibliothek exhibition rooms open daily 10am-6pm.*

PHILOSOPHENWEG HIKING TRAIL

The favorite stroll of famed thinkers Goethe, Feuerbach, and Junger, stretches along the Neckar, high on the side of the **Heiligenberg,** and offers spectacular views of the Schloβ opposite and the city below. Many benches and small gardens along the path make for great picnic spots. Go beyond the Philosophenweg and continue up to the top of the Berg to find the ruins of the 9th-century St. Michael Basilika, the 13th-century Stefanskloster, and an amphitheater built under Hitler on the site of an ancient Celtic gathering place.

 # The standard loop begins a few blocks north of the Theodor-Heuss-Brucke, runs up along the side of the mountain and then descends via stone-walled footpath to the Karl-Theodor-Brucke. For the longer route up the mountain, don't take the stairs down and just keep going up.

KARL-THEODOR-BRÜCKE BRIDGE

On your requisite (and worthwhile) trip between the schloβ and the Philosophenweg, you'll cross this bridge, also known as the Alte Brucke. On the southern side, Disney-style towers stand as a gate into the Altstadt, with plump (read: entitled) statues of the bridge's namesake, the prince who commissioned the bridge in 1786 as a symbol of his modesty, standing guard. Along the northern edge a brass monkey is also poised, holding a mirror intended to teach tourists humility. Rub the monkey's outstretched fingers for wealth, the mirror to return to Heidelberg, and the mice for lots of children. At night, the bridge provides an excellent view of the accompanying illuminated Schloβ.

 # Toward the eastern end of the Altstadt.

KURPFÄLZISCHES MUSEUM ⊛♿ MUSEUM

Hauptstr. 97 ☎06221 583 40 20 🖳www.museum-heidelberg.de

Built for Palatinate Germany fanatics, this enormous maze of a museum features an extensive collection of oil paintings by local and regional artists from the 18th and 19th centuries, as well as an archaeology exhibit in its bottom levels. You'll be amazed when you see just how many portraits of Renaissance-era German nobility can fit in a single room. Also on hand are Roman tombs and a cast of Heidelberg's oldest resident, the Heidelberg Man.

 # 1 block west of Universitätspl. on Hauptstr.; look for the flags outside. $ €3, students €1.80. Su €1.80/€1.20. ⏰ Open Tu-Su 10am-6pm.

HEILIGGEISTKIRCHE (CHURCH OF THE HOLY SPIRIT) ⊛♿ CHURCH

Hauptstr. 189 ☎06221 211 17 🖳www.heiliggeistkirche.de

Built in the 14th century, Heiliggeistkirche is the embodiment of an identity crisis. Originally built as a Catholic church, the church switched multiple times between Catholicism and Protestantism. Eventually they erected a wall to divide the church so that both denominations could use the church simultaneously. The 200-year-old wall came down in 1936, and Protestants now have full use of the church. The church is now also the final resting place of several of Heidelberg's electors, and no visit is complete without browsing through all the small souvenir stands that surround the church. Vista-holics will also appreciate the panoramic view at the top of the tower, though height-aholics might complain that a trek to the terrace of the schloβ would give a higher altitude.

 # In the middle of the Marktpl. ℹ The church often hosts concerts; visit www.studentenkantorei.de for a complete schedule. $ Church entry free; trip to the top €1.50, students €1. ⏰ Open M-Sa 9am-6pm, Su schedule varies.

FOOD

Being the big student town it is, Heidelberg is no stranger to cheap and tasty food. That said, being the big tourist town it is, Heidelberg also has its fair share of overpriced food (mostly along the Hauptstr.). Veer off the central road, especially around Universitätspl., for a sampling of the cheap international fare that Heidelberg has to offer. Grocery stores like **Penny Markt** *(Plöck 13, 1 block southeast of Bismarckpl. ⏰ open M-F 8am-10pm, Sa 7am-10pm)* and **Aldi Süd** *(Poststr. 11, 1 block west of Bismarckpl. ⏰ open M-Sa 8am-8pm)* offer some of the best deals, while fresh fruits and vegetables can be found at **Rewe City** *(Kurfürstenanlage 6, 1 block south of Bismarckpl. ⏰ open M-Sa 8am-midnight).*

FALAFEL
MIDDLE EASTERN ❶

Heugasse 1 ☎06221 21 61 03 03

Tucked away from the busy Hauptstr., this Lebanese falafel shop offers delicious and affordable meals. Get a piping hot falafel or spicy chicken rolled in bread with fresh mint leaves, lettuce, tomato, and sauce. Be sure to try the free tea.

Turn onto Heugasse from Hauptstr., two blocks east of Universitätspl. $ Wraps €3-4.50. ⏰ Open daily 11am-11pm.

MERLIN
INTERNATIONAL ❷

Bergheimerstr. 85 ☎06221 65 78 64 www.cafe-merlin.de

The tables of this calm cafe spill out onto an untouristed sidewalk well away from the rush of the Altstadt. The sorcery-themed breakfast menu includes the **"Harry Potter"** and (of course) the "Merlin," while daily lunch specials *(€6.80)* and numerous happy hour deals with generous portions will give you enough energy for another day of exploring. A variety of tofu wraps also make the place vegetarian-friendly.

From Bismarckplatz, take Bergheimerstr. west for four blocks. $ Entrees €5-16.50. ⏰ Open daily 10am-1am.

PERSEPOLIS
PERSIAN ❶

Zwingerstr. 21 ☎06221 16 46 46

Right across the street from the **Bergbahn** stop, Persepolis is the perfect place for a delicious and cheap post-schloβ meal. The rotating menu, posted outside the door, always offers five tantalizing dishes, including one vegetarian option.

From Heiliggeistkirche, take Hauptstr. east and turn right onto the far side of Kornmarkt, then follow the road as it curves to the right. $ Entrees €3.50-5. ⏰ Open M-F 11am-8pm, Sa-Su noon-8pm.

YUFKA'S KEBAP
TURKISH ❶

Hauptstr. 182 ☎06221 485 98 30

So what if it's right in the middle of the Marktpl.—despite its touristy location, locals still tout the wonders of this joint for its tender and juicy meat. Try the *Yufka Spezial (€4.50)*, for an explosion of flavor in your mouth offset by the soft and chewy *yufka* bread.

On Hauptstr. just off the Marktpl. $ Entrees €3.50-9.50. ⏰ Open daily 11am-2am.

RAJA RANI
INDIAN ❶

Mittelbadgasse 5, Friedrichstr. 15 ☎06221 244 84, 06221 653 08 93

This cafeteria-style Indian joint serves up the best Indian food in town for unbelievable steals. Small portions are large enough for a simple meal; the chicken *korma (small €3.90, large €6)* is especially tasty, and the menu features a whopping 27 vegetarian dishes. Come by on weekdays 3-5pm for the best deal of all: a free and refreshingly delicious mango *lassi* with any purchase over €3.

From Bismarkpl., head down Hauptstr. and either turn right just before the Kurpfälzisches Museum onto Friederichstr., or turn right just past the Heiliggeistkirche onto Mittelbadgasse. $ Small portions €2.50-5. Large €4-8. Fish and tandoori specialties €6-14. ⏰ Mittelbadgasse open daily 10am-10pm. Friedrichstr. open daily 11am-11:30pm.

MALECÓN ⊛⊗¥ CUBAN ❶

Mittelbadgasse 3 ☎06221 433 93 83 ▨www.cubamarket-caravana.de

Forget Cuban sandwiches—at Malecón you get authentic Cuban (as well as Persian, Japanese, and Kurdish) rice dishes for cheap. Take advantage of the student discounts on its daily specials *(served M-Sa 11:30am-5pm)*, and you'll have a full stomach with money to spare for a tantalizing mojito.

✦ *From Bismarckpl., head down Hauptstr. past the Heiliggeistkirche, and turn right onto Mittelbadgasse.* ⓘ *Attached store also sells Cuban goods.* Ⓢ *Entrees €5-12. Daily specials €3.60-€5.60. Additional student discounts.* ⓩ *Open daily 11:30am-1am. Kitchen open 11:30am-11pm.*

CAFE ROSSI ➤⊗¥⌂ ITALIAN ❸

Rohrbacherstr. 4 ☎06221 974 60 ▨www.caferossi.de

The food here at this Bismarckpl. institution is good and the summer atmosphere in the outdoor beer garden is remarkable, but Cafe Rossi's real draw is the delicious espressos and cappuccinos that you can get for a measly €0.85-0.95 at the bar. This deal is only for people who savor their cups of joe at the bar, so get your mid-afternoon jolt on a stool at the gorgeous veneered bar.

✦ *Directly south of Bismarckpl.* Ⓢ *Entrees €9.80-17.80.* ⓩ *Open June-Aug daily 9am-1am, Sept-May M-W 8am-midnight, Th-Sa 8am-1am, Su 10am-midnight.*

MÉDOC ⊛⊗¥⌂ CAFE ❷

Sofienstr. 7b ☎06221 204 68 ▨www.medocs-cafe.de

Though its Bismarckpl. location and bilingual menu might put you on the tourist trap lookout, Medoc is a classic student watering hole. On weekends, erudite youngsters flock to this eatery for the cheap and tasty *schnitzel* deals *(Sa-Su after noon €5.50-6)*, and the summer patio is perfect for snickering at confused tourists looking for their buses across the street.

✦ *Across the street from the Bismarckpl. fountain.* ⓘ *M salad special €6. Th after 8pm mixed drinks €4. F after 8pm bigger mixed drinks €3. Sa after 8pm shooters €2.* Ⓢ *Entrees €7.50-14.* ⓩ *Open daily 10am-1am.*

NIGHTLIFE 🔥

Heidelberg's nightlife scene is rife with students looking for good times, so you can hardly go wrong. Downtown, skip the touristy bars along the Hauptstr. and walk one block north to **Unterestr.,** where you'll find a dense pack of bars where drunken revelers fill the narrow way until 1 or 2am. **Steingasse,** off the Marktpl. to the Neckar, is a bit less rambunctious but equally lively earlier in the evening. Nightclubs are not as concentrated there, but with the sheer variety of parties thrown every night of the week, you're guaranteed to find a good time. For a more mellow experience, pack up a barbeque and take it to the parks along the northern shore of the Neckar, west of the Theodor-Heuss-Brüke, and join locals spending the evening convening by their beloved river.

SONDER BAR ⊛⊗¥⌂ BAR

Unterestr. 13 ☎06221 252 00

A glorious ▨**Betreutes Trinken,** "drink with someone who will take care of you" sign overshadows the name of this bar—here, you're always among friends. The alternative music, selected from the piles of CDs and LPs behind the bar, only adds to the ambience as the late-night crowd, increasingly packed in a cramped space, takes to the tabletops. After all, with over 150 whiskeys, 25 absinthes, and even the totally whacky cobra-infused shot (ask to see it), who wouldn't take it to the floor...er...tables?

✦ *From Hauptstr., turn opposite Universitätspl. onto Unterestr.* Ⓢ *Beer from €2. Mixed drinks €5.* ⓩ *Open M-Th 2pm-2am, F-Sa 2pm-3am, Su 2pm-2am.*

BILLY BLUES IM ZIEGLER ⊛⊗¥ CLUB

Bergheimerstr. 1b ☎06221 253 33 ▨www.billyblues.de

Heidelberg's most mainstream club right next to Bismarckpl. is a popular choice for students just looking to dougie. The W salsa parties, starting at 10pm, are exceedingly popular, and the fusion food is top-notch. Weekends see a mix of funk, soul, oldies, and mainstream.

➡ Half a block southwest of the Bismarckpl. ℹ Student entry free Sa before 11:30pm. Cover €3-5. $ Drinks from €6.50. Snacks €5-12.50. ⏰ Open M 5pm-1am, Tu-Th 5pm-2am, F-Sa 5pm-4am, Su 5pm-1am.

DESTILLE 💳🚫♿🍸 BAR

Unterestr. 16 🖥www.destilleonline.de

A tree (fake, but you'd never guess it) grows out of this forest-themed bar, one of the few spots in town that is lively on the daily. Students drink themselves silly with quirky shots, including vodka with Pop Rocks; be sure to check out the illustrations on the menu. Just do it.

➡ From Hauptstr., turn opposite Universitätspl. onto Unterestr. $ Beer €1.70-3.50. Shots €2-8. ⏰ Open M-Th noon-2am, F-Sa noon-3am, Su noon-2am.

CAVE54 🚫💳♿🍸 JAZZ CLUB

Kramergasse 2 ☎06221 278 40 🖥www.cave54.de

Heidelberg's legendary student jazz club, opened in 1954, has seen all the greats: Louis Armstrong, Ella Fitzgerald, Dizzy Gillespie, the works. Add your name to that list by participating in Tusesday evening jam sessions, where everyone is welcome to play. Or just come to listen to great music and enjoy the ambience of the club, a cavernous dungeon connected to the tiny entry by a tight spiral staircase.

➡ Opposite the Heiliggeistkirche on the other side of Hauptstr. $ Cover €3. Mixed drinks €2.60. ⏰ Open daily 10pm-3am, from 8:30pm during live shows. Jam sessions from Tu 8:30pm.

DIE MOHR 🚫💳📶🍸⛅ BAR

Unterestr. 5-7 ☎06221 212 35 🖥www.der-mohr.de

The bartenders may modestly say that there's nothing special about Die Mohr, but students buzz to this watering hole like flies to honey, creating the rambunctious atmosphere made ever so slightly upscale by the framed black-and-white prints against the dark red walls. Sit at the bar and make a few new friends. A smaller lounge next door lets you recover from the hubbub, and the free Wi-Fi gives you a nice place to send some enthusiastic emails during your escapades.

➡ From Hauptstr., turn opposite Universitätspl. onto Unterestr. ℹ M trivia night (in English on request), Th ladies' night with free champagne. Free Wi-Fi. $ Beer €3.70. Big mixed drinks from €5.80. ⏰ Open M-Th and Su 6pm-2am, F-Sa 6pm-4am.

HALLE02 🚫💳🍸 CLUB

Güteramtsstr. 2 ☎06221 338 99 90 🖥www.halle02.de

Halle02 (and its smaller cousins Halle01 and Halle03) recycled some once-sketchy abandoned warehouses by the train tracks to create one of Heidelberg's most popular nightclubs. Multiple venues in one, Halle02 hosts concerts and parties, and even features an outdoor summer beach **(Zollhofgarten)**, complete with lounge chairs and volleyball nets. A frequent venue for student-sponsored parties, here's one place where you're bound to find people your own age ☞**getting after it**.

➡ From the Hauptbahnhof, take bus #33 to Czernyring, then follow the crowds. $ Cover varies with each event and venue; €0-5 (parties) and €10-25 (concerts). ⏰ Zollhofgarten open May-Oct M-F 6pm-1am, Sa 3pm-1am, Su 3pm-11pm. Opening times at Halle02 vary; check website for details.

TANGENTE 🚫💳♿🍸 CLUB

Kettengasse 23 ☎06221 16 94 45 🖥www.t-club-hd.de

One of the only dance clubs in Altstadt, Tangente still remains a popular choice for students who dance (or hook up) the night away amidst the orange-washed walls. Popular parties include the enigmatic Thursday night "Orange Obsession" and the Saturday "Sound Deluxe."

➜ From Hauptstr., turn right onto Kettengasse, located between Universitatspl. and Marktpl. $ Beer from €3. Mixed drinks from €6. ⏰ Open Tu-Sa 10pm-3am.

NACHTSCHICHT 💳♿🍸 CLUB

Bergheimerstr. 147 ☎06221 43 85 50 💻www.nachtschicht.com

Though some locals will say that Nachtschicht is overrated and overhyped, it is still a popular club, appealing more to Heidelberg's younger crowd. Be prepared to dance. Thursday nights are hip-hop; Friday and Saturdays are house music.

➜ From the Hauptbahnhof, walk through the Kurfürsten Passage, cross the street, and walk through the parking lot past the Lidl in the brick building and follow the crowds. $ Cover €4-8. Beer €2-3. Cocktails €5-8. ⏰ Open Th 10pm-late, F 8pm-late, Sa 10pm-late.

ARTS AND CULTURE ♫

Winter visitors should see the **Faschingsparade** (Mardi Gras Parade) cavort through the city on Fat Tuesday. In warmer weather, the first Saturdays in June and September and the second Saturday in July draw giant crowds for fireworks in front of the Schloβ. The **Handschuhsheim Fest** lures revelers the third weekend in June, while the **Schloβfestspiele Heidelberg** *(💻www.heidelberg-Schlossfestspiele.de)* features a series of concerts and plays at the castle from late June to early August. For the last weekend in September, the **Heidelberger Herbst** brings a medieval market to the Altstadt, which later hosts the **Weihnachtsmarkt** during the month before Christmas.

When it comes to concerts, on the other hand, Heidelberg lacks large venues to hold the sort of crowds drawn by top-name artists, and many of the concerts advertised throughout Heidelberg actually take place out in Mannheim at the **SAP Arena** *(💻www.saparena.de)*. Classical concerts can usually also be found in the churches scattered throughout the city.

STADTHALLE 🚫💳♿🍸 AUDITORIUM

Neckarstaden 24 ☎06221 14 22 60 63 💻www.heidelberger-kongresshaus.de

This 1250-seat auditorium boasts magnificently ornate gold details and an enormous pipe organ behind the stage. Local ensembles, including the Heidelberg Philharmonic and student orchestras, regularly perform here, as well as comedians, dancers, and other guest artists. The space also serves as Heidelberg's convention center, hosting many of the intellectual symposia that take place in the town.

➜ Along the river, halfway between the Theodor-Heuss and Alte Brückes. $ Ticket prices vary. ⏰ Box office opens 1hr. before curtain.

SHOPPING 🛍

Heidelberg's main shopping street, the **Hauptstr.**, has enough stores to fulfill anyone's wildest makeover fantasies. The more scholarly will enjoy the bookstores full of Old World charm and English books.

ANTIQUARIAT HATRY 💳🚫♿ USED BOOKS

Hauptstr. 119 ☎06221 262 02

With four floors packed with used books, Antiquariat Hatry is a student's dream come true, both for the selection and the great deals *(4 books €10)*. The eclectic collection has a small section of English books in the front. You'll also find more academically-oriented English-language books mixed in with the German books organized by subject throughout the shop.

➜ Right off the Universitatspl. ⏰ Open M-F 10am-8pm, Sa 10am-6pm.

PRESENCE WITH WORD BOOKS

Plöck 93 ☎06221 18 30 01

Mix and mingle with Heidelberg's expats in this cozy little shop with English-language books in a variety of subjects. Most books are used, though a small selection of new books is also available.

🚶 *From Haupstr., turn away from the river onto Friederichstr, the street before the Kurpfälzisches Museum. Bookstore is at the corner of Friederichstr. and Plöck.* ⏰ *Open M-Sa 11am-7pm.*

VINYL ONLY MUSIC

Hauptstr. 133 ☎06221 16 88 16 🖥www.vinylonly.eu

Despite the deceiving name, Heidelberg's go-to place for new and used music also carries CDs. Pretty much all genres are available, including a large classical section. It seems like the store will burst at any minute from the number of things crammed inside.

🚶 *Off the Universitätspl.* ⏰ *Open M-F 10am-8pm, Sa 10am-6pm.*

be welcome

The **Heidelberg Be Welcome Card** *($€11 per day, €13 per 2 days, €16 per 4 days)* provides discounts at many of Heidelberg's attractions (including free admission to the Schloβ) and restaurants, as well as public transportation coverage within the Heidelberg area.

ESSENTIALS

Practicalities

- **TOURIST OFFICES:** Located outside the Hauptbanhof *(Willy-Brandt-Platz 1. ☎06221 194 33. 🖥www.heidelberg-marketing.de $ City guide map €1, downloadable from the website. Self-guided audio tour €7.50 for 3hr, €10 per day. ⏰ Open Apr-Oct M-Sa 8am-7pm, Su 10am-6pm; Nov-Mar M-Sa 9am-6pm)*, inside the Rathaus on Marktpl. *(⏰ Open M-F 8am-5pm, Sa 10m-5pm)*, and at Neckarmünzpl. *(⏰ Open daily June-Sept 9am-5pm, Oct-May 10am-4pm).*
- **CURRENCY EXCHANGE: Reisebank.** *(Located in the Hauptbahnhof. ⏰ Open M-F 7:30am-8pm, Sa 9am-5pm, Su 9am-3pm.)*
- **LAUNDROMAT: Waschtrommel.** *(Rohrbacherstr. 10, off the Bismarckpl. toward Rewe City. ☎06221 48 57 75. $ Wash €4.30. Dry €2.70. ⏰ Open M-F 9am-9pm, Sa 8:30am-8:30pm.)*
- **INTERNET:** All cafes in Heidelberg that have Wi-Fi offer it for free with any purchase. **Poc@.** *(Bahnhofstr. 9-11, a block southwest of the Bismarckpl. ☎06221 650 82 09. $Internet terminals for €1 per hr. ⏰ Open M-Sa 9am-10pm, Su noon-8pm.)*
- **CITY-WIDE LOST AND FOUND:** *(☎06221 65 37 97.)*
- **TOILETS:** A number of Heidelberg businesses in the Altstadt have a sticker of a square red smiley face in their window, which means that you can go use the bathroom there for free without making any purchases.
- **POST OFFICE:** *(Sofienstr. 8-10, 1 block south of Bismarckpl. ⏰ Open M-F 9:30am-6pm, Sa 9:30am-1pm.)*
- **POSTAL CODE: 69115.**

Emergency!

- **EMERGENCY:** *(☎110.)*
- **FIRE AND AMBULANCE:** *(☎112.)*
- **AFTER-HOURS PARAMEDICS:** *(☎06221 192 92.)*

Getting There

The **Hauptbahnhof** is located in the town's west side and serves a number of destinations, including **Frankfurt** *($ €15-25. ⏰ 50 min., 2 per hr.);* **Mannheim** *($ €6.50. ⏰ 12-20min., 2 per hr.);* **Stuttgart** *($ €30-50. ⏰ 1-1.5hrs., every hr.);* and **Munich** *($ €30-90. ⏰ 3-4hr., 2-3 per hr.).*

walka walka

Heidelberg is relatively small and incredibly walkable, especially if you stay in the Altstadt. Public transportation is reliable, but not quite as frequent as tourists might like; your best bet is probably to join the legions of bikers on the roads.

Getting Around

The RNV (Rhein-Neckar-Verhehr GmbH)

The town of Heidelberg is served by **trams** and **buses.** Single ride passes are around €2, depending on how far you're traveling. Day passes *($ €5.20 single, €9 for up to 5 people)* are also available. The **S-bahn** primarily moves between towns.

By Ferry

Cruise up and down the Neckar with the **Rhein-Neckar-Fahrgastschifffahrt** *(☎06221 201 81)* to Neckarsteinach with commentary in German, English, and French. Boats leave from the southern bank in front of the Kongresshaus *(3-hr. round trip, €12.50 adults, May-Sept. 19 daily every hr.10am-4pm, M until 2pm; Apr and Sept 20-Oct 17 every hr. M-F 11am-2pm, Sa-Su 10am-2pm).* For an eco-friendly trip, take a ride with the **Heidelberger Solarschiffahrts,** the world's largest and entirely silent solar-powered ship. *(Leaves from the southern bank of the Karl-Theodor-Brüke. $ €6.50 per person. ⏰ Open Mar-Nov Tu-Su 10am, 11:30am, 1pm, 3pm, 4:30pm, and 6pm.)*

By Taxi

Taxi stations are located at the **Hauptbahnhof** and **Bismarckpl.** *(☎06221 30 20 30 or ☎06221 73 90 90.)*

By Bike

Eldorado rents bikes for €15 per day or €5 per hr. Discounts are available for three or more days of rental. *(Neckarstaden 52 ☎06221 6 51 89 67 🖥www.eldorado-hd.de ⏰ Open Tu 10-noon and 2-5pm, W-F 10-noon and 2-6pm, Sa 10am-6pm, Su 2-6pm.)*

By Boat

Bootsverleih Simon *(☎06221 41 19 25 🖥www.bootsverleih -heidelberg.de)* is located on the north shore of the Neckar by the Theodor-Heuss-Brücke. *($ 3-4 person paddle boats €8-10 per 30min; and motorboats €14-16 per 30min. ⏰ Open M-F 2-8pm, Sa-Su 11am-8pm.)*

stuttgart ☎0711

While Stuttgart may not immediately come to mind when one lists prominent German cities, the capital of **Baden-Württemberg** is home to one of the most important German exports: cars. Probably thanks to the **Mercedes-Benz** and **Porsche** headquarters in Stuttgart, the streets practically overflow with luxury vehicles, and even the most modest-looking homes will have sleek sports cars parked outside. That luxury is matched by the spectacular museums and well-preserved palaces of the old city. The city's famous mineral baths draw old and young alike (though more old than young) to their healing waters, bucolic forests, and lush vineyards are only a short train ride away.

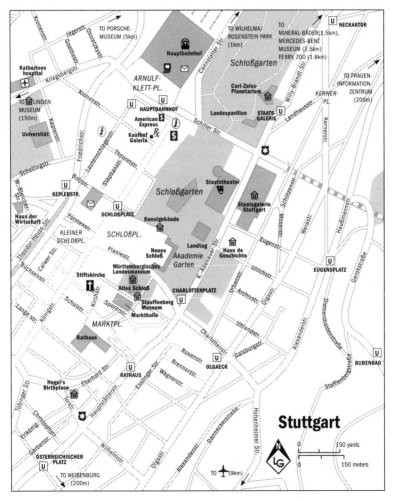

ORIENTATION

At the heart of Stuttgart is an enormous pedestrian zone cluttered with upscale establishments that run south from the Hauptbahnhof. **Königstrasse** and the smaller **Calwerstrasse** are the main pedestrian thoroughfares, while a number of smaller passages connects a whole network of consumer-type places. For those afraid of traffic, the streets are easily accessible from the Hauptbahnhof via an underground passageway called the **Arnulf-Klett Passage,** also home to a number of shops. Running parallel to and west of these streets is the bustling **Theodor-Heuss-Strasse**—the site of Stuttgart's hippest nightclub district. If clubbing isn't quite your thing, turn left from the Hauptbahnhof to get to the **Schloßgarten,** a green expanse lined with some of Stuttgart's best museums. Further south lies the **Schloßplatz,** a more urban retreat with fountains and statues dotted with sidewalk cafes. Walk even further south and you'll reach a more wallet-friendly part of town, with plenty of *döner* stands and reasonably-priced cafes around the **Rotebühlplatz.** Nearby, a host of cafes and bars surround the **Hans-im-Glück** fountain, named after the fabled Brothers Grimm tale.

ACCOMMODATIONS

👍 INTER-HOSTEL — HOSTEL ❷

Paulinenstr. 16 — ☎0711 66 48 27 97 💻www.inter-hostel.com

This small, new hostel boasts an exceptionally friendly and helpful staff, many of whom live in the hostel, and a great location only a few blocks from the bustle of Konigstr. Though its entrance under the highway leaves something to be desired, the living room-esque lounge, complete with board games and a coffee machine, give the space a homey feel. Cheapest laundry you'll ever find, but skip the pricey *(€6.50)* breakfast.

🚏 U1 or U14: Österreich-Pl. From the station, turn right down Paulinenstr. (under the bridge). Alternatively, S-Bahn: Stadtmitte. At the station, take the Sophienstr. exit, follow Sophienstr. for two blocks, then turn left onto Tubingenstr. and right onto Paulinenstr. ℹ Wi-Fi and linens included. Laundry €2, including detergent. $ Singles €39; doubles €27-32; quads €22; 6-beds €19.50-23.50. ⏰ Reception open 6:30am-11pm.

ALEX 30 — HOSTEL ❷

Alexanderstr. 30 — ☎0711 838 89 50 💻www.alex30-hostel.de

Spacious, clean rooms with textured orange walls make this hostel simple yet stylish, but no laundry facilities and limited keys per room are slight inconveniences. The backyard *biergarten* is a great place to hang out. Don't bother with the expensive breakfast buffet; there are plenty of cheaper bakeries nearby.

🚏 U6 (dir: Möhringen), U5 (dir: Leinfelden), U7 (dir: Ostfildern), U15 (Fernsehturm), or U8 (Nellingen): Olgaeck. From the station, turn left and walk up to hill along Alexanderstr. ℹ Wi-Fi €1 for your entire stay. Linens included. $ Singles €35; doubles €28; 3- to 5-beds dorms €23. ⏰ Reception 24hr.

JUGENDHERBERGE STUTTGART (HI) — HOSTEL ❷

Haußmannstr. 27 — ☎0711 664 74 70 💻ww.jugendherberge-stuttgart.de

Perched high in the hills, this hostel has quite the entrance: a bridge leads to a glass elevator that takes you down to the reception area on the fifth floor. Recently renovated, this enormous, impeccable hostel has all the standard HI amenities: a bistro, internet cafe, pool, and foosball. Each room has a separate toilet and shower, making life more convenient.

🚏 U15: Eugenspl. From the station, walk uphill and follow the street as it bears left. ℹ Breakfast and linens included. Wi-Fi in bistro only, €5 for 24hr. Laundry €4. $ Dorms €23.80 first night, €20.50 per night subsequent nights. ⏰ Reception 24hr.

JUGENDGÄSTEHAUS STUTTGART (IB) — 💳🚭📶 HOSTEL ❷

Richard-Wagner-Str. 2 ☎0711 24 11 32 🖥www.hostel-stuttgart.de

This quaint hostel exudes old-fashioned charm, right down to the sloped ceilings and slightly worn wooden furniture. With a 10% ISIC discount, they have the cheapest beds in town, though make sure to book early—summers during the week are usually filled a month in advance.

🚏 U15: Bubenbad - IB Jugendgästehaus. From the station, turn right onto Richard-Wagner-Str. ℹ Breakfast and linens included. Wi-Fi €1 per hr., €3 per day., €15 per wk. $ Singles €21.50; doubles €19; triples €16.50. Additional €2.50 for a single night's stay, €2.50 for private sink, €5 for private bath. ⏰ Reception 24hr.

CAMPINGPLATZ CANNSTATTER WASEN — 💳 CAMPGROUND ❷

Mercedesstr. 40 ☎0711 55 66 96 🖥www.campingplatz-stuttgart.de

This campground by the Cannstatter Volksfest area is a little out of the way from public transport, but during non-festival times the grounds are tranquil and serene.

🚏 S1, S2, or S3: Bad Cannstatter. From the station, take a right and another right at the rotary onto Daimlerstr. When it ends, head across the street and past the train tracks and large field to campground. ℹ Tent €4.50. Car €2.50. Laundry wash €4, dry €3.30. Electricity €0.50/1kW. $ €6.50 per person; ages 3-14 €3.50. ⏰ Reception open daily 7am-noon and 2pm-10pm.

SIGHTS 👁

✍ MERCEDES-BENZ MUSEUM — 💳♿ MUSEUM

Mercedesstr. 100 ☎0711 173 00 00 🖥www.mercedes-benz.com/museum

Take a comprehensive journey through the history of the automobile in this sleek museum. A century's worth of gleaming automobiles—from Gottlieb Daimler and Karl Benz's first experiments to the showy prototypes of tomorrow—will make even the most lukewarm car enthusiast drool. The included audioguide is creepily high-tech, starting segments on its own as you pass through each room.

🚏 S1 (dir: Kirchheim): NeckarPark (Mercedes-Benz). ℹ Audioguide available in 12 different languages. $ €8, students €4, under 15 free; half-price after 4:30pm. ⏰ Open Tu-Su 9am-6pm.

SCHLOßPLATZ/SCHLOßGARTEN — ♿ PARK

Because almost 20% of Stuttgart is under a land preservation order, the city is known for its urban green spaces, the crown jewel of which is the Schloβgarten. Join the hordes of locals that come to lie on the grass and sunbathe in the *Unterer*, *Mittlerer*, and *Oberer* (Upper, Middle, and Lower) areas. Beyond the Oberer Schloβgarten is the central Schloβplatz, a touristy but delightful plaza with ornate fountains and perfectly trimmed hedges. To the east of the plaza is the elegant Baroque **Neues Schloß**, where mythological figures guard the bureaurcrats working inside. To the south is the **Altes Schloß**, now home to the **Landesmuseum Wurrtemburg**. The glass-cubed **Kunstmuseum Stuttgart** is also recognizable by the German-flag-colored Alexander Calder statue in the front.

🚏 Parks throughout the city. $ Free.

KUNSTMUSEUM STUTTGART — 🐾♿ MUSEUM

Kleiner Schloβpl. 1 ☎0711 216 21 88 🖥www.kunstmuseum-stuttgart.de

Stuttgart's art museum, housed in a minimalist glass cube set among the ornate palaces around the Schloβplatz, contains an excellent collection of 20th-century masterpieces. The permanent collection, located on the ground floor and basement, includes a large number of works by **Otto Dix,** known for his grotesque paintings in response to Nazism and World War II. In the basement, follow your nose past a display of color books to a room made entirely of beeswax, and meditate in the serenity. The upper floors are reserved for temporary exhibits.

Even if you don't make it into the museum, take the elevator to the top floor (pretend you're heading to the restaurant) and enjoy the view from the top of the glass cube.

🚆 U5, U6, U7 or U15: Schloßpl. ℹ 1hr. tours in German on W and F 6pm, Sa-Su 3pm. $ €5-8, students €3.50-6.50, under 13 free. ⏰ Open Tu 10am-6pm, W 10am-9pm, Th 10am-6pm, F 10am-9pm, Sa-Su 10am-6pm.

TURMFORUM ♿ TOWER, MUSEUM

Arnulf-Klett-Pl. 2 ☎0711 20 92 29 20 💻www.das-neue-herz-europas.de

Take the elevator or stairs up to the top of the Hauptbahnhof's glistening 10 story tower, where you can get the best free bird's-eye view of the city. Position yourself right under the enormous spinning Mercedes-Benz logo and be sure to admire the neat rows of vineyards in the surrounding hills. Inside the tower is a free interactive exhibit (propaganda campaign) about Stuttgart 21, the highly controversial and expensive railway project that involves the construction of a new Stuttgart station and high-speed line to Ulm, ultimately linking Paris and Vienna. The exhibit, however, fails to mention the fact that the project took over 20 years of incubation to reach citizen approval, and even today, anti-Stuttgart 21 stickers are popular street art.

🚆 Inside the Hauptbahnhof, take the elevator at the South exit ("Südausgang," look for the "Turmforum"). ℹ Most exhibits in German, but English-language pamphlets and a trilingual video presentation are available. All floors wheelchair-accessible except the observation deck. $ Free. ⏰ Open M-W 10am-6pm, Th 10am-9pmand Sa-Su 10am-6pm. Observation deck open Apr-Sept daily 10am-9pm, Oct-Mar M-W 10am-6pm, Th 10am-9pm, Sa-Su 10am-6pm.

WILHELMA 🎟♿ ZOO

Wilhelma 13 ☎0711 540 20 💻www.wilhelma.de

Watch young penguins, llamas, and polar bears in this wildly ornate zoo. The complex also houses botanical gardens on grounds constructed by King Wilhelm as a summer retreat. With over 8000 different animals and 6000 species of plants, Wilhelma is perhaps the largest and prettiest zoo you'll ever visit, making it worth a trek even for those who don't particularly love smelly beasts. Make sure to attend the sea lion feeding *(daily 11am and 3pm).*

🚆 U14: Wilhelma or U13: Rosensteinbrücke. $ Tickets €12, with public transportation ticket €11; students €6/€5.50. Tickets available at the counter until 4pm, afterwards from vending machines. ⏰ Open daily May-Aug 8:15am-6pm, Apr and Sept 8:15am-5:30pm, Mar and Oct 8:15am-5pm, Nov-Feb 8:15am-4pm. Animal houses remain open 45min. after close, plant houses 30min. Aquarium open May-Aug M 9am-6pm, Tu 9am-5:45pm, W-Su 9am-6pm; Apr and Sept M 9am-5:30pm, Tu 9am-5:15pm, W-Su 9am-5:30pm; Mar and Oct M 9am-5pm, Tu 9am-4:45pm, and W-Su 9am-5pm; Nov-Feb M 9am-4pm, Tu 9am-3:45pm, W-Su 9am-4pm.

SCHWABISCHE STERNWARTE 👍🚫 OBSERVATORY

Seestr. 59a ☎0711 226 08 95 💻www.sternwarte.de

On a clear night, skip the cheesy planetarium shows and take a short hike through the hills to this hidden retreat, where chipper astronomists and multiple telescopes introduce you to the secrets of the night sky. The main observatory, complete with a wood-domed roof, is over 100 years old but still functions as good as new. Moons, constellations, and planets are viewable in textbook splendor. The undiscovered nature of this gem allows you several chances for telescope-hogging.

🚆 U15: Heidehofstr. From the station, take a small hike up the hill. ℹ Group explanations are in German, but the astronomers all speak English and will gladly translate. $ €3, students €2. ⏰ Open daily Jan-Apr and Sept-Dec from 9pm; May-Aug M and W-Sa from 10pm.

STAATSGALERIE STUTTGART 👍♿ MUSEUM

Konrad-Adenauer-Str. 30-32 ☎0711 47 04 02 50 💻www.staatsgalerie.de

A comprehensive collection in two wings: the stately paintings in the old wing date from the Middle Ages to the 19th century, while the new wing has a first-rate collection of works by Picasso, Kandinsky, Warhol, and Dali. Ironically, the old paintings are housed in the modern building, while the new paintings are housed in the older building. Each room always has an anachronistic "which of these is not like the other" theme.

🚇 *U1, U2, U4, U9, or U14: Staatsgalerie.* *i Explanations in both English and German.* Ⓢ *Permanent collection €5, students €4, under 12 free. W and Sa free. Special exhibits €10, students €7, ages 13-20 €2.* 🕐 *Open Tu 10am-8pm, W 10am-6pm, Th 10am-8pm, F-Sa 10am-6pm.*

PORSCHE MUSEUM
🌊♿ MUSEUM

Porschepl. 1 ☎0711 91 12 09 11 🖳www.porsche.com/museum

With its new building—a futuristic bastion of polished metal—the Porsche Museum displays some of the world's most stylish and expensive cars, with a large, glorified showroom exhibiting the rich history behind the three generations of Porsche. Much emphasis is also placed on the company's sportscars, and you can stand below the futuristic listening pods to get a feel for the sounds of the company's greatest automobiles.

🚇 *S6 (dir.: Weil der Stadt): Neuwirsthaus/Porschepl.* *i Audio guide (available in 7 languages)* *€2.* Ⓢ *€8, students €4, under 14 with adult free.* 🕐 *Open Tu-Sa 9am-6pm, last entry 5pm.*

LANDESMUSEUM WÜRRTEMBURG
🌊♿ MUSEUM

Schillerpl. 6 ☎0711 89 53 54 45 🖳www.landesmuseum-stuttgart.de

A must-see for every archaeology buff, the Landesmuseum, fittingly situated in the *Altes Schloß*, houses artifacts from the stone age, along with many royal treasures and the crypts of several previous kings and queens. Unfortunately, many of the exhibits are under renovation to prepare for the museum's 150th anniversary in 2012, but the dizzying array of arrowheads, prehistoric jewelry, and woodworking tools on display are enough to please even the pickiest enthusiasts. The third floor is dedicated to a hands-on kids' exhibit, while the basement houses an impressive glass collection, also arranged from prehistoric relics to the present-day cups.

🚇*U1, U2, U4, U5, U6, U7, or U15: Schloßpl.* *i Ticket includes entry into the musical instrument collection at Schillerpl. 1. English-langauge audio guides available.* Ⓢ *Reduced entry fee (due to construction) €3, students 2; other special temporary exhibits may have additional costs.* 🕐 *Open Tu-Su 10am-5pm.*

HAUS DER GESCHICHTE
🌊♿✳ MUSEUM

Konrad-Adenauer-Str. 16 ☎0711 212 39 89 🖳www.hdgbw.de

Continuing on where the Landesmuseum left off, the Haus der Geschichte chronicles the history of Baden-Württemberg from the Napoleonic era to the present day, with impressive exhibits with bright colors, snazzy lighting, and other artsy doodads. Unfortunately, exhibit explanations are all in German, and English-only guests are condemed to the long-winded but necessarily informative audioguide, a cheesy dialogue between the charmingly ignorant Lucy and the joyfully avuncular Dr. Askme, complete with sounds of their footsteps as they accompany you through the museum. Cleanse your mind afterwards in the lounge, a hyper-modern space with suspended pod seats and a 360° multimedia presentation.

🚇 *U1, U2, U4, U9, or U14: Staatsgalerie. Look for the blue and purple fountains; the museum is the building on the right.* *i Free audioguides in English.* Ⓢ *€3, students €2, younger students free.* 🕐 *Open Tu-W 10am-6pm, Th 10am-9pm, Su 10am-6pm.*

MINERALBÄDER (MINERAL BATHS)
🌊♿ HOT SPRINGS

Leuze: Am Leuzebad 2-6 Leuze: ☎0711 2164210
Berg: Am Schwanenpl. 9 Berg: ☎0711 2167090 🖳www.stuttgart.de/bader

Join geriatric Germans as they soak in Stuttgart's renowned mineral baths, filled from Western Europe's most active mineral springs. The 40 million liters of spring water pumped out every day are said to have curative powers, and bathers flock from far and wide to soak in pools, saunas, and showers supplied by the stuff. While you could collect the water in bottles, give yourself a more luxurious treatment by lolling in the Mineralbad Leuze or the less expensive (and less luxurious) Mineralbad Berg. Just be careful—while buffs might tout the benefits of drinking the stuff, it actually tastes like carbonated metallic saltwater.

 # U1 or U14: Mineralbäder, then turn left for Mineralbad Leuze or right for Mineralbad Berg. i Spa treatments also available at each facility. $ Leuze day pass €14.60, students €10.40; Berg day pass €7.10, students €5.60. ⏰ Leuze open daily 6am-9pm. Berg open May-Sept daily 8am-8pm; Oct-Apr M-Sa 6am-9pm, Su 8am-5pm. Last entry to both 1hr. before closing.

FERNSEHTURM STUTTGART ♿ TOWER

Voted by residents the most important landmark of the city, Stuttgart's TV tower was the first of its kind when built in 1954 and served as a model for future towers all around the world. Standing at 217 meters, you can take an elevator up to the observation deck to get the most spectacular view of the city, with stunning sunsets against the neighboring hills.

 # U7, U8, or U15: Ruhbank (Fernsehturm). $ Trip to the top €5, ages 3-15 €3. ⏰ Open daily 9am-11pm, last entry 10:30pm.

CARL ZEISS PLANETARIUM ♿ PLANETERIUM

Willy-Brandet-Str. 25 ☎0711 162 92 15 💻www.planeterium-stuttgart.de

Stuttgarters stargaze at the oddly right-angled city planetarium, named after one of the most famous lens manufacturers in the entire galaxy. Enjoy shows with German voiceovers, visual effects, and spacey background music. Alternatively, head to the observatory for a more intimate, natural introduction to the universe.

 # U1, 2, 4, 9, 14: Staatsgalerie, then turn left onto Schillerstr. and wander into the Schloßgarten. $ Tickets €6, students €4. ⏰ Shows Tu and Th 10am and 3pm; W and F 10am, 3pm, and 8pm; Sa-Su 2pm, 4pm, and 6pm. Sa laser show 7:15pm.

FOOD

Fast-paced and cosmopolitan, Stuttgart is known for its excellent international cuisine. While every bakery under the Stuttgart sun serves up the signature *brezel* (pretzels), and a number of Swabian restaurants will give you your fill of *spätzle* (thick egg noodles) and *maultaschen*—pasta pockets filled with meat and spinach, known as the "Little Cheaters on God" for a sneaky way of eating meat on Fridays during Lent)—some of the best dinners might be a little less traditional. Reasonably-priced restaurants lie along the pedestrian zone between **Pfarrstr.** and **Charlottenstr.,** while **Rotebuhlpl.** and **Kronenstr.** have plenty of *Imbiss* (snack bars). More stylish but still inexpensive options for fresh sandwiches and vegetarian wraps can be found in the **Eberhardstr.** area near the Hegelhaus. For grocery stores, check in the basement of the **Kaufhof Galeria** *(Königstr. 6 or Eberhardstr. 28⏰ Open M-Sa 9:30am-8pm, Eberhardstr. location Sa 9am-8pm)* or, for discount groceries, try the **Aldi** on Marienstr. 11 *(open M-Sa 8am-8pm).*

ARSLAN'S KEBAP TURKISH ②

Marienstr. 28 ☎0711 674 13 24 💻www.arslanskebap-stuttgart.de

For the city's best *döner* kebab, head to this tasty joint, also home to a restaurant proper on the second floor. The key here is the bread—while most places just give you thin, chewy pitas, the *döner* bread at Arslan's is thick, fluffy, and laden with tasty sesame seeds.

 # S1, S2, S3, S4, S5, or S6: Stadtmitte. From the station, take the Marienstr. exit. $ Doner

€3.50. Entrees €7.50 ⏰ *Open M-Th 9am-midnight, F-Sa 9am-1am, Su 10am-midnight.*

VEGI VOODOO KING 🌿 VEGETARIAN [1]

Steinstr. 13 ☎0711 259 93 34

A cult favorite, this vegetarian and vegan outpost offers tasty falafel and other pita-inspired sandwiches, soups, and amazing hand-cut fries in an Imbiss-style eatery. Though you might want to take it to go, beware that all of those delicious sauces piled on top are likely to get messy.

🚏 *From the Hegelhaus, go under the walkway down Steinstr. to restaurant on right.* $ *Sandwiches €3-4.50.* ⏰ *Open M-W 11:30am-12:30am, Th 11:30am-2am, F 11:30am-4am, Su 1pm-12:30am.*

DELI 💳🚭🍸❄⛅ GERMAN [2]

Geiβstr. 7 ☎0711 236 02 00 💻www.deli-stuttgart.de

With a posh location right next to the **Hans-im-Gluck fountain,** join some of Stuttgart's hippest youngsters as they chomp on delicious salads and traditional *maultaschen*. Come here for lunch *(daily noon-2pm)* for the special, with pasta or salad of the day and coffee *(€4.90)*. The outdoor area is a prime people-watching location, especially late into the night as all the locals travel to their nightly haunts.

🚏 *S1, S2, S3, S4, S5, or S6: Stadtmitte. From the station, walk down Rotebühlpl. toward Eberhardstr. and turn left at the Hegelhaus toward the fountain.* $ *Entrees €5.90-13.50.* ⏰ *Open M-Th and Su 9am-1am, F-Sa 9am-3am.*

REISKORN 🌿🚭🍸❄⛅ ASIAN [2]

Torstr. 27 ☎0711 664 76 33 💻www.das-reiskorn.de

The enclosed courtyard in the back of this Thai-inspired restaurant offers an oasis from the usual bustle of outdoor seating. Sit under a straw umbrella amidst the bamboo plants and savor the exotic flavors of your heaping bowl of the house favorite, red curry chicken *(€8.90)*. For a drink, the ginger limeade is especially refreshing and comes steeped in slices of fresh lime and ginger.

🚏 *S1, S2, S3, S4, S5, or S6: Stadtmitte. From the station, walk down Rotebühlpl. toward Eberhardstr. to restaurant on right.* $ *Entrees €8.20-15.90.* ⏰ *Open M-Sa 11:30am-11pm, Su 5pm-11pm.*

ASIA WOK 🌿 ASIAN [2]

Silberburgstr. 149 ☎0711 365 11 88

This family-owned Chinese eatery has delicious, cheap no-frills stir fries, like the rice plates, complete with miniature egg rolls *(€5.50)*. Try the mouthwatering plate of chicken and sprouts. Dessert includes fried bananas in a delightfully light batter with honey *(€1)*, and if you have a great conversation with the owners, you might even get it for free—we wok that.

🚏 *S1, S2, S3, S4, S5, or S6: Feuersee. From the station, turn left onto Silberburgstr.* $ *Entrees €5.50-7.* ⏰ *Open M-Sa 10am-11pm, Su 11am-11pm.*

KESKIN KEBAP 🌿🍸 TURKISH [1]

Marienstr. 14

This small hole-in-the-wall joint serves up your average *döner* at not-so-average prices: for the fully stuffed pita, chock full of meat and veggies *(€1.50)*. While it's not quite as good as *döner* elsewhere, the price can't be beat, and you'll often find long lines of people waiting for the cheapest dinner in town.

🚏 *S1, S2, S3, S4, S5, or S6: Stadtmitte. From the station, take the Marienstr. exit.* $ *Doner €1.50. Entrees €6.* ⏰ *Open M-Sa 10am-midnight.*

NIGHTLIFE

Stuttgart's nightlife runs the gamut from calm lounges to techno clubs. The somewhat pricey sit-down cafes along **Königstr.** and **Calwerstr.** are packed in the early evening. For the real nightlife follow a chic, Benz-driving crowd to the innumerable sidewalk lounges on **Theodor-Heuss-Str.** The club scene doesn't pick up until after midnight, and when it does, **Rotebühlpl.** and **Eberhardstr.** are the most popular areas. **Tips 'n' Trips** publishes comprehensive guides to nightlife in German and English. For more on current events, buy a copy of *Lift* (🖥*www.lift-online.de)*, also available at Tips 'n' Trips *(€2.20).* For gay and lesbian nightlife, check out the shelf of GLBT publications located in the *i-Punkt* in the small corridor to the right of the ticket office; *Queer* (🖥*www.queer-bw.de)* is a monthly magazine that focuses on GLBT events in Baden-Württemberg.

CLUB SCHOCKEN
🐵⊗ ♈⅋ CLUB

Hirschstr. 36   🖥www.club-schocken.de

Enjoy the purple flames along the walls of this alternative indie dance club, with three floors for hanging out. Come on weekend nights for live concerts or dancing with the crowded masses of the city's student population in one of Stuttgart's few clubs without a cover charge.

✈ *S1, S2, S3, S4, S5, S6, U1, U2, U4, or U14: Stadtmitte. From the station, walk along Königstr. and turn left onto Hirschstr.* Ⓢ *Beer €2.80-3. Mixed drinks from €6. Small panini and cakes (served only on Sa) €3.* ☒ *Open M 3pm-1am, Tu-W 3pm-2am, Th 3pm-3am, F 3pm-5am, Sa 11am-5pm, Su 5pm-1am.*

SKYBEACH
🐵♿ ♈⅋ BEACH BAR

Königstr. 6   ☎0163 818 23 20 🖥www.skybeach.de

In good weather, young Germans flock to this club to lounge in bikinis, drink mojitos, and watch the occasional live fire show in a faux-tropical atmosphere. Get a tan while you nap in a hammock and forget that you're actually on the top floor of the parking garage of a department store.

✈ *From the Hauptbahnhof, walk across the street into Stephanstr. and take the Galeria Kaufhof elevators to level D2, then turn left.* Ⓢ *Mixed drinks €7.* ☒ *Open daily 11am-late. Fire shows on some weekend nights; check the website for schedule.*

PALAST DER REPUBLIK
🐵♈⅋ PUB

Friedrichstr. 27   ☎0711 226 48 87

A wooden pavillion with a bar blasts music for fresh-air fans and after-hours aficionados. On weekends, the crowd overflows onto the sidewalk with alarming density.

✈ *From the Schlossplatz, take the stairs between the Kunstmuseum and the Konigpassage and keep walking forward for about two blocks.* Ⓢ *Beer €2.50-3.30.* ☒ *Open M-W 11am-2am, Th-Sa 11am-3am, Su 3pm-1am.*

OBOLOMO
🐵♈⅋❀⅋ BAR

Torstr. 20   ☎0711 236 79 24

Quirky, circular protrusions on the ceiling and bright blue walls give this popular bar the impression of an underwater haven. Its chill atmosphere and late hours means local bartenders often hang out in the wee hours of the morning, gossiping about their evening's encounters. The best seats are at the top of a ladder on a cushioned loft, but you'll have to get there early to stake out a spot.

✈ *U1, U2, or U4: Rathaus. From the station, walk south on Eberhardstr. and turn left onto Torstr.* Ⓢ *Mixed drinks €3-8. Snacks €3-6 (served 3pm-3am).* ☒ *Open M-Th 3pm-5 or 6am, F-Sa 3pm-9 or 10am, Su 3pm-5 or 6am.*

MATA HARI
🐵♈⅋ BAR

Geißstr. 3

Graffiti-drenched bathrooms and overstuffed couches make this bar the down-to-earth student hangout-of-choice amidst the more posh locations nearby. Grab yourself a beer and chat with locals at the communal picnic tables outside or plop yourself down in the living-room style interior—you're sure to make some new friends.

By the Hans-im-Glück fountain: walk past Deli and look for the long benches. $ Mixed drinks €5.50-8. Panini €3.50-4.50. ⏰ Open M-Th 2pm-2am, F-Sa 2pm-3am, Su 2pm-2am.

ZWÖLFZEHN BAR, CLUB

Paulinenstr. 45 ☎0711 658 17 99 🖥www.zwoelfzehn.de

Don't let the tacky tiki garbage distract you from the alternative awesomeness of this club. No mainstream music here: Friday nights are throwback music nights—with 60s, soul, and classic rock—while Saturday nights bring anything from indie rock to electro and hip hop. Live concerts during the weekends also add spice to the mostly-student crowd who dance the night away here. The party usually picks up between 1-2am, so come by then.

S1, S2, S3, S4, S5, or S6: Stadtmitte. From the station, walk down Rotebühlpl. toward Paulinenstr. and look for the aloha-esque sign across the street. ⏰ Open M-Th 8:30pm-1 or 2am, F-Sa 8:30pm-5am, Su 8:30pm-1 or 2am.

SUITE 212 BAR

Theodor-Heuss-Str. 15 ☎0711 253 61 13 🖥www.suite212.com

The streets and couches in front of this upscale bar-lounge stay packed with beer-guzzling and martini-sipping hipsters. Relax with a quieter crowd sitting outside during the day, often including mothers with strollers. The open spaces both inside and out, dotted with stylish cube seats, provide a welcome respite from the typical crowded bar. Don't be intimidated by the bouncers touting their faux bulletproof vests.

S1, S2, S3, S4, S5, or S6: Stadtmitte. From the station, walk down Theodor-Heuss-Str. $ Beer €2.50-3. Mixed drinks €6.50-8. ⏰ Open M-W 11am-2am, Th 11am-3am, F-Sa 11am-5am, Su 2pm-2am.

BETT BAR, CLUB

Friedrichstr. 23a ☎0711 284 16 67 🖥www.bett-lounge.de

Translucent glass brick walls surround a 20-something and younger crowd filling the dance floor of this bar/club late into the night. The canopied beds out back are crowded with perennial late-night loungers (after all, the motto here is, "Relaxing=Clubbing"), and film projections on the walls give the space an artsy feel.

U9 or U14: Friedrichsbau. From the station, look for the large "Filmhaus" sign across the street. $ Mixed drinks €6.50-9. ⏰ Bar open daily 3pm-1am. Club is open 11pm-late.

ARTS AND CULTURE

Connoisseurs of luxury and pleasure, Stuttgart's residents know how to have a good time. The **Stuttgarter Weindorm** (Wine Village) is the largest wine festival in Germany. From late August to early September, wine lovers descend upon **Schillerpl., Marktpl.,** and **Kirchstr.** to sample Swabian specialties and 350 kinds of wine. Beer gets two weeks in the spotlight during the 160-year-old **Cannstatter Volksfest,** Germany's second largest beer festival (dwarfed only by Oktoberfest), held annually on the Cannstatter Wasen *(last week of Sept. and the first week of October).* The **Christopher Street Day** gay and lesbian festival occurs in the last week of July *(🖥www.csd-stuttgart.de).* In late November and Decemer, the spectacular **Christmas Market** lights up the entire town.

Tickets and listings for shows (everything except opera, theater, and ballet) can be found at the **Kartenvorverkauf** desk, a ticket office located within the tourist office, *(⏰ open M-F 9am-8pm, Sa 9am-4pm).* Student discounts vary, but usually musicals can be seen for as little as €5 and classical concerts for half-price.

STAATSTHEATER STUTTGART 🎫♿ THEATER

Oberer Schloßgarten 3 ☎0711 203 20 🖥www.staatstheater.stuttgart.de

Located right across the plaza from the Neues Schloβ, the Staatstheater is one of Germany's most impressive theaters and the heart of the city's cultural vibrancy. Home to Stuttgart's opera, ballet, and theater companies, the performances include impressive modern interpretations of classic operas, stunning ballets, and top-notch plays in German.

🚶 From the Hauptbahnhof, turn left onto Schillerstr. and into the Schloßgarten; the theater is the one past the reflecting pool with the big columns. $ €8-155, student tickets (must be picked up in person before the performance with valid ID) from €8. ⏰ Box office open M-F 10am-6pm, Sa 10am-2pm, and 1hr. before performances.

LIEDERHALLE 🎫♿ MUSIC

Berlinerpl. 1 ☎0711 202 77 10 🖥www.liederhalle-stuttgart.de

With its varied exteriors, the Liederhalle is a complex of five theaters and multiple conference rooms that plays host to mostly classical music concerts but also to musicals and world music groups.

🚶 U2, U4, U9, or U14: Berliner Platz. $ Ticket prices vary. ⏰ Box office open an hour before performances, but visitors are encouraged to order tickets online.

SHOPPING

EINKLANG MUSIC

Christophstr. 7 ☎0711 234 87 71 🖥www.einklang.de

A glorious mecca for all classical and jazz enthusiasts, Einklang offers a treasure trove of both new and old recordings, along with two listening rooms to test out the tracks before you buy.

🚶 U1or U14: Österreichischer Platz. From the station, take the Christophstr. exit. ⏰ Open M-F 10am-8pm, Sa 10am-6pm.

FLAMING STARS 🎫 CLOTHING

Nesenbachstr. 48 ☎0711 620 21 17 🖥www.flamingstar.eu

Want to take a little piece of Stuttgart home with you? Head to this punkster alternative store, where you can find shirts with "Don't F*** with Stuttgart" and other, wittier phrases. Bags, jewelry, and other accessories all observe the same punk-rock-skateboarder theme.

🚶 U1 or U14: Österreichischer Platz. From the station, take the Hauptstatterstr./Christophstr. exit, head down Christophstr. and take a right onto Nesenbachstr. $ Most T-shirts €25. ⏰ Open M-F noon-8pm, Sa 11am-6pm.

PICADILLY ENGLISH SHOP 🎫🍸 BOOKS, GIFTS

Schellingstr. 11 ☎0711 226 09 02 🖥www.piccadilly-english-shop.de

Recognizable by the stereotypically English phone booth outside the door, Picadilly is your one-stop shop for everything Britannia, from digestive crackers to Paddington Bear. There is also a book section with an extensive collection of cheap Dover edition classics, as well as all the bestsellers.

🚶 U9 or U14: Friedrichsbau. From the station, exit to Schellingstr. ⏰ Open M-Sa 10am-8pm.

BUCHHAUS WITTWER 🎫♿🍸 BOOKS

Konigstr. 30 ☎0711 250 70 🖥www.wittwer.de

Stuttgart's very own bookstore has a large selection of English-language books on the ground floor by the elevator (look for the British and American flags).

🚶 U1, U2, U4, U5, U6, U7, or U15: Schloβpl. From the station, go to the other side of the glass-cubed Kunstmuseum. ⏰ Open M-Sa 9am-8pm.

ESSENTIALS

Practicalities

- **TOURIST OFFICES: i-Punkt.** *(Königstr. 1A, by the escalator leading up to the Klett-Passage. ☎0711 222 80. 🖥www.stuttgart-tourist.de $ City guides €1-2.50. [i] ATMs available.)* i-Punkt organizes a walking tour *($ €8 per person ⏰ Apr-Oct daily 11am-12:30pm)* and a 2.5hr bus tour *($ €18 per person, students €14.50 ⏰ Open Apr-Oct daily 1:30pm-4pm.)* Another location in airport Terminal 3 *(⏰ Open M-F 8am-7pm, Sa-Su 9am-1pm and 2-6pm).*
- **YOUTH INFORMATION: Tips 'n' Trips** offers youth-oriented information on the hottest clubs, affordable lodgings, and popular cafes. *(Lautenschlagerstr. 22. ☎0711 222 27 30. 🖥www.tipsntrips.de $Internet access €0.50/15 min. ⏰ Open M-F noon-7pm, Sa 10am-2pm.)*
- **GLBT RESOURCES: Weissenburg.** *(Weissenburgstr. 28a. ☎0711 640 44 94. 🖥www.zentrum-weissenburg.de ⏰Office open M-F 7-9pm. Cafe with pool table and resources open M-W and F 7-10pm, Th 5-10pm, Su 3-10pm.)*
- **WOMENS RESOURCES: Fraueninformationszentrum (FIZ).** *(Urbanstr. 44 . ☎0711 239 41 24 ⏰ Open M-F 9am-2pm.)*
- **LAUNDROMAT: SB-Waschsalon Trieb** is located right behind the Tourist Office. *($Wash €4, dry €1 per 6 min. ⏰ Open daily 5am-midnight.)* The dry-cleaning center across Königstr. also has a 24hr. wash center. *(⏰ Open M-F 7am-7pm, Sa 7am-3pm.)*
- **PHARMACY:** Located in the Hauptbahnhof, down the escalators past track 12. *(⏰ Open M-F 6:30am-8:30pm, Sa 8am-6pm, Su 10am-5pm.)* Alternate location in the Klettpassage. *(⏰ Open M-F 7:30am-8pm, Su 9am-5pm.)*
- **INTERNET: Level One Cyberbar.** *(Konigstr. 22 $€1 per 20min. ⏰ Open M-F 9am-midnight, Sa noon-midnight.)* There are also a few terminals between the post office and Coffee Fellows inside the train station *(€5 per hr.).*

Emergency!

- **POLICE:** *(Hauptstätterstr. 34, or by the lockers in the Hauptbahnhof. ☎0711 259 98 48. Emergency ☎110.)*
- **FIRE:** ☎112.
- **HOSPITAL: Katharinenhospital (Klinikum-Stuttgart)** is located near the train station. *(Kriegsbergstr. 60. ☎0711 27 80.)*

Getting There

By Plane

Flughafen Stuttgart *(☎01805 94 84 44 🖥www.flughafen-stuttgart.de)* has arrivals and departures from a variety of domestic and international cities. Take the S2 or S3 to **Flughafen/Messe** (30min. journey from Hauptbahnhof).

By Train

Stuttgart is the transportation hub of southwestern Germany, and when the Stuttgart 21 project is completed in about 10 years, it will (supposedly) become the "new heart of Europe." Currently, trains run to **Berlin** *($ €130-150. ⏰ 6 hr., 2 per hr.);* **Frankfurt** *($ €40-90. ⏰ 1-3hr., 2-3 per hr.);* **Munich** *($ €40-70. ⏰ 2-3hr., 2 per hr.);* **Basel, CHE** *($ €40-100. ⏰ 3hr., 2-4 per hr.);* **Paris, FRA** *($ €70-160. ⏰ 4-8hr., 1 per hr.);* **Prague, CZ** *($ €75-140. ⏰ 9hr., 1-3 per hr.).*

Getting Around

By Public Transportation

Stuttgart's S-bahn and U-bahn systems have perhaps the most complicated, though artsy, map you've ever seen. The **S-bahn** is run by Deutsche Bahn, and is thus accessible with a **Eurail, Interrail,** or **German Railpass.** The **U-bahn** tram and bus system is run by the Verkehrs- und Tarifverbund Stuttgart (VVS, 🖥www.vvs.de). Trains and tarms run between 5am and 1am daily, while a night bus system exists for those partiers staggering home late at night.

Central Stuttgart is split into two zones, 10 and 20. Beyond that, the zones are split like a concentric roulette board, but most tourist attractions are located within the two zones. A single ride ticket within the same zone is €2, or a 4-ride **Mehrfahrkarte pass** is available for €7.10. The best deals, though, are either the single day pass *(€5.95 in the city, entire network €12.30)*, group day pass *(€9.95, entire network €16.20; includes up to five adults and any of their children under 17)* or the special tourist three-day pass *(€10.30, entire network €13.90; includes one adult and two children, only available at the tourist office or in hotels and hostels)*.

The tourist office offers a special **Stuttcard** that has 3-day discounts to a host of attractions. You can get the card for €9.70, or combine it with a 3-day transportation pass *(city center and airport €18, entire network €22)*.

You can get unlimited transportation within the entire province for just €20 per person or €28 per group of 5, valid from 9am-3am the following morning with the **Baden-Wurttemberg Ticket.**

By Ferry

Cruise up and down the Neckar to visit other scenic outposts with **Neckar-Käpt'n** *(☎0711 54 99 70 60; 🖥www.neckar-kaptn.de)*. Boats leave the Bad Cannstatt dock by Wilhelma Zoo. Take U14 (toward Remseck) to Wilhelma. Ships cuise the Neckar between Easter and Oct. 3-4 times a day for €6.50-26. Return ticket €6.

By Car

Offices in the Hauptbahnhof at track 16 for: **Avis** *(☎0711 223 7258);* **Budget** *(☎1805 21 77 11🕰Open M-F 7am-9pm, Sa 8am-4pm);* **Hertz** *(☎0711 226 29 21 🕰Open M-F 7:30am-8pm, Sa 8am-3pm, Su 10am-2pm);* **Sixt** *(☎0711 223 7822 🕰Open daily 7:30am-9pm);* **EuropCar** *(☎0711 954 6960 🕰Open M-F 8am-9pm, Sa 8am-5pm, located outside track sixteen down one flight of stairs).*

By Bike

Due to Stuttgart's hills, biking is not the most popular way of getting around, and you'll find that most streets lack bike lanes. That said, resources do exist: Deutsche Bahn's **Call a Bike** is organized in Stuttgart, with actual drop-off stations rather than the usual arbitrary roadside bike surprises. Procedures, though, are still the same: register online *(🖥www.callabike.de)*, retrieve unlocking code by phone *(☎0700 05 22 55 22)* or online, €0.08/min or €15/day, first 30min. free.

Bikes can also be rented from **Rent a Bike Stuttgart.** *(Tips 'n' Trips, Lautenschlagerstr. 22.🖥www.rentabike-stuttgart.de $ Rentals €12 per 7hr., €16 per 24hr., €23 per weekend, €49 5 days; students €9/12/16/33. **i** All bikes come with lock and helmet, require an ID and €50 deposit. Cash only. 🕰Open M-F noon-7pm, Su 10am-2pm.)*

By Ride Share

Mitfahrzentrale Stuttgart West, Lerchenstr. 65 *(☎0711 194 48)*. From Hauptbahnhof, take bus #42 (toward Schreiberstr.) to Rosenberg-Johannestr. Open M-F 9am-6pm, Sa 10am-1pm.

ludwigsburg ☎07141

ORIENTATION

Just 15 min. outside of Stuttgart lies the quaint town of Ludwigsburg, which sprung up around the legendary palace. To get the full experience for a little less, consider getting combination tickets to the Schloßes (⑤ *ResidenzSchloß + Schloß Favorite €8, students €4, with museums €12.50/6.30, with Blühendes Barock €15/€7.50*). If you're lucky, you can catch almost-daily performing arts shows and literature readings inside the castles during the Ludwigsburg Schloßfestspiele, held every June-July.

SIGHTS

▩ RESIDENZSCHLOß   ♦& PALACE

Schloßstr. 30   ☎07141 18 20 04 █www.schloss-ludwigsburg.de

Originally conceived as a small hunting lodge for the Duke Eberhard Ludwig, the lodge morphed into a full-blown estate where he could spend more time with his mistress. Though Eberhard, poor dear, died during the 30-year-long construction of the estate, the quarters were enjoyed by his posterity and are now preserved for tourists. The interior of the palace can only be seen on a guided tour, in which well-versed tour guides sardonically play up the enormous size of King Friedrich I (over 6'7" and 400 pounds!) who later lived there. Also on site is an extensive **Ceramics Museum,** displaying ancient earthenware to modern art, the restored **apartment** of Duke Karl Eugen, the "scandalous duke" who had so many mistresses that he made the women that he'd had wear blue shoes so that he could keep track, a **Mode Museum** (Fashion Museum), in which models exhibit the fashions of yesteryear, and a **Theater Museum,** a German-only guide to the history of Würrtemburg theatricals. The museums are all accompanied by a no-frills audio guide.

⚑ *From the train station, take bus #421, #427, #430, #443, or #444 to ResidenzSchloß, or head down Myliusstr. until it ends and then turn right onto Wilhelmstr, then turn left onto Schloßstr.* ⓘ *Make sure to also visit the surrounding gardens (Blühendes Barock).* ⑤ *Tour €6.50, students €3.30. Museums €3.50/€1.80.* ☑ *Grounds open daily 10am-5pm. Tours mid-Mar to mid-Nov in German 10am-5pm; in English M-F 1:30pm, Sa-Su 10:30am, 1:30pm, and 3:15pm; mid-Nov to mid-Mar in German M-F 5 per day, Sa-Su 9 per day; in English daily 1:30pm.*

BLÜHENDES BAROCK   ◉ GARDENS

Mömpelgardstr. 28   ☎07141 97 56 50 █www.blueba.de

More than 70 acres of perfectly-manicured gardens adorn the grounds around the **ResidenzSchloß,** with flowers more spectacular than your average botanical garden. A must-see for anyone with a green thumb, the gardens also feature the kid-favorite Märchengarten, where German toddlers chant at voice-activated exhibits. Ask the mirror on the wall who is the fairest one of all (*Spieglein, Spieglein, an der Wand...*), or open the stone caves to glimpse at the treasures of Ali Baba (*Sesam öffne Dich!*), and relax with a boat tour around the grounds and into the mouth of the whale that swallowed Gepetto.

⚑ *From the ResidenzSchloß, take the east exit to enter the gardens.* ⑤ *Day pass €7.50, students €3.60.* ☑ *Bluhendes Barock open daily 7:30am-8:30pm; Märchengarten open daily 9am-6:30pm.*

SCHLOß FAVORITE   ♦& PALACE

This smaller yet just as ornate "favorite" hunting lodge of the Duke Eberhard Ludwig also maintains an impressive collection of restored rooms and royal artifacts ready for your viewing pleasure. Only viewable via guided tours, German-speaking tour guides make the interior a less likely destination for

English-speakers, but the stunning architecture still make this a picture-worthy destination. Afterwards, take a stroll around the surrounding **Favoritenpark**, where you can pet wild deer (at your own risk).

 # Located directly behind the ResidenzSchloß. $ Tour €3.50, students €1.80. ⏰ German tours every 30min., mid-Mar to Oct daily 10am-12:30pm and 1:30-5pm; Nov to mid-Mar Tu-Su 10am-noon and 1:30-4pm.

FOOD

ASIA GOURMET IMBISS — 🍴🍸 ASIAN [1]

Seestr. 17 — ☎07141 992 56 56

Join the trend of takeout-box-toting Germans with a €3 *schülerbox* from this cheap eatery. Choose between rice and noodles, five kinds of meat, and five kinds of sauces for your quickly-made creation. The price can't be beat, even if the food can.

 # From the train station, head down Myliusstr., make a right on Mathildenstr. then take a left onto Seestr. $ Entrees €3.60-5.90. ⏰ Open M-F 11am-10pm, Sa-Su noon-9:30pm.

EIS OLIVIER — 🍴 ICE CREAM [1]

Wilhelmstr. 10 — ☎07141 92 45 06 💻www.olivier.de

During the summer months, the inside and outside of this ice cream parlor are packed with tourists and locals alike partaking in the century-old tradition of Olivier's famous gelato. With some of the cheapest cones you'll find *(€0.70 per scoop)*, take a moment to cool off with some of Ludwigburg's pride and joy.

 # From the train station, head down Myliusstr. until it ends, and take a right onto Wilhelmstr. $ Scoop €0.70. Sundaes from €2.20. ⏰ Open M noon-10pm, Tu-Th 10am-11pm, F-Sa 10am-11:30pm, Su 10am-11pm.

ESSENTIALS

Practicalities

- **TOURIST OFFICE:** *(Marktpl. 6 ☎07141 91 75 55 ⏰ Open M-F 9am-6pm, Sa 9am-2pm.)* Free maps and guides, as well as listings for local festivals, are available here.

Getting There

From Stuttgart, take the S4 *(dir: Marbach)* or S5 *(dir: Bietigheim)* to **Ludwigsburg.**

MUNICH

No trip to Germany is complete without a voyage to friendly Bavaria, and the populous city of Munich, a city probably responsible alone for your beer-soaked, festive image of German life. The city and its surroundings are as different as can be from modernist Berlin or industrial Hamburg. Munich's Catholic heritage—the city's name comes from the Benedictine monks who founded it, and who also built the magnificent abbey and brewery combo in **Andechs,** just a short daytrip away—has always lent the city a merrier feel. Get merry yourself in the traditional pubs or festivals, or in the thumping clubs of the Schwabing, the university area. Recuperate with a trip to the glorious countryside of **Starnberg am Starnberger See,** and try out the cold lake water if you're still feeling the night before.

greatest hits

- **DRINK IF...** Play drinking games under the stars with 7999 other fun people at Europe's largest beer garden, Hirschgarten (p. 267).

- **BEAMER, BENZ, OR BENTLEY.** Sport the classiest threads you own, and head to the BMW Welt to test drive a new whip (p. 266).

- **A CHILL HANGOUT.** Redeem your free drink voucher and relax in the winter garden hammock at Wombats (p. 254).

- **DOWN IN ONE.** Pace yourself on the Maß and avoid using the vomitorium at Munich's most famous beer hall, Hofbräuhaus (p. 277).

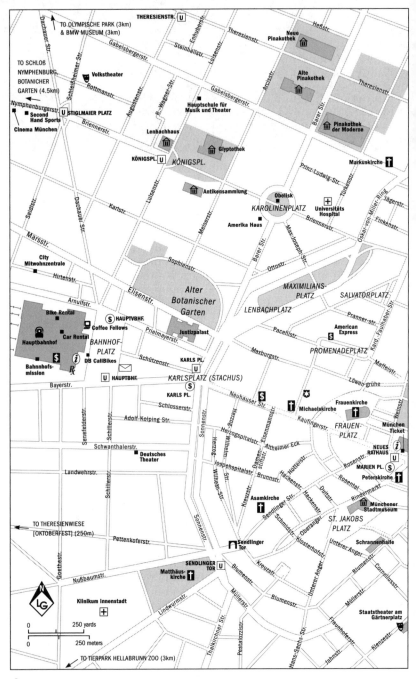

THERESIENSTR. U

TO OLYMPISCHE PARK (3km)
& BMW MUSEUM (3km)

TO SCHLOß
NYMPHENBURG,
BOTANISCHER
GARTEN (4.5km)

Neue Pinakothek

Alte Pinakothek

Hauptschule für Musik und Theater

Volkstheater

Second Hand Sports

Cinema München

STIGLMAIER PLATZ U

Lenbachhaus

Pinakothek der Moderne

Glyptothek

Markuskirche

KÖNIGSPL. U   KÖNIGSPL.

Antikensammlung

Obelisk

Universitäts Hospital

KAROLINENPLATZ

Amerika Haus

City Mitwohnzentrale

Alter Botanischer Garten

MAXIMILIANS-PLATZ

SALVATORPLATZ

LENBACHPLATZ

Bike Rental

HAUPTVBHF. S

Coffee Fellows

Car Rental

Hauptbahnhof

BAHNHOF-PLATZ

DB CallBikes

Bahnhofs-mission

Justizpalast

American Express

PROMENADEPLATZ

KARLS PL. U

HAUPTBHF. U

KARLSPLATZ (STACHUS) S

KARLS PL. S

Neuhauser Str.

Michaelskirche

Frauenkirche

FRAUEN-PLATZ

München Ticket

NEUES RATHAUS

MARIEN PL. S

Peterskirche

Deutsches Theater

Asamkirche

Münchener Stadtmuseum

ST. JAKOBS PLATZ

Schrannenhalle

TO THERESIENWIESE
[OKTOBERFEST] (250m)

Sendlinger Tor

SENDLINGER TOR U

Matthäus-kirche

Klinikum Innenstadt

Staatstheater am Gärtnerplatz

0   250 yards

0   250 meters

TO TIERPARK HELLABRUNN ZOO (3km)

munich

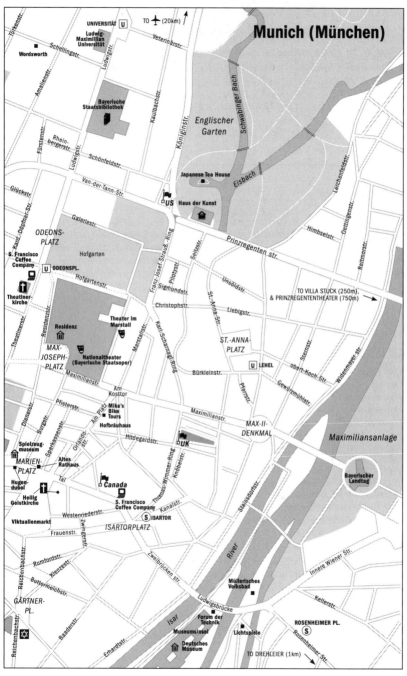

Munich (München)

UNIVERSITÄT

TO ✈ (20km)

Ludwig-Maximilian Universität

Wordsworth

Bayerische Staatsbibliothek

Englischer Garten

Schwabinger Bach

Japanese Tea House

Eisbach

US

Haus der Kunst

ODEONS-PLATZ

Hofgarten

S. Francisco Coffee Company

ODEONSPL.

Prinzregenten str.

TO VILLA STUCK (250m), & PRINZREGENTENTHEATER (750m)

Theatiner-kirche

Residenz

Theater im Marstall

ST.-ANNA-PLATZ

MAX-JOSEPH-PLATZ

Nationaltheater (Bayerische Staatsoper)

LEHEL

Maximilianstr.

Am Kosttor

Mike's Bike Tours

Hofbräuhaus

Maximilianstr.

MAX-II-DENKMAL

Maximiliansanlage

UK

Spielzeug-museum

MARIEN-PLATZ

Altes Rathaus

Canada

Bayerischer Landtag

Hugen-dubel

Heilig Geistkirche

S. Francisco Coffee Company

ISARTOR

Viktualienmarkt

ISARTORPLATZ

GÄRTNER-PL.

River

Innere Wiener Str.

Rumfordstr.

Müllerisches Volksbad

ROSENHEIMER PL.

Isar

Ludwigsbrücke

Forum der Technik

Museumsinsel

Lichtspiele

Rosenheimer-Str.

Deutsches Museum

TO DREHLEIER (1km)

munich

While the majority of budget accommodations can be found in the City Center and Neuhausen, the university area is buzzing with young people and the shops and eateries that they frequent. Marienplatz is the energetic hub of the neighborhood. The major S- and U-Bahn junction—a major pedestrian zone in Munich—is frequented by equal parts student, tourist, and political demonstrator. Coat your stomach with spicy chorizo or the tortilla pie from **Bar Tapas** before hitting the actual bars—both **Alter Simpl** and **Schelling Salon** boast great nightlife scenes and history to boot.

munich

If you ask the average traveler about this Bavarian capital, you'll hear beer, beer, and more beer. The birthplace of **Oktoberfest,** Munich (pop. 1,350,000) prides itself on making some of the world's finest brews, providing beer gardens and halls with the source of merriment and pleasure. Yet those who look past the city as a bastion of alcohol will find that it has much more to offer. As the third largest city in Germany, Munich is also a thriving center of European commerce, and some residents even call the city "Toytown" for its relative wealth and ease of living. World-class museums, parks, architecture, and a rowdy art scene mix the archaic with the modern in a city that is, contrary to some misconceptions, not drowning in booze. Most of the time. Many Mucheners (not Munchkins) also head to Salzburg for a day (only 1½hr. away by train).

ORIENTATION

City Center

The city center is the hub of all tourist activity in Munich. Most of Munich's historical sights and name-brand stores are jam-packed into the few blocks between **Marienplatz** and **Odeonsplatz.** Struggle through the throngs of ubiquitous international camera-flashers and get yourself the stereotypical Bavarian experience, complete with a night at the infamous **Hofbräuhaus** and a stroll through the **Residenzmuseum** and the adjoining **Hofgarten.** South of Marienplatz is the neighborhood **Isarvorstadt,** once home to the city's underground nightlife scene. Today it's more a bustling, yuppie neighborhood, but the bars have retained their original bohemian splendor. This neighborhood also houses Munich's GLBT district. To its west is **Isarvorstadt-Ludwigvorstadt, Theresienwiesen,** otherwise known as the Oktoberfest field, or what we call the stuff of legend. Immediately north of that is the **Hauptbahnhof,** Munich's central train station, where numerous hostels provide an excellent atmosphere for meeting fellow travelers.

University Area

Hear "university area," think culture and retail. Many of the city's impressive art museums dot **Maxvorstadt,** home of the **Königsplatz,** as well as fancy-pants restaurants, quaint coffee houses, and secondhand shops. **Schwabing,** to the north, is a student's dream district; Ludwig-Maximilian Universität erudites make the area trendy and cozy and keep the upscale bars and eateries running with their patronage. To the west of Schwabing everything goes greener with the charming **Englischer Gartens** and Munich's beloved beer gardens by the **Chinesischer Turm** (Chinese pagoda).

Southern
Germany

Olympic Area

The 1972 Olympics was Germany's chance to prove itself in the international spotlight after the sour memories of the 1936 Berlin Olympics under the Nazi regime. However, its success was largely shadowed by the killing of 11 Israeli athletes by Palestinian terrorists. Now known as the **Munich Massacre,** it was immortalized through Steven Spielberg's 2005 film *Munich.* Today, you can visit the **Olympiapark** and marvel at the site of the Games. The imposing **Olympiaturm** (Olympic Tower) is the highest point in all of Munich at 291 meters, and the iconic **Olympiastadion's** (Olympic Stadium) curtains of acrylic glass drape over lime green seats. Also on-site are all things **BMW,** with a museum, factory, and showroom, and the enormous shopping mall, **Olympia-Einkaufzentrum,** for all your food and fashion needs.

Au-Haidhausen

These two neighborhoods across the Isar used to house laborers before WWII bombing nearly demolished Au, though Haidhausen was left surprisingly intact. Today, these regions play a large role in Munich's cultural scene. **Gasteig** cultural complex contains the Munich Philharmonic, a conservatory, the main branch of the public library, and an experimental theater all in one. On the flip side, staples of Munich nighlife line **Westbahnhof** station, with enormous clubs dedicated to all things glitter and party. Talk about being on the right side of the tracks.

Neuhausen-Nymphenburg

Neuhausen remains one of Munich's hidden gems, relatively undiscovered by tourists, so it still actually has character. Take Tram 17 toward Amalienburgstr. and you'll find some of Munich's prettiest landscapes, from the world's largest beer garden at **Hirschgarten** to the beautiful and extravagant **Schloß Nymphenburg** to the tranquil **Botanischer Garten**. For a more urban feel, head to **Rotzkreuzplatz** and meander down Nymphenburgstr. for the city's best cafes and ice cream, then end your night with a rousing chorus at the **Lowenbräukeller** beer hall.

Thalkirchen

This quiet and relatively unexplored neighborhood is actually the Circle of Life. Well, not really, but Thalkirchen's **Tierpark Hellaburn** is the world's first zoo to put animals in their "native habitats." Today, the zoo remains a delight for children and wildlife photographer wannabes, while others take in the beauty of the **Isar River** with extended rafting trips on floating beer gardens and kayaking or rafting along a few legendary whitewater patches.

ACCOMMODATIONS

As a city of beer, Munich sees its fair share of young philanthropists looking to aid the local industry. With that, of course, comes a proliferation of clean and reasonably-priced hostels smack in the city center. The impeccable and convenient public transportation also makes it easy for those looking to stay at cheaper and quieter accommodations elsewhere. The outrageously high demand for rooms during Oktoberfest means that you should probably book months (up to a year) in advance, and beware that rates do increase 10-20% during those 16 magical days. The summer months, crowded with vacationers, will also see rises in demand and price, so again make sure to book days in advance.

City Center

WOMBATS 💳♿📶🍸 HOSTEL [2]

Senefelderstr. 1 ☎089 59 98 91 80 💻www.wombats-hostels.com/munich

With its bright fluorescent colors and curvy lobby furniture, Wombats caters to hip hostel-hoppers. Redeem the free drink voucher you got at check-in at the bar while you play a few games of pool with some new friends, and relax on a hammock in the sunny winter garden. Many rooms facing the winter garden have poor ventilation, though the noisy fans (provided) offer a little respite. All rooms have private bathrooms, high-tech key-card lockers, and clothing hangers.

🚇 S1, S2, S3, S4, S5, S6, S8, U1, U2, U4, or U5: Hauptbahnhof. Across the street from the Hauptbahnhof (south side). ℹ Linens included, but you'll have to make and strip your own bed. Wi-Fi in the lobby (spotty connection in rooms) included. $ 4- to 10-bed dorm rooms from €12-27; doubles €35-38. ⏰ Reception 24hr.

EURO YOUTH HOTEL 💳⊗📶🍸 HOSTEL [2]

Senefelderstr. 5 ☎089 59 90 88 11 💻www.euro-youth-hotel.de

Cozy rooms, good company, and knowledgable staff define this centrally-located hostel, which also offers complimentary tea and coffee for its guests. The 12-person dorms are a bit cramped, but doors to the outdoor terrace provide excellent (and much-needed) ventilation. An outlet at each bed lets you charge your electronics overnight with ease. With its 360-degree wrap-around bar, the lounge here is a popular hangout and final stop for many beer tours through Munich.

🚇 S1, S2, S3, S4, S5, S6, S8, U1, U2, U4, or U5: Hauptbahnhof. Across the street from the Hauptbahnhof. ℹ Shared and private bathrooms available. Free Wi-Fi. $ 12-bed mixed dorms €18.80-22.00; singles €50-52. Doubles, triples, quads, and quints also available. ⏰ Reception 24hr.

JAEGERS HOSTEL 💳⊗📶🍸 HOSTEL [2]

Senefelderstr. 3 ☎089 55 52 81 💻www.jaegershostel.de

With its sleek orange walls, this spotlessly clean hostel sports a large variety of rooms. For the ultra-budget experience, pack some earplugs and get a bed in the 40-person room, but be forewarned—there are only six showers for 80 people! All other dorms, though, have ensuite bathrooms, and you can even keep the boys away with female-only dorms.

🚇 S1, S2, S3, S4, S5, S6, S8, U1, U2, U4, or U5: Hauptbahnhof. Across the street from the Hauptbahnhof. ℹ Private bathrooms in each room. Wi-Fi and linens included. $ Singles from €55; 10-person dorms €23; 40-person dorms €17; 2-, 4-, and 6-person rooms also available. Women-only dorms from €25. ⏰ Reception 24hr.

MEININGER'S HOSTEL AND HOTEL 💳⊗📶🍸 HOSTEL ❷

Landsbergerst. 20 💻www.meininger-hotels.com

Graffitied walls, communal kitchen, TV lounge, and a ping-pong table in the basement give Meininger's a college-dorm feel—there's even a refrigerator with a free-for-all shelf. The rooms, though, are much more spacious than any of those you probably saw in college, and its convenient location close to Theresienwiese makes it a top choice for Oktoberfest.

🚇 S1, S2, S3, S4, S5, S6, or S8: Hackerbrücke. Turn right onto Grassenstr. and then right again onto Landsbergerstr. ℹ Wi-Fi and linens included. Women-only dorms (max. 6 beds) available. $ 3-14 bed dorms from €25; singles from €75. ⏰ Reception 24hr.

THE4YOU 💳♿📶🍸 HOSTEL ❷

Hirtenstr. 18 ☎089 552 16 60 💻www.the4you.de

This hostel sits removed from other area hostels, and with its private bar it's perfect for those looking for a little more peace and quiet in an ideal location. A full German breakfast buffet is also included. Wire-frame rolling storage lockers are provided under each bunkbed.

🚇 S1, S2, S3, S4, S5, S6, S8, U1, U2, U4, or U5: Hauptbahnhof. Exit the Hauptbahnhof toward the north, walk forward one block and then turn left onto Hirtenstr. ℹ Linens and Wi-Fi (available in the lobby) included. $ 8-bed dorms from €22; shared-bathroom doubles from €32; 4- and 6-bed dorms also available. ⏰ Reception 24hr.

IN VIA MARIENHERBERGE 🚫⊗📶🍸 HOSTEL ❸

Goethestr. 9 ☎089 55 58 05 💻www.invia-muenchen.de/1-wohnen/marienherberge/

This female-only hostel is an appealing escape from the rowdier hostels a block away. Popular for German girls doing short-term internships in Munich, the rooms at the Marienherberge are sunny, clean, and homey enough for your mother's approval. There's even a free piece of chocolate for you when you arrive!

🚇 S1, S2, S3, S4, S5, S6, S8, U1, U2, U4, or U5: Hauptbahnhof. Exit the south side of the Hauptbahnhof to Goethestr.; look for the colorful IN VIA sign on the left side of the street, and buzz the "Marienherberge" telecom for entry. ℹ Linens and Wi-Fi (available in the lobby) included. 2 communal kitchens. $ 1- to 4-bed dorms from €30 per night. Call to make reservations with the English-speaking staff. ⏰ Reception 10am-11pm; guests 18+ receive a key for 24-hr. access.

A AND O HOTEL AND HOSTEL MUNICH 💳⊗📶🍸 HOTEL ❸

Bayerstr. 75 ☎089 555 785 💻www.munich-hotels.com

Look beyond the tacky orange-and-yellow decor to find plenty of budget rooms geared toward families with small children; most rooms combine a double bed with a bunkbed in a spacious arrangement. Although this branch of the A and O also has a 14-bed and 10-bed dorm in the basement, even the staff advise against those rooms for their summertime humidity and limited bathrooms. Instead, hostel-seekers should try the Neuhausen location, just on the other side of the train tracks. Reserving individual beds in the quads is possible, but discouraged.

🚇 S1, S2, S3, S4, S5, S6, S8, U1, U2, U4, or U5: Hauptbahnhof. Exit the Hauptbahnhof to the south and turn right onto Bayerstr.; hotel will be a few blocks down on the left. ℹ Internet access €1 per 20 min., €5 per 24 hr., €8 per week. Private rooms have TV, bathrooms, and linen. $ Singles from €32; doubles from €20; quads and dorms from €12. ⏰ Reception 24hr.

CREATIF ELEPHANT HOTEL

●❀⊗⟨⟨ᵖ⟩⟩ ⁺ HOTEL ❸

Lämmerstr. 6 ☎089 55 57 85 ▣www.munich-hotels.com

With its cheeky bright-colored walls and location amongst other hostels, the Creatif Elephant combines a youthful chic attractiveness with more luxurious hotel amenities. Most rooms are recently renovated with funky, modern furniture and include flatscreen TVs. Ask the approachable staff for recommendations.

✈ *S1, S2, S3, S4, S5, S6, S8, U1, U2, U4, or U5: Hauptbahnhof. Exit the Hauptbahnhof to the north and walk one block before turning left onto Hirtenstr. Hotel will be on your right; you can't miss its bright colors.* ⓘ *Wi-Fi included. Best rates if booked online. Parking €10. Breakfast buffet €9.* Ⓢ *Singles from €30; doubles from €60.* ⓧ *Reception 24hr.*

HOTEL JEDERMANN

●❀⊗⟨⟨ᵖ⟩⟩ ⁺ HOTEL ❸

Bayerstr. 95 ☎089 54 32 40 ▣www.hotel-jedermann.de

Relax at this simple hotel just minutes away from the Hauptbahnhof. Some older rooms have small cube-shaped televisions and retro orange carpeting from the 80s, but the newly renovated rooms enjoy a swanky lacquered wood furniture with flatscreen TVs. Rates include an all-you-can-eat breakfast in the sunny and elegantly decorated breakfast nook.

✈ *S1, S2, S3, S4, S5, S6, S8, U1, U2, U4, or U5: Hauptbahnhof. Exit the Hauptbahnhof and turn right onto Bayerstr., hotel will be on your right.* ⓘ *Cable television includes channels in English, French, and Italian. Wi-Fi included. Computer available for free use. Parking €8.* Ⓢ *Private singles €49-139, with shared bathroom €35-59; doubles €69-189/49-89. Additional bed €15-30.* ⓧ *Reception 24hr.*

University Area

PENSION AM KAISERPLATZ

●❀⊗⟨⟨ᵖ⟩⟩❀ PENSION ❸

Kaiserpl. 12 ☎089 34 91 90

Each elegantly decorated room in this 10-room pension has its own unique period style, from Victorian to Baroque, with every detail down to the patterend bedsheets from Italy selected meticulously by the owner herself. The quiet neighborhood is slightly removed from the touristy hubbub of the city center, but only a stone's throw from the student-infested Schwabing.

✈ *U3 or U6: Münchener Freiheit. Walk past Vanilla Lounge down Herzogstr., then turn left onto Viktoriastr.; the pension is on the right at the end of the street.* ⓘ *Breakfast (served in-room) included. Rooms fill up quickly, so book in advance.* Ⓢ *Singles from €31, with shower €47; doubles €49; triples €72; quads €92; quints €110; 6-bed rooms €138.* ⓧ *Reception 8am-8pm.*

PENSION ISABELLA

●❀⊗⟨⟨ᵖ⟩⟩❀ PENSION ❹

Isabellastr. 35 ☎089 271 35 03 ▣www.pensionisabella.de

Each room offers plenty of space and seating areas, with unique decor and in-room sink. Bathrooms are shared, but they're large and clean.

✈ *U2: Hohenzollernpl. Walk west on Hohenzollernpl. and turn left onto Isabellastr.; it's on the right.* ⓘ *English-speaking owner. Wi-Fi included.* Ⓢ *Singles €38-53; doubles €30-40; triples €26-36; quads €22-32.* ⓧ *Reception 8am-8pm.*

Olympic Area

HAUS INTERNATIONALE

●❀⊗⟨⟨ᵖ⟩⟩ ⁺❀ HOSTEL ❷

Elizabethstr. 87 ☎089 12 00 60 ▣www.haus-internationale.de

Clean rooms, an expansive cafeteria, and serene courtyard make this quiet and out-of-the-way hostel a good bet if you're in the area. A discotheque downstairs, open until 1am, pretty much makes up the local scene since the only thing nearby is a gas station across the street. Haus Internationale has 573 beds, so you're sure to meet other travelers, though most of them are with large groups.

✈ *U2: Hohenzollernpl., then Bus #53 (dir.: Aidenbachstr.) or Tram #12 (dir.: Romanzplatz):*

Barbarastr. ℹ *Breakfast, linens, towels, and Wi-Fi included. Single beds in dorms not available, you must book the entire room.* $ *Singles €33-49; doubles €29-39; triples to 7-bed rooms €30-26. Packages with lunch and dinner (half and full board) also available.* ⏰ *Reception 24hr.; after 11:30pm show room key to security guard for entry.*

CAMPINGPLATZ NORD-WEST
CAMPGROUND [1]

Auf den Schrederwiesen 3 ☎089 150 69 36 🖥www.campingplatz-nord-west.de

A little isolated, but it's basically your standard campground with plenty of shady lots. On-site restaurant provides food if you're too lazy to head out.

🚇 U1or U3: Olympia-Einkaufzentrum, then bus #175: Ludwigsfeld (Campingplatz). $ *€5.20 per person, under 14 €3.70, under 6 €2; €4-8 per tent; €4 per car. Showers €1.50. Laundry €3.50 per wash.* ⏰ *Office open May-Sept 8am-1pm, 3pm-9pm; Oct-Apr 8am-11am, 5pm-8pm.*

Au-Haidhausen

MOTELONE
HOTEL [3]

Orleansstr. 87 ☎089 59 97 64 90 🖥www.motel-one.de

Turquoise is no longer only Tiffany's. Indeed, MotelOne has taken over the brand's signature shade for their interior decor for their mostly business traveler clientele. Despite translucent tables in the lounge or dramatic black-and-white floor-to-ceiling photos of Munich's greatest sights, the building does not even remotely resemble the famous shop. Cozy rooms are decked out in—you guessed it—turquoise blankets and upholstery.

🚇 S1, S2, S3, S4, S5, S6, S7, or S8: Ostbahnhof. Turn right onto Orleansstr. ℹ *Free Wi-Fi in lobby, or €5 per room. No phones in rooms.* $ *Singles from €59; doubles from €74.* ⏰ *Reception 24hr.*

GOLDEN LEAF HOTEL ALTMÜNCHEN
HOTEL [3]

Mariahilfpl. 4 ☎089 45 84 40 🖥 www.golden-leaf-hotel.de

Clean, spacious rooms in a quiet part of town (except for the chimes from the church across the street). Decor is old-fashioned but comfortable, and the beds come with luxurious goosedown comforters.

🚇 S1, S2, S3, S4, S5, S6, S7, or S8: Ostbahnhof, then Bus #152 (dir.: Rotkreutzplatz): Schweigerstr. Hotel is directly across the street from the side of the church. ℹ *Rooms include hair dryer, TV with English channels. Wi-Fi €8 per 1hr., €13 per day. 3-bedroom apartment also available.* $ *Singles €48-180; doubles €58-200. Cheapest rates on weekends.* ⏰ *Reception 6:30am-10pm.*

HOLIDAY INN
HOTEL [5]

Hochstr. 3 ☎089 480 30 🖥www.munich-meeting-centre.de

"Hotel, Motel, Holiday Inn..." This chain's more positive connotations these days have to do with Pitbull, but Holiday Inn is actually one of Munich's nicer hotels. The Holiday Inn is conveniently located close to an S-bahn stop, comes with an attached mall, and is only a few minutes' walk away from the city center. Its amenities remind you that you're not in a hostel anymore; you can choose from five different firmnesses for your pillow, make yourself free coffee and tea, and have a dip in the sunny indoor pool.

🚇 S1, S2, S3, S4, S5, S6, S7, or S8: Rosenheimer Pl. ℹ *Wi-Fi free in lobby, otherwise €22 per 24hr. cycle (starting at noon).* $ *Singles from €100; doubles from €130.* ⏰ *Reception 24hr. Pool open daily 6am-10pm.*

Neuhausen

JUGENDLAGER KAPUZINERHOLZL (THE TENT)
HOSTEL/CAMPGROUND [1]

In den Kirschen 30 ☎089 141 43 00 🖥www.the-tent.com

When Munich prepared to host the 1972 summer Olympics, the government kicked out all the hippies camping out at the English Gardens, who then skipped out to the northeast corner of town to set up a permanent camp. There the Tent was born. Sing songs with other campers around the large bonfire before heading to bed in the giant 160-person tent, or get a floor mat (provided) and set yourself up in the unfurnished tent next door. Bathroom facilities are much cleaner and well-maintained than your summer camp ever was, and, true to hippie culture, the cafeteria serves almost exclusively organic foods. A communal kitchen also makes cooking for yourself a breeze.

🚉 Tram 17: Botanischer Garten, take a right onto Franz-Schrankstr. and a left at the end of the street. ℹ Wi-Fi included. Free street parking available (first-come first-served). $ Floor €7.50 (including blankets and floor pad), bed €10.50. Camping €5.50 per person with additional charge from €5.50 per tent. Credit card required for advanced reservation, but only cash payments accepted. ⏰ Reception 24hr. except between 10:30-11:30am and 5:30-6:30pm. Quiet hours begin at 1am.

A AND O HACKERBRÜCKE 💳🚫📶🍸 HOSTEL ❶

Arnulfstr. 102 ☎089 45 23 59 58 00 🖥www.aohostels.com

With its quiet location away from the central hostel scene at Hauptbahnhof, the A and O has plenty of beds for those who don't mind being a little farther away from the buzz. Rooms are clean and simple, but not always the most well-maintained; don't be surprised if your bedside lamp doesn't work. In some rooms a foyer with an extra door separates the bathroom and the bedroom, providing more privacy and separation for those staggered midnight returns.

🚉 S1, S2, S3, S4, S5, S6, S7, or S8: Hackerbrücke; turn left upon exiting the station and then left again onto Anulfstr. Or Tram 16 or 17: Marsstr. ℹ Internet access €1 per 20 min., €5 for 24hr., €8 per week. All rooms have private bathrooms, TV, and hair dryer. Linens only included in single and double rooms, otherwise €3. $ Singles from €29; doubles from €16; dorms from €12. ISIC discount. ⏰ Reception 24hr.

JUGENDHERBERGE MÜNCHEN NEUHAUSEN ◆Ⓧ⁽ᵗ⁾ HOSTEL ❷

Wendl-Dietrich-Str. 20 ☎089 20 24 44 90 🖳www.muenchen-neuhausen.jugendherberge.de

This old-fashioned hostel doesn't offer the bells and whistles (read: bar) of other area hostels, but with it comes a tranquility essential for the overwhelmed traveler. Rooms are bright and homey, and the multiple buildings on the property cater to different types of travelers, from individuals looking for a bed in a large dorm to school groups with a teachers' suite on the same floor.

✈ *U1 or Tram 12: Rotkreuzplatz; go past the Galeria Kauhof down Wendl-Dietrichstr. to hostel on right.* ⓘ *Requires Hostelling International membership (www.hihostels.com). Breakfast and linens included. Wi-Fi €5 per 24hr.* Ⓢ *Rooms from €24.50; doubles or 27+ guests €28.50.* 🕒 *Reception 6am-11pm; afterwards security guard on duty will only let you in if you have a key.*

CAMPINGPLATZ OBERMENZING ◉Ⓧ CAMPGROUND ❷

Lochhausenerstr. 59 ☎089 811 22 35 🖳www.campingplatz-muenchen.de

Just your average hedge-lined campground, with the lack of accessibility via public transportation to match. Watch out for the surcharges—a shower costs €1, electricity costs €0.5 per kW per hr.; at that rate you might as well check into a more centrally located hostel.

✈ *S2: Untermenzing, then take bus #164: Campingplatz. Bus comes every 20min.; last bus at 1am.* Ⓢ *€5 per person; under 14 €2; €4.50 per tent, with car €8.50.* 🕒 *Open Mar 15-Nov 1. Reception 7:30am-10pm.*

G HOTEL ◆Ⓧ⁽ᵗ⁾❄ HOTEL ❸

Leonrodstr. 11 ☎089 18 95 90 🖳www.ghotel.de

Just half a block away from Rotzkreuplatz, this three-star hotel has value-priced rooms that won't design or comfort. Each room, decked in royal blue upholstery and veneered wooden furniture, comes with plenty of closet space and even a small kitchen. Had too much beer and bratwurst? Work it off in the 24hr. fitness room, equipped with cardio machines and weights. Handicapped rooms on the second and fourth floors.

✈ *U1 or Tram 12: Rotkreuplatz.* ⓘ *Internet for a small fee, although access on the lobby laptop is free.* Ⓢ *Singles €45-55; doubles also available. Up to a 20% discount with stays longer than 4 weeks. Breakfast buffet €12.* 🕒 *Reception 6:30am-11pm.*

Thalkirchen

▨ JUGENDHERBERGE MÜNCHEN PARK (HI) ◆♿⁽ᵗ⁾♥❄ HOSTEL ❸

Miesingstr. 4 ☎089 78 57 67 70 🖳www.muenchen-park.jugendherberge.de

This recently renovated hostel is the Hilton of hostels, with brightly-colored, well-designed rooms, each named after a prominent German scientist. Ample shelving and storage make unpacking a real possibility, and glass-enclosed hangout spaces with smart orange sofas encourage relaxation. No bar, but there is a giftshop full of gimmicky jewelry and all sorts of HI memorabilia. A "family room" on the first floor includes a ball pit and slide for youngsters, as well as a spotless kitchen.

✈ *U3: Thalkirchen, take the Fraunbergstr. exit and then follow the signs.* ⓘ *Breakfast and linens included. Wi-Fi €5 per 24hr. In-room lockers require a €2 deposit.* Ⓢ *Singles €38-41; doubles €69-74; 4- to 6-bed dorms €24-30. Age 26+ additional €4 per night.* 🕒 *Reception 24hr.*

CAMPINGPLATZ MÜNCHEN-THALKIRCHEN ◉ CAMPGROUND ❶

Zentrallandstr. 49 ☎089 723 17 07

The surrounding woods, meandering paths, and nearby river give this large campground a rustic feel, though the on-site lounge, restaurant, and supermarket for convenience's sake take away any excur for that "I'm stuck in the middle of nowhere" feeling.

✈ *U3: Thalkirchen, then Bus #135: Campingplatz.* ⓘ *Laundry wash €5, dry €0.50 per 10min.* Ⓢ *€4.70 per person, under 14 €1.50; €3-8 per tent; €4.50 per car. Showers €1 per 6 min.* 🕒 *Open mid-Mar-late Oct. Reception 7am-11pm.*

SIGHTS

Beyond the usual beer and Oktoberfest sights, Munich has a wealth of castles, museums, and other historical sights well worth a visit. The best day to visit museums is Sunday, when most of them are either free or reduced priced. Those reduced prices also usually mean that you'll have to pay for the audio guide, but it's still a good deal over paying the regular price.

City Center

MARIENPLATZ ♿ SQUARE

Marienpl. 1

Towering spires surround this social nexus, major S- and U-Bahn junction, and pedestrian zone of Munich. The **Mariensäule,** an ornate 17th-century monument of the Virgin Mary, sits at the center of this large square as a tribute to the city's near-miraculous survival of both the Swedish invasion and the plaugue. To the north sits the equally ornate **Neues Rathaus,** the new city hall, built in the early 20th century in a neo-gothic style. Camera-touting tourists can always be found staring at its central tower during the thrice-daily **Glockenspiel** mechanical chimes display, considered to be one of the most overrated attractions in all of Europe *(daily 11am and 12pm, in summers also at 5pm).* To the right of the Neues Rathaus is the **Altes Rathaus,** the old city hall, which now houses a toy and teddy bear museum, **Spielzeugmuseum,** *(open daily 10am-5:30pm, €3, under 15 €1, family €6).* A busy open space, Marienplatz is also often used for political demonstrations.

🚇 S1, S2, S3, S4, S5, S6, S7, S8, U3 or U6: Marienplatz. $ Free. ⏰ Square open daily.

ALTER PETER ♿ CHURCH

Rindermarkt 1 ☎089 260 48 28

An enormous Gothic-inspired church sitting right in the city center, Alter Peter was severely damaged during WWII. It was meticulously rebuilt with true German precision, down to original cannonballs lodged in the church wall (walk around the outside of the church to the back, take the steps leading up to Cafe Rischart, and look around the top right corner of the window frame). Nowadays a 306-step climb to the top of the 92m tower offers the best birds-eye view of Munich: on clear days, you can see over 70 miles.

🚇 S1, S2, S3, S4, S5, S6, S7, S8, U3 or U6: Marienplatz. $ Church entry free. Climb to the top €1.50, students and children €1. ⏰ Tower open M-F 9am-6:30pm, Sa-Su 10am-6:30pm.

RESIDENZ AND HOFGARTEN ♿ MUSEUM

Residenzstr. 1 089 26 06 71 💻www.residenz-muenchen.de

Once the quarters of the Wittelsbach dynasty, the Residenz is now a museum aptly called the Residenzmuseum displaying all its lavish treasures. Get ready for blinding gold leaf gilded rooms decked out in the Baroque, Rococo, and Neoclassical styles. Highlights include the Rococo **Ahnenglerie,** hung with over 100 family portraits tracing the royal lineage, the spectacular **Renaissance Antiquarium,** the oldest room in the palace, replete with stunning frescoes, and large and in charge Chinese and Japanese porcelain. On the same property is the **Treasury,** which houses royal crowns and jewels, and the **Cuvilliés Theatre,** the stunning royal theater that saw the premiere of several Mozart operas. The treasury and theater require a separate ticket for entry. Directly behind the museum is the **Hofgarten**, popular for post-dinner strolls and ballroom dancing under the central pavilion on weekend evenings.

🚇 U3, U4, U5, or U6: Odeonsplatz. ℹ Free audio tours available in German, English, French, Italian, and Spanish. Many of the rooms, including those in the Königsbau (King's Tract), will be under renovation for another few years. $ Residenz and Treasury each €6, seniors €5, free for students and children; Residenz and treasury ticket €9/€8/free; Theater €3/€2/free. Combination of all three €11/€9/free. ⏰ Residenz and treasury open daily Apr-mid-Oct 9am-6pm, mid-Oct to

Mar 10am-5pm. Theater hours vary based on season schedule; check the website for details. Last entry 1hr. before close.

ODEONSPLATZ ⊗ SQUARE

This large central square share is flanked by three main attractions: **Theatinerkirche**, the **Feldherrnhalle**, and the **Residenz.** Commonly mispronounced by some ignoramuses as ✪ "Tina Turner Church," the Theatinerkirche was built by the Elector Ferdinand Maria on a bargain with God. Heirless and aging, Ferdinand prayed for a son, upon which he promised to build the most magnificent church known to man. Lo and behold, a son was born, and in 1690 the magnificent mustard-yellow Theatinerkirche was erected. Sitting between the church and the adjacent Residenz is the Feldherrnhalle monument, built in 1844 to honor the Bavarian army. Two lions flank the steps leading to the platform, one looking at the church with its mouth closed (never speaking against the church) and one looking to the Residenz with its mouth open (always speaking against the government), though Germany's most infamous dictator probably didn't approve of the latter. The Feldherrnhalle was also the site of open gunfire during Hitler's infamous Beer Hall Putsch in 1923, and if you walk around the side of the Feldherrnhalle toward the Residenz, you can see the four corners of an imprint where a Nazi plaque honoring their "fallen heroes" once hung.

🚇 U3, U4, U5 or U6: Odeonsplatz. $ Free.

ASAMKIRCHE ⊗ CHURCH

Sendlingerstr. 32 ☎089 23 68 79 89

Escape the chaos of materialism surrounding Asamkirche and enter the divine through its heavy doors. Built as a private church but forced by the public to make it, well, public, the 11-pew Asamkirche has long been regarded as perhaps the most extravagant example of the Baroque style. The church's patron saint, John of Nepomuk, was thrown in the Moldau River by order of the emperor for refusing to violate the confidentiality of confession; ceiling frescoes tell the entire story with amazing detail. Immediately to either side of the church stand the residences of the two Asam brothers, Cosmas Damian and Egid Quirin, who financed its construction. Their houses are still connected to the church balcony.

🚇 S1, S2, S3, S4, S5, S6, S7, S8, U3 or U6: Marienplatz, then 4 blocks down Sendlingerstr. $ Free. ⏰ Open daily 9am-5:30pm except during services.

FRAUENKIRCHE ♿ CHURCH

Frauenplatz 1 ☎089 290 08 20

A vestige of the city's Catholic past, the Frauenkirchen was built in the late 1400s in a mere 20 years, a feat unheard of during that time. According to the legend, the architect made a pact with the devil: if he built visible windows to the church, the devil would see to its rapid completion. The architect, however, simply cleverly positioned the windows behind columns such that they remained hidden from the devil's vantage point at the entrance. The devil, upon realizing the sham, stomped his foot at the entrance, leaving an imprint—a men's size 9 footprint—that you can still see today. An elevator ride to the top of the tower gives great views of the city.

🚇 S1, S2, S3, S4, S5, S6, S7, S8, U3 or U6: Marienplatz. $ Tower €3, students and children over 6 €1.50. ⏰ Church open daily 7am-7pm, tower open M-Sa 10am-5pm.

MÜNCHENER STADTMUSEUM ♿ MUSEUM

St.-Jakobs-Platz ☎089 23 32 23 70 💻www.stadtmuseum-online.de

For an in-depth look at Munich's history, look no further than this hidden museum, where you'll find paintings, furniture, and even plastic food honoring Munich's culture and traditions. While Munich-exclusive exhibits take up much of the museum, the top floor also houses an impressive array of native and foreign musical instruments (gamelan, anyone?) as well as a small concert hall. Motion-sensored dancing skeletons one floor below will both inspire and terrify. The adjacent **Film Museum** also shows international films in their original languages, offering a host of both classic and recent English-language films *(tickets from €4).*

⇞ S1, S2, S3, S4, S5, S6, S7, S8, U3 or U6: Marienplatz, turn right onto Rindermarkt. ℹ Explanations for most exhibits in German only, so bring your imagination. $ €4, students €2. Su free. ⏰ Open Tu-Su 10am-6pm.

JEWISH MUSEUM AND OHEL JAKOB SYNAGOGUE 👍♿ CHURCH

St.-Jakobs-Platz ☎089 22 39 60 96 🖥www.juedisches-museum-muenchen.de

The Munich Jewish Museum is a well-designed museum with informative exhibits on Jewish life in Munich. The permanent exhibit catalogs Jewish history in the city, with a separate section dedicated to each of the five senses; particularly impressive is the a large carpet map of Munich, which serves as a geographic basis for photos lining the adjacent walls. The architectural marvel **Ohel Jakob (Jacob's Tent) Synagogue** was inaugurated in 2006 after the original synagogue nearby was destroyed in 1938. Jews are always welcome, though non-Jews can only enter on guided tours or with a Jewish friend.

⇞ S1, S2, S3, S4, S5, S6, S7, S8, U3 or U6: Marienplatz, turn right onto Rindermarkt. ℹ All exhibits in the museum in both German and English. $ €6, children and students €3, family €9. Guided tours of the synagogue €5. ⏰ Museum open Tu-Su 10am-6pm.

THERESIENWIESE ⊛⊗ OKTOBERFEST VENUE

When King Ludwig I of Bavaria got hitched in 1810, he decided to throw his bride a party. There would be a prestigious horse race, an audience of international royalty, and this being Bavaria, all sorts of alcoholic merriment. The horse race was to take place a little outside the city, on a large field known as Theresienwiese, aptly named for his bride Theresa. Over the years, the horse race lost its glamor, but the drinking never stopped, and every October colonies of tourists make the unholy pilgrimage in true Bavarian form. While there's not much but a big empty field during the other months, you'll be sure to find all of Munich doing the Oktoberfest jig: drink, sleep, repeat. To one side of the field stands a large statue of **Bavaria**, the region's secular patron saint. You can climb up to the top of this cast-iron statue, but claustrophobes beware the narrow and practically windowless space. The view is virtually nonexistent and on hot days it gets ridiculously muggy.

⇞ U4 or U5: Theresienwiese. ℹ During Oktoberfest, be sure to arrive before 4:30pm to get a table. $ Bavaria admission €3, students €2. ⏰ Bavaria open March-Oktoberfest 9am-6pm, during Oktoberfest until 8pm. Last entry 30min. before close.

DEUTSCHES MUSEUM 👍♿ MUSEUM

Museumsinsel 1 ☎ 089 217 91 🖥www.deutsches-museum.de

One of the world's most comprehensive museums of science and technology, the Deutsches Museum has an overwhelming array of exhibits on everything from steam engines to genetic engineering. Relics marked throughout the museum as "Masterpieces" include the workbench on which Otto Hahn first split an atom, the world's first electron microscope, and the first automobile ever produced. High-tech touchscreen displays give most explanations in both German and English. The subterranean labyrinth of mining tunnels are especially intriguing, even if they don't impart too much academic knowledge. The museum's 50+ departments cover over 17km, so don't expect to see it all in a day—be strategic and bring some good walking shoes.

⇞ Tram #18: Deutsches Museum, or S1-8: Isartor and walk across the river. ℹ Free guided tours in German; English-language guide book (€4) available in vending machines throughout the museum. $ Tickets €8.50, students €3, children under 6 free. Planetarium €2 more. ⏰ Open daily 9am-5pm, last entry an hour before.

museum combo

The Deutsches Museum also operates two other museums in Munich: the Verkehrszentrum *(Theresienhöhe 14a, take U4/5 to Schwanthalerhöhe)*, a collection of vehicles and other exhibits exploring the history of mobility and transport, and the Flugwerft Schleissheim *(Effnerstr. 18, take S1 to Oberschleissheim)*, an enormous display of airplanes, engines, and other things having to do with space travel. Unless you're really into these things, it's probably not worth your time, but they're just examples of how amazingly extensive the Deutsches Museum network is.

Both museums are open daily 9am-5pm and are €6, students €3. A combo ticket for all three museums is available for €17.

University Area

The Kunstareal *(🖥www.pinakothek.de)* is a museum district near the edge of Maxvorstadt that comprises the overwhelming majority of Munich's art museums, making it home to a veritable buffet of art. Like all buffets, you can get too much of a good thing and be left feeling nauseated, so try to take in a few each day to truly appreciate the offerings. Most of these museums are free *(all state-run Pinakotheks and the Museum Brandhorst €1)* or reduced price on Sundays (though you will also have to pay for the audio tour, which is usually free every other day), while on other days combination tickets can gain you entry for a discount. A ticket (€12) will get you into the three Pinakotheks, the Museum Brandhorst, and the Sammlung Schack for a day, while €29 will get you into them for 5 days, allowing you to time digest between courses.

KÖNIGSPLATZ ♿❄ SQUARE

Literally "The King's Square," Konigsplatz was comissioned by King Ludwig I to be Munich's cultural center. What resulted is a field with three enormous Greek buildings: the **Propyläen,** an ornate gateway, the **Glyptothek,** houses the king's collection of Greek and Roman statues, and the **Antikensammlung,** housing royal antiques. While World War II transformed this "German Acropolis" into a center for Nazi rallies and offices, the entire area was restored back to its original splendor in 1988, and you can now visit both the Glyptothek *(☎089 28 61 00)* and the Staatliche Antikensammlung *(☎089 59 98 88 30 🖥www.antike-am-koenigsplatz.mwn.de)* for their incredible works of ancient art.

🚏 U2 or Bus #100: Königsplatz. $ Each museum (Glyptothek and Antikensammlung) €3.50, students €2.50. 🕐 Museums open Tu-W and F-Su 10am-5pm, Th 10am-8pm.

ENGLISCHER GARTEN ♿ GARDEN

Stretching majestically along the city's eastern border, the Englischer Garten (English Garden) is one of the largest metropolitan public parks in the world, dwarfing both New York's Central Park and London's Hyde Park. The possible activities here are numerous, from nude sunbathing (areas are designated FKK, Frei Körper Kultur, or Free Body Culture, on signs and maps) and bustling beer gardens to pick-up soccer games and shaded bike paths. On sunny days, all of Munich turns out to fly kites, ride horses, and walk their beloved dogs. The main park ends with the **Kleinhesseloher See,** a large aritifical lake, but the park extends much further and becomes ever more wild, although the fiercest thing you might see is a roaming flock of sheep. Several beer gardens on the grounds as well as a Japanese tea house offer respite, while the Chinese pagoda and Greek temple make the park an international cultural festival. Need some American spirit? Don't miss the surfers illegally riding the white-water waves of the Eisbach, the artificial river that flows through the park (near the Haus der Kunst, on the southwest corner of the park).

U3: Universität, Giselastr., or Münchner Freiheit, and head east.

NEUE PINAKOTHEK MUSEUM

Barerstr. 29 ☎089 23 80 51 95 www.neue-pinakothek.de

Built by Ludwig I to house his private collection, the Neue Pinakothek is devoted entirely to 19th-century art. Special attention is given to German art in "overlooked" movements, though the most popular pieces in the collection today are the French Impressionist paintings. Monet water lilies and Van Gogh sunflowers brighten the museum. Follow the room numbers to get a sense of the progression of art during this period.

U2 or Bus #100: Königsplatz. $ €7, students €5. Audio guide €4.50 Su. Open M 10am-6pm, W 10am-8pm, and Th-Su 10am-6pm.

ALTE PINAKOTHEK MUSEUM

Barerstr. 27 ☎089 23 80 52 16 www.alte-pinakothek.de

Find Munich's finest 14th- to 18th-century art is at this world-renowned museum where Northern European artists are especially well-represented, including Dürer, Cranach, Brueghel, Rembrandt, and Rubens. Look for Rubens' gigantic *The Last Judgment*—the museum's galleries were sized to accommodate this enormous canvas. French, Italian, Spanish, Dutch, and Flemmish masterpieces are also on display through the museum's two floors. Wind down after all that art with a game of pick-up soccer on the expansive lawn.

U2 or Bus #100: Königsplatz. i The special exhibit usually cost extra. $ €7, students €5. Audio guide Su €4.50. Open Tu-W and F-Su 10am-6pm, Th 10am-8pm.

PINAKOTHEK DER MODERNE MUSEUM

Barerstr. 40 ☎089 23 80 53 06 www.pinakothek-der-moderne.de

In a sleek metal and concrete museum designed by Munich's own Stephan Braunfels, this Pinakothek displays a rich collection of 20th-century art. Big names' paintings share the art space, with engaging contemporary sculpture and video installations. The design section, covering the basement floors, has something for everyone, tracing the development of furniture and appliance design through history with innovative exhibits displaying everyday objects on a giant conveyor belt. The museum's two other departments feature graphic art and architecture.

U2 or Bus #100: Königsplatz. $ €10 adults, students €7; audio guide on Sundays €4.50. Open Tu-W and F-Su 10am-6pm, Th 10am-8pm.

MUSEUM BRANDHORST MUSEUM

Theresienstr. 35a ☎089 238 05 22 86 www.museum-brandhorst.de

This colorful building houses the collection of 20th and 21st century art of Udo and Anette Brandhorst, heirs of the German powerhouse company Henkel. An airy wooden staircase (complete with padded handlebars) joins the three stories of this museum. Over 100 works by Andy Warhol are exhibited in the basement, including a portrait of Marilyn Monroe. Much of the second floor is dedicated to American artist Cy Twombly, with one room full of giant roses inspired by snippets of poetry. Also look for the haunting sculptures by Damien Hirst about the formidable forces of modern medicine, such as the *in this terrible moment we are victims clinging helplessly to an environment that refuses to acknowledge the soul*, an enormous cabinet displaying pills in all manners of shapes and sizes. After your visit, grab some gelato from Balla Beni across the street.

U2 or Bus #100: Königsplatz. $ €10, students €7. Audio guide Su €4.50. Open Tu-W and F-Su 10am-6pm, Th 10am-8pm.

HAUS DER KUNST 🚌♿❄ MUSEUM

Prinzregentenstr. 1 ☎089 21 12 71 13 💻www.hausderkunst.de

Originally built by the Nazis as a "Hall of German Art" and a center of visual propaganda, this enormous building somehow survived the Allied bombing unscathed. Bucking the hyper-nationalism of its creators, the enormous halls now play host to many world-class, contemporary temporary exhibitions that pass through Munich. Three exhibitions generally populate the museum at any given time.

⇆ Bus #100: Königinstr., or U4-5: Lehel and then tram #17 for 1 stop (dir.: Effnerpl.). $ Each exhibition €8, students €6, with combination tickets available; ages 12-18 €2, under 12 free. ⏰ Open M-W 10am-8pm, Th 10am-10pm, and F-Su 10am-8pm.

ALLIANZ ARENA 🚌♿❄ SPORTS COMPLEX

Werner-Heisenberg-Allee 25 ☎089 200 50 💻www.allianz-arena.de

Germany's most famous soccer complex looks like an organized clump of iridescent bubbles. Opened in 1972, the Allianz Arena was the first stadium to have a complete color-changeable exterior, with a red glow on FC Bayern game nights and a blue glow on TSV 1860 game nights. The stadium seats nearly 70,000 screaming fans, while the third floor houses a retail complex where you can buy fan gear for either team in their respective megastores or take a break in the Lego Spielwelt (Lego Gameworld).

⇆ U6: Fröttmaning. $ Tour €10, students €9, ages 4-12 €6.50. ⏰ English-language tours offered daily (except on match days) at 1pm. Stadium open 10am-6pm except on match days.

fütball faithful

I am An American Who Doesn't Watch Soccer. Yes, one of those. Back home, there are millions of us people who don't much care for eleven sweaty men kicking a ball around to each other, with the ninety minute drone of sporting monotony punctuated (if you're lucky!) once or twice by the excitement of a goal. My brother and I watched the past two World Cup tournaments periodically; we considered a game a success if we managed to pay attention long enough to see a goal scored.

But on Sunday night, I decided to go undercover as A German Who Would Follow Her Team to the Edge of the Earth. The city of Berlin was broadcasting the first game against Australia live outside Olympic Stadium, to a crowd of 200,000 bloodthirsty (and beerthirsty) Deutschelanders.

Blending in was surprisingly easy. Even if I sometimes feared that the 199,999 people standing around me would suddenly collectively figure me out, I managed to conceal my nationality for those three crazy hours. I sang along to cheers whose words I didn't understand, I jumped up and down with people I'd never met, and I drank good beer in the spirit of international cooperation.

The night couldn't have gone better. Four times Germany scored on Australia, and every time the crowd went absolutely wild. I'd actually never seen anything like it. And that was all it took. I'm hooked. I love soccer. Actually, no—I love *fütball.* I'm swapping in my Birkenstocks for cleats, and I'm never leaving my hostel without my shin guards. And I'm carrying around a red card for the next German that says Americans don't care about soccer.

-Sophia Angelis

Olympic Area

OLYMPIAPARK
👍 SPORTS COMPLEX

☎089 30 67 27 07 💻www.olympiapark.de

Built for the 1972 Olympic Games, the lush Olympiapark offsets the curved steel and transparent spires of the impressive **Olympia-Zentrum** and the 290m tall **Olympiaturm,** Munich's tallest building. A 1-3hr. self-guided audiowalk gives highlights of the entire park. Otherwise, three English-language tours are available. The 90min. **Adventure Tour** gives an introduction to the history and construction of the entire park with a walk through the Swimming Hall, site of Mark Spitz's then-record 7 gold medal win, the Olympic Hall, and the Olympic Stadium. The 1hr. **Stadium Tour** details the large stadium. The **Roof Climb,** a daring two-hour exploration of the stadium with a rope and hook, is for adrenaline junkies only. Tourists can also marvel at the view from the top of the tower and stroll around the **Rock (and Roll) Museum** at the top.

🚇 U3: Olympiazentrum. ℹ Other tours available in English upon reservation; see website for details. $ Adventure Tour €8, students 5.50. Stadium Tour €6/4. Roof climb €39/29. Tower and Rock Museum €4.50, under 16 €2.80. Discounts with receipt from admission to Sea Life, BMW Welt/Museum. ⏰ All tours offered daily Apr-Nov. Adventure Tour: 2pm, Stadium Tour 11am, Roof Climb 2:30pm (weather permitting). Tower and Rock'n'Roll Museum open daily 9am-midnight. Audiowalk hours vary on season, generally 9am-4:30pm (winter) to 8:30am-8pm (mid-summer); check the website for details.

SEA LIFE
👍♿ AQUARIUM

Willi-Daume-Pl. 1 ☎018 05 66 69 01 01 💻www.sealifeeurope.com

Seahorses and stingrays and sharks, oh my! This extensive aquarium showcases organisms from many different environments, including Nemo's cousins and fat, ugly groupers. Discovery stations along the way allow you to feel the textures of different aquatic creatures for yourself, and the grand finale—a 10m shark tunnel—will leave you humming Jaws for the rest of the day.

🚇 U3: Olympiazentrum, head toward the tower and then follow the signs. $ €15.50, students €14.50, age 3-14 €9.95; €5 discount if you book online. ⏰ Open Apr-Sept daily 10am-7pm; Oct. M-F 10am-6pm, Sa-Su 10am-7pm; Nov-Mar M-F 10am-5pm, Sa-Su 10am-7pm. Last entry 1hr. before closing.

BMW WELT AND MUSEUM
👍♿ MUSEUM

Petuelring 130. ☎018 02 11 88 22 💻www.bmw-welt.com

A marvel of architectural daring, the enormous steel and glass spiral of the BMW museum houses state-of-the-art interactive exhibits detailing the history, development, and design of Bavaria's second-favorite export. Illuminated frosted glass walls and touch-sensitive projections lead visitors past engines, chassis, and concept vehicles with exhibits in both English and German. The award-winning kinetic sculpture features 714 suspended metal balls in a variety of shapes, many of them of historic and current BMW vehicles. Visitors can also tour the adjacent **production factory** with a tunnel that runs through the entire production line, or enjoy the video games and customizable test cars in the **BMW Welt** building.

🚇 U3: Olympiazentrum. BMW Welt will be the large steel structure on your left; a ramp accessible from inside the building will lead you across the street to the museum. ℹ Factory and museum tours available by appointment only. $ Museum €12, students €6. BMW Welt free. Special discounts with Olympiapark ticket or the City Tour Card. ⏰ Museum open Tu-Su 10am-6pm; BMW Welt open daily 9am-6pm.

Au-Haidhausen

VILLA STUCK
⊛♿ MUSEUM

Prinzregentenstr. 60 ☎089 45 55 51 25 💻www.villastuck.de

This elegant villa, designed by Munich artist Franz von Stuck, provides a sophisticated backdrop for the art of the early 20th-century German Jugendstil, a movement that celebrated nature and the smooth lines of the body. Gold mosaic arches, marble fireplaces, and recessed black ceilings offset the colorful landscapes and still lifes. For contrast, rotating exhibits in the basement highlight contemporary artists.

🚏 Bus #100 or Tram #18: Friedensengel. 💲 €6, students €3. ⏰ Open Tu-Su 11am-6pm.

Neuhausen

👍 SCHLOß NYMPHENBURG ♿❄ CASTLE

Schloβ Nymphenburg ☎089 17 90 80 🖥www.schloss-nymphenburg.de

The breathtaking Schloβ Nymphenburg, a favorite summer residence for Bavarian royalty modeled after Versailles, was built in 1662. Now open to the public, the palace opens with the lavish two-story **Stone Hall,** bursting with extravagant Rococo decor and Neoclassical themes. Make your way through electors' apartments, including the bedroom in which King Ludwig II was born, and feast your eyes on the portraits in the Gallery of Beauties, featuring 36 women King Ludwig I considered to be the most beautiful in all of Bavaria. Situated in the expansive landscaped gardens are four other equally ornate pavilions: the **Amalienburg, Badenburg,** the grottoed **Magdalenenkrause,** and the oriental **Pagodenburg.** Summertime brings plenty of classical concerts to the park grounds; check kiosks for details. German-speaking science enthusiasts will not want to miss the **Museum Mensch und Natur** *(Museum of Man and Nature, to the right of the palace, 🖥www.musmn.de),* a two-story tribute to natural history with superb interactive exhibits.

*🚏 Tram 17: Schloβ Nymphenburg. **i** The gardens are free, so you'll often see morning joggers or bikers traversing the grounds. 💲 Palace €5, students €4; porcelain museums €4/3; pavilions each €2/1; combination ticket for palace and porcelain museums €10/8, €4/3 for all pavilions. Audio tours (English available) €3.50. Museum Mensch und Natur €3/2, Sundays €1. Everything free for under 18. ⏰ Entire complex open daily Apr-Oct 15 9am-6pm, Oct 16-Mar 10am-4pm. Badenburg, Pagodenburg, and Magdalenkrause closed in winter. Museum Mensch und Natur open Tu-W 9am-5pm, Th 9am-8pm, Fr 9am-5pm, Sa-Su 10am-6pm.*

piggy backing

Schloβ Nymphenburg and the Botanic Garden are connected through their back gates, so you can get the best of both in just one trip.

BOTANISCHER GARTEN ♿ GARDEN

Menzingerstr. 65 ☎089 17 86 13 16 🖥www.botmuc.de

Next door to Schloβ Nymphenburg, the immense Botanic Garden bursts fauna with palms and orchids, an alpine lake, and other exotic landscapes. The English language audio tour of the 11 different greenhouses will inspire you with a wealth of information about everything from the meat tenderizing properties of the papaya to the differences between male and female cycads.

🚏 Tram 17: Botanischer Garten. 💲 €4, students €2, under 18 free; alpine garden €2. Audio tour €3/2.50. ⏰ Open daily May-Aug 9am-7pm; Apr and Sept 9am-6pm, Feb-Mar and Oct. 9am-5pm, Nov-Jan 9am-4:30pm. Greenhouses close 30min. before close.

HIRSCHGARTEN ♿🍸❄ PARK, BEER GARDEN

Hirschgarten 1 🖥www.hirschgarten.com

This seemingly modest park filled with playful children and zen sunbathers is also home to Europe's largest Biergarten, seating a whopping 8000 jolly clinkers. Grab a *Maβ*, and take a seat in the boisterously delightful atmosphere, and have your heart melted by all the cute kids running around the premises. During the summer, the carousel is a constant source of joy. To think, if only you had grown up in a beer garden.

Tram 17: Romanplatz, then walk south to the end of Guntherstr. i Credit cards accepted in restaurant. $ Entrees €7-14. Maβ €7.20. ⏰ Kitchen open 11am-10pm.

HERZ-JESU-KIRCHE ♿❄ CHURCH

Romanstr. 6 ☎089 13 06 75 26 🖳www.herzjesu-neuhausen.de

A stunning glass cube encases this unforgettable church, opened in 2000 to replace the previous church that had burned down. Sitting in the middle of a residential neighborhood, the Herz-Jesu-Kirche adds a refreshing view to the otherwise bland apartment buildings that surround it. Look closely at the front face of the church and you'll notice that the blue hue comes from a pattern of nails; on festival days, the entire 14-meter front opens in a U-shape, exposing the wooden interior. Inside, wooden slats let shining rays of light bedazzle the congregation, and more tricks of the light reveal the pattern of a cross on the wall behind the altar. The sleek and simple organ plays host to many free concerts during the summer.

Tram 12: Renatastr. Head south on Renatastr. for one block and turn right onto Lachnerstr. to church on left. $ Free entry; tours in German €5; English guide books €3.50. ⏰ Open daily 8am-noon and 2-7pm. Tours during the summer on Sundays at 2pm.

Thalkirchen

In the summertime, Thalkirchen plays host to flurries of visitors floating (in every sense of the word) down the Isar River. The *Flosslände*, a natural wave along the river (from U3 Thalkirchen, take Bus #135 toward Campingplatz), sees its share of surfers and kayakers. In warm weather, look for kayak rentals along the river. Serenity-seeking visitors instead take a *Flossfahrt*, a day-long trip down calmer waters on an enormous rafts, complete with food, drink and music for a beer garden on the water. Most of these actually begin south of Munich and float to the *Flosslände* as the final stop, see 🖳www.isarflossfahrten.biz for more information.

TIERPARK HELLABURN ⊛ ZOO

Tierparkstr. 30 ☎089 625 08 34 🖳www.tierpark-hellabrunn.de

Munich's zoo was created in 1911 as the world's first "Geo-zoo," meaning that animals are separated by their original geographic locations and kept in environments as close possible to their original habitats. Dodge the screaming four-year-olds and wander around the four continents represented. Flock with flamingos, elephants, and elks, and make sure to stop in Villa Dracula for the bat house. Vending machines distributing portions of food *(€0.50)* let you get up close and personal with your favorite creatures.

U3: Thalkirchen, or Bus #52 from Marienpl.: Tierpark. i All explanations in German only. For a more interactive experience, check the feeding schedule at the front gate. $ €9, under 14 €4.50, students €6. ⏰ Open daily Apr-Sept 8am-6pm, Oct-Mar 9am-5pm. Animal houses close 30min. before zoo.

Outside Munich

NEUSCHWANSTEIN CASTLE ♿ CASTLE

Neuschwansteinstr. 20, Schwangau ☎083 62 93 08 30 🖳www.neuschwanstein.de

The "Cinderella castle" upon which Disney based their theme park creations, Neuschwanstein was built on a dream that ended in anything but happily ever after. The prodigal King Ludwig II's fetishes contributed to the construction of his ultimately unfinished masterpiece. Neuschwanstein, literally "new swan stone," and the fabled **Schwansee** (Swan Lake) on the castle property hints at the first fetish. Swans are incorporated into even the door handles. Interestingly, actual swans have never been seen on the property. Ludwig also got hooked on Wagner's extravagant Romantic-era operas after hearing Lohengrin, an opera about (surprise) a swan, and appointed Wagner the official royal opera-writer, a pretty obscure profession. The painted murals on the walls of each room in Neuschwanstein tell the opera stories. Finally, while hardly alone in his money fetish, Ludwig took it to the next level, continuing to build his elaborate castles even after he had sunk the royal treasury into debt. Ludwig II had fantastic visions of wealth, having grown up on the stories of the flashy medieval kings. In this theme, his **Throne Room** looks like a Byzantine chapel (read: lots and lots of gold) with a 2000-ton crown-shaped chandelier.

Unfortunately for Ludwig, in 1873 the government staged a coup and declared the king mentally insane, forcing him to abdicate the throne. A few days later, both Ludwig and his psychiatrist were found face-down in a lake in Munich. The circumstances behind their deaths remain a mystery to this day. Construction of Neuschwanstein, only one-third complete, was immediately halted after his death, which conveniently left the third floor unfurnished for the cafe, gift shop, and theater for a free 20-minute historical film alternating in English and German. In a classic act of German efficiency, six weeks after the coup the cash-strapped government opened up the castle as a museum, and Ludwig's paragon of perfection has remained a point of inspiration to visitors and Disney-lovers ever since.

No visit to this castle is complete without a walk across **Marienbrücke,** a slightly rickety wooden-bottomed bridge built by Maximillian, Ludwig's father, for his wife Mary. The bridge sits over a slim and elegant waterfall and gives a stunning side view of Neuschwanstein. Also on-site at Neuschwanstein is the yellow **Hohenschwangau,** King Ludwig II's favorite summer retreat in his youth. Here you can see Ludwig's bedroom, with inlaid crystals on the ceiling to represent stars in the night sky, and the piano and bed that Richard Wagner used during his visits.

🚏 DB: Füssen (about 2 hrs.); once there, walk right across the street to take either the 73 or 78 bus (10 min., 2 per hr., €1.90 per way or free with the Bayern ticket): Königsschlößer (Royal Castles). To get to the castle, you can either walk up the hill (many routes available; 20-50min.), take a bus (up €1.80, down €1, and round-trip €2.60; 10 min.; drop-off behind Neuschwanstein between the castle and Marienbrücke), or take a horse-drawn carriage (up €6, down €3; 15min.). ℹ Purchase tickets for tours at the main ticket office located a 3-minute walk uphill. Tours available in 14 different languages, last 35min., and are required for entry into the castle. The summer months bring loads of fairy-tale-seeking tourists, so get there early to reserve your spot. Make sure to save time for some hiking to the Marienbrücke (15min. from Neuschwanstein) and other mountaintop-top destinations. Special wheelchair-accessible tours available with advance registration on Wednesdays. $ Guided tours of castle €9, students €8, under 18 free with an adult. Tickets can also be reserved in advance via phone for an extra €1.80 per ticket. The two castles share a ticket office, though the Hohenschwangau office is open 30min. after Neuschwanstein's closes; combination tickets for the two castles are available (€17/15). ⏰ Castle open Apr-Sept 9am-4pm, Oct-Mar 10am-4pm; ticket office open an hour before opening and closing.

DACHAU CONCENTRATION CAMP MEMORIAL SITE 👍♿ MEMORIAL SITE

Alte Römerstr. 75, Dachau ☎081 31 66 99 70 🖥www.kz-gedenkstaette-dachau.de

The first thing prisoners saw as they entered Dachau was the inscription *Arbeit Macht Frei*, "work will set you free" on the iron gate to the camp. Dachau was the Third Reich's first concentration camp, opened in 1933 to house political prisoners on the former grounds of a WWI munitions facotry. After Hitler visited the work camp in 1937, it became a model for over 30 other camps through Nazi-occupied Europe and a training ground for the SS officers who would work at them. Those who volunteered for medical experiments in hopes of release were frozen to death in hypothermia experiments or infected with malaria, all in the name of "science." The barracks, designed for 5,000 prisoners, once held 30,000 men at a time - two have been reconstructed for visitors, and gravel-filled outlines of the other barracks stand as haunting reminders. The camp's crematorium and gas chambers have also been restored. On the site are also Jewish, Catholic, Lutheran, and Russian Orthodox prayer spaces, each designed to offer guidance and solace to visitors. The museum at the Dachau Memorial Site, in the former maintenance building, examines pre-1930s anti-Semitism, the rise of Nazism, the establishment of the concentration camp system, and the lives of prisoners through photographs, documents, videos, interactive exhibits, and artifacts. An additional display in the bunker chronicles the lives and experiences of the camp's most prominent prisoners, including Georg Elser, the SS officer who attempted to assassinate Hitler in 1939.

*🚆 S2 (dir.: Petershausen): Dachau (4 stripes on the Streifenkarte, or get a €7 Munich XXL ticket to cover all transportation for the entire day), and then bus 726 (dir.: Saubachsiedlung): KZ-Gedenkstätte (1 stripe, €1.20, or free with Munich XXL ticket). **i** Due to graphic content, museum not recommended for children under 12. All displays have English translations. There is a small cafeteria at the welcome center, but the grounds are extensive, so bring a snack [$] Audio guides in English, French, German, Italian, and Hebrew €3.50, students €2.50. Tours €3 per person. Museum and memorial grounds free. ⏰ Open Tu-Su 9am-5pm. Tours (2.5hr.) in English daily at 11am and 1pm, in German at noon. 22min. documentary shown in German at 11am and 3pm, English at 11:30am, 2pm, and 3:30pm.*

FOOD

Ubiquitous *Biergärten* (beer gardens) serve savory snacks and booze throughout Munich. For an authentic Bavarian lunch, spread some *brezeln* (pretzels) with *leberwurst* (liverwurst) or cheese. *Weißwürste*(white veal sausages) are another favorite, served with sweet mustard and a soft pretzel on the side; real Müncheners only eat them before 11am. Slice the skin open and devour their tender meat. *Leberkäse*, a local lunch, is a pinkish mix of ground beef and bacon. *Leberknödel* are liver dumplings served in soup or with *kraut* (cabbage). *Kartoffelknödel* (potato dumplings) and *semmelknödel* (bread and egg dumplings) should be eaten with a hearty chunk of meat. Vegetarians can enjoy *käsespätzle* (egg noodles baked with cheese) or a plate of *spargel* (asparagus) with a *germknödel* (a sweet, jelly-filled dumpling topped with vanilla sauce) for dessert. For traditional brews, simply ask for *"ein Bier"* to get the house specialty on tap. You can also specify the type of beer you want, as opposed to the brand,such as *Weiß* (white), *Dunkel* (dark), or *Hell* (bright) to get the house version. The quarter of Munich's population born outside of Germany supplies the city with Turkish, Pakistani, Ethiopian, and Japanese cuisines.

City Center

You'll find plenty of tourist-friendly eateries here, serving up pricey traditional Bavarian delights (read: pork, potatoes, and beer) with easy-to-read English menus. Those on a budget are better off grabbing a döner *kebab* or a *lamacun* from one of the many Turkish cafes around the Hauptbahnhof, like **Ali Baba** *(Schillerstr. 6 [$] döner kebab €3)*,grabbing some picnic fixings from cheap grocery stores like **Lidl** *(Schleißheimerstr. 85-87)* and **Aldi** *(Schleißheimerstr. 468)*, or noshing on fruit from a stand on warm sunny days. Many grocery stores are also located near subway stations, so keep your eyes peeled. Sandwich stands like **Yorma's** (many locations within Hauptbahnhof) offer hearty pre-made sandwiches *(€2-3)*, and chains such as **Vinzenzmurr** *(Sonnenstr. 8, among other locations)* have traditional Bavarian food fast-food style. For a slightly fancier and more expensive farmer's market experience, head to **Viktualienmarkt** *(southeast of Marienplatz by Alter Peter, open M-Sa 7am-8pm, summer M-F 7am-8pm, Sa 7am-4pm)* and chomp away with some beer in the garden by the towering maypole.

AUGUSTINER BEERHALL AND RESTAURANT

●&♥♨ GERMAN ❸

Neuhauserstr. 27   ☎089 23 18 32 57 ▣www.augustiner-restaurant.com

Get your hearty authentic German standards here; try two *weißwurst (white sausages; €4.50)* with a bowl of fresh asparagus soup *(€3)*, or go for gravy-laden roasted pork with a giant potato dumpling and sauerkraut *(€10.50)*. Watch out: the pretzels at your table will actually set you back a little *(€0.90)*. Enjoy the subdued beer-hall ambience in either the main hall or the picturesque courtyard with a .5L Augustiner Edelstoff *(€3.60)*. Though this place may seem like a tourist haven with its multilingual staff and menus, rest assured that most patrons are actually faithful locals.

♯ *SB or UB: Karlsplatz (Stachus), walk past the fountain and under the arches to Neuhauser Str.; restaurant will be on right.* **i** *Multilingual menu.* ⑤ *Entrees €4-24.80.* ② *Open daily 9am-midnight.*

WEIßES BRAUHAUS

●⊗♥♨ GERMAN ❸

Tal 7   ☎089 290 13 80 ▣www.weisses-brauhaus.de

Weißes Brauhaus has been serving up excellent renditions of traditional fare since 1540. Try the pork, braised in Aventinus beer, with a selection of house Tegernseer Hell beer *(0.5L €3.50)*. Minimizing on meat? The Weißes Brauhaus salad *(€8.90)* offers a refreshing balance between leafy greens and crispy meat.

♯ *S1, S2, S3, S4, S5, S6, S7, S8, U3, or U6: Marienplatz; walk past the arches or Altes Rathaus to restaurant on the left.* **i** *Multilingual menus available.* ⑤ *Entrees €6.30-13.50.* ② *Open daily 8am-1am; kitchen open until 11pm.*

CAFE RISCHART

●&♥❀♨ CAFE ❶

Marienpl. 18   ☎231 70 03 10 ▣www.rischart.de

Locals complain endlessly about the hordes of tourists that crowd their beloved Cafe Rischart, known for its baked goods and gelato. Thankfully for them, Cafe Rischart has several other locations around the city, but its Marienplatz location is undoubtedly the most iconic. Grab an enormous melt-in-your-mouth slice of butter cake as you people-watch from the patio. In addition, delicious sandwiches *(€3-4)* and pretzels *(€1)* make a great lunch. Definitely do not leave without a scoop of gelato *(€1)*! The sit-down menu is considerably more expensive than take-away, so make a picnic out of it.

♯ *S1, S2, S3, S4, S5, S6, S7, S8, U3, or U6: Marienplatz; located in the SE corner of the square.* ⑤ *Entrees €4-9.* ② *Open M-Sa 7am-8pm, Su 9am-7pm.*

KAIMUG

●⊗♥ ASIAN ❷

Sendlingerstr. 42   ☎089 20 60 33 27 ▣www.kaimug.de

For a break from all food Deutsche, try this little gem located right next to the Asamkirche. With excellent curry and cheap stir-fry, Kaimug doesn't sacrifice atmosphere or portion size. Desserts with coconut or mango make you swear off jelly-filled anything. Entrees also come in multiple sizes, so eat your fill. Vegetarian entrees galore.

♯ *U1, U2, U3, or U6: Sendlinger Tor. walk down Sendlingerstr. to restaurant on left.* **i** *Multiple locations throughout Germany.* ⑤ *Entrees €6.50-8.* ② *Open M-Sa 11am-10pm; kitchen closes at 9pm.*

PRINZ MYSHKIN

●⊗&♥❀♨ VEGETARIAN ❹

Hackenstr. 2   ☎089 26 55 96 ▣www.prinzmyshkin.com

Considered Munich's best vegetarian restaurant, Prinz Myshkin is pricey but well worth the splurge. The soy imitations will have you proclaiming "I can't believe it's not meat!" in only the most elegant of voices suited to the restaurant's high arched ceilings and arboreal tapestries. The delicious zen sticks appetizer *(€8.50)* comes with an arugula salad and is filling enough to be an entree.

♯ *U1, U2, U3, and U6: Sendlinger Tor, and walk down Sendlingerstr. to restaurant on left.* **i**

English menu available. Vegan offerings marked. $ Entrees €9-16.50. Daily lunch specials €5.50 ⏰ Open daily 11am-12:30am.

LAPORTE CONFISEUR 🚭 🍸 DESSERT ❷

Heiliggeiststr. 1 ☎089 291 61 21 12

This little chocolate shop, run by a charming elderly French couple, sells gourmet sweets and tasty crepes. The real attractions, however, are the sugar sculptures of the Eiffel Tower, Sacre-Coeur, Frauenkirche, and other sights, all meticulously hand-crafted by the owner himself.

➡ S1, S2, S3, S4, S5, S6, S7, S8, U3, or U6: Marienplatz. Walk past Alter Peter to Viktualienmarkt. Storefront (not free-standing) is located beyond Nordsee. $ Chocolates €6 per 100g. Crepes €2.30-3. ⏰ Open M-F 10am-6:30pm, Sa 10am-5pm.

HAXNBAUER 💳 ♿ 🍸 ❄ ☀ GERMAN ❹

Sparkassenstr. 8 ☎089 216 65 40 💻www.kuffler-gastronomie.de/haxnbauer

Vegetarians beware: Haxnbauer's iconic spits daily spin hundreds of *haxn*, Munich's specialty pork knuckles, having tantalized diners with its secret marinade and grilling strategy since the 1960s. With expensive fare like the ½ pork knuckle w/ sauerkraut *(€14.90)*, Haxnbauer is not so much for the everyday *Münchener*, but it makes a worthwhile treat. Portions are enormous, so bring a friend!

➡ SB, U3, or U6: Marienplatz; walk past the Altes Rathaus and turn left onto Sparkassenst. i Multilingual menu. $ Entrees €12-32. ⏰ Open daily 11am-midnight.

University Area

👍 **BAR TAPAS** 🚭 🍸 ☀ TAPAS ❷

Amalienstr. 97 ☎089 39 09 19 💻www.bar-tapas.com

Dark red walls and candlelit tables set the tone at this romantic Iberian outpost. Grab a pen and a slip of paper from the bar to make your selections from the displays of tapas. Especially recommended are the spicy chorizo and the tortilla pie with cheese, potatoes, and onions. The place fills up on the weekends, so get there early.

➡ U3or U6: Universität. Turn west (left) onto Adalbertstr. i 2-4 tapas recommended per person. Cocktails €5 daily after 10:30pm. $ Each tapas dish €4.20. ⏰ Open daily 4pm-1am.

CAFE IGNAZ 🚭 ☀ VEGETARIAN ❸

Georgenstr. 67 ☎089 271 60 93 💻www.ignaz-cafe.de

Newton's third law states that for every reaction there is an equal and opposite reaction. In the land of meat and potatoes, that equal and opposite reaction comes in the form of this quaint vegetarian and vegan cafe, its carrot logo the antithesis of Bavarian cuisine. The pastries are delicious, and the savory gnocchi and crepes are guaranteed winners.

➡ U2: Josephsplatz. Take Georgenstr. west for two blocks. i English-language menu. $ Entrees €7-12. Breakfast buffet M and W-F 8am-11:30am €7 including warm drink. Lunch buffet M-F noon-2:30pm, €6.90. Happy hour M-F 3pm-6pm, one entree for €6. Brunch buffet Sa-Su 9am-2pm, €9. ⏰ Open M, W-F 8am-11pm, Sa-Su 9am-11pm.

LO STUDENTE 🚭 🍸 ☀ ITALIAN ❷

Schellingstr. 30 ☎089 27 37 54 47 💻www.lo-studente.com

As the name may suggest, Lo Studente was made for students, and this popular eatery is always filled with young people getting their fill. The gourmet pizzas are made in a wood-fire oven, and unlike other similar restaurants in the area, here you can get pizza by the slice. Weekday lunch specials make for fat portions on a skinny budget.

➡ U3 or U6 to Universität, then turn right (east) onto Schellingstr. $ Slice €2.50, whole 32cm pizzas €3.50-10. Lunch specials €5-7.50. ⏰ Open daily 11am-midnight.

ECLIPSE ISRAELI ❷

Hessestr. 51 ☎089 522221 🖥www.eclipse-grillbar.de

Serves Edward Cullen on a plate. Just kidding, but the exotic wonders of Israel are a more-than-worthy substitute. Come here to find Munich's best falafel sandwich to-go *(€6)*, rich and flavorful with authentic Middle Eastern spices, or try the *Schipud-Kebab (€5.50)*, made from beef and lamb laden with fresh herbs and pine nuts.

U2: Theresienstr., then north on Augustenstr. for one block and left onto Hessenstr. [i] English-speaking staff. $ Entrees €5.50-16. ⏰ Open daily 5-10pm.

STEINHEIL 16 GERMAN ❷

Steinheilstr. 16 ☎089 52 74 88

Schnitzel is the subject here, as the kitchen rapidly churns out plate upon plate of enormous fried and breaded goodness covering an equally gargantuan mound of fries. The wooden tables are crammed with hungry students, feasting on the relatively cheap plates of fried deliciousness as frantic yet superbly organized waiters fly around the eatery to take care of even the pickiest appetites. Get here early and hungry, and leave stuffed and satisfied.

U2: Theresienstr., then take Augustenstr. south one block and turn left onto Steinhielstr. [i] Always crowded, so get there early or make a reservation. $ Schnitzel with fries and salad €9.40. Entrees €6-14. ⏰ Open daily 10am-1am.

SHIVA INDIAN ❷

Augustenstr. 96 ☎089 523 28 88 🖥www.shiva-muenchen.de

The scent of incense and bright colors envelope you as soon as you enter this Indian restaurant. Delicious curries and midday specials make this a hopping lunch spot.

U2: Theresienstr., then take Augustenstr. 1 block north. [i] 10% discount if you get takeout. $ Entrees €10-17. M-F 11:30am-2:30pm 24 different dishes €6.50-10. ⏰ Open daily 12:30-2:30pm and 5:30-11pm.

BEI RAFFAELE ITALIAN ❸

Luisenstr. 47 ☎089 52 15 19 🖥www.bei-raffaele.de

Be mesmerized by the practiced hands of the chefs making your pie right in front of your eyes. Just a few minutes later, your personal pizza is ready, hot, steaming, with a sweet doughy Neapolitan crust and the freshest ingredients possible. This family-owned restaurant has been around for over 25 years now, so they must be doing something right. Weekday lunch specials can get you an entire 32cm pizza *(€6)*, show and all.

U2: Theresienstr., head down Theresienstr. toward the University, and then take a right onto Luisenstr. [i] The staff might not speak English, but they do have an English-language menu on hand. $ Pizza and pastas €6.60-13, Entrees €13-19. 3-course prix-fixe €27. ⏰ Open Tu-Su 11:30am-12:30am.

LARA 44 TURKISH ❷

Schellingstr. 44 ☎089 39 29 50 45 🖥www.lara44.de

Lara 44's super fancy pillows make it look like an overpriced döner kebab joint, but the mouthwatering kebabs, lahmacuns, and other Turkish staples actually come at competitive prices *(from €3)*. Take it to go, or sit back and bask in the fanciness.

U3 or U6: Universität, then turn right onto Schellingstr. $ Entrees €3.50-10. ⏰ Open daily M-Sa 8am-8pm.

TÜRKENHOF GERMAN ❸

Türkenstr. 78 ☎089 280 02 35

With enormous portions and a daily student special *(€5)*, Türkenhof is packed with hungry students and thirsty locals sitting around the wooden bar, decorated by a giant pair of wooden eagle wings over it. The hipster vibe is crystallized by metallic vintage posters along the wooden-planked walls. Try the *Türkenhofschnäppchen*, a rotating snack-of-the-day featuring munchies like two weiβwurst with a pretzel and beer *(€6)*.

U3 or U6: Universität, then turn right onto Schellingstr. and right again onto Türkenstr.; restaurant on right. $ Entrees €6.70-12.60. ⏰ Open M-Th and Su 11am-1am, F-Sa 11am-2am.

L'OSTERIA PIZZA E PASTA ITALIAN ❷

Leopoldstr. 28a ☎089 38 88 97 11 🖥www.losteria.info

Enormous pizzas and tasty pastas await you in this small haven on the busy Leopolstr. On summer nights, the strings of lights hanging over the treetops give the lively courtyard a backyard party feel. The pizzas are too large for one, so most folks split them as waitresses carry around plates upon plates of semicircular dough to eager customers. The crowd varies from casual students to suit-wearing businessmen.

U3 or U6: Giselastr. $ Pizza and pastas €8-12. ⏰ Open M-Sa 11am-midnight, Su noon-midnight.

BALLA BENI ICE CREAM ICE CREAM ❷

Theresienstr. 46 ☎089 18 91 29 43

The wait's long, the portion's small, and the price is high, but you can always count on a large crowd outside this tiny ice cream joint, rain or shine. That's because Balla Beni makes the city's smoothest and creamiest homemade gelato. Only 12 flavors are featured daily, but they range from the luscious commonplace vanilla to the more exotic chocolate ginger. The frugal only go for one scoop, but you can always ask for small tastes of other flavors to be added into your edible bowl.

Tram 27 or Bus #100: Pinakotheken. Across the street from Museum Brandhorst. $ Each scoop €1.20 ⏰ Open daily mid-Feb.-mid-Oct. 10am-11pm.

MAO CHINESE ❸

Schleissheimerstr. 92 ☎089 54 35 67 12 🖥www.mao-muenchen.de

This restaurant takes it's name seriously. Little Red Books, in German, alas, litter every table, stereotypically Chinese photographs decorate the walls, and popular communist phrases title each section of the menu ("Fish: Mao Swims in the Yangtze"). The real attraction is the upscale overpriced kitsch, not the solid food, that you'd be hard-pressed to find elsewhere. Plenty of vegetarian entrees, like "Budda rises in the west" are available.

U2: Josephspl., then south on Josephspl., turn right onto Görresstr., and left onto Schleissheimerstr. $ Entrees €7.50-18.80. ⏰ Open M-Sa 11:30am-2:30pm and 5:30pm-11:30pm, Su 5:30pm-11:30pm.

Au-Haidhausen

WRITSHAUS IN DER AU GERMAN ❹

Lillienstr. 51 ☎089 448 14 00 🖥www.wirtshausinderau.de

Writshaus in der Au claims to serve the largest dumplings in all of Munich, both in size and variety. Try the Original Münchner Knödel, an enormous hash of pretzel dough, roast pork, and—of course—beer *(€10.50)*. Other favorites include the *Hofente*, Bavarian-style duck fresh from the oven *(€13.80 per portion, €17.90 per half duck)*, and the chocolate dumplings served with a berry compote *(€6.90)*.

Tram 18: Deutsches Museum, then cross the bridge and head past Museum Lichtspiele to turn right onto Lillienstr. i English menu available. $ Entrees €7.70-18.80 ⏰ Open M-F 5pm-1am, Sa-Su 10pm-1am.

CAFE VOILA CAFE ❸

Wörthstr. 5 ☎089 489 16 54 🖥www.cafe-voila.de

Locals flock here, maybe because they can sit in the sunny atrium and wonder at the color-changing sign behind the bar over breakfast. Or, more likely, it's the over 100 cocktail choices.

⇟ Tram 19: Wörthstr., or S1-8 or U5: Ostbahnhof, head straight out through the entrance onto Wörthstr. one block past the small park between the roads. ℹ Happy hour M-Th and Su 5pm-1am: all cocktails €5. $ Breakfast €4-10.50. Entrees €5.50-21.50. ⏰ Open daily 8am-1am.

CREPERIE BERNARD AND BERNARD ❀⊘🍸❄ FRENCH ❷

Innere Wiener Str. 32 ☎089 480 11 73

Sing along with the chipper French waiters as you settle in for some authentic crepes. There are over 30 different options, but stick with the sweet over savory. For the ultimate treat, get yourself a flambee and watch the flames right in front of your eyes.

⇟ Tram 18: Wiener Pl., or U4 or U5 to Max-Weber Platz and turn onto Inner Wiener Str. ℹ Not much English, but French spoken. $ Entrees €4.10-10 ⏰ Open M-F 5:30pm-midnight, Sa 6:30pm-1am, and Su 5:30pm-midnight.

HOFBRÄUKELLER 💳⊘🍸❄⛅ GERMAN ❸

Innere Wiener Str. 19 ☎089 459 92 50 🖥www.hofbraeukeller.de

A favorite beer garden east of the Isar, Hofbräukeller serves all the usual German favorites with both a beer hall and a beer garden in a space shared with a not-so-German Sausilito's, complete with sand and lawn chairs. A children's playplace offers a painting table and ball pits so parents can drink in peace. Free Wi-Fi throughout the complex gives you even more incentive to stay.

⇟ Tram 18: Wiener Platz. ℹ English menu available. $ Entrees €9.10-13. ⏰ Open daily 10am-midnight.

CHOPAN II ❀⊘🍸❄ AFGHANI ❸

Rosenheimerstr. 6 ☎089 44 11 85 71 🖥www.chopan.de

Dark red walls, gold designs, and light shades creating intricate patterns on the ceiling, Chopan makes the ambience romantic. The food does less so—it's pretty mediocre.

⇟ Tram 18: Deutches Museum, cross the bridge to restaurant on right. ℹ Another location in Neuhausen at Elvirastr. 18, one block south of the Mallingerstr. U-Bahn stop. English menu available. $ Entrees €9.50-15. ⏰ Open daily 5pm-11pm

L'ANGOLO DELLA PIZZA ❀⊘🍸❄⛅ ITALIAN ❷

Breisacherstr. 30 ☎089 448 89 79 🖥www.langolo-della-pizza.de

Located on a quiet side street locals seat themselves against an exposed brick backdrop, while the candlelight on the tables flicker shadows on their faces, highlighting their delicate bone structure. There they can enjoy piping hot, though unextraordinary, wood-oven pizzas and pastas. But remember, it's all about the incandescent lighting and the bone structure.

⇟ S1-8: Ostbahnhof, then head north on Orleanstr. and turn left onto Breisacherstr. ℹ Special discounts on pizza on M, pasta on W. $ Pizzas €3.50-10. Pastas €6.30-8. 0.5L Beer €2. Lunch menu from €5.50. ⏰ Open M-F 11:30am-2pm and 5:30pm-12:30am, Sa-Su 4pm-12:30am. Kitchen open until midnight.

Neuhausen

RUFFINI ❀♿🍸⛅ CAFE ❷

Orffstr. 22-24 ☎089 16 11 60 🖥www.ruffini.de

This whimsical cafe on a quiet residential street buzzes with locals catching up with each other or the morning paper. Expert baristas churn out perfect cups of frothy cappucino; order yours with a flaky croissant *(€5.70)* and take it to the sunny rooftop terrace. Downstairs, sample some wines at the bar from an extensive menu *(.25L €4.60-7.400)*, or practice your German reading comprehension with the provided magazines.

⇟ Tram 12: Neuhausen, then turn perpendicular to tram route such that park is immediately to

the left. Cafe is two blocks down Ruffinistr. ℹ *Rooftop terrace is self-service, so order downstairs before you sit down. Small bakery attached, entrance on Ruffinistr.* $ *Breakfast entrees €5.70-8.30* ⏰ *Open Tu-Fr 8:30am-6pm, Sa 8:30am-5pm, Su 10am-5pm.*

AUGUSTINERKELLER GERMAN [3]

Arnulftr. 52 ☎089 59 43 93 🖥www.augustineerkeller.de

Augustiner is widely viewed as the most prized of Bavarian brews since its birth in 1824, and its beer garden is no less precious. Clinking beer glasses resound as early as 11am at this favorite, where residents enjoy enormous pretzels and dim lighting beneath century-old chestnut trees. The restaurant serves up authentic Bavarian dishes, though the real attraction is the namesake beer.

S1, S2, S3, S4, S5, S6, S7, and S8: Hackerbrucke; turn right onto Anulfstr. $ *Maß €7.20. Restaurant entrees €9-23. Beer garden is cash only.* ⏰ *Beer garden open daily 11:30am-midnight, restaurant open 10am-1am.*

SCARLETTI'S CAFE [1]

Nymphenburgerstr. 155 ☎089 15 53 14 🖥www.scarletti.de

The Scarletti family has been the creme de la creme of Munich's ice cream scene for generations. Choose from 60 flavors for your cone, or sample one of the 57 different shake and sundae creations. Come with ravenous friends to tackle the 18-scoop Coppa Bombastico, mixed with fresh fruit and cookies *(€22)*. The cafe also serves a few entrees, including a soft and savory spinach-and-feta quiche *(with salad; €5)*.

U1 or Tram 12: Rotzkreuzplatz. $ *Single scoop to-go €1. Shakes and sundaes €4.20-11.50. Lunch entrees €3-6.70.* ⏰ *Open Feb and Sept 9am-8pm, Mar-Apr and Oct 9am-11pm, May-Sept 9am-11:30pm.*

CAFE FREIHEIT CAFE [3]

Leonrodstr. 20 ☎089 13 46 86 🖥www.cafe-freiheit.de

An excellent people-watching spot on the busy Rotzkreuzplatz, Cafe Freiheit serves up delicious fare in a posh, newly-renovated space. The lunchtime patronage is less novel, with Neuhausen's aging population as the main clientele, but don't be afraid to stay and try their daily lunch specials *(€7)*.

U1: Rotzkreuzplatz. ℹ *Check online for specials; M-F 8-10am all hot non-alcoholic beverages €1.90. 10% off for all takeout.* $ *Breakfast €5.50-9.90. Lunch €6.90-16.50. Dinner €15.50-16.50.* ⏰ *Open daily 8am-11:30pm. Kitchen open 8am-9:45pm.*

RICK'S CAFE MEXICAN-AMERICAN [2]

Wendl-Dietrich-Str. 5 ☎089 16 04 43 🖥www.ricks-cafe.biz

Tex-Mex isn't quite what you think of when you think Southern German cuisine, but Rick's Cafe is a great place to satisfy those burrito cravings. Popular with students from the hostel down the street, the cafe is known for its cheap, large-portioned lunch specials *(€5.80)*.

U1: Rotzkreuzplatz, then walk down Wendl-Dietrich-Str. to restaurant on left. $ *Entrees €5.80-11.60.* ⏰ *Open daily 11am-1am.*

THE BIG EASY AMERICAN SOUTHERN [4]

Frundsbergstr. 46 ☎089 15 89 02 53 🖥www.thebigeasy.de

The Big Easy recreates the relaxed jazzy swank of New Orleans' upper crust. Bask in the candlelight to the soft strains of live jazz every Thursday, and snack on crawfish while you draw in some southern comfort. Hopefully the seafood is more local than the Gulf Coast.

Tram 12: Neuhausen, then turn perpendicular to tram route such that park is immediately to the left. Cafe is two blocks down Ruffinistr. ℹ *Su jazz buffet brunch €18.50 per person.* $ *Entrees €9.20-14.50* ⏰ *Open M-Sa 5pm-1am, Su 10am-1am.*

Thalkirchen

ALTER WIRT IN THALKIRCHEN
🚭🍸 GERMAN ❷

Fraunbergstr. 8 ☎089 74 21 99 77

This traditional Bavarian kitchen also cooks up various international classic cheap eats like burgers and quesadillas. But you didn't come to Germany for that, and honestly you're better off sticking to the traditional stuff. Cheap and hearty food with large portions make this a local favorite.

U3: Thalkirchen, then head down Fraunbergstr. ℹ *Specials include Schnitzel Thursdays (enormous plate of schnitzel with fries, €5.10 with the purchase of a drink).* $ *Entrees €7-16.* ⏰ *Open Su-Th 9am-1am, F-Sa 9am-3am. Kitchen closes at midnight.*

MANGOSTIN RESTAURANTS
🚭🍸 ASIAN ❹

Maria-Einsiedel-Str. 2 ☎089 723 20 31 💻www.mangostin.de

Half kitschy, half classy, the orientally-inspired Mangostin cooks up pricey Germanized "Asianese" food in a Japanese garden setting. The other restaurants on the same premises also feature artful decor. You're definitely paying for the miraculous cultural fusion, not the food.

U3: Thalkirchen, take the Tierpark exit and you'll see it on the corner. $ *Entrees €12-25.* ⏰ *Open 11:30am-midnight, though each restaurant's hours may vary.*

NIGHTLIFE

Bavaria agreed to become a part of a larger Germany on one condition: that it be allowed to maintain its beer purity laws. Since then, Munich has remained loyal to its six great labels: **Augustiner, Hacker-Pschorr, Hofbräu, Löwenbräu, Paulaner,** and **Spaten-Franziskaner.**United, they provide Müncheners and tourists alike with all the fuel they need for late-night revelry. Four main types of beer are served in Munich: **Helles,** a standard light beer with a crisp, sharp taste, **Dunkles,** a dark beer with a heavier, fuller flavor, **Weißbier,** a smooth, cloudy blond beer made from wheat instead of barley, and **Radler or Russ'n** a "shandy" or "cyclist's brew"; half beer and half lemon soda with a light, fruity taste. Munich's beer is typically 5% alcohol, though during Starkbierzeit, the first two weeks of Lent, Müncheners traditionally drink Starkbier, a dark beer that is 8-10% alcohol. Daring travelers can go for a full liter of beer, known as a 👍**Maß** *(€5-7).*Specify if you want a *halb-Maß (.5L, €3-4),* since only Weißbier is almost exclusively served in 0.5L sizes. While some beer gardens offer veggie dishes, vegetarians may wish to eat elsewhere before a post-meal swig. It's traditional to bring your own food to outdoor beer halls—drinks, however, must be bought at the Biergarten. Bare tables usually indicate cafeteria-style *selbstbedienung* (self-service).

City Center

While many students prefer to stay in their own hostel bars and seasoned Germans prefer their beer halls, those more adventurous take advantage of the ripe new nightlife scene that has recently formed around Gärtnerplatz. Once home to a more exclusive, artsy underground scene, the area's newfound popularity has since made it much less exclusive but just as much fun. The gay district is also located in the vicinity, with most of the city's gay bars along Müllerstr. between Gärtnerplatz and Sendlinger Tor.

👍 HOFBRÄUHAUS
♿🍸 BEER HALL

Platzl 9 ☎089 29 01 36 0 💻www.hofbraeuhaus.de

No trip to Munich is complete without a trip to its most famous beer hall. Steeped in history, Hofbrauhaus remained royalty-only until the King Ludwig I opened it to the public in 1828. Seat yourself at one of the crowded benches and make some new friends. Beer here only comes in liters *(€6.90);* if you ask for anything less, they'll chortle and bring you a *Maß* anyway. By the end of the night, you'll be singing at the top of your lungs with complete strangers, and if you're not feeling so well, ask to visit the celebrated vomitorium, an ergonomic device built for those occasions.

S1, S2, S3, S4, S5, S6, S7, S8, U3 or U6: Marienplatz. Take a left right before the Altes Rathaus onto Burgstr., walk past the Alter Hof courtyard, and take a right onto Pfisterstr. Restaurant will be on your right. i Get here early to guarantee a spot, especially for large groups. $ Entrees €7-14. ⏰ Open daily 9am-11:30pm.

CAFE AM HOCHHAUS — CLUB

Blumenstr. 9 — ☎089 290 13 60 🖳www.cafeamhochhaus.de

One of the first clubs in the area, Cafe am Hochhaus defines itself by its musicality, with DJs spinning anything alternative, from jazz to funk. This draws an assorted clientele, and on any given night you might run into some of Germany's most famous models or the 50-year-olds who practically live there. Dance under the vodka-bottle-shaped disco ball, and pause to contemplate the quirky wallpaper. Sunday nights are gay-friendly, though straights are always welcome.

U1, U2, U3 or U6: Sendlinger Tor. Walk toward the tram stop such that the brick arches of Sendlinger Tor are behind you, and turn left onto Sonnenstr. The road will turn into Blumenstr. and curve multiple times before you reach the cafe on your right. i No food. $ Shots €3-5. Cocktails €7-8. ⏰ Open daily 8pm-3am, later on the weekends. The party usually doesn't get started until 10pm.

KSAR BARCLUB — CLUB

Müllerstr. 31 — ☎089 55 29 84 79 🖳www.ksar-barclub.de

Usually the subdued bar atmosphere turns into an electronic and minimalist tunes dance party by 10pm. The crowd veers to the older side, but that only adds to your new-found maturity, while you perch on a black leather cube and sip your drink. Watch the award-winning bartenders juggle their tools as they make your cocktail. A flatscreen TV and a projector broadcast major sports shows.

Directly behind Cafe am Hochhaus (above); look for the Smirnoff logo on the canopy. i Try the signature raspberry mojito (€8). $ Cocktails €7.50-8.50. Coffee made from a hardcore espresso machine also served. ⏰ Open in summer W-Sa 6pm-3am, in winter M-Sa 8pm-4am.

NED KELLY'S AUSTRALIAN BAR AND KILIAN'S IRISH PUB — CAFE-BAR

Frauenpl. 11 — ☎089 24 21 99 10 or 089 24 21 98 99 🖳www.nedkellysbar.com, www.killansirishpub.com

Venture "down under" to Ned Kelly's and Kilian's subterranean digs. These two bars, which share an outdoor entrance, have long catered to Munich's ex-pat community. Live music daily, but on weekends it's barely audible over the chatter of patrons handling Guinness *(0.5L €4.40)* or Fosters *(0.5L €3.90)* and the homestyle Australian and Irish fare. Make sure to cheer for your favorite teams during live broadcasts of rugby and ice hockey games.

S1, S2, S3, S4, S5, S6, S7, S8, U3, or U6: Marienpl., find it directly behind the Frauenkirche. i Free Wi-Fi. Credit cards €25 minimum. $ Entrees €8-17.10. ⏰ Open M-Th 11am-1am, Fr-Sa 11am-2am, Su 12am-1am.

CAFE SELIG — CAFE-BAR

Hans-Sachs-Str. 3 — ☎089 23 88 88 78 🖳www.einfachselig.de

According to one area bartender, most of the city's young gays would rather go to straight clubs than gay clubs. For them, Cafe Selig was born. An upscale Viennese coffeehouse serving in-house roasted cups of joe by day, a mainstream club for all orientations by night, with weekends basically staked out by gay men. Go ahead and order a beer *(0.5L €3.10)*, but most people prefer the aperol-spritz—a concoction of half white wine, half water, and a dash of the orange-flavored aperol *(€3.40)*.

U1 and U2: Fraunhoferst., head down Fraunhoferst. toward Frenzy, turn left on Müllerstr. and left again onto Hans-Sachs-Str. $ Entrees €6-12. ⏰ Open M noon-1am, Tu 5pm-1am, W-F noon-1am, Sa-Su 9am-3am. Kitchen closes daily at 10pm.

BAU

♦⊗♈✿♨▼ GAY CLUB

Müllerstr. 41 ☎089 26 92 08 🌐www.bau-munich.de

The unmissable glorious rainbow wrapped around this bar's exterior announces the orientation. Different nightly themes bring a diverse crowd to Bau. The music is usually less diverse, unless you attend German oldies night or film music night. Show off your moves on the two levels of the galvanized-steel construction-themed dance floors.

⚥ *U1, U2, U3 or U6 to Sendlinger Tor, walk down Blumenstr. and turn right onto Müllerstr.* ℹ *Women (rarely seen) are welcome on all nights except for certain events (check website for details).* Ⓢ *Beer from €3. Shots €2.50-3. Cocktails €7.50.* ☾ *Open daily 8pm until the party dies down (usually 3am or later).*

K AND K

⊗♿♈✿ CLUB

Reichenbachstr. 22 ☎089 20 20 74 63 🌐www.kuk-club.de

It's a *Pretty Woman* kind of story. Once upon a time, a traditional Bavarian restaurant, K and K (or "K u K" as the locals call it) got a makeover of subdued walls, neon-colored lights, and cube seats was, and became one of the hottest nightlife spots in Munich. Beer-drinking was replaced with cocktail-sipping and chain-smoking. Tu-Sa local DJs play anything from house to hip hop to rock, making this restaurant a versatile keeper.

⚥ *U1 or U2: Frauenhoferstr.* Ⓢ *Beer €3.40. Shots €2.50. Cocktails €7-10.* ☾ *Open daily 8pm-2am, Tu-Sa until 3am.*

MORIZZ

♦⊗♈✿♨▼ BAR

Klenzestr. 43 ☎089 201 67 76 🌐www.club-morizz.de

The patrons' lively chatter reverberating along the mirrored walls gives this bar a comfortable living room feel. Many frequent for the scrumptious Thai food and mixed drinks. During the summer, try the strawberry daiquiris, sweet and tangy with fresh strawberries *(€8.50).*

⚥ *U1 or U2: Fraunhoferstr.* Ⓢ *Thai dishes €11.20-17.50. Cocktails €7.50-11.* ☾ *Open M-Th 6pm-2am, F-Sa 6pm-3am, and Su 6pm-2am.*

HOLY HOME

⊗♈✿♨ BAR

Reichenbachstr. 21 ☎089 201 45 46

Holy Home is, as the name suggests, for its faithful clientele. The arched ceilings might bring ancient monasteries to mind, but the decor and crowd is definitely not. Once a staple of Munich's underground scene, Holy Home now occupies the neighborhood bar niche, where new friends, who encourage getting beyond tipsy, are made.

ℹ *Su is the Smoker's Club, the only day smokers can whiff indoors.* Ⓢ *Beer €3.20. Shots €2-8.* ☾ *Open daily 6pm-1am, Th-Sa until 3am.*

DIE BANK

⊗♈✿♨ CLUB

Müllerstr. 42 ☎089 23684171 🌐www.die-bank.com

Local artists' work adorn the walls of this stylish yet non-exclusive bar, where DJs spin anything from funk to house and live bands regale the crowd on Su. F-Sa cocktails are concocted with fresh fruit juices; try the apfelstrudel shot *(€3.50).* While you're at it, visit the neighbors upstairs and get yourself some pizza *(F-Sa €2.50-3 per slice, or €6-12.50 for a whole pizza)*, a haircut *(Th-Sa 8pm-2am, laura@die-bank.com)*, or have a jam sesh in the music room, complete with guitars, celli, and other miscellaneous instruments *(W, F, and Sa from 8pm, 🌐www.klangduche.net).*

⚥ *U1, U2, U3 or U6: Sendlinger Tor. Walk down Blumenstr. and turn right onto Müllerstr.* Ⓢ *Beer from €3.20. Shots €5-10. Cocktails €7.50-11.50.* ☾ *Open M 5pm-2am, Tu-Th 4pm-2am, F 4pm-5am, Sa 5pm-5am, and Su 5pm-2am.*

BAADER CAFE

⊗♈✿ CAFE-BAR

Baaderstr. 47 ☎089 201 06 38 🌐www.baadercafe.de

Located on a residential street, the Baader Cafe has been a favorite go-to for locals, serving up a good time for 25 years. The boho vibe makes it a chill hangout by day, especially during brunch with food like buttermilk pancakes with fresh fruit *(€5.10)*,while by night the young mostly-student crowd turns the place into a "baad"-ass busy bar. Come by for happy hour daily from 6-8pm for cocktails *(€5)*. Try the elderberry blossom spritzer, especially popular during the summer. The bar is more popular in the winter.

🚇 U1 or U2: Fraunhoferstr., walk toward the river (away from Frenzy) and turn left onto Baaderstr. $ Food €3.30-8.50. 0.5L Beer €3.30. Cocktails €7. ⏰ Open daily 9:30am-whenever the party ends.

FRENZY ❁🚭🍸☀ CAFE, BAR

Fraunhoferstr. 20 ☎089 20 23 26 86 💻www.frenzy-family.de

The dizzying neon pink and green decor and floral wallpaper make this a popular spot for women,who comprise 90% of Frenzy's clientele during the week. Weekends feature a 50/50 mix. Frenzy's environmentally conscious mantra means only organic foods and humanely-raised meats. Popular items include the *Heiße Ziege*, a salad with goat cheese, honey, sunflower seeds, and homemade dressing *(€9.50)*.

🚇 U1 or U2: Fraunhoferstr. Restaurant is across the street. ℹ English-speaking staff, but don't expect to find too many tourists here. $ Cocktails €5.50-8. ⏰ Kitchen open M-Sa 9am-1am, Su 9am-midnight. Sa-Su bar closes at 2am.

University Area

👍 **ALTER SIMPL** ❁🚭🍸❄☀ BAR

Türkenstr. 57 ☎089 272 30 83 💻www.eggerlokale.de

Once a second home to Munich's bohemian artists and intellectuals, Alter Simpl today contains all the cozy fixings of a neighborhood bar, with a rich history to boot. Founded in 1903, the bar takes its name from an old satiritical magazine called "Simplicissmus," with the magazine's iconic logo of a dog breaking the chains of censorship reworked into a dog breaking open a champagne bottle. Coupled with great Bavarian food and a lively student scene, what's not to love?

🚇 U3 or U6: Universität, then turn right on Schellingstr. and right onto Türkenstr. $ Beer 3 per .5L. Snacks and entrees €5.50-14. Daily lunch specials €7.77. ⏰ Open M-Th 11am-3am, F-Sa 11am-4am, and Su 11am-3am. Kitchen closes 1hr. before.

👍 **SCHELLING SALON** ❁🚭🍸❄ BAR

Schellingstr. 54 ☎089 272 07 88 💻www.schelling-salon.de

Schelling has been a Munich institution since 1872. Rack up at the tables where Lenin, Rilke, and Hitler once played *(€9 per hour)*. The walls, filled with newspaper articles and other memorabilia, attest to the salon's cred. Unwind with a cheap beer and friends after a hectic week of real drinking.

🚇 U3 or U6: Universität, then head away from the Siegestor and take a right onto Schellingstr. ℹ Foosball and ping pong also available. $ Breakfast €3-6, German entrees €5-12, beer 0.5L €2.90. ⏰ Open M and Th-Su 10am-1am. Kitchen open until midnight.

FLASCHENBAR ❁ BAR

Schleissheimerstr. 43 ☎089 99 01 36 36 💻www.flaschenbar.com

With a special *(€1)* on bottled beers and a live DJ every Th (8-10pm), the Aaschenbar attracts hordes of young people looking for a good time on the cheap. The space, with its washed-out red walls and custom-made beer bottle chandeliers, is so cool that it's often rented out for private parties on weekends (call ahead to check). Despite its popularity, the bar has a homey (albeit crowded) attitude, where you can casually strike up a conversation with anyone.

🚇 U2: Theresienstr., turn west on Theresienstr. and walk a block to the end, then turn right onto Schleissheimerstr. ℹ No food served, but you can bring your own or ask the bartender to order a pizza. $ Beer usually €2.70 per botle. Shots €2.50. ⏰ Open M-Sa 8pm-3am or later.

EAT THE RICH
💳⊗🍸❄ BAR

Hess-str. 90 ☎089 18 59 82 💻www.eattherich.de

Walk past the gauche leopard-print curtains into this trendy yet still kitschy bar, jam-packed with attractive young people. Sit under the floral glass chandelier and go psychedelic in the colorful glittery lights. Forget that *halb-Maß* of *Weissbier;* here at Eat the Rich you can get half a liter of your favorite cocktail and you'll be surprised at just how quickly the night goes by.

🚇 U2: Theresienstr., turn west on Theresienstr. and walk a block to the end, then turn right and take your first left onto Hessenstr. $ Cocktails €10-13; for 0.5L add €2.50. ⏰ Open Tu-Sa 7pm-3am. Kitchen closes at 2:30am.

VANILLA LOUNGE
🚫⊗📶🍸❄⛅ CAFE-BAR

Leopoldstr. 65 ☎089 38 66 68 36 💻www.vanilla-lounge.de

This popular hub manifests the flavor: smooth, simple, and sweet. The day begins with laptop-bearing students lounging about, completing assignments courtesy of the free Wi-Fi, but the nighttime scene transforms it into an ambient club lounge complete with purple hues and hopping beats. Tee-totaling? Not a problem—the lounge offers a whopping 20 alcohol-free cocktails *(€7.50)*,and with a 24-page cocktail menu, there's something for everyone.

🚇 U3 or U6: Münchner Freiheit. ℹ Free Wi-Fi. All coffee products are lactose-free. $ Mixed drinks €7.50-8.50. ⏰ Open M-F 8am-2am, Sa-Su 8am-3am.

CAFE MOCCA
🚫⊗ HOOKAH

Herzogstr. 2 ☎089 33 03 97 81 💻www.mocca-munich.com

This Lebanese *shisha* (hookah) bar, is pervaded by a sweet vanilla hookah scent envelops the cafe and its surroundings. Park yourself in the draped interior, or grab a seat in the outdoor lounge that to enjoy a puff under the stars. Also, the fact that this cafe is next to Vanilla Lounge makes this street sound like a 20-something's Candy Land.

🚇 U3 or U6 to Münchner Freiheit, directly behind the Vanilla Lounge. $ Hookah standard €7, deluxe €10. Mixed drinks €5 after 4pm. Daily lunch specials €7. ⏰ Open M-Th 11am-2am, F-Sa 11am-3am, and Su 11am-2am.

THE MARTINI CLUB
💳⊗🍸❄⛅ BAR

Theresienstr. 93 ☎089 52 01 29 24 💻www.the-martini-club.de

You know a place is serious when the drink menu is 59 pages long. Modeled after the original prohibition-era Martini Club in New York, the Munich version recreates its exclusive and upscale splendor. Th live piano jazz adds to this ambiance, and the customers here range from well-dressed students to respectable bankers who can actually afford the luxurious Ultimate Champagne Cocktail (€333).

🚇 U2: Theresienstr., head one block west on Theresienstr. to restaurant on left. ℹ W ladies' night with 2 selected martinis €2. $ Mixed drinks generally €9-13, though the "liquid luxury" section will have you paying extensively more. Entrees €7-18. ⏰ Open Tu-Su 6pm-4am. Kitchen closes 3:30am.

Au-Haidhausen

👍 MUFFATWERK
🚫♿ LIVE MUSIC

Zellstr. 4 ☎089 45 87 50 10 💻www.muffatwerk.de

This former power plant hosts techno, hip-hop, spoken word, jazz, and dance performances. The massive performance hall features international DJs and artists, while the attached beer garden and cafe provide a more relaxed venue for enjoying the afternoon or evening.

🚇 Tram 18: Deutsches Museum, then cross the bridge and turn left (follow the signs). $ Cover generally €5-9, though many events are free; concert tickets vary in price. Check website for events. ⏰ Shows generally begin between 9-10pm with entry one hour earlier. Beer garden open M-Th 5pm-1am, F-Su noon-1am. Clubbing nights generally begin between 10-11pm.

OPTIMOLWERKE AND KULTFABRIK CLUB COMPLEXES

Friedenstr. 6 ☎089 450 69 20 💻www.optimolwerke.de

Grafingerstr. 6 ☎089 45 02 88 99 💻www.kultfabrik.de

In adjacent lots lie **Kultfabrik** and **Optimolwerke**, two powerhouses of adolescent fury, each with enormous candy-store assortments of smaller venues. Many locals complain that the enormity of these complexes lends an impersonal feel, and their location in abandoned factories by the train tracks is just gritty, but here's where you'll find Munich's youth into the wee hours. Hours, covers, and themes vary between each of the invididual venues, which range from the fun-in-the-sun **Bamboo Beach** (Kultfabrik), complete with imported sand, to the darker **Drei Turme** (Optimolwerke) with its castle-like interior. Also within Kultfabrik is **Kalinka**, where you can fill up on vodka and party it up against a giant 7ft. bust of Lenin *(open F-Sa)*. Kultfabrik also offers a monthly publication with schedules that you can find in many hostels and other places where young people congregate.

🚋 S1, S2, S3, S4, S5, S6, S7, or S8: Ostbahnhof, then walk through the underground tunnels past all the tracks to the back of the station and follow the crowds. $ Prices vary, but covers are generally around €5 and cheaper if you go earlier in the night. ⏰ Hours vary, but most parties begin between 10-11pm; check online for directories for each club.

WASSERWERK BAR BAR

Wolfgangstr. 19 ☎089 48 90 00 20 💻www.wasserwerk.org

Munich's first punk rock bar (exposed pipes and airbrushed cars on the ceilings included) now hosts a lively underground scene, complete with gourmet cocktails. The easygoing bartenders will happily create personalized drinks based on your specifications.

🚋 U4, U5 or Tram 15, 18, 19, or 25: Max-Weber Pl., then head east on Kirchenstr. and turn right onto Leonhardstr. $ Cocktails €7.50-9.50, happy hour daily 6pm-8pm with cocktails €5.80-6.50. ⏰ Open M-Th 6pm-2am, F-Sa 6pm-3am.

Neuhausen

The citizens of Neuhausen tend to be slightly more seasoned (read: older), so aside from a few celebrated beer halls, nightlife is much tamer than what you'd find in other parts of town. That said, while it may be difficult to find a dance party, there are plenty of bars with character and ambiance.

LÖWENBRÄUKELLER BEER HALL AND GARDEN

Nymphenburgerstr. 2 ☎ 089 54 72 66 90 💻www.loewenbraeukeller.com

Marienplatz has Hofbräuhaus, and Neuhausen has Löwenbräukeller. Across the street from the Löwenbräu distillery, Löwenbräukeller is easily identifiable by its elaborate tower of green and the characteristic Lowenbrau lion sitting on the terrace. Renovated in 2008, Löwenbräukeller offers the best of all worlds—an ornate indoor beer hall, a relaxed rooftop terrace, and a 1000-seat beer garden. Dine on traditional Bavarian fare while downing Löwenbräu lager under the stars, and sing your way back home in the company of new friends.

🚋 U1: Stiglmaierpl. ℹ English menu available. $ Maß €7.80. Entrees €8-20 ⏰ Open daily 10am-midnight.

BACKSTAGE BAR

Wilhelm-Hale Str. 38 ☎089 126 61 00 💻www.backstage.eu

Housed in a converted gas station, Backstage features music, often live, from the indie underground scene. Local crowd varies depending on the evening's act, but during the summer you can always expect a crowded *Biergarten* with one of the best beer deals in town *(Maß €4.80)*.

🚋 SB: Hirschgarten, or Tram 16 or 17: Steubenpl. ℹ Check the website for details. $ No cover for most events. ⏰ Summer Biergarten open M-Th 6pm-2am (or later), F-Sa 6pm-4am, Su 6pm-2am (or later). Check website for specific events; nightly dance parties usually start between 10-11pm.

BAAL OSTERIA MIT PASTA AND TAPAS 💳🚫♿ CAFE-BAR

Kreittmayrstr. 26 ☎089 18 70 38 36 💻www.osteria-baal.com

The LeTtErInG is so middle school, but Baal has some intelligence so let it pass. A literary watering hole boasting bookshelves overflowing with classics and a statue of Homer by the bar, Baal attracts students and Bohemians alike with its cheap daily pasta specials *(ask for the TIPP, €5 at lunch and €6 at dinner)*, enormous salads, inventive tapas, and smart cocktails. Dine on the terrace while the sunset gleams through the adjacent Sankt-Benno Kirche's stained-glass windows, then retreat inside for a game of pool *(30min. €4.50, 1hr. €8)* or a conversation in the candlelit library-bar.

🚏 Tram 20 or 21: Sandstr., then cut across the small park and turn onto Kreittmayrstr. ℹ Free wireless, just ask for the password. $ Entrees €8.80-10.80. ⏰ Open M-F noon-1am, Sa-Su 7pm-1am.

BAVARIA BOWL 💳🚫♿🍸💳 ENTERTAINMENT

Lazaretstr. 3 ☎089 427 41 90 💻www.olympia-bowling.de

While the overall design of this bowling alley looks like it hasn't changed since the 80s, bowling has remained a timeless and classic form of German entertainment. Young and old alike try their hands at the small alley's 10 lanes, equipped with that classic bowling alley scorekeeping software that reminds you of the same decade. Saturday after 8pm is "Limelight," Bavaria Bowl's version of glow bowling, or come on Sunday for "Bowling and Breakfast," an all-you-can-eat affair with three games of bowling *(€15)*.

🚏 U1: Mallingerstr., and turn onto Lazarettestr. to bowling alley on left. ℹ Food and drinks also offered. $ Price varies depending on date and time; generally €22 per lane per hr. ⏰ Open Tu-Th 4pm-1am, Fr 2pm-2am, Sa 1pm-2am, Su 9:30am-11pm.

ARTS AND CULTURE

Though the culture here seemingly centers around beer, you're never at a loss for world-class music and theater. For comprehensive listings of performances, check out *Munich Found* (*🖥www.munichfound.de $€3 at newsstands*). Tickets for most events can be purchased at *München Ticket*, a counter at either of the tourist offices (*☎018 054 81 81 81 🖥www.muenchenticket.de*).

Theater, Opera, and Classical Music

As a Wagnerian capital, Munich has a thriving classical music and opera scene, especially in the summertime, as many historic attractions host their own concert series. Get a taste for King Ludwig II's Wagner obsession by attending an opera yourself; the opera festival (*🖥www.muenchener-opern-festspiele.de*) in July features performances in the Pavilion 21 Mini Opera Space, a contemporary expanse of angular steel set up at the square behind the National Theater, as well as Oper für Alle (Opera for All), free open-air concerts and Jumbotron-broadcasted operas under the summer stars.

NATIONAL THEATER 🎫♿ OPERA

Max-Joseph-Pl. 2 ☎089 21 85 19 20 🖥www.bayerische-staatsoper.de

Built by Max Joseph to bring opera to the people, this magnificent theater is now home to the Bayerische Staatsoper and has soaring white balustrades, an enormous chandelier, and rich velvet seating. Student tickets (*from €9*) sold 1hr. before shows at the entrance on Maximilianstrand or two weeks in advance from the box office at Marstallpl. 5 behind the theater. Tickets can also be purchased online.

🚇 U3 or U6: Odeonspl. or Tram 19: Nationaltheater. ℹ Subtitles in German. ISICs not accepted for student tickets; bring alternate forms of ID. $ Guided tours €5, students €4. ⏰ Box office open M-Sa 10am-7pm and 1 hr. before shows. Guided tours of the theater almost daily in the summer in German; English-language tours offered four times a year in July. All tours start at 2pm and last 1hr. See website for details.

STAATSTHEATER AM GÄRTNERPLATZ 🎫♿ THEATER

Gärtnerpl. 3 ☎089 20 23 86 84 🖥www.gaertnerplatztheater.de

This theater in the nightlife hub of Gartnerplatz shows a mix of comic operas, musical theater, and, true to the cultured bohemian atmosphere of the area, artsy-fartsy works from the early 20th century. The steps outside are also a popular hangout spot, perfect for people-watching over a meal on the go.

🚇 Tram 17 or 18: Reichenbachpl. $ Tickets generally €4-60; students always get half price, or certain shows have "KiJu" €8 student tickets. ⏰ Box office open M-F 10am-6pm, Sa 10am-1pm.

PRINZREGENTENTHEATER 🎫♿ CATEGORY

Prinzregentenpl. 12 ☎089 21 85 02 🖥www.prinzregententheater.de

A magnificent theater built as a festival hall for the performance of Wagner's operas, the Prinzregententheater now houses the Bayerische Theaterakademie and shows a number of productions ranging from theater, classical music, opera, to ballet.

🚇 U4: Prinzregentenplatz. $ €8 student tickets available for most shows at the door. ⏰ Box office open M-F 10am-1pm, 2-6pm; Sa 10am-1pm.

GASTEIG KULTURZENTRUM 🎫♿ THEATER

Rosenheimerstr. 5 ☎089 48 09 80 🖥www.gasteig.de

This enormous complex of glass and brick has three concert halls and an ultra-chic black box theater for small, experimental productions. Resting on the former site of the Bürgerbräukeller, where Adolf Hitler launched his failed Beer Hall Putsch, the complex also has a conservatory, a folk music academy, and the renownd Munich Philharmonic. Check out the swirly tuba and piano fountain in the back.

🚇 S1, S2, S3, S4, S5, S6, S7, or S8: Rosenheimerpl. or Tram 18: Am Gasteig. $ Student tickets

for select shows from €8. 🕐 *Building open daily 8am-11pm. Box office open M-F 10am-8pm, Sa 10am-4pm.*

DEUTSCHES THEATER
THEATER

Werner-Heisenberg-Allee 11   ☎089 55 23 44 44 ▣www.deutsches-theater.de

Set in a complex of tents in the outskirts of town, the Deutsches Theater gives off the impression of a traveling circus. Here, though, it's the shows rather than the venues that move, and the 1700-seat Deutsches Theater plays host to many traveling broadway and cabaret musicals making their pit stop in Munich, many in their original English versions.

⚑ *U6: Frottmaning.* 💲 *Student tickets available 30min. before showtime for €25.* 🕐 *Grab your tickets online or from München Ticket; the box office is currently undergoing renovations.*

Film

English films are usually dubbed in German—look for "OV" (original language) and "OmU" (subtitled) on posters or listings. Pick up some facts on the world's most obscure (and some not-so-obscure) topics at Munich's Internationales Dokumentar-filmfestival (▣www.dockfest-muenchen.de), a weeklong international documentary competition held every May. For the more mainstream, the broader Filmfest München (▣www.filmfest-muenchen.de) takes place in mid-summer and is spread out in theaters all across the city. Listings for these festivals, as well as some of the larger cinemas in Munich, can be found in *in München*.

CINEMA
MOVIE THEATER

Nymphenburgerstr. 31   ☎089 55 52 55 ▣www.cinema-muenchen.com

This theater plays almost exclusively English-language films, along with live satellite broadcasts of operas and concerts from all around the world. Sip a *bier* during the movie to remember you're in Munich, or grab some Ben and Jerry's and pretend you're back at home.

⚑ *U1: Stiglmaierpl., then 2 blocks west on Nymphenburgerstr.* ℹ *Reserve tickets online, as movies often sell out.* 💲 *€7.50-8.50, students €6.50-7.50. Matinees M-F before 5:30pm €4.50/€3.50.*

MUSEUM LICHTSPIELE
MOVIE THEATER

Lilienstr. 2   ☎089 482403 ▣wwwmuseum-lichtspiele.de

This cute, quirky little theater is perhaps best known for their weekly showing of Rocky Horror *(F-Sa 11:30pm)*, a tradition that has continued for 34 years. Films are all shown in their original versions, with most of them in English.

⚑ *Tram 18: Deutsches Museum, cross the bridge, and head to the right.* 💲 *Tickets vary by day and time, ranging from €5.50-7.50. Student tickets generally €1 less.*

Other Music

Big-name pop stars usually perform at the Olympiahalle and the Olympiastadion. These being outdoor venues, though, you can always sit on the grass at the Olympia-park and enjoy the music for free. Smaller venues for less mainstream artists can be found at Muffatwerke and Backstage.

🖼 TOLLWOOD FESTIVAL
FESTIVAL

Olympiapark South   ☎0700-38 38 50 24 ▣www.tollwood.de

Munich's annual culture festival attracts a young and active German audience for hundreds of concerts, theatrical productions, and circus shows from the world's leading performers. These spectacular presentations compete for attention amid Oktoberfest-style tents serving delicacies, including Munich's own sweet nectar, beer. Tollwood Magazine, available from the tourist office, lists performances, many of which are free.

⚑ *U3: Olympiazentrum, or take the special MVV bus (Tollwood 99) that runs from Westfriedhof (U1) and Schiedplatz (U2 and U3).* 🕐 *Held mid-June-mid-July and late Nov-Dec. Festival grounds open M-F 2pm-1am, Sa-Su 11am-1am.*

GLOCKENBACH WERKSTATT BÜRGERHAUS ⊕ COMMUNITY CENTER

Blumenstr. 7 ☎089 26 88 38 ▣www.glockenbachwerkstatt.de

By day, this community center hosts a kindergarten and other kid-friendly courses, including dance, soccer, and African drumming. By night, the place transforms into a hub that showcases local talent, with open mic nights, jam sessions, live concerts, and DJ dance parties. A summer courtyard cafe is a choice snack spot for many locals.

✦ *S1, S2, S3, S4, S5, S6, S7, S8, U3 of U6: Marienpl., then wrap around Viktualienmarkt, turn right onto Reichenbachstr., right onto Frauenstr., which turns into Blumenstr. when the road curves.* *i* *Events vary widely from day to day, so check the schedule online.* Ⓢ *Cover charges free-€8.* Ⓩ *Open daily; nighttime events start between 5 and 10pm.*

JAZZCLUB UNTERFAHRT ⊕& JAZZ

Einsteinstr. 42/44 ☎089 448 27 94 ▣www.unterfahrt.de

This subterranean venue hosts the best in the jazz and world music scenes at concerts each evening in a relaxed atmosphere. Performers occasionally also include young talent from local music schools.

✦ *U4 or U5: Max-Weber Pl., then east on Einsteinstr.* *i* *Reservations recommended.* Ⓢ *Entry fee generally €14-16, with student tickets half price.* Ⓩ *Club open daily 7:30pm-1am, F-Sa until 3am; concerts always begin at 9pm.*

Oktoberfest

Every autumn, colonies of tourists make the unholy pilgrimage to Munich to make merry in true Bavarian form. From noon on the penultimate Saturday of September through early October, participants chug five million liters of beer after eating 200,000 Würste. Oktoberfest is the world's largest folk festival—in fact, it has gotten so large and so out of hand that the city has stopped advertising it. Those who plan on attending better have some close Bavarian friends with extra beds, as most budget accommodations are booked up to a year in advance and prices can double or triple depending on the venue.

Oktoberfest began on October 12, 1810, to celebrate the wedding of the future king **Ludwig I** of Bavaria. Representatives from all over Bavaria met outside the city gates, celebrating with a week of horse racing on fields they named Theresienwiese in honor of the bride (U4 or U5: Theresienwiese). The bash was so much fun that Munich's citizens have repeated the revelry (minus the horses) ever since. An agricultural show, inaugurated in 1811, is still held every three years, and a panoply of carousels, carnival rides, and touristy souvenirs continues to amuse beer-guzzling participants.

The festivities begin with the Grand Entry of the Oktoberfest Landlords and Breweries, a parade that ends around noon with the ceremonial drinking of the first keg, to the cry of "O'zapft is!" or "It's tapped," by the Lord Mayor of Munich. Other special events include international folklore presentations, a costume and rifleman's parade, and an open-air concert. Each of Munich's breweries set up tents in the Theresienwiese. The Hofbräu tent is the rowdiest. Arrive by 4:30pm to get a table. You must have a seat to be served alcohol. Drinking hours are relatively short, about 10am-10:30pm, depending on the day, but fairground attractions and sideshows are open slightly later. Those who share a love of alcohol with their kin will appreciate the reduced family day prices every Tuesday noon-6pm.

SHOPPING

When it comes to shopping, Munich is overrun by international chains. You can find just about anything you ever imagined in the city center with its three main shopping streets. **Neuhauserstr.** and **Kaufingerstr.** are connected pedestrian-only streets that run between Karlsplatz (Stachus) and Marienplatz and have no more than four separate H and M's within a half-mile. **Maximilianstr.** is Munich's latest seen-and-be-seen rip-off avenue with shops the likes of Prada and Louis Vuitton and cafes with €12 cups of coffee.

Malls

OLYMPIA-EINKAUFZENTRUM — 💶♿ MALL

Hanauerstr. 68 ☎089 14 33 29 10 🖥www.olympia-einkaufzentrum.de

Set in the outskirts of town, the Olymipa-Einkaufzentrum is your typical mall and the largest in Bavaria. Shops range from the low-end equivalents of dollar stores to mid-level shops like Zara and H and M, and a large food court covering a diverse array of cuisines.

🚇 U1 or U3: Olympia-Einkaufzentrum. ⏰ Open M-Sa 9:30am-8pm.

INGOLSTADT VILLAGE — 💶♿ OUTLET MALL

Otto-Hahn Str. 1 ☎084 18 86 31 00 🖥www.ingolstadt-village.de

This largest outlet center in Germany stocks surplus and slightly damaged name brands for 30-60% discounts. While the prices are not that great compared to American outlet shops, this is a great place to get European name brands not readily available elsewhere. With over 100 stores, it's a great place to exercise your use of plastic on a daytrip.

🚇 A shuttle from Munich runs every Th and Sa, departing from outside the Karstadt by the Hauptbahnhof at 9:30am and outside of San Francisco Coffee Company at Odeonspl. at 9:45am; return to Munich at around 4pm. €15, under 16 free. ⏰ Open M-Sa 10am-8pm.

Electronics

SATURN — 💶♿❄ ELECTRONICS

Neuhauserstr. 39 ☎089 23 68 70 🖥www.saturn.de

This electronics megastore carries everything from stereo systems to headphones, computers to cameras. Cheap finds in the big bins on the ground floor, with an enormous collection of music and DVDs in the basement.

🚇 S1, S2, S3, S4, S5, S6, S7, S8, U4, or U5: Karlsplatz (Stachus). Go past the fountain under the arch to store on right. ℹ Branches throughout Germany. ⏰ Open M-Sa 9:30am-8pm.

Souvenirs

👍 MÜNCHNER GESCHENKE-STUBEN — 💶⊗ SOUVENIRS

Marienpl. 8 and Peterspl. 8 ☎089 22 16 71 🖥www.bavarian-shop.de

Everyone's gotta get some souvenirs, and here's the cheapest place to get it. Ornate steins, postcards, pins, and other trinkets are offered here at half the price of some other nearby souvenir stands.

🚇 S1, S2, S3, S4, S5, S6, S7, S8, U3 or U6: Marienplatz. Locations in the Rathaus (left side) and by Alter Peter. ℹ €20 min. for credit cards. ⏰ Open M-F 9:30am-6:30pm, Sa 10am-6pm.

GALERIE NISCHKE — 💶⊗ PHOTOS

Baaderstr. 52 ☎017 43 22 28 43 🖥www.nischkemuc.com

You'll come here more to ogle than to actually buy, but a tour of this gallery, laden with gorgeous black-and-white panoramic photos of Munich, is definitely worth it. Forget those postcards and get something a little more memorable, if you can afford it.

🚇 U1 or U2: Fraunhoferstr., then turn left (with the river ahead of you) on Baaderstr. [$] Large calendars start at €50. ⏰ Gallery open M-F 2pm-7pm, Sa 11am-4pm.

Books

👍 THE MUNICH READERY — 💶⊗ USED BOOKS

Augustenstr. 104 ☎089 12 19 24 03 🖥www.readery.de

This cozy nook shelves thousands (more like 15,000+) of secondhand books in English, from the latest mystery thrillers to Let's Go guides from 1982. Plop onto one of the comfy black leather sofas and ask the homey staff for some tea.

‡ *U2: Theresienstr., then walk north on Augustenstr.* ℹ *The only used English-language bookstore in southern Germany.* $ *Used books generally €5-10, but frequent sales see prices dropping to as little as €1 per book.* ⏰ *Open M-F 11am-8pm, Sa 10am-6pm.*

WORDS' WORTH BOOKS

Schillingerstr. 3 ☎089 280 91 41 💻www.wordsworth.de

Words' Worth has a large selection of books (including many academic titles) and gift items all in English in their location next to the university.

‡ *U3 or U6: Universität, then a right onto Schillingerstr.* ⏰ *Open M-F 9am-8pm, Sa 10am-4pm.*

HUGENDUBEL 💳♿📶❄ BOOKS

Marienpl. 22 ☎ 089 30 75 75 75 💻www.hugendubel.de

This glorious seven-story bookstore smack-dab in the middle of the city stocks titles on everything you could ever imagine (the *Twilight* series knows no language barriers). The size of the shop offers anonymity if you want to just grab a book and start reading on a stylish red pod. There's a large section of books in English and other languages, as well as language reference materials, on the 5th floor.

‡ *S1, S2, S3, S4, S5, S6, S7, S8 U3, or U6: Marienplatz, in the SE corner of the square.* ℹ *Free Wi-Fi.* ⏰ *Open M-Sa 9:30am-8pm.*

K PRESSE AND BUCH 💳♿📶 NEWSTAND

Hauptbahnhof 1 ☎089 55 11 70

This chain has locations all throughout Munich and the rest of Germany, but one of the branches (there are at least three) in the Hauptbahnhof offers English-language books and periodicals.

‡ *In Hauptbahnhof, across from tracks 24.* ⏰ *Open daily 7am-10:45pm.*

ESSENTIALS ℹ

Practicalities

- **TOURIST OFFICES: EurAide** is Deutsche Bahn's English-speaking office. Staff books train tickets for all European destinations for free. Tickets for public transit and discounted tickets for English-language walking, bus, and bike tours also available. Pick up a free copy of the helpful brochure *Inside Track. (Inside Hauptbahnhof.* ☎*59 38 89.* 💻*www.euraide.com* ⏰ *Open daily May-Sept M-Sa 8am-noon and 2pm-6pm, Su 8am-noon, Oct-Apr M-Sa 8am-noon and 1pm-4pm, Su 8am-noon.)* English-speaking staff books rooms for free with a 10% deposit. Also on-site at each tourist office is Muenchen-Ticket, a booking agency for concerts, theater, and other events. *(Bahnhofsplatz 2, Marienplatz 2.* ☎*23 39 65 00* 💻 *www.muenchen-tourist.de* $ *English city guides €2, and maps €0.40.* ‡ *Take a right out of the main Hauptbahnhof entrance (Bahnhofsplatz), or find it at the base of the Neues Rathaus (Marienplatz).* ⏰ *Gahnhofsplatz loc. open M-Sa 9am-8:30pm, Su 10am-6pm. Marienpl. loc. open M-Sa 10am-8pm, Su 10am-4pm.)*

tours

All of these tour companies offer Third Reich tours, as well as daytrips to Dachau and Neuschwanstein, which always include the cost of transportation. Check out the Sights section for more information on those.

- **BIKE RENTAL AND TOURS:** Pedal, laugh, and down a few beers as you pick up some creative history on one of 👍**Mike's Bike Tours.** *(Bräuhausstr. 10.* ☎*089 25 54*

39 88 *www.mikesbiketours.com* Ⓢ *English city guides €2, maps €0.40. Hefty backpackers' discount with receipt from stay at certain hostels (see website for details).*✠ *S1, S2, S3, S4, S5, S6, S7, S8, U3, or U6: Marienplatz. Tours start at by the tower of the Altes Rathaus.* ✪ *Tours daily from mid-Apr to Aug 11:30am and 4pm, Sept-mid-Nov and Mar-mid-Apr 12:30pm. Office open mid-Apr-Oct 7 10am-8pm; Mar-mid-Apr and Oct 8-Nov 18 10:30am-1pm and 4:30-5:30pm when not raining.)* **Radius Tours** offers historical walking tours of the city in English, including a 2hr. tour of the Altstadt. Bike tours also available. *(Opposite track 32 of the Hauptbahnhof.* ☎*089 55 02 93 74* *www.radiusmunich.com* Ⓢ *Bike tours €18.*✠ *S1, S2, S3, S4, S5, S6, S7, S8, U3, or U6: Marienplatz. Look for the guides in blue and white checkered shirts.* ✪ *Office open Apr-Nov M-F 9am-6pm, Sa-Su 9am-8pm. Tours offered Apr-Oct daily 10:45 and 11:45am. Bike tours May-Oct, every Tu, Th, and Su at 10:30am.)*

- **CONSULATES: Canada** *(Tal 29.* ☎*089 219 95 70* *www.canadainternational. gc.ca* ✠ *S1, S2, S3,S4, S5, S6, S7 or S8: Isartor; look for the gold door to the righ of Conrad.* ✪ *Open M-Th 9am-noon.)* **Ireland** *(Dennigerstr. 15.* ☎*089 20 80 59 90* *www.dfa.ie* ✠ *U4: Richard-Strauss Str.* ✪ *Open M-F 9am-noon.)* **UK** *(Möhlstr. 5.* ☎*089 21 10 90.* *www.ukingermany.fco.gov.uk* ✠ *Tram 18: Effnerpl.* ✪ *Open M-Th 8:30am-noon and 1pm-5pm, F 8:30am-noon and 1pm-3:30pm.)* **US** *(Koniginstr. 5.* ☎*089 288 80* *www.munich.usconsulate.gov* ✠ *U3, U3, U4, U5, or U6: Odeonspl.* ✪ *Open by appointment only.)*

- **CURRENCY EXCHANGE: ReiseBank** has decent rates and Western Union money-wiring office. *(at the front of the Hauptbahnhof.* ☎*089 55 10 80* *www.reisebank. de* ✪ *Open daily 7am-10pm.)* **Exchange AG** will cash travelers' checks with a hefty commission. *(Peterspl. 10.* ☎*089 235 09 20.* ✪ *Open M-F 10am-6pm.)*

- **LUGGAGE STORAGE:** Available at the airport. *(*☎*089 97 52 13 75.* *www. munich-airport.de.)* Also available at the Hauptbahnhof. *(*☎*089 97 52 13 75.)*

- **LOCKERS:** Accessible in the main hall of Hauptbahnhof. *(*Ⓢ *€3-5 per 24hr. for up to 3 days.* ✪ *Open from 4am-12:30am. A staffed storage room in the main hall is open M-F 7am-8pm, Sa-Su 8am-6pm.)*

- **LOST PROPERTY:** Anything lost in the Hauptbahnhof or on DB or S-Bahn trains will find its way to the **DB Lost Property Office.** *(In the Hauptbahnhof by track 26.* ☎*089 13 08 66 64.* *www.fundservice.bahn.de* ✪ *Open M-F 7am-8pm, Sa-Su 8am-6pm.)* Those searching for lost property on the U-Bahn subway lines will be taken to the **Infopoint Office of the MVV.** *(In the Hauptbahnhof.* ☎*089 21 91 32 40.* ✪ *Open M-F 8am-noon and 12:30pm-4pm, Sa-Su 9am-12:30pm and 1pm-5pm.)* **Official Lost Property Office.** *(Ötztalerstr. 17.* ☎*089 23 39 60 45.* *fundbuero.kvr@muenchen.de* ✪ *Open M 8am-noon, Tu 8:30am-noon and 2-5:30pm, W-F 8am-noon.)*

- **GLBT RESOURCES:** Munich is home to a large and liberal gay population, with most of the community centered around Mullerstr. and Gartnerpl. in the Glockenbachvertel. Every summer a pride festival is a popular event along Hans-Sachs-Str, complete with vendors, performances, and plenty of fun. **Leo,** the queer magazine of Bavaria, is published monthly and includes gay-interest articles as well as an events listing. **Blu** is geared toward a younger crowd and reads like a fashion magazine, also with events listings in the back *(**www.blu.fm).* **Rosa Muenchen** is a quarterly directory of all things gay, covering everything from shops to pharmacies to escorts to gay sports teams.

- **GLBT HOTLINES: Gay Services Information.** *(*☎*089 260 30 56* ✪*Open daily 1pm-midnight.)* **Lesbenberatungsstelle LeTra.** *(Angertorstr. 3.* ☎*089 725 42*

72 🖳www.letra.de ⏰ Hotline open M 2:30-5pm, Tu 11:30am-1pm, W 2:30-5pm, Th 7-9pm.) **Schwules Kommunikations und Kulturzentrum,** also called the **"sub,** " has a wealth of resources, counselors, and also staffs a small cafe and library for gay men. English spoken. *(Müllerstr. 43. Information Hotline ☎089 260 33 20. Violence Hotline ☎089 192 28 ⏰ Center open M-Th 7-11pm, F-Sa 7pm-midnight, Su 7-11pm. Their information hotline is staffed daily 7-11pm and their violence hotline is staffed daily from 10am-7pm.)*

- **HOME SHARE: Mitwohnzentrale Wolfgang Sigg GmbH/An der Uni** offers apartments available by the month and a helpful multi-lingual website. *(Fendstr. 6 ☎089 330 37 40 🖳www.mrliving.de ⇄ U3 or U6: Munchener Freiheit. Walk south on Leopoldstr., turn left onto Fendstr. At #6, ring buzzer, and go through the corridor to the 2nd building. ⏰ Open M-F 9am-noon, other hours by appointment.)* **City Mitwohnzentrale** rents apartments for a stay of over 4 days. *(Lämmerstr. 6 ☎089 592 51 01 🖳www.mitwohn.org $ Sublets usually for €300-400 per month. ⇄ By the Arnulfstr. exit of the Hauptbahnhof.)* **Studentenwerk** offers inexpensive housing options for students, though you usually need a university affiliation. *(Leopoldstr. 15 ☎089 38 19 62 83 🖳www.studentenwerk.mhn.de ⇄ U3 or U6: Giselastr.)* **Apartment-Börse Studentenstadt Freimann** offers temporary dormitory housing. *(☎089 324 32 88 🖳aboerse@gmx.de ⇄ U6: Studentenstadt. ⏰ Open M-F 6-8pm.)*
- **VISITOR PUBLICATIONS: New in the City** is an annual publication in German and English covering everything from apartment registration to popular nightlife. Available at local newsstands *(🖳www.newinthecity.de).*
- **WOMEN'S RESOURCES: Kofra Kommunkationszentrum für Frauen** offers job advice, knowledge on lesbian politics, books, magazines, and a small cafe. *(Baaderstr. 30. ☎089 201 0450 🖳www.kofra.de $ Internet €1 per hr. ⏰ Open M-Th 4-10pm, F 2-6pm.)* **Frauentreffpunkt Neuperlach** offers venues and services for women, including an international coffeehouse and English conversation nights. Check website or call for dates and times. *(Oskar-Maria-Graf-Ring 20-22. ☎089 670 64 63 🖳www.frauentreffpunkt-neuperlach.de.)* **Lillemor's Frauenbuchlader** is a women's bookstore. *(Barerstr. 70. ☎089 272 12 05. ⏰ Open M-F 10am-7pm, Sa 10am-2pm.)*
- **DISABLED TRAVELERS: Info Center für Behinderte.** *(Schellingstr. 31. ☎089 211 70. 🖳www.vdk.de/bayern ⏰ Open M-Sa 9am-8pm, Su 10am-6pm.)*
- **TICKET AGENCIES:** Advance tickets are available at **München Ticket**'s retail locations within the tourist offices in the Rathaus in Marienpl. and at the Hauptbahnhof. *(☎018 054 81 81 🖳www.muenchen-ticket.de $ Phone €0.14 per min. ⏰ Rathaus location open M-Sa 10am-8pm, Marienplatz location open M-F 10am-8pm, Sa 10am-4pm.)*
- **LAUNDROMATS: Waschomat** is a bright and cheery laundromat with English-language instructions. *(Parkstr. 8. $ Wash €3.90 (soap €0.40), dry €0.60 per 5min. high-spin or €0.80 per 15min. Happy hour daily 6am-9am wash €3.30. ⇄ Tram 18 from Hauptbahnhof (dir.: Gondrellpl.) or 19 (dir.: Pasing): Holzapfelstr. Turn onto Holapfelstr., take the second right onto Schwanthalerstr., and then turn left onto Parkstr. ⏰ Open daily 6am-midnight.)*
- **INTERNET: San Francisco Coffee Company.** *(Im Tal 15, with other locations throughout the city. $ Free Wi-Fi with the purchase of a coffee.)* **Coffee Fellows Cafe** has an internet cafe on the second floor. *(Schuetzenstr. 14. $ Free Wi-Fi for an hour with any €5 purchase. Wireless or PC use €1.30 per 30min or €2.50 per hour. Black-and-white printing €0.30 per sheet. Faxing €0.50 per sheet within the*

country, €1.00 outside the country.) **Bayerische Staatsbibliothek** has over 8.3 million books, magazines, and newspapers, as well as temporary exhibits. Computers and internet access available, but you'll have to get a library card. *(Ludwigstr. 16 .* ☎*089 28 63 80* ◾*www.bsb-muenchen.de* ⚒ *U6: Universität.* 🕐 *Reading room open 8am-midnight.)*

- **POST OFFICE:** *(*☎*018 03 00 30 08* ⚒ *The yellow building opposite the Hauptbahnhof.* 🕐 *Open M-F 8am-8pm, Sa 9am-4pm.)*

- **POSTAL CODE:** 80335.

Emergency!

- **POLICE:** ☎110.

- **AMBULANCE AND FIRE:** ☎112

- **EMERGENCY MEDICAL SERVICE:** ☎089 19 222

- **EMERGENCY ROAD SERVICE:** ☎089 018 02 22 22 22

- **RAPE CRISIS SUPPORT: Frauennotruf München** *(Gullstr. 3.* ☎*089 76 37 37.* ◾*www.frauennotrufmuenchen.de* 🕐 *Available daily 6pm-midnight.)*

- **AIDS HOTLINE:** In German. *(*☎*089 194 11 or* ☎*089 23 32 33 33* 🕐 *M-F 7-9pm.)*

- **PHARMACIES:** *(Bahnhofpl. 2.* ☎*089 59 98 90 40.* ⚒ *On the corner of the Hauptbahnhof; take a right upon exiting.* 🕐 *Open M-F 7am-8pm, Sa 8am-8pm.)*

- **MEDICAL SERVICES: Klinikum Rechts der Isar.** *(Across the river on Ismanigerstr.* 🕐 *Open 24hr. for emergencies.)* **Münchner Aids-Hilfe e.V.** offers free risk analysis and advice for AIDS and other STDs. *(Lindwurmstr. 71.* ☎*089 54 33 30.* ◾*www.muenchner-aidshilfe.de* Ⓢ *Most tests require a small fee.* 🕐 *Open M, W, and Th 5-8pm.)*

Getting There

Transportation to Munich is never a problem, with direct flights arriving daily from many international locations. In addition, many European cities are accessed with the **Deutsche Bahn,** the German railway system, with trains arriving at the Hauptbahnhof (central station).

By Plane

Munich's international airport, Flughafen München *(Nordalee 25* ☎*089 975 00* ◾*www.munich-airport.de)* is a 45-minute train ride from the city center. Take S1 or S8 to Flughafen *(runs every 10 min.).*

By Train

Munich's central train station, **München Hauptbahnhof,** *(Hauptbahnhof 1* ☎*089 130 81 05 55* ◾*www.hauptbahnhof-muenchen.de)* has arrivals and departures to a host of European cities. All major trains arrive at the HBF. Take S1, S2, S3, S4, S5, S6, S7, S8, U1, U2, U3, U4, or U5 to Hauptbahnhof. Connected cities include **Berlin** *(*Ⓢ *€79.* 🕐 *6hr., 2 per hr.);* **Frankfurt** *(*Ⓢ *from €50.* 🕐 *3hr., 2 per hr.);* **Köln** *(*Ⓢ *from €120.* 🕐 *5hr., 2 per hr.);* **Füssen** *(*Ⓢ *from €20.* 🕐 *2hr., every 2hr.);* **Hamburg** *(*Ⓢ *from €60.* 🕐 *4hr., every hr.);* **Hanover** *(*Ⓢ *from €50.* 🕐 *5hr., every 1hr.);* **Düsseldorf** *(*Ⓢ *from €40.* 🕐 *3hr., 2 per hr.);* **Dresden** *(*Ⓢ *from €80.* 🕐 *6hr., 2 per hr.);* **Bonn** *(*Ⓢ *from €70.* 🕐 *6hr., 4 per hr.);* **Leipzig** *(*Ⓢ *from €60.* 🕐 *4.5hr., 1 per hr.);* **Innsbruck, AUT** *(*Ⓢ *from €30.*🕐 *2hr., ever 2hr.);* **Salzburg, AUT** *(*Ⓢ *from €20.*🕐 *2hr., every hr.);* **Zurich, CHE** *(*Ⓢ *from €50.* 🕐 *5hr., 4-5 per day);* **Prague, CZR** *(*Ⓢ *from €60.* 🕐 *6hr., 4 per day);* **Paris, FRA** *(*Ⓢ *from €129.* 🕐 *6-10hr., 6 per day);* **Amsterdam, NHE** *(*Ⓢ *from €50.* 🕐 *8-12hr., ever 1hr.).* The station also serves as a hub for the city's own public transportation system (the **MVV**).

Getting Around

Munich's pubilc transportation system consists of four integrated components: the **S-bahn,** a surburban train; the **U-bahn,** an underground municipal train; **trams,** and **buses.**

Deutsche Bahn

The S-bahn is under the operation of the Deutsche Bahn network, so Eurail, Inter-Rail, and German railpasses are vaild. S-Bahn to the airport starts running at 3:30am **Ticket Validation:** Before you begin your journey, validate your ticket by getting it stamped in the blue boxes. Plainclothes officers often check for tickets, and those without properly validated tickets are charged a hefty €40 fine. Don't get caught!

MVV Network

The U-bahn, trams, and buses are all part of the city's MVV network (☎089 41 42 43 44 ▨www.mvv-muenchen.de) and require separate ticket purchases. Pick up maps at the tourist office or at the MVV Infopoint office in the Hauptbahnhof. The MVV network runs M-Th 5am-12:30am, F-Sa 5am-2am, and Su 5am-12:30am. Separate NachtTrams (night trams) run every 20 minutes and go to just about everywhere in the city. Tickets come in multiple forms based on how far you're traveling and how long the pass is valid. The simplest form is the single Einzelfahrkarte ticket (€2.40), which is good for two hours for a trip in one direction. All other trips depend on the distance, for which the Munich area is split into 16 different zones of concentric circles around the city center. For short trips (within the same zone), get a Kurzstrecke (€1.20). For multiple rides, buy a stripe ticket (Streifenkarte) which usually comes with 10 stripes (€11.50). Cancel two stripes per zone or one stripe if traveling within the same zone. The zones are further grouped into four different groups for which you can get one-day or three-day passes and single or partner tickets (covering up to 5 adults or children and a dog, with 2 children = 1 adult). There are several cards available.

- **ISARCARDS:** An IsarCard is a week- or month-long pass only available for single travelers that costs only a little more than the 3-day passes. IsarCards, however, only run during the week or month proper (e.g. weekly passes work from Sunday to Sunday, and monthly passes are bought for each specific month), so plan accordingly.

- **CITY TOUR CARD:** This card gets you transportation along with some discounts to Munich attractions. That said, most of these attractions are actually not the more popular ones, and the discounts are tiny. Unless you are planning on going to most of these attractions with a partner ticket, it's probably not worth it.

- **BAYERN TICKET:** The Bayern Ticket gets you access to any public transportation within Bavaria for an entire day (M-F 9am-3am, Sa-Su midnight-3am). The ticket also covers bordering cities including Ulm and Salzburg, making the ticket perfect for day trips to Salzburg and Neuschwanstein. A single ticket costs €20, which is already a considerable savings, but get a group of 5 friends together and pay only €28, which comes to only €5.60 per person.

By Taxi

Taxi-München-Zentrale (☎089 216 10 or 194 10 ▨www.taxizentrale-muenchen.de). A large oasis of taxis waits immediately outside the Hauptbahnhof, or call them directly from one of the 130+ taxi stands located throughout the city (tram and subway maps will usually indicate which stops have taxi stands). Call ahead to make special requests for pet-friendly or large-capacity cars.

By Car

Upstairs at the Hauptbahnhof (opposite track 24) are **Budget** (*i* Online reservations only. ⏰ Open M-F 7am-9pm, Sa-Su 8am-5pm), **Avis** (☎01805 55 77 55 ⏰ open M-F 7am-9pm, Sa-Su 8am-5pm), **Europcar** (☎01805 8000 ⏰ Open M-F 7am-9pm, Sa-Su 8am-7pm), **Hertz** (☎1805 33 35 35 or ☎089 550 2256 ext. 2.⏰ Open M-F 7am-9pm, Sa-Su 9am-5pm), and **Sixt** (☎1805 26 02 50 ⏰ Open daily 6am-9pm).

RADIUS BIKES

➔ BIKE RENTAL

☎089 55 02 93 74 ◼www.radiusmunich.com

Bike rentals available for an hour or longer.

⚑ *Opposite track 32 of the Hauptbahnhof.* ℹ *Helmet included. Deposit €50.* Ⓢ *Bike rental €3-7 per hour, €14.50-18 per day.* 🕙 *Open Apr-Nov M-F 9am-6pm, Sa-Su 9am-8pm.*

MIKE'S BIKE TOURS

BIKE RENTAL

Bräuhausstr. 10   ☎089 25 54 39 87 ◼www.mikesbiketours.com

Bike rentals available for one day or longer.

⚑ *Behind the Hofbräuhaus. From Marienpl., go past Altes Rathaus onto Tal, then turn left onto Hochbrückenstr.* ℹ *Helmet, map, lock, and other accessories included.* Ⓢ *Rental €12 per first day and €9 per day afterward.* 🕙 *Open mid-Apr-Oct 7 10am-8pm; from Mar-mid-Apr and Oct 8-Nov 18 10:30am-1pm and 4:30-5:30pm when not raining.*

DB CALL A BIKE

BIKE RENTAL

☎0700 05 22 55 22 ◼www.callabike.de

DB Call a Bike is a Deutsche Bahn service available by phone after registering online.

ℹ *€5 deposit.* Ⓢ *Rental €0.08 per min. €15 max.*

SECONDHAND SPORTS

➔ BIKE SALE

Nymphenburgerstr. 29   ☎089 59 70 74 ◼www.secondhand-sport.de

This shop sells used bikes from €50 with buyback options. Good selection of outdoor adventure gear, snowboards, skis, and helmets. English-speaking staff also services bikes with a speedy turnaround.

⚑*U1 to Stiglmaierpl.* Ⓢ *Rental €0.08 per min. €15 max.* 🕙 *Open M noon-7pm, Tu-F 10:30am-7pm, Sa 10:30am-4pm.*

starnberg am starnberger see ☎081

ORIENTATION

The beautiful small town of Starnberg, situated at the northern end of the Starnberger See just 20km south of Munich, has been a favorite vacation spot for Germans since the Wittelsbach family named the city its summer destination of choice in the 16th and 17th centuries. Today, leafy forests and shimmering waters of the pristine Starnberger See, capped by the manificent Alps to the south, draw visitors to this oasis of quiet beauty. The town offers a self-guided walking tour, indicated by plaques along the road, to all the main highlights, though the information is only provided in German. The tourist office is located at Wittelsbacherstr. 2c. (☎081 519 06 00 ◼www.sta5.de).

SIGHTS

SEE PROMENADE BOARDWALK

Park benches line the shore, making for excellent people-watching and relaxation. Restaurants along the promenade also offer outdoor seating, perfect for a picturesque coffee break. Basically, an excellent place to sit your arse down all day and feel like you're making something out of it.

⚑ *Exit the train station and take the underground pathway toward the lake.* Ⓢ *€3, students €2.* 🕙 *Open Tu-Su 10am-5pm.*

MUSEUM STARNBERGER SEE

➔& MUSEUM

Possenhofenerstr. 5   ☎081 514 47 75 70 ◼www.museum-starnberger-see.de

Following the signs to the museum, make your way up the steps, and past the rustic houses to this fascinating, all in German, set of exhibits chronicling the rich history of the small town. The more modern **Heimat Museum,** the history museum, includes the "Delphin," the last ship to be comissioned by Ludwig I, complete with a glass cabin. Walk across the glass tunnel to the Lochmann-Haus next door, where budding interior decorators can "ooh" and "ahh" at floorboards dating back to 1474, while history buffs can explore the objects of everyday life in medieval Germany. The objects are all cool, but the information gets lost in translation, so unless you speak German, the museum probably isn't worth your money.

Ⓢ *€3, students €2.* Ⓠ *Open Tu-Su 10am-5pm.*

SAINT JOSEPH KIRCHE

CHURCH

Schloβbergstr. 3

Ready yourself for some serious steps and head uphill to this church, the unique interior of which blends the styles of Baroque, Rococo, and Classical. Yellow arches and rainbow pastel columns support a frescoed ceiling. The white marble altar, designed by famed Rococo master Franz Ignaz Gunther, epitomizes the his penchant for extravagant decoration in gold and silver. Outside, the meticulously manicured gardens and cemetery offers a breathtaking view of the city and the lake below.

Ⓠ *Usually open 9am-5pm, though hours vary sporadically during the winter and in bad weather.*

SCHLOβ STARNBERG

CASTLE

Schloβbergstr. 12

From the other side of the church, take a left past a stone bridge over a wooded lot to see Schloβ Starnberg, once a favorite vacation stop for the Wittelsbachs and now home to government financial offices. The gardens, however, are always open for wandering. Continue down the steps that wrap around the right side, and head onto the sloping roof terrace of the Stadt Starnberg (City Hall). There, admire the juxtaposition of its curviness against the rustic right angles of the Schloβ overhead.

FOOD

If you're hungry, grab a bite at one of the many cafes and restaurants that dot the lakeshore, or try some more traditional beer gardens up the hill in the town itself.

CAFE RESTAURANT CITY

GERMAN ❷

Zweigerstr. 2

☎081 51 64 10

Generous portions of seafood, grilled specialities, and traditional Bavarian food in a quaint setting.

Ⓢ *Entrees €5-12.* Ⓠ *Open daily 11am-10pm.*

SCHINDLER DELIKATESSEN

CAFE, DELI ❸

Maximilianstr. 2   ☎081 51 44 68 89 50 ◫www.schindler-delikatessen.de

This upscale bistro serves up delicious soups, salads, and quiches, as well as picnic-making supplies for a meal along the promenade.

Ⓢ *Entrees €7-14.* Ⓠ *Deli open M-F 9:30am-6:30pm, Sa 9am-2pm. Restaurant open M-Sa noon-10:30pm.*

UNDOSA

ITALIAN, GERMAN ❹

Seepromenade 1   ☎081 51 99 89 30 ◫www.undosa.de

Rich fare is served at this Mediterranean-inspired terrace right on the water's edge. Unparalleled views, live music, and a marble dance floor make this former bathhouse dating from 1888 worth the splurge.

Ⓢ *Entrees €11-19.* Ⓠ *Open daily 10am-11pm.*

ESSENTIALS

Getting There

Take S6 toward Tutzing to Starnberg with the Munich XXL card, (€7.00). The train stops right in the center of town, with the lake to one side. Information listed above is for the tourist information office, which will also book rooms for those looking to stay overnight (🕑 *Open May-Oct M-F 8am-6pm, Sa 9am-1pm*).

Getting Around

Boating on the river is a popular attraction, and you can take an hour-long or three-hour ferry ride offered by the **Bayerische Seen-Schifffahrt** (☎*08151 8061*▣*www. seenschifffahrt.de.* ***i*** *Check board for schedule.* Ⓢ *€8.80-16*) or power it yourself on a kayak or canoe (many vendors along the lake post their prices at the door). Another way to get around the lake for a tour is on a bicycle, popular with tourists in the summer (▣*action-funtours.de*). While you're there, make sure to check out the colorful floating obelisk on the lake to your left before turning to the right and heading onwards to the museum.

andechs ☎081

ORIENTATION

Andechs, a picturesque monastery atop Heiligenbeg hill on the Ammersee, has been a pilgrimage destination since the Middle Ages mostly due to its valuable collection of relics like branches from Christ's thorns and a victory cross from Charlemagne. Learn more at the tourist office (*Bergstr. 2* ☎*081 52 37 60* ▣*www.andechs.de*).

SIGHTS

ANDECHS MONASTERY
👣♿ MONASTERY

Its first cloister dates to 1392, but it gained nortoriety in 1455, when Albrecht III founded a Benedictine monastery here. Albrecht is buried at Andechs, along with a number of 20th-century Wittelsbachs. Shut down during the 1803 secularization of church property, Andechs was bought back by Ludwig I for an outrageous sum and reopened in 1843. Today, around 20 monks are part of the monastery, with seven of them living on the hill.

 ⚑ *After exiting the tourist information office, turn right and walk into town, and follow the brown signs along the stream. Keep following the stream along Kienbachstr., then Andechstr., at the end of which you can turn left onto the Kientalstr., a path that follows the river Kien through a wooded valey, or turn right onto Leitenhöfe and follow the longer 5km scenic route.*

ANDECHS CHURCH
👣♿ CHURCH

The beautiful sundial and onion-topped domes of the pink and white Andechs Church sit stately atop the steep hill leading up to the monastery. The church was built after a fire destroyed its predecessor and was refurbished in spectacular, full-blown Rococo style for the 1755 tercentenary. The sprawling ceiling frescoes and gold accents complement the mural above the altar by Johann Baptist Zimmermann. Also in this church are the celebrated relics, but those are only accessible via a privately guided tour, which, unless you're really into the relics, is probably not worth it. A small chapel on the left houses the remains of the composer Carl Orff, most known for the rousing cantata **Carmina Burana** and an annual summer festival in Andechs that pays homage to his music.

 Ⓢ *Entry free.* 🕑 *Free 30min. German-language tours offered mid-Apr-mid-Oct M-Sa noon, Su 12:15pm. English-, French-, and Italian-langauge tours available by reservation only for private tours (60 min., includes the chapel with the relics, €54 for up to 12 people, or €4.50 per person for more than 12; add €25 for non-German).*

ANDECHS BREWERY — BREWERY

Modern-day pilgrims are motivated by the monks' famous Andechs brew, the sale of which has financed the Benedictines' good works since 1455. The brewery produces 100,00 hectoliters of delicious beer a year, known mostly for its high alcohol content: the Helles is 11.5%, while the Doppelbock Dunkles reaches a dizzying 18.5%.

$ 60min. brewery tours €4.50 per person and includes a €1 voucher for the pub. ⏰ Tours run mid-Apr-mid-Oct every Tu-W at 11am. English-, French-, and Italian-language tours available by reservation only for private tours (60min., €54 for up to 12 people, or €4.50 per person if more; add €25 for non-German).

HERB GARDEN — GARDEN

An herb garden on the premises showcases medicinal and homeopathic plants. Great for a scenic walk.

$ Free. ⏰ Open 24hr. except for a brief break during the winter.

FOOD

BRAUSTUBERL — BEER GARDEN ❷

Join the imbibing crowds of locals for the boisterous atmosphere and panoramic views from the lively terrace. The beer *(from €5.40)* is cheaper than in Munich proper, and the enormous fresh-baked pretzels with butter *(€3.50)* from the monks' dairy farm are definitely worth trying.

$ Meat dishes €1.75 per 100g. ⏰ Open daily 10am-8pm, hot dishes 11am-6:30pm.

KLOSTERGASTHOF — RESTAURANT ❹

Those wanting a more sit-down experience can grab a proper meal here, with even cheaper beer *(from €3.60)* but more expensive entrees.

$ Entrees €6-18. ⏰ Open daily 10am-11pm, kitchen closes at 10pm.

SHOPPING

KLOSTERLADEN — SOUVENIRS

Don't leave without getting some souvenirs from your trip. In addition to the usual trinkets, you can also bring back some Andechs brew *(4 bottles €8.20)*, including the schnapps that the monks produce with herbs, apples and pears, berries, and honey *(500 ml €13.75; 20ml nips €1.95)*. English guide books are also available here.

⏰ Open Feb-Dec M-F 10am-5:30pm, Sa-Su 10am-6:30pm.

ESSENTIALS

Getting There

Take the S8 to Herrsching *(⏰45 min. i Use a €10.40 Gesamtnetz Tageskarte)*. Once in Herrshing, check with the Tourist Information office across the street on MVV bus schedules; there is also a **private bus** *(⏰ runs every 30min. $€2.20)*. You can also bike or hike the 3.5-km. trails to Andechs.

VIENNA

Vienna is a city where you can live in both the past and the present. While half of the city floats majestically along in the 17th and 18th centuries, the other half zooms into the 21st, creating a fusion of time and space that will transport you from one age to the next in a blink of an eye.

First and foremost, Vienna is a city of the arts. After all, it seems that every classical music genius lived and worked in Vienna; Mozart, Beethoven, Schubert, Strauss, Brahms, and Haydn all came to Vienna at some point in their lives. Walk by an apartment building in the Inner Stadt, and you will probably hear the practice of a violin coming from within. Or just walk down a major street and lose track counting theaters with nightly music, theater, and dance performances.

Famous thinkers like Sigmund Freud met to pore over controversial ideas, while artists like Hundertwasser, Klimt, and Schiele painted so many masterpieces that Vienna has enough museums to last a lifetime, and in just a few days you can barely scratch the surface.

The cobbled streets of Vienna's Inner Stadt conjure an Old World romance that is still reflected in the people's love for tradition—where else in the world do people waltz en masse on New Year's Eve? Yet, for its upcoming generation, Vienna offers the modern shopping, dining, and wnightlife of any cosmopolitan city—clubs cluster under the brick train track archways, and small cocktail bars craft drinks as an art form. Walk through Belvedere and see modern art sculptures or to drink wine overlooking vineyards and the Danube—the old and the new, the city and the country—all of it is within reach.

greatest hits

- **THE HIGH GROUNDS.** Wander around Schloß Schönbrunn—an imperial summer residence with a French garden that harkens to Versailles (p. 312).

- **DRINK LIKE A FISH.** Sip some of the strongest cocktails of your life at First Floor, where a modern fish aquarium runs the length of the bar (p. 320).

- **PLEASE DON'T STOP THE MUSIC.** Gorge on food, drink, and free music at Donauinsel Fest, held every June on Danube Island (p. 326).

- **ONE-NIGHT STAND.** Buy a €5 standing-room ticket to Mozart's *Don Giovanni* at the gorgeous Staatsoper (p. 325).

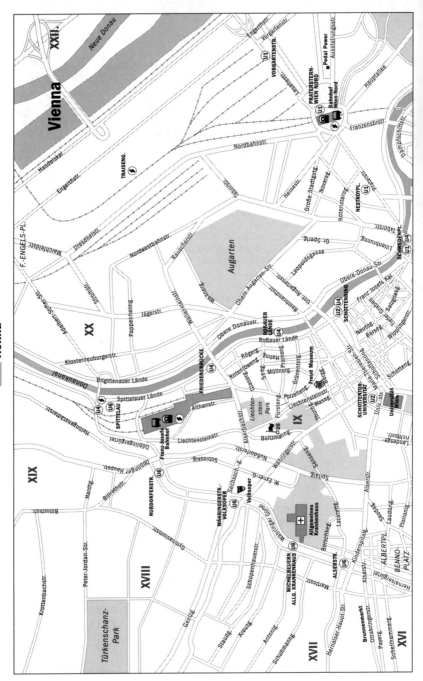

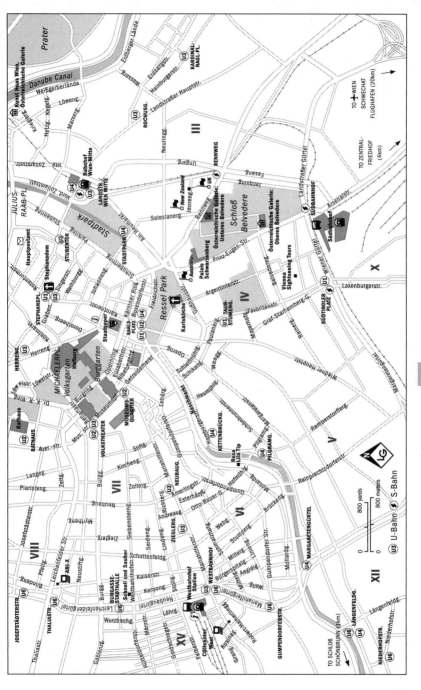

vienna

Leave your hostel in Mariahilf or Neubau, and pick up some bargain breakfast at **Naschmarkt**—an open-air market stocked with delicious ingredients and prepared meals alike. After refueling, split from the Core Districts, and head for the Inner City. Pick up a sexy librarian tour guide at Nationalbibliothek, then people-watch at Franziskanerplatz with a cappuccino from **Kleines Cafe.** When the sun sets, head to **First Floor** for some drinks with other Viennese youth, or get your culture on at Staatsoper, where standing room tickets start at just €2.50. Head to **Shakespeare and Company Booksellers** when you've exhausted the city, and find discover your next destination in their extensive travel section.

orientation

INNER CITY

Vienna's Inner Stadt is the city's heart and soul, and if you are only visiting for a few days, you will undoubtedly spend most of your time here. Named a UNESCO World Heritage Site in 2001, this historical area measures a mere 1.4 sq. mi.—it's hard to believe so much is crammed into such a small space. At the center of the district is the grand, gothic **Stephansdom** at Stephanspl., from which the district's main arteries extend— **Rotenturmstrasse** leads toward the Danube canal and the nightlife of the "Bermuda Triangle," while in the opposite direction, the shopping thoroughfare of **Karntner Strasse** paves the path toward the Opera House. The grandest of all is **Graben** with its historic facades (ignore the McDonald's golden arches and the H and M signs), connecting to **Kohlmarkt** and eventually leading to the **Hofburg Palace,** the Hapsburg Empire's former headquarters. Though a museum, church, or palace is literally around every corner, the real pleasure of the Inner Stadt is getting lost in its winding streets of Baroque, medieval, and Jugendstil architecture. You will pass cafes with patrons overflowing into the streets, and then suddenly find yourself in a quiet grassy plaza with a few benches. The clickety-clack of horse shoes on cobblestones can't help but transport you to another time, even if the tourist hustlers dressed up as Mozart remind you every now and again that it is in fact the 21st century.

CORE DISTRICTS

If the crowds of tourists in the Inner Stadt are driving you camera-crazy, the Core Districts offer a series of lesser known, but just as interesting, sights that are really not as far away as they may seem on the map. These districts (numbers II-IX) are also home to the majority of local Viennese and city inhabitants and offer a modern-day flavor and diversity that may have originally seemed to fall through the cracks in the Inner Stadt cobblestone streets.

Across the Danube canal to the east is the gritty second district, **Leopoldstadt,** which, although home to the overly photographed Prater Reisenrad and Augarten, is otherwise rather un-picturesque. In a C-shape around the Inner Stadt, districts III through IX fan out in a counter-clockwise direction. The third district, **Landstrasse,** to the south, is home to the sweeping grounds of Schloβ Belvedere with the famous Klimt collection, and color-crazy, quirky Kunsthaus Wien and Hundertwasser Haus. The fourth, **Weiden,** and the fifth, **Margareten,** offer some of the greatest palate pleasures; the tasty **Naschmarkt** and **Gumpendorfer Strasse,** with their collections of cafes, restaurants, and coffeehouses, have some of the city's best dining experiences.

If you are booking a hostel, it's likely you will be staying in the sixth, **Mariahilf,** or the seventh, **Neubau.** Mariahilf is named after the city's longest shopping throrough-fare, Mariahilferstr., with more H and M branches than can be counted on two hands as well as many other international chain stores, ice-cream shops, and shoe stores. The seventh district stretches west from the Museum Quartier and is refreshingly non-mainstream next to Mariahilf. Many of the city's young artisans have set up high-end boutiques with creative clothing and jewelry, the nightlife is vibrant, and the for-mer red-light district of Spittelberg offers some cobblestoned character to the area. Behind the Rathaus (City Hall), the eighth district of **Josefstadt** is a comparatively quiet residential area, with the exception of the nightlife hot spot along the **Gürtel** (the Belt Road). Here, the bars are built into the structure of the Stadtbahn, where the U6 runs, creating a funky underground vibe where DJs spin and the drinking never ends. **Alsergrund,** the ninth district, is mainly home to the university campus and a wealthier enclave. The spectacular spires of **Votivkirche** accompany some more notable museums, including the **Lichenstein.**

OUTER DISTRICTS

The Outer Districts (numbers X and up) encircle the core districts starting from the south in a clockwise direction and include far fewer sights and way more locals. Welcome to suburbia, baby. The southernmost districts, **Simmering (XI), Favoriten (X),** and **Meidling (XII)** are not terribly interesting and are generally avoided by tourists, with the exception of the Zentralfriedhof. Locals consider these blue-collar neigh-borhoods the underbelly of the city, and this may be the only area with the potential for danger.

By far the most popular draw for tourists in the Outer Districts are the grounds and imperial rooms of **Schloβ Schonbrunn** in the 13th, one of the most spectacular sights in the whole city. In the 14th, Otto Wagner's **Kirche am Steinhof** glistens among a

backdrop of green hillside in one of the city's wealthier districts, Hietzing.

Just beyond the Gürtel in the 15th and 16th, a number of additional hostels lie along and around the top portion of Mariahilferstr., around Westbahhof. With the exception of the commercial Mariahilferstr., this area tends to feel either industrial or strictly residential, and even dining options become more limited. The 15th, **Rudolfsheim-Funfhaus,** houses much of the immigrant population, including Turks and Serbs.

A gem of the Outer Districts is **Dobling (XIX)** and, in particular, the *heurigers* (wine taverns) of **Grinzing,** where you can spend an evening dining (and drinking) and arrive back in the city happily tipsy. Over the past few years, this has become a popular stop for tourists wishing to get a bit of the countryside, and so at times there is the inevitable eyesore of the coach tour buses. If you can Photoshop those out of your mental picture, Grinzing is a pleasure, with quiet tree-lined streets and cobbled plazas. There are still many fine dining options and *heurigers* without the tourist souvenirs; be sure to find one with a spectacular view out into the vineyards and over the Danube.

accommodations

INNER CITY

There are no budget accommodations in the Inner City. Be prepared to spend your life savings here.

ALMA BOUTIQUE HOTEL
💳♿📶🍸❄ HOTEL [5]

Hafnersteig 7 — ☎1 533 296 10 🖥www.hotel-alma.com

All 26 rooms at the Alma have been newly renovated into sleek, modern singles and doubles with private baths. The decorations are "Viennese Art Noveau," tasteful splashes of red and large designs in gold manage to be professional and not cross the line into tacky. From the flatscreen TVs and Wi-Fi to biscuits on your pillow, this hotel offers all the comforts of home and more.

🚇 U1 or U4: Schwedenpl.; Tram 1 or 2. ℹ Breakfast included. $ Singles €87-122; doubles €127-188. ⏰ Reception 24hr.

PENSION PERTSCHY
💳♿📶 PENSION, HOTEL [5]

Habsburgergasse 5 — ☎1 53 44 90 🖥www.pertschy.com

This pension is the closest you'll come to living in an imperial-style room at a reasonable price. The singles and doubles (some of which can actually accommodate three or four people) are traditionally decorated with gold-trimmed cabinets and hanging chandeliers. Size varies greatly, so consider booking a superior or deluxe double room if you want extra legroom.

🚇 U1 or U3: Stephanspl. ℹ Breakfast included. $ Singles €79-122; doubles €119-188. Extra bed €23-38. ⏰ Reception 24hr.

HOTEL POST
💳♿📶 HOTEL [5]

Fleischmarkt 24 — ☎1 51 58 30 🖥www.hotel-post-wien.at

Mere steps away from the bustling Schwedenpl. and all the other Inner Stadt sights, these rooms are a great price for the location, especially in comparison to the other first district hotels. The hotel was recently refurbished, and the rooms feel clean, though the decor leaves something to be desired.

🚇 U1 or U4: Schwedenpl.; Tram 1 or 2. ℹ Breakfast included. $ Singles €42-51, with bath €73-87; doubles €68-79/100-130; triples €87-103/120-157. ⏰ Reception 24hr.

PENSION RIEDL
💳♿📶 PENSION [5]

George Coch Pl. 3 — ☎1 512 79 19 🖥www.pensionriedl.at

Located on the fourth floor of a beautiful Inner Stadt building (sweeping staircase, gated elevator) on a quiet plaza, this pension offers single and double rooms. Each of the 10 rooms is different—some are more spacious while others have balconies, and four are soon to be renovated. The already newly renovated rooms have larger showers and fancy beds.

🚋 *Tram 1 or 2: Julius Raab Pl.* ℹ *Breakfast €8.* Ⓢ *Singles €50-77; doubles €70-110.* 🕑 *Reception 7:30-11:15am and 4-8pm.*

CORE DISTRICTS

▧ BELIEVE-IT-OR-NOT HOSTEL ⊛⊗⁽ᵞ⁾ HOSTEL ❸
Myrthengasse 10, Apt. 14 ☎676 55 000 55 💻www.believe-it-or-not-vienna.at

Don't let the entrance fool you—this hostel has more spunk, character, and free stuff than you will believe. As an apartment that has been converted into a hostel, Believe-It-Or-Not has a full living room and kitchen for use, and the rooms of only four or eight beds are styled like a ski lodge. Spiral stairs lead up to the top bunks in the four-person rooms. Be sure to sign your name in gold or silver on the black furniture in the foyer—it's the guestbook!

🚌 *Bus #48A.* Ⓢ *8-bed dorms with shared bath €24; 4-bed dorms with private bathroom €28.* 🕑 *Reception 8am-noon, 24hr. availability over intercom.*

WESTEND CITY HOSTEL ⊛♿⁽ᵞ⁾⌂ HOSTEL ❷
Fuegergasse 3 ☎1 597 67 29 💻www.westendhostel.at

Westend City Hostel will welcome you to Vienna with a helpful English-speaking staff and a variety of room types to choose from. Every room is different, though most have a table and chairs and all have an ensuite toilet and shower. All kinds of amenities are available... even alarm clocks for rent.

🚇 *U3 or U6: Westbahnhof.* ℹ *Breakfast, linens, and Wi-Fi included.* Ⓢ *4- to 12-bed dorms €20.50-27; singles €52-70; doubles €31-44. Rates increase during summer and holidays.* 🕑 *Reception 24hr.*

PENSION KRAML ⊛⊗⌂ PENSION ❹
Brauergasse 5 ☎1 587 85 88 💻www.pensionkraml.at

This family-run pension is the epitome of hospitality. All of the rooms are sparkling clean, spacious, and plush with wall-to-wall carpeting. Some have shared bath but still have a sink in the room. This prime real estate includes a buffet breakfast, and is definitely worth the extra moolah if you can afford it.

🚇 *U3: Zieglergasse or U4: Pilgramgasse.* ℹ *Breakfast and Wi-Fi included.* Ⓢ *Singles €35; doubles €56-66, with bath €76-87; triples €78/76-87; family apartment (3-5 people) €99-135.* 🕑 *Reception 24hr.*

K AND T BOARDINGHOUSE ⊛⊗⁽ᵞ⁾❋ PENSION ❺
Mariahilferstr. 72 ☎208 35 48 💻www.ktboardinghouse.at

Located directly off the bustling Mariahilferstr., these apartment-style rooms are classically decorated with curtains, light wood floors, and additional furniture such as a table and chairs. If this location is booked, there is a brand new K and T Boardinghouse 2 just a few steps away *(Chwallagasse 2)* where extremely spacious beige-toned rooms come with large comfy couches.

🚇 *U3: Neubaugasse.* ℹ *Inform reception of arrival time when making a booking. A/C €10 per night.* Ⓢ *Singles €79; doubles €79; triples €99; quads €119.*

HAPPY HOSTEL ⊛⊗⁽ᵞ⁾⌂ APARTMENTS, HOSTEL ❷
Kurzgasse 2 ☎1 208 26 18 💻www.happyhostel.at

Renting out one of Happy Hostel's apartments will certainly make you and your group of travelers happy. The apartments have kitchens and ensuite baths as well as spacious living areas with TVs and couches. In a newer building across the street, the limited dorm rooms are more standard with bunk beds, shared bathrooms, and wooden floors.

🚏 *U3 or U6: Westbahnhof.* *i* *Internet access included.* Ⓢ *3- to 6-bed dorms €15-23, with kitchen and bath €18-27; singles €33-36; doubles €44-52/54-72; apartments €42-48 per person.* ⏰ *Reception 24hr.*

JUGENDHERBERGE MYRTHENGASSE HOSTEL ❷

Myrthengasse 7 ☎1 523 63 16 💻www.hihostels.com

Highly popular with HI regulars, the 3- to 4-bed dorms in this hostel book up quickly in the busy summer months. The linoleum-floor rooms are not particularly homey, but they do have a private showers (toilets in the halls) and are kept extremely clean. Lockers, great lounge spaces, and an outdoor courtyard complete this dependable hostel, and there is a hearty daily dinner offered for €6.

🚏 *Bus 48A.* *i* *Reservations recommended in summer months. HI card required.* Ⓢ *Dorms €16.50-17.50; doubles €19.50-20.50.* ⏰ *Reception 24hr.*

PANDA HOSTEL HOSTEL ❶

Kaiserstr. 77, 3rd fl. ☎1 522 25 55 💻www.panda-vienna.at

Located on the third floor of an apartment building, Panda Hostel feels like staying in a large apartment with dormmates. The rooms have high ceilings (with really tall bunk beds), but they are spacious and have tables, chairs, or couches for extra seating. The small kitchen has no stove, so don't anticipate high-quality cooking, but there is a refrigerator and microwave.

🚏 *Bus 48 A. Tram 5.* *i* *2-night min. stay.* Ⓢ *5- to 7-bed dorms €15.* ⏰ *Reception 8am-2pm. Check-in until 11pm. Lockout 10am-2pm.*

HOTEL PENSION WALZERSTADT PENSION ❹

Zieglergasse 35 ☎1 523 71 22 💻www.walzerstadt.at

Pensions, unlike hostels, have a few extra comforts for a few extra euro. Walzerstadt offers these extra bits (and you don't have to feel guilty about walking in at 3am and waking your dormmates), in addition to the desirable location amid nightlife. The ridiculously clean rooms have simple decorations and are sometimes small or oddly shaped, but all have private bath and Wi-Fi.

🚏 *Tram 49.* *i* *Breakfast €5.50. All rooms have private bath Ring bell for reception.* Ⓢ *Singles €68-75; doubles €98-110; triples €132-144. Extra bed €25.*

BAG AND MAP APARTMENT GUESTHOUSE APARTMENT ❷

Wimbergasse 31 ☎1 957 69 34 💻www.bagandmap.com

Hidden on a quiet residential street, Bag and Map Apartment Guesthouse is on the top floor of an old, traditional building. Many of the rooms are apartment style, including a convenient private kitchen for cooking. While this is not for travelers who want to meet their neighbors or make new hostel friends, you will certainly be comfortable here.

🚏 *U6: Burrgasse. Tram 18.* *i* *All rooms and apartments have private bathrooms. Ring bell for reception.* Ⓢ *Doubles €52-58; triples €69-78.*

LABYRINTH HOSTELS HOSTEL ❶

Lindengasse 4 💻www.hostelworld.com

When the receptionist says, "the rooms are nothing special" it might not really encourage you to stay here. So, we guess that's what you can expect—basic bunks in plain rooms. Despite that, the location, in the heart of the artsy Neubau district with cool boutiques and bars at your doorstep, is a major selling point.

🚏 *U3: Neubaugasse.* Ⓢ *16-bed dorms €13; 10-bed dorms €15 6-bed dorms €17; 4-bed dorms €19.* ⏰ *Reception 9am-midnight.*

OUTER DISTRICTS

HOSTEL RUTHENSTEINER HOSTEL ❷

Robert Hamerlinggasse 24 ☎1 89 342 02 or 1 89 327 96 💻www.hostelruthensteiner.com

With its quiet flowered courtyard, countryside-style living room, and even a bar made out of solid cherry-wood, this hostel will undoubtedly feel like home. The rooms have a rustic feel, with wood-plank doors and prints from famous Vienna artists like Klimt and Hundertwasser on the walls, and many also are off the balcony overlooking the courtyard. To add to its character and charm, there is a free book exchange and musical instruments for guest use.

🏃 *U3 or U6: Westbahnhof. Walk down Mariahilferstr. away from the train station and take a left on Haidmannsgasse. Your 1st right will be Robert Hamerlinggasse, and you will see a sign for the hostel.* *i* *Wi-Fi and lockers included. Book exchange and musical instruments available. Credit card surcharge 3%.* Ⓢ *8-bed dorms €15-20; 3- to 5-bed dorms €17-22. Doubles €25-27, with bath €28-30.* Ⓩ *Reception 24hr.*

WOMBATS CITY HOSTEL—THE LOUNGE 🏄♿📶♈ HOSTEL ❷
Mariahilferstr. 137 ☎1 897 23 36 🖥www.wombats.eu

Just 50m from Westbahnhof, Wombat's newest Vienna hostel is young, social, and in the know. The receptionists will gladly assist you in getting settled in your bunk, where your magnetic key card also automatically locks your locker, so you don't have to worry about a clunky padlock. The rooms are all ensuite and immaculate—a few years ago, the Lounge was elected as the cleanest hostel worldwide. From 6pm onward, meet new friends and grab cheap drinks in the womBar downstairs.

🏃 *U3 or U6: Westbahnhof.* *i* *Wi-Fi, lockers, and luggage storage included. Breakfast €4.* Ⓢ *4- to 6-bed dorms €16-29; doubles €29-39.* Ⓩ *Reception 24hr.*

HOSTEL SCHLOßHERBERGE 🏄⊗♨ HOSTEL ❷
Savoyenstr. 2 ☎1 481 0300 🖥www.hostel.at

Located on the outskirts of the District XVI on the grounds of an old palace, this hostel is certainly not your average city hostel. Heck, it's practically in the woods, as you will see when you take the bus to the top of the hill, after also riding the U-bahn. The large grassy space overlooks the city, with plenty of room for sunbathing, a volleyball net, and even a minigolf course. The rooms are all ensuite, with bunks and locker space. Keep your fingers crossed that you end up in one of the first-floor rooms with the doors that open directly onto the lawn with the spectacular view.

🏃 *U3: Ottakring. From the stop, take Bus 46A or 146A: Schloß Wilhelminenberg* *i* *Breakfast, parking and Wi-Fi included. Notify reception if you plan to arrive after 10pm.* Ⓢ *4-bed dorms €19-27; 3-bed dorms €22-32.50. Singles €50-60; doubles €57-73.*

DO STEP INN 🏄⊗📶♨ PENSION, HOSTEL ❸
Felberstr. 20 ☎699 19 23 27 69 🖥www.dostepinn.at

Many of these double and triple rooms have beds with frames (no bunks!), lending this pension the professionalism of a hotel. The rooms are all ensuite and have sparkling new wood flooring, yet, possibly to some inconvenience, you must rent by the room, not by the bed. The common spaces and kitchens are adorned with colorful mosaics and potted plants that emphasize the old-style building and spiral staircase. While the locale is not ideal, the walk to more bustling streets is not too strenuous.

🏃 *U3 or U6: Westbahnhof. Exit from the upper platform, turn left on Felberstr.* *i* *Luggage storage, lockers, and Wi-Fi included. Credit card surcharge 4%.* Ⓢ *Singles €35-39, with bath €45-49.50; doubles €44-48.40/52-70; triples €51-55.50/66-75; quads €60-66/75.60-76.60.* Ⓩ *Reception open daily 8am-9pm. Ring bell for entrance.*

WOMBATS CITY HOSTEL—THE BASE 🏄♿📶♈♨ HOSTEL ❷
Grangasse 6 ☎1 897 23 36 🖥www.wombats.eu

The original Wombats hostel in Vienna is a few blocks off Mariahilferstr., and is not quite as shiny and spunky as its younger sibling. The bright blue building feels a bit grittier, with darker masculine tones and slightly smaller rooms, though the cleanliness standard is still A+. The Base has all the same perks as the Lounge (Wi-Fi, ensuite rooms, etc.), and as an added bonus, there is a terrace bar to enjoy drinks outside on warm summer nights.

🚇 U3 or U6: Westbahnhof. Follow Mariahilferstr. until no. 152, then turn right into Rosinagasse. Take your second left. ℹ Wi-Fi in common spaces, lockers, and luggage storage included. Breakfast €3.50. Ⓢ 4- to 6-bed dorms €14-29; doubles €50-78; triples €60-87. ⏰ Reception 24hr.

HOSTEL HUTTELDORF
💳♿🌳 HOSTEL [2]

Schloßberggasse 8 ☎1 877 02 63 💻www.hostel.at

Located off the western end of the U4 line, Hostel Hutteldorf is not for party animals who plan on having late nights (unless, of course, you are a party animal that will keep going until the Ubahn opens the next morning at 5am). The majority of the four- to six-bed rooms are located in the high-rise building that has views of the city and the hills, and it's worth booking ahead to reserve this rather than being stuck in the 20-bed dorm (which is, strangely enough, the same price as the 6 bed-dorm). The hostel highlight is the large grassy backyard lawn surrounded by trees—great for a lazy afternoon of sleeping and sunbathing.

🚇 U4: Hutteldorf. Exit to Hadikgasse, then follow the signs to the hostel. ℹ Wi-Fi, luggage storage, lockers, and breakfast included. Ⓢ 6- or 20-bed dorms €13-22; 4-bed dorms €16-27; 3-bed dorms €17.50-30. Singles €28-50; doubles €40-72. ⏰ Reception 24hr.

A AND O WIEN
💳♿📶🍸🌳 HOSTEL [1]

Lerchenfelder Gürtel 9-11 ☎1 49 30 480 39 00 💻www.aohostels.com

The Vienna branch of A and O's hostel chain is located on the busy Gürtel road, closer to the outskirts of the city. Inside, don't expect coziness; the rooms are basic with metal-framed bunks and lockers in a tall high-rise building. Luckily, the large windows offer plenty of light and air. Despite the lack of homey decor, A and O does offer all the other necessities such as Wi-Fi, luggage storage, easy bike rental, and plenty of brochures to guide you around the city.

🚇 U6: Burggasse Stadthalle. ℹ Breakfast €4. Ⓢ 8- to 10-bed dorms from €12, with bath from €13; 4- to 6-bed dorms from €13/15; doubles with bath €25; singles with bath €39. ⏰ Reception 24hr.

HOTEL HADRIGAN
💳♿📶 HOTEL [3]

Maroltingergasse 68 ☎1 604 00 00 💻www.hadrigan.com

Just as long as you are not expecting the Marriott, the facilities of this budget hotel should suit your stay in the city just fine. The rooms are cleaner and fresher than the common spaces, with new coats of paint and simple decorations for a homey feel. Ignore the faux-oriental rugs in the hallways and the dim lighting and focus on the clean sheets and comfy pillows.

🚇 U3: Ottakring. Ⓢ Singles €40-64; doubles €44-69; family rooms (3-4 beds) €64-99. ⏰ Reception 24hr.

HOTEL GEBLERGASSE
💳♿📶 HOTEL [3]

Geblergasse 21 ☎1 406 33 66 💻www.geblergasse.com

While the lobby and common spaces have seen better years, the newly renovated rooms are surprisingly crisp, clean, and very white—white sheets, white walls, white curtains. The location is a toss-up: there is a sex shop around the corner, but it's also within close distance to public transportation and you will not be bothered by noise or traffic at night.

🚇 U6: Alser Str. ℹ Free Wi-Fi, safe and TV in room. All rooms ensuite. Ⓢ Singles €34-89; doubles €49-99; family rooms (3-6 beds) €79-139. Parking €9 per day. Rates vary greatly, so check website. ⏰ Reception 24hr.

PENSION ELIZABETH
🚫🚫 PENSION, APARTMENTS [2]

Holochergasse 17 ☎1 983 56 34

These apartment-style rooms are quite off the beaten track; you are literally staying in extra rooms in a residential apartment building a good 10 blocks beyond Westbahnhof. Instead of any cohesive decor scheme, rugs, refrigerators, leftover beds, and mismatched dining furniture seem haphazardly thrown together to furnish these sometimes cramped or oddly shaped spaces. There won't be the opportunity to meet other travelers here because the rooms are entirely self-sufficient, and at most you will share a kitchenette or bathroom with one other room.

🚏 U3 or U6: Westbahnhof. Exit from the upper platform, then turn left on Felberstr. Turn right on Holochergasse (it will be after the 2nd bridge on your left). ℹ Rooms must be rented by the room, not bed. Ring bell. $ 2- to 6-bed rooms €19.50-29 per person.

sights

INNER CITY

STEPHANSDOM — ♿ 📷 CHURCH

Stephanspl. ☎1 515 52 35 26 🖥www.stephanskirche.at

Monolithic by day and ethereal by night, this Gothic masterpiece is one of Vienna's must-see sights. Its massive towers and colorful tiled roof depicting the Hapsburg crown punctuate the city skyline, dwarfing the plaza and people below. Inside, the high-vaulted ceilings and arches offer a somber darkness, broken only by the rustling of tourists and their cameras. You can enter the cathedral at the back for free, while the €3 ticket will get you up close to the nave and stone-carved pulpit.

🚏 U1 or U3: Stephanspl. $ Church admission €3, with audioguide €4.90. Catacomb tour €4.50, children €1.50. Tower and bell €4.50/1.50. All-inclusive ticket €14.50, students €12. ⏰ Church open M-Sa 6am-10pm, Su 7am-10pm. Bell and tower open daily 8:15am-4:30pm. Tours M-Sa 9-11:30am and 1-4:30pm, Su 1-4:30pm.

ALBERTINA — 🎟 ♿ 🍸 ⛅ MUSEUM, STATE ROOMS

Albertinapl. 1 ☎1 534 830 🖥www.albertina.at

A ticket to the Albertina grants you access to all the impressive museum floors in addition to a series of plush state rooms (which are, dare we say, nicer than the main Hofburg complex, and far less crowded). The permanent art collection on the top floor encompasses all the modern art greats, including Degas, Picasso, Miro, and Kandinsky, to name just a few. The remaining exhibits rotate every few months, and temporary exhibits on Picasso, Michaelangelo's drawings, and South African artist William Kentridge will be presented through early 2011.

🚏 U1 or U3: Stephanspl. Or U1, U2, or U4: Karlspl. $ Adults €9.50. Seniors and Vienna card holders €8, under 19 free. Audioguide €4. ⏰ Open M-Tu 10am-6pm, W 10am-9pm, Th-Su 10am-6pm.

HOFBURG PALACE — 🎟 ♿ 🍸 MUSEUM, IMPERIAL APARTMENTS

Heldenpl. ☎1 533 75 70 🖥www.hofburg-wien.at

A visit inside the Hofburg consists of three parts: the Imperial Silver Collection, a museum about Empress Elisabeth, and the Imperial Apartments where Franz Joseph and Elisabeth lived. The Silver Collection is an extensive display of cutlery, plates, bowls, and centerpieces—gold, silver, porcelain—in every shape, size, and design imaginable. In this portion of the museum, the audioguide is particularly helpful (and concise) at guiding visitors through what would otherwise be one packed display case after the next. The Sisi Museum then delves into the life of Empress Elisabeth Sisi, from her childhood to tragic death, with artifacts and stunning replicas of her gowns and jewels. Finally, the Imperial Apartments, the most interesting part of the Palace, you can see where Franz worked, slept, and ate and even where Elisabeth bathed.

🚏 U3: Herrengasse. Or, U2 or U3: Volkstheater, then Tram 1 or 2. ℹ Audioguide free with entrance

ticket. $ *Tickets for each sight €10, students €9, ages 6-18 €6. Sisi Ticket (entrance to all 3 Hofburg venues plus the Furniture Collection and Schonbrunn Palace) €22.50, students €20, ages 6-18 €13.50, family (2 adults, 3 children) €47. Tours €2.50, children €1.* ⏰ *Open daily July-Aug 9am-6pm; Sept-June 9am-5:30pm.*

NATIONALBIBLIOTHEK/STATE HALL — LIBRARY

Josefpl. 1 ☎1 534 10394 🖥www.onb.ac.at

Bookworms should not miss this stunning Baroque library, one of the most beautiful historical libraries in the world. Commissioned by Emperor Charles VI, the library has double-story nutwood bookcases, marble statues, rose-and-cream marble floors and pillars, and pastel ceiling frescoes that stretch to every corner. Today, the library holds over 200,000 volumes that can still be accessed in the adjacent reading room and also has two temporary displays per year that focus on some bookish theme; the exhibit at the time of research explored "Intercultural Dialogue in Old Writings" and displayed magnificent manuscripts in Hebrew, Arabic, Greek, and Latin. Warning: you might have to get a neck massage afterward from all the craning to look up.

U1, U2, or U4: Karlspl. Or U3: Herrengasse. $ *€7, students €4.50.* ⏰ *Open Tu-W 10am-6pm, Th 10am-9pm, F-Su 10am-6pm.*

KUNSTHISTORISCHES MUSEUM — MUSEUM

Maria Theresien-Pl. ☎1 525 240 🖥www.khm.at

This stunning building houses the city's most extensive and impressive collection of work, including art from the 15th to 19th centuries, Greek and Roman antiquities, one of the five largest coin cabinets in the world), and halls of Egyptian and Near Eastern works. Start at the picture galleries so you don't run out of steam, and pace yourself—Room X, devoted to Bruegel's works, is worth spending some time in. Don't miss the Rembrandt self-portraits and Canaletto's cityscapes, the latter of which elegantly show how much the city has changed.

U2 or U3: Volkstheater, tram 1, 2, D. $ *Adults €12, with Vienna card €11, students under 27 €9, under 19 free.* ⏰ *Open Tu-W 10am-6pm, Th 10am-9pm, F-Su 10am-6pm.*

STADTPARK — PARK

Main entrance from Johannesgasse

Nestled into the Ringstr., this large green space filled with benches, walkways, and statues of musicians (10 points for spotting the gilded Johann Strauss) beckons to all on summer afternoons. Enter through the stone collonades, then wander until you find the perfect spot for reading or a picnic. Drool from afar at Vienna's most acclaimed restaurant, Steierereck, where a meal will set you back over €100, and avoid the Kursalon, whose nightly dinner-music deals ooze tourist tackiness.

U4: Stadtpark or U3: Stubentor, tram 1 or 2. $ *Free.* ⏰ *Open 24hr.*

SECESSION — EXHIBITION HALL

Friedrichstr. 12 ☎587 53 07 🖥www.secession.at

This square building with a golden laurel-leaf dome will certainly catch your eye as you wander through the Naschmarkt and Karlspl. area. The inside spaces are used for rotating art exhibits (check the current program online), but most people go just to see the basement room housing Gustav Klimt's *Beethoven Frieze.* Said to be an interpretation of Beethoven's *Ninth Symphony*, it depicts mankind's search for happiness on three walls of the rectangular room.

U1, U2, or U4: Karlspl. $ *€5 (groups of 8 or more €4 per person), students and seniors €4 (groups of 8 or more €2.50 per person). Tours €1.50.* ⏰ *Open Tu-W 10am-6pm, Th 10am-8pm, F-Su 10am-6pm.*

FRANZISKANEKIRCHE — CHURCH

Franziskanerpl. ☎1 512 45 78 🖥www.franziskaner.at

In a chill, charming, and cobblestoned plaza slightly hidden from tourist hordes at Stephanzpl., Franzikanerkirche is worth a quick visit and photo op. While the interior has two rows of ornate wooden pews, the church is perhaps best experienced from the outside. Sit in the square at the outdoor seating of Kleines Cafe and relish in the pale blue exterior and pretty fountain.

U1 or U3: Stephanspl. $ Free. Church guide booklet €4.70. ⏰ Open daily 6:30am-5:30pm.

HAUS DER MUSIK MUSEUM

Seilerstätte 30 ☎1 513 48 50 💻www.hdm.at

The four floors of this interactive world of music could take 5hr. to fully explore. The journey begins with information about Vienna's premier philharmonic orchestra, where you can watch (in HD) the previous year's New Year's Eve concert. In the Sonosphere (second floor), sound becomes the focus, as you learn about what we hear and how we hear it through electronic computer and headset stations. The third floor of "Great Composers" has cleverly arranged displays on the lives and work of the many musical geniuses who worked in Vienna. There is a free audio tour, but it is more of a joy to read the English placards with Beethoven, Mozart, or Haydn playing in the background. The final Futuresphere offers interactive sound games that kids will love.

U1, U2, or U4: Karlspl. $ €10, students €8.50, ages 3-12 €5.50. Combined ticket with Mozarthaus €15, children €7. ⏰ Open daily 10am-10pm.

MAK (MUSEUM FUR ANGEWANDTE KUNST) MUSEUM

Stubenring 5 ☎1 711 360 💻www.mak.at

Antique junkies and architecture aficionados will love this museum's brightly colored walls and hanging glass cases filled with everything from Venetian glassware and lace to architectural models of 20th- and 21st-century buildings. Klimt's *Stoclet Frieze* is one of the few paintings in a museum otherwise devoted entirely to applied arts. The MAK also boasts one of the most famous and comprehensive collections of oriental carpets in the world.

U3: Stubentor, tram 1 or 2. $ €8, students €5.50. Children and under 19 free. Family €11. Free for all Sa. Tours €2. ⏰ Open Tu 10am-midnight, W-Su 10am-6pm. English tours Su noon.

BURGGARTEN PARK

Entrance on Burgring

Because of the prime location amidst the Inner Stadt sights, this green space is most frequented by tourists sitting on benches and eating gelato. There is a Mozart statue with flowers in the shape of a treble clef, though you will have to sneak past the scalpers selling concert tickets to snap your photo. Stroll behind the Hofburg or drink coffee in the majestic Palmenhaus restaurant overlooking the park.

U1, U2, or U4: Karlspl.; Tram 1, 2, D. $ Free. ⏰ Open daily dawn-dusk.

MOZARTHAUS MUSEUM

Domgasse 5 ☎1 512 17 91 💻www.mozarthausvienna.at

This apartment is the only surviving Mozart house, and was where the musical genius composed *The Marriage of Figaro* at the height of his wealth and fame. The first floor of the museum speculates how Mozart lived during his time there, and much of the building and surrounding streets remain as they were. The second and third floors focus on his life history and music, but unfortunately many of the displays don't do the composer or his music justice. You might also find yourself wishing the audio tour had more of his music and less commentary.

U1 or U3: Stephanspl. From the stop, walk down Singerstr. and turn left on Blutgasse. i Audio tour in English included with ticket price. $ €9, students and seniors €7. Combined ticket with Haus der Musik €15, children €7. ⏰ Open daily 10am-7pm.

PETERSKIRCHE CHURCH

Peterspl. ☎1 533 64 33 💻www.peterskirche.at

Established by the Fraternity of the Holy Trinity and supported by the Opus

Dei (*Da Vinci Code*, anyone?), Peterskirche's turquoise dome glows eerily, especially when illuminated at night. The soft beige-rose marble walls balance out the otherwise ornate interior and are accented by the royal purple curtains on the confessionals.

🧭 U1 or U3: Stephanspl. From the stop, head down Graben on the left. $ Free. ⏰ Open M-F 7am-8pm, Sa-Su 9am-9pm. Free organ concerts M-F 3pm, Sa-Su 8pm.

JÜDISCHES MUSEUM (JEWISH MUSEUM) 🎟♿ HISTORY MUSEUM

Dorotheergasse 11 ☎1 535 04 31 💻www.jmv.at

While the Jewish Museum has a wide collection of prayer books, scrolls, Torah curtains, and other artifacts—many of which are quite beautiful—the lengthy historical explanations might be a bit dry for those who aren't obsessed with the past. The viewable storage area on the top floor has an impressive number of objects collected over the years from synagogues, prayer houses, and private homes.

🧭 U1 or U3: Stephanspl. From the stop, walk down Graben, then turn left on Dorotheergasse. $ €6.50, students €4. ⏰ Open M-F 10am-6pm, Su 10am-6pm.

NATURHISTORISCHES MUSEUM 🎟♿🛍 NATURAL HISTORY MUSEUM

Burgring 7 ☎1 521 77 💻www.nhm-wien.ac.at

Across from the Kunsthistorisches Museum, in an identically beautiful building, this natural-history museum has two floors that take the visitor on a journey from the beginning of the world and its lifeforms up until modern day. Fossils, mineral collections, and plenty of preserved amphibians floating in glass jars await, as do some impressively large skeletons of dinosaurs and whales. The breathtaking gem collection in Room IV is the most valuable gem collection on the continent, and includes a topaz weighing 250 lb.

🧭 U2 or U3: Volkstheater, tram 1 or 2; bus 2A, 48A. $ €10, students €5, seniors €8, under 19 free. Guided tours €2.50. Scientific tours €6.50. ⏰ Open M 9am-6:30pm, W 9am-9pm, Th-Su 9am-6:30pm. Tours to roof Su 3pm.

CORE DISTRICTS

👍 BELVEDERE 🎟♿❄🛍 MUSEUM, PALACE GARDENS

Prinz Eugen Str. 27 (Upper), Rennweg 6 (Lower) ☎795 570 💻www.belvedere.at

The sweeping grounds of Schloß Belvedere house two magnificent museums, with Vienna's best-known work of art, Gustav Klimt's *The Kiss*. Oberes (Upper) Belvedere houses the Klimt collection as well as a magnificent spread of Beidermeier, Neoclassic, Medieval, and Baroque art arranged over three floors around the grand Marble Hall. From Oberes Belvedere, take a leisurely stroll through the gardens to Unteres (Lower) Belvedere, taking in the manicured hedges, fountains, and the views of Stephansdom and the city in the distance. Unteres Belvedere has rotating exhibits, one in the palace and another (usually contemporary) in the Orangery, accessed though the Marble Gallery and the Golden Room. There is a quiet, private garden in front of the Orangery with views back up to Oberes Belvedere and magnificent arrays of exotic flowers in the summer. On your way out, the multiple museum shops offer Klimt-printed everything—even teddy bears.

🧭 Tram D, O, or 71. $ Unteres (Lower) Belvedere €9.50, seniors €7.50, students €7, under 18 free. Combined tickets (Unteres and Oberes) €14/11/10/free. ⏰ Upper open daily 10am-6pm. Lower open M-Tu 10am-6pm, W 10am-9pm, Th-Su 10am-6pm.

👍 KUNST HAUS WIEN 🎟🚭🍸🛍 MUSEUM

Untere Weißgerberstr. 13 ☎1 712 04 91 💻www.kunsthauswien.com

From an early age, school teachers noticed Friedensreich Hundertwaßer's "unusual sense of color and form," currently apparent in the building of the Kunst Haus Wien and all of his works within. The floor and pipes curve, the stairs are stacked with bright tiles and bits of mirror, and the house is filled with live "tree tenants," making the KunstHaus a cartoonish, magical land. The first two floors of the museum contain Hundertwaßer's spectacular works, with titles including *Stokes, Splotches, and Heads* and *Who Has Eaten All My Windows?* while the third floor is used for rotating exhibits.

🚇 U1 or U4: Schwedenpl. From the stop, Tram 1: Radetzkypl. $ €9, ages 11-18 €4.50, children under 10 free. M (except holidays) €4.50. Combination ticket (Kunsthaus and temporary exhibitions) €12, ages 11-18 €6. ⏰ Open daily 10am-7pm.

KARLSKIRCHE 🚭⊗ CHURCH

Karlspl. ☎1 504 61 87 🖥www.karlskirche.at

One of Vienna's most stunning churches, Karlskirche's gleaming turquoise dome and two elaborately engraved columns reflect in the circular pool in Karlspl. Inside, the cream and pink marble is softly elegant. Take the glass elevator 35 meters up to admire the frescoes from mere feet away. You can also climb additional stairs up into the dome for (slightly obscured) views of the entire city.

🚇 U1, U2, or U4: Karlspl. $ €6, students €4, under 11 free. Groups of 6 or more €5 per person. Audio tour €2. ⏰ Open M-Sa 9am-12:30pm and 1-6pm, Su noon-5:45pm.

LEOPOLD MUSEUM 🎫♿❄☁ ART MUSEUM

Museumspl. 1 ☎525 700 🖥www.leopoldmuseum.org

The Leopold collection has recently been rearranged to guide the viewer through the art, architecture, and design elements of "Vienna 1900." The glistening white walls and large airy rooms provide a cheery setting to view some of the comparitively dark (and depressing) works of Egon Schiele, on whom the collection has a particular focus. There are also works by other prominent Austrian artists ,such as Gustav Klimt, Kolo Moser, and Oskar Kokoschka.

🚇 U2: Museumsquartier. Or U2 or U3: Volkstheater. $ €11, students €7, seniors €8, family (2 adults, 3 children) €23. ⏰ Open M, W 10am-6pm, Th 10am-9pm, F-Su 10am-6pm.

PRATER AND WEINER REISENRAD 🚭♿🍸☁ AMUSEMENT PARK

Riesenradpl. ☎1 729 54 30 🖥www.wienerreisenrad.at

The Prater is home to Vienna's symbolic ferris wheel, the Wiener Reisenrad, which you will have undoubtedly seen on numerous postcards (if not in a certain James Bond film, you die-hard fans). While a corner of the park is devoted to over 250 amusement rides and games and plenty of ice cream stands, the rest is pure, peaceful green space that was formerly an imperial hunting ground. On the weekends, a walk or run through the expanse is a common activity for the local Viennese.

🚇 U1 or U2: Praterstern. $ Park free. Each ride has individual prices. Wiener Reisenrad €8.50, students and Vienna cardholders €7.50, ages 3-14 €3.50, under 3 free. ⏰ Each ride has its own hours. Check the website for rotating schedule.

ST. MARXER FRIEDHOF ♿☁ CEMETERY

III, Leberstr. 6-8 ☎1 4000 80 42

Even bringing along a friend or visiting in the middle of the day won't prevent this spooky cemetery from feeling like a real-life horror film. The gravestones are overgrown with weeds, and the grass comes up to your knees in this ghost town. St. Marxer's claim to fame is as the real resting place of Amadeus Mozart, which is easily spotted as the only manicured tomb in the entire place.

*🚇 Tram 71: St. Marx. Bus 74A. **i** A map of the tombs is located at the entrance. $ Free. ⏰ Open daily 7am-dusk.*

MUMOK (MUSEUM MODERNER KUNST STIFTUNG LUDWIG WIEN)

🎫⊗❄☁ MUSEUM

Museumspl. 1 ☎525 00 1400 🖥www.mumok.at

This modern art museum seems to be hit or miss depending on the current exhibits that rotate every two to three months. The events range from displays of prominent modern art to more obscure installations that experiment with interesting themes such as light, movement, or space. The museum space itself is a grey, square warehouse with glass elevators to swiftly guide you through the museum's five floors.

🚇 *U2 or U3: Volkstheater. Or U2: Museumsquartier.* 💲 *€9, seniors and Vienna cardholders €7, students under 27 free, students over 27 €6.50, families €14, annual pass €33.* 🕐 *Open M-W 10am-6pm, Th 10am-9pm, F-Su 10am-6pm.*

AUGARTEN
&⚐ RECREATION

Entrance on Obere Augartenstr.

Although slightly secluded from the rest of District II, this green space is immensely popular with families and almost overrun with squealing children on the weekends. Tall trees line gravel paths that lead to the park's slightly frightening (and somewhat hideous) Flakturm, tall cement bunkers built during WWII.

🚇 *Tram 21.* 💲 *Free.* 🕐 *Open daily dawn-dusk.*

OUTER DISTRICTS

🏛 SCHLOß SCHÖNBRUNN
♥&⚐ PALACE, GARDENS, IMPERIAL APARTMENTS

Schönbrunner Schloβstr. 47
☎1 811 130 🖥www.schoenbrunn.at

Schonbrunn Palace's gardens rival many a famous French palace garden (ahem, Versailles). The main avenue stretches from the palace to the Fountain of Neptune, behind which the arched structure of the Gloriette stands majestically on a hill. The Gloriette was built to commemorate the return of Prague to Habsburg rule in 1775 and the view of the palace, gardens, and city from here is breathtaking. The palace itself has an extensive set of imperial rooms, the most impressive of which you can view on the Imperial Tour (although the Great Gallery is unfortunately under restoration until 2012). If you have the time and a few extra euros to spare, the Grand Tour has some of the most ornate, albeit smaller, rooms, including the Millions Room, the palace's most valuable room due to the rare rosewood wall paneling.

🏃 *U4, Tram 10 or 58, or Bus 10A: Schonbrunn.* Ⓢ *Admission to gardens and grounds free. Imperial Tour (22 rooms) €9.50, children €6.60, students €8.50, Vienna cardholders €9.50. Grand Tour (40 rooms) €13, students and Vienna cardholders €11.40, children €9. Grand Tour with guide €14.40/13/10.* 🕐 *Open daily Apr-June 8:30am-5pm; July-Aug 8:30am-6pm; Sept-Oct 8:30am-5pm; Nov-Mar 8:30am-4:30pm.*

KIRCHE AM STEINHOF
🌐⊗ CHURCH
Baumgartner Höhe 1
☎1 910 601 12 04

Kirche am Steinhof, built by Otto Wagner, is a shining (literally) example of Viennese Art Nouveau architecture. The copper dome is blindingly bright against the otherwise green hillside where the church resides. The surrounding parkland was formerly a Nazi psychiatry center that played a horrific role in the Nazi euthanasia experiments, but today the whole complex is part of the Otto Wagner Hospital. Four angels stand guard at the entrance to the church, while ornate mosaics, creamy white walls, and stained-glass windows illuminate the interior.

🏃 *U3: Ottakring. From the stop, take 48A: Psychiatrisches Zentrum.* Ⓢ *Tours (50min.) €6, students and children €4, under 15 free. Art Nouveau tour (1½hr.) €10, ages 15-18 €7, students €6.* 🕐 *Viewing Sa 4-5pm. Mass Su and holidays 9am. Tours Sa 3pm. Art Nouveau tour runs Apr-Sept every F at 3:30pm.*

ZENTRALFRIEDHOF
♿☁ CEMETERY
Simmeringer Haupstr. 234
☎1 760 410 🖥www.friedhoefewien.at

Stone cherubim, crosses, and pillars decorate over 2.5 million tombs in Vienna's Central Cemetery. From the main entrance (Gate II), a straight walk down the central aisle will bring you to the most famous inhabitants, including Beethoven, Brahms, Schubert, and Wolf in section 32A, as well as a fake tomb for Mozart (the real one is in St. Marx). In front of the large Dr. Karl Lueger Kirche, the central church, the presidents of the Second Republic are buried in the manicured Presidentsgruft. Gate 1 of the cemetery leads to the large and unfortunately neglected area of Jewish memorials.

🏃 *Tram 71: Zentralfriedhof; the 2nd Zentralfriedhof stop is the main entrance.* Ⓢ *Free. Cars €2.20.* 🕐 *Open daily May-Aug 7am-8pm; Sept 7am-7pm; Oct 7am-6pm; Nov-Feb 8am-5pm; Mar 7am-6pm; Apr 7am-7pm.*

food

INNER CITY

🔖 KLEINES CAFE
🌐⊗⚲☁ CAFE ❷
Franziskanerpl. 3

Kleines Cafe might just be the smallest coffeehouse in the whole city, but you know what they say—small coffee house, big heart. Or is it big feet, big... nevermind. The cappuccinos are piled high with a top hat (not just cap) of foam, and beers and wine are also a popular choice. The outdoor seating in Franziskanerpl. is a delight during the summer, and the cozy, leather interior feels expanded with the clever use of mirrors.

🏃 *U1 or U3: Stephanspl.* Ⓢ *Coffee €2-4. Entrees €5.50-10.* 🕐 *Open M-Sa 10am-2am, Su 1pm-2am.*

IMERVOLL ⊛⊗🍸☁ VIENNESE ❸

Weihburggasse 17 ☎513 52 88

Imervoll is one of the best places to go in the Inner Stadt for traditional Viennese cuisine that's more authentic (and flavorful) than just a schnitzel. The constantly changing menu is a handwritten paper on the glass wall of the entrance, boasting dishes like *Rindsgulasch (beef stew with dumplings and paprika; €9.40)* and *Gebratene Bachforelle (fried trout with onion and salad; €11.70).* In warm weather, customers flock to the outdoor seating in Franziskanerpl., leaving the simple yellow interior quite empty.

⇄ U1 or U3: Stephanspl. $ Entrees €8-17.50. Appetizers and salads €6.50-14.50. ⏰ Open daily noon-midnight.

FIGLMÜLLER 💳♿🍸 VIENNESE ❸

Wollzeile 5 ☎512 617 77 💻www.figlmueller.at

For a *weiner schnitzel* bigger than your head, Figlmüller is undoubtedly the place to come. This family-run restaurant has become well known for its massive schnitzels *(€13)*, so tourists abound, though a table or two of locals still emerge. The recommended side potato salad and greens *(€3.80)* is the ideal schnitzel companion and should not be overlooked. Come hungry, leave with a food baby.

⇄ U1 or U3: Stephanspl. ℹ Additional location at Backerstr. 6. English menu available. $ Entrees €10-15. ⏰ Open daily 11am-10:30pm.

TRZESNIEWSKI ♿⊛☁🍸 SANDWICHES ❶

Dorotheerg 1 ☎1 512 32 91

From Polish origins to a Vienna institution, *Trzesniewski* (try saying that three times fast) offers mini open-faced sandwiches on brown bread *(€1)*. The intriguing flavors, including wild paprika (quite spicy!) and mushroom and egg are definitely for those willing to step out of a PB-and-J comfort zone. Other ingredients include onion, tunafish, and cucumber, and many are vegetarian.

⇄ U1 or U3: Stephanspl. From the stop, walk down Graben, and look for the signs on your left about 3 blocks down. $ Brotchen €1. ⏰ Open M-F 8:30am-7:30pm, Sa 9am-5pm.

EISSALON TUCHLAUBEN ⊛♿☁ GELATO, DESSERT ❷

Tuchlauben 15 ☎1 533 25 53 💻www.eissalon-tuchlauben.at

So creamy, so delicious, and easily the best gelato in the entire city. Look for the bright orange overhangs and the orange cups to match. Sit down at the outdoor patio to indulge in a large sundae or take out a cup or cone for a cheap, sweet thrill. The hazelnut is not to be missed.

⇄ U1 or U3: Stephanspl. $ Cups and cones €1.70-4. ⏰ Open M-F 10am-11:30pm, Sa 11am-11:30pm.

ÖSTERREICHER IM MAK 💳♿🍸☁ CAFE, BAR ❸

Stubenring 5 ☎1 714 01 21 💻www.oesterreicherimmak.at

Serving up modern and traditional Viennese cuisine, Österreicher im MAK has all the appropriate design elements to rival its neighboring museum (yes, the MAK)—a large hanging chandelier made entirely of wine glasses and a combination of oddly shaped high and low bar tables, which admittedly look cooler than they feel. During lunch, if the weather is good, most people enjoy the outdoor patio and take advantage of the bargain daily lunch special *(€6.40)*.

⇄ U3 to Stubentor; Tram 1 or 2. $ Coffee €3-5. Entrees €9-20. Wine by the glass €7-10, by the bottle €20-30. ⏰ Open daily 9:30am-1am.

DEMEL 💳♿☁ CAFE ❷

Kohlmarkt 14 ☎1 535 171 70 💻www.demel.at

Visitors and locals alike will easily name Demel as the one Viennese coffeehouse that shouldn't be missed. Although the prices are steep *(€5.10 for a hot chocolate)*,

the elegance and charm are simply unsurpassable. Be sure to browse through the confectionery on your way out—just don't drool on the boxes of chocolate.
🚇 U1 or U3: Stephanspl. Or U3: Herrengasse. $ Coffee €3-7.80. Soups and entrees €6.20-21.00. Desserts €6.40-8. ⏰ Open daily 9am-7pm.

CAFE DIGLAS 💵♿🍸🌤 CAFE ❷
Wollzeile 10 ☎1 512 57 65 💻www.diglas.at
The popularity of this plush *kaffeehaus* has grown over the years, evident now by the menu offered in every language imaginable. While the crystal chandeliers, velvet booths, and marble tables may feel like a step back in time, the prices do not, so don't rush home and put on your corset just yet. A coffee and dessert alone can set you back close to €10.
🚇 U1 or U3: Stephanspl. $ Teas €3.30. Breakfast €4.20-9.20. Entrees €7.50-15.50. Apple strudel €4.50. ⏰ Open daily 7am-midnight.

LIMES 💳♿🍸🌤 MEDITERRANEAN ❸
Hoher Markt 10 ☎1 905 800 💻www.restaurant-limes.at
Limes serves up fresh salads, pastas and other Mediterranean fare in an "urban chic" interior or out on the patio at the edge of Hoher Markt. Inside, the bar's high white stools seem to contradict the dining room's low, green couches and candelabras; luckily they are separated by wispy strands of green fabric. Decor aside, the food is downright tasty.
🚇 U1 or U3: Stephanspl. Or U1 or U4: Schwedenpl. ℹ Credit card min. €15. $ Entrees €6.50-20.50. ⏰ Open M-Sa 9am-midnight.

1516 BREWING COMPANY 💳♿🍸🌤 PUB ❷
Schwarzenbergstr. 2 ☎961 15 16 💻www.1516brewingcompany.com
If you want some familiar-looking food (read: classic American grub), 1516 has large portions of burgers, soups, and salads in a pub-style restaurant and bar. Its tap beer brewed on the premises is the drink of choice, and the large slab of barbecued baby-back ribs served with potatoes and salad *(€13)* is large enough to share.
🚇 U1, U2, or U4: Karlpl. $ Entrees €8-13. Sandwiches and burgers €5.50-9.20. ⏰ Open M-Th 10am-2am, F 10am-3am, Sa 11am-3am, Su 11am-2am. Kitchen open until 2am.

ZANONI AND ZANONI 💵♿🍸🌤 GELATO, DESSERT ❶
Lugeck 7 ☎512 79 79 💻www.zanoni.co.at
On a hot summer's night, Zanoni and Zanoni is just the thing to make all your gelato dreams come true. With an impressive list of choices, you may as well opt for the large cone with three flavors *(€2.50)* and make your selection easier. If we put these flavors in a milkshake, it would definitely bring all the boys to the yard.
🚇 U1 or U3: Stephanspl. U1 or U4: Schwedenpl. ℹ Another location at Burging 1. $ Small cone (2 flavors) €2. Large cone (3 flavors) €2.50. ⏰ Open daily 7:30am-midnight.

AIDA ♿💳🍸🌤 CAFE, CONFECTIONERY ❶
Singerstr. 1 ☎089 898 82 10 💻www.aida.at
Undoubtedly you will stumble across the coffee and confectionery shop Aida at one of its multiple branches all over the city. You can't miss it; the decor is bubble-gum pink chairs and neon pink signs, for crying out loud. While the melange *(€3)* is a bit on the small side, the Stephanspl. location overlooks the plaza and church, and it's satisfying to sit in the chairs instead of being blinded by them from afar.
🚇 U1 or U3: Stephanspl. $ Coffee €1.80-3. Strudel and torten slices €1.30-3. Sundaes and ice cream €4.30-5. ⏰ Open M-Sa 7am-8pm, Su 9am-8pm.

CORE DISTRICTS

🏛 NASCHMARKT
♨️🚹🍽 MARKET ❷

Wienzeile

This open-air market is the best way to begin a day of sightseeing in the city, as the market feels like a sight itself! Endless stalls of olives, stuffed peppers, dried fruits and nuts, cheeses, meats, vegetables and fruit sell their wares, and on Saturdays, there is a flea market. Running parallel to the stands, sit-down restaurants and cafes offer coffee and more professionally assembled meals, from sandwiches to seafood.

✚ *U1, U2, or U4: Karlspl.* Ⓢ *Prices vary by stall.* Ⓩ *Market stalls open M-F 6am-7:30pm, Sa 6am-5pm. Flea market open Sa 6:30am-4pm.*

🏛 RA'MIEN
🍴🚹🍽🏠 VIETNAMESE ❷

Gumpendorfer Str. 9
☎1 585 47 98 🖥www.ramien.at

You will be worshipping your large bowl of *pho* noodles, *lo mein*, or rice by the end of your meal and craving *gyoza* dumplings (€7) for days afterward. The rice bowls, such as the one with duck, Thai basil, and chili (€8.50), come with a small salad and slice of fruit.

✚ *U2: Museumsquartier.* ⓘ *Credit cards min. €10.* Ⓢ *Entrees €7-14.* Ⓩ *Open Tu-Su 11am-11pm.*

ZUM ROTEN ELEFANTEN
♨️🚹⟨ᵖⱷ⟩🍽🏠 VIENNESE, FRENCH, CAFE ❸

Gumpendorferstr. 3
☎966 80 08 🖥www.zumrotenelefanten.at

The cream-colored walls and dark wooden chairs give this cafe an artsy yet sophisticated flair that is emphasized by the patrons, who sip their coffee particularly daintily. The French-inspired cuisine is flawless, and the lunch menu is an extremely good value. Look for the sign with just the picture of a red elephant.

✚ *U1, U2, U4; tram 1, 2, or D: Karlspl.* Ⓢ *Lunch €8. 2-course dinner €19.* Ⓩ *Open M-F 11:30am-2:30pm and 6pm-midnight, Sa 6pm-midnight.*

GASTHAUS WICKERL
🍴🚹🍽🏠 VIENNESE ❷

Porzellangasse 24A
☎317 74 89

This cozy, traditional *beisel* (pub) has everything from the wooden tables and chairs to the beers on tap. The food is delicious, especially the *Karnter Nudeln* (Viennese dumplings) topped with diced tomatoes and with side salad (€9.10), though if you're really sticking to "tradition," you could always go with the *weiner schnitzel* (€9.50) instead.

✚ *Tram D.* Ⓢ *Salads €5-7. Entrees €7-14.* Ⓩ *Open M-F 9am-midnight, Sa 10am-midnight.*

DER WIENER DEEWAN
♨️♿🏠 PAKISTANI, HALAL

Liechtensteinstr. 10
☎925 1185 🖥www.deewan.at

This well-loved Pakistani buffet lives by the motto, "eat what you want, pay what you wish." The booths with high ceilings and funky painted walls are always packed (and the university is nearby), so come on off hours to ensure you get a table. The buffet always offers meat and vegetarian dishes, and all of the food is halal.

✚ *U2: Schottentor. Or Bus #40A: Bergasse.* Ⓢ *You decide!* Ⓩ *Open M-Sa 11am-11pm.*

HALLE
🍴🚹🍽🏠 CAFE ❷

Museumspl. 1
☎523 70 01 🖥www.motto.at

One of the trendy outdoor cafes in the middle of Museumsquartier, Halle's breakfasts (€5.50-9.40) will set your day on the right track. The lunch special changes daily (eggs and omelettes, crossiants, and extra large cafe lattes; €7.20-8.50), and there is a bar and drink menu for when the sun goes down. If the weather is right, take advantage of the tables on the patio overlooking the bustle of the MQ courtyard.

✚ *U2: Museumsquartier. Alternatively, U2 or U3: Volkstheater.* Ⓢ *Entrees €7-10. Sandwiches €8. Cafe latte €3.50.* Ⓩ *Open daily 10am-2am.*

CAFE SPERL 💳♿🍸🌤 CAFE [2]

Gumpendorfer Str. 11-13 ☎1 586 41 58 💻www.cafesperl.at

Grand, elegant, traditional... yellow? These are some of the words that may be used to describe perhaps the most quintessential of all Vienna's coffeehouses. The pale yellow building and corner entrance overlook a small plateau with shaded outdoor seating, while inside the large expanses of marble and wood are accented by two billiard tables.

🚇 U2: Museumsquartier. Bus #57A: Station Köstlergasse. $ Coffee €2-6. ⏰ Open M-Sa 7am-11pm, Su 11am-8pm.

YAK AND YETI 💳♿🍸🌤 NEPALESE [2]

Hofmühlgasse 21 ☎595 54 52 💻www.yakundyeti.at

Take your taste buds on a journey east for some traditional Nepalese cuisine. Thursdays is "Momo Day" so you can sample all the sauces and fillings in an all-you-can-eat *momo* (Himalayan dumpling) buffet *(€12)*. Or, on Tuesdays, eat *Dal Bhaat* (a rice, lentil, meat, and veggie meal) with your fingers in the traditional style *(all you can eat; €10)*.

🚇 U4: Pilgramgasse. Or bus #13A: Esterhazygasse. $ Appetizers €3-4.25. Entrees €5.50-18. Desserts €3.50-4.50. ⏰ Open M-F 11:30am-2:30pm and 6-10:30pm, Sa 11:30am-10:30pm.

UBL 🚫♿🍸🌤 VIENNESE [3]

Presgasse 26 ☎587 64 37

Just down the street from the Naschmarkt, this Viennese *beisel* holds its own culinary clout in the city dining arena. The traditional Austrian dishes, often with slight influences from other cuisines, have garnered much acclaim and won awards. Enjoy your *schweinsbraten*, *schnitzel*, or *semmelknodel* on the surprisingly peaceful, although narrow, terrace, barricaded from the street by tall, thick trees.

🚇 U4 or bus #59A: Kettenbruckengasse. $ Entrees €8.50-16. ⏰ Open daily noon-2pm and 6-10pm.

ZU DEN 2 LIESERLN 🚫♿🍸🌤 VIENNESE [2]

Burggasse ☎523 32 82 💻www.2lieserln.at

So many *schnitzels*, so little time. This traditional *beisel* certainly offers the Viennese *weiner schnitzel* (pork with a side potato salad), but there is also a fascinating selection of schnitzel specials to choose from—"Cordon Bleu" and "Puszta" are among the list. Enjoy your *schnitzel* in a warm, wood-paneled interior or a pleasant outdoor seating area with large sweeping trees.

🚇 Bus #48A. $ Weiner schnitzels €8.50-13. ⏰ Open daily 11am-11pm.

LUCKY NOODLES 🚫♿🍸🌤 ASIAN [1]

Mariahilferstr. 77

If you are in the mood for fast and easy takeout, you can't go wrong with a steaming box of Lucky Noodles, either with vegetables, chicken, or both. No fance or schmance, just noodles, and the steady stream of people means the noodles are always fresh. Add your own sauces, and even use chopsticks.

🚇 U3: Zeiglergasse. $ Noodles €2.50-3.50. ⏰ Open daily 10:30am-11:30pm.

FRESCO GRILL 💳🚫📶🍸🌤 MEXICAN [2]

Liechtensteinstr.10 ☎660 467 89 83 💻www.frescogrill.at

This is Vienna's version of a Tex-Mex joint—minimal decor, maximum burritos. The ingredients are tasty, fresh, and not as greasy as you would expect, so you can indulge guilt-free. Quesadillas, taco salads, chips and salsa, and beer are all on the menu.

🚇 U2: Schottentor. ℹ 30min. free Wi-Fi access for customers. Can create student account for a 5% discount. $ Burritos €4.60-6.60. ⏰ Open M-F noon-9pm.

NICE RICE

⊛⊛⊘♨ VEGETARIAN, INDIAN ❷

Mariahilfer Str. 45, im Raimundhof 49 ☎1 586 28 39 🖥www.raimundhof.at/nicerice/

Down a cobblestone alley filled with boutiques and cafes, this cheery restaurant offers Indian-inspired all-vegetarian meals. Entrees include basmati rice with hummus and tofu (*€8.50*) or Indian samosas with salad and yogurt sauce (*€9.30*). The outdoor seats are perfect for mango-lassi-sipping (*€2.80*) and people-watching *(priceless)*.

₩ *U3: Neubaugasse or U2: Museumsquartier. The restaurant is down an alleyway off Mariahilfer Str.* Ⓢ *Entrees €4-15.* 🕐 *Open M-Sa 10am-7pm.*

ELEPHANT CASTLE

⊛♿ ❖♨ INDIAN, CAFE ❶

Neubaugasse 45 ☎0699 920 84 59 🖥www.elefantcastle.at

Walk into this tiny cafe and mistake it for someone's kitchen. The Indian-inspired food is made in front of you with a healthy homemade flair. The mango chutney is particularly tasty (in anything!), while the curry dishes are heartier than the simple and slightly small sandwiches.

₩ *U3: Neubaugasse* Ⓢ *Sandwiches €3.50-5.50. Curries €6.50-8.50.* 🕐 *Open M-F 11:30am-3:30pm.*

OUTER DISTRICTS

🏷 HEURIGER HIRT

⊛♿ ❖♨ WINE TAVERN ❷

Eisernenhandgasse 165 ☎1 318 9641 🖥www.zurschildkrot.com

The slightly strenuous trek to reach this hillside *heuriger* (wine tavern) is completely worth the experience of sipping spritzer and looking over the sweeping views of the vineyards, lush hillsides, and the tiny town of Kahlenbergerdorf alongside the Danube. There is no fancy decor, just peeling picnic tables and some hanging lanterns, and you will likely be the only English-speaker there. The self-serve menu changes daily, and you can walk into the kitchen and point at what you want. Bring your own water—there is no drinking water available, only wine!

₩ *Bus #239: Verein Kahlenbergerdorf. From the stop, walk through the small town to your left and up Eisernenhandgasse at the back. It's about a 15min. walk up the hill.* ℹ *The place is popular with locals, so if you plan to come around 7:30 or 8pm, make a reservation. Pay as you go.* Ⓢ *Meat portions €3-6. Salad portion €2-4. Slices of bread or garnishes €0.40 each.* 🕐 *Open Apr-Oct M-F 3pm-late, Sa-Su noon-late; Nov-Mar F-Su noon-late.*

🏷 CAFE DOMMAYER

☞♿ ❖♨ VIENNESE ❷

Auhofstr. 2 ☎1 877 546 50 🖥www.dommayer.at

This traditional coffeehouse has one of the most elegant courtyards in the city—sweeping green and white striped umbrellas shade high hedges, as though made for ladies sipping on tea with pinkies up. The waiters in white button-down shirts, black vests, and in some cases black bowties offer additional elegance, yet somehow the atmosphere is friendly, not stuffy. Take a book, order a coffee and dessert, and spend a few hours.

₩ *U4: Hietzing.* Ⓢ *Coffee €2.30-6. Entrees €4.80-12. Desserts €2.40-3.50.* 🕐 *Open daily 7am-10pm.*

FRANCESCO

☞♿ ❖♨ ITALIAN, BIERGARTEN ❸

Grinzinger Str. 50 ☎1 369 23 11 🖥www.francesco.at

After all the *schwein* and *suppen*, some Italian cuisine is just what the doctor (or chef) ordered. Francesco serves pizzas, pastas, risottos; and at quite reasonable prices, as well as some pricier meat and fish dishes. The large open courtyard is shaded by a canopy of green, while inside the feel is rustic Viennese, with exposed brick, dark wooden tables in cozy booths with low ceilings, and even gold-framed paintings and some statues scattered throughout. Italian food in a Viennese hunting lodge... makes total sense.

₩ *Bus #38A.* Ⓢ *Entrees €6.50-24.* 🕐 *Open daily 11:30am-midnight.*

KENT 🍴♿🍸☁ TURKISH ❷

Brunnengasse 67 ☎405 91 73 💻www.kentrestaurant.at

Kent likes to advertise itself as the "best Turkish food in the world," and it might not be too far off the mark—it's at least the best Turkish food in Austria. At this more casual cafe location (they also have branches in districts X and XV), you can see all the food in trays before you order—see whether the stuffed eggplant or *moussaka* catches your eye. There are also plenty of meat dishes from the grill, salads, and dips.

🚏 U6: Josefstadter Str. $ Entrees €5-11. ⏰ Open M-Sa 6am-2am.

MAYER AM PFARRPLATZ 🍴♿🍸☁ WINE TAVERN ❸

Eroicagasse 4 ☎1 370 12 87 💻www.pfarrplatz.at

This *heuriger* is tourist-friendly without being overly touristy. In other words, there are a few souvenirs for sale but no tourist buses at its tiny plaza location. The long courtyard is filled with wooden tables and flowers, while indoors the restaurant could be your grandma's living room—flowered drapes matching flowered hanging lamps, muted green and rose tones, and even portraits of old ladies on the walls. Order a meal off the menu or frequent the buffet, where you put together your own meal and pay by portion.

🚏 Bus #38A. $ Menu and buffet style offerings from €10. ⏰ Open M-F 4pm-midnight, Sa-Su 11am-midnight.

10ER MARIE 🍴♿🍸☁ WINE TAVERN ❷

Ottakringer Str. 222-224 ☎489 46 47 💻www.fuhrgassl-huber.at

Although it doesn't have its own vineyards, this conveniently located *heuriger* is popular with the locals (especially the above-50 generation) who spend hours drinking spritzer and glasses of white wine. The menu is limited, so it's popular to choose a few portions of meat or salad from the buffet as a snack to accompany your drinks. The no-frills courtyard is backed by the *heuriger*'s pale yellow walls and green picnic tables, while inside the wooden booths and pleasant country decorations are lit by soft yellow lanterns.

🚏 U3: Ottakring. From the station, turn left on Thaliastr., then take a right on Johannes Krawarik. $ Spritzers and wines €1.70-2. Entrees €7-10.50. Buffet offerings €1-4 each. ⏰ Open M-Sa 3pm-late.

STRANDGASTHAUS BIRNER'S 🚭📶🍸☁ VIENNESE ❷

An der Oberen Alten Donau 47 ☎271 53 36

Along the edge of the Obere Alte Donau, the sliver of the Donau that runs through district XXI, Strandgasthaus Birner's is a favorite among locals enjoying the water and sunny weather. Three tiers of seating look out over couples boating and children splashing on the other side and are decorated with bright tablecloths and umbrellas, flowers, vines, and potted plants. Birner's serves traditional Viennese dishes, but the best is an *eis kaffee (cold coffee with ice cream; €4.20)* after a day in the sun.

🚏 U6: Neue Donau. $ Entrees €5.50-14.50. ⏰ Open daily 9am-11pm.

SAIGON 🚭♿🍸 VIETNAMESE ❷

Neulerchenfelderstr. 37 ☎408 74 36 💻www.saigon.at

This Vietnamese restaurant is the real deal—from the crispy, light egg rolls with dipping sauce and mint leaves to the large bowls of noodle soup *(pho.)* The dishes are artistically arranged and garnished with cucumber and tomato slices and a flower-shaped radish, and luckily the meals taste as good as they look. Saigon also has a quick-meal stall in Brunnengasse market (in front of no. 40), with cheap boxes of noodles, rice, and meat for a meal on the go *(€2.50-5).*

🚏 U6: Josefstatter Str. $ Entrees €7.20-15. ⏰ Open daily 11:30am-11pm.

FIGL'S 💳♿🍸☀ VIENNESE, BIERGARTEN ❸

Grinzinger Str. 55 ☎1 320 42 57 💻www.figls.at

This Viennese restaurant at the entrance to Grinzing offers traditional cuisine in a modern restaurant setting rather than a touristy *heuriger* get-up. The refined decor offers crisp wooden tables and booths, as well as a curved wooden bar around a large brass fireplace. The leafy courtyard offers private sections in a gentle slope out back, while the menu is a blend of traditional Austrian dishes as well as a Caesar salad *(€12)* or burger *(€9.50).*

🚏 Bus #38A. $ Entrees €7.50-23. ⏰ Open daily 11:30am-midnight. Lunch menu served M-F 11:30am-4pm.

nightlife

INNER CITY

FIRST FLOOR 💳🚭🍸 BAR

Seitenstettengasse 5 ☎533 78 66

This is one of Vienna's classic bars in district I, with paneling and molding from the 1930s mixed with a modern fish aquarium running the length of the bar. Although the fish are on "permanent holiday," as one bartender put it, the jazzy music and smoky velvet of this bar's interior gives it plenty of good ambience. On an off night the friendly bartenders might even let you mix your own pisco sour.

🚏 U1 or U4: Schwedenpl. $ Mixed drinks €6-9. ⏰ Open M-F 5pm-3am, Sa-Su 7pm-3am.

FLEX 🎵♿🍸☀ CLUB, BAR

Am Donaukanal ☎1 533 75 25 💻www.flex.at

Located in a gritty, unused subway tunnel, Flex boasts the best sound system in the city as well as the most famous name. (In 2003, the magazine *Spex* voted Flex the best club in the German-speaking world.) Though 2003 is actually quite a while ago, people still flood this alternative venue. Come in break it down on the club's dance floor which is attached to cafe's Danube banks (where you can also easily bring your own booze... score!).

🚏 U2 or U4: Schottenring; Tram 1 or 31: Schottenring. $ Free entrance to Flex Cafe. Club cover €4-12. ⏰ Open daily 6pm-4am.

VOLKSGARTEN DISCO ♿🍸☀ CLUB, BAR

Burgring 1, Volksgarten ☎532 42 41 💻www.volksgarten.at

Located on the edge of the Volksgarten green space, this popular club has been a part of the Vienna nightlife scene for almost as long as the 180-year-old building. Okay, not really, but in club-years, definitely so. The mix of indoor and outdoor space is adorned with plants, kidney-bean shaped tables, and colorful benches. The music ranges from R and B to reggae, and there's always plenty of dancing.

🚏 U2 or U3: Volkstheater. $ Cover free-€20, depending on event. ⏰ Open F-Sa 11pm-late; sometimes open during the week for special events.

DICK MACK'S 🎵♿🍸 IRISH PUB

Marc-Aurel-Str. 7 ☎676 706 81 24 💻www.paddysco.at/dickmack

Just beyond Schwedenpl.'s Bermuda Triangle and its pricey beers, Dick Mack's is the Irish pub that all the local university students swear by. The decor is nothing special (it's a typical pub), but the beers are cheap, cheap, cheap. You won't be sorry you began the night here when you leave happily intoxicated and likewise happily not broke.

🚏 U1 or U4: Schwedenpl. $ Beer €2. Mixed drinks €2.80. ⏰ Open M-Sa 8pm-4am.

ONYX
●♿♉ BAR

Stephanspl. 12   ☎1 535 39 69 ▪www.doco.com

The floor-to-ceiling windows of this sixth-floor bar in Haas Haus give unparalleled views of Stephansdom. It feels as though you could literally reach out and touch the roof. The view is to die for and so are the pricey drinks, especially the Frozen Blackberry with vodka and lemon, which mainly draw Vienna's young business crowd to the bar's sleek couches and stools.

⚑ *U1 or U3: Stephanspl.* Ⓢ *Mixed drinks €9-14.* 🕐 *Open daily 9am-2am.*

PLANTER'S CLUB
●♿♉⌂ BAR

Zelinkagasse 4   ☎533 33 93 15 ▪www.plantersclub.com

Low leather chairs, small coffee tables, and palm fronds adorn this colonial-style bar with deep wood accents and soft green and yellow lights. Be prepared to stay a while because the cocktail menu is at least 20 pages, and each one seems to be tastier than the last. There are over 450 single malt whiskeys alone. The place gets crowded around 10pm, so come early to snag a seat. The neighboring restaurant of the same name also comes highly recommended.

⚑ *U2 or U4: Schottenring.* Ⓢ *Mixed drinks €7-15.* 🕐 *Open daily 5pm-4am.*

PASSAGE
●⊗♉ CLUB, BAR

Babenberger Passage.   1 961 88 00 ▪www.sunshine.at

Turn an abandoned, underground pedestrian walkway into a series of clubs and you will get Passage, a stylish, futuristic club where people dress to impress (definitely don't arrive in your hiking gear). The music is mostly mainstream—club, dance, house, and pop—with a sleek bar and dance floor. Don't drink too much or the intricate lighting might make you think you are in a *Star Wars* movie (which could be a good thing, we guess).

⚑ *U2, Tram 1, 2, or D: Museumsquartier. At the corner of Burgring and Babenbergerstr.* Ⓢ *Cover varies depending on event.* 🕐 *Hours vary by event; check schedule online for details.*

CORE DISTRICTS

⬛ STRANDBAR HERRMANN
●♿♉⌂ BAR, BEACH CLUB

Herrmannpark   ▪www.strandbarherrmann.at

This canal-side venue is as close to a beach bar as it gets in Vienna. Parts of the ground have been covered with sand, and there are plenty of deck chairs for sunbathing during the day (although swimming in the canal is generally not recommended). By night, beers are passed around, and there is plenty of live or mixed music to set the scene.

⚑ *U1 or U4: Schwedenpl., exit to Urania. Or U3, Tram 1, 2, or 2A: Stubentor.* Ⓢ *Beer €3.30-4.80.* 🕐 *Open daily 10am-2am.*

CHELSEA
●♿♉⌂ BAR, CLUB, MUSIC VENUE

Lerchenfelder Gürtel/Stadtbahnbogen 29-30   ☎1 407 93 09 ▪www.chelsea.co.at

Back when the area was a red-light district, Chelsea opened in the Stadtbahnbogen, soon to revolutionize the Gürtel nightlife scene. The exterior lacks the glass facades that many of the newer Gürtel venues boast (look for the brick walls covered in posters instead), but that suits Chelsea's down-to-earth plain quality that gives it a pub vibe. With rock, Britpop, and funk blaring, the people are always ready to party. Come early because it gets packed.

⚑ *U6, Tram 46, or Bus #48A: Thaliastr.* Ⓢ *Cover free-€12.* 🕐 *Open daily 6pm-4am.*

BABU
●⊗♉⌂ BAR, CLUB

Stadtbahnbögen 181-184   ☎699 1 175 40 72 ▪www.babu.at

This large restaurant, bar, and club expands over four archways of the Gürtel underneath the train tracks. Inside, it's all glass and air, with a split-level design and crisp white seats. From the top floor, you can look out the windows onto the Gürtel, while below in the bar a gussied-up crowd schmoozes and sips cocktails.

🚇 U6: Nußdorfer Str. ⏰ Open daily 6pm-late.

CHARLIE P'S
🍸 IRISH PUB

Währinger Str. 3 ☎1 409 79 23 💻www.charlieps-irishpub.at

Like Dick Mack's, this Irish pub boasts cheap drinks and a young penny-pinching student crowd who want to drink a lot but spend a little. The upstairs has big tables and benches to sit and talk with a large group of friends, or you can head to the cellar where there is an additional bar, some high tables, and the always-popular karaoke.

🚇 U2: Schottentor. ⏰ Open M-Th noon-2am, F-Sa noon-3am, Su noon-1am.

PRATERSAUNA
♿🍸 CLUB

Waldsteingartenstr. 135 ☎1 72 919 27 💻www.pratersauna.tv

One of the newest clubs in Vienna's "in" scene, Pratersauna is a former sauna converted into a club. A deck and lawn with chairs encircle the pool, which looks temptingly lit up on warm summer evenings, but unfortunately it's not open when the club is in full swing. (And yes, they will kick you out if you try to swim. Also, Let's Go does not recommend swimming under the influence.) The alternative, warehouse-style dance floors reflect the minimalist music that is generally played and is too monotone for anyone who's looking for a dance beat. The high entrance price is mostly due to hype; spend willingly but don't be surprised if you are a bit underwhelmed. Oh yeah, and it generally doesn't get packed until after 2am.

🚇 U2: Messe. Or Tram 1: Prater Hauptallee. 💲 Cover free-€15. Beers €3.80. Mixed drinks €7-9. ⏰ Open W-Sa 9pm-late. Pool open W until 4am.

B72
🍸 BAR, MUSIC VENUE

Hernalser Gürtel, Stadtbahnbogen 72 ☎1 409 21 28 💻www.b72.at

Part of the growing Gürtel nightlife scene (under the railway arches), this small venue regularly hosts national and international DJs and bands, though it's particularly known within the Austrian alternative music world. The venue is cleverly split over two floors—on the ground level, the two bars and stage reside, while on the first level, there are tables and chairs with views down onto the stage.

🚇 U6 or Tram 43: Alser Str. 💲 Cover free-€15. ⏰ Open daily 8pm-4am.

Q [KJU:]
🍸 BAR, CLUB

Währinger Gürtel, Stadtbahnbogen 142-144 ☎1 804 50 55 💻www.kju-bar.at

Frequented by a young, party-going crowd, Q [kju:] is another club venue on the Gürtel nightlife scene, with a rowdy, dance-happy clientele. The red walls with gold and leather accents are adorned with hanging mirrors that make the dance floor seem larger (and also provide a convenient means of checking out your latest dance moves). If you don't feel like shakin' your booty, observe the sunken dance floor from a booth alongside it.

🚇 U6: Währinger Str., Volksoper. ⏰ Open daily 8pm-4am.

PRATERDOME
♿🍸 CLUB

Riesenradpl.7 ☎908 119 29 00 💻www.praterdome.at

The largest club in Austria, Praterdome fulfills every disco-goer's fantasy... within reason, of course. There are four dance floors playing every type of music imaginable and 12 bars to serve you up drinks. While the laser lights and neon colors are cool, the clientele often thinks they are a bit too cool (in other words, trashy). Mentally prepare yourself for a large night out and bring a very very large group of friends—it's likely you will lose a few in this massive party complex.

🚇 U1: Praterstern. 💲 Cover free-€10. ⏰ Open Th-Sa 9 or 10pm-late.

CAFE STEIN
⊛ᕭ℉⌂ RESTOBAR

Währinger Str. 6-8 ☎319 72 41 ▣www.cafe-stein.com

In the warm weather, Cafe Stein's outdoor deck is the best place to enjoy a quiet beer or wine and close conversation with friends; the views of Votivkirche lit up at night provide good food for conversation. During the cooler seasons, the three floors inside offer a more clubby vibe, with many students from the nearby university coming to be merry.

🍴 *U2, Tram 37, 38, 40, 41, 42, 43, 44, or Bus #1A: Schottentor.* ⓘ *Open M-Sa 8am-1am, Su 9am-1am.*

ALL IN
⊛ᕭ℉ BAR, MUSIC VENUE

Währinger Gürtel, Stadtbahnbögen 90-91 ☎1 236 52 89 ▣www.allinbar.com

One of the more recent arrivals on the Gürtel nightlife scene, All In boasts a sleek design that blends the exposed brick of the subway arches with modern glass shelves and geometric furniture. There is a dance floor as well as a long bar with high square stools—dress up a bit and order one of the delicious, fruity cocktails. The music ranges from oldies to jazz to hip hop, so check the website for upcoming events.

🍴 *U6 or Tram 43: Alser Str.* ⓢ *Cover free-€8.* ⓘ *Open Tu-Sa 9pm-4am, Su 10am-8pm.*

HALBESTADT
⊛ᕭ℉ BAR

Währinger Gürtel, Stadtbahnbogen 155 ☎319 47 35 ▣www.halbestadt.at

This intimate, tiny cocktail bar is practically hidden in a single archway of the Stadtbahnbogen. The bar stretches along one side, while on the other side a single leather bench runs the length of the room. Sit with one or two friends for a quiet drink and view the Gürtel through the large glass windows at either end of the bar. Then, when the time is ripe, hit up the crazier clubs nearby.

🍴 *U6, Tram 40, 41, 42, or Bus #40A: Währinger Str., Volksoper.* ⓘ *Open daily 8pm-4am.*

LUTZ BAR AND CLUB
⊛⊗⁽ᵗ⁾℉⌂ BAR, CAFE, CLUB

Mariahilfer Str. 3 ☎585 36 46 ▣www.lutz-bar.at, www.lutz-club.at

This is one of those venues that transitions from day to night seamlessly. During the day, eat breakfast and drink coffee while accessing the free Wi-Fi or reading an international newspaper in your leather armchair. The bar is only a few steps away as the party crowd rolls in. The downstairs club, complete with laser neon lights and a dance floor, is a sure fire way to party. Every night is a different event, such as "Tipsy Tuesdays."

🍴 *U2: Museumsquartier.* ⓘ *Bar and cafe open M-F 8am-late, Sa 9am-late, Su 10am-late. Club open daily 9:30pm-late.*

RHIZ
⊛ᕭ℉⌂ BAR, CLUB, MUSIC VENUE

Lerchenfelder Gürtel, Stadtbahnbogen 37-38 ☎1 409 25 05 ▣www.rhiz.org

This casual, and somewhat cramped, music venue particularly appeals to people with a love of electronic music. Ten years ago, Rhiz was the place for experimental electronic sounds that pushed the boundaries of the music world, while today, live acts ranging from electronic to rock play regularly to packed houses. A warning to those with delicate ears—it can get loud!

🍴 *U6, Tram 2 or 33: Josefstädter Str.* ⓢ *Cover free-€10.* ⓘ *Open M-Sa 6pm-late. DJs start at about 9pm.*

OUTER DISTRICTS

U4
⊛⊗℉ DANCE CLUB

Schonbrunner Str. 222 ☎817 11 92 ▣www.u-4.at

U4 is a club legend in Vienna—everyone has their own story and impression of the place, but all will undoubtedly name-drop that Nirvana once played there. In its dark underground locale, U4 has two dance floors with different music, and the program changes every night. Its far-out location in the district XII eliminates the possibility of club-hopping easily, so everyone commits to the night, often-times taking the first U-Bahn train home in the morning.

✈ *U4: Meidlinger Hauptstr. The club is directly behing the station on Schonbrunner Str.* 🕐 *Open M-Sa 10pm-5-6am.*

arts and culture

THEATER

TANZQUARTIER WIEN
♣♿ CORE

Museumspl. 1   ☎1 581 35 91 🖥www.tqw.at

With an ambitious schedule of new shows every weekend, Tanzquartier Wien has become a premier dance space for contemporary and modern-style dance. Much of it is experimental, and the shows range from one-woman acts to ensemble pieces performed in the studio spaces or the neighboring Kunsthalle theater.

✈ *U2: Musemspl. Or U2 or U3: Volkstheater. In Museumsquartier, walk beyond the Leopold Museum and turn right.* 🛈 *Tickets €11, students €7.50. Open dance classes (professional level) €9.* 🕐 *Box office and info office open M-Sa 9am-8pm.*

THEATER AN DER WIEN
♣♿ CORE

Linke Wienzeile 6   ☎1 588 85 🖥www.theater-wien.at

One of Vienna's youngest opera houses (it opened in 2006), Theater an der Wien becomes *the* opera destination in July and August when its shows keep running even though the normal opera season stops. A new show usually premieres each month.

✈ *U1, U2, or U4: Karlspl.* 🛈 *Tickets €12-160. Student rush operas €15, concerts €10. Standing-room tickets €7.* 🕐 *Box office open daily 10am-7pm. Student-rush tickets are available 30min. before curtain at the box office. Standing room (based on availability) can be purchased 1hr. before showtime.*

VIENNA'S ENGLISH THEATER
♣ CORE

Josefsgasse 12   ☎402 126 00 🖥www.englishtheatre.at

Vienna's English Theater was established in 1963 as a summer theater for tourists, but its popularity enabled it to expand into the traditional theater season (and now it doesn't even run shows during the summer months). In 2004, it was awarded the Nestroy Prize for 40 years of achievement, with appearances by the likes of Judi Dench and Leslie Nielsen and European premieres of plays by David Auburn and Edward Albee.

✈ *U2 and U3: Volkstheater. Or Tram 1 or D: Parliament; Tram 2: Rathaus; or Bus #13A: Piaristengasse.* 🛈 *Tickets €22-42. Students and under 18 20% off. Standby tickets €9.* 🕐 *Box office open Jan-May and Sept-Dec M-F 10am-7:30pm, Sa and holidays 5-7:30pm; on non-performance days Jan-May and Sept-Dec M-F 10am-5pm. Limited number of standby tickets are available 15min. before curtain.*

FILM

ENGLISH CINEMA HAYDN
⊗ CORE

Mariahilfer Str. 57   ☎1 587 22 62 🖥www.haydnkino.at

If you're on the lookout for some good ol' American pop culture, this cinema is one of the few in the city that presents English-language films without subtitles. All the major motion pictures you've heard of and, surprisingly, not too behind the US in terms of release dates (i.e., you will probably find a few that you haven't seen already).

✈ *U3: Neubaugasse.* 🛈 *Tickets €5.90-8.50, depending on length of film and day of the week.* 🕐

Box office opens 15min. before 1st show and closes 15min. after beginning of last show.

BURG KINO
⊛& INNER

Opernring 19 ☎587 8406 ▨www.burgkino.at

A centrally located theater that shows a mix of mainstream and indie. There are two screens—one reserved for a popular Hollywood movie or cartoon (screened in the original version), while the other, smaller screen offers a rotation of less prominent indie flicks (although still fairly recent and also in the original English versions).

🚃 *U1, U2, U4, Tram 1, 2, or D: Karlspl.* Ⓢ *Tickets M-Th €5, F-Su €6.* ⏰ *Box office opens 30min. before 1st showing.*

ARTIS INTERNATIONAL
⊛& INNER

Schultergasse 5 ☎535 65 70 ▨www.cineplexx.at

This old Inner Stadt cinema shows only recent Hollywood flicks in English and generally without subtitles. There is even an occasional 3D offering. Some movie-goers balk that the screens are too small, especially compared to the uber large, stadium style theaters we are now used to.

🚃 *U1 or U3: Stephanspl. Or U3: Herrengasse.* Ⓢ *Tickets €6-10.* ⏰ *Opens 15-30min. before 1st showing.*

MUSIC

STAATSOPER (STATE OPERA)
⚐ INNER

Opernring 2 ☎514 44 22 50 ▨www.wiener-staatsoper.at

For many visitors, seeing an opera in the gorgeous Staatsoper is a highlight of a trip to Vienna. Hindemith's *Cadillac*, Mozart's *Don Giovanni* and *Le nozze di Figaro*, Janácek's *Kátja Kabanová*, Händel's *Alcina*, and Donizetti's *Anna Bolena* are just six of the newest productions. Opera season runs Sept-June, but during the summer months, operas are shown on a 50-sq.-m screen on the plaza in front of the Opera House for free.

🚃 *U1, U2, U4, Trams 1, 2, D, J, 62, 65: Karlspl.* Ⓢ *Tickets €3-250. Standing-room tickets €2.50-5. Tours €6.50, seniors €5.50, students and children €3.50.* ⏰ *Box office (Operngasse 2 ☎514 44 78 10) open M-F 8am-6pm, Sa-Su 9am-noon. Tours of the Opera House vary based on show schedule, but usually 1-3 per day in the afternoon at 2, 3, and 4pm; check website ahead of time. Tickets include entrance to Opera Museum (except on M). Standing-room tickets are available 80min. before curtains.*

WIENER PHILHARMONIC ORCHESTRA
INNER

Ticket and Ball Office, Kärntner Ring 12 ☎505 65 25 ▨www.wienerphilharmoniker.at

The Wiener Philharmonic Orchestra embodies the musical spirit of Vienna. Strauss, Mahler, Bruckner, and Wagner are some of the famous names that have been associated with the orchestra over the years, which is perhaps why season subscriptions often sell out years in advance. Tickets for their annual New Year's Eve concert performed in the Musikverein has to be lotteried due to such high demand, but they perform at many other venues and times throughout the city.

🚃 *U1, U2, U4, Tram 1, 2, or D: Karlspl.* Ⓢ *Prices vary.* ⏰ *Box office open M-F 9:30am-3:30pm, and 1hr. before the subscription concerts and end-of-year concerts.*

WIENER STADHALLE
⚐&♿ OUTER

Vogelweidpl. 14 ☎1 98 100 ▨www.stadthalle.com

The Stadthalle presents the greatest variety of music, entertainment, and artistic acts of any Vienna venue, as well as some sports and even kid's musicals. Although it's lacking Old World opera house charm (the building resembles a spaceship), it has seen big-name musicians including Guns n' Roses and the Red Hot Chili Peppers.

🚃 *U6: Burgasse.* Ⓢ *Ticket prices vary based on event.* ⏰ *Box office (between Hall D and Hall F) open M-Sa 10am-8pm.*

arts and culture . music

FESTIVALS

DONAUINSEL FEST (DANUBE ISLAND FESTIVAL) DANUBE ISLAND

Danube Island www.donauinselfest.at

This three-day festival is one of the most popular outdoor events in Europe, taking place on the Danube Island and welcoming over 2 million attendees. Free concerts galore with every genre of music imaginable, plenty of food and drink (sometimes too much!), and even a section with amusement park rides and games.

U1: Donauinsel or U6: Handelskai. $ Concerts and music free. Food, drink, and rides vary. ⏰ A weekend in June.

VIENNALE INNER

Siebensterngasse 2 ☎1 526 59 47 www.viennale.at

The Viennale prides itself on showcasing Austrian and international films for young audiences, focusing on documentary films, international shorts, and experimental works. Every year, the festival screens over 300 films and receives over 90,000 visitors and audience members, including about 700 accredited guests from the film industry. Many of the screenings include discussions with the filmmakers, and there are other events such as concerts, book presentations, and cultural exhibitions throughout.

Cinemas throughout the Inner Stadt. ⏰ Festival runs every Oct.

RAINBOW PARADE INNER, CORE

Ringstr. ☎1 216 66 04 www.regenbogenparade.at

Only begun in 1996, the gay pride parade has now become one of Vienna's largest events, sweeping the Ringstr. with the rainbow flags, outrageous outfits and body paint, and lots and lots of glitter. The parade culminates in a free concert with multiple acts, food and drink stands on the streets, and a generally exuberant atmosphere that might seem unexpected in this otherwise traditional city. Be on the lookout for the blow-up, rainbow-colored balloons shaped like male genitalia.

U4: Stadtpark. From Stadtpark to Schwarzenbergerpl. $ Parade and concert free. ⏰ Early in July.

vienna

shopping

CLOTHING

MOTMOT CORE

Kirchengasse 36 ☎1 924 27 19 www.motmotshop.com

T-shirts, T-shirts, T-shirts in every color and style imaginable and with hilarious designs and idioms. If you like surprises, buy a sale bag, which has a mysterious selection of shirts in a brown bag for a fixed, cheap price (male or female is indicated). Other fun accessories like buttons and belts are also available.

Tram 49. $ T-shirts €25-50. Buttons €1. ⏰ Open Tu-F noon-7pm, Sa noon-5pm.

BE A GOOD GIRL ♿ CORE

Westbahnstr. 5A ☎524 47 28 www.beagoodgirl.at

While part of this shop is a hair salon (chic, obviously), the other half has funky bags, wallets, fedoras, and sneakers for sale. There is also an interesting selection of books and notebooks, one of which has Vienna city grids on the pages in the place of regular lines or graph paper.

Tram 49. ⏰ Open Tu-F 10am-7pm, Sa 10am-4pm.

ART POINT

CORE

Westbahnstr. 3   ☎522 04 25 ▧www.artpoint.eu

This store epitomizes the creativity of up-and-coming European designers, whose clothing is sometimes more like a work of art than particularly practical. Art Point is best known for their "two sleeves and one collar," which is as it sounds: two dress shirt sleeves attached to a dress-shirt collar, then wrapped around and tied like a scarf. They come in every pattern imaginable and are made for men and women.

🚋 *Tram 49.* ⑨ *2 sleeves and 1 collar €85.* 🕘 *Open M-F 11am-7pm, Sa 11am-5pm.*

MUSIC

SCOUT RECORDS

CORE

Capistrangasse 3

Stepping into this record store is like venturing into a music-collector's basement. Wall shelves, filing bins, and even cardboard boxes are all packed to the brim with CDs, DVDs, and records. There is a large selection of jazz as well as rock, metal, and classical. Be prepared to spend some time getting lost in the music.

🚋 *U3: Neubaugasse.* ⑨ *CDs from €3. Vinyl records up to €40.* 🕘 *Open M-F 2-7pm, Sa 10am-5pm.*

SUBSTANCE

CORE

Westbahnstr. 16   ☎523 67 57 ▧www.substance-store.com

The pristine rows of CDs and vinyl records are shiny and expensive, making this music store the place to buy new music. The collection is extensive, though the focus is on indie, electronica, and alternative.

🚋 *U3 or Tram 49: Neubaugasse.* 🕘 *Open M-F 11am-7:30pm, Sa 10am-6pm.*

AUDIAMO

OUTER

Kaiserstr. 70   ☎699 95 31 90 ▧www.audiamo.com

It's not too often you can find books on tape when traveling abroad, and in English no less! Audiamo has crime, romance, thriller, biography, fiction, and children's books on tape, as well as some CDs and DVDs for your listening and viewing pleasure. Look for the British flags on the boxes that indicate English-language selections. There is also a pleasant cafe in the shop with coffee and snacks.

🚋 *U6 or Tram 5: Burggasse.* 🕘 *Open M-F 9am-7pm, Sa 10am-5pm.*

BOOKS

▨ SHAKESPEARE AND COMPANY BOOKSELLERS

CORE

Sterngasse 2   ☎1 535 50 35 ▧www.shakespeare.co.at

This store's motto is "Let yourself be found by a book," and there really is no better place to do just that. Located in a nook in one of the oldest parts of the Inner Stadt, Shakespeare and Co. has large English selections of travel literature, fiction, and history books arranged on wooden bookshelves that stretch from floor to ceiling. It often holds book readings and other events open to the public.

🚋 *U1 or U4: Schwedenpl.* ⑨ *Used books from €3. New books from €8.* 🕘 *Open 6 days a week 9am-9pm; call ahead for weekly schedule.*

THE BRITISH BOOKSHOP

CORE

Weihburggasse 24   ☎1 512 19 450 ▧www.britishbookshop.at

Just when you just thought you would never find the perfect vacation read, The British Bookshop is overflowing with more selection than you know what to do with. Choose from fiction, travel (▨**Let's Go** included!), classics, crime, romance, and even business books. Don't miss the sale bin hidden behind the bulletin board next to the cash register.

🚋 *U3, Tram 1 or 2: Stubentor.* ⑨ *Paperback novels €9-12.* 🕘 *Open M-F 9:30am-6:30pm, Sa 9:30-6pm.*

KUNSTHALLE WIEN SHOP

CORE

Museumspl. 1 ☎524 02 20 🖥www.kunsthallewien.at/en/shop

The kooky knick-knacks assembled here will certainly entertain. Because who doesn't need a massive chocolate-bar shaped calculator or kama sutra dice? Pick up hilarious postcards *(€1.20-3.50)* to send home or a new eraser for "Really Big Mistakes."

U2: Musemspl. Alternatively U2 or U3: Volkstheater. In Museumsquartier, the shop is beneath the stairs of the MUMOK. ⏰ Open daily 11am-7pm.

LIFE BOOKS/"BÜCHER FUR'S LEBEN"

BOOKS

Capistrangasse 5 ☎1 587 94 60 🖥www.lifebooks.at

This bookstore has got its motto right, offering all the "life books" you could need, though unfortunately the majority are in German. There is a selection in English that consists of mainstream novels and bestsellers, and the English-speaking staff is happy to recommend their favorites.

U3: Neubaugasse. From the stop, the bookstore is off Mariahilfer Str.. $ English books €8-11. ⏰ Open M-F 10am-6pm, Sa 10am-4pm.

essentials

PRACTICALITIES

- **TOURIST OFFICES:** The Vienna Card, opera and theater tickets, and other brochures are available. *(☎1 24 555 🖥www.vienna.info Located in the Inner Stadt, Albertinapl. across from the Albertina museum, behind the Opera House. $ Hotel reservations €2.90. ⏰ Open daily 9am-7pm.)*
- **EMBASSIES: Australia.** *(IV, Mattiellistr. 2-4. ☎1 506 740 🖥www.australian-embassy.at ⏰ Open M-F 8:30am-4:30pm.)* **Canada.** *(I, Laurenzerberg 2 ☎1 531 38 30 00 🖥www.kanada.at ⏰ Open M-F 8:30am-12:30pm and 1:30-3:30pm.)* **UK.** *(III, Jauresgasse 12 ☎1 716 130 🖥www.britishembassy.at ⏰ Open M-F 9am-1pm and 2-5pm.)* **US.** *(IX, Boltzmanngasse 16 ☎1 313 390 🖥www.usembassy.at ⏰ Open M-F 8-11:30am.)*
- **INTERNET CAFES: künstlerhauskino wien - internetcafé.** *(Karlspl. 5. ☎587 96 63 19 $ €1.60 per 30min. ⏰ Open daily 11am-9pm.)* **Surfland.c@fe.** *(Krugerstr. 10 ☎512 77 01 $ €6 per hr. Photocopy €0.50. Color copy €1. Printing €0.30 per page. ⏰ Open daily Apr-Oct 10am-11pm; Nov-Mar 10am-10pm.)*
- **POST OFFICE:** The main office *(Hauptpotamt)* is located in the Inner Stadt. *(Fleishmarkt 19 ☎0577 677 10 10 ℹ Other branches are located throughout the city; look for the yellow signs and post boxes. ⏰ Open M-F 7am-10pm, Sa-Su 9am-10pm.)*
- **POSTAL CODES:** 1010 (Inner Stadt) through 1023 (District XXIII).

EMERGENCY!

- **POLICE:** *(☎133)*
- **AMBULANCE:** *(☎144)*
- **FIRE:** *(☎122)*
- **PHYSICIAN:** *(☎141)* **Physicians Hotline for Visitors:** *(☎513 9595 ⏰ 24hr.)*
- **EMERGENCY DENTAL:** *(☎512 20 78 ⏰ Service on nights and weekends.)*
- **PHARMACY:** *(☎15 50 ⏰ Open on nights and weekends.)*

GETTING THERE

By Plane

Vienna is centrally located in Europe and as a result is quite easy to reach via plane. **Vienna-Schwechat Airport** *(Wien-Schwechat Flughafen. ☎7007 222 33 💻www.viennaairport.at)* is home to **Austrian Airlines** *(💻www.austrian.com)*, which runs non-stop flights from most major cities in Europe to Vienna multiple times a day. Other airlines that fly to Vienna include **British Airways** *(💻www.britishairways.com)*, **easyJet** *(💻www.easyjet.com)*, **Aer Lingus** *(💻www.aerlingus.com)*, **Lufthansa** *(💻www.lufthansa.com)*, **KLM** *(💻www.klm.com)*, **Air France** *(💻www.airfrance.com)*, and **United Airlines** *(💻www.united.com)*.

One of the least stressful ways to reach the city center after a long flight is with the **City Airport Train** *(CAT, 💻www.cityairporttrain.com)*. It brings you to **Wien Mitte** in a mere 16min., from which you can then connect to the U4 underground line at Landstr. The CAT runs every half hour. *(⏰ From the airport to the city daily 5:38am-11:38pm. From the city to the airport daily 6:05am-12:05am. $ One-way €9, round-trip €16; with a Vienna Card €7.50/15. On board tickets cost €12. Children under 14 ride free.)*

In addition to the CAT, the **Schellbahn** *(S-7 or S-8)* runs into the city as well, though it's a bit trickier. The trains going to the city should read "Wien Mitte," "Wien Nord," or "Florisdorf," while the train to the airport should have a "Flughafen" or "Wolfsthal" sign. *($ One-way tickets (2 zones) €4.40, bought in advance €3.60. With the Vienna card €2.20/1.80.)*

Airport Express Buses also shuttle between various places in the city center and the airport and take about 20min. *(💻www.postbus.at ☎1 7007 323 00, 517 17 $ One-way €6, children €3, Vienna Cardholders €5. Round trip €11/5.50/10. ⏰Every 30min., 5am-midnight.)*

By Train

There are a number of train stations located throughout the city that serve as major hubs for both local and international trains.

Sudbahnhof

If you are wondering where the Sudbahnhof went, in short, it's gone. But don't freak out just yet. Since 2009, the Sudbahnhof has been under construction, and a shining new **Vienna Central Station** will take the place of this defunct station. The VCS is scheduled for completion in 2013. During construction, the eastern portion of Sudbahnhof (Ostbahn) will remain running, serving eastern bound trains to destinations like Bratislava.

Westbahnhof

The Westbahnhof is also undergoing construction and large portions are closed until 2011, but all the normal destinations are still active. This includes trains to other parts of **Austria** (Innsbruck, Salzburg) as well as international destinations including **Hungary** (Budapest), **Germany** (Munich, Hamburg, Berlin), and **Switzerland** (Zurich). The airport buses and taxis ranks still drop off and pick up in from the station, and you can easily connect to the U3 or U6 underground lines as well as tram lines 5, 6, 9, 18, 52, and 58. Westbahnhof also still has ticket windows and machines, an ÖBB Travel Centre, luggage storage, shops, cafes, and an information point in operation.

Wien Meidling

In Vienna's District XII, Wien Meidling lies at the end of Meidlinger Haupstr. and serves international destinations in the **Czech Republic, Poland,** and **Germany.** It has taken over all the local arrivals and departures that previously used the Sudbahnhof and also connects to the U6 Station Philadelphiabrücke, Tram 62, Bus lines 7A, 7B, 8A, 9A, 15A, 59A, and 62A, and S-bahn lines S1, S2, S3, S4, S5, S6, S9, and S15. Wien Meidling has taxi stands, luggage lockers, ticket machines, an ÖBB Travel Centre, and an information desk.

Wien Mitte

The City Airport Train arrives at Wien Mitte, where you can easily connect to the U3 and U4 underground lines and multiple S-bahn lines.

GETTING AROUND

If you are staying in the city, a car is definitely not needed. Save the parking money and buy yourself a drink.

By Wiener Linien

The public transportation system in Vienna—the Wiener Linien *(🖳www.wienerlinien.at)*—is extensive, reliable, and safe. It consists of the **U-bahn** (underground), **trams** (above ground), and **buses.** The **Vienna Card** *(available in hotels and at the tourist information center on Albertinapl. and the airport for €18.50),* gives you 72hr. of unlimited transportation access within the city as well as over 200 discounts on other sights. Other useful transportation tickets include the 24hr. season ticket *($ €5.70),* the 48hr. season ticket *($ €10),* the 72hr. season ticket *($ €13.60),* and monthly *($ €49.50).* A single ride costs €1.80. For the U-bahn, buy your ticket at the multilingual machines and validate it (stamp it) at the little blue boxes before reaching the platforms. Single tickets for trams and buses can be purchased on board for €2.20, coins only. The five U-bahn lines run on weekdays from 5am to midnight, while the buses and trams end a bit earlier. Check the Wiener Linien website for exact schedules of specific lines. In September 2010, the U-bahn lines started to run all night on Fridays and Saturdays in addition to the night buses that already reach a large portion of the city.

By Taxi

Because the public transportation system is so extensive, taxis are not entirely necessary, but they come in handy when the Nightbus is elusive. Some taxi numbers include ☎4000 011 11, ☎4000 010 00 (Inner Stadt), ☎601 60, ☎401 00, and ☎313 00, although the best bet is to pick one on the street. (All accredited taxis in the city are known to be reliable.) In the Inner Stadt, taxis cluster on **Rotenturmstrasse** and **Schwedenplatz** near the nightlife, but they also wait outside other well-known clubs in the core and outer districts. Taxis have set rates for the airport, and there are some that are exclusively airport taxis: **C and K** *(☎444 44)* and **Airportdriver** *(☎22 8 22)* run €35-48, depending on the number of passengers. An Austria-wide taxi number is ☎1718.

By Bike

Because of Vienna's manageable size, bikes are extremely common in the warmer spring and summer months, and there are safe bikepaths (over 1100km total) throughout the city. **Citybike** is a public bike-rental system with over 60 stands located around the city, usually close to public transportation hubs. To rent a CityBike, tourists need the CityBike Tourist card (unless you somehow have a MasterCard or Visa associated with an Austrian bank). **Royal Tours** *(Herrengasse 1-3)* and **Pedal Power** *(Ausstellunstr. 3)* offer the cards for €2 per day, but it's worth asking your hostel or hotel as well. *($ From €4 per hr.)*

By Suburban Train

The suburban train network **(Austrian Federal Railways, ÖBB)** is also extensive and provides swift and easy access to the surrounding towns and countryside. These trains require different tickets than the inner-city public transport, but all the stations have the multilingual machines or ticket counters. Single rides start at €1.80 for nearby towns, such as **Mödling.**

AUSTRIAN ALPS

The hills are alive
with the sound of music
with songs they have sung for a thousand years...
My heart wants to beat like the wings of the birds
That rise from the lake to the trees
My heart wants to sigh like a chime that flies
From a church on a breeze.
                    -The Sound of Music

greatest hits

- **TAKE ME TO THE RIVER.** Take a leisurely boat ride along the Danube through the Wachau valley from Melk (p. 341) to Krems (p. 344).

- **A CINDERELLA STORY.** Slip on some glass pumps and explore the picture-perfect library, salons, and halls of Grafenegg Castle (p. 345).

- **OCEANS 14.** Find a George Clooney-esque gambling buddy and double down at the Grand Casino in Baden (p. 343).

- **YOUR PLACE OR MINE?** Pull on a sweatshirt and take a boat tour through Seegrotte—a former gypsum mine in Mödling (p. 335).

student life

While the Austrian Alps aren't bustling with student culture, there are countless attractions at which you can flash your plastic (student ID card) for great discounts; knock an entire euro off for your studies at Melk's **Schloß Schallaburg.** Stift Heiligenkreuz's abbey and church in Modling will set you back only €3.50, while entrance to Klosterneuburg's **Essl Museum** of art is free for students—be sure to call ahead and ask about the program of visiting artists. Speaking of free, that's how much you'll pay for a walk along the Danube in Tulln. Admission to Baden's **Grand Casino** is free, too, but gambling typically calls for a wallet.

klosterneuburg ☎2243

According to legend, **Klosterneuburg Monastery** was built when Margrave Leopold III found his wife's wedding veil that she had lost nine years earlier. It was hanging from an elderberry tree somewhere between the Vienna Woods and the Danube, and at that moment, the Virgin Mary appeared and commanded Leopold to construct a monastery in her honor. Thus the magnificent Abbey came into being. Over 900-years-old, Klosterneubug Abbey is at the heart of the small city of Klosterneuburg, located 10km up the **Danube** from Vienna. Around it, a selection of streets with shops and cafes have a small-town flavor; there are just enough large grocery stores to prevent the town from feeling as archaic as the abbey. Access to the town is easy via public transportation, making Klosterneuburg a popular daytrip from Vienna.

ORIENTATION

Wiener Str. is the main highway toward the town center, along which the bus #239 drives and the City Train runs parallel. On this street, with the city behind you, the **Essl Museum** will come up first on the right, and the **abbey** will be further ahead on the left. In the town center, Wiener Str. turns into **Neidermarkt,** where multiple bus stops and tourist information center can be found around a small plaza. Neidermarkt then curves left uphill and turns into Stadtpl., another main artery with the city's shops and cafes. Bus #239 runs along Stadtpl. toward **Maria Gugging,** a neighboring town about 8km further into the Vienna countryside.

SIGHTS

KLOSTERNEUBURG ABBEY — CHURCH, WINERY

Stiftspl. 1, 3400 Klosterneuburg ☎2243 44 12 12 www.stift-klosterneuburg.at

The most frequented sight in the town of Klosterneuburg, the abbey houses an elaborate church, the **Verdun Altar,** and Austria's oldest and largest winery below. If you have some hours to spare, it's a good deal to invest in the Stiftsticket, which will allow you to tour-hop the whole day.

It's the huge monastery with 2 towers. i The Sacred Tour including the Church and Verdun Altar is the only tour offered in English. The self-guided "Imperial Tour" through the imperial rooms has English explanations. $ Tours €5-9, students €4-6. Stiftsticket tour €14/10. Open daily 9am-6pm. Sacred Tour Sa and Su 2pm.

ESSL MUSEUM — ART MUSEUM

An der Donau - Au 1, 3400 Klosterneuburg ☎2243 37 05 01 50 www.essl.museum

Agnes and Karlhienz Essl have collected over 7,000 works of art during their lifetimes, and it is their primary wish to share and educate others about the world of contemporary art (hence the free shuttle bus and free entry for students). The Essls are highly involved in the organization of the permanent collection as well as the program of visiting artists (all of whom they have met while traveling). In 2011, look forward to two special exhibits featuring up-and-coming artists from India and from New York.

✈ *A free shuttle bus (25min.) leaves from Vienna at Albertinapl. 2 at 10am, noon, 2, and 4pm. Return shuttle buses to the city leave the museum at 11am, 1, 3, and 6pm.* Ⓢ *Students, retirees, and unemployed free. Adults €5. Family €9. W 6-9pm free.* Ⓩ *Open Tu 10am-6pm, W 10am-9pm, Th-Su 10am-6pm.*

MUSEUM GUGGING
♠♿ MUSEUM, GALLERY

Am Campus 2, 3400 Maria Gugging
☎2243 870 87 🖳www.gugging.at

Museum Gugging was established as a showcase for the artwork of the neighboring Haus de Kunstler, where mentally ill patients are given a voice through artistic expression. Their work—mostly drawing and painting—has revolutionized the field of "Art Brut," popularizing artists such as Johann Hauser. The upstairs museum is paired with the downstairs Galerie Gugging, where visitors can purchase selected artworks.

✈ *U4: Heiligenstadt or bus #239: ART/Brut Center Gugging. Follow the signs for the museum and gallery up the really big hill.* Ⓢ *€7, seniors €5.50, students €5, family €14, children under 6 free.* Ⓩ *Open Tu-Su Jan-May and Sept-Dec 10am-5pm; June-Aug 10am-6pm.*

FOOD

HOTEL ANKER
♠♿♥♨ RESTOBAR ❷

Niedermarkt 5, 3400 Klosterneuburg
☎2243 32 13 40 🖳www.hotel-anker.at

Hotel Anker offers meat, potatoes, and beer at more reasonable prices than the few other sit-down restaurants located in town. Many locals enjoy Hotel Anker as a regular smoking and drinking establishment, so don't expect white tablecloths and crystal wine glasses. The staff will kindly offer you an English menu and satisfyingly greasy french fries.

✈ *Behind the bus stop, across from the train tracks in Klosterneuburg.* Ⓢ *Entrees €6.50-13.* Ⓩ *Open daily 10am-11pm.*

ESSENTIALS

Practicalities

Everything you need is on the main street, **Stadtplatz,** or **Niedermarkt,** where the train and buses drop off. Along Stadtpl., there are a number of 24hr. **ATMs** (*bankomats*) and full-service branches of Bank Austria and Este Bank. **Grocery stores** (Spar, Billa), **pharmacies** (Bipa, dm), cafes and specialty shops are all located along Stadtpl.

- **TOURIST OFFICES:** The tourist office can give you maps and information on rooms. *(Niedermarkt 4 ☎2243 320 38).*

Getting There and Getting Around

If you are planning on visiting the **Essl Museum** in Klosterneuburg, take advantage of the free shuttle to and from the museum. From the Essl Museum, you can walk down the street to Klosterneuburg town center or take the bus #239 one stop. If you are not planning on visiting the Essl, Klosterneuburg is also easily accessible by public transportation. Take the U4 to Heiligenstadt, then pick up bus #239 toward Klosterneuburg/Maria Gugging. The **City Train** *(S40)* also runs to the town and drops off right near the bus stops in the town center.

laxenburg ☎2236

Hop off the plane at LAX...kidding. You can get here via a Metro-bus transfer. The quiet town of Laxenburg sits 17km southwest of Vienna, and to be honest, is really only worth visiting on a sunny day when you can enjoy the grounds of the one and only sight in town—**Schloβ Laxenburg.** Somewhat reminiscent of Schloβ Schonbrunn in the city, Laxenburg is a pale yellow palace with sweeping grounds, and was formerly a spring and summer home of the imperial family. Today, the Schloβ has been converted into the **International Institute for Applied Systems Analysis,** so unfortunately, there are more computers than horse-drawn carriages on the premises. Visiting the Schloβ isn't an option, but you can explore the grounds, which were actually Empress Sisi's favorite escape from the city and where she often enjoyed lengthy horseback rides. Laxenburg was also Empress Sisi's honeymoon destination, but the town never really figured out how to market that, so the destination has remained relatively untouched by tourists.

ORIENTATION

While Laxenburg is not an overly complicated town, if you are one of those people who need a map or else, print one out before taking the day trip. Laxenburg does not have a tourist office, and the few kiosks that sell maps have limited supplies. When you disembark from the bus at **Franz-Josef Platz,** the first notable sight is the pink **Kaiserbahnhof,** an old train station that has been converted into a restaurant. Walking with the restaurant on your left and the street on your right, you will reach **Hofstrasse,** where the bank, grocery store, and very important ice cream shop await. A right turn will lead to **Schloβplatz,** with the **Pfarrkirche, Rathaus,** and **Schloβ Laxenburg.** At the very end of the street through the carpark, a gate marks the entrance to Schloβpark Laxenburg.

SIGHTS

SCHLOßPARK LAXENBURG — PARK, CASTLE

Schloβpl. 1 ☎2236 712 26 www.schloss-laxenburg.at

According to landscape gardening experts, the Laxenburg Palace grounds are a prime example of Romantic period horticulture (read: a really pretty park). Enjoy the endless stretches of winding paths, benches, fields, and woods with hidden monuments, grottoes, temples, fountains, and even a medieval tournament sight scattered throughout. The highlight of the park is **Franzensburg Castle,** surrounded by water and accessed by either a series of bridges or a short ferry ride *(€0.40)* from the front. There is a large playground for children, boats for rent on the lake, and a few cafes inside the grounds.

The entrance to the park is at the end of Hofstr. $ Part admission €1.50. Boat rental on the lake inside €6-10 per 30min. for 1-4 people (prices vary on type of boat). ⏰ Park open daily dawn-dusk. Boat rental open M-F 10am-7pm, Sa-Su 7:30am-8pm.

FOOD

EISSALON LAXENBURG — ICE CREAM, CAFE ❷

Hofstr. 7 ☎2236 727 52 www.eis-laxenburg.at

The dining options in town are limited, so be prepared to fill up on delicious gelato and ice cream sundaes at this popular establishment. Coffee in the morning, ice cream in the afternoon. Who needs real food anyway?

On the corner of Hofstr. and Herzog Albrecht Str. $ Sundaes €4.90-5.20. Ice cream (cone or cup) €1.80-3.40. Coffee €1.70-3.20. ⏰ Open daily 10am-10pm.

ESSENTIALS

Practicalities

Laxenburg is not an overly developed town, and really has no commercial shopping.

- **BANK: Raiffeisenbank.** *(On the corner of Hofstr. and Herzog Albrecht Str. i 24hr. ATM.* 🕘 *Open M and Th 8am-12:30pm and 1:30-6pm; Tu, W, F 8am-12:30pm and 1:30pm-3pm.)*

- **GROCERY STORE: Adeg Activ.** *(*🕘 *Open M-F 7:30am-6:30pm, Sa 7:30am-5pm.)*

Getting There

The 17km trip to Laxenburg is simple and cheap. First, take the U1 to **Sudtiroler Platz** and transfer to the bus terminal—not to be confused with the local city bus stops. This is a much larger bus stop affair, with many gates lettered A, B, C, etc. A painless 30-minute ride on **Postbus #566** (🖳*www.postbus.at* 💲 *€1.80)* leads directly to Franz-Josef Pl. in the middle of Laxenburg. Be aware that the destination of most #566 buses is Eisenstadt, so it will not say "Laxenburg" on the front of the bus.

mödling ☎2258

A small town on the edge of the **Vienna Woods** (*Weinerwald*), Mödling offers a peaceful atmosphere from which to taking hiking trips or explorations of nature. In reality, the neighboring towns like Hitnerbruhl and Heiligenkruez have more desirable sights, including the underground lake of Seegrotte and the picturesque Cistercian Abbey against a backdrop of green mountains. Mödling itself is a low-key town, with pleasant pedestrian streets ideal for an afternoon walk—or a wedding?! According to statistics, Mödling is the marriage capital of Lower Austria, with over 1200 ceremonies each year. If you are ridin' solo, Mödling is better known as the summer destination of Beethoven, who wrote Missa Solemnis at the **Hafner House** at Haupstr. 79. There are a few other museums in town, as well as the swimming pools of **Stadtbad** at Badstr. 25, but these constitute more of a children's water park than a relaxing spa, so it's best to get out into the surrounding wilderness.

ORIENTATION

Exiting right from the Mödling train station, a left at the first intersection with lights will put you on **Hauptstrasse,** the town's main thoroughfare with restaurants, shops, banks, and supermarkets. A walk up Haupstr. (with the building numbers increasing) will bring you through **Jospeh Deutsch Platz** and **Freiheitsplatz** to the network of pedestrian streets and the **Hauptplatz,** where the tourist information office is found.

SIGHTS

SEEGROTTE UNDERGROUND LAKE, CAVE

Grutschgasse 2a ☎2236 263 64 🖳www.seegrotte.at

Set in the Vienna Woods, the former gypsum mine is now Europe's largest underground lake, and attracts more than 200,000 visitors annually (including lots of school groups). The mine experienced its most prominent 15 minutes of fame as the filming location for the 1993 movie, *The Three Musketeers;* parts of the set are still intact to prove it, including a viking-style boat. The caves and lake are only accessible via a tour, which takes you through the mines and on a boatride around the lake. The mines are nine degrees Celsius, so be sure to bring a jacket.

⚑ *Bus #364 or #365: Hinterbruhl Seegrotte. From the stop, continue along the street in the same direction as the bus, then make your 1st right at the Seegrotte cafe. You will see tour buses and the Seegrotte entrance will be down the street in front of you.* 💲 *€9, children 4-14 €6, children under 4 free. Family (2 adults and 2 children) €24. Group rates (20+ people) available. Blanket* *rental €0.50. ⏰ Open Apr-Oct M-Su 8:30am-5pm; Nov-Mar M-F 9am-3pm, Sa-Su 9am-3:30pm. English tours usually at noon.*

STIFT HEILIGENKREUZ ABBEY, CHURCH

Zisterzienserabtei Stift Heiligenkreuz ☎2258 870 31 38 💻www.stift-heiligenkreuz.at

While the grounds and courtyards are free to explore, it's worth taking the tour to see inside this Abbey, currently home to over 80 monks. The tour journeys through the cloister, reading corridor, chapels, chapterhouse, fountain house, and sacristy, culminating in the magnificent Abbey Church which has garnered much attention for its unique blend of Romanesque and Gothic styles. In the sacristy, be sure to look closely at the inlaid woodwork of the cabinets, handcrafted by two monks over the course of 20 years.

Bus #364 or #365. ℹ The Abbey is only accessible via tour. $ €7, students €3.50, seniors €6, family card €13. ⏰ Open Mar-Oct daily 9-11:30am and 1:30-5pm, Nov-Feb daily 9-11:30am and 1:30-4pm. Tours M-Sa 10am, 11am, 2pm, 3pm, and 4pm, Su 11am, 2pm, 3pm, and 4pm. Tours in German unless there's a large percentage of English-speakers, but helpful information cards are otherwise provided.

FOOD

There are not many good food options in this city. One good way of feeding yourself is to go to one of the supermarkets, such as **Spar** *(across from the train station, on Haupstr.)* or **Billa** *(Elizabeth Str. ⏰ Most shops close M-F 6pm, Sa around noon, and closed on Su.).*

KLOSTERGASTHOF STIFT HEILIGENKREUZ INTERNATIONAL [3]

Stift Heiligenkreuz ☎2258 870 30

As the only restaurant near the abbey, tourists make up the majority of the customers, with higher prices to match. However, the meals are large, hearty, and quite flavorful with a range of meat and vegetarian options from a simple salmon steak with rice and vegetables *(€13.60)* to an Indian curry with grilled turkey and rice *(€10.10)*. Vegetarian entrees include fried cauliflower with tartar and salad *(€7.60)*. The pleasant courtyard with fountain and spreading trees is delightful.

Bus #364 or #365: Stift Heiligenkreuz. $ Entrees €7.60-18. ⏰ Open daily 9am-9pm.

ESSENTIALS

Practicalities

- **TOURIST OFFICE** *(in the center of town, off the Hauptpl. at K. Elizabeth Str. 2 ☎2236 267 27 💻www.moedling.at ⏰ Open M-F 9am-12:30 and 1:30pm-5pm.)*
- **PHARMACY:** *(In Friheitspl. Look for the large green cross. ⏰ Open M-F 8am-6pm, Sa 8am-noon.)*

Emergency!

- **POLICE:** *(Joseph Deutsch Pl., off Hauptstr.)*
- **BANKS: Oberbank, Ertse,** and **Volksbank** are scattered along Haupstr. and in the pedestrian streets.

Getting There

Getting to the town of Mödling is incredibly simple. **S-bahn** trains (Vienna's suburban train network) run every 5-10min. from Wien Meidling *(accessible from the U6 Philadelphiabrucke stop)* to Mödling. The journey takes 20min. and a one-way ticket costs €1.80. In Mödling, a less extensive bus network connects to the surrounding towns, including **Hinterbruhl** and **Heiligenkreuz.** Bus #364 and #365 run to both these towns and stop close to, if not at, the main sights there such as the **Seegrotte** and **Stift Heiligenkreuz.** Each one-way journey costs €1.80. Buses run 1-2 times per hour, and up to 4 times per hour around 11am and noon. Check the schedules ahead of time to plan your day most efficiently.

tulln an der donau ☎2272

As the district capital of Lower Austria, Tulln an der Donau (Tulln on the Danube) feels much like a normal city with regular citizens going about their business, all with the flowing Danube as a picturesque backdrop. While the city has a modern feel with plenty of commercial shops and restaurants, there are remnants of the old **Roman equestrian camp** mixed in, such as the oldest structure in town—the **Salzturm**—and the **Roman walls,** now preserved in an underground glass enclosure. The two churches, **St. Stephans** and **Minorite Church,** add their spires to the skyline, while the small **Schiele Museum** and **Roman Museum** give the city more cultural clout. Tulln provides plenty of simple pleasures for a day away from the big city, including fountains, statues, promenades, and gardens. Come for a sunny day and you might find yourself anxiously awaiting to return.

ORIENTATION

From the **Tulln Stadt** train station, a short walk up Bahnhofstr., with the station directly behind you, brings you to **Rathausplatz** and the neighboring **Hauptplatz** with benches, cafes, banks, and a fountain. From the Hauptpl., a number of streets lead toward the **Danube Promenade** along the water, and to a number of the town's notable fountains and sights. From the Hauptpl., Lederergasse brings you to **Minoritenplatz.**

SIGHTS

DANUBE PROMENADE — PROMENADE

along the Danube

Tulln's waterfront location is part of the town's draw, so it's worth walking or biking along the promenade and taking in a few of the sights. Starting from the western end, you can find artist Hundertwasser's boat *Regentag* ("Rainy Day") docked at the Schiffstation. Following the walkway, you will then see the **Nibelungen Denkmal** (fountain) which depicts the meeting of Kriemhild and Etzel in Tulln in the German epic *Nibelungenlied.* Passing the **Donaubuhne** where concerts are regularly held, you will see the **Salzturm** (Salt Tower), which was used as a flank tower when Tulln was a Roman equestrian camp. Short as the walk may be, spending time on the promenade is a highlight of Tulln.

From the train station, walk down Bahnhofstr., through the Hauptpl., straight to the Danube. $ Free.

EGON SCHIELE MUSEUM — MUSEUM

Donaulande 28 ☎2272 645 70 🖥ewww.gonschiele.museum.com

This small, three-story museum is located in the former county jail of Tulln, Egon Schiele's birthtown. The prison rooms are adapted to display over 60 original works—mostly drawings, water colors, and oil paintings—many of which were done early in his lifetime. The first floor also gives history on Schiele's childhood between Tulln, Krems, and Klosterneuburg; be sure to ask for the handy English translation cards.

Along the Danube Promenade; look for signs. $ €5, students €3, seniors €3.50. ⏰ Open Apr-Oct Tu-Su 10am-noon and 1pm-5pm.

DIE GARTEN — GARDENS

Am Wasserpark 1 ☎2272 681 88 🖥www.diegartentulln.at

Opened in 2008, this permanent garden show displays over 50 individually-designed and constructed gardens, some dedicated to pleasure and beauty while others addressing specific structural or ecological issues. Explore the "Japanese garden," "wellness garden," "rosarium," or "farmer's garden," to name just a few. Each garden has an English description and explanation, and many have benches and chairs on which to relax and fully absorb your surroundings. Nearby, there is a treetop path that takes you 30 meters above the garden for a bird's-eye view.

♯ *Walk along the Danube Promenade with the water to your right. Follow the signs.* Ⓢ *€11, students and seniors €9, children under 17 €6, children under 6 free, groups (20+) €7.50 per person. Season passes available.* Ⓓ *Open Apr-Oct M-Su 9am-6pm.*

FOOD

GASTHAUS "ZUM GOLDENEN SCHIFF"

⌗ ♿ ♯ VIENNESE ❷

Weiner Str. 10

☎02272 626 71

This *gasthaus* has a classic wood-paneled interior, simple white and blue checkered tablecloths, and a cozy, no-frills atmosphere. All the classic Viennese dishes are on order, including *gebackene scholle* (*€11.50*), *wiener schnitzel* (*€9.50*), *zweibelrostbraten* (*€12.50*), as well as a selection of soups and side dishes.

♯ *From Bahnhofstr., cross through Rathauspl., then make your first right on to Weiner Str. The restaurant is directly across from the post office.* Ⓢ *Entrees €7-14.* Ⓓ *Open M-F 10am-2:30pm and 5:30-11pm, Su 10:30am-3pm.*

ESSENTIALS

Practicalities

- **TOURIST OFFICES:** The Tourist Info Office staff offers numerous brochures and pamphlets, a train schedule, restaurant listings, as well as an extremely helpful free town map. They will also book rooms in town for a €2 fee. (*♯ Minoritenpl. 2* ☎*2272 675 66,* 🖳*www.tulln.at* Ⓓ *Open Oct-Apr M-F 8am-3pm; May-Sept M-F 9am-7pm, Sa-Su 10am-7pm.*)

- **BANKS:** Erste Bank has a **24hr. ATM** on the back side. (*Rathauspl. 8.* ☎*05 0100-20111.* Ⓓ *Open M-Th 8am-noon and 1-3:30pm, F 8am-noon and 1-4:30pm.*) There are also branches of Volksbank, Bank Austria and Oberbank in the Hauptpl., also with 24hr ATMs.

- **GROCERY STORES: Zielpunkt grocery.** (*Hauptpl. 24* Ⓓ *Open M-F 7:30am-7pm, Sa 7:30am-6pm.*)

- **PHARMACIES: Bipa pharmacy.** (Ⓓ *open M-F 8am-7pm, Sa 8am-6pm.*)

- **POST OFFICE:** The post office also has a **Western Union.** (*Weiner Str. 7-9.* ☎*0577 677 34 30* 🖳*www.3430.post.at*) Ⓓ*Open M-F 8am-6pm.*)

Emergency!

- **POLICE:** (*Nibelungenpl., behind the Tourist Office and next to the Town Hall.*)

Getting There and Getting Around

Trains to Tulln leave about every half hour from Vienna's most northern train station, **Franz-Joseph Bahnhof** in the 9th district. The trip takes 30-35min. and costs €5.40. When you buy your ticket, check to see which station in Tulln the train will stop at, Tulln an der Donau or Tulln Stadt. **Tulln Stadt** drops you closest to the **city center,** accessed via a short walk up Bahnhofstr. If you get iff at Tulln an der Donau, you can easily take a bus (*€1.80*) to the city center or, if you already have a map, walk 15-20 min.

austrian alps

petronell carnuntum and
bad-deutsch altenburg ☎2163

The ancient Roman city Petronell Carnuntum and the neighboring town, Bad-Deutsch Altenburg, are located halfway between Vienna and Bratislava to the east. While all that remains of the Roman city are ruins, the tourist companies have poured money into reconstruction to make you think that Carnuntum may still be worth a visit—as if you can go back in time with reenacted gladiator fights. Rather than succumb to the tourist bus, it is far more enjoyable to explore the Roman ruins that haven't been falsely restored and annotated. **Heidentor** (which remains a symbol of the city) is the large Roman archway built for Emperor Constantius II. It's a bit lost in the countryside of wheat fields and windy country highways and is best reached on bike or by car. Similarly, the nearby Carnuntum **amphitheater** (not to be confused with the tourist site in Bad-Deutsch Altenburg) provides some rock ruins that could provide the setting for a peaceful picnic, and are open to wander through and climb on. Carnuntum and Bad-Deutsch Altenburg could be a peaceful daytrip if you want to go for a bike ride and just enjoy the landscape. Otherwise, stick to the city.

ORIENTATION

The Petronell-Carnuntum train station is about a ten-minute walk from the **Hauptplatz** and **Hauptstrasse** Walk straight behind the train station down Bahnhofstr., which will gradually merge with Bruckerstr. Follow Bruckerstr. to the right until the street ends in a T at Hauptstr. A right on Haupstr. from the T-junction will take you to the Hauptpl. It is possible to walk to all the **Roman ruins** throughout Carnuntum.

If you are arriving in Bad-Deutsch Altenburg, you will also have a 10min. walk to the town center. From the station, follow Hainburger Str. downhill. After the sharp curve to the left, you will find yourself in the Hauptpl. with the clock tower, fountain, and cafes. To the right, Badgasse leads to the Danube and the Museum Carnuntinum, while straight ahead Weiner Str. leads to the amphitheater. Most of the main restaurants and commercial shops (although limited) are along **Weiner Stasse.**

SIGHTS

CARNUNTUM ARCHEOLOGICAL PARK (OPEN-AIR MUSEUM)✒⊗♨ ROMAN RUINS
Hauptstr. 1, Petronell-Carnuntum   ☎2163 337 70 ▣www.carnuntum.co.at

These Roman ruins used to be the civilian quarter of the former Roman city of Carnuntum. For many, the exploration of the area starts here, where you can visit residential buildings and learn the history with detailed English placards. All of the buildings are reconstructed (in fact, the baths were being built at the time of research), and the actual ruins are only foundations, which may bother the history buffs even if the kids don't care.

Ⓢ *Access to museum and amphitheatre €9; children 15-18, students and seniors €7; children 11-14 €3. Guided tours €2.* ⏰ *Open Mar-Oct daily 9am-5pm.*

AMPHITHEATRE ✒⊗ ROMAN RUINS
Weiner Str. 52, Bad-Deutsch Altenburg   ☎2163 337 70 ▣www.carnuntum.co.at

The remains of the amphitheater are a bit underwhelming, especially if you've seen any of the more impressive and extensive Roman ruins in someplace like Italy. During the summer months, there are gladiator reenactments and other historical shows, which might be the only reason to visit. Even then, it might be a bit gauche for anyone other than the kids.

Ⓢ *Admission to ampitheater included in Carnuntum Archeological Park ticket €9.* ⏰ *Open Mar-Oct daily 9am-5pm.*

FOOD

IL CENTRO

🍴♿🍸☀ CAFE ❷

Hauptpl. 21 ☎02163 14 30 90 💻www.il-centro-carnuntum.at

This modern-style cafe with a glass bar and sleek couches seems out-of-place in the otherwise humdrum town of Carnuntum. There is a pleasant outdoor seating area right on the Hauptpl., where you can enjoy a delicious *eis kaffee* (ice coffee) under the sunshine or the shade of a large umbrella. The long hours (compared to other restaurants in town) make this a more flexible option for nourishment throughout the day.

⇞ The Hauptplatz is directly off of Haupstr. in Carnuntum. $ Snacks and sandwiches €2.80-4.50. Iced coffee €3.80. Breakfast €2.90-7.80 ⏰ Open M-Tu 7am-8pm, Th-Sa 7am-10pm, Su and holidays 9am-8pm.

ESSENTIALS

Practicalities

There is not much to the town of Petronell-Carnuntum; it's more of a countryside village with one bank, one grocery, one post office...you get the idea.

- **TOURIST OFFICES:** The **tourist information center** has helpful maps and mostly-German brochures about the region. *(On the corner where Haupstr. meets Taungasse. ⏰ Open M 9am-1pm, Tu-F 9am-4:30pm.)*
- **RAIFFEISENBANK:** *(Haupstr. 35 ☎051066 99 30 00 💻www.raiffesisen.at/bruck-carnuntum) ⏰ Open M 8am-noon and 2-5:30pm, Tu-Th 8am-noon, F 8am-noon and 2-5:30pm.)*
- **POST OFFICE:** *(1 Kirchenpl. ⏰ Open M 7:30am-noon, W 7:30am-4pm, F 7:30am-noon.The 1st W of each month 7:30am-4pm and 5pm-7pm.)*

Getting There

While Petronell-Carnuntum and Bad Deutsch-Altenburg are best explored with a car or on a bike (once you get there), they are both accessible by train from Vienna. From Landstr./Wien Mitte (accessed from the U3 or U4 underground lines), take the S-7 in the direction of "Wolfsthal." The ticket costs €7.20 and will take a little over an hour, dropping you in "Petronell-Carnuntum." One stop further *(€9)* will take you to "Bad-Deutsch Altenburg." The train leaves every hour from Vienna starting at about 4:30am; the last train leaves to return to Vienna around 10pm. Check the schedule for precise times.

melk ☎2752

The distinctive yellow Stift Melk, sitting majestically on top of a cliff overlooking the Wachau region, is undoubtedly what brought the town of Melk onto the tourist radar. There's no doubt about it—the abbey looks pretty freakin' amazing on a postcard. While the current abbey was once a Babenburg palace, the town itself also has just enough history evident to charm its visitors. It's quite simple to walk through the streets and pick out the historic buildings: the old bread shop with the two turrets, the market fountain and *rathaus* (town hall), the Gothic parish church, and the oldest surviving building, Haus am Stein, which means "House at the Stone" because it's literally built on a rock. The cobbled pedestrian streets with shops and the plazas with cafes all bask beneath the glory of Stift Melk, melding past and present into one of the prettiest daytrips from Vienna.

ORIENTATION

From the train station, a walk down **Bahnhofstrasse,** passing the church on your left, will bring you to the **Hauptplatz.** The main pedestrian street, **Hauptstrasse,** leads from here to Rathauspl., where a farther hike up stairs will lead to **Stift Melk** on the hill above. Another important historical street, **Sterngasse,** runs parallel to Hauptstr., as the only street untouched by the fire in 1847. Through Rathauspl., is the tourist information office.

SIGHTS

STFIT MELK — ABBEY

Abt-Berthold-Dietmayr-Str. 1 ☎2752 55 52 32 www.stiftmelk.at

This mustard yellow Abbey looms gracefully over Melk and the Danube, and has become one of the most important cultural sights in the Wachau region. First a residence of the Babenberg family, the Baroque structure became an abbey in 1089 and even today, about 33 monks live, pray, and work there. A ticket to the abbey takes you first through the imperial rooms, where modern exhibits about the Abbey's past are installed. The highlights are the terrace with views over the Danube, the stunning library with gilt books and ceiling frescoes, and finally the gold-slathered Baroque church. Remember to explore the gardens, and look for the 250-year-old linden trees.

Walk up the stairs from the Rathauspl. Follow the signs. i Tickets to abbey automatically include entrance to the park. Nov-Mar visits only possible with a guided tour. $ Tickets €9.50, students €5, family €19, groups (20+) €8.50 per person. With tour €11.50/7/23/10.50. Park admission without abbey ticket €3, students €2, children 6-16 €1. Prices expected to rise in 2012. Abbey open May-Sept 9am-5:30pm; Apr and Oct 9am-4:30pm. English tours daily 10:55am and 2:55pm. Park open May-Oct 9am-6pm.

SCHLOß SCHALLABURG — PALACE

3382 Schallaburg ☎2754 631 70 www.schallaburg.at

Schloβ Schallaburg, only 5km from Melk, is another one of Lower Austria's wondrous castles, situated in the idyllic green hillside. Schallaburg's history in the Middle Ages is clearly reflected in the Romanesque castle and Gothic chapel, with the impressive terracotta mosaics bursting with gods, goddesses, mythical creatures, figures from mythology, and gargoyles. The detailed gardens are rich with flowers and other landscaping work.

There is a direct transfer from the Melk train station to Schloβ Schallaburg. The shuttle leaves the train station at 10:40am, 1:15pm, and 4:45pm and departs Schallaburg at 10:55am, 1:30pm, and 5pm. The trip takes 15min. and costs €4. $ €9, students and seniors €8, family €18. Full-price combination ticket with Melk €15. ⏰ Open M-F 9am-5pm, Sa-Su 9am-6pm.

FOOD

STIFTSRESTAURANT MELK

VIENNESE [2]

Abt-Berthold-Dietmayr-Str. 3 ☎2752 525 55 www.stiftmelk.at

Located in the Orangery directly next to the abbey, the Stiftsrestaurant is predictably filled with tourists, but the food is high-quality and comparably priced with most other restaurants in town. The menu has something for everyone—meat, fish, soups, and salads—and it serves its own wine grown from the Abbey's vineyards. The leaf salad with grilled fish fillet and garlic marinade *(€9.40)* goes spectacularly with a glass of the house white *(€2.30)*.

Next to the entrance to the Abbey. $ Entrees €6.90-14.50. Soups and snacks €3.30-7.40. ⏰ Open Mar-Oct daily 8am-7pm, Nov-Feb daily 9am-5pm.

ESSENTIALS

Practicalities

- **TOURIST OFFICE:** The office has helpful maps and pamphlets on the town and region. If you ask, the receptionist will provide schedules for trains running back to Vienna from Melk and Krems, as well as the current boat schedules. *(Babenbergerstr. 1 ☎2753 52 30 74 20 www.neideroesterreich.at/melk ⏰ Open Apr M-F 9am-noon and 2-6pm, Sa 10am-noon; May-June M-F 9am-noon and 2-6pm, Sa-Su 10am-noon and 4pm-6pm; July-Aug M-Sa 9am-7pm, Su 10am-noon and 5-7pm; Sept M-F 9am-noon and 2-6pm, Sa-Su 10am-noon and 4-6pm; Oct M-F 9am-noon and 2-5pm, Sa 10am-noon.)*
- **BANK: Raiffesienbank.** *(Abbe Stadlergasse. ⏰ Open M-Th 8am-12:30pm and 2-4pm, F 8am-12:30pm and 1:30-4:40pm, and Sa 8:30am-11am.)*
- **24HR ATM: Volksbank.** *(Hauptpl. 7.)*
- **PHARMACIES: Apotheke.** *(Rathauspl.10. ☎523 15.)* There is also a **Bipa** pharmacy across the street.
- **POST OFFICE:** *(Wiener Str. 85. ☎0577 677 33 90 ⏰ Open M-F 8am-6pm and Sa 8am-1pm.)*

Emergency!

- **POLICE:** *(Spielberger Str. 17. ☎059133 31 30.)*

Getting There

By Train

From Vienna's **Westbahnhof,** trains run regularly to Melk *($ €15.40. ⏰ 1¼hr, every 20min).* In many cases, you need to switch trains in St. Polten, so be sure to ask when you purchase the ticket whether your particular train runs a direct trip.

By Bike

The same bike path that runs to Krems continues on to Melk, along both sides of the Danube and passing through other significant towns including Durnstein and Spitz.

By Boat

The **DDSG Blue Danube** *(🖳www.ddsg-blue-danube.at)* and **Brandner** *(🖳www.brandner.at)* boats sail between Krems and Melk 2-3 times per day. Many people choose to take the train to Melk in the morning, take an afternoon boatride to Krems for the afternoon, and then a train from Krems back to Vienna in the evening.

baden ☎2252

Located just an hour outside the Vienna city center, Baden bei Wien is known as "the place with the **spas** and a really big **casino**." And to be honest, that's about all that's there. Unless you crave the healing powers of a **thermal pool** (generally popular with the population over 50) or are a small child craving pool parties (popular with those ages 10 and under), there aren't many people in-between. Aside from swimming and gambling, walking around the Biedermeier and neo-classical style buildings is much like walking around a smaller, quainter version of Vienna. Miniature versions of the same things—a Rathaus, Plague Monument, Stadttheater, and St. Peter's Church—constitute the prominent buildings of a city that at one point was the Empire's resort destination. Baden is also known for a few famous residents; **Beethoven** composed his Ninth Symphony at Rathausgasse 10, and poets **Grillparzer** and **Raimund Nestroy** were frequent visitors.

ORIENTATION

The Badner Bahn lets off in Josephpl., right in the center of the city. From there, the pedestrian street **Frauengasse** leads directly to the **Hauptplatz**, though it is recommended to drop by the Tourist Information Office first. A short walk down **Erzherzog-Rainer-Ring** will lead to another small plaza, and there will be a large green "Tourist Info" sign pointing the way.

SIGHTS

GRAND CASINO AND KURPARK — CASINO, PARK

Im Kurpark ☎2252 444 96 🖳www.baden.casinos.at

The Grand Casino is Baden's claim-to-fame; the building that houses that casino and hotel were once an imperial bath. If gambling isn't your vacation sport of choice, take a walk th344rough the Kurpark and woods up the hills behind the casino. Manicured pathways lead to a Strauss monument and the Beethoventempel, with views over the whole city, and farther up the paths turn into hiking trails through the Vienna Woods.

From Joseph Pl., walk up Erzherzog Rainer Ring. Follow the signs. $ Free admission to casino and park. ⏰ Casino open daily 1pm-late.

ROSARIUM — GARDEN

Entrances on Pelzgasse and Doblhoffgasse 🖳www.baden.at

Austria's largest rose garden, with over 600 types of roses, is open year-round, though the roses are only in bloom in June and October. Take a stroll down the pathways, drink coffee overlooking the pond, or just sit on a bench and chat with a friend. If you feel the urge, there's a jungle gym!

From Josephpl., walk down Pergerstr., which becomes Gutenbrunnerstr. and then pedestrain-only Sclosserg. The entrance will be right in front of you at the end of the street. $ Free. ⏰ Open daily dawn-dusk.

RÖMERTHERME — SPA, THERMAL BATH

Brusattipl. 4 ☎2252 450 30 🖳www.roemertherme.at

With a water area measuring over 900 sq. m, there are plenty of whirlpools or massage streams on which to place your behind. Take a dip in the hot pools or jacuzzi,

or do some leisurely laps in the large pool. The healing waters seem to cater to the extremes of the age range: really old or really young. If it's a nice day, try the Art Deco pool outside at Thermalstrandbad, which has sand and more of a beachy vibe.
Directly adjacent to and slighty behind the tourist information office $ Entrance to pools M-F €9.50, Sa-Su €11.50. Daytickets €14/15.70. ⏰ Open daily 10am-10pm.

FOOD

NEW TOKYO
JAPANESE ❷

Johannesgasse 1 ☎02252 243 03

Located away from the Hauptpl. and pedestrian streets, New Tokyo is where to go to avoid tourists and find reasonable prices, even though you miss out on the town's atmosphere. New Tokyo serves sushi, sitr-fries, and everything in between. The lunch specials are great deals: various stir-fries and bento boxes are all served with miso soup and salad.
Next to the Rosarium front entrance. $ Lunch specials €5-7. ⏰ Open daily 11:30am-2:30pm and 5:30-11:30pm.

ESSENTIALS

Practicalities
A small city, Baden offers everything you may need in and around the pedestrian streets of the Hauptpl.

- **GROCERY STORE: Spar.** *(Behind the Rathaus on Rathausgasse.)*
- **BANK: Volksbank.** *(Hauptpl. ⏰ Open M-Th 8am-3:30pm).* **ATMs** are also scattered throughout the city and in the Grand Casino lobby.
- **INTERNET: @ internet café** on Frauengasse is open until 10pm.
- **TOURIST OFFICE:** *(Brusattipl. 3 ☎2252 226 00 💻www.baden.at ⏰ Open M-F 9am-6pm and Sa 9am-2pm.)*

Getting There
The easiest way to reach Baden is to take the **Badner Bahn,** a blue and white tram, Metro, and train all in one. It leaves from behind Vienna's Staatsoper (next to the U-bahn station) and runs to Baden's Josephpl. Tickets are available at the blue boxes *($ €2.40. ⏰ 1hr).*

krems and stein ☎2732

As the gateway to the Wachau region, Krems and its neighboring town Stein are undoubtedly the most picturesque cities from which to begin exploring the Austrian countryside. Located west along the Danube 64km from Vienna, the narrow cobbled streets of Krems seamlessly blend the old and new—cafes and shops along the commercial thoroughfare hide networks of twisted alleyways, where you will stumble across hidden plazas and doors. Wander from one hallowed church to the next (**Pfarrkirche, Piaristenkriche,** and **Frauenbergkirche** are just a few), and take in the view from the hillside beneath the ancient **Pulverturm.** In addition to its historical foundation, Krems has secured its place in the hearts of art-lovers with the **KunstMiele** (Art Mile) and in the livers of wine-lovers as a premiere wine region.

In the neighboring town of Stein, the main street **Steiner Landstrasse** has the most gorgeous old building facades enlivened with flower boxes and in some cases a refreshing coat of paint. Here in Minoritenpl., the **Minoritenkirche** has been altered into a convertible space for artists to rent and display their work. On a warm summer day, stroll along the Danube back to Krems and then take the boat home, just in time to watch the shadows begin to lengthen over the glistening blue of the Donau.

ORIENTATION

If arriving by train, walk through Bahnhofpl. and down Dinstlstr. to reach the main throroughfare of Krems, **Untere Landstrasse** to the right and **Obere Landstrasse** to the left. At the far end of Obere Landstr., you can pass under the *steintor* (gate) and leave the old city into the town of Und. Here you will find the tourist office, **Krems Tourismus.** Continuing west through Und leads to the picturesque neighboring town of Stein, whose main thoroughfare Steiner Landstr. similarly runs parallel to the Danube.

SIGHTS

GRAFENEGG CASTLE — CASTLE, GROUNDS

Schloß Grafenegg ☎2735 550 05 22 🖥www.grafenegg.com

Enter into your own personal fairy tale à la Cinderella as you explore the grounds and ornate rooms of this gorgeous castle nestled in the Austrian countryside a little ways from Krems. The square tower has four mini turrets with clocks in between, and even though the moat is dry, the luminescent white castle is picture perfect. Inside, explore the library, salons, halls, and dining room—be sure to look up at the hammer-beam ceilings for some of the most elaborate Historist woodwork in all of Austria. Today, the castle also hosts about 30 cultural events per year, either in parts of the castle or at the outdoor stage and auditorium, also located on the Castle grounds.

🚶 The ÖBB (Austrian Rail) runs train services from Vienna; Franz-Josefs, Spittelau and Heiligenstadt stations to the station Wagram-Grafenegg, 2km from Grafenegg Castle. Some taxi companies offer a fixed-price transfer from Krems for €30 (up to 4 people). Call ☎2732 858 83 or ☎664 210 33 55. If you have a car, getting to Grafenegg is much easier. Driving time from Vienna takes around 40min. Take A22 in the direction of Stockerau. Take the Krems/Tulln/St. Pölten exit S5 to the Grafenegg exit. $ €5, students €3, family ticket €7.50, groups (20+) €4 per person. ⏰ Castle open Apr-Oct Tu-Su 10am-5pm.

KARIKATURMUSEUM — ♿ MUSEUM

Steiner Landstr. 3a ☎2732 90 80 20 🖥www.karikaturmuseum.at

The jagged roof and life-size cartoon statues mark this unique Cartoon Museum on Krems' Art Mile. Unlike many cartoon museums, the Karikaturmuseum focuses not only on comic strips and animations but also on political and humor-based cartoons under the motto "laughter is healthy." Most of the exhibits, with the exception of one permanent exhibit, rotate every six months. 2011 marks the 10-year anniversary of the museum, so big (and secretive) plans are in the works!

🚶 On the Kunstmiele (Art Mile). $ €9; children, seniors, and students €8. ⏰ Open daily 10am-6pm.

KUNSTHALLE 🎫♿ ART MUSEUM

Steiner Landstr. 3 ☎2732 90 80 10 🖥www.kunsthalle.at

This convertible art space hosts primarily modern art exhibits, that rotate every 3-4 months. Three new exhibits are in the works, one of which focuses on "New Realism," and its artists, including **Marcel Duchamp.** Another consists of Daniel Spoerri's "object boxes," which innovatively uses multiple materials in different dimensions. The final will be the mixed-media installation *Twelve-O'Clock in London* by an Austrian-American artist.

⇄ *On the Kunstmiele (Art Mile).* $ *€9, students €8, family ticket €18, groups of 10 or more €7 per person.* ⏰ *Open daily 10am-6pm.*

FOOD 🍎

SCHWARZE KUCHL 🚭🚫🍸⛅ VIENNESE [2]

Untere Landstr. 8 ☎02732 831 28 🖥www.schwarze-kuchl.at

This country-style *kuchl* ("kitchen") offers up traditional Austrian dishes at a tiled stove right before your eyes. As though in a country home, the walls are lined with pots, cooking utenstils, and other countryside paraphernalia, though it reads as quaint, not kitsch, and makes Schwarze Kuchl a cozy locale for a hearty meal during your exploration of Krems and Stein.

⇄ *On the main street in Krems town.* $ *Entrees €5.50-14.* ⏰ *Open M-F 8:30am-7:30pm, Sa 8:30am-5pm.*

ESSENTIALS ℹ

Practicalities

Krems' commercial thoroughfare is Untere Landstr./Obere Landstr. (Upper and Lower), where you can find all the necessary shops and practicalities.

- **TOURIST OFFICES:** *(Utzstr. 1. ☎02732 700 11 🖥www.krems.info ⏰ Open Nov 1-Apr 6 M-F 8:30am-5pm; Apr 7-Oct 19 M-F 8:30am-6:30pm, Sa 10am-noon and 1pm-6pm, Su 10am-noon and 1pm-4pm.)*
- **BANK: Bank Austria at Obere.** *(Landst. 19.* ℹ 24hr ATM.*)*
- **POST OFFICE:** *(Brandströmstr. 4-6.* ☎02732 826 0642*)* and *(Steiner Landstr. 68.* ☎057 7677 3504.*)*
- **PHARMACIES: Apotheke.** *(Corner of Untere Landstr. and Marktgasse.)* **Bipa pharmacy.** *(Landstr. 19.* ⏰ Open M-Sa 9am-noon and 1:30-5pm.*)*

Getting There ✈

Krems is a common excursion from Vienna and is easily accessed from the city. By train, the trip begins at Franz-Joseph Bahnhof *($ €13.90. ⏰ 1hr., 25 per day).* In the summer *(May-Sept),* the **DDSG Blue Danube** runs on Sundays from Vienna to Durnstein, departing Vienna at 8:30am. It stops in Krems at 2pm, and picks up again at 5pm. *(🖥www.ddsg-blue-danube.at $ Round-trip €29.50.)* If you are feeling particularly energetic, it is also possible to bike from Vienna to Krems, following the bicycle path that runs alongside the Danube. If you get tired, you can always return via train or boat; in most cases, they allow you to take on a bike free of charge.

ESSENTIALS

You don't have to be a rocket scientist to plan a good trip. (It might help, but it's not required.) You do, however, need to be well prepared, and that's what we can do for you. Essentials is the chapter that gives you all the nitty-gritty you need to know for your trip: the hard information gleaned from 50 years of collective wisdom (and those phone calls to Germany and Austria the other day that put us on hold for an hour). Planning your trip? Check. Staying safe and healthy? Check. The dirt on transportation? Check. We've also thrown in communications info, meteorological charts, and a ▨phrasebook, just for good measure. Plus, for overall trip-planning advice from what to pack (money and as little underwear as possible) to how to take a good passport photo (it's physically impossible; consider airbrushing), you can also check out the Essentials section of ▨www.letsgo.com.

We're not going to lie—this chapter is tough for us to write, and you might not find it as fun of a read as 101 or Discover. But please, for the love of all that is good, read it! It's super helpful, and, most importantly, it means we didn't compile all this technical info and put it in one place for you (yes YOU) for nothing.

greatest hits

- **WORK IT.** You need a visa and a work permit to secure employment as a foreigner in Germany (p. 348).
- **CHANGE WITH THE TIMES.** The introduction of the euro has altered tipping practices in Germany (p. 349).
- **CANCEL THE TEA PARTY.** Ask for a mehrwertsteuer return form and enjoy some tax-free shopping (p. 352).
- **PUFF PUFF PASS.** The possession of small quantities of marijuana is decriminalized in Germany (p. 353).

planning your trip

- **PASSPORT:** Required for citizens of Australia, Canada, Ireland, New Zealand, the UK, and the US.

- **VISA:** Required for visitors who plan to stay in Germany or Austria for more than 90 days.

- **WORK PERMIT:** Required for all foreigners planning to work in Germany or Austria.

DOCUMENTS AND FORMALITIES

You've got your visa, your invitation, and your work permit, just like Let's Go told you to, and then you realize you've forgotten the most important thing: your passport. Well, we're not going to let that happen. **Don't forget your passport!** Citizens of Australia, Canada, Ireland, New Zealand, the UK, the US need valid passports for entrance into Germany and Austria.

Visas

EU citizens do not need a visa to globetrot through Germany and Austria. Citizens of Australia, Canada, New Zealand, and the US do not need a visa for stays of up to 90 days, but this three-month period begins upon entry into any of the countries that belong to the EU's **freedom of movement** zone. For more information, see **One Europe.** Those staying longer than 90 days may purchase a visa at the German mission that covers your residence. A visa costs €60 and allows the holder to spend 90 days in Germany or Austria.

Double-check entrance requirements at the nearest embassy or consulate of Germany and Austria (listed below) for up-to-date information before departure. US citizens can also consult ▣http://travel.state.gov.

Entering Germany to study requires a student visa. For more information, see the **Beyond Tourism** chapter.

Work Permits

Admittance to a country as a traveler does not include the right to work, which is authorized only by a work permit. For more information, see the **Beyond Tourism** chapter.

TIME DIFFERENCES

Germany and Austria are one hour ahead of Greenwich Mean Time (GMT) and observe Daylight Saving Time.This means that they are is six hours ahead of New York City, 9 hours ahead of Los Angeles, one hour ahead of the British Isles, 9 hours behind Sydney, and 10 hours behind New Zealand.

money

GETTING MONEY FROM HOME

Stuff happens. When stuff happens, you might need some money. When you need some money, the easiest and cheapest solution is to have someone back home make a deposit to your bank account. Otherwise, consider one of the following options.

essentials

The EU's policy of freedom of movement means that most border controls have been abolished and visa policies harmonized. Under this treaty, formally known as the Schengen Agreement, you're still required to carry a passport (or government-issued ID card for EU citizens) when crossing an internal border, but, once you've been admitted into one country, you're free to travel to other participating states. Most EU states are already members of Schengen (excluding Cyprus), as are Iceland and Norway.

Wiring Money

Arranging a **bank money transfer** means asking a bank back home to wire money to a bank in Germany or Austria. This is the cheapest way to transfer cash, but it's also the slowest and most agonizing, usually taking several days or more. Note that some banks may only release your funds in local currency, potentially sticking you with a poor exchange rate; inquire about this in advance. Money transfer services like **Western Union** are faster and more convenient than bank transfers—but also much pricier. Western Union has many locations worldwide. To find one, visit ▣www.westernunion.com or call the appropriate number: in Australia ☎1800 173 833, in Canada and the US 800-325-6000, in the UK 0800 735 1815, in Germany ☎0800 180 7732 or in Austria ☎0800 29 6544. To wire money using a credit card in Canada and the US, call ☎800-CALL-CASH; in the UK, 0800 833 833. Money transfer services are also available to **American Express** cardholders and at selected **Thomas Cook** offices.

Despite what many dollar-possessing Americans might want to hear, the official currency of 16 members of the European Union—Austria, Belgium, Cyprus, Finland, France, Germany, Greece, Ireland, Italy, Luxembourg, Malta, the Netherlands, Portugal, Slovakia, Slovenia, and Spain—is the euro.

Still, the currency has some important—and positive—consequences for travelers hitting more than one eurozone country. For one thing, money-changers across the eurozone are obliged to exchange money at the official, fixed rate and at no commission (though they may still charge a small service fee). Second, euro-denominated traveler's checks allow you to pay for goods and services across the eurozone, again at the official rate and commission-free. For more info, check a currency converter (such as ▣www.xe.com) or ▣www.europa.eu.int.

US State Department (US Citizens only)

In serious emergencies only, the US State Department will forward money within hours to the nearest consular office, which will then disburse it according to instructions for a US$30 fee. If you wish to use this service, you must contact the Overseas Citizens Services division of the US State Department (☎+1-202-501-4444, from US 888-407-4747).

TIPPING AND BARGAINING

Service staff is paid by the hour, and a service charge is included in an item's unit price. Cheap customers typically just round up to the nearest whole Euro, but it's customary and polite to tip 5-10% if you are satisfied with the service. If the service was poor, you don't have to tip at all. To tip, mention the total to your waiter while paying. If he states that the bill is €20, respond "€22," and he will include the tip. Do

money · tipping and bargaining

pins and atms

To use a debit or credit card to withdraw money from a cash machine (ATM) in Europe, you must have a four-digit Personal Identification Number (PIN). If your PIN is longer than four digits, ask your bank whether you can just use the first four or whether you'll need a new one. Credit cards don't usually come with PINs, so if you intend to hit up ATMs in Europe with a credit card to get cash advances, call your credit card company before leaving to request one.

Travelers with alphabetic rather than numeric PINs may also be thrown off by the absence of letters on European cash machines. Here are the corresponding numbers to use: 1 = QZ; 2 = ABC; 3 = DEF; 4 = GHI; 5 = JKL; 6 = MNO; 7 = PRS; 8 = TUV; 9 = WXY. Note that if you mistakenly punch the wrong code into the machine multiple (often three) times, it can swallow (gulp!) your card for good.

embassies and consulates in germany

- **AUSTRALIAN EMBASSY IN BERLIN:** *(Wallstr. 76-79, 10179 Berlin, Germany ☎49 30 880 08 80 🖳http://www.germany.embassy.gov.au/beln/home.html ☼ Open M-Th 8:30am-5pm, F 8:30am-4:14pm.)*

- **CANADIAN EMBASSY IN BERLIN:** *(Leipziger Pl. 17, 10117 Berlin, Germany ☎49 30 20 31 20 🖳www.canadainternational.gc.ca/germany-allemagne ☼ Open M-F 8:30am-5pm.)*

- **IRISH EMBASSY IN BERLIN:** *(Jägerstr. 51, 10117 Berlin, Germany ☎49 30 22 07 20 🖳www.embassyofireland.dehome.html ☼ Open M-F 9:30am-12:30pm and 2:30-4:45pm.)*

- **NEW ZEALAND EMBASSY IN BERLIN:** *(Friedrichstr. 60, 10117 Berlin, Germany ☎49 30 20 62 10 🖳www.nzembassy.com/germany ☼ Open M-Th 9am-1pm and 2-5:30pm, F 9am-1pm and 2-4:30pm.)*

- **UK EMBASSY IN BERLIN:** *(Wilhelmstr. 70, 10117 Berlin, Germany ☎49 30 20 45 70 🖳http://ukingermany.fco.gov.uk/en/.html ☼ Open M-Th 9am-1pm and 2-5:30pm.)*

- **US EMBASSY IN BERLIN:** *(Pariser Pl. 2, 14191 Berlin, Germany ☎030 830 50 🖳http://germany.usembassy.gov ☼ Open M-F 8:30am-noon.)*

- **US CONSULATE IN DÜSSELDORF:** *(Willi Becker Allee 10, 40227 Duesseldorf, Germany ☎0211 788 8927 🖳http://duesseldorf.usconsulate.gov)*

- **US CONSULATE IN HAMBURG:** *(Alsterufer 27/28, 20354 Hamburg, Germany ☎040 411 71 100 🖳http://hamburg.usconsulate.gov/)*

- **US CONSULATE IN MUNICH:** *(Königinstr. 5, 80539, München, Germany ☎089 2899 6901 🖳http://munich.usconsulate.gov)*

money · tipping and bargaining

german embassies and consulates abroad

- **EMBASSY IN CAMBERRA:** (119 Empire Circuit, Yarralumla ACT 2600, Australia ☎61 262 70 19 11 ▣www.canberra.diplo.de ✿ Open M-F 9am-noon.)

- **EMBASSY IN OTTAWA:** (1 Waverley St., Ottawa, ON, K2P 0T8 ☎001 61 32 32 11 01 ▣www.ottawa.diplo.de ✿ Open M-F 9am-noon.)

- **EMBASSY IN DUBLIN:** (31 Trimleston Avenue, Booterstown, Blackrock, Co. Dublin ☎353 12 69 30 11 ▣www.dublin.diplo.de ✿ Open M, Tu, and F 8:30-11:30am, Th 8:30-11:30am and 1:30-3:30pm.)

- **EMBASSY IN WELLINGTON:** (90-92 Hobson St., Thorndon, 6011 Wellington, New Zealand ☎64 4 473 60 63 ▣www.wellington.diplo.de ✿ Open M-Th 7:30am-4:30pm, F 7:30am-3pm.)

- **EMBASSY IN LONDON:** (23 Belgrave Square, SW1X 8PZ, London, United Kingdom ☎020 78 24 13 00 ▣www.london.diplo.de ✿ See website for a detailed service schedule.)

- **EMBASSY IN WASHINGTON:** (4645 Reservoir Road, NW, Washington DC, District of Columbia, USA 20007-1998 ☎1 20 22 98 81 40 ▣www.germany.info ✿ Open M-Th 8:30am-5pm, F 8:30am-3:30pm.)

embassies and consulates in austria

- **AUSTRALIAN EMBASSY IN VIENNA:** (Mattiellistr. 2-4, A -1040 Vienna, Austria. ☎43 50 67 40 ▣www.austria.embassy.gov.au ✿ Open M-F 8:30am-4:30pm.)

- **CANADIAN EMBASSY IN VIENNA:** (Laurenzerberg 2, A-1010 Vienna, Austria ☎43 531 38 30 00 ▣www.canadainternational.gc.ca/germany-allemagne ✿ Open M-F 8:30am-5pm.)

- **IRISH EMBASSY IN VIENNA:** (Rotenturmstr. 16-18, 1010, Vienna, Austria ☎43 715 42 46 ▣www.embassyofireland.at)

- **UK EMBASSY IN VIENNA:** (Jauresgasse 12, 1030 Vienna, Austria ☎43 71 61 30 ▣www.britishembassy.at ✿ Open M-F 8am-noon and 1-4pm.)

- **US EMBASSY IN VIENNA:** (Boltzmanngasse 16, 1090 Vienna, Austria ☎43 31 33 90 ▣http://austria.usembassy.gov ✿ Open M-F 8:30am-5pm.)

essentials

not leave the tip on the table; hand it directly to the server. It is standard to tip a taxi driver at least €1, housekeepers €1-2 a day, bellhops €1 per piece of luggage, and public toilet attendants around €.50. Germans rarely barter, except at flea markets.

TAXES

Most goods in Germany and Austria are subject to a Value-Added Tax—or *mehrwertsteuer* (MwSt)—of 19% (a reduced tax of 7% is applied to books and magazines, foods, and agricultural products). Ask for a MwSt return form at points of purchase to enjoy tax-free shopping. Present it at customs upon leaving the country, along with your receipts and the unused goods. Refunds can be claimed at Tax Free Shopping Offices, found at most airports, road borders, and ferry stations, or by mail (Tax-Free Shop-

- **EMBASSY IN CANBERRA:** *(12 Talbot St., P.O. 3375, ACT 2603, Manuka, Canberra, Australia ☎61 262 95 15 33 ▦www.bmeia.gv.at)*

- **EMBASSY IN OTTAWA:** *445 Wilbrod St., Ottawa, ON K1N 6M7 ☎613 789 14 44 ▦www.austro.org)*

- **EMBASSY IN DUBLIN:** *15, Ailesbury Court Apartments, 93, Ailesbury Road, Dublin 4, Ireland ☎353 1 269 45 77 ▦www.bmeia.gv.at/en/embassy/dublin.html)*

- **CONSULATE IN WELLINGTON:** *(Level 2, Willbank House, 57 Willis Street, 9395, Wellington, New Zealand ☎64 4 499 63 93)*

- **EMBASSY IN LONDON:** *(18 Belgrave Mews West, London SW1X 8HU, UK. ☎020 78 24 13 00 ▦www.bmeia.gv.at/en/embassy/london.html)*

- **EMBASSY IN WASHINGTON:** *(3524 International Court Northwest, Washington, DC 20008-30228 ☎(202) 895-6700 ▦www.austria.org)*

ping Processing Center, Trubelgasse 19, 1030 Vienna Austria). For more information, contact the German VAT refund hotline (☎0228 406 2880 ▦www.bzst.de).

safety and health

GENERAL ADVICE

In any type of crisis, the most important thing to do is **stay calm.** Your country's embassy abroad is usually your best resource in an emergency; registering with that embassy upon arrival in the country is a good idea. The government offices listed in the **Travel Advisories** feature at the end of this section can provide information on the services they offer their citizens in case of emergencies abroad.

Local Laws and Police

Certain regulations might seem harsh and unusual (practice some self-control city-slickers, jaywalking is a €5 fine), but abide by all local laws while in Germany or Austria; your respective embassy will not necessarily get you off the hook. Always be sure to carry a valid passport as police have the right to ask for identification.

Drugs and Alcohol

The drinking age in Germany and Austria is 16 for beer and wine and 18 for spirits. The maximum blood alcohol content level for drivers is 0.05%. Avoid public drunkenness: it can jeopardize your safety and earn the disdain of locals.

If you use insulin, syringes, or any perscription drugs, carry a copy of the prescriptions and a doctor's note. Needless to say, illegal drugs are best avoided. While possession of marijuana or hashish is illegal, possession of small quantities for personal consumption is decriminalized in Germany and Austria. Each region has interpreted "small quantities" differently (anywhere from 5 to 30 grams). Carrying drugs across an international border—considered to be drug trafficking—is a serious offense that could land you in prison.

The following government offices provide travel information and advisories by telephone, by fax, or via the web:

- **AUSTRALIA: Department of Foreign Affairs and Trade.** (☎+61 2 6261 1111 🖳www.dfat.gov.au)

- **CANADA: Department of Foreign Affairs and International Trade (DFAIT).** Call or visit the website for the free booklet *Bon Voyage...But.* (☎+1-800-267-8376 🖳www.dfait-maeci.gc.ca)

- **NEW ZEALAND: Ministry of Foreign Affairs.** (☎+64 4 439 8000 🖳www.mfat.govt.nz)

- **UK: Foreign and Commonwealth Office.** (☎+44 20 7008 1500 🖳www.fco.gov.uk)

- **US: Department of State.** (☎888-407-4747 *from the US,* +1-202-501-4444 *elsewhere* 🖳http://travel.state.gov)

SPECIFIC CONCERNS

Natural Disasters

Relatively weak earthquakes occur regularly in Germany and Austria, primarily in the seismically active Rhein Rift Valley or in coal mining areas where blasting can set them off. In the event of an earthquake, drop and take cover if indoors. If outside, move away from buildings and utility wires.

PRE-DEPARTURE HEALTH

Matching a prescription to a foreign equivalent is not always easy, safe, or possible, so if you take **prescription drugs,** carry up-to-date prescriptions or a statement from your doctor stating the medications' trade names, manufacturers, chemical names, and dosages. Be sure to keep all medication with you in your carry-on luggage.

Common drugs such as aspirin (*Kopfschmerztablette* or *Aspirin*), acetaminophen or Tylenol (*Paracetamol*), ibuprofen or Advil, antihistamines (*Antihistaminika*), and penicillin (*Penizillin*) are available at German pharmacies. Some drugs—like pseudoephedrine (Sudafed) and diphenhydramine (Benadryl)—are not available in Germany or Austria, or are only available with a perscription, so plan accordingly.

Immunizations and Precautions

Travelers over two years old should make sure that the following vaccines are up to date: MMR (for measles, mumps, and rubella); DTaP or Td (for diphtheria, tetanus, and pertussis); IPV (for polio); Hib (for *Haemophilus influenzae* B); and HepB (for Hepatitis B). For recommendations on immunizations and prophylaxis, check with a doctor and consult the **Centers for Disease Control and Prevention (CDC)** in the US or the equivalent in your home country (☎+1-800-CDC-INFO/232-4636 🖳www.cdc.gov/travel).

getting around

For information on how to get to Germany or Austria and save a bundle while doing so, check out the Essentials section of 🖳**www.letsgo.com.** (In case you can't tell, we think our website's the bomb.)

essentials

BY PLANE

Commercial Airlines

For small-scale travel on the continent, *Let's Go* suggests 🖥**budget airlines** for budget travelers, but more traditional carriers have made efforts to keep up with the revolution. The **Star Alliance Europe Airpass** offers low economy-class fares for travel within Europe to 220 destinations in 45 countries. The pass is available to non-European passengers on Star Alliance carriers, including Lufthansa, Brussels Airlines, Austrian Airlines, and Swiss Air Lines. (🖥*www.staralliance.com*) **EuropebyAir's** snazzy FlightPass also allows you to hop between hundreds of cities in Europe and North Africa. (☎*+1-888-321-4737* 🖥*www.europebyair.com* 🟊 *Most flights US$99.*)

In addition, a number of European airlines offer discount coupon packets. Most are only available as tack-ons for transatlantic passengers, but some are standalone offers. Most must be purchased before departure, so research in advance. For example, **oneworld,** a coalition of 10 major international airlines, offers deals and cheap connections all over the world, including within Europe. (🖥*www.oneworld.com*)

budget airlines

The recent emergence of no-frills airlines has made hopscotching around Europe by air increasingly affordable. Though these flights often feature inconvenient hours or serve less popular regional airports, with ticket prices often dipping into single digits, it's never been faster or easier to jet across the continent. The following resources will be useful not only for crisscrossing the Schengen area but also for those ever-popular weekend trips to nearby international destinations.

- **BMIBABY:** Departures from multiple cities in the UK to Paris, Nice, and other cities in France. (☎0871 224 0224 for the UK, +44 870 126 6726 elsewhere 🖥www.bmibaby.com)

- **EASYJET:** London to Bordeaux and other cities in France. (☎+44 871 244 2366, 10p per min. 🖥www.easyjet.com $ UK£50-150.)

- **RYANAIR:** From Dublin, Glasgow, Liverpool, London, and Shannon to destinations in France. (☎0818 30 30 30 for Ireland, 0871 246 0000 for the UK 🖥www.ryanair.com)

- **SKYEUROPE:** Forty destinations in 19 countries around Europe. (☎0905 722 2747 for the UK, +421 2 3301 7301 elsewhere 🖥www.skyeurope.com)

- **STERLING:** The first Scandinavian-based budget airline connects Denmark, Norway, and Sweden to 47 European destinations, including Montpellier, Nice, and Paris. (☎70 10 84 84 for Denmark, 0870 787 8038 for the UK 🖥www.sterling.dk)

- **TRANSAVIA:** Short hops from Krakow to Paris. (☎020 7365 4997 for the UK 🖥www.transavia.com $ From €49 one-way.)

- **WIZZ AIR:** Paris from Budapest, Krakow, and Warsaw. (☎0904 475 9500 for the UK, 65p per min. 🖥www.wizzair.com)

BY TRAIN

Trains in Germany and Austria are generally comfortable, convenient, and reasonably swift. Second-class compartments, which seat from two to six, are great places to meet fellow travelers. Make sure you are on the correct car, as trains sometimes

BACKPACKING
by the numbers:

117 photos snapped

41 gelato flavors (3 lbs gained)

23 miles walked (in the *right* direction)

6 buses missed

4 benches napped on

2½ hostel romances

1 Let's Go Travel Guide

0 REGRETS.

LET'S GO

www.letsgo.com

we'd rather be traveling, too.

split at crossroads. Towns listed in parentheses on European train schedules require a train switch at the town listed immediately before the parentheses.

You can either buy a **railpass,** which allows you unlimited travel within a particular region for a given period of time, or rely on buying individual **point-to-point** tickets as you go. Almost all countries give students or youths (under 26, usually) direct discounts on regular domestic rail tickets, and many also sell a student or youth card that provides 20-50% off all fares for up to a year.

rail resources

- **WWW.RAILEUROPE.COM:** Info on rail travel and railpasses.
- **POINT-TO-POINT FARES AND SCHEDULES:** 💻www.raileurope.com/us/rail/fares_schedules/index.htm allows you to calculate whether buying a railpass would save you money.
- **WWW.RAILSAVER.COM:** Uses your itinerary to calculate the best railpass for your trip.
- **WWW.RAILFANEUROPE.NET:** Links to rail servers throughout Europe.
- **WWW.LETSGO.COM:** Check out the Essentials section for more details.

BY BUS

Though European trains and railpasses are extremely popular, in some cases buses prove a better option. Often cheaper than railpasses, **international bus passes** allow unlimited travel on a hop-on, hop-off basis between major European cities. **Busabout,** for instance, offers three interconnecting bus circuits covering 29 of Europe's best bus hubs. *(☎+44 8450 267 514 💻www.busabout.com $ 1 circuit in high season starts at US$579, students US$549.)* **Eurolines,** meanwhile, is the largest operator of Europe-wide coach services. We get misty-eyed just thinking about their unlimited 15- and 30-day passes to 41 major European cities. *(Germany ☎+49(0)69 7903-501. Austria ☎+43 12 98 29 00. 💻www.eurolines.com $ High season 15-day pass €345, 30-day pass €455; under 26 €290/375. Mid-season €240/330; under 26 €205/270. Low season €205/310; under 26 €175/240.)*

BY BICYCLE

Some youth hostels rent bicycles for low prices, and in Germany and Austria, train stations often rent bikes and often allow you to drop them off elsewhere. In addition to **panniers** (US$40-150) to hold your luggage, you'll need a good **helmet** (US$10-40) and a sturdy **lock** (from US$30). For more country-specific books on biking through the Schengen area, try **Mountaineers Books.** *(1001 SW Klickitat Way, Ste. 201, Seattle, WA 98134, USA ☎+1-206-223-6303 💻www.mountaineersbooks.org.)*

keeping in touch

BY EMAIL AND INTERNET

Hello and welcome to the 21st century, where you can check your email in most major European cities, though sometimes you'll have to pay a few bucks or buy a drink for internet access. Although in some places it's possible to forge a remote link with your home server, in most cases this is a much slower (and thus more expensive) option than taking advantage of free **web-based email accounts** (e.g., 💻**www.gmail.com**). **Internet cafes** and the occasional free internet terminal at a public library or university are listed in the **Practicalities** sections of cities that we cover.

Wireless hot spots make internet access possible in public and remote places. Unfortunately, they also pose security risks. Hot spots are public, open networks that use unencrypted, unsecured connections. They are susceptible to hacks and "packet sniffing"—the theft of passwords and other private information. To prevent problems, disable "ad hoc" mode, turn off file sharing and network discovery, encrypt your email, turn on your firewall, beware of phony networks, and watch for over-the-shoulder creeps.

BY TELEPHONE

Calling Home from Germany and Austria

Prepaid phone cards are a common and relatively inexpensive means of calling abroad. Each one comes with a Personal Identification Number (PIN) and a toll-free access number. You call the access number and then follow the directions for dialing your PIN. To purchase prepaid phone cards, check online for the best rates; 🖳www.callingcards.com is a good place to start. Online providers generally send your access number and PIN via email, with no actual "card" involved. You can also call home with prepaid phone cards purchased in Germany and Austria.

If you have internet access, your best—i.e., cheapest, most convenient, and most tech-savvy—bet is probably our good friend **Skype** *(🖳www.skype.com).* You can even videochat if you have one of those new-fangled webcams. Calls to other Skype users are free; calls to landlines and mobiles worldwide start at US$0.021 per minute, depending on where you're calling.

Another option is a **calling card,** linked to a major national telecommunications service in your home country. Calls are billed collect or to your account. Cards generally come with instructions for dialing both domestically and internationally.

Placing a collect call through an international operator can be expensive but may be necessary in case of an emergency. You can frequently call collect without even possessing a company's calling card just by calling its access number and following the instructions.

Cellular Phones

The international standard for cell phones is **Global System for Mobile Communication (GSM).** To make and receive calls in Germany and Austria, you will need a GSM-compatible phone and a **SIM (Subscriber Identity Module) card,** a country-specific, thumbnail-size chip that gives you a local phone number and plugs you into the local network. Many SIM cards are prepaid, and incoming calls are frequently free. You can buy additional cards or vouchers (usually available at convenience stores) to "top up" your phone. For more information on GSM phones, check out 🖳www.telestial.com. Companies like **Cellular Abroad** *(🖳www.cellularabroad.com)* and **OneSimCard** *(🖳www.onesimcard.com)* rent cell phones and SIM cards that work in a variety of destinations around the world.

BY SNAIL MAIL

Sending Mail Home from Germany and Austria

Airmail is the best way to send mail home fromGermany and Austria. **Aerogrammes,** printed sheets that fold into envelopes and travel via airmail, are available at post offices. Write "airmail," *"par avion," "Luftpost"* (German) on the front. Most post offices will charge exorbitant fees or simply refuse to send aerogrammes with enclosures. Surface mail is by far the cheapest and slowest way to send mail. It takes one to two months to cross the Atlantic and one to three to cross the Pacific—good for heavy items you won't need for a while, like souvenirs that you've acquired along the way.

Sending Mail to Germany and Austria

In addition to the standard postage system whose rates are listed below, **Federal Express** handles express mail services from most countries to Germany and Austria. *(☎+1-800-463-3339 🖳www.fedex.com).*

There are several ways to arrange pickup of letters sent to you while you are abroad. Mail can be sent via **Poste Restante** (General Delivery; *"Postlagernd Briefe"* in

To call Germany from home or to call home from Germany, dial:

1. THE INTERNATIONAL DIALING PREFIX. To call from Australia, dial ☎0011; Canada or the US, ☎011; Ireland, New Zealand, or the UK, ☎00; Germany, ☎00.

2. THE COUNTRY CODE OF THE COUNTRY YOU WANT TO CALL. To call Australia, dial ☎61; Canada or the US, ☎1; Ireland, ☎353; New Zealand, ☎64; the UK, ☎44; Germany, ☎49.

3. THE CITY/AREA CODE. *Let's Go* lists the city/area codes for cities and towns in Germany opposite the city or town name, next to a ☎, as well as in every phone number. If the first digit is a zero, omit the zero when calling from abroad to the Schengen area.

4. THE LOCAL NUMBER.

German) to almost any city or town in the Schengen area with a post office, and it is pretty reliable. Address Poste Restante letters like so:

Justin Bieber
Postlagernd Briefe
12345 City
Germany

The mail will go to a special desk in the central post office, unless you specify a post office by street address or postal code. It's best to use the largest post office, since mail may be sent there regardless. It is usually safer and quicker, though more expensive, to send mail express or registered. Bring your passport (or other photo ID) for pickup; there may be a small fee. If the clerks insist that there is nothing for you, ask them to check under your first name as well. *Let's Go* lists post offices in the **Practicalities** section for each city.

American Express has travel offices throughout the world that offer a free **Client Letter Service** (mail held up to 30 days and forwarded upon request) for cardholders who contact them in advance. Some offices provide these services to non-cardholders (especially AmEx Travelers Cheque holders), but call ahead to make sure. For a complete list of AmEx locations, call ☎+1-800-528-4800 or visit ▣www.americanexpress.com/travel.

climate

Germany and Austria have a temperate seasonal climate dictated by the North Atlantic Drift. The climate in the countries is oceanic with maximum rainfall during the summer. To convert from degrees Fahrenheit to degrees Celsius, subtract 32 and multiply by 5/9. To convert from Celsius to Fahrenheit, multiply by 9/5 and add 32.

AVG. TEMP. (LOW/ HIGH), PRECIP.	JANUARY			APRIL			JULY			OCTOBER		
	°C	°F	mm	°C	°F	mm	°C	°F	mm	°C	°F	mm
Berlin	-3/2	26/35	43	4/13	39/55	43	13/23	55/73	53	6/13	42/55	36
Frankfurt	-3/1	26/34	38	4/13	39/55	41	13/23	56/74	53	6/13	43/56	38
Hamburg	-2/2	28/36	61	3/12	37/53	51	12/21	54/70	81	6/13	44/55	64
Vienna	-5/1	23/34	46	3/13	37/55	56	12/23	53/73	99	4/13	40/56	48

°CELSIUS	-5	0	5	10	15	20	25	30	35	40
°FAHRENHEIT	23	32	41	50	59	68	77	86	95	104

measurements

Like the rest of the rational world, Germany and Austria use the metric system. The basic unit of length is the meter (m), which is divided into 100 centimeters (cm) or 1000 millimeters (mm). One thousand meters make up one kilometer (km). Fluids are measured in liters (L), each divided into 1000 milliliters (mL). A liter of pure water weighs one kilogram (kg), the unit of mass that is divided into 1000 grams (g). One metric ton is 1000kg.

MEASUREMENT CONVERSIONS	
1 inch (in.) = 25.4mm	1 millimeter (mm) = 0.039 in.
1 foot (ft.) = 0.305m	1 meter (m) = 3.28 ft.
1 yard (yd.) = 0.914m	1 meter (m) = 1.094 yd.
1 mile (mi.) = 1.609km	1 kilometer (km) = 0.621 mi.
1 ounce (oz.) = 28.35g	1 gram (g) = 0.035 oz.
1 pound (lb.) = 0.454kg	1 kilogram (kg) = 2.205 lb.
1 fluid ounce (fl. oz.) = 29.57mL	1 milliliter (mL) = 0.034 fl. oz.
1 gallon (gal.) = 3.785L	1 liter (L) = 0.264 gal.

language

GERMAN (DEUTSCH)

Most Germans speak some basic English, but you will encounter many that don't. Preface any questions with a polite *Sprechen Sie Englisch?* (Do you speak English?) When out at restaurants, bars, and attractions, a simple *Bitte* (please) and *Danke* (thank you) are obviously important magic words. Even if your handle on German is a little loose, most locals will appreciate your effort.

Pronunciation

German pronunciation, for the most part, is consistent with spelling. There are no silent letters, and all nouns are capitalized.

An umlaut over a letter (e.g., ü) makes the pronunciation longer and more rounded. An umlaut is sometimes replaced by an "e" following the vowel, so that "schön" becomes "schoen." Germans are generally very forgiving toward foreigners who butcher their mother tongue, but if you learn nothing else in German, learn to pronounce the names of cities properly. Berlin is "bare-LEEN," Hamburg is "HAHM-boorg," Munich is "MEUWN-shen," and Bayreuth is "BUY-royt."

Different pronunciations for certain letters and diphthongs are listed below. Different pronunciations for certain letters and dipthongs are listen below. The German "ß," is referred to as the *scharfes S* (sharp S) or the *Ess-tset*. It is shorthand for a double-s , and is pronounced just like an "ss" in English. The letter appears only in lower case and shows up in two of the most important German words for travelers: Straße, "street," which is pronounced "SHTRAH-sseh" and abbreviated "Str."; and Schloß, "castle," pronounced "SHLOSS."

PHONETIC UNIT	PRONUNCIATION	PHONETIC UNIT	PRONUNCIATION
a	AH, as in "father"	j	Y, as in "young"
e	EH, as in "bet"	k	always K, as in "kelp"
i	IH, as in "wind"	r	gutteral RH, like French
o	OH, as in "oh"	s	Z, as in "zone"
u	OO, as in "fondue"	v	F, as in "fantasy"
au	OW, as in "cow"	w	V, as in "vacuum"
ie	EE, as in "thief"	z	TS, as in "cats"

ei	EY, as in "wine"	ch	CHH, as in "loch"
eu	OI, as in "boil"	qu	KV, as in "kvetch"
ä	similar to the E in "bet"	sch	SH, as in "shot"
ö	similar to the E in "perm"	st/sp	SHT/SHP, as in "spiel"
ü	close to the EU in "blue"	th	T, as in "time"

Phrasebook

Nothing can replace a full-fledged phrasebook or pocket-sized English-German dictionary, but this phrasebook will provide you with a few of the essentials. German features both an informal and formal form of address; in the tables below, the polite form follows the familiar form in parentheses. In German, all nouns can take any one of three genders: masculine (taking the article **der;** pronounced DARE), feminine (**die;** pronounced DEE), and neuter (**das;** pronounced DAHSS). All plural nouns also take the *die* article, regardless of their gender in the singular.

ENGLISH	GERMAN	PRONUNCIATION
Hello!/Hi!	Hallo!/Tag!	Hahllo!/Tahk!
Goodbye!/Bye!	Auf Wiedersehen!/Tschüss!	Owf VEE-der-zain!/Chuess!
Yes.	Ja.	Yah.
No.	Nein.	Nine.
Sorry!	Es tut mir leid!	Ess toot meer lite!
EMERGENCY		
Go away!	Geh weg!	Gay veck!
Help!	Hilfe!	HILL-fuh!
Call the police!	Ruf die Polizei!	Roof dee Pol-ee-TSEI!
Get a doctor!	Hol einen Arzt!	Hole EIN-en Ahrtst!

Greetings

ENGLISH	GERMAN	ENGLISH	GERMAN
Good morning.	Guten Morgen.	**My name is...**	Ich heiße...
Good afternoon.	Guten Tag.	**What is your name?**	Wie heißt du (heißen Sie)?
Good evening.	Guten Abend.	**Where are you from?**	Woher kommst du (kommen Sie)?
Good night.	Guten Nacht.	**How are you?**	Wie geht's (geht es Ihnen)?
Excuse me/Sorry.	Enthschuldigung/Sorry.	**I'm well.**	Es geht mir good.
Could you please help me?	Kannst du (Können Sie) mir helfen, bitte?	**Do you speak English?**	Sprichst du (Sprechen Sie) Englisch?
How old are you?	Wie alt bist du (sind Sie)?	**I don't speak German.**	Ich spreche kein Deutsch.

Useful Phrases

CARDINAL NUMBERS										
0	1	2	3	4	5	6	7	8	9	10
null	eins	zwei	drei	vier	fünf	sechs	sieben	acht	neun	zehn

CARDINAL NUMBERS										
11	12	20	30	40	50	60	70	80	90	100
elf	zwölf	zwanzig	dreißig	vierzig	fünfzig	sechzig	siebzig	achtzig	neunzig	hundert

ORDINAL NUMBERS					
1st	erste	**5th**	fünfte	**9th**	neunte
2nd	zweite	**6th**	sechste	**10th**	zehnte
3rd	dritte	**7th**	siebte	**20th**	zwanzigste
4th	vierte	**8th**	achte	**100th**	hunderte

DIRECTIONS AND TRANSPORTATION

(to the) right	rechts	(to the) left	links
straight ahead	geradeaus	Where is...?	Wo ist...?
next to	neben	opposite	gegenüber
How do I find...?	Wie finde ich...?	It's nearby.	Es ist in der Nähe.
How do I get to...?	Wie komme ich nach...?	Is that far from here?	Ist es weit weg?
one-way trip	einfache Fahrt	round-trip	hin und zurück
Where is this train going?	Wohin fährt das Zug?	When does the train leave?	Wann fährt der Zug ab?

ACCOMMODATIONS

Rooms available	Zimmer frei	I would like a room...	Ich möchte ein Zimmer...
No vacancies	besetzt	...with sink.	...mit Waschbecken.
Are there any vacancies?	Gibt es ein Zimmer frei?	...with shower.	...mit Dusche.
Single room	Einzelzimmer	...with a toilet.	...mit WC.
Double room	Doppelzimmer	...with a bathtub.	...mit Badewanne.
Dormitory-style room	Mehrbettzimmer/ Schlafsaal	nonsmoker	Nichtraucher

TIME AND HOURS

open	geöffnet	closed	geschlossen
morning	Morgen	opening hours	Öffnungszeiten
afternoon	Nachmittag	today	heute
night	Nacht	yesterday	gestern
evening	Abend	tomorrow	morgen
What time is it?	Wie spät ist es?	break time, rest day	Ruhepause, Ruhetag
It's (seven) o'clock.	Es ist (sieben) Uhr.	At what time?	Um wieviel Uhr?

FOOD AND RESTAURANT TERMS

bread	Brot	water	Wasser
roll	Brötchen	tap water	Leitungswasser
jelly	Marmelade	juice	Saft
meat	Fleisch	beer	Bier
beef	Rindfleisch	wine	Wein
pork	Schweinfleisch	coffee	Kaffee
chicken	Huhn	tea	Tee
sausage	Wurst	soup	Suppe
cheese	Käse	potatoes	Kartoffeln
fruit	Obst	milk	Milch
vegetables	Gemüse	sauce	Soße
cabbage	Kohl	french fries	Pommes frites
I would like to order...	Ich hätte gern...	Another beer, please.	Noch ein Bier, bitte.
It tastes good.	Es schmeckt gut.	It tastes awful.	Es schmeckt widerlich.
I'm a vegetarian.	Ich bin Vegetarier (m)/ Vegetarierin (f)	I'm a vegan.	Ich bin Veganer (m)/ Veganerin (f).
Service included.	Bedienung inklusiv.	Daily special	Tageskarte
Check, please.	Rechnung, bitte.	Give me a Nutella sandwich.	Geben Sie mir ein Nutel- labrötchen.

essentials

GLOSSARY

ab/fahren: to depart
die Abfahrt: departure
das Abteil: train compartment
Achtung: beware
die Altstadt: old town, historic center
das Amt: bureau, office
an/kommen: to arrive
die Ankunft: arrival
die Apotheke: pharmacy
die Arbeit: work
der Ausgang: exit
die Auskunft: information
die Ausstellung: exhibition
die Ausweis: ID
das Auto: car
die Autobahn: highway
der Autobus: bus
das Bad: bath, spa
das Bahn: railway
der Bahnhof: train station
der Bahnsteig: train platform
der Berg: mountain, hill
die Bibliothek: library
die Brücke: bridge
der Brunnen: fountain, well
der Bundestag: parliament
die Burg: fortress, castle
der Busbahnhof: bus station
die Damen: ladies (restroom)
das Denkmal: memorial
die Dusche: shower
der Dom: cathedral
das Dorf: village
eklig: disgusting
die Einbahnstraße: one-way street
der Eingang: entrance
ein/steigen: board
der Eintritt: admission
der Fahrplan: timetable
das Fahrrad: bicycle
der Fahrschein: train/bus ticket
die Festung: fortress
der Flohmarkt: flea market
der Flughafen: airport
der Fluß: river
das Fremdenverkehrsamt: tourist office
die Fußgängerzone: pedestrian zone
das Gasthaus: guest house
die Gedenkstätte: memorial
geil: cool or horny

das Gleis: track
der Hafen: harbor
der Hauptbahnhof: main train station
der Hof: court, courtyard
die Innenstadt: city center
die Insel: island
die Jugendherberge: youth hostel
die Karte: ticket
das Kino: cinema
die Kirche: church
das Krankenhaus: hospital
das Kreuz: cross, crucifix
die Kunst: art
der Kurort: spa/resort
die Kurverwaltung: resort tourist office
das Land: German state/province
die Lesbe: lesbian (n.)
der Markt: market
der Marktplatz: market square
das Meer: sea
das Münster: cathedral
das Museum: museum
der Notausgang: emergency exit
der Notfall: emergency
der Notruf: emergency hotline
der Paß: passport
der Platz: square, plaza
die Polizei: police
das Postamt: post office
die Quittung: receipt
das Rathaus: town hall
die Rechnung: bill, check
das Reisezentrum: travel office in train stations
die S-Bahn: commuter rail
das Schiff: ship
das Schloß: castle
der See: lake
die Stadt: city
der Strand: beach
die Straße: street
die Tankstelle: gas/petrol station
das Tor: gate
die U-Bahn: subway
die Vorsicht: caution
der Wald: forest
das WC: bathroom
wandern: to hike
der Wanderweg: hiking trail
der Weg: road, way
die Zeitung: newspaper
der Zug: train

essentials

GERMANY 101

history

EARLY GERMAN HISTORY

Blonde Savages

The Romans first identified the German region in the first century BCE with a flattering description of these fierce tribes. The ancient Germans became famous for stopping Roman expansion at the Battle of the Teutoborg Forest in 21 CE, under the leadership of their chieftain Hermann. As Rome weakened, Germany became a highway for tribes making inroads into Europe.

Charlemagne's Conquests

From 772 to 814, Charlemagne, King of the Franks, took over many German territories, forcefully converting thousands of pagans to Christianity. Eventually, the Pope appointed Charlemagne as the Roman emperor, a title that Charlemagne then expanded when he established **The Holy Roman Empire (HRE).** By Charlemagne's death in 814, the HRE spread across a vast area of Europe, including modern Germany. Charlemagne's son, Louis the Pious, inherited the massive empire, and all remained pious (who would have guessed?) under his reign. The empire was then passed on to Charlemagne's grandsons, who hadn't learned that sharing was caring. The squab-

facts and figures

- **POPULATION:** 82,140,043
- **AREA:** 357,021 sq. km
- **BEER BREWERIES:** 1234
- **NATIONAL PARKS:** 14
- **DRINKING AGE FOR BEER:** 16
- **DAILY BEER CONSUMPTION PER CAPITA:** .32L
- **AVERAGE LIFE EXPECTANCY:** 79 years

bling heirs fragmented the territory, and the empire slowly eroded.

Disastrous Dynasties

Three Ottos and four Salian rulers later, the German monarchy was once again a prodigious European power. However, following the Salian dynasty, the Hohenstaufens regrettably came into rule from 1138 to 1254. The Hohenstaufen rulers successfully shattered their political power with embittered battles against both German princes and the Catholic church. Matters worsened in 1197 when three-year-old Frederick inherited the kingdom. Wisely, it was decided that Frederick's rule should be handed over to older relations. Thus, Phillip took charge, until a fourth Otto assassinated him. The decades of death and disaster finally diminished in 1273 with the election of Rudolf, a member of the Hapsburg family.

Let the Drinking Begin

In 1516, the oldest food regulation law, the **German Beer Purity Law**, was enacted. This law regulates the production of beer in Germany. According to the law, pure German beer should consist of only barley malt, hops, and water. However, the current regulation is not as stringent, since most beers now also contain yeast.

Now That's a Load of Bull

In 1536, the **Golden Bull of 1536** was drawn up as the empire's constitution. It stated that the seven Prince-Electors would convene to elect German emperor; over time, the Habsburgs monopolized the imperial throne and turned it into a de facto hereditary title. It wasn't until 1806, when people finally realized that the constitution was more bull than golden, and the empire folded beneath the Napoleonic invasion.

RELIGIOUS RAGE

German Reformation

In 1517, Martin Luther posted his paper, the **95 Theses**, on the door of a local church in Wittenberg, Germany. The paper ranted about the issues of the Church, particularly focusing on the problem of indulgences. Luther's controversial beliefs sparked religious strife across the country. At the **Diet of Worms** in 1521, the emperor and the diet (the representative congress) exiled Luther. On his exit from the country, armed men seized Luther and then removed him to Warthing Castle under the protection of the elector of Saxony. Luther then lived in Germany under the alias of "Squire George."

However, Luther reappeared in 1522, further heating religious controversies. Finally, in 1526, the **Edict of Worms** permanently banned Luther's teachings. Luther's supporters protested so vehemently they were christened Protestants.

Both Catholics and Lutherans turned to war in an attempt to achieve religious superiority. Ultimately, the violence ended with the **Peace of Augsburg** in 1555, which stated that each ruler of a German state could choose the official religion of his territory.

1212
A German boy proclaims himself a prophet; his Children's Crusade embarks on a fun-sized quest to Jerusalem.

1348
Black Plague sweeps through Europe for the first time. 70% of Hamburg dies in the epidemic.

1499
Switzerland and the German empire call it quits.

1620S
The cuckoo clock is invented in the Black Forest.

1749
Johann Wolfgang von Goethe is born.

1813
Napoleon is defeated at Leipzig.

Thirty Years' War

The Peace of Augsburg brought little peace to Germany. Religious conflict soon led to the devastating **Thirty Years' War**. The lengthy war ravaged the country, as most of it was fought on German soil; up to a third of the German population died in the conflict. The war ended with the **Peace of Westphalia** in 1648 that left greater Germany a patchwork of independent states, Catholic or Protestant.

SHIFTING TERRITORIES

German Confederation

After German armies helped to defeat Napoleon in 1813, European powers met in Vienna to reorganize Europe. As a result of the meeting, the **German Confederation** was founded. The Confederation was a union of 39 states under Austrian leadership. However, this loose association fell apart in 1867. From 1867 to 1871, a transitional government, the **North German Confederation**, was put under the control of Prussia.

The Otto Era

Guess who's back? Another Otto. Otto Von Bismarck finally unified Germany in 1871 forging a new German Empire. His main priority was to build up Germany's power by carefully crafting European alliances. Not even Bismarck could manage under-the-table agreements, and the alliances eventually dissolved, leaving Germany to its own devices, which wasn't all that bad: Germany was quickly on its path to becoming the greatest industrial power in the world, led by companies like Krupp and Bayer. The university of Berlin became a model for the modern research university.

THE BEGINNING OF INSTABILITY

World War I

In 1914, World War I erupted after a Serbian nationalist shot the heir to Austro-Hungarian throne, **Archduke Franz Ferdinand**. Germany promised to support Austria's fight against Serbia. Germany united with Austria-Hungary, Bulgaria, and the Ottoman Empire to form the **Central Powers**. They fought against the **Triple Alliance** of Britain, France, and Russia. Germany tried to defeat France and Russia with its dual-action **Schlieffen Plan**. However, stalled military action in France rendered the plan unsuccessful, and both sites settled into trench warfare. The United States entered the war with the Triple Alliance in 1917, shortly after Germany declared its new policy of unrestricted submarine warfare. The **Treaty of Versailles** followed in 1919. The Treaty called for harsh reparations for Germany and its defeated allies. The Treaty also unwisely forced the defeated countries to accept sole responsibility for the war. Germany, humiliated and defeated, was also left economically destroyed.

Weimar Republic

In 1919 under the democratic **Weimar Constitution**, Friedrich Ebert became the first President of Germany. However, the **National Socialist German Workers' Party** and the **German Commu-**

1848
Communist Manifesto by Karl Marx is published.

MARCH 14, 1879
Albert Einstein is born. Germany gets a lot kookier.

1932
Volkswagen car is test driven for the first time.

MAY 8TH, 1945
Victory in Europe Day (V-E Day).

AUGUST 1961
The Berlin Wall is built.

AUGUST 25, 1970
Claudia Schiffer is born.

history . the beginning of instability

1988
Steffi Graf wins all
four Grand Slam
singles titles and the
Olympic gold medal.

**NOVEMBER
9TH, 1989**
Berlin Wall is torn
down.

**OCTOBER
3RD, 1990**
West and East
Germany officially
unite.

nist Party did not accept the new government. Because of the increasing popularity of both parties the new democracy never developed strong national support.

ATTEMPTS AT WORLD DOMINATION

Rise of Hitler

As Germany struggled to establish political stability, Adolf Hitler, the leader of the **National Socialist 'Nazi' Party**, took this opportunity to rise to power. In 1933, Paul von Hindenburg, the newly elected President, appointed Hitler as Chancellor of Germany. On February 27th, 1933, the Nazis covertly burned down the Reichstag, the seat of the legislature, blaiming the catastrophe on "communist terrorists." The chaos following the fire was exactly what Hitler had hoped for. Taking advantage of the fear amongst the German people, Hitler took charge and passed the **Enabling Act of 1933**, which essentially made Hitler the dictator of Germany. When Hindenburg died on August 2, 1934, Hitler made himself Führer, or supreme leader. He began his extensive territorial conquests in 1938 by entering and annexing Austria. By 1939, Hitler and his Nazi army were attempting to control all of Europe. Concurrently, the Nazi's racial progrom was manifested through a genocide, now known as the **Holocaust**, which killed over 12 million people, including six million Jews.

World War II

When Germany invaded Poland in 1939, Britain, France, Australia, and New Zealand declared war against Germany. On September 27, 1940, Germany, Italy, and Japan united as the **Axis.** The United States claimed neutrality until December 8th, 1941, a day after Japan bombed Pearl Harbor, when it declared war against Japan. Germany declared war on the United State three days later. The **Allies,** whose major players were the U.S., Britain, and the Soviet Union, successfully forced Germany and its Axis allies to retreat over the next four years. Hitler, comprehending his failure, committed suicide on April 30th, 1945. Shortly after, Germany surrendered.

On June 5th, 1945, the victorious Allies divided up Germany and Berlin into four zones. The three most Western zones, controlled by the U.S., Britain, and France, eventually united and became known as the **Federal Republic of Germany.** The one Eastern zone, controlled by the Soviet Union, became known as the **German Democratic Republic**. By the time the the war ended in 1945, over 7 million Germans had died.

REPAIRING A BROKEN NATION

The Road to Recovery

Following WWII, Germany was in ruins. Capitalist West Germany's economy began to improve, and East Germany was rebuilt within the Warsaw Pact. However, East German citizens were subject to communist rule and had no political freedom. The two countries, led by different forms of government, became increasingly distinct and divided, yet the question of reunification was never forgotten.

germany 101

Fall of the Wall

On November 9th 1989, East German citizens were finally allowed to cross border points into West Germany with the destruction of the Berlin Wall. On October 3rd, 1990, East and West Germany officially united. This date is now known as **Unity Day**, a German national holiday that marks the end of a repression in the East. Germany joined the European Union in 1993. After a tumultuous history involving manuy break-ups and make-ups, Germany is finally a centralized country, with a stable political system and a thriving economy.

politics and government

After years of turmoil, the post-WWII German government finally stabilized as a parliamentary democracy. In 1949, the parliamentary council approved the **Basic Law**, the constitution of the **Federal Republic of Germany.** It outlines human rights and freedoms granted to German citizens and specifies government structure.

GOVERNMENT SYSTEM

Germany has a federal government, and 16 regional state governments. The states, called Länder, each have their own parliament and government.

The Federal President is the most important figure in the German political system. However, in reality, he is more of a ceremonial figurehead. As head of the Federal Government and the 16 Federal States, the Federal Chancellor is the real boss.

There are two chambers that comprise the legislative branch of the German government. The first chamber is the **Bundestag.** Members of the Bundestag are elected nationally every four years. The second chamber is the **Bundesrat,** which represents the interests of the Länder. Members of the Bundesrat are elected through regional elections every four to five years.

The German judiciary system is an independent branch of government. The highest court is the Bundesverfassungsgericht. Or, in fewer letters and more words, as the **Federal Constitutional Court.**

people

POPULATION

Germany has a population of about 82 million people, with a population density of 230 people per square kilometer. The main language in Germany is, shockingly, German.

ETHNIC GROUPS

91.5% German, 2.4% Turkish, 1.7% Italians, .4% Greek, .4% Polish, and a sizeable number of refugees from the former country of Yugoslavia.

RELIGION

33% of the population is Protestant and 33% is Roman Catholic. Another 3.5% of the population is Muslim. There is also a small Jewish community in Germany. The large remainder of the population does not identify with a religion.

Wanna bond with the German people? Here are some good conversation pointers and useful words for making your trip easier.

- **KNOW YOUR LOCAL SPORTS TEAMS.** Sports make great conversation starters, and who hasn't heard of the Celtics or the Yankees? Throw Oliver Kahn (recently retired legendary goalie of Bayern Munich) or Arne Friedrich (defender for the Hertha BSC) into the mix and you're all set.

- **LEITUNGSWASSER.** Knowing the German word for "tap water" is useful in multiple ways; free drinks, cheaper living, and a good intermediate between beers.

- **BEER APPRECIATOR.** Germans are always trying to teach you about their favorite drink, which comes cheaper than water. Like beer (try Schumacher, Augustiner, Franziskaner, and Tannenzäpfle) or die trying.

- **WO IS...?** Need an escape route? Try the phrase "where is." And don't promise, "I'll be back"—that robot is Austrian.

land

Germany borders France, Switzerland, Austria, the Czech Republic, Poland, Denmark, Netherlands, Belgium, and Luxembourg. The North Sea and the Baltic Sea border northern Germany. From countryside vineyards to massive mountain ranges and farming flatlands, Germany varies greatly topographically. Northern Germany primarily consists of flat plains, which serve as farmland for wheat, barley (Germany is the leading producer of barley), sugar beet, rye, and potato production. Central Germany has a vast range of plateaus. Farmers grow grains and root crops on the flatlands, and vineyards and orchards cover the sloped areas. Mountainous regions, including the Bavarian Alps and the Black Forest, stretch across southern Germany. Germany's highest mountain, Zugspitze, is in the Bavarian Alps. The Black Forest is a much smaller mountain range, with an average height of about 3,000 feet above sea level. To the west is the Rheinland, which is renowned for its vineyards, rolling countryside, and prime proposal spots alongside astounding landscapes and the Rhein River. Other main rivers in Germany are the Wester, the Elber, the Main, the Oder, and the Danube.

media

NEWSPAPERS

Bild Zeitung is the most popular news and gossip newpaper in Germany. If you want to read about political news and world events, then pick up a copy of *The Faz (Frankfurter Allgemeine Zeitung)*. For business news, there is *Handelsblatt*, a daily business paper. For a lengthy read, *Die Zeit* is a popular weekly newspaper...with over 100 pages of news.

MAGAZINES

Der Spiegel is a reputable newsmagazine that delivers world news weekly. Der Spiegel's competitor, *Focus*, has more pictures and shorter articles that cover everything from sports to cultural events to politics.

TV

While you may not be able to catch the next episode of Jersey Shore in Germany, you will be able to find cable television in most places in the country. The most popular TV channels are Das Erste (ARD), Bayerischer Rundfunk (BR), Zweites Deutsches Fernsehen (ZDF), Radio Television Luxembourg (RTL), Pro 7, SAT-1, and Premeire.

---

hair i am

When I popped from my mother, she said, "I can't love this, it needs hair." It's true, Mother lacked a basic understanding of human growth patterns, but her message about the importance of hair was not lost on me.

Nor was it lost on Berliners who regard locks and waves as something more than just a poof of hair follicles. The head is a temple, and the hair is that temple's grass; and wouldn't you want your temple's grass to be novel and well groomed?

Outside of this city, hair is too often the crud we pull from our shower drains as we convince ourselves it was worth it to let our girlfriend live with us.

But Berliners know better, and never live with their girlfriends.

They also know better on the hair front. It's not uncommon to see 70-year-old women waiting in line at the supermarket with pink blotches in their hair, or businessmen in suits with uneven segments shaved from their heads.

The head challenges the Berliner—what will you do with me? The answers can be pretty novel.

-Nelson Greaves

---

literature

Ever heard of *Steppenwolf, Metamorphosis,* or *Beowulf*? If these titles make you shudder from your college English 101 days, you can thank the German authors of these classics.

The first major German literary movement, **Sturm und Drang**, emerged in the 1770s as a rebellious response to Enlightenment. During this time, Johann Wolfgang von Goethe and Friedrich von Schiller rose to fame with their debut works, *The Sorrows of Young Werther* and *Die Räuber*, respectively. Their pieces, containing juicy plots of love triangles and revolution, fit right in with a scandalous *Gossip Girl* episode. Literary excellence resurged in Germany following World War II. Authors focused on scrutinizing recent national, social, and political turmoil. The most notable writers from this time include Siegried Lenz, Heinrich Boll, and Günter Grass.However, during the second-half of the 20th century, East German authors were forced to write within the constraints of "social realism." Despite this limitation, Christa Wolf, Heiner Müller, and Irmtraud Morgner became prominent literary figures during this time.

film

German film achieved global recognition with the production of **Madame Dubarry**, later retitled **Passion**, in 1918. The government utilized films as a means of propaganda during World War I. After World War I, German filmmakers led the way in the modern exploration of the cinematic form; the best-known example is Fritz Lang's *Metropolis*.

Propaganda films returned during Hitler's Third Reich. Due to the manipulative and controlled nature of the industry, many prominent producers, actors, and writers fled the country. Following World War II, Americans exercised control over the German film industry, which slumped into a series of regrettable film productions.

Finally, German cinema put itself back on the world-stage of film with the 1998 production of **Run, Lola, Run**. Since then, the industry has had a decade-long shift from award-winning comedies to more serious films. Recent films, such as **Goodbye Lenin!** (2003) and **The Lives of Others** (2007), have succeeded partly because they have used German national history to create universally accessible stories.

If you ever plan on having a German film party (obviously a great party theme), then you should show classics like **Metropolis** (1925), **Das Boote** (1982), **Wings of Desire** (1987), and **The Tin Drum** (1982).

art and architecture

ARCHITECTURE

Germany is bursting with an abundance of architecture from all eras. Thanks to the Romans the town of Trier holds remains of the **Abbey Church of St. Michael's**, completed back in 1000 CE. Another Romanesque style landmark is the **Speyer Cathedral**, which now stands as the largest Romanesque church in the world.

Move on to other epochs and Germany still impresses. Most notable from the Gothic period are the **Freiburg** and the **Köln** Cathedrals. The Freiburg Cathedral, completed in 1230 CE, is the only Gothic church tower in Germany from the Middle Ages. The Köln Cathedral, the second largest Gothic cathedral in the world, took over 600 years to complete. From the Renaissance era, Germany boasts **Heidelberg Castle** and **Augsburg City Hall**. If you want to go Baroque, check out **Zwinger Palace**, **Würzberg Residence**, and **Brandenburg Gate**. Brandenburg Gate has particular historical significance as a reminder of the wall that once divided East and West Germany. If more modern art is your thing, look no further than Berlin's **Volkswagon Showroom** and the glass-walled department store **Galeries Lafayette**.

ART

The medieval movement encompassed the art scene in Germany from 200 to 1430. After 1000 years too many, the medieval movement gradually gave way to the Renaissance, which inundated Europe from 1300 to 1602. Prominent German artists of this era include Albrecht Dürer and Han Holbein the Younger.

gnome home

An unusual first that Germany can claim for itself is the production of the first garden gnome. This little lawn ornaments were developed in the mid-1800s by a man named Philip Griebel. He chose the gnome for its kindly reputation among German gardeners: it was said in German myth that gnomes often could help with gardening during the nighttime. The gnomes were a huge hit and spread across all of Germany and into the rest of Europe, until World War II began and discouraged people from buying things like lawn ornamentation. Today, only a few gnome-makers remain in Germany, and Griebel's descendants are one of them. Even still, there are estimated to be around 25 million garden gnomes still residing in Germany!

Neoclassicism took hold in Germany from 1750 to 1830. It was quickly followed by its rebellious successor, the romantic movement. Romanticism rejected rigid reasoning and symmetry, and instead centered around powerful emotions and nature. The paintings of **Caspar David Friedrich** particularly embody the essence of romantic ideals.

Modern art swept through Germany duing the late 19th century and early 20th century, facing major opposition from the National Socialist Party during the 1930-40s. In fact, in 1937, Nazis compiled over 650 pieces of modern art into an art exhibition entitled, **Entartete Kunst**, or "Degenerate Art," to illustrate unacceptable art to the German public. However, the exhibition attracted over three million people, the highest viewership of any modern art show to date. The modern art era made way for contemporary art, represented in Germany by Jonathan Meese and Andreas Gursky.

etiquette and customs

DINING

Traditionally, German restaurants allow self-seating if no host is present. Water with your meal is on request and you must specify if you want tap water. Otherwise, the restaurant will rack up your bill by bringing you expensive bottled water. Also, before you satiate a ravenous appetite with a fluffy roll, consider the unfortunate extra charge for rolls or bread.

the wurst

- **BRATWURST.** This popular sausage is made from a combination of pork and veal.

- **THURINGER BRATWURST.** Think Bratwurst, but spicier.

- **CURRY WURST.** A common fast food delicacy consisting of bite-size pieces of wurst, topped with tomato sauce and a spoonful of curry powder.

- **BOCKWURST.** Similar to a hot dog in appearance, it's typically made with veal or pork and smoked and eaten with mustard and bock beer.

GRATUITY

At the end of the meal, the bill includes gratuity. However, it is appropriate to add a 5% tip for good service, and a 10% tip for exceptional service.

MEET AND GREET

Unlike workaholics in the United States, Germans look down upon working after hours as evidence of poor planning. Germans face tasks at work and in their personal life with an approach of careful scheduling and organization.

When entering a room, shake hands with everyone in the room individually, including children. Until you are told otherwise, address a person with their official title and surname. When entering a store, always greet with a "Guten Tag." Upon leaving the store, even if you did not buy anything, it is polite to say goodbye, or, "auf Wiedersehen."

SO YOU WANT TO MEET THE PARENTS...

If you are invited to a German home, it is best to bring chocolates or flowers as a gift. Since many flowers carry particular stigmas, it is safest to bring yellow roses or tea roses. After all, you don't want to give funeral flowers to your kind host.

Germans eat meals with forks in the left hand and the knives in the right hand. German etiquette requires keeping elbows off the table, although hands should always be visible on the table. Sorry, no under the table deals. When you are finished (try to finish everything on your plate), lay your knife and fork parallel to each other on the right side of the plate. Finally, for all salad lovers out there, always fold your lettuce with your knife, instead of cutting it.

holidays and festivals

DATE	NAME	DESCRIPTION
December 5	St. Nicolas Day	On the eve of December 6th, children leave their shoes outside for Saint Nick to fill with treats
December 21	St. Thomas Day	People late to work have to wear a cardboard donkey all day. Don't be a slow ass on this day!
December 24	Christmas Eve	Shops close early today
December 25th	Christmas Day	Shops closed all day
January 6th	Three Kings Day	Children dress up as kings and participate in parades
42nd day before Easter	Fasching	A Carnival similar to Mardi Gras, celebrated the week of Lent.
Friday before Easter	Good Friday	Shops closed all day
late March/early April	Easter	Shops closed all day
late September/early October	Beerfest	Beer festival with tasting tents and events
October 3	Unity Day	Celebration of the reunification of East and West Germany

FESTIVALS

Karneval

Colorful costumes, blaring pop music, and uninhibited dancing take over Germany during Carnival, also called **Karneval**, **Fastnacht**, or **Fasching**. The Carnival officially starts on November 11th at 11:11 am, but the festivities don't commence until February, coinciding with the start of Lent. A myriad of masquerades and costume parties cumulate with grand parades on the 42nd day before Easter, **Rosenmontag** (known as Rose Monday in the US). In some cities, such as Munich, the wild celebrations hit on Tuesday, when dance parties overflow blocked off streets. The best festivities are found in Munich, Muenster, Aachen, Köln, and Mainz.

Oktoberfest

Where can you drink a one-liter beer at 9am with a million people doing the exact same thing? Only at **Oktoberfest**. Every year, from late September to early October, you can be drunk in Munich for 16 straight days, surviving on enormous pretzels and even larger mugs of beer. Oktoberfest starts with the official tapping of the first barrel of beer at the Schottenhamel tent. For the following two weeks, over six million people attend the festival to pay patronage to beer tents. Beer tents are exactly what they sound like: Massive tents filled with tables, where attendees can settle down and get down to the business of beer. The tents open at 10 am on weekdays and 9 am on the weekends, and close at 11:30pm. Tents only serve beer until 10:30 pm, although you may be passed out on the tent floor by then. If you remain conscious, just remember to bring cash only. Always tip the waitresses (usually a euro per beer), otherwise you might not get seconds. Or thirds. Most importantly, it is difficult to get into a tent without a reservation. One must make reservations directly through the landlord of each tent. Often, a reservation requires a minimum group of six to eight people. If you do not have a reservation, arrive at the tents by noon on weekdays or by 10 am on the weekends. For landlords' contact information, go to ■www. oktoberfest.eu.

sports and recreation

FIELD HOCKEY

Men, the good news is that you can be on an all-men's field hockey team in Germany! Kilts optional.

TENNIS

Due to the worldwide success of tennis aces Steffi Graf and Boris Becker, tennis has become increasingly popular in Germany. While public tennis courts are hard to find, there are many private clay and turf courts around the country. Swimming, on the other hand, is an activity that is commonly open to the public. Many cities have public outdoor and indoor pools.

SKIING

For winter recreational activities, check out one of Germany's many ski resorts. At 2963 meters, Zugspitze is the highest peak in Germany. With 13mi. of runs, the Zugspitze ski area is open from November to May. For cross-country skiers, glide by monasteries and castles on trails in Oberammergau or explore the hundreds of miles of trails through the Black Forest.

SOCCER

With thousands of clubs and millions of fans across the country, Germany's most popular and revered sport is soccer. England may have David Beckham, but Germany has armies of youngsters training to become soccer prodigies.

If foot-eye coordination is not your forte, you will not be shunned from society; just demonstrate your prowess in other popular athletic pastimes, including **basketball, track, skating** and **cycling**.

food and drink

PREPARE FOR THE WURST

Carnivores look no further. Germany beckons your presence with a cornucopia of processed pork and meat, placed under the umbrella term *wurst*. Know how to deal with the wurst when venturing through restaurants and street vendors.

AN APPLE A DAY

The other main food groups in Germany include bread, cheese, and alcohol. If you crave produce to balance your meals, head to the weekly **Wochenmarkt**. The Wochenmarkt opens one to two times a week in most towns and suburbs. Although slightly pricier than the grocery store, the market is always abundant with ripe, local harvest. When shopping at the grocery store, bring your own bag or money to buy them at checkout. Don't look for a bagger either, since you must bag your own groceries.

WE LOVE OUR BREAD, WE LOVE OUR BUTTER

Breakfast, or **Fruhstuck,** typically consists of buttered bread with a topping of cheese, jam, or some variety of pork. Don't look for hot pancakes or crispy hashbrowns here; cooked breakfasts are rare in Germany.

Lunch, or **Mittagessen,** is the main meal, typically served between 12 and 2pm. This one to three course meal starts with everyone proclaiming, "Guten Appetit."

From 3 to 5pm is afternoon teatime. Indulge in desserts like Black Forest cake, marble cake, firm pudding molds, or the infamous Berliners.

Dinner, or **Abendessen,** is from 6 to 8pm. Dinner is ordinarily another carb loaded meal, featuring buttered bread topped with deli meat. At this point, it may be time to consider the Atkins diet.

SHOTS, SHOTS, SHOTS, EVERYBODY

Yes, it is true that Germany is second in the world for beer consumption. But, you will not be zealously chugging from **Das Boot** every time you enter a bar. Normally, **Kleines Bier** is a quarter-liter of beer while **Grosses Bier** is a half-liter. In Bavaria, many places serve a **mass** of beer, which equals one liter.

Germans might be famous for their over 1200 breweries, but there are also plenty of other spirits available. Many Germans enjoy a shot of Schnapps, called **Korn**, with their beer. If you are looking to cut back on sugar, steer clear of liqueurs, which (by law) must contain 100 grams of sugar per Liter.

BEYOND TOURISM

If you are reading this, then you are a member of an elite group—and we don't mean "the literate." You're a student preparing for a semester abroad. You're taking a gap year to save the trees, the whales, or the dates. You're an 80-year-old woman who has devoted her life to egg-laying platypuses and figuring out what the hell is up with that. In short, you're a traveler, not a tourist; like any good spy, you don't observe your surroundings—you become an active part of them.

Your mission, should you choose to accept it, is to study, volunteer, or work in Germany as laid out in the dossier—er, chapter—below. More general wisdom, including international organizations with a presence in many destinations and tips on how to pick the right program, is also accessible by logging onto the Beyond Tourism section of ▣www.letsgo.com. We leave the rest (when to go, whom to bring, and how many changes of underwear to pack) in your hands. This message will ▓self-destruct in five seconds. Good luck.

greatest hits

- **START A NEW LIFE.** German and American governments choose students to participate in a competitive language program. The best part? They pay for airfare and accommodations (p. 380).

- **WORK ON AN ORGANIC FARM.** Get an amazing view of the Bavarian hills while working for an agricultural cause (p. 381).

- **MASTER A NEW TONGUE.** Learn to speak the beautiful (some argue robotic) German language (p. 380).

- **TEACH FOR GERMANY.** Teach English and maybe even pick up some German along the way that involves more than, "Bier bitte" (p. 384).

studying

Still yearning for the cornucopia of beer at college parties but feel like imbibing in a more cultured surrounding? Then Germany is the study abroad country for you. Germany is famous for its vibrant student life, and there are opportunities to travel and study in radically distinct regions of the country (be warned that the food, however, may not differ as much).

Study-abroad programs range from basic language and culture courses to university-level classes, often for college credit (it's legit, Mom and Dad). Costs and duration of the programs also vary greatly. These factors depend on the available housing options a program offers, as well as the location of the program. Although German universities are not officially ranked, there are notable differences in areas of study or campus size and layout that distinguish German universities. Many university-affiliated programs are located in larger cities with multiple housing options, while volunteering programs range from metropolises to rural towns and host family-living options. Consider all the options carefully before you apply to these programs, as there are trade-offs to any choice.

UNIVERSITIES

Most university-level study abroad programs are conducted in German, although many programs offer classes in English as well as opportunities to learn German. The fearless linguist can sometimes directly enroll in a university abroad, but this may make college credit less easily attainable. Start the search for your perfect program by visiting websites like ▣www.studyabroad.com, ▣www.studyabroadinternational. com or, if you're a college or a university student, a study abroad office.

International Programs

AMERICAN INSTITUTE FOR FOREIGN STUDY (AIFS)

River Plaza, 9 West Broad Street, Stamford, CT 06902   ☎+1-866-906-2437 ▣www.aifs.com
Organizes various summer, semester, and year-long study abroad programs. Open to high school and college students. Summer abroad program in Berlin.
Ⓢ *Summer programs cost appropriximately $6000.* Ⓩ *Programs last 6-8 weeks.*

THE EXPERIMENT IN INTERNATIONAL LIVING

PO Box 676. 1 Kipling Rd., Brattleboro, VT 05302   ☎+1-800-345-2929
▣www.experimentinternational.org
Offers summer programs in Germany involving language skill improvement and cultural education.
Ⓢ*$6,500 with international airfare included.*

beyond tourism

visa information

No visa is needed to enter Germany for European Union nationals or US citizens for up to 90 days. To work in Germany, non-EU citizens usually need a residence permit and a work permit. Work permits are difficult to acquire without a job offer. Employees of European Economic Area (EEA) companies who have "Van der Elst" visas are exempt from work permits. Students have three options for student visas: a language course visa that is void when the course is completed, a student visa that must be converted to a residence visa upon university admission, or a one-year student visa along with proof of study.

ARCADIA UNIVERSITY

450 S. Easton Road, Glenside, PA 19038 ☎+1-866-927-2234 🖳www.arcadia.edu/abroad
Summer abroad program in Germany to learn about culture and renewable energy policies and technology.
Ⓢ *$7,600 with airfare included.*

INSTITUTE FOR THE INTERNATIONAL EDUCATION OF STUDENTS

33 N. LaSalle Street, 15th Floor, Chicago, IL 60602-2602 ☎+1-800-995-2300
🖳www.iesabroad.org

Summer, semester, and full year programs in Germany available. Each program focuses on a specific area of study, like Environmental Studies and Sustainability.
Ⓢ *Fees vary.*

EXPERIMENTAL LEARNING INTERNATIONAL

1557 Ogden St., Denver, CO 80218 ☎+1-303-321-8278 🖳www.eliabroad.org
Volunteer and internship programs in various countries, including Germany. Paid internships involving vineyard work from mid-Sept. through Oct. also available.
Ⓢ *Fees range from $1,265-3,365, depending on length of stay, with an application fee of $100* 🗓 *Programs last 2-12 weeks.*

AHA INTERNATIONAL

70 NW Couch St., Suite 242 Portland, OR 97209 ☎+1-800-654-2051
🖳www.ahastudyabroad.org

Offers various study abroad programs in Germany.
Ⓢ *$3,730-6,000.* 🗓 *4-6 weeks.*

GLOBAL LEARNING SEMESTERS

14525 SW Millikan Way #32004, Beaverton, OR 97005-2343 ☎+1-877-300-7010
🖳www.globalsemesters.com

Offer Study in Europe semesters that include German destinations.
i *Minimum GPA 2.5.* Ⓢ *Around $17,000.* 🗓 *Programs last 1 semester.*

THE EXPERIMENT IN INTERNATIONAL LIVING

PO Box 676. 1 Kipling Rd., Brattleboro, VT 05302 ☎+1-800-345-2929
🖳www.usexperiment.org

Take a summer to enhance your German language skills while engaging in community service and exploring the region.
Ⓢ *$6500 for 4 week program, airfare included. $400 for preliminary application.*

LEXIA

6 The Courtyard, Hanover, NH 03755 ☎+1-800-775-3942 🖳www.lexiaintl.org
Summer or semesterprograms in Berlin to study architecture, visual culture, and cultural studies.
i *Applicants must have completed at least 1 year of undergraduate studies and have a minimum cumulative grade point average of B- in their field of study.*

CCIS STUDY ABROAD

2000 P St., NW, Suite 503 Washington, DC 20036 ☎+1-800-453-6956
🖳www.ccisstudyabroad.org

Learn German in summer or semester long programs in Berlin or Heidelberg.
Ⓢ *Semester $5,633-11,453. 8 week summer programs $5,500-6,900.* 🗓 *Semester programs offer studies in business administration, foreign language, politics, and history. Range from 8-16 weeks.*

INTERNATIONAL ASSOCIATION FOR THE EXCHANGE
OF STUDENTS FOR TECHNICAL EXPERIENCE (IAESTE)

DAAD, Referat 514, Kennedyallee 5053175 Bonn ☎228 882 266 🖳www.iaeste.org
The United States also has an office, which you can contact to apply for hands-on

technical internships in Germany. You must be an undergraduate student studying science, technology, or engineering.

⏰ Most programs 8-12 weeks.

German Programs

CONGRESS-BUNDESTAG YOUTH EXCHANGE FOR YOUNG PROFESSIONALS

CDS International, 440 Park Ave. South, New York, NY 10016 ☎+1-212-497-3500 💻www.cdsintl.org/fellowshipsabroad/cbyx.php

Co-sponsored by the German and US governments, this cultural exchange is geared toward 18-24-year-old young professionals. 75 people are chosen to participate in language immersion, classes, and an internsip in Germany; airfare and accommodations are provided.

$ Airfare and accommodations are provided. ⏰ Programs last 1 year.

DEUTSCHER AKADEMISCHER AUSTAUSCHDIENST (DAAD)

871 United Nations Plaza, New York, NY 10017 ☎+1-212-758-3223 💻www.daad.org

Information on language instruction, exchanges, and scholarships for study in Germany. Processes foreign enrollment in German universities. Also distributes applications and information brochures.

LANGUAGE SCHOOLS

As renowned novelist Gustave Flaubert once said, "Language is a cracked kettle on which we beat out tunes for bears to dance to." While we at Let's Go have absolutely no clue what he was talking about, we do know that the following are good resources for learning German. Most of these language programs are specific to Germany. Keep in mind that cost, duration, course intensity, and housing options vary widely.

EUROCENTRES

Seestr. 247, CH-8038 Zürich ☎+41 044 485 50 40 💻www.eurocentres.com

Language programs for beginning to advanced students with homestays in Berlin.

[i] Must be 16+. $ Courses $550-690 for 2 weeks. ⏰ Programs 2-12 weeks.

GOETHE-INSTITUT

72 Spring St., 11th fl., New York, NY 10012 ☎+1-212-439-8700 💻www.goethe.de

Look on the web, contact your local branch, or write to the main office. Runs German language programs in over 10 German cities and abroad, as well as high school exchange programs in Germany.

$ Courses €1,990-2,770.

GERMAN LANGUAGE SCHOOL (GLS)

Kastanienallee 82, 10435 Berlin ☎030 78 00 89 11 💻www.gls-berlin.de

Berlin-based language school offers variety of language courses with on-site accommodation or homestays, internships, high school exchanges,and summer camps in Berlin and Munich.

[i] 18+. $ Standard 5-week course roughly US$810; 5-week accommodation US$2,160.

BWS GERMANLINGUA

Bayerstr. 13, 80335 Munich ☎089 59 98 92 00 💻www.germanlingua.com

Full- and part-time language classes in Munich and Berlin for up to 1 year.

$ Standard 6-week German courses €1030. Various accommodation options available, adding an additional charge of €40-550.

DEUTSCHKURSE FÜR AUSLÄNDER BEI DER UNIVERSITÄT MÜNCHEN E.V.

Adelheidstraße 13b, 80798 München ☎089 271 26 42 💻www.dkfa.de/english

Offers courses for foreigners studying or applying to study in Germany.

$ 8-week course €720.

volunteering

Despite Germany's position as a global economic leader, there is plenty of volunteering to be done in the country. Your help could promote organic farming in the country. Or you can work to rebuild historical sights and public spaces ravaged by time and wars. You can build houses for those in need. You can even promote civil service and be a positive role model for future generations. And of course, there is always more to be done. The options are exhaustive. Begin your search with broader sites like ◨www.volunteersabroadcom, www.servenet.org, and www.idealist.org. The listings below, ranging from broad databases to specific programs to enlist in, can also help you in your search.

Most volunteers in Germany help out on a short-term basis at organizations that make use of drop-in or once-a-week volunteers. However, there are also longer programs that will enlist full-time assistance from any span of time between several weeks to a year. Consider these before applying or signing up to volunteer. A few organizations are religious have religious requirements.

Be aware that many volunteer programs require a fee. But before you throw your hands up in the air, crying out, "must I pay to be an altruist?" and move on to more self-indulging goals, understand that the fees usually help keep the organization afloat. The payment may also cover housing, food, and any other expenses your presence may cost. Fees may also help to build more structured volunteer organizations, which can be ideal for younger volunteeres, who may need more direction. If you're concerned about where your money is being spent, request an annual report or finance account. A reputable organization will not refuse this request.

ENVIRONMENTAL CONSERVATION

- **AGRIVENTURE:** Organizes agricultural exchanges and homestays at farms throughout Europe. Prices vary by program. (*#202A-300 Merganser Drive, Chestermere, Alberta, T1X 1L6* ☎*+1-403-25-7799* ◨*www.agriventure.com*)

- **BIOSPHERE EXPEDITIONS:** Provides a menu of eco-friendly getaways to the Bavarian Alps and other volunteer expeditions. (*PO Box 917750, Longwood, FL 32791* ☎*+1-800-407-5761* ◨*www.biosphere-expeditions.org*)

- **BUND JUGEND:** This eco-friendly group provides informations and organizes events for youth in Germany, including volunteer and internship opportunities. Website in German. (*☎030 275 86 50* ◨*www.bundjugend.de*)

- **EARTHWATCH:** Arranges 1- to 3-week programs in Europe (occasionally Germany) to promote conservation of natural resources. (*Mayfield House, 256 Banbury Road, Oxford, OX2 7DE, UK* ☎*+44 018 65 31 88 38* ◨*www.earthwatch.org/europe.* *i Fees vary based on location and duration, and costs vary by program.*)

- **WILLING WORKERS ON ORGANIC FARMS (WWOOF):** Membership (€20) in WWOOF offers room and board at a variety of organic farms in Germany in exchange for work. (*Postfach 210, 25901263 Dresden* ◨ *www.wwoof.de*)

HISTORICAL RESTORATION AND ARCHAEOLOGY

- **ARCHAEOLOGICAL INSTITUTE OF AMERICA:** The Archaeological Fieldwork Opportunities Bulletin lists field sites throughout Europe on its website. (*656 Beacon St., Boston, MA 02215* ☎*+1-617-353-9361* ◨*www.archaeological.org*)

- **OPEN HOUSES NETWORK:** A group dedicated to restoring public spaces and historical buildings in various regions of Germany. (*Goetheplatz 9 B, D - 99423 Weimar* ☎*036 43 50 28 79*◨*www.openhouses.de*)

volunteering · historical restoration and archaeology

- **PRO INTERNATIONAL:** Since 1949, this volunteer organization has brought together youth from around the world to help reconstruct and preserve sites in Germany. Many of their projects also serve local children and the environment. *(Leopold-Lucas-Str. 46A, 35037 Marburg ☎642 16 52 77 💻pro-international.de. ℹ Ages 16-26.)*

YOUTH AND COMMUNITY OUTREACH

- **AFS INTERKULTURELLE BEGEGNUNGEN E.V. (AFS INTERCULTURAL PROGRAMS):** 6- to 12-month volunteer opportunities to serve local communities available for 18+ travelers. Student exchanges also available for high schoolers over the summer and during the school year. *(In Germany, Postfach 50 01 42, 22701 Hamburg ☎0 403 99 22 20 💻www.afs.de. In the USA,71 West 23rd Street, 17th Floor, New York, NY 10010 ☎+1-212-352-9810 💻www.afs.org)*
- **BIG FRIENDS FOR YOUNGSTERS:** The German arm of the Big Brothers Big Sisters program; provides mentoring for young kids on a longer term basis. *(💻www.biffy.de)*
- **CANADIAN ALIANCE FOR DEVELOPMENT INITIATIVES AND PROJECTS:** Offers diverse 2- to 3-week programs in Germany aiming to promote peace, tolerance, and community. *(2202-1455 Howe Street, Vancouver, British Columbia, V6Z 1C2, Canada. In USA ☎+1-617-502-0400 💻www.cadip.org. $Program roughly €300.)*
- **CAMP ADVENTURE YOUTH SERVICES:** Sends college students to 118 camps in 16 countries to serve as counselors for children of US military. Airfare, housing, travel, food stipend of $22 per day, and 12 units of undergraduate credit provided. *(1223 W. 22nd St., Cedar Falls, IA 50614 ☎+1-319-273-5960 💻www.campadventure.uni.edu. $Participation fee of $285.)*
- **HABITAT FOR HUMANITY INTERNATIONAL:** Volunteers build houses in over 83 countries, including Germany. Periods of involvement range from 2 weeks to 3 years. *(121 Habitat St., Americus, GA 31209 ☎1-800-422-4828 💻www.habitat.org)*
- **UNITED PLANET:** Sends volunteers ages 18-30 to perform a wide range of community service work. Long-term (6-12 months) volunteer abroad program in Germany available. *(11 Arlington St., Boston, MA 02116 ☎+1-617-267-7763 💻www.unitedplanet.org)*
- **SERVICE CIVIL INTERNATIONAL VOLUNTARY SERVICE (SCI-IVS):** Arranges work experience in German civil service camps from 2 weeks to 12 months for 18+ individuals. (*In Germany, SCI - Deutscher Zweig e.V., Blücherstraße 14, D-53115 Bonn ☎ 0228-212086/7 💻www.sci-d.de. In the USA, SCI USA, 5474 Walnut Level Rd., Crozet, VA 22932 ☎+1-434-336-3545 💻www.sci-ivs.org. $Program fees apply.)*
- **FREUNDE DER ERZIEHUNGSKUNST RUDOLF STIEINERS E.V. (FRIENDS OF WALDORF EDUCATION):** 75 placements for 7-12 months and 1-2 years to volunteer with disabled or eldery people. *(Neisser Str. 10, D-76139 Karlsruhe ☎0 721 35 48 06120 💻www.freunde-waldorf.de/en/voluntary-services/in-germany. ℹ No participation costs, but airfare is expected to be paid by volunteer. Group housing included and stipend of €150.)*

beyond tourism

SOCIAL AND POLITICAL ACTIVISM

- **AMNESTY INTERNATIONAL:** Human rights organization with various internship and volunteer positions available. *(Sektion der Bundesrepublik Deutschland e.V., 53108 Bonn ☎0 228 98 37 30 💻www.amnesty.de)*
- **INTERNATIONALE BEGEGNUNG IN GEMEINSCHARTSDIENSTEN E.V.:** Brings together Germans and foreigners to promote mutual understanding while working on projects 30 hr. per week to serve local communities. *(Schloßerstraße 28, 70180 Stuttgart ☎ 0 711 649 02 63 💻www.ibg-workcamps.org)*

- **ICJA FREIWILLIGENAUSTAUSCH WELWEIT, E.V.:** A non-profit organization that promotes sociopolitical commitment by organizing practical 2 to 12-month long volunteer peace projects. *(Stralauer Allee 20E, 10245 Berlin ☎ 030 21 23 82 52 🖳www.icja.de)*
- **MOBILITY INTERNATIONAL USA:** Matches people with and without disabilities to staff international community service projects and to champion disability rights. *(132 E. Broadway, Suite 343, Eugene, Oregon 97401 ☎+1-541-343-1284 🖳www.miusa.org)*

FOR THE UNDECIDED ALTRUIST

- **VOLUNTEERS FOR PEACE:** Hosts project directories for individuals, teenagers, and families that want to volunteer in various areas. *(🖳www.vfp.org/directory.htm)*

EDUCATION

- **GEOVISIONS:** Live with a German family while teaching them English for 15 hr. per week. *(63 Whitfield St., Guilford, CT 06437 ☎+1-203-453-5838 🖳www.geovisions.org/pages/723_conversation_corps_munich.cfm)*
- **INTERNATIONAL VOLUNTEERS:** Assist at a daycare, senior citizen, or youth center in the Western German town of Enkenbach-Alsenborn. *(🖳www.internationalvolunteers.org/index.php/countries/germany.* ℹ Programs are 2-12 weeks. $ Costs start at $1265.*)*
- **AMERISPAN:** A study abroad program that also offers volunteer placement opportunities in several countries, including Germany. *(1334 Walnut St, 6th Floor, Philadelphia, PA 19107 ☎+1-800-879-6640 🖳www.amerispan.org)*
- **WORKAWAY:** A website that lists various opportunities to work in exchange for food and accommodations. *(🖳www.workaway.info)*

working

We understand, money doesn't grow on trees. Luckily, English speakers are a hot commodity for both long- and short-term jobs, especially in the tourist industry and other establishments like hotels and restaurants. Remember that some jobs require degrees and specific skills, especially in the sciences.

The recruitment of non-EU workers is strictly regulated in Germany. You can consult local, federally run employment offices. These fall under the umbrella of Bundensanstalt für Arbeit (Federal Employment Service), through which you can find local agencies. The best tips on jobs for foreigners often come from fellow travelers or resources at hostels and tourist offices. Another great way to start is to look up web listings, many of which are listed in **Other Long-Term Work.** Also note that working abroad often requires a special work visa.

more visa information

All visa applications cost €60 and require valid passports for identification. Remember that short-term visas can take 2-10 days to process, while long-term visas can take up to 3 months. Visa applications should be sent to the German embassy. For additional visa information, refer to Documents and Formalities.

LONG-TERM WORK

If you plan to spend a substantial amount of time, over 90 days, working in Germany, search for a job well in advance. International placement agencies can find employment abroad, especially for those interested in teaching. Internship and professional training programs are another way to ease into working abroad. Some internships are even paid, albeit not well, and many cite internships as good learning experiences. Be wary of advertisements for companies requiring a fee to get you a job, as many of the same jobs can be found for free online or in newspapers.

Teaching English

If you're more into the emotional fulfillment and satisfaction than income, teaching may be the job for you. Additionally, several programs in Germany provide a daily living expense stipend. Teaching in rural regions of Germany also means lower living costs (translate: extra money in your pocket). In most cases, at least a bachelor's degree is necessary for a full-time teaching position. Due to a high demand for native English-speaking teachers, a bachelor's degree serves as a sufficient qualification for teaching in Germany; hence freelance teaching is a popular option for recent college graduates.

Many schools require teachers to have a Teaching English as a Foreign Language (TEFL) certificate. Some positions do not require this, but they tend to be lower-paying. English-speakers without knowledge of the German language can also be hired for English-immersion classrooms in private schools. Various placement agencies and university fellowship programs are the best resources to find teaching jobs. The alternative is to contact schools directly and try your luck.

- **INTERNATIONAL SCHOOLS SERVICES (ISS):** A non-profit corporation that builds and manages international schools where they offer teaching and administrative positions. (15 Roszel Road, P.O. Box 5910, Princeton, NJ 08543 ☎609-452-0990 ▣www.iss.edu)

- **TEACH INTERNATIONAL:** Offers TESOL (Teaching English to Speakers of Other Languages) in New Zealand, Australia, and Canada to be certified to teach English abroad. (Level 2/370 George St., Brisbane, 4000, Australia ☎+1 617 32 11 46 33 ▣www.teachinternational.com)

- **INSTITUTE OF INTERNATIONAL EDUCATION:** This highly competitive program sends college graduates to teach in Germany. (809 United Nations Plaza, New York, NY 10017 ☎+1-212-883-8200 ▣www.iie.org)

- **TEACHING ENGLISH AS A FOREIGN LANGUAGE:** Lists various job opportunities to teach English abroad. (▣www.tefl.com)

- **OXFORD SEMINARS:** Offers TEFL programs and job placements in Europe. (244 5th Avenue, Suite J262, New York, NY 10001-7406 ☎+1-212-213-8978 ▣www.oxfordseminars.com)

Internships and Professional Training

- **CA EDUCATION PROGRAMS (CAEP):** Coordinates paid internships and other educational experiences with agricultural organizations. Jobs range from farming to wine-making. College credit also available. (112 E. Lincoln Ave., Fergus Falls, MN 56538 ☎+1-218-739-3241 ▣www.caepinc.org)

- **INTERNATIONALE WEITERBILDUNG UNT ENTWICKLUNG GGMBH:** Professional training for students and young people from Germany and abroad. (Inwent - Capacity Building International, Germany, Friedrich-Ebert-Allee 40, 53113 Bonn ☎228 446 00 ▣www.inwent.org)

- **CDS INTERNATIONAL:** Offers professional development programs and long-term paid internships in several countries, including Germany, for students and recent graduates of accredited US colleges and universities. *(440 Park Avenue South, New York, NY 10016 ☎+1-212-497-3500 🖳www.cdsintl.org)*

- **RESEARCH INTERNSHIPS IN SCIENCE AND ENGINEERING (RISE):** Offers summer internship programs in which German PhD candidates are paired with North American undergraduates. Stipend provided. *(Section 316, Kennedyallee 50, 53175 Bonn ☎022 888 24 25 🖳www.daad.de/rise)*

- **INTERN ABROAD:** Search engine for internships abroad. *(🖳www.internabroad.com)*

Au Pair Work

Au pairs are typically women aged 18-27 who work as live-in nannies, caring for children, and doing light housework in foreign countries in exchange for room, board, and a small stipend. The job allows you to explore Germany and local culture without the high cost of traveling. However, you might face mediocre pay, long hours, and the possibility of not getting along with your assigned family. Stipends and salaries can vary greatly, but expect somewhere between €50-95. The au pair agencies listed below are great places to start searching for a family, especially since much of your experience depends on who you're placed with.

- **AUPAIRCONNECT:** Database of families looking for aupairs as well as available au pairs. *(🖳www.aupairconnect.com)*

- **AU PAIR CARE CULTURAL EXCHANGE:** Provides au pair opportunities in Germany. *(AYUSA International e.V., Giesebrechtstr. 10, 10629 Berlin ☎308 439 39 20 🖳www.aupaircare.de/inbound)*

- **INTEREXCHANGE:** Provides listing of teaching and au pair jobs in Germany. *(161 6th Ave., New York City, NY 10013 ☎+1-212-924-0446 🖳www.interexchange.org)*

- **CHILDCARE INTERNATIONAL:** Lists au pair opportunities available across the globe. *(🖳www.childint.co.uk)*

Other Long-Term Work

- **TESALL.COM:** The original search engine for jobs abroad maintains the most extensive, if hard-to-navigate, database. *(🖳www.tesall.com)*

- **INTERNATIONAL COOPERATIVE EDUCATION:** Finds summer jobs for students ages 18-30 in Germany. Semester- and full year commitments also available. Costs include a $250 application fee and $900 placement fee. *(15 Spiros Way, Menlo Park, CA 94025 ☎+1-650-323-4944 🖳www.icemenlo.com)*

- **MONSTER:** An extensive job search engine. *(🖳www.monster.de)*

- **JOBSAFARI:** Similar to Monster (above), Jobsafari is a German job search engine that finds jobs by occupation and location. *(🖳www.jobsafari.de)*

- **EUROJOBS.COM:** And one more extensive job search engine, geared toward jobs in Europe. *(🖳www.eurojobs.com)*

SHORT-TERM WORK

A popular option is to work for an allotted amount of time at a hostel in exchange for room and board. High turnover in the tourism industry can also present short-term job opportunities. If you're at all bi- or multi-lingual, you may find jobs faster in the translation fields. If you don't feel like trying your luck once you're in Germany, try the websites below for ideas and posted job listings.

- **EASYEXPAT.COM:** Provides job listings and guides to getting short-term work in Germany. *(🖳www.easyexpat.com)*

working . short-term work

- **DEUTSCH-AMERIKANISCHES INSTITUT TÜBINGEN:** Offers teacher training, lists of events and German-American programs in Germany, and freelance teaching positions for those with BA or MA degrees. (✉*www.dai-tuebingen.de/en/index. php?sec=news*)

- **BUNDESAGENTUR FÜR ARBEIT:** The federal employment bureau, which handles student applications from abroad, can connect you to various job opportunities. German fluency required. (✉*www.arbeitsagentur.de*)

- **TRANSITIONS ABROAD.COM:** Lists various short-term work opportunities, including au pair jobs, farmwork, and other summer jobs. (✉*www.transitionsabroad.com*)

tell the world

If your friends are tired of hearing about that time you saved a baby orangutan in Indonesia, there's clearly only one thing to do: get new friends. Find them at our website, ✉www.letsgo.com, where you can post your study-, volunteer-, or work-abroad stories for other, more appreciative community members to read. There's also a Beyond Tourism section that elaborates on non-destination-specific volunteering, studying, and working opportunities. If you liked this chapter, you'll love it; if you didn't like this chapter, maybe you'll find the website's more general Beyond Tourism tips more likeable, you non-likey person.

INDEX

a

Albertina 307
Alter Peter 260
Andechs 295
  essentials 296
  food 296
  orientation 295
  shopping 296
  sights 295
Andechs Brewery 296
Austrian Alps 331
  Baden 343
  Klosterneuburg 332
  Krems and Stein 344
  Laxenburg 334
  Melk 341
  Mödling 335
  Petronell Carnuntum and Bad-
    Deutsch Altenburg 339
  Tulln an der Donau 337

b

Beatles 92
beer gardens 270
  Augustinerkeller 276
  Cassiopia 70
  Englischer Garten 263
  Heinz Minki 72
  Hirschgarten 267
  Hofbräuhaus 277
  Hofbräukeller 275
  Hugo's 222
  Jägerklause 69
  Prater Garten 67
  ResidenzSchloß Darmstadt 218
  Tempelhofer Park 51
Belvedere 310
Bergstrasse Wine Road
  Heppenheim 216
Berlin 11
  accommodations 20
  arts and culture 73
  essentials 79
  food 52
  nightlife 62
  orientation 14

shopping 75
  sights 34
beyond tourism 377
  studying 378
  volunteering 381
  working 383
Bonn 181
  accommodations 181
  essentials 184
  food 183
  sights 181
budget airlines 355

c

Cafe am Hochhaus 278
Camsdorfer Brücke 158
Carmina Burana 295
castles and schloßes
  Dom 168
  Früh am Dom 173
  Grafenegg Castle 345
  Heidelberger Schloß 227
  LandgrafenSchloß 220
  ResidenzSchloß 247
  Schloß Charlottenburg 34
  Schloß Moritzburg 137
  Schloß Nymphenburg 267
  Schloßplatz 40
  Schloß Schönbrunn 312
  Shloß Bellevue 42
  Stephansdom 307
Charlottenburg 14
Checkpoint Charlie 51

d

Dachau Concentration Camp
  269
Donauinsel Fest (Danube
  Island Festival) 326
Dresden 120
  accommodations 121
  arts and culture 133
  essentials 135
  food 129
  nightlife 131
  orientation 120

sights 125
Düsseldorf 184
  accommodations 186
  arts and culture 196
  essentials 197
  food 192
  nightlife 194
  orientation 184
  shopping 196
  sights 188

e

embassies
  Austrian 353
  German 352
  in Austria 352
  in Germany 351
entrance requirements 348
environmental conservation 381
essentials 347
  climate 359
  getting around 354
  keeping in touch 357
  language 360
  measurements 360
  money 348
  planning your trip 348
  safety and health 353
euro 349
European Union 349

f

film
  in Berlin 74
  in Munich 285
  in Vienna 324
Frankfurt 201
  accommodations 202
  arts and culture 211
  essentials 213
  food 208
  nightlife 209
  orientation 201
  shopping 212
  sights 203
Frauenkirche 125
Friedrichshain 18

index

g

German Reformation 366
Germany 101 365
  art and architecture 372
  etiquette and customs 373
  film 371
  food and drink 375
  history 365
  holidays and festivals 374
  land 370
  literature 371
  media 370
  people 369
  politics and government 369
  sports and recreation 375
gnomes 372
Goethe, Wolfgang von 225,
  228, 371
Große Freiheit 36/Kaiserkeller
  104

h

Hamburg 92
  accommodations 94
  arts and culture 107
  essentials 108
  food 102
  nightlife 104
  orientation 92
  shopping 108
  sights 97
Heidelberg 225
  accommodations 225
  arts and culture 232
  essentials 233
  food 229
  nightlife 230
  orientation 225
  shopping 232
  sights 227
historical restoration and
  archaeology 381
how to use this book 10

i

international calls 359

j

Jena 157
  accommodations 157
  essentials 161
  food 159
  nightlife 160
  orientation 157
  shopping 161
  sights 158

k

kabaret 147
KaDeWe 75
Köln (Cologne) 164
  accommodations 165
  arts and culture 177
  essentials 179
  food 173
  nightlife 175
  orientation 164
  shopping 178
  sights 168
Kolumba 169
Kreuzberg 20

l

language 360
  phrasebook 361
  pronunciation 360
language schools 380
Leipzig 138
  accommodations 139
  arts and culture 147
  essentials 149
  food 144
  nightlife 145
  orientation 138
  shopping 148
  sights 141
long-term work 384
Lübeck 112
  acccommodations 112
  essentials 116
  food 115
  sights 113
Ludwigsburg 247
  essentials 248
  food 248
  orientation 247
  sights 247

m

Marburg 219
  accommodations 219
  essentials 222
  food 221
  orientation 219
  sights 220
Marienkirche 113
Marienplatz 260
Mathildenhöhe 217
memorials
  Dachau Concentration Camp 269
  Homosexual Memorial 38
  Memorial to the Murdered Jews of
    Europe 38
microbreweries 59
monuments
  Berliner Mauer Dokumentationzen-
    trum 47
  East Side Gallery 49
Moritzburg 137
  essentials 138
  food 138
  orientation 137
  sights 137
Mozart, Wolfgang Amadeus 309
Munich 252
  accommodations 254
  arts and culture 284
  essentials 288
  food 270
  nightlife 277
  orientation 252
  shopping 286
  sights 260
museums
  Bauhaus Museum 152
  Beethovenhaus 181
  Deutsches Technikmuseum Berlin 50
  für Kunst und Gewerbe 97
  für Moderne Kunst 203
  Hamburger Kunsthalle 97
  Haus der Geschichte 182
  K21: Kunstsammlung Im
    Ständehaus 188
  Käthe-Kollwitz-Museum 34
  Kunst Haus Wien 310
  Ludwig 169
  Mercedes-Benz 237
  Museumsufer 206
  Neue National Gallerie 45
  Nietzsche Archiv 154

index

Pergamon Museum 37
Topography of Terror 37
music and opera 73
  in Berlin 73
  in Munich 284
  in Vienna 325

n

Neuschwanstein Castle 268
Nordrhein-Westfalen 163

o

Oberbaumbrücke 50
Oktoberfest 286

p

parks
  Grunewald and the Jagdschloß 36
  Park an der Ilm and Gartenhaus 152
  Tempelhofer Park 51
  Tiergarten 43
  Volkspark 48
pins and atms 351
Planten un Blomen 97
Potsdam 85
Potsdamer Platz 45
pre-departure health 354
  immunizations and precautions 354
Prenzlauer Berg 18

r

rail resources 357
Reichstag 42
Residenz and Hofgarten 260
Rhein 164

s

Schokoladen Museum 172
Schöneberg and Wilmersdorf 14
short-term work 385
soccer 265
Spreewald and Lübbenau 82
Städel 206
St. Andreas Kirche 188
Starnberg am Starnberger
  See 293
  essentials 295
  food 294
  orientation 293
  sights 293
Stuttgart 235
  accommodations 236
  arts and culture 243
  essentials 245
  food 240
  nightlife 242
  orientation 236
  sights 237
suggested itineraries 5

t

taxes 352
teaching English 384
theater
  in Berlin 74
  in Munich 284
  in Vienna 324
Thirty Years' War 367
time differences 348
travel advisories 354

u

Universität (Heidelberg) 227

v

Vienna 297
  accommodations 302
  arts and culture 324
  essentials 328
  food 313
  nightlife 320
  orientation 300
  shopping 326
  sights 307
visa information 378, 383

w

walking tour 41
Weimar 150
  accommodations 151
  essentials 156
  food 154
  nightlife 155
  orientation 151
  shopping 155
  sights 152
working 383
World War II 368
wurst 373

index

MAP INDEX

Berlin	12-13
Berlin Mitte	16
Charlottenburg and Schöneberg	15
Dresden	118-119
Dresden Altstadt	122
Dresden Neustadt	123
Düsseldorf	185
Frankfurt	200
Hamburg	90-91
Heidelberg	224
Köln (Cologne)	166
Kreuzberg	19
Leipzig (Innenstadt)	139
Munich (München)	250-251
Nordrhein-Westfalen and Hesse	165
Northern Germany	93
Prenzlauer Berg	17
Southern Germany	253
Stuttgart	235
Vienna	298-299

MAP LEGEND

- ▪ Sight/Service
- ✈ Airport
- ⌂ Arch/Gate
- 💲 Bank
- 🏖 Beach
- 🚌 Bus Station
- ✪ Capital City

- ♜ Castle
- ✝ Church
- ⚑ Consulate/Embassy
- ⛪ Convent/Monastery
- ⚓ Ferry Landing
- (347) Highway Sign
- ✚ Hospital

- 🖥 Internet Cafe
- 📖 Library
- Ⓜ〉Ⓜ Metro Station
- ⛰ Mountain
- ☪ Mosque
- 🏛 Museum
- ℞ Pharmacy

- ♣ Police
- ✉ Post Office
- 🎿 Skiing
- ✡ Synagogue
- ☎ Telephone Office
- 🎭 Theater
- ⓘ Tourist Office
- 🚆 Train Station

The Let's Go compass always points NORTH.

Pedestrian Zone

Stairs

Park

Water

Beach

map index

LET'S GO!

THE STUDENT TRAVEL GUIDE

These Let's Go guidebooks are available at bookstores and through online retailers:

EUROPE
Let's Go Amsterdam & Brussels, 1st ed.
Let's Go Berlin, Prague & Budapest, 2nd ed.
Let's Go France, 32nd ed.
Let's Go Europe 2011, 51st ed.
Let's Go European Riviera, 1st ed.
Let's Go Germany, 16th ed.
Let's Go Great Britain with Belfast and Dublin, 33rd ed.
Let's Go Greece, 10th ed.
Let's Go Istanbul, Athens & the Greek Islands, 1st ed.
Let's Go Italy, 31st ed.
Let's Go London, Oxford, Cambridge & Edinburgh,
    2nd ed.
Let's Go Madrid & Barcelona, 1st ed.
Let's Go Paris, 17th ed.
Let's Go Rome, Venice & Florence, 1st ed.
Let's Go Spain, Portugal & Morocco, 26th ed.
Let's Go Western Europe, 10th ed.

UNITED STATES
Let's Go Boston, 6th ed.
Let's Go New York City, 19th ed.
Let's Go Roadtripping USA, 4th ed.

MEXICO, CENTRAL & SOUTH AMERICA
Let's Go Buenos Aires, 2nd ed.
Let's Go Central America, 10th ed.
Let's Go Costa Rica, 5th ed.
Let's Go Costa Rica, Nicaragua & Panama, 1st ed.
Let's Go Guatemala & Belize, 1st ed.
Let's Go Yucatán Peninsula, 1st ed.

ASIA & THE MIDDLE EAST
Let's Go Israel, 5th ed.
Let's Go Thailand, 5th ed.

ACKNOWLEDGMENTS

SARAH THANKS: Germany/BPB runs on Fun Pod. Bro-tastic Colleen (i.e., bear) for always being patient with her freshman Ed. Meagan for musicals "busting out all over" on the daily. Matt for his melodic Jamaican Patois. Daniel for the jajajas. Marykate for fielding questions despite disagreements on cuisine. Joey G for the bear hugs. Prod for solving multiple computer issues while jamming on the ukulele and sharing stories. Ashley, Nathaniel, and Joe for the inspiration and comedy, the best combination an employee could ask for. Everybody else at Let's Go; you're all incredible. My researchers for putting their best foot forward for this book. My friends who dealt with the antics and rain checks. Big sis' Becca, who's a trooper and a role model, and little sis' Nina, the light of my life. My parents for going the extra mile for me. And for feeding me, which is a full-time job.

COLLEEN THANKS: My RWs for killer copy and staying in touch. Sarah for supering (and being super). FUN POD. Daniel for pep talks. Matt for letting me be Ari. Meg for Massachusetts and summer theater. Marykate for laying the smackdown at Crema. Nathaniel for hiring me. Joe for family dinners. Joe for marketing moves. Sara and Dan for fixing my lazy RIVER. Edward-Michael for treats on crebit. Trace for loving life and being a bestie. Iris for labbits. Aaron for tweeting at me and reminding me that my boyfriend is gay. Court and Cathy for being all-star Gato Girlz. Travis for that free drink (call me!). Unos for snack hours and karaoke. Winnie and Logan for SF. Katie for NYC. Mr. Cronin for my first Red Sox game. My proctees for being good. Brendy for buying great birthday presents. Mom for everything.

DIRECTOR OF PUBLISHING Ashley R. Laporte

LET'S GO masthead

EXECUTIVE EDITOR Nathaniel Rakich

PRODUCTION AND DESIGN DIRECTOR Sara Plana

PUBLICITY AND MARKETING DIRECTOR Joseph Molimock

MANAGING EDITORS Charlotte Alter, Daniel C. Barbero, Marykate Jasper, Iya Megre

TECHNOLOGY PROJECT MANAGERS Daniel J. Choi, C. Alexander Tremblay

PRODUCTION ASSOCIATES Rebecca Cooper, Melissa Niu

FINANCIAL ASSOCIATE Louis Caputo

DIRECTOR OF IT Yasha Iravantchi

PRESIDENT Meagan Hill

GENERAL MANAGER Jim McKellar

ABOUT LET'S GO

THE STUDENT TRAVEL GUIDE

Let's Go publishes the world's favorite student travel guides, written entirely by Harvard students. Armed with pens, notebooks, and a few changes of clothes stuffed into their backpacks, our student researchers go across continents, through time zones, and above expectations to seek out invaluable travel experiences for our readers. Because we are a completely student-run company, we have a unique perspective on how students travel, where they want to go, and what they're looking to do when they get there. If your dream is to grab a machete and forge through the jungles of Costa Rica, we can take you there. If you'd rather bask in the Riviera sun at a beachside cafe, we'll set you a table. In short, we write for readers who know that there's more to travel than tour buses. To keep up, visit our website, www.letsgo. com, where you can sign up to blog, post photos from your trips, and connect with the Let's Go community.

TRAVELING BEYOND TOURISM

We're on a mission to provide our readers with sharp, fresh coverage packed with socially responsible opportunities to go beyond tourism. Each guide's Beyond Tourism chapter shares ideas about responsible travel, study abroad, and how to give back to the places you visit while on the road. To help you gain a deeper connection with the places you travel, our fearless researchers scour the globe to give you the heads-up on both world-renowned and off-the-beaten-track opportunities. We've also opened our pages to respected writers and scholars to hear their takes on the countries and regions we cover, and asked travelers who have worked, studied, or volunteered abroad to contribute first-person accounts of their experiences.

FIFTY-ONE YEARS OF WISDOM

Let's Go has been on the road for 51 years and counting. We've grown a lot since publishing our first 20-page pamphlet to Europe in 1960, but five decades and 60 titles later, our witty, candid guides are still researched and written entirely by students on shoestring budgets who know that train strikes, stolen luggage, food poisoning, and marriage proposals are all part of a day's work. Meanwhile, we're still bringing readers fresh new features, such as a student-life section with advice on how and where to meet students from around the world; a revamped, user-friendly layout for our listings; and greater emphasis on the experiences that make travel abroad a rite of passage for readers of all ages. And, of course, this year's 16 titles—including five brand-new guides—are still brimming with editorial honesty, a commitment to students, and our irreverent style.

THE LET'S GO COMMUNITY

More than just a travel guide company, Let's Go is a community that reaches from our headquarters in Cambridge, MA, all across the globe. Our small staff of dedicated student editors, writers, and tech nerds comes together because of our shared passion for travel and our desire to help other travelers get the most out of their experience. We love it when our readers become part of the Let's Go community as well—when you travel, drop us a postcard (67 Mt. Auburn St., Cambridge, MA 02138, USA), send us an email (feedback@letsgo.com), or sign up on our website (www. letsgo.com) to tell us about your adventures and discoveries.

For more information, updated travel coverage, and news from our researcher team, visit us online at www.letsgo.com.

THANKS TO OUR SPONSORS

- **HOTEL HANSABLICK.** Flotowstr.6, 10555 Berlin, Germany. ☎49 030 390 48 00. ▨www.hansablick.de.

- **ALETTO KREUZBERG.** Tempelhofer Ufer 8/9, 10963 Berlin, Germany. ☎49 030 25 96 04 80. ▨www.aletto.de.

- **ALETTO SCHÖNEBERG.** Grunewaldstraße 33, 10823 Berlin, Germany. ☎49 030 25 96 04 80. ▨www.aletto.de.

- **HELTER SKELTER HOSTEL.** Kalkscheunenstr. 4-5, 10117 Berlin. ☎0049 0 30 280 44 99 7. ▨www.helterskelterhostel.com.

- **SUNFLOWER HOSTEL.** Helsingforser Str. 17, 10243 Berlin. ☎0049 0 30 440 44 250. ▨www.sunflower-hostel.de.

- **HEART OF GOLD HOSTEL.** Johannisstr. 11, 10117 Berlin. ☎0049 0 30 29 00 33 00. ▨www.heartofgold-hostel.de.

- **ODYSSEE GLOBETROTTER HOSTEL.** Grünberger Str. 23, 10243 Berlin. ☎0049 0 30 29 0000 81. ▨www.globetrotterhostel.de.

- **FIVE ELEMENTS HOSTEL.** Moselstr. 40, 60329 Frankfurt. ☎0049 0 69 24 00 58 85. ▨www.5elementshostel.de.

- **EASY PALACE CITY HOSTEL.** Mozartstr. 4, 80336 Munich. ☎0049 0 89 55 87 97 0. ▨www.easypalace.de.

- **CITYSTAY HOSTEL.** Rosenstrasse 16, 10178 Berlin-Mitte. ☎49 30 23 62 40 31. ▨www.citystay.de.

HELPING LET'S GO. If you want to share your discoveries, suggestions, or corrections, please drop us a line. We appreciate every piece of correspondence, whether a postcard, a 10-page email, or a coconut. Visit Let's Go at **www.letsgo.com** or send an email to:

feedback@letsgo.com, subject: "Let's Go Germany"

Address mail to:

Let's Go Germany, 67 Mount Auburn St., Cambridge, MA 02138, USA

In addition to the invaluable travel advice our readers share with us, many are kind enough to offer their services as researchers or editors. Unfortunately, our charter enables us to employ only currently enrolled Harvard students.

Maps © Let's Go and Avalon Travel
Design Support by Jane Musser, Sarah Juckniess, Tim McGrath

Distributed by Publishers Group West.
Printed in Canada by Friesens Corp.

ISBN-13: 978-1-59880-707-3
Sixteenth edition
10 9 8 7 6 5 4 3 2 1

Let's Go Germany is written by Let's Go Publications, 67 Mt. Auburn St., Cambridge, MA 02138, USA.

Let's Go® and the LG logo are trademarks of Let's Go, Inc.

quick reference

YOUR GUIDE TO LET'S GO ICONS

☎	Phone numbers	⊗	Not wheelchair-accessible	❄	Has A/C
▣	Websites	((ᵠ))	Has internet access	⇌	Directions
💳	Takes credit cards	⛱	Has outdoor seating	*i*	Other hard info
⊛	Cash only	▼	Is GLBT or GLBT-friendly	Ⓢ	Prices
♿	Wheelchair-accessible	⚲	Serves alcohol	⏰	Hours

PRICE RANGES

Let's Go includes price ranges, marked by icons ❶ through ❺, in accommodations and food listings. For an expanded explanation, see the chart in How To Use This Book.

GERMANY	❶	❷	❸	❹	❺
ACCOMMODATIONS	under €15	€15-25	€26-35	€36-50	over €50
FOOD	under €5	€5-9	€10-14	€15-22	over €22

IMPORTANT PHONE NUMBERS

EMERGENCY: ☎112			
ISOS Alarm Center	☎+49 6102 358 81 00	ISIC Hotline	☎+44 20 87 62 81 10
Domestic Operator	☎0180 200 10 33	English language crisis line	☎01 47 23 80 80

CURRENCY CONVERSIONS

These rates are current as we go to press. Who knows how much they might have changed.

AUS$1 = €0.70	€1 = AUS$1.42	UK£1 = €1.20	€1 = UK£0.83
CDN$1 = €0.76	€1 = CDN$1.30	US$1 = €0.79	€1 = US$1.25
NZ$1 = €0.56	€1 = NZ$1.77	EUR€1 = €1	WOAH!

TEMPERATURE CONVERSIONS

°CELSIUS	-5	0	5	10	15	20	25	30	35	40
°FAHRENHEIT	23	32	41	50	59	68	77	86	95	104

MEASUREMENT CONVERSIONS

1 inch (in.) = 25.4mm	1 millimeter (mm) = 0.039 in.
1 foot (ft.) = 0.305m	1 meter (m) = 3.28 ft.
1 mile (mi.) = 1.609km	1 kilometer (km) = 0.621 mi.
1 pound (lb.) = 0.454kg	1 kilogram (kg) = 2.205 lb.
1 gallon (gal.) = 3.785L	1 liter (L) = 0.264 gal.